Let me
count the ways

letters of friendship, love, and deception

PERLA FOX

DEVORA
PUBLISHING
NEW YORK◆JERUSALEM◆LONDON

Let Me Count the Ways
Published by Devora Publishing Company
Text Copyright © 2008 by Perla Fox

COVER DESIGN: www.pushingtheenvelope.com
TYPESETTING: Koren Publishing Services
EDITORIAL AND PRODUCTION MANAGER: Daniella Barak
EDITOR: Michael Dickel

Hard Cover ISBN: 978-1-934440-07-0

E-mail: publisher@devorapublishing.com
Web Site: www. devorapublishing.com

Printed in the United States of America

First, this book is dedicated to
Louis and Celia
my parents,
whose love & support inspired
me throughout my life.

It is also dedicated to
my wonderful husband,
Jules

to my children
Jordan, Kenneth and Judy

and to my grandchildren
Benjamin, Rebecca and Liana

I hope these pages will enlighten them
about our family lore and encourage
them to reach for the sky.

Many Thanks...

I want to acknowledge the help that family and friends have given to me over the years in preparation for this book. To Perry Hamburg for his tales about Jacob Kanster as a youngster in Jerusalem, meeting Pauline Berger in the tenements of New York, the bit about the stills and about Sarah Henna in Czarist Russia; to Hillel Abrams for his remembrances of Benjamin Grossberg; to Graenum Schiff for the piece about Jacob in Florida; to Nan Rudin about Mom and Pop buying Bakala; to Shoshana for "My Mommy and Daddy don't do that"; to Nat and Jack Abrams for their contributions; to Sylvia Brilliant for the story about the haunted house and her brother Avraham Dov; to Paula Lippman for her contributions; to Ruth Slonim for photos of her mother, Esther, and aunt Kitty; I also want to thank Harry Hamburg and Robin Kitay for offering photos. Thank you to all the others who contributed tidbits to this story as well. Not all contributions made it into the final book, but they all added to the whole and are gratefully acknowledged.

I also want most sincerely to thank Yaacov Peterseil, the publisher of Devora Publishing, who had faith in my manuscript when others could not see its potential; Michael Dickel, my editor, who worked so tirelessly with me from Jerusalem; Batsheva Pomerantz, the proofreader, who tidied up all the loose ends and Daniella Barak, of Devora Publishing, for her skill and patient managing from manuscript to finished book. I also want to thank my dear husband, Jules, for encouraging me

v

and preparing so many meals while I was busy working. My children also deserve many thanks for not complaining during their visits that I was too engrossed to spend more time with them. That will all change. And, thanks to you readers who have decided to experience this journey with me.

Perla Fox

Introduction

*M*y daughter Judy helped me get my children's picture book, *The Wooodles: Stretching your Imagination*, off the ground. She inspired me to try again with this book. About 10 years before my parents passed away, Judy and her children, Benjamin, Rebecca and Liana frequently asked my parents and me to repeat family stories they had heard over the years. Whenever my husband Jules and I returned from Israel to visit, I sat with my parents and took notes. It seemed like a good idea to get as much information as possible before it was too late. I had no intention, at that time, of publishing a book.

When the material began to repeat itself, I said to my father, "You and Mom saved your courtship letters. Would you let me use them in this memoir?" I wanted Mom to read them to Pop first, to make sure it was O.K., his eyesight no longer permitting him to read them himself. I also thought it would be a sweet way for my parents to relive the past. Surprisingly, Dad, for his part, said it was all right with him. When my mother did not have the strength to read many letters to him, I read a few.

My father passed away on October 27, 1995, at the age of 97, a day before their 67th wedding anniversary. A few days later, I saw Mom reading some of the letters. She laughed and she cried, and finally said, "Go ahead and use them." She had nothing to worry about since she taught me never to put anything in writing that I would not want printed in the Washington Post. She passed away on August 4, 1997, at the age of 94.

There were 451 courtship letters neatly tied in ribbons. Not only had they kept each other's letters, Dad even kept carbons of those he sent to Mom. This gave me an unprecedented look into the lives and times of my parents' courtship beginning in 1926 until their marriage in 1928. My father also kept copies of letters between him and his sisters, brothers, cousins and friends going back to 1915. Among these, there were 265 letters between my father and his former accounting partner, Dave Glushak.

The latter letters outlined a business deal during the depression years, which held great promise for their futures despite fraudulent dealings on the part of the parent company.

When all the material was entered into my computer, I had over 2,000 pages. Editing this down to a manageable length was quite a challenge. While the words of the letter writers remain their own, including deliberate misspellings, the repetitious and irrelevant material was removed in the editing process. Some names of third parties were changed for privacy as well. This includes the company name, Argomite – the company existed under a different name.

This has been a labor of love for over 23 years. During the process, I learned how very special my parents were and how lucky I was to have been their daughter.

PART ONE

In The Beginning God Created

My father, Yekutiel Leib Grossberg, known as Louis C., was the fourth in a family of ten living children. His name should have been Kitay, since that was the family name before his father, Benjamin, decided to opt out of the Czar's army. In those days, Russia controlled Lithuania, and a young man was likely to be drafted for a period of twenty years. So, Benjamin Kitay decided to take advantage of one reprieve from such a fate. He became the only son of a widowed mother. The real Mrs. Grossberg had lost her only son at the age of three but death records, like birth records in their town of Hazenput, County of Kovno Gubernia, were not always a matter of public record. Thus, Benjamin Kitay become Benjamin Grossberg.

My grandparents, Benjamin and Sarah Henna, were quite elderly when I was a child and spoke little English. They lived across town and my father visited them regularly. Grandpa was short and slim with dark brown hair and eyes. He had a regal air about him that commanded admiration and respect. His voice was soft and when he spoke, people listened. Grandma was also short though slightly taller than her husband. She was a little plump and always wore a pleasant smile. Her hair and eyes were also very dark, as was the case with all the children. People who knew the family often remarked about the Grossberg eyes – large, black and very good-looking. I don't know why or when Benjamin moved to Grobin, Latvia, but there he married Sarah Henna Effenbach around 1890. At some point they moved to Libau and that is where the children were born.

My mother, Celia Kanster Grossberg, was the eldest of five children. I had a closer relationship with Jacob Kanster, my mother's father, than with Benjamin, even though Jacob lived in New Jersey and we lived in Washington, DC. His English was quite good. Papa, as everyone called him, was dark-complexioned with a voice that almost crackled. He suffered from asthma but smoked anyway. He looked like the brother of Anwar Sadat – the resemblance was that close. Papa never seemed to get angry. In fact, he always had a smirk on his face as if he was about to say something funny, which he often did. Mother took me with her whenever she went to visit. I never knew my mother's mother, Pauline (Paula) Berger. She died a few months before I was born and I was named after her, an Ashkenazi (Eastern European) custom among the Jews. The custom among Sephardic (Spanish) Jews was often to name after the living. Jacob was half Sephardic. According to the few pictures I have, taken shortly before she died, Paula was on the heavy side with short blond hair. Her children said she was beautiful and this was evident in her engagement photo with Jacob, from 1900.

According to my cousin, Perry Hamburg, Papa told a story that when Pauline Berger came to America she lived with an aunt in a tenement on the Lower East Side of Manhattan and worked as a cigar maker. Papa lived in the same building. When she caught his eye, he romanced her by playing his accordion on warm summer nights on the roof of the building. Because of his good looks, suave complexion and long moustache, he was considered quite a "catch." Pauline, or Paula as he called her, won the prize.

My father Louis, was born in Libau and his memories of it were surprisingly good, though he left for America when 11-years-old. He remembered his mother making meat sausage to sell and the small house in which he lived. His niece, Sylvia, remembered her mother Esther saying no one in the village wanted this old house because it was haunted. Since there was nothing better, she took it. The first night she heard eerie voices and footsteps, so the next day she recited prayers and attached *mezuzahs* (scrolls with Torah text) to all the doorposts. That ended the ghostly visits.

Orthodox Jews do not ride on the Sabbath nor do they handle

money. One Sabbath in Latvia, when Louis was about 6-years-old, he was walking to synagogue with his father and spied a coin on the ground. Louis stooped to pick it up.

"No, don't touch the coin. It is *Shabbos*," his father said.

Disappointed, Louis left it there. About a block later they came upon a beggar in the street.

Grandpa leaned over to the beggar and said, "If you will go back a block you will find a coin."

The man took off to find it. Louis was pleased that someone in real need would have the money.

Louis also remembered Riga, swimming in the Baltic Sea near his home and the cold, cold winters. His job was fetching small bits of coal that fell from the unloading docks. Louis and his cousin, Herman Freudberg, would also collect pieces of coconut – considered prized delicacies – that fell from containers.

One day when my young son Jordan complained about having to walk to elementary school in the snow, a distance of a half-mile, my father said, when he was a child, he had to walk 5 miles in bitter cold weather. He admitted, however, that the children in Latvia loved the wintertime when the lakes froze over. He would put on one ice skate and off he'd go. Why only one? Because one of his siblings needed the other. When the countryside was lush with spring and summer foliage, he might go on the back of a mule. Jordan said, "I wouldn't mind going to school that way, but we don't have any mules in Chevy Chase."

In Libau, my grandfather, Benjamin Grossberg, was a peddler for The Singer Sewing Machine Company, going from town to town with his horse and wagon. He would be gone for days at a time. Making a living in Latvia was always difficult, and in his case dangerous. With nine children to feed, he worried that bandits would do more than just rob him, leaving his wife and children destitute. On one such trip, he barely escaped with his life, and as a valued employee, he was offered a better position in the office, but this required him to work on the Sabbath, which he refused to do. The time had come for him to change occupations. Yet, how many jobs were there for a pious Jew in a town filled with pious Jews? Fortunately, the job he found was right up his alley. He became a *masgiach* (a kosher supervisor) on board a ship plowing its way between Riga and New York.

7

In the years around 1907, thousands of Jews emigrated from Europe to America and, being religious, needed the services that Benjamin was eminently qualified to perform. Not only was he a pious Jew, he was also a Talmudic scholar and was often asked to settle religious disputes. My grandfather knew the difference between custom and religious law, and scoffed at those who confused the two. In later years in America, he had running arguments with his eldest daughter, Esther, who thought that her friends' religious practices were Jewish law rather than custom.

During one voyage when Benjamin was away at sea, the police came to the door of their house. Louis' mother, Sarah Henna, answered it with a baby in her arms and several little ones hiding behind her skirt. She politely asked what they wanted. They were looking for Benjamin in order to send him back to Lithuania, along with his children. Sarah Henna could remain since she was born in Latvia but Benjamin was a foreigner.

She told the police that her husband was not at home and added sweetly, "If the children are not allowed to remain here, then take them with you, all 9 of them!"

Then she called her children to come at once but the police, thinking better of it, turned and abruptly left.

In those days, Latvia was either controlled by Germany or Russia, depending upon the political divisions of the time. Since children retained the nationality of their father, this meant that legally, the children were also Lithuanian, regardless of the fact that all had been born in Latvia. On January, 15, 1898, when my father was born, the town was in German hands, but was later taken over by the Russians.

Sarah Henna was considered a very knowledgeable healer – better than doctors, if you could find one. She was fond of putting onions at the foot of the bed, garlic around the neck, or feeding chicken soup to cure what ails you. Many of these folk remedies later were proved therapeutic.

Her powers were sorely tested when her year-old twins caught diphtheria. The girl was even sicker than the boy. The doctor told her that the girl, Eleanor, would not last the night and to concentrate her efforts on the boy. Sarah Henna was frantic. Thinking that the boy would survive, she began working on Eleanor. She did not intend to let one of her children die if she could help it. Her diligent efforts were successful in saving the girl. Tragically, the boy died.

At the end of each ship's voyage, my grandfather, Benjamin, went to all the passengers to sign a document stating their satisfaction with the quality of food aboard ship. Signing this paper was a formality for the passengers, but a requirement for my grandfather. A good report reflected positively on the ship's captain. My grandfather loved his job. Even though it took him away from home for weeks at a time, he was in his element. Passengers would engage him in conversations of a religious nature or on topics of the day, and he felt needed and appreciated.

On his last voyage from Riga to New York, a few passengers had a serious disagreement with the ship's personnel having nothing to do with the food. Since their passage was prepaid, there was little they could do to gain satisfaction. Along came Benjamin with his document requesting signatures that the food served on board was satisfactory. The passengers decided they had found their means of retribution and refused to sign his paper. Instead, they wrote that the potatoes were cold, the meat wasn't any good and besides, there wasn't enough of it, etc. Though Benjamin pleaded with them, they would hear none of it. Benjamin went to the captain to explain the situation.

"It's not my fault that the passengers won't sign. They told me the food was good. Their argument is with you, not me."

"That's too bad," answered the captain. "When I get ashore, I have to hand in your affidavit to the company, signed or unsigned. If you can't get the passengers to sign, I'll have to get another *masgiach* who can get the signatures on the next voyage."

Benjamin was devastated. What was he to do stranded in America with his family in Latvia? For a while, he stayed with relatives who had emigrated earlier. They tried to persuade him to remain and bring his family over to join him. His initial reaction was no, he considered America too *treif* – not kosher – for him. But the arguments grew more intense.

"Bunim" they said, using his Yiddish name, "Life was no picnic in Latvia – being separated from your family, the pogroms. You don't want to raise your children in such a place. Bring them all to America."

After much coaxing he gave in.

"O.K.," he said, but it's so expensive. How will I manage? I have no job and no money?"

"Don't worry," they answered. "We will help."

And they did.

One of the most active in that regard was 16-year-old Leo Freudberg, a favorite cousin of Louis', living in Washington, DC since 1907. He began raising money to bring the Grossberg family to America. Though only a boy himself, he wanted his cousins to join him.

When Sarah Henna learned that instead of her husband returning to Latvia, she and the children were to travel to America, she was very apprehensive. A new country? A new language? How would they make a living? However, on the positive side, she would be reunited with relatives now in America and would not have to worry when her husband left the house that he might never return. Sarah Henna began to prepare for the long voyage.

Fortunately, many years earlier, Benjamin had purchased U.S. Citizenship in Latvia for a nominal sum, when it was possible to do so. Little did he realize that that inexpensive piece of paper would come in handy one day.

Once, when Czarist Russia ruled the area, Sarah Henna had heard a radical activist on a soapbox preaching the virtues of communism and atheism. She roundly chastised him for his un-Godliness.

"With God's help, we'll get rid of people like you when we're in power!" The activist said.

While many relatives immigrated to the United States, some remained in Latvia. The family in America corresponded over the years with those relatives who remained in the old country. In 1943 the letters suddenly stopped. It is assumed that they did not escape the Holocaust. I look upon my grandfather's job loss as *beshert* (foreordained). Had Benjamin remained in Latvia with his wife and children, they might have suffered the fate of other family members and millions of Jews.

My father had less than fond memories of the ocean passage to America. Steerage was cold, damp, noisy and dirty. Everyone was crammed into small spaces. A copy of the ships manifest details all manner of requirements that the passengers promised to adhere to – like how many bundles each one could bring on board, permissible food and various other rules and regulations. Quoting from some of the more notable ones, "each emigrant over 12-years of age is entitled to a separate berth with mattress, pillow and blanket. For children under the age of 12 one berth with mattress, pillow & blanket will be allotted to two children." The Russian East Asiatic Steamship Company Ltd., would supply their meals "with table utensils, drinking water and water for washing." The baggage taken on board, presumably in kilograms, was 77 for Sarah Henna, Esther and Willie and 38.5 kilograms for everyone else. Only 2 kilograms were registered for Joseph, the youngest, who was listed as six-months old though he was really two.

The only things saved from the voyage were three Hebrew books Louis brought with him. One was *Bere'shit* (Genesis), published in 1865 in Warsaw. The other two were *Shemot* (Exodus), 1874, Vilna and *Tehilim* (Psalms), 1834, Vienna. They now reside on my bookshelf.

Passengers could not bring any luggage containing "anything that is inflammable, corrosive, or malodorous, nor wines nor spirituous liquors." Each passenger needed enough funds to provide for his or her needs once landed in New York. But the crowning touch was the oft-mentioned restrictions of immigration as stated in Article 14 of the ship's manifest:

> According to American laws (see art. 321 of the Act of March 1903) the following classes of aliens are not admitted in the United States: Persons with bodily defects rendering them incapable of work, persons afflicted with a contagious disease, idiots, insane persons who have been insane within five years previous, paupers, professional beggars, persons who have been convicted of capital crime, polygamists, anarchists & prostitutes. All such persons are sent back by the same steamer on board of which they arrived in America.

Any child aged 12 or under was allowed on at half fair. Babies up to 1-year could travel free. The eldest child, Esther (Rochel), was 17 and could not pass for 12 so her age was listed as 16. The others, however, were biologically impossible. While the children were approximately two years apart, Willie (Wolf 15) and Kitty (Keile 13) were listed as 11-year-old twins. Louis (11) passed as 9-years-old, Eleanor (Elke, 9) as 6, Pauline

(Pesse, 7) as 4¾, Miriam (6) as 4, Solomon (Schleime, 4) as 3 and the youngest, Joseph (Yosse, 2) was listed as six-months and traveled free. It was probably common practice to fudge the ages to save money, and fortunately no one questioned the manifest.

My father didn't remember being seasick but he did remember being sick of the stewed prunes that were served as dessert every meal. It was years before he would eat prunes again. He also remembered his excitement at arriving in New York on July 4, 1909. Where else in the world would they have such spectacular fireworks just to welcome him to America? Actually, the records show that they docked on July 7. Either the ship arrived early or that was an exceptional year.

Ellis Island was a memorable experience. Everyone was weary, many sick from the motion of the ship and all bedraggled remnants of humanity. After standing in the interminable lines, Sarah Henna and children finally approached the processing area. Doctors and nurses checked each passenger for health problems. Even such minor ones as eye infections doomed the immigrant to return to his place of origin. How many families had to take a return voyage because one of the children took ill on the ship?

When it was Sarah Henna's turn, she was first asked, "Where are you going to live?" When she replied, Washington, DC, the immigration officials lost all interest in the family. They didn't even check their eyes, which fortunately were healthy. The officials were so happy that here was a family that was not going to swell the hordes of New York that they sent them on their way without further examination.

The accommodations in Washington were little better than the ship. How many relatives could find space for a family of eleven? The solution was to divide them up. My father and two of his siblings were doled out to Aunt Rochel Hoddas, his mother's sister, while others were put up hither and yon.

Cousin Leo was ecstatic that all his efforts had finally paid off and his best pal, Louis, was finally in America. At the time of their arrival, my father was reunited with Leo's brothers, Herman, also 11, and Isadore Freudberg, then 13. He remembered the occasion well. It was the first time Louis was introduced to a banana. He took a bite, but he couldn't swallow it.

Now in America, Esther, the eldest child, acted like a queen bee and enjoyed bossing all the younger children. She would give them 2¢ for school lunch every day. Since Sarah Henna would not have allowed her children to eat non-kosher food, most likely the money was for something extra, like an apple or an orange.

At 11-years-old, Louis began Jefferson Grade School in America. His languages were Latvian, Russian, German and at home his mother tongue was Ashkenazi-German Yiddish. He had yet to master English. Before classes began, he tried to learn a few words from Cousins Helen and Rebecca Hoddes, his Aunt Rochel's daughters, but found English spelling and pronunciation illogical.

"Why isn't 'snow' pronounced like 'now'?" he cried. "It should be 'snauw'."

His knowledge of languages probably made it easier for him to learn English, for within a few years his English was excellent. On his first day of school, the principal needed to place him in his proper grade. However, Louis couldn't understand her questions.

He was asked, "How much is 7 and 8?"

Louis thought she had asked, "How much is 7 times 8?" and answered, "56."

That answer told her to place him in 4th grade. For the longest time, though, he thought he was in the 3rd grade. Louis saved most of his report cards. He attended the Gales School from grades 6 through 8 and graduated *Cum Laude*.

Initially, his grades were only average but his deportment was always excellent. As his English improved, so did his grades. He soon became an E (Excellent) student academically.

Yet, when he brought home his report cards, his father would say, "There is only one E in each square. I see room for at least two."

His father expected excellence yet never praised him for it. Yet to his buddies in *shul* (synagogue), Benjamin would show the report card to everyone and *kvell* (brag) with pride. This may be why my father rarely praised my own achievements directly. I think he was afraid I would stop working hard. It wasn't until I was an adult that I heard someone tell me how my father would boast about me to them, but to my face – never.

As for my mother, she had no reservations about telling me when she was pleased. My talents went in the direction of art, not math or science. Since my father was excellent in both, he could not understand why I had difficulties. When I was in grade school, I made the mistake of asking him to help me understand long division. He sat me down to see how I was approaching the problem.

Within a few moments he complained, "Your way doesn't make any sense to me. This is how you should do it."

He then wrote an upside down curlicue and zip, zip, zip came up with the answer. I had no idea what he was doing.

"That's not the way the teacher told us to do it." I moaned. "What is that strange upside-down sign?"

"This is the way I learned to do it in Latvia and it's the easiest way to do it. I still do it this way today."

I gave up in tears and he gave up in exasperation. That was the last time I asked him to help me.

Honor Thy Father and Thy Mother

Babe, my father's youngest sibling, was the only one born in the United States. Officially, his name was Israel, but being the baby of the family, he was forever known as Babe, which later annoyed his wife, Myra. She was the only one who called him "Iz." As the last remaining sibling, he died December 28, 2003, at the age of 93. The way my father told it, Babe was born in 1910, nine months after my grandmother and the nine children arrived in America. Now the family once again totaled ten children.

Somehow, my grandparents managed to raise all those children without Dr. Spock. Discipline was left to Grandma. Grandpa never hit any of them. Actually, she never hit them either. She relied on a *ritter* (a thin bundle of twigs tied together with a string). The ritter hung prominently on the wall for all to see. If a child misbehaved, she would point to the ritter and say, "Do I need to use that on your *tush* (back side)?"

Considering that my grandfather was so religious, it would have been natural to expect him to be autocratic, but he was not. His view of life and family was very pragmatic. Discipline was maintained by the enormous respect and love that the children had for their parents, who were always approachable. It was so important not to disappoint them that the worst punishment was having their father say, *"far a Yid, past dos nit,"* meaning in Yiddish, it was "unbecoming for a Jew to behave that way."

When the children left home, he never questioned their ritual observances. He might not eat in their homes, but he would never reproach them for their relaxed kosher kitchens. His excuse for not eating was, "I'm not really hungry. Maybe a glass of tea." The one thing he occasionally did eat in my parents' kosher home was ice cream. I guess he knew that commercial ice cream was not prepared with meat.

Louis' brother Sol used to work at Kitty's and Al's canteen from about 1920 to 1932. Once at about 1:30 PM, there was only a soldier left, eating ice cream in the back room. Sol was preparing a ham and egg sandwich for his lunch. Just then Benjamin unexpectedly stopped in.

Seeing Sol taste something on the griddle, he asked, "*Shmect gut?* (Taste good?)"

Upon seeing the frying pan he asked, "For whom are you making this?"

Thinking fast, Sol pointed to the soldier. When the food was ready, he took it to the soldier, who protested that he did not order it.

"Take it, it's on the house," Sol told him.

Benjamin must have known that the meat was not kosher. Whether or not he believed the story that the meal was for the soldier is debatable, but it was quite characteristic for him to say nothing about it.

One day Benjamin came to see Louis and Sol in a third floor office they shared for a time. After the visit he left to go downstairs. My father assumed he would take the elevator. When he escorted his father out the office door, he watched him head for the winding stairs.

"What are you doing, Pa?" he asked. "Let me call for the elevator."

"No, don't do that," he replied. "When I came I had to use the elevator. I couldn't climb up three flights of stairs, but I don't want to bother the elevator man now. I can walk down by myself."

And so he did. Neither Benjamin nor Louis ever asked anyone to do something he could possibly do himself. My father would annoy us at the dinner table by getting up for something rather than asking for it to be passed.

Driving on the Sabbath was a strict no-no. In later years, during tax season, Saturday was the only day when my father took a brief rest from work to visit his father. Grandpa had to know that my father did not walk seven miles to drop in for a spot of tea. My father was careful to park the car around the corner and walk the rest of the way to the apartment. He would be greeted with all the warmth and affection that an old man could extend to a busy son who took the trouble to visit after working day and night. Never would he ever suggest that my father had done anything wrong. They would sit together, kibitz in Yiddish about this and that and tell each other jokes. Since I couldn't understand Yiddish, I rarely went along. If I had been a fly on the wall, I might have heard my grandfather tell this joke.

GABRIEL

Jake dies, goes to heaven and meets Gabriel who gives him a tour. They come to a big gate, which Gabriel opens. Jake sees lots of people, some dancing, playing cards, gambling, etc. Gabriel closes the gate and Jake asks him who those people were. Gabriel says they are the Reform Jews. Then they go on to another big gate. He opens it and Jake sees the people there are more demure, reading, studying, debating and quietly dancing, but no gambling or rowdiness. Gabriel closes the gate and tells Jake those people are Conservative Jews. A third gate appears and before he opens it, Gabriel tells Jake that they must be very quiet. Gabriel opens the gate and Jake sees all the people are studying, praying seriously and discussing the Bible. No TV, dancing or any amusements. When Jake asks who are those people, Gabriel says they are the very Orthodox who are so religious that they think they are the only ones in heaven.

Yiddish was rarely spoken in our house, only when my parents didn't want me to know what they were saying. Occasionally, though, they would decide this was a significant lack in my education and carried on a conversation in hopes that I would pick it up by osmosis. When they tried to "teach" it to me, I would put my hands over my ears and refuse to listen.

"That is why you never learned it," they admonished.

The fact that my Mother's Yiddish was not that good was beside the point. She could understand it pretty well, but her speaking left something to be desired. While I picked up some phrases and expressions, it was only when I was in high school that I felt I was missing something. I wanted to understand my grandfather. For two years, I studied German for just that reason and did manage to get the gist of their conversations. German was just close enough to Yiddish for that to be useful. Unfortunately, by the time I had achieved some limited proficiency, Grandpa died. I forgot German altogether.

How did the Grossberg family manage to survive, with a father and mother who couldn't speak English and ten children to feed? My grandfather Benjamin (or Bunim to everyone) could not have made it without the help of his children. There were no safety nets then. Immigrant families could not rely on one breadwinner, since most of the parents were not native English speakers.

Grandpa got a job as an agent in the Hebrew Relief Society, where Yiddish was commonly spoken, a job my father took over in later years. It paid him 25% of what he collected, which earned him $6.00 a week. Louis helped out with collections after school, usually speeding along on one roller skate – a skill he picked up in Latvia no doubt. I don't know if he ever had the luxury of using two skates. When Louis was not in school or collecting money for the Hebrew Relief Society, he was selling apples, oranges, gum and shoe strings on the street. He learned the importance of maintaining the rights to "his" corner.

In fact, all the children helped to earn money in any way they could.

When money was saved, the family moved to a small three-story row-house on K Street, NW between 6th and 7th Streets. One or two of the upstairs bedrooms were used for paying guests who wanted kosher food and a few days of lodging. In that way, Sarah Henna contributed to the family coffers.

On one occasion, a guest who was familiar with the junk business suggested to Grandpa that if he would invest about $100.00 they could open a junk shop in partnership. Though $6.00 a week in those days kept a family from starving, it did little to ensure their prosperity. Grandpa agreed and the two men rented a store on the corner of 6th and K Streets and called it Chicago Junk Company.

After a year or so, the partner left and Benjamin was in business by himself. Grandpa needed his eldest daughter, Esther, to help run the business. Esther was seventeen when she arrived in America and stayed in school the shortest time, so she was only marginally useful in the shop. She had little opportunity to learn to write or spell English properly. She was also the most *frum* (pious), and in 1917, she married Harry Abrams, a very religious man who boarded at their house when visiting from New York. He was also in the junk business and dealt with my grandfather's shop on a regular basis.

Another guest was young Rabbi Yalow, or "Yale," as he preferred to be called. Although he had *Smicha* as a *Rav* (was ordained as a rabbi), he preferred to be a businessman. He had experience in the wholesale bag business, bags that held coffee beans, sugar, nuts, etc. He induced Grandpa to open a side business with him and call it the Grossberg Yale Bag Co. He didn't want to use his own name. The Rabbi Yalow Bag Company didn't have quite the right ring to it.

In 1917–1918, Louis drove a Model T Ford light truck and traveled throughout nearby Maryland buying feedbags and burlap from farmers. Farmers knew rotting bags were worthless and didn't mind if Louis tried to tear them. Yalow bought mixed bags from junk shops and taught Louis to distinguish the different grades. The bags were then sorted and shipped to wholesalers. Coffee beans came in bags worth five times as much as bags containing potatoes. There was a distinct profit involved in knowing the difference between mixed burlap bags and bags of the same kind.

Before Esther's marriage in 1917, her *tnoyim* (engagement party) was held at the home of her parents, where a table was set up for about 20 people. Among those attending the festivities were a number of rabbis, including Rabbi Yalow. Some of the people made speeches and Rabbi Yalow decided to say a few words. He was a brilliant man, and with great ease pointed to each person in the room and made up a rhyme about each one. Sometime later, one of the other attending rabbis, Gadalya Silverstein, wrote a book entitled, *Speeches I Made*. Included among his speeches was the speech Yale made at the engagement party.

When Yale found this out, he said to my grandfather, "From whom did this rabbi steal a speech? From a bagman!"

I Am the Lord Thy God

The first synagogue the family joined was Ohev Shalom at 5th and I Street, NW. The service was Orthodox, all in Hebrew, and Rabbi Silverstone, the city rabbi, mostly functioned as its rabbi. When Benjamin wanted to move his junk shop to larger quarters, he found a site on 5th Street, right next door to Ohev Shalom. A coal yard had been located there before, but they had vacated the premises and the space was available for rental. DC law required that no junk shop could be housed in a location without the approval of the nearby neighbors, so the synagogue had to give its approval.

Benjamin went to the powers-that-be to get their consent, but they refused. Why? They were afraid that a junk shop would disturb their Sabbath prayers.

Benjamin said, "Look, I am a member of this congregation. My shop would be closed on *Shabbos* (religious way of pronouncing Shabbat, meaning Sabbath) and on every other Jewish holiday."

"No," they said, "promises are not enough," and they refused to allow his junk shop to move next door.

Benjamin was so incensed that he left the synagogue and moved the whole family a block away to Adas Israel Congregation on 6th and I Street, which later became the most important Conservative synagogue in the city. At the time, the new synagogue was almost as Orthodox as the prior one and Benjamin was happy. He became the *shammas* (sexton), and worked at that job until his retirement.

As a boy, Louis was a member of the Choir at Adas Israel, and Mr. Glushak was the cantor. One day Benjamin asked the cantor how Louis was doing in the choir.

"He's a bum like the rest of the bums," the cantor replied as several people were standing around.

He said this because some of the kids threw spitballs and misbehaved during rehearsals, though he didn't know which ones and obviously didn't care. My father claimed he never did this, but to Mr. Glushak, everyone was guilty. The accusation was a great insult to Benjamin and when he got home he slapped Louis. This was the only time he ever laid a finger on him.

Mr. Glushak went on to become a Rabbi. His son, Dave, and daughter, Fanny, played prominent roles in my parents' lives in years to come. Rabbi Glushak even officiated at the wedding of Louis and Celia.

Thou Shalt Not Take the Lord's Name in Vain

In 1911, Louis prepared for his bar mitzvah. On the appointed day, Louis was treated to an extra piece of cake for dinner. There were no parties, no gifts and certainly no big fuss over the event. Not like what goes on today. With the bar mitzvah over, he was now a man, at least religiously speaking.

As was his custom, Benjamin went to Synagogue every day. Synagogue life was often stimulating and Benjamin was highly involved as the *shammas*. As an adult, Louis was frequently involved as well.

Rabbi Silverstone officiated at Ohev Shalom, the 5th and I Streets Synagogue, which was strictly orthodox. One day the rabbi decided he would like to live in Palestine and left Washington, DC. His stay in Palestine was brief and when he returned to Washington, he attended services at Adas Israel Synagogue at 6th and I Streets.

When the President of the congregation saw him, he invited the rabbi to sit on the dais. Similarly, when Benjamin Grossberg saw Rabbi Silverstone attending his Talmud class, he invited him to teach the class. Benjamin felt that the students might prefer to be taught Talmud by a rabbi. He was only the shammas, though probably more qualified to teach Talmud than this Rabbi.

The Talmud class attendees must have disagreed with Benjamin, because they did not like the change and complained to the President that they wanted Mr. Grossberg to continue teaching. His response was that they had to take it up with the board of governors.

Timing is everything and it happened to be *Rosh Hashanah* – the Jewish New Year, when it is customary to blow the *Shofar*, or ram's horn, during services at the synagogue. At Adas Israel, the number of blasts on the Shofar was about 20, whereas at more orthodox synagogues the number was 100. Rabbi Silverstone, sitting on the dais and noting the cessation of blasts made a fuss, insisting that 80 more were in order. He was politely asked by the President to sit down.

Ten days later was *Yom Kippur* – the Day of Atonement – and shortly thereafter a meeting of the synagogue. Two complaints were offered and discussed. One, that Rabbi Silverstone should not be permitted to sit on the dais because he disrupted the *Rosh Hashanah* service and another, regarding the daily Talmud class, that it should not be taught by Rabbi Silverstone, but by Mr. Grossberg. These two items were expressed in the form of resolutions. Louis, as the recording secretary, was asked to take care of the matter of the resolutions.

After much deliberation, Louis decided to write two letters. On November 8, 1923, he sent the first to Mr. M. Garfinkle, President of *Agudas Hakhilos* – the organization of Jewish congregations:

"It has come to the attention of the Adas Israel Congregation, 6th & I Sts. NW that Rabbi G. Silverstone has returned to this city and desires to become the officiating rabbi of Washington. It is noted that a mass meeting has been arranged under the auspices of Agudas Hakhilos to be held at the Fourteenth Street Shul on next Sunday for the purpose of taking action in this matter.

"You are hereby advised that the Adas Israel Congregation is unalterably opposed to the election of Rabbi Silverstone to this post. Furthermore, this Congregation desires it to be distinctly understood that as a member of the Agudas Hakhilos it disapproves the action of that body in calling a mass meeting on Sunday for the purpose stated; that it deems any election of that meeting illegal and without force; and that it will not recognize Rabbi Silverstone as Chief Rabbi of Washington in the event of his being elected.

"By direction of the Board of Directors"

The second letter was sent to Rabbi Silverstone. Louis tried to be diplomatic:

Please be advised that at a meeting of the board of Governors of the Adas Israel Congregation, 6th & I Sts., NW, the following resolutions were passed:

1. Resolved that no persons other than President and Vice President and the officiating Rabbi and Cantors of the Congregation shall be permitted to occupy a seat on the Rostrum of our Synagogue during *Shabbat* (Sabbath) and Holiday Services. The Secretary is directed to advise Rabbi Silverstone that the Chair previously occupied by him will be removed from the Rostrum in accordance with the terms of this resolution.

2. Whereas it appears that in accordance with his usual custom Mr. B. Grossberg is contemplating resigning his leadership in the study of the Torah on Saturday and Week Day afternoons in favor of Rabbi Silverstone and, Whereas, a number of members of this Congregation have voiced a preference for Mr. Grossberg's leadership, be it therefore, Resolved that the duties of Mr. B. Grossberg, the Shammas of this Congregation be and they hereby are increased to include the teaching of the Torah to all members desiring to take advantage thereof, as has been his practice for the last few months.

The Secretary is instructed to advise Mr. B. Grossberg and Rabbi G. Silverstone of this resolution.

Rabbi Silverstone was never seen again at Adas Israel.

After Pop heard me read the letters of November 23, 1923, he told one of Benjamin's jokes. Until then, I had no idea my grandfather had such a sense of humor:

THE GUEST

A traveling salesman stayed overnight in various places but always went home for Shabbat. Friday morning as he was ready to leave, the innkeeper said,

"My daughter is to be married tomorrow evening and I very much want you to attend."

The sales clerk said, "I am very sorry but I can't stay because my wife is expecting me home for Shabbat."

The innkeeper replied that he would send a messenger to inform the man's wife that her husband would not be home because he would be attending a wedding. The salesman agreed. In order to stay for the wedding he had to remain in the inn two extra nights. When the wedding was over and he prepared to leave, the innkeeper presented him with a bill, which included charges for the extra two nights. The salesman protested loudly that he had only stayed the two extra nights to be able to attend the wedding to which he had been invited and didn't think it was fair to charge him for this.

The innkeeper said that the guest had stayed two extra nights and used the services and food of the lodging place and he must pay. Finally, the innkeeper said to the salesman that even though he insisted on payment, he was willing for both of them to go to see the local rabbi and let him be the judge. The salesman agreed.

When they told the rabbi the story, the rabbi said that there was no question that the guest must pay the bill since he had used the innkeeper's services. The guest was very unhappy but he paid the innkeeper and departed for home. After about half an hour, the innkeeper rode up to the salesman on his horse and gave him back the money for the extra two nights. The salesman was astonished and even a little angry.

"Why did you carry on so about my owing you for the extra days and even involved the rabbi in our disagreement when you planned to give me back my money? What kind of a trick is this?"

The innkeeper replied, "I just wanted to show you what kind of a rabbi we have in this town."

Until Sarah Henna could no longer accompany him, she joined Benjamin at synagogue, too. But at the age of 80, my grandmother passed away. During the last days of her life, Grandpa would sit with her, and pray to God that it was time to take her. He could not bear to see her suffer. It was 1948 and I was at summer camp. I remember visiting them before I left. She did not know me. I watched my grandfather sitting by her bedside, holding her hand. By now, he was the only one she still recognized, and it gave her comfort to know he was there. I was speaking to my cousin Hillel Abrams one day and asked him some questions about our grandparents. He told me that years ago, he lived a few blocks away from them and it was easy to visit Grandma and Grandpa frequently. His strongest recollections were also of them sitting together on the sofa holding hands. Grandma died on *Rosh Chodesh Av* (the first day of the Hebrew month *Av*).

When Sarah Henna died, Grandpa called my father on the phone and reminded him that for 25 years before her passing, she accompanied him to the synagogue every weekday morning, rain or shine and sat in front of a little mahogany table on which she rested her *Siddur* (prayer book). One day, he noticed the table had a broken leg. Grandpa asked Pop if he could have it fixed because he wanted to keep it for sentimental reasons. My father knew that Louie Barnes, an excellent cabinetmaker, could do the job and took the table to his shop on Rockville Pike, in Maryland.

Two weeks later, Barnes called Pop to say his shop had suffered a catastrophic fire. It was so hot it melted his metal roof, steel lathes, steel saws, and every stitch of lumber and cabinet work on the premises. The only thing left standing unharmed, was my grandmother's mahogany table that he had repaired. "What the Hell got into that table, I don't know. Come pick it up. I don't want to touch it!" So my father promptly retrieved the table.

After a time, Grandpa was terribly lonely. He was ten years older than she, but still in good health. He dreaded a future alone without his beloved wife. Finally, he decided the answer to his problem was companionship. The only proper thing to do was to marry again, by which time he was 98-years-old. How many women do you think were waiting in the wings for just this sort of opportunity?

The synagogue continued to offer him solace. There, Benjamin learned of a widow who might be amenable to a proposal. She was 83, a mere spring chicken. Contrary to what people might have thought, his children had no objections. The wedding was a very private affair. However, it didn't take Benjamin long to realize his new wife was nothing like Sarah Henna.

When he heard people ask about the new Mrs. Grossberg, he answered, "*Vu kump sie, Mrs. Grossberg*?" Meaning: "She's not Mrs. Grossberg. She will *never* be Mrs. Grossberg!"

His new wife complained to Louis, Sol, Babe and a grandson, Hillel, that her husband would not leave her alone. Shortly thereafter, Benjamin went to Hillel and then to Sol, both lawyers, and said, "What can

I do with her? She is impossible to live with. I want a divorce." Somehow Sol talked him out of it, but soon afterwards she left to live with her children.

"Good riddance." Benjamin said.

Within two years she died. Problem solved.

In 1944 Benjamin Grossberg retired as the *shammas* of Adas Israel Congregation. His eyesight was failing and he could no longer conduct the *Minchah* (afternoon) and *Maariv* (evening) services. He also had to leave the group of about a dozen men who attended his daily Talmud classes.

Benjamin asked the president, Joe Wilner, for severance pay of $5,000. Wilner replied, "Why are you entitled to a pension? You got paid while you were working and now that you are not working, you're not entitled to any money." Benjamin was then 85-years-old and asked to speak to the board of governors and this was arranged. He told the board that for 22 years he rendered services far beyond what was required by his job as shammas. He mentioned the money saved by taking over duties the Synagogue previously had to pay for, like for part time helpers, which amounted to far beyond the $5,000 he was requesting.

Benjamin was then asked to leave the room while the board took up the matter. The board rejected the appeal for $5,000 but taking his age into consideration, voted him a pension of $150 a month for life. This was accepted.

At the end of his life, Benjamin lived alone with full-time care. He lost his eyesight, but never complained. His children visited him regularly, did everything necessary to make him comfortable, and went to great lengths to hide the expense of his nursing care. He still believed prices had changed little over the past 30 years. Had he known the truth, he would have refused to accept it. Louis, Sol and Miriam paid his bills. In the end, he made out much better than the synagogue board anticipated, because he lived to be 104, an additional 19 years, and received a total of $34,200 over that period.

Perhaps Pop would have told the following joke here:

THE GIFT

A rabbi, who was greatly beloved by his flock, was given a valuable gift every year. One year, they ran out of ideas of what to give the rabbi, and one of the members came up with the story that he saw an ad where a mechanical horse was advertised for sale. After investigating, the committee decided to buy the horse, and told the rabbi they had a horse for him.

"What am I going to do with a horse? I have no stable to lodge him nor do I know how to take care of a horse." The chairman then trotted out the mechanical horse, and told the rabbi that no food and no stable were required.

"All you need do is get up on the horse and use 4 words. To make him trot say, danken Gott *(thank God). To make him gallop say,* danken Gott, danken Gott, *and to make him stop say,* oy gevalt *(oh what calamity)." To try it out the rabbi got on the horse, said* danken Gott *and the horse trotted along, being steered by the reins.*

"That's great," said the rabbi and he decided to really try out the horse the next day. Bright and early the following morning, the rabbi got on the horse and said, "danken Gott," to which the horse responded beautifully. He trotted along for a while, heading for the countryside, where he really wanted to do some galloping. "Danken Gott, danken Gott," said the rabbi and the mechanical horse raced quite a distance. To try out the stop, he said, "oy gevalt" and the horse came to a sliding stop. Satisfied, the rabbi continued at a fast gallop until suddenly he saw a big ditch in front of him and yelled, "oy gevalt." The horse again responded with a sliding stop two inches before the precipice. Drying his perspiration, he then said, "danken Gott."

In 1962, a year before Grandpa died, Rabbi Kotler came back to Washington, DC. This was 47 years after he had stayed at my grandparents' home while raising funds for his institution. The rabbi remembered Benjamin Grossberg and learned he was still alive at the age of 103. He inquired if someone in the Grossberg family would lend a kosher home for one evening where he could speak to the rabbis of the community. He was informed Pop had the right home.

My father picked up the rabbi at the train station, where a multitude of rabbis had come to greet him. My father was asked if it would be possible to visit my grandfather. Pop said yes and took him to Grandpa's apartment where he lived with nursing care.

Grandpa remembered Rabbi Kotler and said he was happy to see him because he was very disturbed by something and hoped the good rabbi could put his mind at ease. What was the problem?

Grandpa said, "It is written that when a person reaches the age of 100 he is *putter fun mitzvos* (meaning, he is no longer required to observe the religious obligations of a Jew). Secondly, if a person uses the name of the *Oberster* (God) in vain, it is a *neveira* (a sin). All my life I have observed all the religious commandments and tried passionately not to sin, but here I am, over 100-years-old, sinning before the Lord. I can not put a morsel of food in my mouth without washing my hands and making a *Bracha* (a blessing) – and therefore using the name of the Lord. Since I am no longer required to make this Bracha, I am using the name of the Lord in vain and thereby sinning. Is it my fault I am still alive?"

The rabbi listened patiently and finally said, "It is true that when a person reaches the age of 100 he is putter von mitzvos. Before the age of 100, the burden of proof is on him to show he is unable to perform the *mitzvoth* (commandments). After he reaches 100, the burden of proof switches. He now is presumed to be unable to perform the mitzvoth and thus is not required to do so. The mistake you make is in thinking you are not permitted to pray after age 100. If you are able, you are certainly allowed to perform all the mitzvoth required of persons less than 100, and if you do so you are not sinning." This was a tremendous relief to Grandpa.

Then my father showed Rabbi Kotler the table that had survived the fire, telling him the story of the fire. He asked the rabbi's opinion of how such a thing could have occurred. Quick as a flash the rabbi said, "The answer is simple. I will give you two reasons. Number one, you fight fire with fire. There was so much fire in that table at which your wife prayed for 25 years, the fire in the table was stronger than the fire in the shop so it could not burn. Secondly, God looks after those who truly and honestly observe his commandments."

Rabbi Kotler well remembered my grandmother and what a pious and wonderful woman she was. "There is no doubt God looked after her property and wouldn't allow anything to happen to it."

After Grandpa died, Pop put the table in his recreation room and now that he is gone, it resides in our daughter Judy's house. If you look underneath it, you can see scorch marks.

Sometime in the 1700s, the Kansteroom family immigrated to Palestine and settled in Jaffa. Turkey, then part of the Ottoman Empire, was in control of Palestine until General Allenby and the British forces defeated them in 1917. The British were granted control by the League of Nations in 1919. This Mandate ended with the creation of the State of Israel, May 14, 1948.

Papa was born in Jerusalem at a time when there were only 2,000 people in the city, most of them Jews. Jacob, known to all as Papa, had a great sense of humor. I don't remember him telling jokes as such but his stock in trade was to play harmless pranks on other members of the family. He had a great rapport with the nephew and cousins of his wife, Paula. They constantly played tricks on each other. Just listening to him talk had everyone laughing. From where he got his sense of humor, we don't know. Jules and I lived in Israel for 30 years and as far as we could tell, none of the other family members there could match him.

My mother, Celia Kanster was born September 10, 1902 or 1903. She was the second child. The first child, a boy, died of brain fever when he was 1-year-old – most likely from meningitis, although perhaps from what was then called "summer complaint," a gastro-intestinal ailment most likely caused by contaminated milk. Her family lived at the time in a tenement flat on Manhattan's heavily Jewish Lower East Side.

There is some question about Celia's date of birth. She claimed that when her mother was questioned during the census her English was poor and she gave incorrect information. Celia's birth certificate was reissued on December 9, 1952, probably for passport purposes. The Certificate of Birth says it was a delayed registration. It shows Celia Kanster's date of birth as September 10, 1902. Place of birth: 144 Monroe St., New York. Mother: Pauline Berger, Age: 22, Birthplace: Russia, Occupation: housewife, Father: Jacob Kanster, Age: 25, Birthplace: Palestine, Occupation: sheet metal worker, Total number of children born alive prior to this one: one. Jacob Kanster signed it, December 3, 1952. Celia may never have had an original birth certificate.

Coincidentally, both of my sets of grandparents lost a child who died very young.

In order to apply for a birth certificate from the Bureau of Vital Statistics, Celia furnished them with her parents' marriage certificate. It showed that she was the daughter of Jacob and Caroline Konsta (Pauline Kanster), and that she was 3-years-old in 1905. At that time, the family lived in Spring Valley, New York.

In those days Spring Valley was an isolated area in the country and the school was very far away. Originally, Celia and her sister Edith, who was 13 months younger, were put in the same class because they only spoke Yiddish. After Celia learned enough English, she was put in her proper grade. Cousin Perry Hamburg remembers his mother, Sarah, saying the children then had to speak only English at home because their mother insisted upon it, no doubt influenced by the girls' problems at school.

After Sarah was born in 1907, the Kanster family moved to Paterson, New Jersey where Ruthie was born in 1909. From there they briefly settled in Newark – New Jersey's predominantly Italian and very tough North Ward. On the first day of school, Edith got into a serious fist fight after a classmate from the notorious LaMorte family ridiculed "Kanster" as "can of tomatoes," making Edith go ballistic.

The Federal Census of 1910 shows Celia, daughter of Jake and Pauline Kanster, age 8 years, born in New York. Regardless of whether Celia was born in 1902 or 1903, at least September 10 was accepted as her birthday. She herself claimed it was in 1903, since her parents were married in 1900 and there had been one child born before her.

My maternal grandfather, Papa (Jacob Kanster), was born about 1877. It is believed that his Sephardic forebears left Spain during the Spanish Inquisition in the 1490s, when everyone had to convert to Catholicism or leave Spain. Various countries welcomed the Jews, like Greece, Turkey, Yemen, Egypt and Holland. Papa's family fled to Holland, where the Kanster name picked up the "-oom" to become Kansteroom.

I found my grandmother's naturalization certificate, issued to Pauline Kanster nee Berger, September 28, 1914. She was 39-years-old. Height: 5'7"; Color of hair: Black; Residing at: Paterson, NJ; Children: Celia age 12, Edith age 10, Sarah age 7, Ruth age 5 and George age 2; Husband, Jacob Kanster; Issued in: Passaic County; Previous subject of: Turkey.

Jacob recalled to my cousin Harry Hamburg his experiences growing up in Jerusalem in the 1880s and 1890s. The problems between the

Jews and the Arabs went back a long time. When the Jewish children were let out of school, the Arab men sitting on the parapets would take pot shots at them as they ran through the streets. This was done for sport. Jacob and his brother Louis were short in stature but ran very fast. They took off first and ran in zigzag fashion through the alleys at top speed. While the Arab riflemen leaned over trying to get a good shot, other boys would dash up to the roof and push the Arabs over the ledge. At least, that was the story.

Jacob Kanster was asthmatic and could not tolerate the climate in Palestine. The blowing sand was a constant irritant. In the late 1890s, he left a large family behind, including three sisters, but no one there to carry on the Kansteroom name. He and his two brothers immigrated to the United States.

Jake, as some called him, spent a year or so in Paris before coming to America. There he worked in a leather tannery and lived in what was essentially a flophouse for young single Jewish men. He had fun cavorting with Parisian women during that exciting "Belle Epoch" period, but would never be more specific about those days. Pity.

In 1898, when the Spanish-American War broke out, Jacob tried to enlist in the United States army but was rejected. Probably because of his asthma.

Jacob remained very close to his brother Louie and they both eventually settled in Passaic, New Jersey. Upon his arrival in America, his name was shortened to Kanster, though other members of his family retained the name Kansteroom. Jacob and Louie set up a business making pots and pans from copper and tin. His tinsmith trade began as a sheet metal worker, installing gutters and leaders on Jerusalem roofs.

Prohibition entered the picture with the signing into law of the Volstead Act, authored by Andrew J. Volstead. The 18th Amendment to the Constitution enacted in January 16, 1920 ushered in a bonanza for business and criminal activity that lasted for 13 years. Like thousands of others during this time, Jacob and Louie took advantage of this opportunity to add another dimension to their trade. They made "stills" for the illegal bootlegging of liquor.

When Revenue Officers traced the stills to Jacob and Louis, the men struck a deal. They agreed to become informers. The brothers were smart enough to realize that they had created a cottage industry. They would manufacture the equipment, install it, and then give the police the location. The police would raid the stills, destroy them and the bootleggers would return to their source for more equipment. A nice business, no? It never occurred to the bootleggers where the police got their information.

Perry recalled Papa saying that during one of his deliveries, Pauline accompanied him. A traffic cop who noticed the illicit cargo in the back of the truck stopped them, but Pauline magically talked him into letting them go.

After Prohibition was repealed, Louie and Jacob moved to Newark, New Jersey. Louie opened a shop selling coal-burning stoves for heating and cooking. Jacob started a company with his new son-in-law Sam Hamburg to make tin and copper items for home and industry. The factory name was the Kanster-Hamburg Manufacturing Company. Considering the connections they made during prohibition, Papa was able to expand on those contacts. Tavern owners needed to keep their beer chilled so he supplied them with beer coolers.

By all accounts, Jacob's wife, Paula, was an excellent cook. Every weekend, relatives would descend just to taste her delicacies. On one particular Sunday morning, the bell rang and there they were. They had come from Brooklyn. Traveling back and forth to 842 Hunterdon Street, in Newark, New Jersey, was not a simple thing. They had to take an elevated train to New York and another train to New Jersey.

These visits were often unannounced. They just appeared at the door and were welcomed with open arms. Though the children were saddled with helping in the kitchen, they didn't mind because they knew they were in for a treat. When evening approached, Uncle Louie Cohen and Cousins Morris Shapiro and Henry Berger, prepared to leave for the train. It was wintertime and Papa brought their overcoats.

Once on the train, they settled in for the ride home but the train was crowded and they could not sit together. Soon, a passenger in front of Uncle Louie moved so Cousin Henry took that seat. Then the passenger next to Louie left and Morris joined him. Within a few more minutes, the people in front and in back moved also. The men looked around to see if there was something better to be seen out the windows a few rows away or across the aisle. It was then they sensed something amiss.

"Do you smell that?" Morris asked, when he became aware of an incredibly bad odor. "Where is it coming from?"

They looked around and at each other. Nothing was suspicious. After a while more people moved away.

"We better move too," said Henry, but each time they moved, others moved too.

The smell in the train was overpowering. They were relieved to arrive at their destination and descended from the train. It was very cold and they had escaped at last. When they got to Henry's house, his mother sniffed the air.

"What did you step in?" she asked, "What is that horrible smell?"

With that, the men examined each other more thoroughly. In Louie's coat pocket was a little package neatly wrapped and tied with a string.

"Ah," said Louie, "that's just leftovers from lunch."

Paula often gave them a small bag to take along on the train. After all, they might get hungry.

"Open it up," said their mother.

Sure enough it was food. It was Katchkeval cheese. This cheese is a mild delicacy when fried up in Paula's kitchen and was much prized by her family. However, in its raw state, like Limburger, it is uncommonly foul smelling.

Papa thought it would make a nice, if humorous, parting gift.

My mother, Celia, neither kept memorabilia of her childhood nor any records of past events, as had my father, Louis. I always knew she was very artistic, a trait she probably inherited from both her parents. Her father was a tinsmith, and her mother, the family dressmaker. Her father by now had his own factory, where he produced various things like radiator covers, kitchen cabinets and children's lunch boxes. Mom regretted not keeping even a lunch box as a memento.

Her mother, Paula, recognized quality when she saw it. She was also an excellent seamstress and made all the children's clothing including coats. She even made her own wedding dress. Whenever she bought material, if she could only afford to make one new garment, it had to be made with the best fabric available.

When Celia was 10-years-old in grade school, she won a statewide contest to design a pattern for use in all the New Jersey schools. Her Dogwood blossoms, the State national flower, was chosen and reproduced on all the curtains and stationery throughout the school system. Her woodcut hung in the principal's office for years. Unfortunately, she did not keep a sample of that either.

Celia grew up appreciating and collecting all objects of art and learned to tell what was worth owning and what was not. Her instincts were remarkable. She had a knack for spotting which artists' work to collect before they were recognized by the art world.

My mother had limited art instruction but was so naturally talented that she painted beautifully, made gorgeous flowers from Formosa wood fiber and expressed herself in many artistic endeavors. All the things she valued, she made sure I took lessons to learn. From my earliest memories, she schlepped me to art classes, drama classes and even swimming lessons.

She regretted never learning to swim. Louis learned as a child and even saved the life of one of his cousins. When 17-years-old, he and his cousin Sol Naiman went to Ocean City for a vacation. Sol was a big, strong and very powerfully built young man. He had once lifted a horse up by its front feet. The day was hot and the water looked inviting, so the pair rented a canoe and went boating. When they had gotten out a ways, Louis decided to take a dip.

He knew Sol could not swim so he said, "It's not deep here. I'll go in and see if it's safe."

While in general it was not deep in that particular area, dredging had been done to replenish the beach and it was very deep indeed. When Louis jumped in, he found to his great surprise that he could not stand up.

"Sol," he yelled when he came up, "Don't jump in, it's too deep, I can't touch bottom!"

With that, Sol panicked and immediately leaped into the water. Louis was dumbfounded. Why would Sol do such a stupid thing? Sol began to thrash about wildly, gulping water and screaming for dear life. Fortunately, by the time Louis reached him, Sol was unconscious, which was lucky because Sol was at least twice Louis' weight and a good 6 inches taller. During his struggle to save Sol, he was afraid they both would drown. With Sol passed out, though, Louis was able to bring him to shore where he was resuscitated. The canoe, however, floated away. After hearing this story, my mother decided I must have swimming lessons.

Thou Shalt Have No Other Gods Before Me

One day, Rabbi Aaron Kotler came to Washington, DC, for a week to attend a rabbinical conference. He was the Dean of *Beth Midrash Gevoah*, the Rabbinical Graduate School in Lakewood, New Jersey. Naturally, he wanted to stay with my grandparents where he knew the food was kosher. Having rabbis at the house was a delight for Grandpa. He so much enjoyed the long discussions of minute points of Jewish law and history. For instance, the reasons for *kashrut*, or kosher laws, are not explained in the Bible. The law governing which animals can be eaten includes only those which chew their cud and have cloven hoofs. Thus a cow may be eaten but a horse may not. Not one word is said as to why. Most likely, it was to separate the Jewish people from the idolaters around them. While many have their own rationalizations, these are mere speculations. In the words of my grandfather, speculations are not worth a *shuske pulver* (a little powder) – that is, they are worthless.

Before Rabbi Kotler agreed to the lodging arrangements he wanted to ensure that Grandma would accept his room rent because, as he told her, "I am not a charity case and this is not just for one night like on other occasions when you refused to accept any money."

"Rabbi, I will allow you to pay on one condition. You must tell me what you like to eat so that I will prepare your meals to your satisfaction," Sarah Henna said.

"That will be acceptable," replied the rabbi.

Every day he told her what he wanted to eat and Sarah Henna obliged. When the time came for Rabbi Kotler to leave, he asked for the bill.

My grandmother told him, "There is no bill. Put your money back in your pocket, Rabbi. I will not take it."

"What?" cried the Rabbi. "We had an agreement. You promised to accept payment and now you won't. I would never have stayed otherwise."

"I know Rabbi, we had an agreement but I had no intention of taking your money. I said I would take your money on condition that you would tell me what you wanted to eat every day. If I had told you I would not accept your money, you would not have told me what you liked to eat and I wanted you to feel at home."

"But, you promised, Sarah Henna."

"That's right, Rabbi, I promised, but I didn't promise positively."

Of all Louis' siblings, he was closest to his sister, Kitty, two years his senior. At least as children that was the case. Her Yiddish name was Kayla and in all their interactions, they often called each other by pet names. Louis' English name was Louis Cassel, so Kitty shortened it to his initials, L.C. or Lucy. In letters to each other they made up other names depending on the circumstances.

Even if there was a traveling rabbi in the guestroom, Louis and Kitty found ways to do their thing unhindered. They were especially fond of sneaking out on a summer night when everyone was asleep.

Kitty might slip into Louis' bedroom and whisper, "Let's go out for corn."

Louis would immediately get dressed and very quietly they would leave the house. Nearby was an all night fruit and vegetable stand where they bought half a dozen ears of corn. When they returned home they snuck into the kitchen and cooked the corn, laughing and eating together – but very quietly. They must have cleaned up very carefully because as far as Louis knew, no one ever found out.

World War I began in Europe in 1914, and while the United States was not yet involved, Congress was not immune to its implications. Because he needed to work, Louis was very disappointed that he could not participate in the Reserve Officers Training Corp (ROTC). In all Washington high schools the pre-army cadets wore uniforms, used unloaded riffles, and marched in official parades. No doubt the uniforms were a big attraction, especially as far as the girls were concerned, and of course the marching was very impressive. This was considered a very important part of a male student's life. High schools would have contests to determine the best marching unit and by implication, the best high school. Every boy had to join the cadets unless he had an excuse, such as participation in other athletic sports or if he had to work after school. Officers were picked for accomplishments heavily weighted on scholarship. Had he been a cadet, Louis would have been an officer, but he was needed in the family junk shop after school.

Louis was so disappointed he never forgot it. Maybe this led him to revive "The Agora Society," his high school debating team. As president, he organized debates not only in his school but inter-scholastically as well. His grades also had to be kept up. Those good grades became an embarrassment to his brother Sol when he went to high school. The math teacher announced in class one day that Sol's brother Louis, was in her class 8 years earlier and he earned a grade of 110%.

"How do you get more than 100%?" She was asked.

"When I offered 8 problems to be answered out of 10," she replied, "Louis brought in the answer to all 10 correctly."

Sol never forgave Louis for preceding him in school.

Maybe Louis' involvement with The Agora Society was beshert. All through his life he was able to express himself clearly and with great humor. His speeches were masterpieces, as were his letters. During 10 years at summer camp, every day I received a post card or short note from my mother but only once during each season did I receive a letter from my father. Those letters made up for their infrequency by being 10–14 pages long. He could write a fascinating letter without saying anything at all.

The other campers would watch me reading and laughing at my long letter and when I got through they asked, "So what did he say?"

"Nothing," I answered, "but he said it so well."

One of the earliest pieces of writing that Louis saved was a composition he submitted to his English teacher on January 25, 1916, with the teacher's comment – "Very good" scrawled across the top. My father, who came to America without any English turned out to be a better speller than his daughter.

THE LOST ADDRESS

Fritz Preiser, having saved up a sufficient sum of money to join his wife in America, stepped out of the New York customs building in high spirits. It was three years since he had seen his beloved Gretchen and his little baby. Now, that he had come, he must lose no time in getting to them.

He hailed a passing cabman and began fumbling in his pockets for the address. He turned every pocket inside out, but to no avail. The address was gone. Knowing no living soul in that city, he was utterly helpless. Hoping against hope, he asked the cabman whether he knew the address of his wife, but that gentleman, of course, had never heard of Gretchen Preiser. He was driven to a cheap hotel where he remained overnight.

Next morning he went to the German quarter and tried to locate his beloved ones. But all in vain. His wife and child could not be found, try as he might. As he walked the street aimlessly, an idea struck him. He would steal something, or otherwise commit a crime. His wife, reading of his arrest would then come to him. The more he thought of the idea the better he liked it.

Having planned the details of his robbery, he walked into the nearest grocery store and, after purposely glancing from right to left, appropriated a loaf of bread and started for the door. The proprietor, noticing this, called him back and, giving him his sympathies and a dollar bill bade him good-bye and good luck. Not at all daunted, he decided to try again. At the corner he noticed a big automobile. With his penknife he cut one of the tires. The chauffeur, hearing the escape of the air, stepped out of his seat to investigate. To the great surprise of Preiser, the chauffeur handed him a quarter, saying that he gets two dollars for every tire he buys.

At this Fritz became desperate. He swore he would not fail again. He would break one of those large show windows. With a stone in his hand, he proceeded to locate a suitable subject for his vengeance (sic).

He soon found a window to his liking. With all his might he threw the stone at the pane of glass which, naturally, was shattered. A crowd immediately assembled, and before he had decided what to do next, Fritz found himself on the outskirts of the crowd. He tried to force himself to the window and confess his guilt, but he only got some hard knocks for his pains.

Such a state of affairs was entirely unlooked for by him. It had never occurred to him that he would encounter difficulties in obtaining his arrest.

Tired, disappointed, and discouraged, he turned his weary footsteps towards his hotel, where he heard the cry of a child. He turned and saw a pretty little child of scarcely more than four years of age crying for its mother. He took the child in his arms intending to find its house. Suddenly he heard a cry of "Murder! Police! Kidnapers!" At the sound of the voice he turned quickly. "*Ach, Gott!*" he cried, "*Mein Gretchen! Mein Gretchen!*"

By 1919, my Grandparents, Benjamin and Sarah Henna (Effenbach) Grossberg, applied for U.S. citizenship. The original American citizenship Grandpa bought in Latvia was probably not sufficient now. Their Certificate of Naturalization, # 1147605, Volume 30, Number 3016 was found in Pop's old office files after his death. It was for his father and mother. "Sarah, age 49 with husband. Height – 5′4, Color – white, Complexion – dark, Color of eyes – brown, Color of hair – brown. Children at home, Louis – 20, Eleanor – 18, Pauline – 16, Miriam – 14, Solomon – 13, Joseph – 11 and Israel – 8 years; with parents; Benjamin Grossberg, whose previous nationalization was a subject of Russia. Applied March 3, 1919." It was issued on December 30, 1919.

My grandfather's original family name was Kitay. The Kitay name has an interesting background. Between 1534 and 1538, Petrok Maly built fortifications of walls and towers in Moscow. They were the old Kitay-Gorod, built to protect the enlarged population of Moscow in case of a siege. These fortifications resemble the Kremlin. The Kitay-Gorod was a business and commercial center filled with various workshops. Ivan the Terrible later built a bazaar there called Gostinny Dvor. People erroneously thought that the name of Kitay-Gorod was derived from China (Kitay). The real meaning of Kitay comes from an Old Russian word meaning "wattle," a form of construction using slender branches woven around a stout log. Earth and clay was built up around this construction. The word for town was "gorod" which meant fortress. So they named the fortress Kitay.

All the rest of Louis' family retained the Kitay name and a branch of that family lived in Paterson, New Jersey. I have no idea if the family originated from that Russian area, but names were often acquired this way. When people moved from one town to another, their family name became the name of the town from whence they came.

PART TWO

Before They Meet

Louis got his drivers license in 1915. He didn't have a car so one wonders why he needed a license. Maybe it was a popular thing to do since cars were such a novelty. He was 17-years-old. His high school homeroom teacher was Alice Deal, a math teacher, he thought. One day Alice Deal told Louis that she had just bought a new car but didn't know how to drive it yet. She had graduated from a teachers college in Baltimore and wanted to attend a reunion. She asked Louis if he would drive her and he agreed. This was a big honor, being asked by his teacher to drive her new car. I can't imagine that Louis had that much experience but there were few things he thought he could not do. The streets in Baltimore were covered with cobblestones, making driving very difficult. When they arrived, Louis was told to stay a few hours at the home of her friend, an English teacher. While he waited for the reunion to be over, the English teacher asked him how he liked Baltimore. He replied that he didn't like it. She then gave him a lecture about "talking down" someone else's hometown. Alice Deal must have been a very special teacher. The junior high school that I attended in Washington, DC, was named after her.

The first correspondence Louis saved was from his friend David Glushak, son of the rabbi who had caused Louis to get his one and only slap from his father. Dave and Louis became friends in grade school and this warm relationship continued through adulthood. They studied accounting together, went into the Internal Revenue Service together, opened an accounting partnership and tried to make their fortunes together in what was then the first appearance of detergent soap. Nothing turned out quite the way they planned.

This letter was dated February 4, 1915. David must have been a year or two older since he was already in college. He was at a farming and agricultural school and tried to encourage Louis to join him there.

> Dear Louie:
>
> I received your letter and I thank you very much for it. There are quite a lot of things I want to tell you. First. What my cousin told you was bull. If you are a non-resident of the state it costs $20.00 extra that's all. If you have 100 dollars, you can easily get through the first year because you could & would get work to do for your room & board. It costs 10 dollars a semester to register and then it costs for laboratory and books but that's all. No paying the profs. for extra help. They are like boosters for you. Help you all you want. This year it cost me 50 dollars lab fees and books and other incidentals. It will cost you 70 and train fare is 29. Therefore I say it will cost you $100. The summer you can work on a farm as that is required and you can make $80. So you see Abe doesn't know what he talks.

In another letter, David said, "I made some fine grades, not like yours but good for this place. To change the subject, I'll tell you that that cow was killed by the Univ. as she was old and they wanted to experiment with her. They found a great deal new that helped the dairy science. The big cow we now have is worth at least $2,000. Some price. I am very pleased to hear that you are making high grades. If you keep it up you will be exempt from many fees in this University. That will save you a good 20 dollars. It's all bull about papa not being able to pay for me. I'll work during summer and then work here also. I'm not trying to work for my board this year. But I will next year. Cornell is a great school but there is not much chance of getting work out there. We have many fellows from New York working their way through. Your dear friend, David"

Shortly thereafter began a correspondence between Louis and Rose Bersh, a first cousin on his mother's side. Rose was tall and slim and slightly resembled a good-looking Eleanor Roosevelt. From her home in Paterson, New Jersey, she wrote on May 1, 1915.

> Dear Louis,
>
> What is it that keeps you from writing. Is it because you have forgotten my address? If so, write to me and I will tell you what it is. I am sure you would recollect that you owe me a letter. If after you recollect that fact and don't care to write, I wish you would drop me a line and tell me so! Your cousin Rose.

Apologetically, he answered that he was terribly busy with school and the shop. "Not as busy as I am," she retorted. "Besides, I've been sick allot (sic)."

> Dear Louis,
>
> I spoke to my father and told him that you were studying for agriculturist and he said that you should consider that step very carefully because you might get a post so far from home. Oh, yes, before I forget, I must tell you that *my* father bought a new Overland touring car and if you come out in the summer, we shall give you a ride. How is Willie?
>
> I want to tell you this little incident. Across the street from us there is an Atlantic & Pacific Tea Store. There are two clerks employed here. Last Saturday night about 9 o'clock, two well dressed young men entered the place. They pointed revolvers at the clerks and asked for the cash. One of them refused so they hit him on the head with the revolver inflicting a severe wound, opened the register and walked out with $200 in cash. They ran down the street by our house and as the snow was quite heavy on the ground soon disappeared. Nothing has been heard of them since. The Doctors put a few stitches in the clerk's head and he is alright now but all Totowa was frightened. Rose

"Willie," in Rose's letter, was Louis' older brother William, who was 15 when he came to America and too old to go to public school. He did attend some night classes and learned to read and write English. Willie suffered from being the oldest brother of very smart siblings. Without the education and, probably the ambition, he could not compete, though he was not lazy and tried to help when he could. As an adult, Willie worked as a clerk in many stores and at one time worked for the Pennsylvania Railroad Company where he traveled on trains and sold drinks and candy to the passengers. In his later years he had a little grocery store in a very poor neighborhood and was briefly married. When asked about his love life with his new wife he said, "*Zie vill nicht und Ich ken nicht* (she don't want it and I can't do it)."

Rose graduated from Paterson High School in January 1916 and made sure to write Louis that she was the brightest girl in her department so he needn't be ashamed of his cousin. She was going to Normal School to prepare herself to be a teacher. "I haven't seen Willie for quite a while. The last time I was in New York was last month and then my father and I went with him to buy a suit. Listen, Lou are you taller than Willie? I hope so, for if not I stand head and shoulders above you. Oh well, never mind. Napoleon was small but believe me I wish you his fame. Professor Smith offered me a free scholarship in Drake University, Des Moines, IA. He said it is some honor to go there and I guess it is. I told him Iowa was too far for me."

Most of Rose's letters dealt with her experiences at school. She was very nervous about her exams and being able to teach, even though she knew the material. References were made to Willie and Grandpa. Presumably, Willie had been visiting and times were difficult for Grandpa. Business was not going well. "Don't worry there is nothing at all the matter with Willie. He is perfectly well. Did your father get my mother's letter? What is he going to do?"

Then on July 17, 1916, "You are to be congratulated upon having received such excellent marks. You wanted to know about my school. There are about 100 girls in the school, 19 of whom are my classmates. There is only one boy. In the beginning of the term there were three such nuisances – all of them Jewish. Two left and one still lingers. The one who left in the middle of the term likes me quite well and gave me to understand that I was the object of his most obnoxious affections even while at High School. The remaining lunatic, shall I say, also knows how to play the part of cavalier but has dropped off practicing his designs on me and is now highly infatuated with a good-looking gentile girl."

A year later, July 22, 1917, Rose wrote she was tired with vacation already, especially after returning from the beach on Staten Island where they were held up by the ferry. "We were the 110th machine when we came. There was one ferry, taking eight machines at a time and going every 20 minutes. After waiting four hours, we got a ferry and came home at 1 AM. When we left there were about 300 machines waiting. Tell me, Louis, do you still expect to come out here this summer? When do you think you will come? Esther wrote and told me you had a scholarship. I hope you intend to use it this fall but is that possible?"

On April 6, 1917, the United States was dragged into the First World War and Rose wondered how it would affect Louis.

Dave Glushak did not experience military service. As a college student, he was exempt. His letters extolling farm life kept coming in his efforts to persuade Louis that farming was the wave of the future. His letters were voluminous, 10–14 typewritten pages as he outlined which courses Louis should take in school and which farm journals he should read

"Hang around farms and get all you can. *The Country Gentleman, Successful Farming,* and *Brudan's Gazette* are good papers. Try to learn all you can about gasoline engines and try to become a good all around mechanic. The real reason that farmers don't make good is nearly always due to their carelessness and non-mechanical ability. Farming is being done more and more by machinery and it is much better and easier on the man also as it is cheaper."

Why a city bred, religious Jewish boy would be attracted to that occupation Louis could not fathom. In any event, he finally declined to join him. Louis wrote he was now driving and presumably told him about his little jaunt to Baltimore. Dave answered, "Dear pal, I am glad you got your driving license and therefore I wish you would return me mine as soon as possible. What kind of a truck is that Pullman? What is its capacity? How old is it? And give me all the details."

The truck referred to was the Model T he needed to go out into the countryside with "Yale" to buy bags.

Dave continued, "I am working hard on the farm. I have ploughed some, cut wheat and oats and am now making hay. Have you seen my brother lately? Have you seen to my brother's car. What is the Chevrolet doing in Wash. Are they selling the Monroe car also? It looks exactly like the Chevrolet."

"I am only hoping for the day that you'll come here to MO. There are several boys from New York here. Save all the money you can, boy, for you'll need it. You will be able to get a job here during hours that will pay you through but boy, try and do your best." He enclosed a picture of himself in full dress army uniform and added, "I told you that we all had to take one year of military here in the university. If you were a cadet in Tech and you got a sergeant position before you graduate you would be able to get your uniforms free and 20 dollars a year here in the university. Also give my love to Esther and baby. From your best pal, David." Esther had become a mother and she and Harry were living in upstate New York.

When Louis graduated from McKinley Manual Training High School in February of 1917, he won a 4-year scholarship to the Chemical Engineering faculty of the University of Pennsylvania. He had graduated valedictorian. Letters flew back and forth between Louis, the university registrar and his high school principal. All the papers were in order when the roof fell in.

Kitty got married. Eleanor, only sixteen, could not cope with both school and the business, too. This meant that the bulk of the responsibilities fell on Louis. He would take the orders, pay the bills and write letters signing his father's name. If Kitty were there, he could accept the scholarship and monitor the junk business at the same time. Now, he could not leave unless someone took his place. Maybe he could get a reprieve and enter the university the following year.

Louis took a train to Philadelphia to plead with the registrar. He even offered to pay for the first year. The registrar's response was, "If you don't show up for the first day of classes, your scholarship will be given to the next in line." Classes started in September and Louis was heartbroken. Here was an opportunity to get a free college education and he had to turn it down. Grandpa's English was poor and keeping business records was beyond him. Only Louis was in a position to do this. Unfortunately, his older brother Willie was not capable of stepping into Kitty's shoes.

Rose asked in her letter of July 22, 1917, "Friday, the day of draft, was quite an exciting day. How was it in Washington?"

When war broke out, the army had a branch called the "Students Army Training Corp." In brief, SATC was jocularly called the "Saturday Afternoon Tea Club." This was a branch of service leading to a commission in the army. To be eligible, one had to be a college student. Louis applied then for entrance to George Washington University and was accepted. This made him a college student and exempt from the draft. He enlisted in the SATC.

Yale didn't stay very long in the bag business. He suddenly decided that being a bagman in the army was not nearly as sacred as being a rabbi out of the army – clergymen being exempt. He once again donned the mantle as Rabbi Yalow and took a pulpit in Syracuse, New York. Thereafter, Louis took his brother Willie to help when he drove around for burlap and bags.

Leo Freudberg, Louis' cousin on his father's side, continued to be his good buddy. They spent as much time together as they could and enjoyed all the pleasures the city had to offer. Washington, DC, has always been one of the most beautiful cities in the world and whenever possible, the boys would go to Haynes Point and bicycle around the Tidal Basin of the Jefferson Memorial. The loveliest time was in the spring when the cherry blossoms were in bloom.

On September 8, 1917, Rose wrote that she had a poem accepted in a local newspaper and would start teaching kindergarten the following week. She was to graduate as a teacher in February of 1918. Shortly after that, she wrote, "Paterson looks pretty empty now so far as the young men are concerned. Everyone is either enlisting or has already gone to war. Elsie's friend is on his way to France just now. She has a heart broken. My children in school are very enthusiastic about all sorts of war activities. Today we head the school list. We have nearly 100% so far as war gardens are concerned – I have about 200 pupils knitting through my department for the Red Cross and in our spare moments we are constantly kept busy making snippings for soldiers pillows and gunwipes for soldiers to use. My children have searched thru libraries and brought some splendid books to school to be sent out for the soldiers. Then too, my father gave me all the tangled wool he had in the store and we made cootie strings for the soldiers in the trenches. So you see I too am trying to do my bit and I am thankful to be rather well situated so I can do it.

"Louis, I must ask you one frank question what did your teachers do to you when detaining you after school had become to you not a punishment but a pleasure? I can't chase my boys home after school and that's a standing joke around School No. 4. One of my boys works in the Empire Theatre selling chocolates. During the day, I sent him from my room and at noon, he came to ask me if he might apologize. In the evening I went to the theatre and during the last intermission, Charles sent a large box of chocolates to me with the other candy-boy. Later when I met him on the street and talked to him about it, Chas. stood there saying, 'Aw gee, Miss Bersh, What's the matter – can't a fellow give away a box of fancy if he want to?' So of course I took them and Charlie has become my adopted baby since and he is pretty proud of it. He is a big, tall handsome boy and he really enjoys it when I call him a baby. I wish you could see my kiddies. Some of them are only 3 or 4 yrs. younger than their teacher and they are very good for me."

Louis really missed Kitty when she married and left home. He felt like half of him had gone away but they managed to stay in touch by writing letters. She frequently threw in Yiddish expressions. Kitty and her husband Al were now living in Detroit, Michigan. Kitty probably had the wittiest personality of all the siblings. She was small like the other Grossbergs, had short, dark, curly hair and an impish smile. Al, on the other hand, was tall and had a temper. He was a man to be reckoned with but in those honeymoon days, this trait was yet to fully develop.

October 30, 1917. Kitty writes, "To Louis, *Mine Hartz* (my heart): Yes, there is a reason why I am writing to-day to you, being as how you are still *stummer wie a flonken*, (as speechless as a piece of meat). The reason is a letter from Esther which has in it a sentence, running thusly: 'Mamma writes that she has to make the furnace all by herself and at the end of the day she is so tired and worn out that she doesn't hardly enjoy the very existence.'

"Well, you can imagine how that struck me. Louis, you will probably not believe me when I say that I have had a horrible lump in my throat ever since this morning, when I received Esther's letter. She says she is worried. Naturally, being away from home the same as I, and knowing *now* the real worth of a mother, she should be worried. But, upon second thought, I figured out that worry will do no good and that something will have to be done. So I ups and get an idea. I wouldn't ask you and Willie to take care of the furnace because it is too hard for you. Naturally, if it is too hard for you two *bundes* (bandits) it surely is for Ma and Ma shall never have to make the fires herself if you will help me. This is the scheme.

"See if Brooks or any other honorable Shocker will come twice a day or 3 times, if necessary and take care of the furnace. Offer from $1.00 to $1.50 per weak (sic) for the services. You can get it for that. Then, every weak (sic) I will send you $1.00 with which to pay him and if it costs 50¢ more, you pay for the difference. I am sorry that $1.00 per weak will be all I can possibly spare for the present, anyway, for I am a poor *bettler* (meaning unclear) myself. But from the last I would spare $1.00 per weak if I know Mamma will not have that work to do.

"Louis, believe me, you do not know what a mother means to you. You cannot know, because you have not gone through what I am going through right now. Away from everyone I love even from my husband most all weak (sic) long.

"Dr. White told me that Ma should not work so hard. Please do what I have asked even if Ma & Pa protest. I hope you will do it as soon as you get this letter and answer me immediately so I can begin to send the weekly dollar. But, whatever you do, do not let Esther know of my offer because she may think I am trying to show off or something like that. Do not mention the fact that I wrote about it, savvy?

"Well, now I surely deserve an answer, don't I? If you do not care to write yourself, will you let your typewriter do it? You owe me 4 letters and 16 apologies already. Your loving Sis, Kit."

My father could not understand why his mother wrote such a thing to Esther since he remembered tending to the furnace. This next letter from Kitty in Detroit to her sister Eleanor, came to be among Pop's papers probably the same way many other letters found their way to his house. After Kitty died, he seemed to be the repository for family records. There were also receipts and tax records from his sister Pauline after she died. People commonly kept copies of their correspondence, especially if they used a typewriter. Remember carbon paper?

> Oct. 30, 1917
> Dearest Ella:
> Your letter received and sorry to hear that you have nothing to write and are doing so. By golly, girl, you surely do beat me in saying nothing on a whole page. What I want to know is how things are at home, such as business and health and things in general. The fact that I am so far from home makes it that much more interesting to hear from you about everything. I want to know how the children are getting on in school, how you and Sollie are doing with your music and how Mamma feels and how Papa feels and if you all have warm clothes for the winter and coal and eats. – By heck, there are a million and one things you could write about, so get busy, kiddo, and write a 64-page letter as soon as possible.
> By the way how is the weather in Washington? It has been snowing here all day today and it is cold too. Well that's all. Be good and give love to all. Sis, Kitty

When my parents had a house on Garrison Street, Sol came over one day and sat down at our piano. My sheet music was out and he was able to play something with little trouble. This was remarkable since he had no piano at his house and probably had not played in years. As for Eleanor, I only remember seeing her once, when she appeared one day from California with her husband. She was wearing a large brimmed hat, so it must have been summer time. I have a photograph of Eleanor as a beautiful bride, so when I see that photo I can picture Eleanor in her hat as well. Funny, how I can remember a hat but not the person wearing it. Her husband Maury was a likable fellow who fancied himself a songwriter. He never published anything and hardly earned a living. My father often sent them money.

The first few years after Kitty married Al Cohen, they lived in Michigan. Later they moved to Virginia where Al had a canteen next to the army base in Ft. Meyer, Virgina, close to the cavalry post. Pop recalled that Kitty was a wonderful dancer, very light on her feet. She would light up a room when she entered. Unfortunately, Al was very jealous and considered dancing an embrace. He even disliked it when my father danced with his own sister.

Kitty led a difficult married life. Al never made much of a living, and today would probably be called an abusive husband and father. While I don't know that he ever hit Kitty, he certainly made her life miserable verbally. I remember as a young child, going to their house in Virginia one afternoon with my mother. We had been invited to lunch. Kitty was an excellent cook and baker. For dessert, she served a delicious lemon meringue pie, my favorite. It was so good that I asked for a second piece.

Al immediately said, "No!" in a loud voice.

He didn't approve of anyone asking for seconds. It had to be offered first and I gathered he was not about to offer any more. I know that my mother was upset and Kitty was very embarrassed.

Al had little use for religious rituals. His behavior at the Seder table at Passover lives long in my memory. Until my grandmother, Sarah Henna, could no longer prepare this feast for the family, we all gathered at their home on M Street. In the kitchen sat a large barrel with the wine my grandmother made. The Seder table took up the entire area of their narrow dining room with extensions to the end of the living room. There were 25 to 30 people seated around it with most of the men congregated at its head. There they sat chanting the service in Hebrew. Since no one could understand what was going on, the rest of the attendees chatted amongst themselves.

The restless children left the table to carry on mischief around the periphery. It seemed to go on forever. Al behaved like one of the children, making faces and tossing bits of matzo across the table. While this was amusing to us children, it was very annoying to the adults.

It is important to add here, that while Al was very dismissive of religious ceremonies, he did have a change of heart. During his later years, Al became the building chairman of the Arlington-Fairfax Jewish Center where services were conducted on Shabbat and Holidays. He also worked actively for a hospital and was remembered favorably by those who knew him. Al died a couple of years before Kitty of a bone marrow disease. But my most notable memory was of Al Cohen being a clown at the Seder table.

This experience prompted my father to conduct his Seders differently. At our house, each of us was called upon to read part of the service in either English or Hebrew and, since we never knew who would be called upon next, we all stayed attentive.

Cousin Rose, the ever-faithful correspondent, wrote on November 15, 1917, that she was "dreadfully tired. Gosh! but those cherries were good. Thanks ever so much, Louis. I have been quite ill all week and so I know you'll excuse me. Well, Louis, I'll thank you again for sending me that 'sweet gift.'"

Louis sent Kitty sweets as well. On December 27, 1917 came a letter from Kitty. "*Gott sie danken ongekummen* (Thank God what came). Oh boy, what joy, can be obtained from bonbons. You are a darling, no use talking. I surely thank you for it 100% more than if you hadn't sent it at all. Even now, I am devouring a 2 oz. piece of Mrs. Velaties concoction and your letter too pleased me quite a bit. Only it was so awfully short. What's the matter, you can't write a long letter any more. I am afraid, I'll have to resort to violence and write only short ones too. Yes, dear boy, that makes me 16, but sorry to say, on only one side. The left one. The right side has years all of its own. Nevertheless, I am still a spring chicken with the accent on the *ing. Notice.*

"Say, brooder, how would you like to go out in 5 below zero weather and ice skates? Well, that's what we have here, that's what I am enjoying; only I am omitting the ice-skating. Oh, I suppose you can guess why but anyway I am enjoying the five below. Boy, this is some country. You know, Canada is just across the bridge from here, and when you go downtown, you can see the Scotch Kilties, freezing in their short skirts and socks, some cute bunch.

"By the way, tell me, the 15th of Jan. makes you according to American records 20 or 21. Please let me know that as it has weighed quite heavily on my dome here lately. I'd hate to see you leave the U.S.A. just yet. Do not forget to answer me that and soon too if you do not want me to have any worryment.

"By the way, I want to tell you something and ask for your advice in the matter. You know that I have $50 in the German American Bldg. Assn. at Wash. Well, I had expected to use it when the new addition arrived but as long as Al doesn't know a thing about it and being as how it am none of his business either, I had decided that I will be able to do without it. Only I should like to have about $10 or $15.00 to apply on a baby carriage. So, I have decided to withdraw that amt., sent it home and have Ma send it to me as a present for the Kidd. The rest of the money I'll keep for Ma for a suit and hat for the summer so she can come visit me. Well, will that be O.K. with Ma, ask her please. When you answer this be sure you write it on something separate from the big letter as Al likes to read your letters, too. Also your age on that same paper, too. You see, I am 21-years now, and we can't both be that young, can we.

"Something else, I was going to buy a shirt for Pa for his birthday, but we got a letter from Sadie telling me about the sugar shortage in Wash. so as it happened, I got hold of 20 lb. of sugar and am sending it to you so you all may not have to worry about it for a time. So, I had to postpone the shirt for a while, but will send it on the 15th with something for you too. You know how things happen at times with the best of us. Just a little shortage in the dough, that's all. Please caution Ma not to mention anything to Cones about the sugar. They get all they need from their relatives. Tell Ma to excuse me for not writing to her personally, but I am quite busy now.

"Let me see, was there anything else I wanted to say to you – Oh yes, ask Celie if I may send her an order for some few things I need. She has so far disregarded my existence entirely. No more to write my boy. Be real nice to me and answer me a real long letter soon. I was happy all day after reading your little one. A long one could make the happiness last a whole week."

Celie Freudberg and her sister Dora owned The Embroidery Shop in Washington, DC. They lived together with a third sister, Annie, who was deaf and mute. Annie was a sweet soul who understood a good deal and was able to communicate remarkably well considering that she had no training. These three ladies were Leo Freudberg's sisters. The Embroidery Shop was a very important institution in the city. Anyone who fancied needlework went there to find the best selection of thread and canvases to embroider. All the fashionable ladies knew this was the place for fine linens.

As for the Valatie's, this was another Washington institution. These caramel candies were so unusual that everyone for miles around knew the name. Some were chewy and some crumbly, some dark and some

light, with and without nuts. They became a favorite gift for every occasion. I remember Pop bringing them home to Mom and my husband,
Jules, bringing them home to me.

Cousin Rose Bersh wrote Louis December 28 that she had given up cro-
chet needles for knitting needles. "There have been other forms of Red
Cross work, such as the seals, and getting members for the organization.
Besides I have served on food committees, on lunchroom committees,
on sugar committees and on coal committees. I have received so many
requests from old friends, and school friends who are on active service
abroad to write to them. I had a severe injury in the 'gym' class. I broke
a blood vessel. I missed two weeks from school and it was mighty fortunate for me that our schools had to close a week before the regular
holiday because of the coal shortage."

A business letter arrived for Louis to handle, dated January 8, 1918,
from Whitmore, Lynn & Alden Co., 1225 F Street NW, Washington, DC,
Jewelers and Silversmiths. It was addressed to Chicago Junk Company,
515 K Street, Washington DC.

> Gentlemen:
> Is this a joke for surely there is a mistake somewhere as the
> last time this paper was hauled out we were allowed thirty five
> cents per hundred and as you quote seven hundred and eighty
> pounds of waste paper, as per your memorandum of January
> Eighth, we think you forgot some figures that belong on your
> check. Kindly let us hear from you in reference to same as we feel
> there must be a mistake. Awaiting your reply, we beg to remain,
> Very truly yours, Whitmore, Lynn & Alden Co.

Louis responded January 9, 1918.

> Gentlemen:
> Speaking of jokes, we wonder whom the joke is really on. If
> you will take the trouble to inquire of any dealer in town you will
> find that ten cents per hundred is the present market price for
> baled waste paper. Within the last few months waste paper has

dropped in price from forty to ten cents a hundred pounds. It may interest you to know that our share of your paper, the profit, is exactly the same as yours – seventy-eight cents.

But where the 'joke' comes in is with your so called excelsior. You can readily see that it does not pay us to haul small quantities of paper for ten cents a hundred pounds. Your mention of excelsior, however, is what caused us to send for your waste, as good clean excelsior is salable at present. We sent our men to you with instructions to haul the excelsior directly to the concern which buys it of us.

Our men removed two loads of this packing from your basement. A little later we were informed that the excelsior could not be used, as it was mixed with paper, straw, etc. Excelsior so packed, we were told, should be hauled to the city dump. This, then, makes three loads for seventy-eight cents. Don't you think you have struck a rather good bargain?

Kitty's next letter said she didn't have time to write very much. "I only want you to let me know what you have done about the arrangements for making the furnace for our house. Please, if you do not wish to write to me yourself, let Ella or Pauline tell me, or there will be no birthday present for honorable Louis C. Grossberg on Jan. 15.

"Another favor I ask of you. Morris referred a bonding Co. to Pa for reference because he needed eight people for a reference. Please give a favorable reply to them in case they write as it will not make you liable for anything and only help Morris. He needed a bond. So long Jew baby & answer if only a few words."

January 24, 1918 – Kitty uses her pet name for Louis C.

Dear Lucy:

Just a line to tell you that I have just sent you P.P. 2 prs. hose as a small token of my remembrance to your honorable birthday, may you have one every year for the next 100 years or more. It is but a humble gift indeed, but you may be sure that a heart full of good luck & best wishes, mixed with real true love is interwoven in every stitch. I see that it is nearly 2 weeks past due, but the terrible cold weather kept me from going downtown (I am a very delicate woman now). Please, observe the soft pedal when acknowledging receipt of the package. Savvy.

February 2, 1918 – Kitty is now the mother of a son, Robert.

Dearest Lucy:

Thanks, old boy for the wire. But sorry I cannot go just now. The reason being that our treasury is quite empty at present. Yes, quite empty. You know the moving has taken everything we had to get as many things for our home you can't imagine, and yet we need at least $100 worth of stuff more. Such things as dishes, kitchen utensils, and many other things I can't think of right now. So you see, I can't possibly indulge in pleasure trips, much as I would want to.

Lucy dear, I owe you a letter and by Gimminy Crickette (sic), you'll get one as soon as I can possibly do it. We came back from Detroit Sunday night and went right to our bungalow. So yesterday evening Mrs. Finch brought me the letter from Celie. The package has not as yet arrived. Please call up Celie and tell her I received her letter yesterday and will write to her in a day or two, as soon as I get straightened up in the bungalow. Will also write to you then. How is business? I hope you are all doing well. Robert says he would like to see you. How is Willie? Is he working and making something. Give him mine and Robert's love. No, I don't mean the love we gave you, but other love.

By the way, how did Pa & Ma happen to go to Syracuse now! Who footed the bill?

Yours as ever, Kitten, 104 Sunnyside Court (Muddyside when it rains)

February 4, 1918 – Rose writes:

Dear Louis:

Just today, each girl in the class was called separately into the office and told whether she passed or failed. I think everyone around could hear my heart beat. As soon as I knew I phoned home. I shall send this special delivery so that you may get it in time to come to my graduation on this Wednesday evening, Feb. 6. I'm afraid I'm dreaming to imagine anyone coming or caring to come from the Capital to see a school marm graduate. I would love to see Esther and Kitty. They must be divinely happy. Celie Freudberg was here and we surely were tickled to see her. I am so sorry she couldn't stay until Thursday. It was just great of her to come out here. I think for a while I shall stay home doing nothing and then I'm going to coax to go out of town to teach. I don't know if my mother will let me but –

I feel real sick tonight. Three of my classmates flunked and they carried on something terrible. When I got home I felt so blue that I went to bed and just now, 9 PM I got up. So at last, Louis, I'm a real teacher. Does my profession still awaken in you the old latent antagonism? We took our oaths today, that we would teach Americanism and its meaning and we were told that we are about to enter the most wonderful profession on earth – that of teacher.

Rose wrote again on February 7, 1918. "Thank you ever so much for your kind wishes. Let me thank you once more for your remembrance and tell you how sorry I am you weren't able to come to the graduation."

And again on February 24, she said, "You can just bet I admire your taste but what ever made you give me anything that is far too pretty to use? All I could do with those handkerchiefs was to look at and admire them, show them proudly to my friends and then put them away, of course. Without joking, Louis, they are beautiful and I appreciate them but you mean just as much to me without a gift. You should not spend your money so foolishly.

"Well here I am teaching at last. Just when I had been fully persuaded to stay at home a while and take things easy, fate, much stronger than reason comes along and sweeps me into a little crowded classroom with forty little kiddos. Heaven knows how long I'll be there for their regular teacher has pneumonia. Many of the children are Jewish and they are all rather bright. On Thursday I was teaching them *My Shadow*, by Robt. Louis Stevenson. Their former teacher must have told them the poet's name because when I announced the wonderful fact that I was going to tell them who wrote the poem, one boy in the front seat raised his hand and said, 'I know.' All right, Abie, what is it? As quick as a flash he said, 'Rabbi Lewis Levenson.'

"I was offered a permanent position in the schools of NY and would have accepted but my parents wouldn't let me. Gee, Louis, but you hate my profession, and womanlike I almost think if I ever began to rate it, you would be the last person I should ever confess it to. At present, I am not perfectly happy, not even near to it but this state of mind does not spring from the fact that I'm a teacher. I want to tell you how glad I am that you are about to resume your studies. That you will make a great success as a lawyer I haven't the slightest doubt, for I remember how forcefully you put forth your arguments against teaching as a profession for me; that you will always win I am sure if you follow this advice. Never have as your opponent a woman. If you do, you are bound to lose. You just couldn't keep it up long enough to win, could you?"

When I read this letter to Pop, he said he didn't know where Rose got the idea that he was going to study law.

Kitty sent this April 15, 1918, letter from Jackson, Michigan. The latter part was missing but on the back was Louis' response. Kitty is writing what Al is dictating.

"Dear Lou C:

"I am leaving my present position in a few days to go into the tire and accessory business for myself. This may appear strange and startling to you, for, whoever saw a millionaire go into such a petty business. However, I am going into it on a rather large scale, being in a position to obtain very liberal credit on my good looks.

"It would be impossible for me to operate a business of this kind without outside help, so naturally I would either have to hire a man to stay in the store during my absence or get a partner in the business. Before doing either of the two things, I have a little proposition to offer you and heartily believe it to be a wonderful opportunity to get into the biggest business in this country to-day.

"I believe that it would be foolish for me to attempt to explain your end of the proposition in this letter." Al offered a small drawing account to start and an interest in the business later. "My initial stock when opening will be somewhere between 5 & 10 thousand dollars. The experience that I have gotten."

This is the draft of a letter or most likely a telegram to Al Cohen at Sunnyside Court, written on the back of the above letter. "Am greatly flattered by your proposition and am proportionately sorry I cannot accept it. Realize it is wonderful opportunity but am securely tied to home. Pa needs me here. Would suggest you start without partners if possible. Go to it kid and make good. Am pulling for you. Love, Louis"

April 27, 1918, Louis wrote to the editor of *The WASHINGTON TIMES*, Munsey Building, Washington, DC, evidently to settle a dispute. Louis asks for the best estimate as to the increase in population in Washington, since the United States entered the World War and enclosed an SASE for reply. The reply was dated April 30, 1918 and is included here for historical reasons.

> My Dear Mr. Grossberg:
>
> In re of the 27th.
>
> The Police Census last November gave Washington 395,547 population the Civil Service Commission states the employees which are under their classification are coming at the net rate of about 1,000 a week. About 1,600 actually come: but about 600 refuse to stay, or others previously here insist on going – because *they cannot get housing accommodations. So the net increase is 1,000 a week*, from that source, making it about 425,000 six months later. After 1 year it should be 477,000 and after 2 years – 529,000. Congress is appropriating $10,000,000 for temporary housing in the District at $600 per worker…Sincerely, John E.

May 28, 1918, Rose wrote again. "I cannot help wondering whether you would rather hear from Rose Bersh, substitute teacher in the second grade or from Rose Bersh, instructor and supervisor of Fine Arts of School No. 4 and that's who I am at the brilliant age of twenty. I received my appointment on the Ides of March about two years sooner than I should have been appointed and without special art training. I was told that the position was given to me on my merit and for my artistic and disciplinary ability.

"I instruct all the upper grade classes in the entire school and am responsible for the aesthetic development of about 700 pupils in 13 different classes. There was a pretty hot fight put up by the many unappointed teachers in the city when I 'landed my job.' Since then I have been offered a High School teachers position in Pennsylvania and am wondering whether or not to accept. Do you expect to go to college in Sept. I was all prepared to go to Columbia this summer but that is out of the question until I am well again."

The only letter from Pop's sister Eleanor was dated June 25, 1918. She was the fifth child, born two years after my father. Louis was 20-years-old when he received it. He remembered Eleanor as a very happy little girl. Copies of this letter were sent to several of her siblings. She wanted everyone to remember her birthday.

ATTENTION TO THE GENTLE FOLKS?

Did any of you ever learn of the fact that a birthday is on its way to 614–M St.? I have received a telegram stating that it will arrive on the 15th of July. Now in order so as to make it welcome, is to dress the newcomer in its best of style and that is as follows:

1. One very fine middy blouse
2. One and only one pair of white shoes
3. A pretty dress
4. And one thing more a pair of silk hose

Kindly don't forget the hose because if you wouldn't get the hose the shoes wouldn't be satisfied so whatever you do by any means satisfy the shoes, and the rest I will leave to you. Thank you, the Birthday which is on its way. Ella

War is hell, whether you are attacking the enemy or defending yourself. Yet oddly, it did not seem so terrible to the young people, except to those who had experienced it themselves. On the home front, there were no TV sets to bring the horror to the living rooms of the American people on a daily basis. True, there were black and white newsreels at the cinemas and stories in the newspapers, but for some reason, they were romanticized. Color photos were not available.

In fact everyone, boys and girls alike, wanted to be part of it. America did not enter the war until April 6, 1917, and it was all over by November 11, 1918. By the time enough of our troops began reporting back about the true nature of war, all chances of participating in that great heroic episode had vanished. Even at the end, there were still a great many who felt they had missed an exciting opportunity to be patriotic overseas.

Leo Freudberg was the first to enlist. His letters now joined others that flowed to Louis through the U.S. postal service. They were usually very long, very verbose, often written in longhand, but filled with glimpses of army life that were often amusing. Being stationed Stateside gave him the opportunity to come home to Washington for visits. In his very long letter of July 14, 1918, he wrote from his base on stationery of the Army and Navy Young Men's Christian Association. Across the top was penned, "Some place in Charlotte" and "With The Colors."

My Dear Louis,

You Poor Gazoop, you little bit of sawdust, you piece of rotten herring, you shrimp, how you was and how you knocken them. Well so you had a fine time on the straw ride. Well I am glad you did & how did you like Miss Cohen (no relation), don't you think she is sweet? Isn't she some chicken? O boy, and listen you grain of sand if you wrong or don't treat her right or anything happens to her I will hold you responsible, so beware and look out for the USM (United States Marines), or I will bark. I know when you will read this you will shiver your timbers.

I will start with reveille, that's another definition for morning of course – you haven't the brains to know it yourself so I'm taking the trouble to explain. After we jump from our hammocks a matter of about 7 feet from the ground, we proceed to dress which takes us about 5 minutes and then the darn old bugle blows again to fall in line. We then march to the parade grounds go through a morning drill. That takes about fifteen minutes and then we proceed to double hoof it back to camp a matter of about 3 long blocks we proceed to wash up and take our bedding out for an airing, hang it out over the railing. After that we proceed to fall in line for breakfast. Now I must tell you an interesting event, they made me a kitchen police in other words I am chief cook and bottle washer. Here I must stop for I am called to a sacred strong duty and that is to peel onions…

Well after we get through with our breakfast we proceed to do what we damn please. Sleep, sing, dance, play, write or anything that's mischievous. At 12 o'clock we proceed to march to mess hall & eat again. I proceed to clean up. After that we proceed to do anything we chose except leave the place. And then at six we eat again. Pretty soft for them. I mean for me. After supper we continue doing nothing. About 7 PM we proceed to undress naked to the skin, you know how you first came into this world and walk from bunk to the shower a half a block and proceed to rub myself down. After my rub down I proceed to recline as best as my feeble body will permit me to my lofty hammock and rock from side to the other. As the boys start coming in we start raising hell telling jokes and some of us start singing. I was elected sing leader of the bunk but Lou, we have a good time all nice boys. Training camp is a vacation.

In another letter, Leo says, "You asked me about my vaclosin (probably vaccine)? Or shot as you call it. Well they both gave me Hell especially the second one which I received Monday the 21. I was laid up in bed all day Tuesday and could not move an inch. But Wednesday it got O.K. You ask too damn many questions. I get $66 a month, that is I am supposed to get it. So far I haven't received any dough yet."

Leo was in quarantine for twenty-one days and was then sent to school for two or three months. He hoped to go north to New York or Philadelphia rather than Florida so he could go home occasionally before seeing foreign service.

August 9, 1918 – Rose writes:

Dear Louis,

I understand that you intend to make me a personal visit very shortly when you go on your vacation and since I'm not going away this summer, you are more than welcome. I guess your parents must be almost home by now and I certainly hope they had a great old time.

Listen Louis, I resigned my position and I want very much to enlist for 'overseas service!' I have been inquiring from several sources for a place which I can fill. I only hope my chance to go comes real soon. In the meantime, I am knitting socks. I can well imagine how busy you must be. You surely have earned a vacation.

It is unlikely Louis' parents went on a vacation in 1918. Money was tight. Maybe they visited their daughter Esther in Syracuse, New York. In later years, his mother did go to Atlantic City, usually in the spring after *Pesach* (Passover). The children would save up to send her for a rest after the holidays.

Leo managed to get this entire message on a postcard. Dated August 28, 1918, from "Applicants Camp, USMC, Paris Island, South Carolina."

> Dear Louis,
>
> Don't fool yourself if you think you are working hard. Why boy, you are having a tea party every day. Yesterday was inspection day and so natch the movie rolled out at 4:30, made up bunk, cleaned it with kerosene, wee, I am good at that, swept up the bunkhouse, then mopped it. Then to the kitchen, served on the table, washed the dishes, cleaned & mopped the mess hall and then chow (eats), even the Willard (Hotel) is *no* comparison. And now it was light and the day's work was *attempted*. From peeling onionskins to cleaning the latrines. The life is great, if you don't weaken. All this is mere circumstance to what will be when we go to the training camp. The sergeants and corporals are old timers, 5 to 15 years in the service and the type can be imagined. Tell your folks I am awfully sorry not to have been able to say goodby. So long old boy and WRITE. Yours, Leo

Dave's father, Rabbi Glushak, was originally from New York. He officiated in a Washington synagogue for many years and when offered a better position in New Jersey, decided to return with his wife and daughter Fanny. Fanny was heartbroken but she was too young to be left behind. Dave remained with relatives in Washington to finish school. Fanny wrote Louis of her unhappiness at leaving all her friends and, indeed, everyone who knew Fanny was sorry to see her go. She was charming, witty and little seemed to hold her down. No party was a success without Fanny and her departure left a big void in the social life of her peers. Kitty, another live wire, was a terrific dancer and taught him all the current dance steps. He sorely missed her not being there to continue this part of his social education. It seemed like his favorite people were out of sight and the only way to keep in contact was to write.

Once Fanny arrived in New Jersey in 1920, she started making new friends immediately. One of them was Ida, whom she introduced to Louis. Not only was Louis writing to Rose, Kitty and Leo on a regular basis, he now added Fanny and Ida to his list. Ida met Dave Glushak through his sister Fanny, when he visited his family in New Jersey. Later Dave and Ida married and as far as my father could tell, the marriage was a solid one. In the early days, Ida was very agreeable, but after a while, her darker side appeared. She hated Washington and had few, if any, friends. Even her own sister didn't get along with her. Ida was a very jealous woman and almost ruined the wonderful relationship between Louis and Dave. She also came close to causing the breakup of my parents just before their marriage.

However, on August 8, 1918, Ida was friendly. She sent a postcard to Louis on which was written: "Dear Lew: Had a 'swell' time until today, but – I'm over the mumps now! Don't know what Colonial Beach looks like yet. Will see this week. Sincerely, Ida." On the front of the card Fanny added, "No gentleman would swear before a lady – always let the lady swear first. I'm Fanny."

It appears from the letters that Louis felt compelled to enlist. Maybe he expected to be drafted and hoped to have some say as to how he would serve. Not being in the ROTC had a bigger impact on him than anyone thought. Kitty certainly was at a loss to understand her brother when she wrote him September 13, 1918. Pop couldn't remember any interest in the Navy, but thinks it may have been because his cousin Herman Freudberg was in the Navy. Herman was Leo's brother and later lived in Philadelphia. He owned a jewelry shop and Pop bought my mother's wedding rings from him ten years later.

Dear Louis:

Just a few lines. Ma wrote us that you are waiting to enlist in the navy. Well, I really don't see why you will not be exempt being that you can prove you are nearly ⅔ the support of the family. However, I suppose you know what is best.

Now, you know, I am your Sis & Al your Bro. so under the circumstances we have a rather keen desire to see you before you ups and goes to fight for us so we have decided to import you to our humble domain for as long a period as you can stay. Naturally it is but fair and befitting that you, our main object of delight, should get yourself all ready, brush up your 'Sunday go to meeting' suit, give yourself one of those famous knickel (sic) shoe shines, thereby scoring the honorable knickel, and *kun sech sehn* (come and see).

Of course, Al will send the round trip fare as soon as we get your answer that you are coming. We would very much like to have you for *Shukes* (Sukkot, a fall festival holiday) so please, I hope we will not be disappointed. I suppose poor Ma & Pa must feel just terrible. I know how I feel, and I am but a *Makite* (another pet name Louis used for Kitty). It really seems to me you could get off. Really, I don't see what they will do in the shop without you. Tough luck, Damn the Kaiser.

You know this little verse, don't you?

Good-bye Pa, Good-bye Ma,
Good-bye mule with your old hee hah
I don't know what this war is about
but I'll bet you by gosh I'll soon find out.

Good-bye Sweetheart don't you fear
I'll bring you a King for a Souvenir
I'll bring you a Turk and a Kaiser too
And that's about all one fellow can do.

Love to all, tell ma I received her letter and am sorry to say that Robert does not crawl yet. However, he is some boy just the same. You will see.

In another undated letter, "Hello Once Again: I was just talking to Al and he says that he has a hunch you can get exempt here as the small town board will listen more to your story. Perhaps you can come to work here and say you send the money home. My goodness, I don't know what Ma will do without you. Anyway, you come on over and we will see what can be done. Well, so long and let us hear from you immediately if not sooner. Suppose you address your letter to the store. Kit"

This condensed 10-page letter from Leo, our Marine hero, was dated September 22, 1918.

Hello Old Top,

You are entitled to a letter and I'll try to write one in 20 minutes I have while waiting for the corp. to come back. I am cleaning up the mule stable this morning. God bless those mules. They take their own good time. So far I have been all about every kind of a job we have on this Island. I have not chopped wood yet, but am very hopeful that I'll get that sometime very soon.

Here they are great believers in keeping the machine going at all times. A marine, they say, never gets tired. He must either be down or up. If he is up he does things and if he is down, he goes to the hospital. It will be 3 weeks since I landed in this particular camp and damned if I can see what I've accomplished. I consumed a good deal of chow, washed a hell of a bunch of shirts and drawers, cleaned enough garbage to feed ⅓ of Belgium and got enough cussing out to last me another 25 years. Some call this life pretty tough but I don't seem to be affected by it at all. The only time it is hard is when I have to get up, especially now. It is rather cold at nights now. The cold wind blows thru the tents and believe me it takes about 8 hours to get warmed up…

I am beginning on the 5th page and have not written a damn thing. Louis, I am glad to be here and meet farmers, butchers, bums, roughnecks, hawkers, singers is an experience. Here a fellow has a fine chance to study psychology, philosophy, cussing, washing, cleaning and what not. When I get through I expect to be chief of the street cleaning and garbage dept. at DC. Oh I guess I could hold down a job as a dishwasher at the Willard (an elegant hotel in Washington, DC).

We get the finest beans and rice in the morning and the best rice and beans for dinner and oh boy, for supper well that is all a new menu, a new series of rice and lima beans. Some weeks there is not a bean in sight, then the eats are pretty good, tomatoes and soup and stew beef, that is if you can imagine well about finding the beef in the stew. Bread, coffee and H_2O we get a plenty. Prunes and stewed peaches or apples and chocolate pudding make their appearance when the cook feels well. You know, I'll have a hard time with my table manners. I do as the Romans do. I grab too because my appetite is the best ever. When I am at home and a meal should be ready, I'll be the 1st there not much left for the others by the time they get to the table…

I met Eckhart, of your class today. He is a corporal a very nice fellow and he asked me lots about you. He wants me to send you his best regards. He looks very good and military like. Been here 9 mos. and is crazy to go *over*…They call this training boot training and it is well named. We are handled like a bunch of boots. After I get through here in about 3 months I go up to the quartermaster school for 3 or 5 months which will mean that I may not see old sweet home for one hell of a long time. There are days when I am crazy to walk by 14th and NY Ave. and have a decent meal but there is little time to think about this…So far I have not beheld the looks of a fair maiden…I hope when you get this you'll know where you stand concerning the army.

Kitty's letter of September 23, 1918, mentions *Tante* (Aunt) Lena's boys – meaning Leo and Herman Freudberg. She says that she's happy that Willie is doing well in the shop, though Pop did not remember him working there at all.

So far, no one has told me anything regarding Tante Lena's boys. Please would you mind to tell me in what branch of the service they are in and how they like etc. etc. Also, do not fail to let me know in what branch you will enlist and when and how and why and if so, who. How about the Student's Corps. Don't you like that?

About the fruit dish. I had it taken to a Jeweler who says he does not know how much it would cost to replace it, nor can it be put in absolute perfect condition again. The post officer is now in possession of the dish. I'd rather they would give me the money for it so I could get something else with it. There are quite a few things I'd much rather have than that dish. You understand. Suppose you go into some store and price a dish like that. Or else have the Post Office do it. You can offer some excuse for not knowing the price. Savvy.

Well sir lady, about business is rather a difficult thing. Both, the terrible rainy and mean weather of the past 2 weeks, coupled with the gas less Sundays has kind of hit this kind of business in the head, but then, the sun has come out lovely this morning and so, lets hope for better business.

So glad to hear that Willie is doing nicely in the shop. I always knew that if that fellow were given a good chance he would make good. I shall write him a letter the first chance I have. Believe me, if Willie's brother will have to go over there, you can absolutely rely on Willie to do his best. When did he come home and how did he enjoy his visit with Esther? Give him love & regards.

My father saved a photograph of his brother Willie standing with a baby. I have only two pictures of Willie, except for large group photos with him in the background. On the back of this one is written, "Mr. W. Grossberg with Miss R. Abrams on July 18, 1918, Syracuse, New York." Willie was visiting his sister Esther in Syracuse when her daughter Sylvia Rebecca was a baby. Pop didn't remember that Willie ever went to Syracuse and wondered where he got the money to go. Was it through his railroad job?

Cousin Herman was stationed at Camp Charleston, SC, and writes, on October 9, 1918:

Dear Sir:

I shall not mince words with you any longer. Nor shall I waste any of my valuable time with such as you. You low highbrow. Trying to tell me he wrote me a postal card and two letters. What makes you lie to me so? Now listen young man I wrote you a sixteen-paged letter a few weeks ago. Now shake it up and answer it.

Well kid I hope you passed in your exam. If you write me a
longer letter I have some real dope...

Louis' military service was brief indeed – less than three months before
the war ended. In fact, it was briefer than that because shortly after en-
listment he caught the flu. Thousands of Americans died of the disease.
Boys from farming areas seemed to be hit the hardest. They had less
immunity than city boys who had been exposed to more illnesses prior
to their military service. The flu took millions of lives worldwide.

Louis was at a training camp for about a month when he went
home for the weekend. He didn't remember if he was feeling sick at
the time, but when he got home, he really took ill. A doctor was called
to the house and found Louis in bed, and a hot brick wrapped up in a
vinegar-saturated cloth placed at his feet.

Knowing of Sarah Henna's reputation for healing, the doctor said,
"I can't do anything for him. You can probably cure him better than I."

The flu caused Louis to lose much of his hair. His temperature was
106° for a week and without his mother's expert nursing, he might have
become another statistic. The doctor later said Louis survived because
his mother had nursed him so well. He had seen others much less sick
that died. The doctor then asked her for some of her home remedies
which seemed to work better than his. One was to burn wool and let
the smoke smolder to heal a wound.

As per instructions, Louis tried to notify his unit but was too sick
to make contact for a couple of weeks. At that point, the officer in charge
ordered him back to be treated by army doctors on base. When Louis
told him there was no way that he could make it back, the army gave
in and said to stay home and recover. It probably didn't take too much
persuasion since the army doctors were overwhelmed with patients, if
they were not sick themselves.

Louis received this post card to which he finally responded by phone
to avoid being AWOL.

Oct. 29, 1918,

> WAR DEPARTMENT to Louis Grossberg, 614 M St. NW.
> **BE ALERT** *Keep in touch with your Local Board*
> *Notify Local Board immediately of change of address*
> Until able to report for duty, have condition reported each
> day by phone to Sergeant Freedman Wist. Bring doctor's certifi-
> cate when reporting.

Rose recounted her family's experience with the flu in her letter of October 11, 1918. It had already affected her sisters Isabelle and Naomi.

"Everything in this city is closed on account of the epidemic. We are
losing so many people here it scares you to death. Isabelle and Naomi
both have the Influenza. Belle is getting better and I hope in a few days
Naomi will feel all right. This morning when the doctor came, he said
I was next in order for it so I was inoculated and my arm is beginning
to feel mighty funny." Rose was now teaching art in high school and
added, "The pupils, many of them, are very nearly my own age and I
do have a glorious time."

Kitty's husband Al was sick too. A letter from his brother, Hyman,
was dated October 23, 1918. Evidently, Al's father went to help and Hyman offered to go from Washington if necessary. Hyman also offered to
send clothes from their store, to be paid off later. Kitty wrote to Louis
in early November.

> Dear Elsie – or was it L.C.? Schkoos please,
>   Your letter pleased me more than you may think. I am glad
> that you have enlisted, and funny or strange as it may seem to you
> I, too, wish that you may be able to go across and do your duty.
> Just think, if you had a chance to go to France and by God's help
> to come safely back, why my dear, you would almost be a *Fran-*
> *zewate Schnookele.*" (I have no idea what "Franzewate" means.
> "Schnookele" is an endearment.)
>   Kiddo, you just work hard and attend to your duties and I feel
> confident that you will get what you want. I had hoped so terribly
> hard that you would be able to run up here during the Christmas
> Holidays for a visit. I had hoped that we would be able to spare
> the cash, but if things continue as they are now, in the face of the

obvious cold weather setting in, I am afraid it will be beyond question. Can you guess how sorry I am, being as how you will probably go overseas without as much as a fat juicy fair-well kiss from your own Makite. I say Lou, what's the use of living?

By this time no doubt you will have started your studies at the ASTC (SATC) and probably you have already been promoted to the honorable and much sought after rank of KP (Kock in Pot). If so, why, and if not, why not?

If the latest reports are correct, your *Sister*, mind you, spell it with a capital S, is a full fledged citizen of the U.S.A. and acknowledged as a person. Just think, I can now vote to my hearts' content, and suffer, by golly, and Jimene Chriskes. From now on you may take your hat off and bow low to me for in this regard I am far above you, being as how you are only a District of Columbian, which doesn't count. I hope you will have the proper respect for me from now on. And that is not all, my power has risen to such an extent as to almost make it possible for Al and me to be real political enemies during election time. Just imagine, supposing I am inclined to vote Democratic and Al Republican and he trying to make me vote his way and I voting the way I please: Oh, Christophor...

By the way, tell me what has become of the Flu that you had? I hope it has flown away. I get quite worried because I haven't had a letter for nearly 2 weeks from home...

Business with us seems to be pretty good on some days and not so good on other days. Now if we can hold out until Spring... I am sorry I cannot send you a prepaid invitation for Christmas Holidays but remember, old Pal of mine, you of the 2-story ice cream cones, remember, that, if we will have plenty of dough, I will be able to bake lovely bread and there will be prepaid invitations and prepaid return trips galore. Just you wait.

I think this is a long enough letter for you so *Verbleibe hartz lich gegrusst und gekusst von diene dich ewig liebende Schwester* (in my heart I remain your loving sister). Kitty

Pop's brother Sol remembered this story about Kitty. While she didn't have enough money to pay for Louis' visit to Michigan, she did send

25¢ a week so that the kids remaining at home could go to the movies every week. There were five children then and the cost was 5¢ apiece. One week Kitty sent 45¢ so that her parents could go along too and see their first movie. The adult price was 10¢ each. On the way to the theater, their father asked how much it cost to go to the movies and when told it would be 45¢, he said, *"Finf und fiftzik cent! Mir ken kaifen neun leiben broit. Lommer gehen ahaim!"* (Meaning: "Forty five cents! I can buy nine loaves of bread. Let's go home!") With that, he gave the children 3 cents to buy some apples and pocketed the rest. They never forgot what their sister Kitty's generosity to their parents cost them.

During the war, even though Louis had citizenship from his father, the Lieutenant in his Company suggested he get citizenship papers of his own because for persons applying for officer status, the 5-year waiting period for aliens was waived. The Lieutenant and Louis went to court and he became a citizen in 1918. The judge asked the officer how long he had known Louis. The officer said 3 years, though the truthful answer would have been 1 month. So, the judge signed the citizenship papers.

After my father passed away, I found this affidavit in his filing cabinet. LCG Naturalization paper dated Dec. 10, 1918, Supreme Court of DC #1129194, Petition volume #2562 M. His Social Security number was #577–03–7006. His father's Citizenship was #1147605.

Louis' cousins, Leo V. Freudberg and Rose Bersh, were themselves distant cousins through marriage, but they had not met previously. Louis' mother and Rose's mother were Effenbach sisters. Louis probably introduced Leo to Rose when she visited Washington during one of Leo's furloughs. Leo's middle name was Victor, which Rose adopted for him.

Rose Bersh wrote Louis from Paterson, New Jersey, September 1918, asking him to come out no later than the Friday before the New Year, as she would be home then. "I am glad Victor feels as though he can say he had a good time. I really hope he did. It is not very difficult to please him."

Up to this time, Louis wrote most of his letters in longhand and no copies remained. He was in the habit of keeping carbons of his typed letters. Louis never expected anything to develop between Rose and Leo. Yet, Leo corresponded with Louis hoping to find out what Rose thought of him and Rose did the same about Leo. Louis was very circumspect.

He relayed as little information as he could and let nature take its course. This first carbon of a letter was of one he sent to Rose after he visited her in Paterson, New Jersey. He also called Leo – Victor, or Vic.

"I came in at precisely 10:47:07 o'clock on Thursday Evening. Pa and Ma were asleep. Of course after the usual how-do-you do kisses I had to sit down and tell the kids all about it. Friday evening Vic and I held our usual pow-wow. Of course we were glad to see each other. He thanked me for your kind regards. Naturally we had quite a little talk about Paterson and Totowa…We talked about your poetry and other such interesting topics, but as I told you in Paterson not a word about personal matters. Now that I think of it, it strikes me as rather curious that since that Friday Evening and following Saturday we have hardly spoken a dozen words about you. I am sure Leo thinks often of you and I know that he cannot possibly think more often of you than I do, yet as I say we seldom mention your name together. It is the same with many other acquaintances. We very seldom if ever discuss an acquaintance. Don't you think that is a very much better way than to dissect a person and to examine every part of him? What do you say?" He teased.

The Massachusetts Mutual Insurance Company sent a letter on November 7, 1918, evidently before it knew Louis was in the Army. It says they are in receipt of notification that Louis has enrolled in the Students Army Training Corps and they must advise him that they need an extra premium when he is transferred to a central officers school or to the Army or Navy.

The World War I ended November 11, 1918, and Louis was discharged a few days later. He was 20-years-old and mustered out of the army shortly after returning to base from his near death experience with the flu. Now he had to think about his future. He did not plan to remain a junk and bag dealer forever, but in the meantime, that was his main concern. His brother-in-law Harry Abrams, Esther's husband, had taught him a lot about the business and Louis represented the Abrams Bros. Company in Washington, DC, not only for purchasing Army waste materials but from other junk dealers in the area.

College was out of the question now, for Louis could not afford to go to school in the daytime, at least not full time. He and other discharged soldiers discussed options among themselves. One of them suggested a coming new field, accountancy. None of the colleges Louis knew of had such courses, but on further investigation, he discovered that there was one correspondence school, Pace Institute, that offered a diploma as a graduate accountant. They had a branch in Washington, DC, and their classes were taught at night. This suited him perfectly.

When Louis applied for enrollment, he told the manager that he didn't know a "debit from a horse."

The manager replied, "That's great. You won't have to unlearn anything you picked up in the past."

Eleanor at 18 was becoming useful in the shop but was not ready to take over the reins of the business. Though Louis had years ahead of him before he could step aside, Kitty and Al had other ideas for him. In her letter of November 18, 1918, Kitty writes:

"Did you know that the war was over, and I am afraid you have no chance to go abroad? You did eh, well, listen to this – I savvy that you are a very dutiful son with a poor Pa what wants to do the very best by his blooming offsprings, but can't, no dough. Well, do you and Pa & Ma also realize that you ought to have a chance to make a *tachless* (something) of yourself...If the war had continued and you would have had to go abroad, they would have managed without you. Well, from good sources I learn that after the war the auto accessory business will come into its own. Al will undertake to teach you the accessory business from A to Z. He will pay you $20 per week with board & room, naturally for the start, and as you go along, you get a quarter raise here and there.

"From the $20 per you send Ma $15 regular as clockwork and at the end of say, a couple of years, Al says, when you want to start in for yourself, absolutely he will give you a chance. Considering that Willie can manage at home if he got a chance, you ought to take it.

"Al is going to hire a man to attend to the store while he goes to see the wholesale trade. Believe me, Lou, it pains me to think that a fender man will learn the business where you ought to be. You will be surprised to see how much Al knows of this business. Even now 2 accessory stores and 2 garages here in town do a lot of their buying from Al because Al can sell them cheaper than they can get elsewhere and still make a fairly good profit. You see, Al gets a lot of things at jobber's prices. Please, don't let me wait for an answer. Talk it over with Pa & Ma, and really, Louis, this is a good chance."

Remember Cousin Sol Naiman, the lifter of horses who nearly

drowned while canoeing with Louis? Notification arrived at the Grossberg house dated December 2, 1918, from Headquarters, 313ᵗʰ U.S. Infantry, that Sol Naiman was wounded in action September 30, 1918. Sol Naiman lived with the Grossberg family for a time and probably used that address for army records. He was a member of the American Expeditionary Forces for over 6 months, so received one gold service chevron. There was no record in my father's files of what became of him after that.

Kitty wrote on December 17, 1918, from Jackson, Michigan:

Your little 1 page letter reached me amidst a hurdle burdle of confusion and glamour. You wouldn't guess what was happening. So, being as I am a conscientious believer of limitation of suspense I will stop long enough to explain. There was a mouse in the kitchen so Al tried to catch him and preserve him in a milk bottle. Do you get the meaning? Oh, I see, you don't, well, neither do I…

Somehow, dear Elsie, Your letters put a new pep in my existence. I wait for them with my whole heart and stomach and when they come, I generally wait until all of my work is done before opening them, else my work doesn't get done that day. I get to feeling so happy, reminiscing like that I hate to go back to the ordinary tasks of dishwashing.

So you are now a common ordinary private citizen even as Al and I. Since last you saw me I have become a Mother, and that's something, considering the fact that Bobbie is the cause. Oh boy, you should see your nephew. Some kid, yes indeed, some kid. Right now, he happens to be the proud possessor of an artistically black eye. He bumpt himself yesterday and I begin to suspect the rascal has a baby yellow *hinten* (rear end) if you know what I mean. Smells like it, I hear.

We have a strap for (Bobby) that makes it impossible for him to fall out of the carriage. I generally keep it under his coat and when he stands up and commences to wiggle around everybody thinks in a minute he will fall and you should see the women run to catch him, with a genuine real for sure laugh from the honorable Bobby. Yes indeed, he is some kid.

I suppose you must think Esther's baby is *the thing*. Better wait until you see my handiwork, before passing out the jelly…

You know, Louis, I wish you would do me a favor. Go and have your picture taken and send me one. A postal will do. If you haven't the cash I will be really glad to send it. Often, when I cook corn or *pasechdike knadlech* (Passover dumplings) I would enjoy it 100% more if I had you to look at while I am devouring it.

The 24th of this month is my (22d) Twenty-tood (sic) birthday and if you will manage to let me have the picture I will thank you one quarter of an inch worth. These here are hard times, I am sure, and you may not be in a picture taking mood, but when you think of your Makite and recall that F St. fruit store, I know you'll do it. Thanks in advance.

Lucy dear, I am really & truly sorry I cannot send you fare to come to visit us as we planned. I hope you will understand. As regards to the proposition we spoke of, I must advise you that you can't pay us enough to let you come. As Ma explained it, you are needed to home and that's where you will stay. I hope and wish the very best for you in Washington...

Tell me, Lou, have I a successor in Ella or Pauline or Mary (perhaps Miriam) who share with you those little hopes and pains and laughs and dances and ball games with you? And oh yes, and *peanuts*? Tell me, Lou, Have I? Ma sais the girls are quite developed. I wish you would write me a real long letter about you and home and Aunt Hena's family – Rose included, and have it here by my birthday, Louis, my *heartz* (heart), mine *gidule* (big guy), my bro.

We have lovely weather right now, just like spring and I am oh, so lazy and oh, so lonesome, and Louis, could you come for a visit for Christmas and oh Louis, how about a game of checkers? Here I am, jumbling this letter up to pieces. It's my mood, Iwanchutocom. I hope Ma has clothes and Pa too and the children and Grandma. How is grandma, anyway?

Is Esther still as pretty as she was when she was single? I understand she has taken on a little averdupois (sic). Oh, by the way, Lou, where were you born and where did you live last before coming to the U.S.A.?

Bobby's story was a sad one. He did not get on well with his father. Often he would run away from home and on one of those occasions he enlisted in the army. Bobbie was killed during World War II in the Japanese theatre.

The grandma referred to in Kitty's letter was Minnie Effenbach, her mother's mother who came alone to America about 1912, when she was already 89-years-old. She would attempt to get up to give Louis a seat whenever he entered the room but he would not let her. She lived with the Grossberg family until her death. A hired woman lived in and cared for her and her last days were very difficult. Minnie Effenbach lived to be 98-years-old. Louis never knew his mother's father, Wolfe (Ze'ev) Effenbach, who died in 1869. Records show that when he died, he left his widow with seven children, the youngest being my grandmother, Sarah Henna, who at that time was only 1-year-old. As for Louis' grandparents on his father's side, he never met them. They lived in a different part of Russia or Poland.

Kitty's reminiscing brought to mind another story my father told. Not only did he and Kitty steal away in the night to buy corn during their childhood, but also Kitty was a very vivacious young lady with a mind of her own. Ottenberg's Bakery was on 7th Street, close to 614 M Street where the Grossberg family was living at the time. Mrs. Ottenberg was a tough old lady. One day Kitty walked into the bakery.

Pointing to some cookies, she said, "Give me ½ dozen of those *judemecranks*," whereupon Mrs. Ottenberg gave her a lecture on using such names on God's food.

So Kitty said, "O.K. *mame*, let me have ½ dozen of those *judemecranks*."

Louis, as an agent for his brother-in-law, Harry Abrams, dealt with the Government for the sale of surplus materials. After the war, the Government had a lot of excess supplies they no longer needed. In the Washington area, they appointed a cavalry officer who knew all about horses and maybe something about war but nothing about waste materials. He didn't know the difference between iron and copper. Because there was a great deal of merchandise to be bid on, Louis became acquainted with him by phone and visited him in his office a number of times. On every visit, Louis brought him a cigar though he himself did not smoke at that time. On one visit, the officer handed Louis a cigar, which he could not refuse. Louis had to smoke it and disliked it intensely. Unfortunately, that dislike did not last long. At age 21, Louis was a skinny youngster whom the officer called frequently to ask the prices for the week. He was very helpful to Louis and even allowed him to change his bid occasionally, which was against regulations.

In 1986, when I first started working with Pop on these memoirs, we sat downstairs in the recreation room. He was still smoking cigars. His big concession to the Surgeon General's reports was to give up cigarettes. Periodically he would take a break and go upstairs to smoke, away from me. Even my mother, who was not a smoker, asked him to limit his smoking to the living room where he had an easy chair and a "talking books" machine. In my youth, Mom's smoking was an annual event much attended by those in the house at the time. Four or five years before my father died, he stopped entirely, due either to our urging, Dr. Sislen's or because he lost the taste for it. This made life much better for all concerned.

My father was a joke teller and those who knew him, rarely left his presence without hearing one during their conversations. One of his favorite people to share jokes with was our family doctor, Maurice Sislen. This was especially true in the later years when my parents' health caused them to be seen frequently. Most of the time in the examining room was taken up by exchanging jokes. After one particular visit, Pop told me he had been put into a room where a very large brassiere was hanging on the inside of the door. When the good doctor came in Pop asked,

"Where did that come from?"

"Darned if I know," replied Maury. "It was found hanging there one day but for the life of me I can't remember who left it." I think the bra hung there for quite some time, either to amuse other patients or in hopes that the owner would recall where she had left it.

When Pop was 97 years old he took a big elaborately decorated box of chocolates to the doctor's office. When it was his turn to be escorted from the waiting room, he handed the box to Jill, Maury's very efficient black nurse.

"Who is this for?" she asked.

"It's for you," he said with a smile.

"Why for me?" she asked.

Pop replied, "Every time I come to this office I bring you a urine specimen, so this time I wanted to bring you something nice."

Certain letters I read to Pop would elicit a chuckle and he'd say, "Have you heard this one?"

The cigar he received from that cavalry officer back in 1919 did not start him on tobacco. He may have been a smoker then, but it was of cigarettes and occasionally pipes. Though he was never a heavy smoker, he smoked every day except Shabbat most of his life. As a child, I remember being terribly affected by this. It did nothing for my allergies. When he added cigars to his repertoire, it really made things worse. Of course, in those days, until Americans learned of the hazards of smoking, everyone accepted it. I remember as a child, riding in the car on frequent motor trips, complaining bitterly. His response was, "Just give it a little time and you'll get used to it." Well, I never did!

Honor the Sabbath Day and Keep It Holy

In Louis' dealings for Harry Abrams, he was once asked to put in a bid for copper wire. He learned on Friday that his bid was too high and could have had it changed Saturday morning against regulations. Louis' good friend, the cavalry officer, wanted to accommodate him. Louis tried to call Harry on Friday night and the reply he got was that Mr. Abrams was not in and could not be reached until after the Sabbath, which ended sundown Saturday night. Louis had to let the bid stand, which cost Abrams Bros. about $2,000 extra. Harry remarked upon learning of this, "$2,000 is a cheap price to pay for my Jewishness."

Louis disliked the manner in which the junk shop had to dispose of its merchandise. There was only one wholesaler in the area – N. FRANK & SONS. One of the sons, Nathan, was the manager of the Washington branch and paid somewhat less than the going wholesale rate. To overcome this, Louis made contact with some metal mills in order to ship large quantities of copper, brass, bronze, tires, waste paper, etc. The quantities worth shipping were larger than his shop had, so he went to the other local dealers and offered them a better price than Frank paid and shipped them to the mills directly.

Not only did he get a better price for his own merchandise, but he also made a little profit on the merchandise he bought from the other junk dealers because the price the mills paid Louis was the same price

Frank was getting from the same mills. Naturally, Frank didn't like this and decided to get back at Louis. One day there was an auction of Government waste materials. Most of the junk dealers in town went to the sale and bid on it. There was one batch of uniform buttons made of a lead base with an iron cover. They had the insignia of the uniform on them. Louis bid $25.00.

Frank shouted, "Grossberg! $30.00."

Louis said, "$35.00."

Frank yelled, "Grossberg! $40.00."

He drove the price up to $80.00, which Louis paid.

Afterwards, Frank walked over to Louis and said, "You can't sell this. The only thing that has any value is the lead. But in order to sell the lead, you must remove the iron cover."

Undaunted, Louis went next door to an iron shop, owned by an old man named Frank Snyder. Snyder manufactured iron grills, fences, etc. When Louis took the buttons over there, he told the old man he needed to remove the lead from the iron covers in order to salvage his disastrous purchase.

"That's no problem at all," said Frank. "I'll make you an iron grate with a trough. We will put a sheet over a contraption where we can make a fire and when we set these buttons on top, the lead will melt and run down the trough into a container."

Louis sold the molten lead for $275.00. When he got the check, he showed it to Frank of FRANK & SONS and had the last laugh. Later, Frank became friendly with Louis and told him in a fatherly fashion to get out of the junk business because it was no place for a man with his capabilities.

One of the few letters to Kitty where Louis kept a carbon copy was this one dated December 20, 1918. Louis and Kitty loved to corrupt the English language with made up words and fanciful spelling. It was not always clear that Kitty knew the difference, but Louis certainly did. Louis writes:

What's this! What's this! Am I informed correctly that you have selected December 25th, or some such ungodly date for your birth anniversary, I mean sary? If so I want to know what you mean by that. Is this a birthday epidemic or are you all just copying me. Ansfer me at once.

But I bethought me that, as the saying goes, 'There must be fire behind all this smoke.' It occurred to me that if I wished to be on the safe side it behooves me to take no chances. Well and good. But what is to be done. Ella said, 'Buy her a present.'

'What shall I buy?

'What do you want to buy?' she asks. Did you ever hear of such a thing? What do I *want* to buy? Why I want to buy you a bee-eautiful house with a most magnificent aftomobile and a million dollar bank account and God's guarantee of a hundred years' health and happiness and – and – everything else which you yourself wish for. But *bettler wos redst du* (what are you saying)? It isn't what you want to buy it is what you can afford to buy, right?

Hence and therefore your future children's uncle betook himself to the place where he knows good candy can be obtained. There a gonglomeration of sweets obstructed his view. *Kaum mit zores und gezaeres* (come and go with difficulty) he selected his select and presto in the form of bambonx is making its speedy way towards its destination. May the things which I 'want' to buy you be contained by your darling hubby and may you both live happily *yor ein yor* (year after year) for a generation. Amen. By the way I almost forgot. Conscratulate on your birthday. This makes you sixteen, doesn't it?

Dear Madam I wish to inform you that I have taken heed of your threat as to what would happen, or rather, would not happen on January 15 (Louis' birthday), or thereabout if a certain matter of which I believe you are quite aware is not attended to at once, and have the pleasure to inform you that a certain gentleman is kept busy for periods of not less than twenty minutes per twice a day furnishing the comforts of warmth to our most spacious abode, for which service (he) is duly remunerated every Saturday night of each fifty second of an annum by the antecedent of the above perpendicular pronoun.

I shall now proceed to stop, cease, quit, desist, and defer from further writing. Because why? You owe me a letter. Very Frequently yours…

Leo remained in the service longest. His job now was to help men leave the armed services. His letter began, "today 1919," was from War Camp Community Service, Washington, DC, Contagious Ward and was hand written. Leo asked Louis to deliver and pay off part of a note for him until he got out of confinement. He may have been sick with the flu.

> I am having it pretty soft in this 'camp' as long as I lay in bed. I am up and about however. If your mother does not know she need not know, because she may accidentally tell it to my own mother. Drop around some afternoon. I can talk to you from the porch. Kindest regards old top, Vic

The photo that Kitty requested in December was sent in short order. Her response was dated January 7, 1919.

> Thanks very much indeed for the Velaties. You are sure a pal of mine. But really, old top, don't you think you should have spared yourself the money for things you may need for yourself, such as – tooth accessories, a new pair of *Zizes* (underwear) or *Albekaufus*, as it is most commonly called, or perhaps some new two in one shoe polish. These are all very necessary things for a young man of your caliber to need. Howsoever I thank you and hope to be able to receive a duplicate of that most delicious and long eaten up box of caramels at my next birthday.
>
> I received just a few minutes ago your picture and the note and must give you credit, old top, for thee (sic) art handsome, but short. But really, don't you feel ashamed of yourself for having the audacity (if that's spelled right) to send me such a little cheep (sic) picture, *to me*, think of it, *to me*. You will absolutely have to do better, that's all.

A letter, probably written by Louis as a favor to Leo, was dated February 15, 1919, and addressed, "Dear Parents, Quantico, VA." The war was over but soldiers were not discharged yet and Leo felt lucky to be working in an office instead of on the drill field. His job was to locate marines and route letters to them that were inadequately addressed. He said he missed his mother and didn't appreciate her until he left home.

Ben, probably the soldier who suggested accountancy, wrote June 11, 1919, from Paterson, New Jersey, on stationery of War Department, Port of Embarkation, New York, saying he was not satisfied with his job in Hoboken, New Jersey, and had received papers from the Pace Institute. He looked forward to one day realizing their ambition of forming the Corporation of Expert Accounts that they spoke of a while ago. Signed, "Yours until the next trial balance, Ben."

In the middle of 1919, after studying bookkeeping, his first course at the Pace Institute, Louis applied for a job in the Government Accounting Office and flunked the exam. Six months later, he applied for a position as an auditor in the Income Tax Division of the Internal Revenue Service and passed that exam. He then became a Government employee in 1920, checking income tax returns. He stayed in the Government until January 1, 1924.

Louis' friend, David Glushak, joined him in studying accounting after getting his BS degree in Agriculture. Dave decided that farming was not the glorious occupation he envisioned and returned to Washington to join Louis at Pace. At some point, Dave married Ida, who would not have made a good farm wife. In fact, it may have been due to her that Dave gave up on the farm dream.

Both Louis and Dave worked in the Income Tax Unit at the same time. Their experience with taxes was of tremendous value to them in their later accounting practice because at that time few accountants were familiar with Income Tax Law and practically no lawyers had any knowledge of that field.

Ben wrote again, July 16, 1919. Place, God's Country.

My dear (Ditto on the BUM),

You wonder where I get the time to write so many letters. In the first place, did you ever know of a Government employee who is always working? Well, I am not that kind. I always work, if it is not for the benefit of the Government, it is for my own.

At the present writing I am employed in the inventory and Audit Section of the Supplies. In other words I am an accountant. I run an adding machine, check up figures, you know, juggle figures and *everything*. As to my study in accounting, I gave it up for the hot months, but intend to enter either NYU, or else stick with Pace and Pace.

Here is a funny one. Last Sunday, another fellow and myself, went canoeing up the Passaic River. Everything went along nicely until about 5 o'clock, when we were on our way home. All of a sudden a voice is heard. My eyes met the gaze of a young lady on the opposite shore whom I soon recognized as one of my neighbors. We were asked if we would not be so kind as to row her over to the other side so that she might be able to take the car and proceed homeward. We immediately agree. This young lady was attired in her prettiest Sunday dress. We were dressed in our bathing suits with our clothes lying at the bottom of the canoe. We drew close to the shore (and) beckoned for her to approach, which she did. The scene, one foot on the shore and the other foot resting on the canoe. The boat was given a gentle push, the young lady doing the split, plunging into the water, in so doing she upset the boat also turning us into the water, wetting our clothes. The lady was pulled out, soaked to the skin. Everyone laughing…

Act two: Scene camp fire. Also in scene a clothesline. A fire is made so that the wet clothes may be given a chance to dry. Two other girls are hurried back to Paterson to get some dry clothes for the almost drowned one. Clothes almost dry after waiting almost two and a half hours. The girl is attired in her dry clothes. No applause. The scene shifts, the drowned parties meet, and they lived happily ever after. My regards to all…Just tell Dave that he owes me a letter and also Fanny (Dave's sister).

Ve zien de kinder? (How are the children?)

Doss is goot (That is good).

How do you like my Yiddish?

A reissued Birth Certificate for Edith Cohen, Kitty and Al's daughter, born in DC, October 2, 1919, was originally filed on October 9, 1919. Kitty's birthplace was listed as Germany, which is consistent with what Pop told me – that when he was born, Latvia was part of Germany. The reissued birth certificate was dated March 7, 1952.

In a September 14 Western Union Telegram from Kitty to Louis, she wrote: "Missed railroad connections will arrive 7:15 tonight, Kitty." No more mention of this visit is recorded except that she left some items in Washington, which she hoped Louis would bring with him to

Richmond. The following undated letter from Kitty was posted from Richmond, Virginia, where they moved after leaving Michigan. "We received your letter & are certainly glad to hear that you are coming for a visit. Oh boy. Be sure to let us know on what train you are coming so Al can meet you, and, incidentally I might see to it that I have some grub ready, and perhaps the house in order, when you come. I wish you would bring along a few things I have left home. Namely a small doily, a couple of pillowcases, and Pauline. Also Al's tube of Pepsodent Tooth Paste. Al sent the handbag Parcel Post to-day, and insured for $15.00. I had inside two suits of underwear that are too small or too large for Al. Perhaps Momma can use it for Pa or? Give it to somebody in the shop. In a way I am sore as the dickens at you. Here it was, a perfectly legitimate and proper birthday of mine, a birthday that really demands the respect and reverence of a youngster as you, and nary a letter or an all day and night sucker. For shame, thou 10¢ Pie face. But, as you are coming here, I excuse you for that. Love to all the family. Waitingly, Kautche…"

Among the goods that Louis bought for Harry Abrams were bales of woolen rags. In such bales, 15% of the weight was allowed for cotton included in the wool, such as from men's vests, which included part cotton and part wool. Also, men's coats had cotton linings. This could make up the allowable 15%. When this shipment arrived in Syracuse, the Abrams Company discovered that instead of 15% "Outthrows", the shipment contained 30%. They rejected the shipment and returned it to Washington, demanding a return of the purchase price. The local company refused to accept these bales and they were put in storage.

At that time, whenever Louis needed a lawyer he used SIMON, KOENIGSBERGER & YOUNG. (KOENIGSBERGER later became the sole judge of the DC tax court.) Louis called Koenigsberger to represent Abrams Bros. in suing the seller. In order to save storage charges they sold the bales of woolens for the best price they could and sued for the balance. Before selling the bales, Louis had a couple of witnesses check one of the bales to verify the Abrams Bros. findings. It was Harry's suggestion that they dispose of all but one bale so that they might take it into court to prove to the judge at the trial that there were too many "Outthrows." The lawyer pooh-poohed this suggestion and so they sold all of them. At the trial a year later, the witnesses were so vague that the court threw out their case. So, Harry had been right.

Around the corner from the junk shop was the bag business, which closed up after Yalow left, though the junk shop continued until 1922. In April of 1920, Louis was already working for the Internal Revenue Service. For 2½ years after she graduated from High School, his younger sister Eleanor helped at the junk shop also. One day Louis had a disagreement with Stein & Company, of Atlanta, Georgia. The subject was tires. On November 3, 1919, he sent the following letter.

Gentlemen:

Your letter of Oct. 30th to hand and note with regret that you have shipped another car of tires. The local party for whom I am buying these tires claims that your tires are picked. As proof, he states his pickers can get but 10 to 15% suitable tires out of your lot. For his use unpicked tires yield from 75 to 80% suitable. I personally spent an hour in his yards watching his pickers and verified his statements. With such a low percentage of pickings, your tires are handled at a loss.

Since he bought *unpicked* tires, my principal refuses to accept any more of your tires. Accordingly, I telegraphed to you on Saturday to ship no more tires. Unfortunately, my telegram reached you too late. Inasmuch as you have shipped this car, I will take it for $3.00 per hundred F.O.B. Atlanta, have it picked in my own yard, and take the risk of loss. My principal will not even accept them for $3.00. If this is satisfactory to you, kindly have your bank recall your draft and send another for 95% at $3.00 per hundred. Or you may send me a check for $80.00 and I will take up your draft as drawn.

I regret exceedingly the turn of affairs. The fact, however, remains that your tires have been picked. No doubt your customers have had them run thru before shipping to you. You can readily see that at the present condition of the scrap rubber market it does not pay anyone to buy auto tires mixed including stripped and road worn at a cost of $3.85 per hundred FOB Washington, *unless* the percentage of picking is normal as it should be.

Under no circumstances can I accept any more of your tires, unless subject to report. I have tried to be as fair with you as is possible. I have induced my principal to pocket the loss on your first car and I am willing to chance a loss on the one last shipped. Very truly yours, Louis C. Grossberg

The Stein Company sent the Postal Telegraph Company this letter of November 6, 1919.

Gentlemen:

We are advised by Louis C. Grossberg that he sent us the following telegram: Washington, DC Nov. 1, 1919

Rush: My principal claims your tires are picked. Ship no more. We did not get the above message either by phone or mail, as a result of which we have been caused considerable loss. Please investigate and let us know what you find. Very truly yours, Stein & Company

The Stein Company responded to Louis, November 6, 1919, at 521 K. St. NW, Washington, DC.

Dear Sir:

Your letter of the 3rd inst. was received by us late yesterday afternoon. When we sold you the tires we told you 'our tires are unpicked, except that once in a while a vulcanizer comes and gets a few.' That is a fact, so that you have no ground for your claim.

When we received remittance and settlement of balance due on the first car, we were justified in assuming that the tires shipped were satisfactory. However, had we received your telegram we would not have shipped another car, as we do not want to have dealings that will lead to controversies, but the fact is that we did not get your telegram at all; and while we are willing to cancel your order for the two additional cars of tires, we expect you to pay the price agreed upon for the second car we shipped and will thank you to take care of draft.

You will note that we have written the telegraph company to find out why message was not delivered. If investigation proves them to be at fault, they will be liable for any loss you may sustain, and you will be able to collect from them, since we could have stopped the car before it left Atlanta if telegram had been received. Very truly yours, Stein & Company

Louis then sent a telegram to Stein & Company on November 10, 1919.

Car tires arrived this evening has been rejected by my principal. Will stick to my previous offer and accept car at three cents Atlanta. Wire bank to change draft ninety five percent at three cents. Will accept no other arrangement. If dissatisfied wire instructions as to disposal of car. Louis C. Grossberg

Pop didn't remember what happened with the disagreement in the end, but said he was sure the outcome was satisfactory as far as he was concerned.

Frank Snyder, the ironmonger who helped Louis with the buttons was a kindly old man. Louis' sister Eleanor not only worked in the junk shop, but managed to find time to assist Mr. Snyder as well. She answered his phone, wrote his checks and did whatever she could to be helpful. Louis did his part by preparing Mr. Snyder's income tax returns free of charge.

A few years later, Louis Harrison, who had worked in the junk shop, bought the business in its entirety. Until the purchase was made, Harrison had earned $1.00 a day and was paid daily. Later Harrison founded Harrison Bros. Plumbing Supplies Corporation from which we bought our plumbing supplies in 1972, when building our house in Israel. We found a letter of contract from the Chicago Junk Co. that said the selling price was $250.

After the junk shop was sold, Louis made it a point to keep in contact with Mr. Snyder. One day, Mr. Snyder asked Louis to stop by to see him. He said he was not long for this world and would like to leave $1,000 in cash, "which I give you and Sol to hold as trustees, for Eleanor. You can use it in the meantime if you wish, but when I die I want you to give the money to Eleanor." Mr. Snyder was afraid to leave the $1,000 in his will because Eleanor was only 24-years-old and it might not look good to his family. Louis deposited the money in the Building

Association for interest. This was a godsend. Eleven years later, in 1934, he used this money to help build his house on Garrison Street. Mr. Snyder lived a long time, but when he died, Louis gave Eleanor the $1,000 plus interest.

On November 11, 1919, Rose Bersh wrote Louis, thanking him for remembering her birthday. She was now teaching again and had just arrived home after seeing a parade. "I wonder whether you did not don your uniform this morning to pass before the eyes of an admiring throng. I have the seventh grade and I do get a great deal of fun out of it. I suppose you will be glad to know I drive our car. Last Thursday I got my license and I passed both tests – driving and written – with 100%. Now, aren't you proud of your cousin? What are you doing now? Still at college I take it and as usual, at the head of the class.

"Is Kitty still in Washington? How is she? And how is Al? I think I wrote to her after she had already left Jackson. You are an Uncle, now all right. I can just about imagine you foundling the babies. If you are as affectionate to them all as you were with Bobbie, you have a job on hand..."

Louis used benefits available to him from the Unites States Civil Service Commission because he'd been in the Army. He received a letter addressed to Louis C. Grossberg, 614 M St. NW, Washington, DC, dated November 10, 1919. It said, "That hereafter in making appointments to clerical and other positions in the executive branch of the government in the District of Columbia or elsewhere preference shall be given to honorably discharged soldiers, sailors, and marines, and widows of such, and to the wives of injured soldiers, sailors, and marines who themselves are not qualified but whose wives are qualified to hold such positions."

There was an amusing pamphlet from December 18, 1919, distributed by the BUREAU OF INTERNAL REVENUE regarding work rules, including one stating it was illegal to resign from the service unless the party has worked there at least a year. "The administration of the war revenue laws has been seriously hampered during the last two years by an almost continuous exodus from the Internal Revenue Service of its more experienced officers and employees who have generally sought to commercialize the special knowledge and ability with which their experience in the service had equipped them. The places of many of the persons who thus left the service were filled temporarily by persons who were induced to enter the service as a patriotic duty."

On January 4, 1920, a letter from cousin Minna Kitay, in Paterson, arrived.

> I received your most welcome letter and father wishes me to thank you for your kind and immediate efforts to help him. It surely was a strange coincidence to find that you were going to bed after you wrote it and I was getting up when I received it. At present dad is at the mill. I am hoping he decides to come to Washington. Leave it to me and I'll surely come with him. I surely would love to come along to see the great capital and above all see you and my other dear cousins, auntie and uncle. One thing Louis dear, I would like to ask you if you will send me the names of my dear cousins. I know one's name is Ella but much to my regret I have forgotten the others. I would very much like to write to them once in a while.

Louis' sister, Esther Abrams, wrote from her home in Syracuse, New York.

> January 8, 1920
> My dear Louis:
> I guess you'll say *what's this*, when you got my letter for we are, sadly to say not in the habit in corresponding with each other, never-the-less I shall take the privilege in doing so this time and I mean to get an answer, *pronto, understand.*
> To make this letter short, I want to know everything you told Unka and Aunt Bersh about the money we loaned (borrowed) from Mr. Snyder, how much interest you have to pay in short everything relating to this matter. Now you'll want to know why I ask you all this. I am sorry I can't tell it to you now, maybe sometime when I'll see you all. At present I want you to tell me all about it, and do not mention it to anyone. I am sorry you have been bothered but that can't be helpt any more. Answer right away. Write.

Louis' 22nd birthday was on January 15, 1920, and his sister Pauline sent him a telegram. She included a poem she wrote and said she had baked him a cake. She would have been 18-years-old at the time. She had a coloratura voice Pop said gave him goose pimples every time he heard her sing. In her singing class was a doctor's wife. The doctor frequently attended their recitals. In his opinion, of the entire class, Pauline was the only one with a gorgeous voice and could have a professional future.

According to my father, of all the Grossberg children, Pauline was the most unfortunate. One day when she was about 15-years-old, she returned from a visit to the library and had an epileptic seizure. This was the beginning of a lifetime of *tsoras* (troubles). No doctor could do much for her. On January 10, 1921, Louis wrote a letter to The Rockefeller Foundation, New York City, 61st & Broadway about his sister Pauline, who suffered from fainting spells. He asked for their help but never received a reply.

I have often read in the newspapers and magazines of the wonderful work your institution is doing for humanity thru your research in medical science. Thinking that you may be able to help us, if you will, I am making this appeal to you.

My sister, 19 years of age, is suffering from fainting spells. One doctor said it was apoplexy. When a spell comes upon her, she froths at the mouth and kicks her feet violently. She almost always bites her tongue. The first of these spells dates back about 6 years. Since then, they have been occurring with varied frequency.

We are of very limited means and have found it impossible to take her to specialists. We have, however, consulted a number of local physicians. She had been receiving treatment from Dr. Hopkins, late of the Washington Sanitarium, Tacoma Park, Maryland, until about eight months ago when he left for his home in Wisconsin. While he could not cure her, he did manage to keep the spells a good bit apart. Now, however, they have been occurring with alarming frequency, about every ten days.

They come upon her at various times with but slight warning. She is very conscious of this affliction and is mortally afraid of it. She has had a few spells in bed and will not go to sleep unless there is someone in the room. Mother has aged ten years in the last three. I am five years older than this sister, Pauline, and am a government employee. All of my salary goes toward helping to provide for our family as does that of a 17-year-old sister. There are five dependent children and an old grandmother. We have never before asked for any aid of whatever nature of anyone. I am, therefore, turning to you, in the hope that you can do something for her. If yours is humanitarian work, surely this is a fitting subject. Won't you please advise us?

In later years, Pauline became very dependent upon her brothers and sisters. She also required frequent hospitalizations, which my father attributed to her need for attention. Pauline's health did improve over time and, in fact, I never remember her having any seizures. When young and her health permitted it, she was helpful to the family. Miriam felt that it was her responsibility to look after Pauline and Pauline took advantage of this. Whenever Miriam wanted to go on a vacation, Pauline would get "sick," go to the hospital and return to Miriam's house to recuperate. Finally, when Miriam was in declining health herself, her son Mark put his foot down and told Pauline she was not allowed to go to his mother's house after leaving the hospital. At one point, Pauline's health plan refused to pay for these admissions so the financial burden fell upon my father, Miriam and Sol.

Cousin Herman Freudberg wrote Louis from Columbia, South Carolina, January 23, 1920. He must have been out of the service by that time.

I am still heading South and going strong. Expect to be in Jacksonville Florida some time next week...I am covering the whole South. And I expect to end up by way of Chicago and Detroit. Have you been away yet? Give my love to all...Ever the same, Herman

Herman figured in my father's life in a number of ways. After reading this letter, Pop told me this story. His cousin sold jewelry. When Herman was 25-years-old and still living in Washington, DC, he went to Baltimore to sell some pearls. After dealing with a certain jewelry store, he returned home and discovered that one string of graduated pearls was missing. Herman was frantic. He told Louis about his loss and the two hatched a scheme to get them back. The next day, both men went to Baltimore. Louis walked into the store and told the owner that he wanted to see some pearls because his mother was having a birthday.

"I would like to see graduated pearls," he said. From Herman's description, he recognized the stolen necklace. After looking them over carefully he said, "Before I make this purchase, I need to ask my mother if she would like pearls for her birthday. If she says yes, I'll return later and buy them."

Around the corner, Herman waited for the report. Louis told Herman he thought the pearls were his. About an hour later, Louis went back and asked to see the pearls again. The man produced the string and within a few minutes, Herman walked in. Louis then identified himself as a private detective and pointed to Herman as his client. The merchant turned white. Louis asked Herman if he wanted to prosecute but Herman said no, he just wanted his pearls back, which were quickly returned to him. The jewelry man was relieved, Herman was relieved and Louis was happy to have been of assistance.

Years later, when my father proposed to my mother, he took her to Philadelphia to see Herman for an engagement ring.

After Pop told me this story, he added another tidbit. When he and Herman were children, they played at Herman's house from time to time. One day they went out to the garage and discovered an old Rolls Royce parked inside.

"What's this?" Louis asked. "Where did it come from?"

"Oh, that's Aaron's new car," said Herman. Aaron was his older brother. "Do you want to get in?" he offered.

"Sure," answered Louis. After horsing around a bit, Herman yelled, "Hey, I just lost a coin. It fell out of my pocket and I think it rolled under the car." This was not to be dismissed. Coins were too hard to come by. With that, they scampered out and Herman dove under the car. Unfortunately, there wasn't enough light and he couldn't find the coin. Herman had a bright idea. He took out a match to see better and before Louis could stop him he lit it. What happened next was predictable. The oil under the car caught fire and so did Herman's pants.

"Quick," Louis yelled. "Roll out, roll out!"

Luckily, the fire was extinguished before it could envelop them.

However, how did they explain the charred pants to Herman's mother, Tante Lena?

When my grandfather, Benjamin Grossberg, wanted to get out of the junk business, he needed to borrow some money. He asked his nephew H.B. Kitay for a loan of $50.00 but was refused, no doubt because he was considered a poor credit risk. The Kitay family in Paterson, New Jersey, was quite rich and snobbish. They looked down on their poor Grossberg relatives in Washington, DC. The Kitays owned a large store called "Kitays Over The River." Years later, when Louis and his youngest brother Babe had made it financially, they decided to pay these Kitays a visit. Both men happened to be in New York and decided to hire a taxi to drive them to Paterson. The taxi was instructed to wait right in front of their house so they could be driven back to New York City. Babe wanted them to see that they had arrived in style to show these relatives that the Grossberg family had prospered despite the fact that H.B. Kitay had no faith in them.

Thou Shalt Not Commit Adultery

The Kitays were not the only family members to consider the Grossberg's poor risks. The Bersh family, from whence came Rose, must also have had grave reservations. Esther wrote few letters but this undated one says a lot. She tells Louis off about the junk business, and has words about Al, Kitty's husband, and their Bersh cousins, too.

> Your last letter has surprised me a little. You ask why should not you have gone to Paterson to visit Unkle Bersh. Well, my dear if you have not seen it for yourself so far than Rose's last visit ought to have shown you enough that they want nothing of us.
>
> About the money, I do not know what to think was Unkle's idea in telling you that he wanted to give Papa a few hundred to help him, he said nothing of the kind to us. Harry (Esther's husband) wrote to him that Papa has to buy a house and as he has not a cent of his own, and with money that Harry will give him will not be enough as they ask a big first payment, he told him much, and all the surcumstances (sic), and also offered him as a security a mortgage on the house as well as yearly interest on the money, it was a plane (sic) business proposition, where we did not want him to think that Harry espect (sic) him to just make Papa a present of same.

Well the answer which came two weeks later was such that I was absolutely ashamed to show it to Harry, that Papa's only sister here should answer such a letter in sircumstances (sic) Pa was in at the time. Believe me if it had not been on a Saturday when that letter arrived I would not have shown it to Harry, for him to see the kind of relations we have. I hope to our allmighty that Papa will never need any help from any of our relations.

Harry felt very bad about it for some time, even now when he remembers it hurts him to think of it. So we better leave it with the past. At present I hear that your business is very bad, what do you intend to do? Harry says you don't want to bother with a lot of goods if you can't make a lot on it. I should think it's better a little profit than nothing as long as you have no other thing to do that brings you any profit. Why don't you buy up clips it is very high now, and there are plenty of people that make a nice living in dealing only in clips.

So I do not see what's the matter with you, why should not you be able to do what anyone else can? You are having an advantage over a lot of men in the same sircumstances (sic), who haven't half the education that you possess. The main trouble with you is, you have no pride or ambition if you only had a little of either you would be making money.

Now do not be angry at me for telling you that. I would tell you a lot more, if I only thought that it would be of any help to you. The same with Al. Harry told him to buy a business of vulcanizing tires from our brother-in-law he wanted to sell one of his businesses because he was not able to attend to them. Harry was going to go in with him and furnish all the money necessary, but Al? Oh no! That place was not nice enough for him and he had the best little City in the Country and all the customers he could attend to for the whole year around.

Why he was going to become Rockafeller (sic) in a few months, and it would not pay him to waste his time here. That little Golden City was Jackson, Mich. if you know. And what happent, Katie had all the suffering she could stand, had to take in washing, and God only knows what she did. And the store here you'll ask, well I can only tell you that the same man won't sell it, for any money, he has bought the whole place where that store is located and paid over $30,000 for it, and is making a fortune in it an not ashamed a bit because it has no show windows, that shows that a man who cares not how a place looks or how much he has to work at the start will always make good.

If Al had taken that place then he would by now have been a made man, but now he is looking for something else. I hope for Katie's sake he finds it. So far I have only received woefull (sic) letters from Katie, and to tell the thrut (sic) I don't remember the time when I got a few happy lines from her.

By the way have you had the honor of meeting Celie's future husband (Shultz)? So far I haven't heard from her. I hope she is happy although her silence contradicts that.

Celie might or might not have been happy at the time of this letter, but her husband, Schultz, was later run out of town when it was discovered that he was a bigamist, but not before he fathered a daughter, my cousin Reeva. Reeva grew up, married Max Goldberg and had three children. Reeva's mother and Max's mother were first cousins.

In the 1920s, life was very difficult. There was no social security, no unemployment insurance and no U.S. government guarantees on bank deposits. What little welfare existed was for the truly destitute. To ask for or need this assistance was considered shameful. It was truly a day-to-day struggle to make ends meet. Kitty and Al were not immune from financial woes either, but Al had no trouble suggesting solutions for his father-in-law. In a February 4, 1920, letter from Kitty, she suggested that since Al found out how bad the junk business was, they suggested her father should go into the butcher business instead. Kitty did not want to mention it so she asked her brother-in-law, Harry Abrams, to suggest it. Here she explains the situation to Louis.

"Say about Harry's letter, that's a shame. Did he make it awfully strong, well, 'tain't my fault. I'll tell you what happened. Al came home from Wash. and told me that business with you all is p-u-n-k? We talked about it, worried some over it, and finally decided that Papa ought go into some other kind of business. And what kind, well, in short we decided about a butcher shop after arguing pro-and-con. We decided that since my advise (sic) could hardly carry any weight with it, being as how I am but a poor and insignificant piece of female humanity, I decided to let Harry do it. Straightway I sat me down and wrote to his royal highness.

"I even as much as made all the plans and left it to him to do the submitting. I figured out that a butcher can be hired to do the butchering. You to look after the delivering and getting the orders. Ella to take the money and Papa to Masgee (from the noun *mashgiach*), and to greet the ladies as they come in for the hunks of meat.

"Now what's wrong about that? Nothing as far as I can see. But here I get 3 perfectly good letters, one from you, one from Ma & one from Pauline each pointing a finger to me and saying 'why?' Yes, why? Really, Elsie my boy, I hadn't meant any harm. I meant to write to Ma & Pauline now but Edith just woke up and I must feed her. Please tell them what I had to say about Harry's letter and ask them to please scuse. I hadn't meant no harm."

Ben from the Army wrote Louis again on February 7, 1920.

Dear Looy:

What is there new in Washington? Have you become an accountant (DPA) yet? That is have they come to your terms? As an accountant I guess I will make a good loafer. By the way is Dave married yet? Are the Glushaks going to move to Newark, NJ? Are you making up for lost time just now in the way of recreation, or are you still plugging away at the books that you don't look at? As an accountant you ought to be a good junk salesman…

Well, old top, you want to be very careful this year as it is leap year and prohibition…The office is full of the fair sex, and they have been trying to vamp me for a long time. What luck have you had with them? I guess that you don't want to have any luck with them just now. Not until you become an APA.

On February 11, 1920, Ida sent a postcard with a 1-cent stamp, inviting Louis to her wedding. "Are you going to keep your vow or aren't you!!! You're expected at the Wedding Sunday 3 PM. Don't forget! Ida"

For some reason Louis could not go to the wedding after all. He sent telegrams February 15, 1920, from himself and the Grossberg family to Mr. & Mrs. David A. Glushak, Brooklyn, NY.

> #1 Congratulations. Best wishes for life long happiness. Sorry can't attend now. Expect me at your diamond wedding. Louis
> #2 Congratulations. May your journey thru life be studded with health and happiness. The Family Grossberg

Pop said Ida managed not to attend his wedding either, though Dave did put in an appearance. Ida was not one to forget an imagined slight. Both men were extremely close, a relationship that made her very jealous. They used to exchange small gifts on their birthdays until Ida put a stop to it for a time. Pop said that once he sent Dave a pair of socks and Ida made Dave return them. I suspect that the yearly letters on their birthdays thereafter were not always shared with Ida.

Finances were getting desperate for Kitty and Al. They had moved to Richmond, Virginia in hopes of a better future but on March 11, 1920, Kitty writes:

> Please, dear Elsie, I wish you would do us a favor. Cunningham owes us $133.29. Will you go up to him and tell him that you are going to Richmond and was asked by Al to go in to Cunningham and get either the money or the goods. We can sell the goods here in a jiffy. The fact is, we need the money. You know that appearance often makes a very big difference in the impression a man makes when trying to sell a customer.
>
> Al is dilapidated. He needs a suit the worst kind of way, also shoes & hat, shirts & perhaps *unterhoisen* (yet another word for underwear) too, who knows. If we get the money from him or else the stuff we can get the necessary clothes. Please don't put it off. Either get the money or the merchandise. Attend to this at once please, thus when you come to see us I'll give you one swell feed of flapjacks and what not. Don't forget, either the money or the goods.

Another letter from Kitty was dated March 15, 1920.

> I wrote you Thursday asking to go to Cunningham. Please, Lucy dear, if you haven't done it as yet, do so *now*. We need the money in the worst kind of way. You see, we don't get the money from the Acheson Co. until the end of the month and the truth to tell you we are broke right now though we have money coming to us from the Acheson. So please, don't forget. The gas bill is due Friday and is for $18.00. You see, this is the first bill we got and is for 3 months and a plenty at that, I reckon. Well, we use the gas for heating too, so it's not much when you think to come of it. Besides, we must live. Don't forget, old top.
>
> By the way, I wish that if you are coming you would hurry up & do so. Whenever someone rings the bell Al thinks it's you and then gets disappointed when it's not you. I wish you'd come up for the weekend. I'd try to make you enjoy the trip. Write me in reply at once if not sooner. Yours in debt & in *Schloores* (*tsoras*) & in Richmond, Kit

Harry Abrams' fortunes were not much better. On March 15, 1920, Louis wrote to him:

> Enclosed is B/L and Invoice for shells I shipped to you today. Have shipped in your name to Watertown, NY. As you know, this stuff costs me 12 cents. I bought on your offer of 13¢. Have billed this to you at 13¢. This gives me 1 ¢ profit. If you cannot stand it, say so. It is useless to ask you for a price on goods shipped because you do not answer. Would have shipped before but embargo held me back. Regarding the money I owe you, now a little over 700 dollars, can send our note if you want it. I don't know whether we'll be able to pay it when it's due, but that you may be able to raise some money, with it, will send you it tomorrow.
>
> We are still on a house hunt. There are plenty offered for sale, but somehow there is always something the matter with each one. Maybe if we keep on looking we'll find something eventually. Real Estate seems to have gone crazy here. It is going up daily. What seemed a large price one day, is a bargain the next. Regards to snooks and the rest of the family.

It took until July 30, 1920 for the Grossberg family to find their new home. It was titled to Sarah H. Grossberg and cost $8,000. There were two existing mortgages on the house at 614 M Street, NW, payable at $33.00 a month. The deed was issued August 3, 1920. After a down payment of $150.00, the total auxiliary costs came to $56.20. Examples of such costs were: Tax certificate – 50¢, Preparing deed – $5.00, Recording deed – $1.10, Preparing trust – $5.00, Recording trust – $2.75, Notary fee – $1.00 and Revenue stamps – 60¢.

Three days later, March 18, 1920, Kitty writes again.

I can't understand why you don't answer my letters. I have written you twice since last Thursday asking you to please try & get some money for us from Cunningham but you seem to just simply ignore my letters. I swear, I don't know what we'll do if we don't get a check by Saturday. I suppose Al will have to hock his watch or my ring, otherwise they will shut off the gas and water. Damn it anyhow, it's tough when one has to depend on favors. At least, Louis, can't you answer me, if only to say, *Kirsh Mir in Hinten* (kiss my behind).

Just the same, I wish you had answered me and let me know if you could go over to Cunningham or not, so we would have tried to do something else. As it is, I am worried sick. The grocery man may ask some money any minute and if we don't pay the Gas & Water bill within 5 days they shut it off. Will you please, Louis do us this favor & try to let me know right away what the outcome is. Write so I'll get it Saturday morning and if it's necessary for us to patronize the 3 ball artist (pawnshop), we might as well do it Saturday.

Fortunately, Louis followed through. On March 20, 1920, Kitty thanked him for sending the money.

I am awfully sorry I have been so hasty in writing that last letter. I really & truly didn't mean to be nasty & scratchy and unappreciative, but I felt so badly about you not answering me. I thought you didn't think it important enough. Imagine how I felt, when I realized that the precious gas & water might be cut off, to say nothing of our bread & butter baskets, until the check from the Acheson should choose to arrive. I was worried, that's all. But thank the Lord, you think more of us than I gave you credit for. Now I am all for begging your pardon & for sending a few thanks for granting me the same.

The 25 iron gentlemen (dollars) on your private check was pretty. I like your handwriting on papers like them there ones. Much obliged, old top, and let me tell you here & now that you'll get it back as soon as we get the stuff from Cunningham. In the meantime it helps out a heap. $18 of them have today been transferred to the gas Co. (Nasty people they are, by the way. They threaten to strike & refuse to work just because we wish to owe them a few dollars, can you beat it? And us being honest folks, too. Oh well, what can you expect of such lowlifes.) $10 took the second train to the grocery store and wished itself applied on account. So lovely, and all smiles too.

Al had to have some money and there you are. Louis, I am ready for more. But, this time I won't scold or anything. If you send the stuff out by express Monday or Tuesday we'll get it by Thursday & that'll mean that on Friday we'll have again money. But by all means, please answer this and tell me of developments as soon as you get it so we'll know what to do. You see, we didn't get any money for Feb. on Acct. of Al not making any sales. He was working on the catalogue, consequently, this strain. But don't worry, all will be fine after April 15th. We hope so, anyway. But please, write me anyway, favorable or not.

Al tells me that Tante Lena is terribly ill. Please tell me about her too. And please, Louis, I'd rather have the truth. I'd rather know the worst now, than have to find out anything terrible when I come home. I hate to think of it. Poor Dora & Annie, I can just feel with them. I hope Tante is better & if you are permitted to see her, Kiss her for me.

Tante Lena Freudberg was the mother of Leo, Dora, Annie and Celie "Shultz." In fact, Leo came from a family of ten children: Rahle, Tsila (Celie), Dora, Berawolfa, Nachman, Ore, Annie, Leopold (Victor), Isadore and Herman. The first six names make a rhyme. That is how Louis remembered them – Rahle, Tsila, Dora, Bera, Nachman, Ore (pronounced Ora). Tante Lena was also a sister of my grandmother, Sarah Henna Effenbach.

Pop didn't remember when he began his classes at Pace and Pace, but it had to have been prior to receiving this letter, dated April 3, 1920. "Members of the Unit are especially requested not to enroll in coaching courses conducted by private schools for the announced purpose of preparing them for the internal examinations conducted by the Income Tax Unit." On April 20, 1920, he was informed: "It is understood that this salary carried with it the annual bonus granted by Congress, which is $240 for the fiscal year beginning July 1, 1919."

By April 30, 1920, J.E. Harper, Chief, Division of Appointments wrote:

> Sir: By direction of the Secretary and having been certified by the United States Civil Service Commission as eligible, you have been appointed an Auditor at $1,400 per annum, wr, in the Office of the Commissioner of Internal Revenue, the appointment to take effect from the date of oath." This was the beginning of a lifelong career. Obviously, Pace and Pace did not prevent him from being offered a job.

My mother, Celia Kanster, went to Central High School where she took business courses including bookkeeping. After graduation, she looked too young to be employed, so she went to Drakes Business College for a year and a half. She didn't need to take bookkeeping again but she did take shorthand and typing. When the Fidelity Union Trust Company needed a capable person, they asked the college to send them someone. Celia's skills were so good that the college recommended Celia for the position of stenographer. When she told the bank that she hadn't graduated yet, they told her that she didn't need to graduate; she was already proficient enough to qualify for the job. She was 18- or 19-years-old at the time. Celia progressed rapidly and was entrusted with certifying checks, a very big responsibility. Ultimately she became a "floater," one who can do any job at the bank. For someone so young, and Jewish, this was quite remarkable in those days.

While Dave Glushak continued to live and work in Washington, his sister Fanny and parents had left the area and moved to 305 Hunterdon Street in Newark, New Jersey. This happened to be a few doors away from where Celia Kanster and her family lived.

If Celia did not meet the Glushaks when they moved, she did meet Fanny when Fanny came to work at the bank where Celia worked. Fanny was later instrumental in introducing my father to my mother. Mr. Hollander brought Rabbi Joseph Glushak to Newark to officiate at his synagogue. Mr. Hollander was also a member of the board of Fidelity Union Trust Company. When the Rabbi was contemplating his move from Washington, he told Mr. Hollander that he wanted to find employment for his daughter, Fanny, so that she would be less resistant to the move.

"Don't worry," answered Mr. Hollander. "I have connections at a bank and I'm sure they will be willing to hire her."

When Fanny arrived at the bank, Celia was called upon to teach her the ropes, and they became fast friends. Now there were an unprecedented two Jewish young ladies at the bank.

On a letter with 2¢ postage, Fanny wrote Louis, April 17, 1920, on the stationery of the Talmud Torah Hebrew School:

> Now that everything is settled I have the opportunity of writing to my friends. I suppose you'll want to know how I like Newark, etc. At the present moment, I don't like it for the reason that it separates me from my two brothers and also friends that have meant a lot to me. The first night I couldn't sleep at all. I don't believe I ever cried so much in my life and my only wish was to be back in Washington. However, I'll try to make the best of things for a while. I intend going over to New York next week and try my luck in that city. Until then, I'll say good-bye and also send my regards to the Grossberg Family. If you have any spare time a letter will be greatly appreciated if sent from Louis to Fannie.

Louis was very fond of Fanny and on May 3, 1920, he sent this reply.

> Dear Fandel,
> Good Morning. When in the course of human events it becomes expedient, necessary and wise for one L. Castleton

Grossberg to write an answer to a letter sent Him by one Fannie G. some time since, it behooves such L. Castleton Grossberg to 'Get a wiggle on' and commit himself to pen and ink. However, out of consideration for your time, eyesight and good humor, I am giving my Oliver (Olivetti typewriter) the honor of transmitting the message.

It pained me considerably to read of your loss of precious optic fluid, on the first night of your stay in Newark. Believe me, Newark isn't worth it. And Fannie, do you know, you cry beautifully. That night at the station I saw you cry for the first time; and you looked real nice. What I cannot understand is, why did you have to pick out so public a place as the Union Station to ventilate your emotions – I mean, I could suggest a better place, say some nice evening on a park bench in the company of two, I and the moon. Isn't that much cuter? By this time I presume you have explored the mysterious metropolis of New(enious) York(us). I hope you don't like it.

Here things are slightly less lively than they were when you left, for the obvious reason that you left. Otherwise, things are normal. Washington is still in the United States despite all the Suffrage for Washington League is doing to deny the fact...Let me commend you on your good taste. I have reference to that line in your letter which states, 'and my only wish was to be back in Washington.'

You, I trust will be more prompt in answering this little bit of nonsense than I have been in answering that letter of yours.

Louis and Dave worked together in Washington, as did Celia and Fanny in New Jersey. Fanny decided to introduce her friend Celia to Louis, so she sneaked a photo out of Celia's album, gave it to her brother and asked him to show it to Louis. Fanny had an instinct that fate was about to play a role in her friends' lives and wanted to be a *shadchun* (matchmaker). She hoped to make a *shiddach* (a match). She felt that Celia and Louis belonged together. Her brother evidently agreed.

Unfortunately, the photo was not a good one and showed Celia all suntanned at the beach. She was wearing one of those bathing suits we now think of as unfashionable. However, the bathing suit didn't bother Louis; the sunburn did. He liked his women lily white.

"Forget it," Louis told Dave. "I'm not interested!"

Fanny was very disappointed but she could not do anything about it. It took five years before he finally did meet Celia.

Louis and Dave were very busy with tax work. In addition, they picked up some clients for what they called, "Sundown Accounting," meaning they worked on the side. Maybe the government frowns on this now, but it was permissible then. One day Fanny told Louis that he had missed the boat because Celia had become engaged to a William (Bill) Lifchitz. He had given her a 4-karat diamond ring.

The engagement was a long one, four years – maybe because of the little things that bothered Celia. For a long time, Bill wanted to get married, but Celia kept putting him off. She always found a reason – lack of money, being too busy, family matters or any number of other excuses. Celia, her sisters Sarah and Edith, their husbands and Bill Lifchitz often went out to a restaurant for a midnight snack. The group insisted that their mother, Paula Kanster, accompany them since she was so well liked and fit right in with the young people. Every time they ate out William invariably ordered bacon and eggs. This was very offensive to the girls and their mother, but they never said anything. While Paula did not keep a strictly kosher house, she would never bring in pork nor eat it out. In fact, when her doctor prescribed bacon for her diabetes, she would prepare it in the basement and cry as she ate it. Why bacon was considered good for diabetics is a mystery but in those days, they did the best they could. However, insulin was only discovered in 1921, and its purity, strength and effectiveness took time to be established.

Among her many accomplishments, Paula Kanster was a marvelous cook. In contrast, Bill's mother was a terrible cook. Even Bill preferred eating at Celia's house, and his mother became very jealous every time she heard him rave about Paula's cooking. Not only was his mother a terrible cook, but also every time Celia ate at her house she got sick. His mother prepared everything with a lot of fat. It was nothing for her to fry up steaks in beef fat in the morning and let them stay on top of the stove until dinnertime. One evening when Celia was invited for dinner, she got sick again. His parents were sitting on the porch when she made a mad dash for the bushes and threw up in front of a tree. After that, Bill's mother forbade him from eating at Celia's house.

Harry Abrams heard from Louis on June 12, 1920. Apparently,

Esther was in a Washington, DC, hospital at the time. It is not clear why.

"I am happy to say that Esther is doing very nicely. She has the first room on the first floor and as companion, a patient, an old lady. She gets a fine breeze from the window, which is at the head of the bed. We took, I mean Miriam and Ella and Brother Boy to see her today and he was too darling for anything. Why, the nurses were just crazy about him. Don't you worry one bit about Esther because she has all the conveniences she desires. She has no private nurse because it is not necessary to have one, as I said before, there is no need to worry."

Miriam added: "P.S. Snooks (Sylvia) is getting fatter every day, says 'Bye-bye' and plays all thru the night. She plays around so long that she just falls asleep wherever she is."

Who "Brother Boy" was remained a mystery to me until I read an August 11, 1925, letter Louis sent to Dave from Florida. He was Esther's second child, Avraham Dov, born May 29, 1919, died from lymphatic leukemia August 7, 1925. Nowhere in the letters was he mentioned by name or was his death mentioned. His sister, Sylvia, recalls that when Avraham was in the hospital he called his parents over, put a hand from each on his chest and said he was dying. He wished them well and then said goodbye.

Louis began a correspondence in 1922 with Esther Borenstein in Baltimore, Maryland. She was a friend of the Grossberg family, particularly of Kitty and Louis. In this letter of August 24, 1922, Kitty is visiting Esther Borenstein and writes Louis. Esther had invited Eleanor for Sunday dinner so Kitty wanted Louis to come too.

> I have just returned from Keith's Matinee where I have a perfectly rotten time. The reason being 'you.' To think that once in 3 months when I have an opportunity to entertain you for a day you find all kinds of excuses why you ought not to come. Why don't you just say you don't want to go out of your way to see me as you do Herman or anyone else you choose to visit. I reserve the right to feel hurt and by gosh, I do.
>
> I haven't seen you for a long time and I am sure you would be glad to see me too but I see I made a mistake. Honest, if you knew how you made me feel, you would come over Sunday, dinner or

no dinner, meeting or no meeting. Come to think of it, I believe Al was right last Monday when he said he believed you have no use for him. That hurts me awfully bad. I remember in the old days when you and I were chums. After I was married you kept telling me how my absence made your heart feel fonder, and all that kind of stuff and all about how you would have married me yourself if I were someone else's sister instead of yours and now a visit to me is an ordeal.

Well, allright (sic), if that's the way you feel stay home. But please, if you don't feel that way come over Sunday for the day and to be sure no one ensnares you into eating an unwelcome dinner, eat it at home. And *zu alle zores*, (with all the *tsoras*, troubles) I still have the same bundle of pride I used to be proud possessor of. I went so far the other day as to boast that when I ask you to come over to see me wherever I may be, you would come as quickly as your 'goers' would carry you. And now to have proven myself a *liegner* (liar)…

And it would certainly have been in good taste for you have paid a visit to Bobby since he returned from the Hospital. That's all the mean things I can think of saying right now…

P.S. If you want to prove to me that you are sorry you made me cry, come & tell me so and as a special peace offering besides yourself bring me a box of Velaties. –XXX, Kit

There is no record of how this ended.

Esther Borenstein herself wrote to Louis, October 3, 1922.

Your letter was indeed a surprise to me. Thanks, very much, for your kind wishes. It is quite an honor to be sent to attend the conference of the Keren Hayesod (a charitable society support-ing Jewish communities in Palestine) but honor is given to those who deserve it. It must be fine to know that you are partaking in the heart of society's affairs…

In reference to your visit in Baltimore, I wish to extend my sincere invitation.

Louis had saved his 1920 tax return, which illustrates the importance he placed on charity. His income was $996.39. His personal deduction was

$1,000 so no tax was required. A Schedule K was attached for charitable contributions. Even though he was practically supporting his whole family, he still gave money to help others:

Red Cross – $3.00

Salvation Army – $3.00

Congregation Adas Israel – $5.00

There was a blue *pushkee* – a charity box for Palestine – and boxes for other causes in his home for as long as he could remember. Louis was among the founders of almost every important Jewish philanthropic organization in the Washington metropolitan area. Regardless of his income, money was always put aside to help others less fortunate. In later years, when his finances permitted, he contributed to hundreds of causes around the globe. In 1948, he created a private charitable foundation that he controlled until his death.

At the age of 24, Louis was already deeply committed to Jewish education and synagogue life. On October 29, 1922, he wrote Mr. Dinowitz, an officer of one of the synagogues, in his capacity as the Recording Secretary of Adas Israel Congregation.

"A very serious problem confronts the Jewish community of this city in the matter of giving our children a proper Hebrew education. It is a well-known fact that the Talmud Torahs of the various Jewish congregations in this city are not conducted along proper lines and that there is room for vast improvement. The subject is one that is serious and demands our prompt attention." He proposed that a meeting be held with representatives of the city's synagogues to address the situation.

On November 6, 1922, Louis invited Esther Borenstein to his graduation.

When I left Baltimore, I fully expected to see you in Washington in a few days. I must admit, however, that your reasons for staying in Baltimore over the Holidays were sound. I can well sympathize with your daddy's desire to have his *Freulein Elst* (eldest girl) at his table on the Holidays…

I become officially designated an accountant next Friday evening. Although I completed my course of studies about one and one half years ago and have been practicing as a Public Accountant over a year, yet I have no evidence in the form of a diploma.

In the first place I can not find any entertainment in taking final examinations, and in the second place the writing of a thesis has never appealed to me.

Since we cannot always avoid the distasteful things in life, I took the finals last March and the thesis was then the only thing that stood between me and the coveted sheepskin. It was so easy not to write a thesis, that I allowed eight months to slide noiselessly by. Saturday morning's (October 28) mail brought a considerable shock: turn in a thesis by the following Tuesday and graduate in November or wait for next November. I had expected to take at least one month for the task and here I was suddenly asked to do it in three days. The man who wrote:

> Procrastination, thief of time,
> Had many a man undone;
> He rails at fate and learns too late,
> That NOW reversed is WON.

apparently knew whereof he spake. Now I am glad that it had to be done in such a rush, although one week ago I worked like a Trojan and didn't admit I could do it…

My evening would be perfect next Friday if you would honor me by being present at my graduation. There are no formal invitation cards because of the lack of time, since the exact date was not set until a few days ago. The affair will take place in the Ball Room of the City Club and will be informal. I might add that Saturday, November 11, is Armistice Day and I promise to make the weekend an interesting one for you. I know it will be a pleasant one for me – and the rest of the family. Will you come?

Esther Borenstein declined his invitation on November 8, 1922. Guests were expected and she needed to be with her family.

First of all, I must congratulate you on your graduation, especially after your long delay. Truly chance has favored you by giving you only three days to worry over a thesis…

Your letter was so very cordial, & my desire to go to Wash. is so very great, that I am greatly disappointed at not being able to do so. This may seem flattery, but you have the ability of expressing your thots (sic) in just the fitting way; while poor me, must juggle my words before I can get anybody to comprehend what I ought to say.

Eleanor also invited me over. I alas received a letter from Mrs. Cohen (Kitty) yesterday. Eleanor is just a dear little girl & Mrs. Cohen a fine grown up sister. Is Mr. Glushak still as cheerful as ever? From his description of his wife & all other statements I have heard about her, it seems as if I know her very well & can just imagine how she acts & what kind of a woman she is…Accept my best wishes for your future success in anything you undertake.

Sarah Henna was an unlicensed doctor of folk medicine. Her home remedies were so successful that Louis tried to market one of them. Evidently, he was so impressed with one particular concoction that he sent out a number of letters on November 20, 1922. The first was to Woods Popular Service, Atlantic City, New Jersey.

"I wish to put a herb remedy on the market and am interested in your newspaper advertisement in which you offer to place a one inch ad in 161 magazines, three times, for fifteen dollars. Please let me have particulars relative to your offer. Give the list of magazines and state your price for larger advertisements in other possible combinations of magazines. Thanking you for an early reply, I am, Yours very Truly, Louis C. Grossberg"

He then sent letters to these publications:

Pathfinder Publishing Co., Washington, DC
    American Woman, August, Maine
    Country Gentlemen, Philadelphia, Pennsylvania
    Farmers Wife, St. Paul, Minnesota
    Woman's World, Chicago, Illinois

I wish to advertise a herb remedy for an ailment peculiar to children. Please advise the cost of a one inch advertisement in your periodical.

Before proceeding, Louis wanted to check on the availability and safety of the main ingredient, so he wrote to Parke Davis Co., Detroit, Michigan. Apparently, this remedy was for a urinary infection but was never a marketing bonanza.

> Please quote me your price per pound of Yerby Santa leaves (*Yerba Santa*), otherwise known as Riodictyon (*eriodictyon*). Kindly state what are its chemical properties and especially its action on the bladder. Is it in anyway poisonous? If you have this herb in both pressed leaves and non-pressed leaves, quote me on both if the price is different.

After Louis' sister Eleanor visited Esther Borenstein in Baltimore, Esther wrote him on November 26, 1922, saying, "During Eleanor's stay with me I have grown more fond of her than ever and I know you are very happy to have such a sister." Esther apologized that she could not accept Louis' invitation to come to Washington for Thanksgiving Day.

In his capacity as the keeper of the Grossberg house, Louis had an altercation with the Fitz-Gibbon Company, 1110 F Street, NW, Washington, DC, regarding a leak. On December 5, 1922, he wrote,

> Gentlemen:
> Your letter dated Nov. 27, 1922 in re bill of W. L. Gary & Co. $4.20 against B. Grossberg, 614 M St. NW has been forwarded to me for attention.
> It appears that W. L. Gary & Co. were called in to stop a leak in the furnace coil. This was done in a very few minutes but thru the inefficiency of the Steam Fitter, a further expense of $20.00 was incurred because the coil, being permitted to remain in the furnace without water, burned up. The Steam Fitter was specifically asked whether there was such danger of the coil being destroyed and assured Mr. Grossberg that there was not.
> Aside from this it is considered that the charge of $4.20 for the few minutes work done is exorbitant and out of proportion to the service rendered. However, I am instructed to offer you $2.00 in full settlement of this account in order to close the matter. If this is satisfactory to you, please so advise.

The Fitz-Gibbon Co. replied December 6, 1922. "In Re: W.L. Gary & Company vs. Benjamin Grossberg…

> We have your letter of yesterday regarding the above entitled claim, and regret to advise that you are evidently misinformed as to the facts involved.
>
> Our clients inform us that they were called upon, after hours, to repair the coil in question; that they removed the thing, of necessity, and reported that it would cost $15.00 to complete the work; that this sum of money was refused; and that the sum we now ask is just and equitable for and in consideration of the labor involved in behalf of the debtor indicated.
>
> We regret that we can not accept a compromise, and ask you to see to it that we have a check in full immediately.

The same day a letter arrived from Esther Borenstein. She finally managed to visit Washington and thanked him for his kindness during her stay. She had begun to read *Vanity Fair* by Thackeray. Esther asked him to thank Mr. and Mrs. Glushak, "for being as nice to me and also for their supper."

Louis answered on Sunday, December 10, 1922, that he was delighted to receive her letter. "I admire your bravery. I tried to read *Vanity Fair* on a number of occasions but I always lost heart after the first few pages. You are very brave."

Louis enclosed a paragraph from Tuesday morning's *Herald*. "I am a great admirer of Brisbane. He is probably the greatest living editorial writer. I like his style of writing as well as his capacity for straight thinking. My views on certain topics sometimes differ from his, but that does not appear to worry him. He seems to be slightly anti-British and I think he is prejudiced in his view on the Ship Subsidy question. The real object of the Subsidy is to subsidize certain ship owners (since) they cannot compete with foreign ship owners especially English. For that reason it is claimed we cannot have an American Merchant Marine. The chief difficulty (is) that only a few ship owners are to be subsidized and not all. The question naturally arises, if you subsidize the ship business why not also subsidize the railroad business, the coal business, or every other business? So this is the Subsidy wrangle in a nutshell.

"I have four days leave coming to me that I intended to take the last week of December. Secretary of the Treasury Mellon, however, has decided that no leave will be granted to anyone during the Christmas to New Year week. This makes it necessary that I take my leave before December 25th or lose it." So, Louis decided to use the next two Fridays and Saturdays for sightseeing.

"I ate waffles at the Glushaks tonight and we talked about you. They thank you for the regards and say that you are welcome to eat a waffle supper there at any time."

The Fitz-Gibbons Company was not through with Louis. It sent a letter on December 11, 1922. "A recent editorial in a local news paper contains a thought worth your consideration. Consequently we pass it on to you:

> A Spartanburg Negro recently escaped from a penal chain-gang and, instead of running from the blood-hound placed on his trail, he waited for his pursuer to find him and made friends with it. Then he chained the animal to a tree and went on his way without annoyance. In commenting upon the incident the editor wrote, 'Many a man, hounded by debt, extravagance, conceit, and similar mental blood-hounds, could tie up the pursuer and be peaceful.'
>
> This unpaid account will cease to be an annoyance to you just as soon as you shall have effected its adjustment. Our office is open to assisting you in this.

December 19, 1922, Louis answered the Fitz-Gibbon Co., as the spokesman for his father, who had no idea of how to deal with any of this.

> Please refer to your letter of the sixth instant. I advised Mr. Grossberg of your client's view of the matter but can only reiterate my previous contention. The coils were not removed but were permitted to remain in the furnace and were destroyed. I am again assured that only a very few minutes was consumed in the repair work. I maintain that $4.20 for the work done is excessive and not reasonable.
>
> I have seen your letter to Mr. B. Grossberg dated December 11, in which the recent editorial concerning the escape of the

Spartanburg Negro from a chain-gang is quoted. I agree with you that the thought contained therein is good. However, it appears to me that in this case the 'shoe is on the other foot.' The fugitive is offering the bloodhounds a compromise with the view to making friends with them but the bloodhounds refuse to be befriended. How then is the fugitive to follow the advice offered in the editorial? Surely not by paying the full amount claimed, for that would be tantamount to capture. There would be no value in befriending the hounds unless by so doing an advantage would accrue to the fugitive.

I have consulted my attorney and am advised that from the evidence at hand Mr. B. Grossberg has an excellent case at court if you care to carry it there for settlement. My two-dollar offer in full settlement is still open for your acceptance. I trust that you will reconsider the matter and accept this offer in compromise. If, however, you find that you still require full payment of the amount claimed, we stand ready to take the matter to the courts.

Extending to you the greetings of the holiday season I am, Very Truly yours, Louis C. Grossberg

Unfortunately, there was no further saved correspondence with the Fitz-Gibbon Co. My father did not remember going to court, so the bill was probably settled.

December 18, 1922, Louis hears from Esther Borenstein again. "I have read 80 lines of *Vanity Fair*. Don't laugh now. To state the truth I like it. The heroine is a very sweet innocent girl and the man she loves is abominably abominable. And then to add interest, there's another man in it, too. He's a strong man desperately in love with the sweet girl, and a staunch friend of the abominable one. Now that's a fine mix-up and my curiosity is all a flutter.

"Since *Vanity Fair* is so long I decided to read *The Magnificent Ambersons* for the sake of variety. It's the story of a spoiled man's life and very good…Thanks for the article."

Louis ordered specially printed stationery from the Minute Service Co., 30 Irving Place, New York on December 23, 1922. He sent a check for $4.85 for three cabinets of their stationery. (The word "cabinet" in this context is not in my dictionary.) He requested a cabinet of gentlemen's stationery, white suede stamped with monogram "D.A.G." One cabinet of ladies stationery, pink paper, stamped "P.E.G." and the city is Washington. Another one stamped "E.E.G." and the address is 614 M Street, NW Washington…"D.A.G." was David A. Glushak, "E.E.G." and "P.E.G.," his sisters Eleanor and Pauline.

Louis saved quite a few cancelled checks. Most were for payments he made to his siblings and to Dave Glushak. It seems he doled out sums on a regular basis. Since he was the main breadwinner at the time, his own share of his earnings must have been quite limited. At the age of 21, Louis was paying for life insurance. He retained records that showed dividends accumulated at Mass. Mutual Life Insurance Co. were $8.80 in August of 1919 and increased to $26.05 in 1922.

Even though Benjamin Grossberg was portrayed as the purchaser of record for their home, Louis actually wrote the letters and paid the bills. Coal furnaces were the major means of heating and on September 8, 1922, there was an Application for the Purchase of Coal. In a letter to L. R. White Coal Co., 733 12th Street, Washington, DC, Louis requested 15 tons of coal to be dumped and carried. A $25 deposit was made with a balance to be paid as agreed. They responded, subject to the following restrictions:

1st This order is accepted subject to our ability to get the coal
2nd This order is accepted at the price prevailing at date of delivery
3rd This order is accepted subject to all the rules and regulations of the Fuel Administration, Public Utilities Commission, and any other governmental agency that may be established with reference to the distribution of coal.

After Cousins Leo and Rose were married, they continued corresponding with Louis. This January 15, 1923 draft of a letter may seem confusing at first but read on.

Thanksgiving Day 1921

Dear Newlyweds:

Attached hereto and made a part hereof, although not enclosed herewith is an electric fireless cooker, the medium for the
proverbial female attack upon the male heart via the stomach. May
you use it in peace, harmony, etc. etc.

My letter forwarding the little gift, if indeed were sent would
probably have read somewhat like the above if – this were Thanksgiving 1921. However, it is Thanksgiving 1922, and I am just one
year late. A year is a long time and I am exhibiting considerable
nerve to come in at this late date, but your anniversary, your hubby,
your wife, our friendship will undoubtedly help to smooth the
difficulties.

Shh, don't breath it to a soul. This is not Thanksgiving 1922
but Jan. 15, 1923. Blame it on the coal strike, the rail strike, embar-
goes, freight delays, and poor service. It took 3 mos. to come from
Detroit. I am not nimble-witted enough to 'laugh that off.'

Rose Freudberg thanked Louis on January 19, 1923. She said he should
realize that "in the 1st year of married life neither stoves nor fireless cook-
ers are needed since the first year is lived on love alone but the second
year requires something to sort of help along."

This is to tell you that your lovely note and the fireless cooker came
as a mighty big surprise and that your 'apologies are accepted.' You
surely are much wiser then I ever gave you credit for being since
the only experience you have had as a basis for judging is observation…Hence your gift came at a critical moment and is hailed
as a home saved.

All joking aside though, your remembrance to us surely is a
peach but I really do think you should not have been so extravagant for us. It is by far too much for you to have done. A fireless
cooker – a real honest to goodness electric one like we have now
was something that I looked forward to buying some day when my
ship came in and now look what you went and done! I am making
a close study of it and when I know how to use it properly, I'm hoping to have you come and eat the first fireless cooked dinner in our

home. Anyway, I want you to know that Victor and I were mighty agreeably surprised and feel that such a wonderful gift would have been well worth waiting three or even maybe five years for.

Today we think that preparing for Passover is not a difficult thing – time-consuming yes, but difficult, no. Everything is available in the local super market. In 1923, preparing for the holiday was quite different. Louis wrote to the Redelheim Matzo Company, Chicago, Illinois, to place an order. On February 26, 1923, the Matzo Company responded.

"It is impossible for us to accept this order on any other basis except FOB Chicago. However, if it is acceptable to you, we will have same shipped to you through our Philadelphia agent on the basis of FOB Philadelphia. If this is not satisfactory, please advise us and we will return your check."

Louis responded on March 1, 1923 that the Philadelphia arrangements were satisfactory to him. Among the items ordered were one-hundred forty pounds of Redelheim Matzo for $14.00, thirty pounds of Matzo Meal for $3.30, three pounds of potato flour for 36 cents and six pounds of Horseradish for $1.08. For the ten items ordered, the total price came to $25.15 with a 20% deposit of $5.00.

Again, Esther Borenstein wrote Louis, this time telling of the plays she had seen and the problems of maintaining the Jewish heritage.

It is already March 13, and just two months since I received your last letter. I suppose you think I've forgotten how to write…Do you remember *Bulldog Drummond*? George Arliss is here this week in a play of adventure & I can't decide whether to go or not. Every Saturday afternoon a few of the girls I know & myself go to our shows. Those plays are too good to miss. Recently I have seen *The Sea Woman*, *The Comedians*, *The Circle*, *Tangerine*, & *Kempie*…

Sunday morning we were going to Bible Class. There we had a discussion on inter-marriage. Dr. Lazaras, the rabbi of the temple, said that young people should not go along as mere driftwood, (but) should have definite opinions. For three weeks, he read us the play of the *Melting Pot*. As you would suppose, he is positively opposed to inter-marriage on the grounds that Jews could never be happy with Gentiles because of that instinctive Jewish spirit in us all and (because) the Jewish people as a race have something to give the world, a heritage of ideals & characteristics.

A teacher in the Sunday school at Esther's Temple said that every Jewish child should learn, "what the Jewish people stand for and should grow up with the best ideas. It seems to me that the Jewish race certainly does need more work of this kind, especially the children of the parents who don't care a hang for their religion and don't believe in anything."

The Passover order that Louis placed did not arrive as planned. Evidently, it came late with excess freight charges. Since the delivery service tried to deliver the order on the Sabbath, it was refused. On March 26, 1923, Louis wrote to the Matzo Company in Philadelphia, explaining why the shipment had been refused. He was happy to learn that the excess freight charges would be adjusted: "As you are in a better position than I am to know what the charges would have been had the shipment been made by freight, I shall leave the matter to you. The weight is given on the express receipt as 275 lbs. with express charges of $4.39 and COD Return Charge of $.35. It will be entirely satisfactory to me to have you send the sugar and other unfilled items, if any, as per the original order."

Louis answered Esther Borenstein on April 8, 1923. "You are very fortunate to be able to see so many shows. One every Saturday would just about cover all the shows that are worth while. Since *Bulldog Drummond*, the only shows I saw were David Warfield in the *Merchant of Venice* and the much advertised melodrama, *The Bat*. The first was good from an artistic point of view but very poor from the point of view of the Jew. I am unalterably opposed to the staging of that play because it breeds anti-Semitism. It is a pity that David Warfield and David Belasco, Jews, should be responsible for the showing of this play in the face of the many protests by Jewish organizations and societies.

"*The Bat* is much like *Bulldog Drummond* – mysterious, creepy, and entertaining – for those who like such plays. That lets you out, doesn't it? Personally I do not care much for that type of play (as there) is nothing to take home and think about.

"You write of Jewish ideals, education, problems. It seems that the Jewish youth of the present day are totally ignorant of the history and religious beliefs and achievements of their race. Pesach, Succoth,

Synagogues, Zionism mean nothing to them. I most certainly agree with you that we need more of the type of lectures conducted by your Rabbi...

"Have you ever seen President and Mrs. Harding? One of America's great institutions is the National Game of Baseball. The season's opening is a gala day for Washington. Every seat at the park is always filled. The president (sic) of these United States is the official opener of the baseball season. The official act consists of throwing out the first ball. No other game is quite as attractive as the first." Louis had secured two seats for the opening game and invited Esther to go with him. He offered to pick her up in Baltimore in his "Elizabeth, Lizzie, for short," on April 26, and return her home.

Two days later, Esther reluctantly refuses this invitation. She didn't have the nerve to ask her parents for permission. "Today, Dr. Cameron gave the training school girls permission to visit Wash. to see the Japanese cherry trees. Of course it stands to reason that I would be saving about $1,000 by going to Wash. instead of Japan, but someday I'll go to Japan instead. Thanks again for your wonderful invitation & I hope you enjoy the game."

Esther refused another invitation on April 22, 1923 because she didn't want to miss a day or two of school. "Besides, as I wrote Kitty, my brother is on the road now & Mama is the kind that misses everyone so much. On Friday night, as we all sit around the table & Papa says the prayers, we all feel a certain loss & I should feel dreadful if I were away too. Mama is such a dear little person & I should hate to leave her now. If I did, it wouldn't seem very nice. Not the idea of coming home late, but the whole idea of going to see a boy in another city. I feel that you may be quite angry with me now, but I think you're a nice friend anyway."

As long as the Grossberg family lived on M Street, Louis was responsible for all the repairs around the home. Mr. Heckinger, the owner of their house was also the owner of a large hardware store that sold lumber and plumbing supplies. When the steps on the porch of the house were in dire need of repair, Louis offered to do the work himself if Heckinger would supply the lumber. Heckinger refused, so Louis bought lumber and fixed the steps on his own. However, on April 25, 1923, he wrote a letter concerning other repairs that were needed. Since the lease on the property was to expire May 9, 1923, he did not want to renew unless he could clear up some issues. The house had been leased for three year and Louis had made considerable repairs himself.

"During the term of the lease I papered the house thruout, made repairs to the plumbing, and spent about $150.00 on the furnace. Despite this excessive expenditure on the heating plant, I burned seventeen tons of hard coal this Winter at an average cost of $17.50 per ton.

"Without question the consumption of seventeen tons of coal in Winter indicates that something is radically wrong with the furnace. I feel that inasmuch as the heating plant is a permanent improvement to the property, the owner should make the repairs especially since I have already expended a large sum of money on it." Louis agreed to renew the lease for another two years if the owner would undertake to repair the plumbing and fix the heating plant. When Mr. Heckinger refused to do anything for them, the family decided to move.

Many of Louis' and Dave's clients, who started out as grocers and other tradesmen, later became quite well to do. As auditors, they frequently served as treasurers of various charitable organizations and did this work gratis. It formed a part of their charitable contributions. Due to their influence, their clients also became involved and in time, large contributors. On May 17, 1923, Louis sent a letter to Mr. Simon J. Levin in Baltimore about a Keren Hayesod meeting. This charity was to host Dr. Chaim Weitzman, later to become the first President of the State of Israel. He was expected in Baltimore in ten days and they hoped to raise $5,000 in pledges to give him. As secretary of the organization, Louis requested expense money for administrative costs. He had already donated $3.00 to $4.00 for postcards but needed money for printing and stamps.

"Donations can be sent to Mr. Glushak at 704 M St. NW and payment would be applied to the Weitzman account." He also requested an additional seat at the banquet for Esther Borenstein, who had accompanied him the year before.

That same day, Louis invited Esther to attend the event as his guest. "Dr. Chaim Weitzman, President of the world Zionist Organization and without question the greatest figure in Jewish life today, is coming to Baltimore on Sunday May 27th to open the Keren Hayesod Campaign in your city…As you no doubt know, Dr. Weitzman is a famous scientist and the inventor of TNT, the explosive extensively used by the Allies in the recent unpleasantness over there which Dr. Weitzman gave to the English Government. He is a wonderful personality and a gifted talker. I can assure you a very interesting evening.

"Just a word about that ball game. I was, of course, very much disappointed (but) the reasons you gave did not seem funny to me at all. I could not help admiring your consideration for your parents, even though I was the victim of that consideration.

"Washington is very busy preparing for the Shrine visitors. While you could go to Japan to view the cherry Blossoms, you could not go anywhere to find such a monster affair as the Shriners are planning. As you have a standing invitation to visit us as well as Kitty, to say nothing of Mrs. Glushak, who by the way has recently given birth to a cute baby girl, you should have no difficulty in finding accommodations, a matter that will worry many of our visitors."

Esther accepted this invitation and on May 23, 1923, writes, "I don't know anything about the character of the affair Sunday night, but if you think it proper for me to attend I shall be very glad to accept your invitation."

Louis invited Esther for a different event but on June 27, 1923, she reluctantly declined. However, she was happy to relate she had successfully passed her exams and would be teaching in the fall. Esther studied at a "Normal School" to become a teacher. This was the practice at the time rather than at a college or university.

It didn't take Ida Glushak long to exhibit her unflattering character traits. An example of her temper shows up in these letters she exchanged with Louis. For some reason, she included a picture of Dave in uniform in her July 12, 1923 letter in which she accepts Louis' apology for a minor incident. The second letter from Louis crossed in the mail. He frequently visited the Glushak house, which was near their office.

On one visit, a small incident suddenly grew into a whirlwind. Louis used some hairbrushes from their bathroom, either theirs or ones of his that he kept there. Ida became furious and threw him and the brushes out of the house. Louis didn't understand why she had gotten so angry and tried to make up because of his great bond with Dave. He didn't want such a small thing to spoil their long time relationship. Most likely Dave prompted this letter from Ida.

Lou, I phoned you at 9:40 and 10 – can't get you, so have decided to write. It's my turn to apologize I think. I regret more than I can say my attitude toward your splendid apology this evening which I was too hopping mad to accept in the spirit given. I would feel that this was a black letter day indeed if it were permitted to remain as the date when the unusual unselfish friendship you have always given us ceased to exist.

After all, this is the first dark cloud of misunderstanding that has appeared in our years of friendship – and, doggone it, I wish you'd bring those blamed old brushes back and forget the whole business.

Louis' letter of July 12, 1923, starts out,

Dear Ida,

I was lying in bed mentally writing you a letter when Dave came up and delivered your message. Before I was half thru reading it, my eyes filled with tears and I was gripped in an uncontrollable paroxysm of sobbing that held me for fully five minutes. I don't cry very easily and I don't remember ever having cried that way before. It was like the eruption of a pent-up volcano that had smoldered within me for two hours.

When I left you tonight I drove way out to the District Line and stopped on a dark unfrequented road. I thought the whole matter over and the more I thought the worse I felt. Had you, at the time I offended you, voiced your resentment, I should have immediately apologized and you would have as quickly accepted the apology and all would have been well. Instead however, you permitted the matter to rest with you for two full days and what was at first no doubt of but relatively small moment grew like a cancer until tonight reaching the end of human endurance burst forth thru the medium of those inoffensive brushes. Gad, Ida, that hurt me more than I have ever been hurt before.

I had fondly believed that our friendship was built on solid foundation. But you had returned those brushes! I didn't realize it at first, but as I sat there in the dark the significance of those brushes dawned upon me and my heart was gripped as in a vise of steel. What hurt most was the realization that our friendship meant nothing – was only an empty dream, for otherwise how could so small a thing as a few thoughtless words and a careless tone even shake that structure, let alone demolish it?

I must have sat there over an hour when I finally started for the house, I took out some of my feeling on my car. I just stepped on the gas and flew. Why I did not run into someone or something I don't know. I lost little time in undressing but sleep was out of the question.

When Dave brought your note I know now, that my sobbing was due to joy, joy that after all our friendship was not destroyed, that your action was the result of blind unreasoning anger born of that treacherous cancer that had not been smothered at birth. And you ask that I return the brushes! When I turned the whole matter over in my mind while on that lonely road, I had decided that I would never bring the brushes back. But now, I am ashamed that I construed an angry action as casting a doubt upon the solidity of our friendship. Yes, the blamed old brushes, as you put it, are going back and I feel confident that everything between us will be as heretofore.

It was time Louis settled down. Kitty decided to play matchmaker. She wrote him about a Miss Alshul on August 6, 1923, from Tobyhanna, Pennsylvania where she was spending her vacation. She tried to get Rabbi Glushak involved, as well. It seems that the Rabbi also knew Miss Alshul and Kitty thought she would be a nice addition to the family. Kitty suggested that the young lady should be encouraged to come to the hotel where Kitty was doing secretarial work for a week's vacation on the pretext of visiting Kitty. If everything worked out, Louis would be there the same week.

"You observe her from morning until night and you can easily decide if you care to continue the friendship. Nothing would please me more than to see you happily married. I'll surely do all I can to have you meet her." Unfortunately, we will never know what happened because there were no other letters on the subject and my father had no recollection of having met Miss Alshul.

Louis left the IRS on December 31, 1923, since he felt there was no future in the Government tax service. Rumors abounded that Excess Profit taxes might be repealed as well as the personal income tax laws and many revenue agents were laid off or sent to other parts of the country. The tax laws were vital for financing the First World War. This was especially the case for excess profits taxes on large companies that were enacted for just this purpose. These corporate taxes ran up to 85% above certain exemptions. This was very complicated work and very few accountants and lawyers knew anything about it. As predicted, the Excess Profit taxes were repealed and large corporations and investors heaved a sigh of relief.

By 1922, the WWI bills had been paid and the Personal Income Tax Laws, which were passed in March 1, 1913, looked like they might also go by the wayside. Louis and Dave, like most other revenue agents, expected taxes to decline or be eliminated and figured their government days were numbered. It used to take up to two weeks to audit a large company's records but with the end of the Excess Profits tax laws, it was expected that revenue agents would not have much work to do just auditing simple income tax records. The remaining tax work would be for regular businesses, keeping their records and filing their taxes. They decided to go into an accounting practice partnership. They remained in government until January 1, 1924 and then opened their new office. The name was determined by the toss of a coin. It became Glushak & Grossberg.

The letterhead on the Glushak & Grossberg business stationery was very impressive. Aside from their names and local address, there were four other addresses – New York City; Syracuse, New York; Cleveland, Ohio; and Youngstown, Ohio. These were window dressing. The firm had arranged with other accounting firms to handle work if clients had need of such services in those cities. This practically never happened.

The accounting practice got off to a slow start but Glushak & Grossberg managed to pay their bills – barely. The two men took office space on the third floor of the People's Life Insurance Company Building at 14th and I Streets, NW. While Louis and Dave always got along famously, this was not the case between Dave and their clients. Most of them preferred that Louis handle their affairs. Dave was so bright that he found it difficult to put up with other people's foibles. If someone made an inaccurate statement, regardless of the subject matter, Dave would correct the speaker. Clients did not like this and complained to Louis, who was much more diplomatic. He preferred to ignore unimportant things, but Dave could not let mistakes slide.

After the First World War and before the years of the depression, there was a time of great expectations. Though the accounting practice was doing relatively well, it was not profitable enough to comfortably support Louis and Dave. Dave was now married with a child and was more in need of money than Louis, who continued to live at home. Consequently, Louis turned over most of the business profits to Dave. This could not continue indefinitely, though. Something had to be done to bring in more income. At various times, each of the partners tried to find additional work elsewhere and in 1925 Louis went off to Florida in search of a better future for both of them.

Letters from the men flowed between Miami Beach and Washington, DC. Dave was every bit as good a letter writer as Louis and their correspondence was punctuated with interesting comments and observations. As a joke, they often addressed each other in affectionate terms associated with writing to sweethearts. On August 11, 1925, Louis wrote Dave from the Cortez Hotel in Miami Beach, Florida. The letter was written in longhand but he kept a carbon copy. Louis stayed with his cousin Aaron Freudberg, who was also looking for greener pastures.

"I was much amused over your wire. It does seem from afar that things are aflame here, and that is not altogether wrong. From my observations in some communities, real estate is worth just what it can produce, in other words the income determines the value. Here there is no such thing. A piece of ground is worth just as much as the next fellow will give for it." Louis was encouraged to open an office. A potential client wanted tax work done, but Louis would have to do bookkeeping, too. Though it would only take 3 or 4 hours a week, he considered charging $15 or $20 a week. He was much encouraged about prospects in Florida.

"Office space is a thing to dream about. I hear that about 10 office bldgs. of large size are going up and all rooms were taken before the foundation was in. Living conditions are a matter of small satisfaction to me unless I can make real money. I'd rather stay in Washington. We occupy what is known here as a garage apartment. Aaron calls it our stable. The place is 3½ miles from the center of activities. I have been in a general state of *zutummel* (all mixed up) since I got here."

Louis wanted Dave to come to Florida for a week to investigate "the building game. We may find (that) we cannot swing it, but I don't want to pass up the chance and it is one of a lifetime – just because of the cost of the fare. Sometimes when I begin to think of what will be the outcome of all this crazy speculation in real estate, I can see only ruin for the last man, but on the other hand, there are sky-scrapers going up everywhere around here, railroads being built. Most houses here are temporary structures. One doesn't know what to put up. Your residential property might in a month be so valuable that the improvements on it are ridiculous by comparison with the real estate. Our apartment garage is on a lot which our landlady asks $35,000 for. The house and garage stable can be put up for $2,000. The houses are put up out of wood and plaster. I haven't seen a scrap of wallpaper here. There are no cellars and no furnaces. I am homesick for a chimney. Hills and mountains are not known hereabouts. Construction work outside perhaps of labor shortage seems to offer little or no complications."

Louis had visited Hollywood and Coral Gables and thought they might be the best places to build. "When real estate values will have reached their peak those companies in business at that time will be overrun with construction work. Right now, no sooner the plans for building are made, then the place is sold. The demand for improved property is simply unheard of. How long do you think I would tolerate living in a stable at $50 a month for two out in the country, if I could get some place better. What will happen in November to April when the season is on? I can't imagine a worse rooming shortage. To the far-sighted builder a gold mine is knocking at the door.

"This is my impression of the building possibilities, and you know that I am no builder. For us, with no capital it looks like a hard problem. But where our chance lies is in what we know of building. I have in mind the formulation of a company of about $100,000 cash to begin to build here. The money might be raised in the East. Aaronson would probably come in. Your relatives and mine might back us. All we need is a start. When the real boom comes – and it must, or all these millions upon millions of dollars sunk into Florida will be lost – we should be right in the thick of the game. If J.B. could do it in Wash. without capital and with not 1/50th the boom, why can't we?"

Louis asked Dave to come see for himself and then to go back East to raise capital. "Imagine, in Miami Beach where Joe Stein is, there was not a soul last summer. To-day, stores cannot be gotten and rooms ditto. Joe tells me that he has an apartment with one bed roomette, kitchenette and bathette in an apartment house a good ways from the Beach. He paid $45 a month. Saturday he was informed that the place has been sold and his rooms for the coming month cost $100. In season, they are about $500 a month. Do you blame me for not being able to sit down to accounting work?"

On September 9, 1925, Louis bawled Dave out for writing only once a week. He ran into Mr. Jeffrey who said he was not doing so well on his Miami purchase and would fill him in later. "It will probably surprise you to get this letter typewritten.

"I spent two hours giving legal advice to a potential client when he asked me, how much do I owe you?

"25 simoleons (sic)," I replied.

The man hesitated a bit and then said, "'O.K., send a bill and we will send you a check.'

He then added, "Why last year it only cost me $25.00 for making out my entire return and the fellow worked all day."

"That doesn't mean anything," says I, "because it may cost you $5,000.00 more just because you had a cheap guy make out your return."

The man agreed and again told Louis to send a bill and he would pay it. Later Louis thought about reducing the bill to $15.00 for goodwill. Then that morning he ran across another member of that firm who said that the advice given was worth its weight in gold. When Louis said the other partner had been hesitant about the bill so he was considering reducing it, the man replied, "Oh that Frenchman would think ten dollars too much if that was the first thing you asked him. It is in his nature to bargain, but don't mind him. It was worth $25 to me to find out about the partnership alone. Just send the bill and we'll pay it." Thus, he had money to buy a typewriter.

Louis sent another letter to Dave on September 12, 1925:

Every line of business opening here is doing good. Junk business is also a business and should be no different. I would suggest this: If the Fainberg Co. is really interested in opening a branch here, I should be glad to make a thoro (sic) investigation of the conditions and report my findings to them. Knowing the junk business as I do and having the further advantage of knowing the town of Miami, I could make the investigation in a minimum amount of time. Of course they would first have to authorize such an investigation which would cost them between $100 and $150. Regular audit rates here are $40 a day and I couldn't afford to spend the time otherwise.

In Louis' letter, September 13, 1925, he is hoping to return to Washington for Yom Kippur. "I can't do much here before my office gets built. Somehow General Delivery for a business address is not very impressive even in Miami." Dave had written that Leo's little girl Gracie had been in an accident and Louis was very concerned. "I suppose Leo has given up the idea of coming to Florida. This trouble of his will probably change things for a while anyway.

"Your suggestion about using part of the office for sleeping quarters has been duly considered long before your thoughts on the subject. It would suit me fine if only it could be done. There might be objections from the management of the office building. You can't imagine the handicap of no office." Louis had to interview bookkeepers in the client's office, which he felt cheapened him. He was also disappointed by the lack of money being made available for the bright prospects he hoped would materialize.

"So our building plans are all to be classed with the dreams of the artist. It is a damn shame. This is the first opportunity in the lives of either of us for a turning point in our fortunes and we find our hands shackled. We just have to buckle down and go back to the business of making a living instead of a fortune.

"O yes, our rent has been raised to $60 bucks. You are glad it isn't a 100 and let it go at that. She promises that there will be no raises any more."

Dave apologized to Louis on November 14, 1925, for not writing more often, claiming he was too busy. "The check for $100 came in very nice and handy I thank you. However, insofar as your real estate deals are concerned, you're down there in Florida, you know your own business and, as we said, whatever surplus you have, put it into land, take the darn chance of a lifetime. If we're sunk, we're sunk. If we win, we win, so we should worry. In the mean while do the best you can on that deal."

Dave complained of needing help, both for regular office work and for preparing letters to show clients about investing in Florida. Louis needed letters of his own written, so Dave suggested, "In regard to the letters you want sent out to prospects in Miami, but which you cannot because you haven't a stenographer, how about sending me a list of names and addresses together with the letter you want written and let Ida do it here, dating them far enough ahead. After they are written they can be shipped back to you, and you can mail them in Miami. And, by the way, just had Ida's Hamilton wristwatch which was lying in the drawer converted into a wristwatch for me. Sent it to the Hamilton factory and now I've got a wristwatch. It's a dandy. It costs $55, but it cost me considerably less. Anyway, my ambition of a lifetime has now been realized. I've got a Hamilton wristwatch. I also got a suit from the honorable Mr. Wilner, costs plenty but what say. It's some suit."

Joseph Wilner owned a men's clothing shop on the first floor of their office building. He was also a client, and the same man who later became president of Adas Israel Congregation and didn't want to give Benjamin Grossberg $5,000 as severance pay when he retired.

Louis tells Dave on November 16, 1925 that he really needs an adding machine, which must be the $88.00 model. "Don't forget the long rear legs and the little back attachment for narrow paper." In another letter, dated November 18, 1925, "Business with me is very weak. For this week I have been able to click off only $150.00. I am putting all my spare time into Meredith but I consider this as no cash business. Of course, I expect to cash in on that too some day."

On December 17, 1925, Louis wrote:
"Darling David, every now and then comes the worry of what next. This here white boy is not got a job and this week is a very poor one." While the building business in Florida was going splendidly, he

was unable to take advantage of it without capital. "Nice lots are going for $4,000 and with houses for $15,000. One would think that business would be there for the picking. Unfortunately, not the case. So that's that. Only trouble is that I am absolutely broke. Got fifty cents in my pocket and don't know how my bank account stands. Everybody owes me money and if I don't get some damn soon I'll have to make a call or two for funds." Louis had chalked up only $105.00 for the week.

Even with no money to spare, Louis was already involved in a new branch of the Miami Zionist District. In his letter, December 22, 1925, he said they hoped to raise $100,000 for the United Palestine Fund, "which for a small community is quite a chunk – but we may get it. As to ourselves, I don't know. Seems that we will have to give jointly, you there and I here."

Dave has difficulty finding clients, too. One minute he complains that there is too much work and the next that there isn't enough. December 23, 1925, Louis writes, "Sorry that you find you have nothing to do. I, too,…am a bit short cliented. This week looks even worse than the last with so far only $60.00 to my credit and no visible clientele in the offing. 'Tis true that I have not solicited. Maybe will throw away a ten dollar bill or more on advertising in the daily papers."

Louis again asks Dave to reconsider coming to Florida. He is sure that once Dave sees the possibilities, the two of them could make a go of it. "Otherwise, I have had a feeling for some time that I would like to bid this place good by after March and go back to Washington to stay. I hate this place and feel that all this time has been just this much out of my life. Of course, I do not doubt that your stay here should be profitable because there is plenty of work here for us."

The next day, December 24, 1925, Louis writes Dave again.

Your long letter of consolation and woe, telling me at once that I should not be homesick and that butterless bread is much more painful than nostalgia, (was) received and I am sure you haven't ever been homesick. As to leaving the office alone for a month, I guess you can do that. Figure on leaving immediately after having visited all the customers, that is both of them. Don't he, by the way owe you something like five hundred simoleons? Tell him that an accountant's service is necessary to keep him out of trouble and

139

make him think he'll go bankrupt without us. Personally I have spent a very miserable coupla days walking the streets in the hope that someone will approach me and ask me do I install systems. So far no one has. In fact I gotta get something now that you fear for your butter on that there pumpernickel. Merry Kishekes and Happy Kugel

Louis wrote Dave on December 30, 1925:

"First the sad news that I have as yet no work at all. Let us hope that the New Year will bring many new and cash paying clients both here and at Washington, principally in Washington." Louis told of an acquaintance he met, a product of Pace and Pace, who had an arrangement with a New York CPA firm that sounded interesting. "Maybe if I and you ever work together in the same town we will try it. And yet I really do not feel that I want to be head of a great concern of nationally known accountants unless we can be in the same town together, that's how much I love you.

"I am planning a very quiet New Year's Eve. In fact the thing will be so quiet that I guess I'll stay home and read a book of some kind. But I have planned (to) go away for three days with a nice young lawyer. We will jump in my bus and take a run out to the central part of the State say about 160 miles. There we will rough it a bit – go out fishing, hiking, and whatever our hearts will dictate, anything but worry about the lack of business out here."

By the time I started reading these Florida letters to Pop, he was no longer smoking and we would sit upstairs in either the dining room or the dinette. This was probably about 1993. The old book boxes would be stacked on the end of the table and, as I read to him, we could look out the picture windows and enjoy the view. Years earlier they had bought the adjoining small lot between their house on the corner and the house next door.

Their house was perched on a hillside overlooking Albemarle Street. They had divided the extra lot to put in a driveway up to their main entrance level. The driveway included a parking area for about eight cars, used weekly by Pop's pinochle buddies. The rest of the lot was left wooded with a winding slate stairway up to another rise where a white birdbath sat nestled amongst the azaleas and rhododendrons.

Very old tall trees remained on the lot and the garden portion, probably no more than 20 feet wide, gave the feeling of seclusion and serenity. My mother had designed the garden and we enjoyed watching squirrels playing among the trees. Someone's cat came every day to bask in the sun as if she owned the place.

It was during these Florida letters that I asked him if he had anything to add to this period down South. He said that at the time his biggest regret was not having the money to establish a practice there or to invest in property. If he could have done so, things would have been very different. Then he stopped and thought for a moment. "But if we had been successful in Florida, I would not have returned to Washington. I probably would not have met your mother. So you see, things really turned out for the best. It must have been beshert. Where would I be now without Mom?" To which I added, "And where would I be?"

Leo Freudberg wrote Louis on January 5, 1926, announcing that he was at home, "with an attack of tonsillitis for why else would a guy write in longhand. I understand that you are cleaning up these days. You certainly could not spend the winter in a more summery place. Honestly how are you making out? Do you think I should be there?"

Leo was also involved in Synagogue politics. "Well boy there has been great fire works in shul matters of late. The chief topic for this weeks meeting will be the raising of dues; $5 per month is what we want. Try to get it. If we don't, Rabbi and *Chasan* (*Chazan*, cantor) must go. There is talk of 14th St. and us combining and pooling our habitats and build a 2,000 seater uptown. Also there was a big meeting to build a $100,000 *Talmud Torah* (religious school), made me Secretary and in a moment of thoughtlessness I accepted. I got plenty leisure to repent. Since you put me in Jewish politics, I attended 6 Jewish business affairs – every evening and so forth."

Louis answers Leo, January 10, 1926. "The slogan here is that it is always June in Miami, which slogan was originated by the real estate-nicks who, as you no doubt know, NEVER lie (but) that is not what I came out here for. The result is quite a yearning to be up where it is cold and where they play pinochle of Saturday nights by the heat of the oil burner. (Yet,) imagine going out swimming on Christmas and New Year's days. Only yesterday it was so warm that a vest was uncomfortable beneath the jacket. Out in the country there are oodles of groves of oranges, grapefruit, tangerines, and what will you have? It is green all over all the time. No skiddy mornings, no freezy radiators, no heavy overcoats, in fact no semblance of winter. Those who can come down here in luxury and splendor really enjoy life.

"There is every kind of work. Civic work aplenty...You can work for a shul, a *Talmud Torah*, on the $150,000.00 Keren Hayesod drive soon to be launched here. In fact, us Floridians can give you anything you want that you can pay for – and you better have plenty jack.

"Business? Not so very *glantzig* (great) with me of late. I haven't earned my board and lodging. It costs me every bit of forty dollars a week...

"My observations are those who are engaged in a business enterprise are doing exceedingly well. My obstacle (is) being cursed with a profession. If I had a little cash when I first came here and any kind of business I would be much better off than I am."

As for the land bust that had erupted, "People who had purchased land were trying to unload it. The hope was that winter visitors would want to purchase these properties but word had gotten out and prices had dropped. Still, there were no purchasers.

"The craze is all over and sanity has at last come into its own. The buyer of to-day wants to know what income there is possible from the property he is about to buy. In other words, the standards that prevail in other communities where real estate is concerned are beginning to govern local property. It's the old story, 'He who has, gets' is still as true as ever it was...

"You say, scheduled for the coming week (is) a display of first class fireworks at the shul meeting. Sorry indeed to miss it. I always did enjoy a fight at the shul and the prospects of a good one always made my mouth water. The *Chazan* has always been lazy as hell but I don't know if I blame (him) so much for not wishing to do any teaching of kids. Here there is also a very nice shul but oh the farce of it. The *Chazan* of the shul has recently been ousted. He has become too commercial and has diverted too much of his time to the real estate business..."

On February 19 Dave asked Louis to explore the feasibility of a business deal in Miami Beach for a client who was interested in investing in a 10-story combination garage and hotel complex that would accommodate 1,000 cars a day. Dave compared it to a YMCA hotel in Chicago where the customer paid 35 cents to 50 cents a night. The proposed Miami rate would be 75 cents. After investigating the deal, Louis found it to be too risky.

Dave, reporting on local shul politics, started his February 24, 1926 letter by describing the fund raising event that took place at the Jewish Community Center. The previous accountants charged $230 or $300 and Dave decided to charge $200 or $250 and turn it in as a donation. "It probably is the cheapest form of advertising."

Dave reminded Louis that their $250 note at the bank was due in a few days. Paying it off would leave their balance too low so he went to the vice president in the Commercial Bank and Trust Company and said, "I absolutely had to have $500. I told him that I had about $800 coming in, but that my clients weren't coming across and that I needed the money. I told him I ran an average balance of $400, so he doesn't do another thing but simply takes out a note makes it out for $500." Dave also arranged for a client to receive a substantial loan. "If you can introduce a client to a bank and have a vice president there accept my word for a loan it certainly shouldn't hurt us."

As for the Grossberg & Glushak prospects, "over here you can make a nice living, over there in a few years you will get wealthy. I personally feel this way about it. If in a couple of years the business with you down in Florida is really justifiable, I will be very happy indeed to leave this office in the hands of a junior on partnership basis and come down and settle with you permanently so that we will be together anyway."

On March 8, 1926, Dave wrote:

"I am enclosing a trial balance of our own *tsoras* in this town in Washington. There is only one way I can see in which you can save some income tax money and that is to divide up the net profits in the proportion of ⅔ for me and ⅓ for you." This was the financial arrangement that existed, more or less, anyway. "You of course can also claim auto dept. and expenses as in my case were it not for the business, I would get rid of the damn thing at once. I have discovered that a machine is a blooming luxury that only a rich man can afford. The damn thing is costing me $19.00 a month for gas, oil and garage. That does not include tires, repairs…"

Dave had a lucky escape from an accident that morning. A Western Union messenger on a bicycle suddenly darted out in front of his car. He immediately stopped, "but not till I had nocked (sic) the kid down. He got up absolutely unhurt but the hind wheel was busted. I tell you he had one narrow escape.

"Well, of course the cop came up and I was pretty sore, and after taking down the number of my car etc. he asked me what I was going to do about it. I told him that I would do nothing, as it was not my fault. Then turning to the kid he asked him what he would do about it, so he said he would fix the wheel. Upon hearing the kid's name, I discovered him to be a Jewish boy, so I told the cop that I would pay ½ of the cost of the repairs. Well that seemed to please the cop and this evening the kid brought around the bill for $3.00 whereupon I have him $1.50 and called the deal off. Now the funny thing is, I did not have $1.50 to give my car a much needed wash yet I did have it for that other purpose. *Nu* (so) you know how that works out anyway."

On June 30, 1926, Dave's letter began, "Yesterday I was considerably horrified to receive from you three letters. Three is a whole lot of letters to be getting in one day. My advice to you is that you drive back. It will cost you $85 to send the car back. At that price you can buy a new set of tires at Montgomery Ward…The weather now is good, you may run into a few bad roads in Georgia but it's not bad as it isn't rainy season and all through Florida the roads are good, North Carolina and all the way up is very good territory. I will get you the exact route and mail it to you. You don't have to race. The trip is 1,500 miles. You should average 300 miles a day. I think you can drive straight traveling about 15 hours a day. You should be able to average 20 miles an hour easily because your car ought to be able to do 30 and 35. I think you can cover the distance in 10 days. It'll take you a day or two to rest…"

I read an article in the newspaper outlining the history of road travel in America in the early 1920s and 1930s. Where roads existed, they were generally only two lanes and few were properly paved. To get from Florida to Washington, DC was a monumental ordeal. Restaurants and lodgings were few and far-between. Cars broke down frequently, with gas stations and repair shops rare. It could take days to find someone to fix a car. There was no air conditioning, and often no windows, so weather played a major role in everyone's travel plans. Where Dave says the trip would be 1,500 miles, this was due to a lack of bridges and proper roadbeds. Today the trip is about 1,000 miles, so one can imagine the added driving necessary to complete the journey.

My father's brother, Joe, rode down with him on one of the trips. At one point they came to a spot where for one long block, all was mud. Louis put the car in low gear and kept moving. When he finally reached the other side, the radiator was boiling hot and they had to stop awhile to cool off. As they were waiting, they saw a chauffeur-driven limousine drive to the middle of the block and get stuck. To help them out, Louis stopped at the first farmhouse and asked them to send some horses to pull out the car.

Farther down the road in Georgia, they came to a section of about two blocks under water. Joe got out of the car, took off his shoes and socks, rolled up his pants and walked ahead so Louis could judge the depth of the water. This too they navigated safely.

On July 12, 1926, Dave wrote:

> It is a devil of a note to think that you now have to waste time do-ing nothing but waiting for collections when I am rushed to death here. Insofar as the tires are concerned I think $90 for two tires is an absolutely outrageous sum of money.

Louis writes Dave on July 27, 1926, as he is about to leave Florida. The purpose of his return to Washington is to raise money in order to quit the accounting business and invest in real estate. For those who had money and some wisdom, it was possible to do very well in Florida despite the bust. However, many who tried this did not have Louis' or Dave's business background and lost everything.

"I am in the midst of packing away in Lord only knows where, such of my local troubles as will not find its way into the waste basket. But as *helft kein teretz* (excuses don't help), one must just buckle down to the task and do it. On top of all this I have yet to go home and finish the bookkeeping that I started for Aaron last night." Louis settled his ac-count with some clients but had to take a 60-day note for a payment of $150. "I suppose it is good if they have the money. Right now they don't have that there dough-dough, but it is the best that can be done under the circumstances." He also sold his $88 adding machine for $50.

"I have gotten two tires and tubes at a cost of $43.00 and I am getting another tire and tube to-morrow at the same rate because I find that the rear tires which I was going to put on the front were and still are worse than I had at first thought."

When Louis later returned to Florida, his fortunes did not improve. Ida wrote to Louis on September 16, 1926, with unusually good common sense, by telling him of Dave's great difficulty in trying to raise money. "I know you're well – you know we're all O.K. – so I'll cut out the preliminaries and get down to brass tacks in re: your indestructible desire to go into building, which in calmer fashion is our constant dream, too.

"Dave wrote to his brother-in-law, Al, who didn't even consider it necessary to acknowledge his letter. From his brother, Leo Glushak, Dave yesterday received a letter in which he says, 'Your project requires a great deal of money to finance and a highly experienced builder.' From your brother-in-law Harry, and your relatives in Paterson you can expect nothing, including the Kitays with whom you are in communication.

"There is another thing to consider – that any promoter – the one who has the needed funds in his possession – controls the bag of tricks, and can let you and Dave slide gently out of the whole thing and tie up with some one else. The above sums up the doubts in the case. When Dave, many weeks ago told me that Leo Freudberg was certain that he could raise $450,000 I said, 'I'll believe he can when he has the money.' People don't hand over $1,000 just like that to be turned over to a couple of young accountants with a zeal for building in a far off state. If both of you want to go into building you must get the needed funds yourself. This Washington office must be continued. It supplies the bread and butter.

"Now you in Florida tell everybody as Dave will here, that you're going to stick to accounting. If you can accumulate a decent amount of money and you are sure that you're in building to stay, you can then throw up the Washington office, if you so decide but not before. In the meantime, no one should know you're still dreaming building. Dave and you must talk accounting but in your thoughts well, your thoughts are your own. With best wishes for a happy New Year during which our hopes will be realized, I am, Yours for success, Ida"

The Florida boom of the 1920s was one of the most colorful land rushes in American history. When the First World War was over, Calvin Coolidge saw prosperity on the horizon and people began spending their newly gained riches on cars and other luxury items. Roads were expanding to formerly remote areas and people started flocking to Florida to enjoy the temperate climate. Land was being sold to eager buyers before it was cleared of vegetation or drained of swamp water. In fact, much of it was still underwater, but that did not deter those with cash in hand. In 1924, Florida amended its constitution to abolish inheritance and income taxes. To entice more people, even drivers licenses were not required. Speculators bought land in the morning that they sold in the evening for outrageous profits. With the extension of rail lines, there seemed to be no limit to the riches that awaited the lucky purchasers. However, all good things end, and by 1927 the boom turned into a complete bust. Actually, Louis recognized the impossibility of the outlandish land speculations way before that. It was probably a good thing that neither Louis nor Dave had the money to invest there.

Dave's sister, Fanny Glushak, worked with Celia Kanster at the New Jersey bank until she married Alexander Simpson and moved to New York. Two years later, she returned to the bank for a visit and all the clerks were delighted to see her. By this time, Celia was being badgered by William and his family to get married already. She finally ran out of excuses and the wedding date was set for September 1926. Even though Fanny now lived in New York, she returned periodically to visit her parents on Hunterdon Street, the same street where Celia lived. Her father, Rabbi Glushak, also officiated at the same Temple the Kanster family attended.

In August, a month before Celia's wedding, she was invited for Sunday dinner at the home of William's aunt.

"I can't understand why your mother allows you to spend a lot of money on a phonograph for the family. And how can you buy yourself a fur coat when you need all the money you earn for your marriage?" Bill's aunt criticized.

Celia was dumbfounded. Buying things for her close family or their house gave her a lot of pleasure. What right did this aunt have to question her motives? Who had the right to tell her how she should spend her own money? Celia expected William to defend her.

Instead, he complained, "The trouble with Celia is that anyone can get anything out of her."

With that, she got up from the table and went out on the porch. William followed her.

"That was very rude to walk out. You must go back in and apologize to my aunt."

Celia looked at him with disgust.

"Me apologize? Your aunt should apologize to me and my mother!"

With that, she demanded to be taken home and refused to talk further. Thoughts pushed to the back of her mind suddenly moved to center stage. She realized that all her procrastinations had been for a reason. William was not the man for her.

Jacob Kanster had gone to bed early, but Celia woke him to say she decided to break the engagement. Rather than being shocked or disappointed, her father was delighted to see his daughter so cheerful. Her mother was visiting her sister, Fanny (Berger) Brickman in Baltimore. When Celia phoned her, her mother said she would take the next train home, arriving that Monday evening. Monday morning at the bank, Celia told the office staff to look at her finger the next day, Tuesday. They all assumed that she would be sporting a wedding ring.

Celia met her mother at the station Monday evening, accompanied by Big Sam (her sister Sara's husband), and Dr. Perlman, a friend of the family. Celia wanted Dr. Perlman along to witness the return of the engagement ring. She didn't want William claiming later that she had not returned it, the way another man had in a newspaper article she had read recently. From the station, they went directly to William's house where Celia gave back his ring with these words: "It would never work out."

William was speechless and turned white. And that was the last they saw of each other.

The next day at the bank, everyone wanted to see Celia's wedding ring. Instead, she showed them her bare finger. When they saw her smiling face and how relaxed she was, they were happy for her. For days, William would go to the bank looking for Celia but she would sneak out the back door. Her office friends were on the lookout and protected her. Two weeks later, he finally gave up. Later, when Celia married Louis, William told everyone the reason she called off the wedding was because she had found someone else. The truth was that she did not meet Louis until six months later.

One Saturday in February, Celia and her sister Edith went to New York for the day. Celia mentioned she would like to talk to Fanny (Glushak) Simpson, but was annoyed that Fanny had stopped calling her even though they had been such close friends. Edith decided to call her anyway since they were just around the corner from Fanny's house. When Fanny heard they were in New York, she insisted they come right over. During this visit, Fanny learned of Celia's broken engagement.

"Celia, please come back next Sunday. My husband, Alexander, will be away at a meeting and we could spend a lovely day together," Fanny offered.

"I can't," Celia replied. "I have an appointment with Edith. Maybe some other time."

Later, Fanny took Edith aside and told her she had someone she wanted Celia to meet, so Edith told Celia they could postpone their plans.

The very next day, Fanny set the wheels in motion, and Louis responded in a letter dated February 11, 1927:

"Bright and early this morning our mutual friend Ida called me on the telephone and informed me of your kind invitation to visit you next Sunday afternoon, February thirteenth. If I were superstitious I should waver a bit in my enthusiasm, but since Fridays, ominous numbers, and black cats hold no terrors for me I am delighted to accept your invitation.

"I have heard it rumored that your very dear girl friend, of whose charm and pulchritude Dave and Ida have spoken many times, will be on hand to greet your brother's friend and partner. I am all buoyed up to have a grand time.' Grand times being unusual occurrences for this time of year in the lives of slaving accountants."

The following Sunday, Celia went to Fanny's house and was surprised to find Alexander there. Fanny said he had changed his plans at the last minute.

"I hope you don't mind but we have a visitor coming from Washington, DC," she added.

When Louis arrived, Alexander began to hum, *Here comes the bride*. Celia didn't know what was going on. Then Louis walked into the room and laid eyes on Celia. At this meeting, he knew immediately that she would become his wife.

Obviously, the visit went well as Louis reported to Fanny on February 14, 1927:

I told Dave of your desire to be here and to spend a few weeks in your old home town and he was genuinely pleased. (But don't forget to bring Celia along.)

I want to thank you, Fanny as well as Al, for your kind interest in me and for the very cordial welcome that you both accorded me. I had a mighty enjoyable day of it. Celia is certainly a lovely girl. Say, Fan, what's the chances of getting a word or two from you as to Celia's impressions? Huh – if you could only be believed!

PART THREE

Louis and Celia

In his first letter to Celia, dated February 16, 1927, Louis composed two single-spaced typed pages of elaborate verbiage comparing the Washington, DC, train station and the station in Newark, New Jersey. She never forgot it:

> Dear Celia,
>
> I trust you don't mind my addressing you by your given name. Anything less personal would sound stilted coming from me to Fanny's chum. Besides, I like the name. By way of getting even you may call me Louis. Fair exchange, you know.
>
> First permit me to express in words some of the thanks that filled my bosom – or whatever other part of one's anatomy is given over to the sensation of gratefulness – during the short wait prior to the arrival of my train Sunday night. I only waited about twenty minutes, (and am) thankful to you for the invitation to come up and spend time in your company.
>
> The civic pride your expressions of admiration for our Union Station Depot awoke in me suffered a bit of dampening when I saw your own depot. I wondered if you were not impressed more by contrast than by actual architectural beauty. To me your station afforded a type of beauty that one finds in things of great utility even tho it might suffer from a scrimping of aesthetics.

Consider the late arrival to catch his train. One minute has often cost a man his train. At your station things are built for speed. One step from the door is the ticket office and two steps from the ticket office is the train platform. To enter the depot on time means to catch the train on time. I call that systematic beauty. Our magnificent station is frightfully inefficient when compared to the standards I touched upon above. The distance from the main entrance to the train platform is variously from one mile to ten depending upon the time you have before train leaving. Of what avail, then, is a splendid structure to the poor chap who missed his train if the cause of his disappointment – assuming it was his last weekend train to his sweetheart – is inherent in the splendor of the edifice? As for me, give me a beautiful library and an efficient railroad station.

All this, as you may have guessed, is intended to prove to you that your station is beautiful in another sense and to console myself with the thought that since the two structures are not comparable for lack of being on the same plane, no contrast can exist; which has the effect of assuring me that you really thought our depot beautiful thereby restoring in me the civic pride heretofore mentioned. The fact is that I was just now thinking of a certain dimpled chin and paying scant attention to that mass of nonsense, my typewriter keys were hammering out. Please forgive me.

The train chug-chugged up to the platform at 2:54 sharp. I got into the nearest day coach and started to walk in the direction of the sleepers. I mean the sleeping cars – sleepers were all about me sprawled out in the most inelegant postures that it has ever been my experience to witness. Now that I think of it, I had never before seen a day coach in action at that hour. Men, women, young and old were stretched out on the seats with mouths for the most part wide open and noses busily engaged in vying with each other for the snoring championship of day coach number 762.

I was just about to smile out loud when it occurred to me that I might shortly be forced to join them in competition. It is surprising how quickly my amusement changed to apprehension. Why should all these people ride in a day coach, thought I, if there were sleeping berths to be had for a relatively small price?

The answer would seem to be that there were no more sleepers. Altogether I passed thru three-day coaches all of which were generously occupied with sleepers both as to the quantity of occupiers and quality of occupation. Finally and at last, I reached the first of the sleeping cars and accosted the porter with a nonchalant demand for a lower berth. I was choicy in my desires – and why not?

Let's start a new paragraph. 'Boss,' (he) answered in an equally nonchalant manner, 'they isn't any vacant berths on this ca. Yo' all kin try the next one. Good night sah.'

In the 'next ca' every berth seemed occupied, at least all the portieres were drawn, and I could not locate either the porter or the Pullman conductor. The Third car too was fully occupied. I began to count the hours from three to eight thirty. The result was a greater number of hours than I cared to spend in a day coach. Resolutely I trudged into the fourth and last of the Pullman cars. I am not like that boy who, in an attempt to locate his missing movie money, searched thru every one of his pockets save only the right hand trousers pocket. When asked why he didn't look also in that one he answered, 'Cause ef it ain't there I'll drop dead.'

The first upper berth of the fourth car was vacant. I looked no further but stepped sprightly in search of the porter or conductor. I found the former in the men's lounge industriously shining the shoes of those lords and lordesses fortunate enough to be the proud – perhaps unappreciated – occupants of sleeping berths. 'Cap,' I said, 'How about an upper berth?' I didn't feel that I could stand too great a disappointment. The berth I saw vacant might have been reserved for another station.

'Righto! Got only two uppers left in the car. Fix you right up.' Was I happy? YES, Miss. The next thing I knew I was silently cursing the porter for waking me at such an ungodly hour as eight o'clock. Such is the gratitude of the human animal.

What a wonderful day and night was Sunday! I should have been happy for those wonderful twelve hours to have stood up on my feet thru the ride back to Washington. And then she says to me, 'It is an imposition for me to permit you to take me to Newark.' Washington – Newark – two hundred fifty miles. A long distance, but only twenty-four hours by mail. You'll write, won't you?

Later, after they become engaged, Louis reviews his and Celia's court-ship letters and mentions this first one, among others. The courtship letters began February 16, 1927, and ended after their marriage, October 28, 1928. My father also kept some letters beyond their marriage date, from when one or the other was out of town. In addition, over 260 let-ters exist between my father and Dave through the wedding date. I have included some beyond that date because they concerned the Argomite business deal that figured so prominently in their lives. My father did not tell Mom about many of the problems with the business deal at the time, because he wanted to spare her any anxiety. Later she learned more of the details.

Both Louis and Celia kept most of the letters they received and Louis kept carbons of those he sent. Most were dated and easy to read. My father typed his on his office stationery and retained the carbons. My mother's letters were also typed, usually on the stationery of the Fidel-ity Union Trust Company where she worked. Some were handwritten on family stationery, and those exist as originals only.

"February 19, 1927," Celia wrote.

Dear Louis:

Thanks for permitting me to use your given name. I will say the same regarding the usage of your first name inasmuch as you are an intimate friend of the Simpson's, and a partner of a Glushak, for forgetting the fact that at one time you were the Rabbi's pupil.

You evidently had a hard time getting a berth. As for me, I didn't experience any trouble whatsoever, I had already reserved my berth on the third floor of #842 (her house) and at 2:30 o'clock I had entered the realm of dreamland and at 8:00 o'clock the next morning I was on the way to the bank.

On the bus ride home your experiences pertaining to your trips down Florida were interesting and at that time I decided to learn the art of driving. You can imagine how surprised I was, when my father came home Wednesday evening and told us of his purchase of a Dodge Sedan and how he had made arrangements with an instructor to teach me how to drive. I was surprised at myself for not refusing the offer as I had done several times before but had acquiesced and the next evening found me a pupil, driving on a deserted road. I will say this for the instructor; he must be a hero for daring to sit in the car with poor me at the wheel. My ability to stall, driving on the left side of the street and clipping of corners is a rare treat. I frankly admit I am a bit nervous but I surmise that will wear off.

I too, spent a very pleasant afternoon and evening in the company of the Simson's, Glushaks and yourself. I don't believe Ida was harsh with me, but you have me guessing as to what she had to say.

February 21, 1927

Dear Louis:

It had occurred to me after I posted my letter to you that I did not sign my name. Of course, there is a possibility that I did, but in the event that I did not, I am sending this letter to right the wrong. Sincerely, Celia

February Number 23, 1927

Dear Celia,

Just a word or two to thank you for the letter that reached me this morning. Even tho the letter was a mighty short one – I don't like them short – it was quite welcome. The funny part about this note of yours is that it reached me at a time when it was not feasible for me to read it. I had to put it in my pocket. I don't know whether or not you can imagine the speculative effects such a note in ones pocket can have on a fellow. Not being a male fellow, you probably cannot.

I began to hope and even actually to expect that the letter contained an announcement that you are ready to begin your automobile tour of the country and will make your appearance at 304 Peoples Life Insurance Building in the very near future. I think they call it day dreaming, don't they? Yet so strong is the power of auto-suggestion that I should not have been very much surprised to have seen you walk in here.

I too hate to owe things. You felt that you were indebted to me to the tune of one signature and promptly proceeded to liquidate the indebtedness. That is mighty fine. I wonder tho, if, when a cop will leave a ticket for over parking in your car, you will feel an urge to pay up. I don't.

This building closes at 10:30. The first light has flashed ten minutes ago, which means that in another five the lights go out for the night. Lest I be forced to spend the night here I better stop, cease, quit, etc. from further writing at once.

With many thanks for the unexpected little note, I am, Disappointedly, Louis

Louis follows this with a letter, dated Washington's Birthday 1927:

Dear Fellow-Motorist,

'Congratulations'. Certainly happy to greet a convert to the joys, trials, and tribulations of those who drive their own. I don't know whether to take credit for having unknowingly influenced you to the study of the art, as you call it – of driving or to keep my part of it a secret. You see, I have very little faith in the ability of the average woman driver to keep her head in an emergency. Of course, there are the exceptions, only I do not happen to know any of these exceptions. Here is your opportunity to change my opinions on the subject.

I am afraid that my prejudice was born some six or more years ago when I saw a woman drive her car into a lamppost by the simple expedient of taking her hands from the steering wheel and trusting to luck. She was indeed very lucky because she might have hurt more than her own machine and the lamppost. The funny part about it was that there was no apparent reason for her action. Maybe she was in love and couldn't keep her mind on her job, I don't know. Of course, such a thing could never happen to you. I can't conceive of your becoming so engrossed in anything, even love, to the exclusion of the immediate work at hand. A levelheaded person never does.

Permit me to make a prediction. Within a few months after you have learned all about the car to your own satisfaction, you will develop a liking for driving that you never thought you could.

I never so enjoy a ride in an automobile as when I am the controller of the car's destinies. You will be the same.

You want to know about Ida. I believe I better not tell you. I have learned to be very careful about transmitting statements that women make. You never know just what they say and a man can make no graver mistake than to misquote a woman. These are mere generalities. The specific words that Ida used I have forgotten and in accordance with the sentiments I have expressed above, I shall make no attempts to substitute my own, aside from the bare expression of regret at having been deprived of the pleasure of a visit from you. I suggest that you write to Ida and ask her what she said. Her reply should be interesting as she is a very interesting young lady.

I see by the calendar that it is Washington's Birthday. Once upon a time, it meant something by way of a holiday for me. Now it is merely another opportunity for working at the office. The day seems beautiful enough for a holiday even tho there is snow in spots all over the streets. If I had an inducement I believe, I should proclaim this a holiday. But with you in Newark, I might as well work. Let me know how you are getting along with your driving. I'm pulling for you.

Hearing the letter about driving reminded my father of another joke.

THE TAXI RIDE

The Pope was in a cab with a companion in New York City when he asks the driver if he can't go faster because he has a very important appointment. The driver says, "Sir, this is 5ᵗʰ Ave. and they are very strict here. If I exceed the speed limit I will get a ticket and it will cost me a lot of money." At that point, the Pope tells the driver to go sit in the back seat and he will drive. Sure enough, after speeding along, a cop pulls him over. When the cop asks to see his driver's license, he realizes that the driver is the Pope. He then phones in to his chief and says, "Captain, I have some very important people who were speeding in a car. What shall I do?" The Captain asks who were these people. The policeman says, "I don't know, but the Pope was driving."

February 25, 1927

Dear Louis:

No doubt I too would have been disappointed had I received a short note from you. Had I thought you would have been so disappointed I never would have sent it.

You must think a lot of my driving ability if you expected to hear of my driving to Washington. Maybe some day when the boss says 'Yes,' I will take a trip but I think I have to learn how to drive a little better than I do at the present time. I only stalled twice yesterday, so I have all the qualifications of a driver I'm told. Here is hoping I may be able to change your views on women drivers. Do you think I have a possible chance?

I listened to a program from Washington which included a speech by Calvin (Coolidge) and music by the Army Band. The program reminded me of the few I have the pleasure of knowing in that City.

Fanny invited Celia to act as her chaperone on a trip to Washington next month. "I think she wants to paint the town. I doubt very much if I will be able to accommodate her as our bank is moving into new quarters and they need the cooperation of all their clerks."

February 26, 1927

Dear Celia,

Your letter, I am happy to note – received, read, and put away. You are a wonderful little correspondent. You answer letters. I am quite a bit surprised at myself, too. I really have a very poor reputation as a letter-writer.

It seems so easy to write to you. Then again, I know that in order to expect any letters from you I must first write. Since I most certainly want mail from you I suppose it is the natural thaing (you don't mind and extra 'a,' do you?) that I should be unusually diligent in the promptness of my replies to you.

Do I think you have a chance to change my mind on the ability of women to drive? Do you mean for the better or the worse? That wasn't very nice, was it? No, it was not; and let me say right here that if you drive up or rather down to Washington, or even half way (I would meet you at Philadelphia and drive the rest of the way) I'll forget all about my prejudices and start all over again with no opinion on the subject at all. Fair, isn't it?

So Fanny needs a chaperon! I'm afraid that we'll have to provide a chaperon for the chaperon. However, don't let that stop you because we have plenty of chaperons right here in this town. If necessary I will volunteer to act as yours. How's that?

Next month, that's March. Make it after the fifteenth and then the Income Tax worries will be all over and we shall help both Fannie and you to paint the town red, green, or any other color you two choose to paint the thing. As for your boss and the bank, who cares? There are plenty of bosses in the country and quite a few banks.

Celia wrote on March 3. "My father had to go to the shop this past Sunday morning and asked me if I cared to drive down. Being a good opportunity to get a little practice I said, yes. I got in the car stepped on the gas, rode a block and turned to the left, a car coming from the opposite direction barely missed the fender and in order to avoid hitting another car I heard my father say in less than a second, take your foot off the gas, put left foot on clutch, right on brake, stop, stop, I said stop. (All in one breathe). He then pulled the emergency brake and I stopped just one inch from a telegraph pole. My father got very nervous and demanded the wheel. Not so good for a start. Since then I have had three lessons and have greatly improved and expect to take my test next week and hope everything will be okay."

A girl Celia was training to work in her absence became ill, which increased her workload dramatically. It would now be impossible to accompany Fanny to Washington.

Inauguration Day 1927

Dear Celia,

It is just six o'clock of Friday afternoon or perhaps I should say evening which in this town makes it on the brink of *Shabes* (*Shabbat*). At our house this means that all the family must gather for the eating of the gefillte fish and such other standard *gerichter* (correct things) that help to make Friday nights assume the aspect of Shabes. It has been that way at home ever since I can remember, and I pray to Heaven that it may remain so as long as there is a Grossberg home.

You should not have written to me about your attempts to break up the new car. A skeptic such as I am on the subject of the rights of women for the freedom of the streets in their driving escapades must be fed with glowing reports and not with hair-raising episodes of near-smash-ups. You are not furthering your cause of changing my mind on the subject by telling me of these experiences. Still, things are not so bad. The fault in that last exhibition lies absolutely with your dad. Nothing will confuse a beginner as much as an excited jumble of instructions in the face of a tight squeeze. If your father was willing to let you drive, he should also have been willing to take all the accidents that might go with such a privilege. I'm sure I would. Besides, what's a lamp-post more or less?

That Saturday, Celia had to tell Louis the good news. "I passed my drivers test yesterday afternoon. I expected to take it next week but the instructor thought the time ripe and entered my name to the list. Well anyway, I am glad it is all over and being the fond possessor of a license card makes me feel like a kid with a new toy. Today is very beautiful. I am waiting for my sister Edith and together we will go for a long ride. Maybe as far as Washington. Would you care to go riding with me? Really, I am not a bad driver.

"My sister is calling me. She has the car started. She is gone, I think, to get some gas. Are you very busy at your work? The accountants here seem to be rushed. Trusting you are likewise, Truly, Celia"

March 7, 1927

Dear Celia,

Congratulations! A permit, I understand is the first rung of the ladder of the successful motorist. A successful motorist, I will have you know, is one who breaks all the laws of the Traffic Bureau without getting pinched for his pains. The first thing one of the guardians of the safety of the pedestrians want to see is the little license card you have worked so hard to secure. And, Miss, if your cops are in any way related to our own, you better have it to exhibit. It is only too often a mighty weak weapon, but without it, he is sunk. Moral: carry the darned thing with you always.

If the weather holds the present warmth our annual blooming of the Japanese 'Cheery' Blossoms will be ready for exhibition in about three weeks.

You may not know what this cherry blossom business is all about (but) the Japanese, in a spirit of goodness assisted by a burst of unusual generosity, donated to the Federal Government a young forest of trees called the Japanese Cherry Blossoms. These blossoms are strung out all along the speedway known as the mall. Every spring these trees burst out into bloom and for sheer beauty there is little to rival it anywhere in the country. These blossoms are in full bloom for a period of about two weeks, sometimes even less. During those days, it is almost impossible to drive thru the speedway for the crowds that go there to see them. Many people from out of town come here just for the purpose of getting a peep at those beautiful trees. Here is your excuse to your boss. Tell him that you just gotta go see those cherry blossoms in Washington. He can't produce them in Newark or New York or anywhere else excepting in Japan and in Washington.

Would I like to go riding with you? Certainment! And why not? In case of danger, I can always change the driver and then you will be riding with me. I'll have to begin figuring out a good reason, for the benefit of my partner, why I have business in New York. If you won't come here I'll have to go to Newark, for how else am I to examine your driving?

March 10, 1927 In School
Dear Lou,
The teacher of our Art class stepped out of the room a few moments ago, judging from the noise in the room one would think they were in a foundry instead of a school. The saying holds good here, 'When the cat is away the mice will play.'

I finished my painting a half hour ago and thought it would be a good opportunity to write to you. (Pardon the drawing paper.) You made me wish I was in Washington again when you painted the picture of the Japanese Cherry Blossoms. One Sunday last September I had the pleasure of seeing those trees along the speedway (though not in bloom) and was told of their rare beauty and also the tale about their presence in the Capitol City. Though I would like very much to take the trip, frankly admit I am a bit shy. Maybe sometimes soon.

Surely you won't find it a difficult task to tell Dave of some sort of engagement that needs your attention up here and I will drive you about or you do the driving whichever the case may be. Oh, pshaw, there goes the bell. That reminds me I haven't an envelope for this letter. Will stop in the office and buy one if it isn't too late. S'long, Celia

March 14, 1927
Dear Celia,

Some time ago you expressed the wish that I be very busy making up tax returns and the etc. Your wish came true but I do not thank you for it. Of all the jobs I don't care for, making out tax returns is at the top of the heap. The worst of it is that there is no money in it, that is to say for us – the government is doing very nicely, thank you. You see, we can't collect from our regular clients they pay us a stipulated sum every month for taking care of their accounting troubles of which the Income Tax is one. This means that at the close of the year and until March 15th we are heads over heels in work and the monthly stipend is no more nor less than at any other time.

Last night-Sunday – the gang went to see the Habima players present their *Golem* in Hebrew. Have you seen it, or them? For my part I was tremendously entertained. There were many in the audience who were disappointed particularly because they didn't understand the speech. But then they should not have come, since they knew or should have known that the talk will be in Hebrew.

The Acting was superb. The whole thing (is) so different from what one ordinarily sees and lauds as good acting. There was considerable of the bizarre in it. The speech itself had a thrilling effect on me. I suppose I am more Jewish at heart, tho hardly to be considered the least bit *froom* (*frum*), than many of my acquaintances who saw the play. I had never before heard any Hebrew plays and the language had a very pleasing sound to my ears. The enunciation was perfect. I wish I knew more Hebrew.

Dave was in his seventh heaven. He misunderstands about the same quantity of the language as I do. At any rate, a glorious time was had by the entire firm anyway.

Saturday afternoon was a most glorious time. I took a nice long ride thru the park and was happy to observe that the buds are beginning to peep out of their wintry havens. I shall try to run over to New Jersey some time soon to let you show me the beauties of Newark.

On March 18, 1927 Celia writes: "Too bad about you not wanting any income tax work. Don't you realize if you didn't have any returns to make out you wouldn't have any accounts? Sorry I can't help you in any way. Here I was ready to have you make out my income tax return but realizing the amount of work you had on hand I decided to make it out myself, making it as simple as possible, no deductions were made because the poor Government needs the money.

"I haven't seen the play *Golem* but will if it comes to Newark. My folks plan to visit Baltimore and Washington is not far from Baltimore. I will try and get to see the City again. Should you come to Newark you will be shown feminine, artistic, inanimate or any other kind of beauty you care to see, provided of course you promise to forget about Washington, because I realize you have all sorts of beauties in your City.

"I can't wait until I get home and have my fill of *humentashen* (*homantaschen*, triangular pastries filled with poppy seeds or fruit) in such forms as cookies and *taglachs* (pastry balls covered in sticky syrup), sorry *Purim* (a Jewish holiday) comes once a year."

Louis writes in his reply of March 22, 1927: "By the way those cherry blossoms of ours will have been here and gone before many more days have elapsed. By April third, the party should be in full blast and that might be an inducement for you to snap into it and do your Baltimore visiting about that time. But let me know about it in advance.

"I agree with you. There is little fun in doing work when you can get some slave to do it for you. But be careful you don't teach your (new) assistant so well that you will do yourself out of a job. Not that you would have any trouble about getting another one. Come over to Washington and I shall get you a nice job. In fact, I have an opening for a good bookkeeper right now. The young lady officiating therein now is too flighty for it. She needs more air and by golly, I'll give it to her just as soon as I can find her successor. This paragraph is a good example of the type of speech one may expect from our honorable Rabbi. I refer to the aimlessness of it.

"So you, too, like Purim. And why shouldn't you like it? *Humentassen, teiglech* (*taglachs*), and the etc. are given us only on these special occasions for the express purpose, it would seem, to make us appreciate those occasions.

"Dave and his Madam walked in to pay me a short visit. Ida just asked me at whom this *megile* (*megilla*, story included in the Bible but not part of the main text – at Purim the *megilla* is the *Book of Esther*) is being fired. I just gave her our blandest of smiles to which David added an 'Aha-a-a-a. Secrets.' Now I know I gotta stop. Remember, I want details as to when you are going to be here so that I may arrange with the weather bureau to make it a time for ideal weather."

March 28, 1927

Dear Lou,

It seems that every photogravure section of a newspaper has at least one picture of the Japanese Cherry Blossom trees in bloom and a few Japanese children in native costume promenading the walk. I wager they just put it in the papers to tease me.

(Just a bit of (*hex*citement) – I went to a Masque party in Brooklyn, NY, a few days ago and had a firing good time. There were one hundred guests at this affair. To top the evening off a newspaper photographer came to take a flashlight picture of the crowd. The chemical stuff they use to produce the flashlight exploded and a fire had started in the room where the guests had assembled, the paper hangings that decorated the ceiling burned more quickly then the time it is taking me to explain it. My sister Edith had a premonition that the hangings would catch fire so dashed out of the room as the picture was taken. Most of the people were cool-headed, those near the door ran for water, others pulled the papers down and trampled on them. What an evening.

Mer darfin benchen gaymel (we should thank God we survived) that it didn't develop into a big fire. It will be a long time before I go to another masque affair.

Every year the Kansters visited Baltimore relatives. This year they picked April 15, Good Friday, but discovered that Pesach started on the 16. Not wanting to be away for the holidays, Decoration Day, May 28 was chosen instead. Celia wrote:

I really thought they were going sooner, my father is getting a number of rush orders on the toys and he can't leave the shop even for a day, of course on a Holiday the shop is closed.

March 31, 1927

Dear Celia, April Fool! It *is* a letter.

That over, permit me to start off by telling you how sorry I am that Pesach mixed in to spoil the plans and the fun. I love Pesach and find it very hard to put all the blame upon that fine holiday. Let's blame it on the calendar then. However, the last of May should be a wonderful time to visit Washington. To get even with you for not coming at this time I might take a little trip Newarkward myself next week and waste you a day or so. However, I am not certain as yet. At any rate keep the Dodge in good order and brush up on your driving. I might show up next Saturday afternoon.

Your story about the near-fire was a very interesting one. Personally I like them and it has often been my desire to play an heroic part of some sort at a real fire. I should like to rescue a fair damsel in one of those most approved movie styles – down the rain spout from the fifth floor. Don't care for any higher floors. Of course, I shouldn't like to get burnt nor do I care to see anyone else burnt. But watching a fire sizzle. Oh, boy!

April 4, 1927

Dear Lou:

Very glad to note that you are coming to Newark this Saturday. I underlined the word 'are' because I am taking it for granted that you are coming; so don't change your mind. Let me know what time you will arrive here, in order that I'll be home at that time, try and make it early. You are cordially invited to stay at my home over the weekend.

April 7, 1927, Louis replies:

I should have written sooner but I waited until I was more certain as to whether or not I am really going to Newark this week. Now that it has been settled, I shall be in the neighborhood of the Lehigh Valley Railroad terminal in Newark, Meeker and Elizabeth Ave. (so the timetable says) at precisely 1:00 PM on Saturday afternoon. If I am there at that hour, I shall very soon thereafter call you on the telephone.

I wish to thank you for your kind and generous invitation to spend the week-end at your home, but I will not permit you to be thus bothered with me. Besides, hotels have to live and who should support them if not visitors. So it is all settled that I shall stay at a hotel Saturday night and spend the daytime and other waking hours with you. All right? Thanks.

On April 12, 1927 Louis wrote Celia:

"I tried to get in a few minutes or so yesterday to write you but during the day I was so sleepy I couldn't." Louis attributed this to the pounding of the wheels under his lower K-1 berth and from staying up most of Friday night, but he felt fine the next morning.

"Dave took me home to supper with him yesterday and, of course, I had to tell what sort of time I had. I reminded him of that kiss (at Fanny's wedding) in connection with something I said at the table and Ida piped up and 'how come I never heard anything about that?' Then she wanted to know whom else Dave kissed while he was away from home. A general grand time was had by all. I want to thank you for the wonderful time I had in Newark and elsewhere in your charming company. I am looking forward with pleasurable anticipation to May 30 when I hope to have the privilege of reciprocating your hospitality in some small measure at my command. In the meantime, lest you think that you are rid of me until then, I am thinking of the early part of May in connection with a possible revisit of Newark. This is neither threat nor promise. Merely the recording of a possibility."

Following Louis' visit to New Jersey, he sent a thank-you letter to Celia's mother, Paula, dated April 13, 1927. (Her name was Pauline, but Paula was the name Jacob used).

Celia's next letter to Louis was dated April 15, 1927:

By the way, I like the idea of yours to revisit Newark the early part of May. Of course I won't consider it a threat, but I can't understand why I can't consider it a promise. We can leave early in the Morning and take a trip to the Delaware Water Gap or Bear Mountains. If that is too far there are a number of interesting places one can visit that are nearer home.

I want to thank you again for your kind invitation that I visit Washington. My father said if I expect to go along I have to get busy and gain more confidence in my driving, because he expects me to drive on the open highway. I took the car out this morning and I drove for ten miles. Edith thinks I have greatly improved.

My mother was very happy to receive your letter and said it was very kind of you to remember her.

Celia's parents were much taken with Louis. He spoke to them in Yiddish, was very respectful and valued Jewish ideals.

On April 18, 1927, Dave left for a Zionist meeting, so Louis had to interview applicants for a cashier's job for one of their clients by himself. He wrote Celia they were coming in at 10-minute intervals which made it difficult to write and interview at the same time. After another "gentlemen" came in, he said, "This bird was easy. Right off the bat he didn't like the salary and that ended that.

"The first two days of *Pesach* have come and gone and so have the *Sedorim* (plural of Seder, the religious Passover meal)." Since they never worked on Saturdays or Holidays, Louis and Dave celebrated the second day of Pesach by going to a ball game. "It was a good game – we won. The score was 4 to 0. The best part of the game was that at no time was the outcome certain despite our four run lead in the first inning. As late as the ninth inning the opposition threatened. There were three men on base, one out and Ty Cobb at bat with only four runs needed to tie the score. A homer would have done that. Was there Excitement? There sure was and with a capital E as written. This was the second game I saw in two years and I like to watch them.

"I must make some comment about my next trip. Frankly I care very little about the exact place we should go to when I come again. If you are a member of the party I am satisfied. Without still calling it a promise – I hate to break promises and for that very reason seldom if ever do – I expect to take the next northern trip on about May 7th or 8th, something like that."

April 21, 1927

Dear Lou:

Such is life, my boss won't even take the hint and give me the afternoon off. I go home for lunch during Pesach and take a vacation for lunch period, and why not. I went out at 11 o'clock yesterday and didn't get back until 2:15 o'clock. When I did get back I was asked to take off my hat and coat and stay awhile in order that the clerks might get acquainted with me, as I seem to be a stranger to them. Our chief clerk passed a moment ago and remarked 'What, another letter?' He wanted to know if I had a few minutes to spare in order that I type a few of his letters. He said I might be able to squeeze them in between writing my personal letters answering telephone calls and the lunch periods. Nevertheless, I get my work done and that is all they are interested in.

Just got back from lunch and Mother complained that I eat like a bird (I think she meant the ostrich). If I eat another *latka* (*latke*, potato pancake) my name won't be Celia. I seem to be feeding up on the above mentioned article and *Matzoh's*.

Do you know how to Bowl? This evening the girls of our Bank are having a practice tournament. I can bowl a little, but it is an effort not to follow the ball down the alley. Tuesday evening we are going to bowl in a novel way, if you hit the head pin all the pins that fall down count, if you should get a strike without hitting the head-pin you are out of luck. To get an average of 80 is called excellent. I never get 80, about 45 is my speed. Quite a number of banks are entering the girls to compete in this tournament.

What do you mean by saying you will be here the 7th or 8th of May, do you realize the 8th is Sunday and surely you are not coming for one day.

A Baltimore cousin came to visit so the family took in a Yiddish show. Celia writes again on April 26, 1927.

> I thought I wouldn't be able to understand the lingo but was quite elated because I understood every thing. It sure is different from the shows of the English speaking stage. I like the difference and think I will go again.
>
> I am inviting you again to stay at my house over the week-end. To quote my mother – 'There is always room for one more.'

Louis was reticent about staying at Celia's house. On April 27, 1927, he again declined her kind offer but hopes she "will not consider it a forfeiture of possible subsequent invitations. This time I shall pick a hotel somewhat closer to 842 Hunterdon Street," and he asks her to suggest one.

> I envy you enlightened folk your daylight saving. We here in Washington tried it some years ago, but owing to some bull-headedness on the part of some of our officials and of Congress we no longer enjoy its blessings. Whatever is done with the time when and after it is all saved up, there has always been a great deal of fun for me. The last year we had it here half the town observed it and the other half did not. It would not have been so bad if the two halves were divided in some sort of geographical manner. We could then have governed ourselves accordingly by considering the one as the spendthrift and the other as the industrious and thrifty half. However, those who observed the daylight saving time were hopelessly intermingled both historically and geographically with those who did not, so that it was not uncommon to see two persons in the same household operating under the dual system of time-keeping.
>
> The newspapers poked fun at it all the time changing the popular name of 'daylight saving' for the time-keeping to 'jazz-time saving.' If I remember correctly, the reason for the condition was that Congress overlooked passing the time changing law for the year that I described above with the result that no one had the

authority to order the moving up of the clock. Half the people – by common consent – moved up the clock as they had done by order of Congress the year before and the stubborn other half (I belong to the first half) insisted on continuing with standard time. So a grand time was had by all.

In his letter from the eve of the second day of Passover, Louis expected to arrive on the 7th or 8th as previously stated. The weather had been so changeable that one day it was 90 degrees in the shade and the next he needed an overcoat. "Crazy weather. But as Mr. Mark Twain once said, 'Nobody ever seems to do anything about it.'

> Do I bowl? The answer to this depends altogether upon what you term 'bowling.' Leaving out of consideration any fancy rules such as your gang is putting up about the head pin, if you call 85 excellent bowling, then I might say that I bowl. But if you call bowling what most of the fellows who bowl mean by that term, then I decidedly do not bowl. All of which, translated into simple *mameloshen* (literally, mother tongue, i.e. simple language), just means that if things go well with me I make about 80 or 85. I have bowled as high as 110, but them days are no more.
>
> Last Monday night we had some cousins from out of town visit us, two fellows, and we stopped at a bowling alley place to see what it feels like to throw the pins away once more. This was my first attempt at this pastime for the last three or four years. We bowled one game – there were four of us – my score was 79. At that I came out second.

April 29, 1927
> Dear Lou:
> My desk is littered with papers and books, one has to look twice to find me. At the end of the month we are usually very busy and I have a lot of work on my hands. My boss was in the midst of detailing work to me when he was summoned into the office on some matters of more importance. He sent word over that he would be back in twenty minutes and not to start on the work

until he got back. With twenty minutes and a letter to answer, what could be sweeter?

Lest you have forgotten, I was entered in the bowling tournament and ran away with third prize. As Explained before, we rolled the novel way, (and) I averaged 188 for the three games. I haven't rolled for quite some time; naturally I was a little stiff. Last but not least the grand prize was $1.13, how they figured that out I don't know.

On May 2, 1927, Louis writes that he must have Spring Fever. The weather is so lovely he can't keep his mind on anything. "Bowling has always seemed to me so symbolical of throwing away money, especially when one rolls the alley way. However, when you bowl and collect cash money in the bargain, well, then, that's different. Seems to me that an average of 62⅔ for you under the conditions as you explained them is a mighty good score. You might almost say, as the boy put it when his teacher told him that his answer of 72 to the problem of 8×9 is 'good,' 'Good Hell! That's perfect.' Yes, indeed, that's a fine score."

Louis was reminded of an incident that occurred some eleven years ago. "My sister Kitty, of whom you doubtless have heard me speak a number of times – she with the jealous husband – and I went together on our vacations that summer to a resort some sixty miles from here, called Braddock Heights, and at that time was right exclusive. There were no swimming or other water sports which reduced the activities to enjoying the scenery, dancing, and there was one bowling alley. In those days bowling was a man's sport and considered rather unladylike for any woman to engage in it. However, time did hang heavy on the vacationists and the alley owner wanted business, so he inaugurated a style of bowling for women. The place was very nice and the people who frequented it were also of the better class.

To make it more interesting they kept track of the scores and at the end of the week awarded a prize to the best man bowler and the best lady bowler. Sister Kitty, being a rather adventurous soul, decided she would try her luck and altho she had never before seen a bowling alley she went in there and made a score of 105. This score was immediately put up on the bulletin board – it was on a Monday – and despite anything any of the others could do to overcome it, she was the high score lady of the week. She bowled again after that many times but never again equaled her first mark.

It so happened that her homesick and lonely beau – now her husband – got a heavy case of *meshugeites* (craziness) and Kitty had to return alone before the week was out. I, as her legal representative, collected the prize. The prize, by the way, was no bagatelle. She was a five dollar gold piece. I don't remember now whether I ever gave it to her or not.

I see by your letter that the only hotel near you and the station is the Riviera. You forget to mention anything about it. Is it good enough or bad enough for me? I want a decent hotel but just to rent a room in it, not to buy the place.

As to the time, oh well, I will call you. Just stick around close to the ting-a-linger Saturday afternoon and we shall talk it over by phone. Anticipating the pleasure of being with you again, I am, Impatiently yours, Louis

Since my parents did not know their daughter would be writing this book, they kept no diaries or notes to fill me in on what transpired during these visits. Only the letters give us clues to the things they did or said to each other. Their letters started out very reserved with my mother signing hers "Celia," then "Cel" and later still, "Ceal." As I read these letters, I could feel the progression from acquaintance, to friends, to lovers and the journey was delightful – tender and sweet.

May 9, 1927,
　　Dear Ceal,
　　Just by way of variety. I'll have to figure out a pet name for you. If you know of any I shall be glad to give due consideration to your suggestions. Went to sleep this morning in my night's compartment and two seconds later a burly arm was thrust thru my draperies – they no naught of doors – The second word in that phrase is 'know' and I felt a tugging at my blankets. 'Seven o'clock, Sah,' someone whispered loudly. I wasn't at all interested and went right back to sleep.

Ten minutes later there was more tugging and louder whisperings. I figured it didn't pay to start any arguments with an uncouth porter. I must admit, however, that the knowledge that the car was to be moved away from that particular place in a few minutes lent a bit of wings to my haste. Was I sleepy? I'll shay she do.

Mother was up and about when I came in and of course there was an extra kiss and hug all ready for yours truly as a result of the telescratches (for telegrams) that were launched from a certain drug store in far away Newark the day before. It developed later – this from Dave – that he was not in at the time the wire reached his home and Ida took it upon herself to carry out the directions of her partner's partner.

Right here I must stop a bit in the narrative to explain that last year my brother Joe, from Jacksonville, sent the prettiest gift to mother. It was a very beautiful box of candy. The candy was good, of course, but the box was a real beauty. When Ida was shown that box of candy she couldn't bear to see Joe beat me out in the matter. Now, when the telegram arrived she decided to get even. She would go out and get a box of candy that would outdo the one Joe sent last year. The result was that she bought mother, for my account as directed, the finest box of candy that she could get in the neighborhood. Mother, of course, didn't know anything about all of this. In fact, she doesn't know yet, but Ida felt satisfied.

It so happened that for some unknown reason nothing showed up for mother from Joe yesterday and mother wondered whether Joe wasn't angry about something or other. As you will recall I told you that he was rather quick on the *feribel* (arguments). So there being practically no competition my box took the cake. This evening when I got in for supper Babe greeted me with a story about a package having come for mother from Joe that was a 'wow'. My heart sank. What do you think? It was a most beautiful box of stationery. I haven't yet seen the box that came from me, but if it beats Joe's box it has to be some box no kiddin'.

I want to thank you most warmly for all your kindness to me and also to all your lovely folks.

May 11, 1927

Dear Lou:

I noticed in the letter that you addressed me as 'Ceal,' as the change consists of a letter being left out, it is okay with me.

I am enclosing the pictures we took Sunday. They are for you. Everybody had a good time laughing at the picture of Sam impersonating the 'Missing Link,' and the pinching episode because it is so typical of Sam (Big Sam Hamburg) to do those things. As a whole, I think the pictures turned out very nicely, don't you? I am not going to say a word regarding my own pictures because it will do no good.

This coming Sunday my mother, father, Sara, Sam and myself expect to drive up to the Delaware Water Gap. It is a very long beautiful ride, country and otherwise. We have decided to take all sorts of silly pictures and there is no telling what shapes Sam will get into then.

One of our auditors asked me a moment ago if I saw the diamond pin his wife gave him for his birthday. Not having seen the pin, I answered 'No.' He opened his palm and showed me a dime and a pin. I thought it was pretty good so am passing it on to you.

Mother wants me to thank you again for the flowers you sent her, (I appreciate it too.)

May 12, 1927

Dear Ceal,

Thanks for the pictures. I believe the greatest credit is due me for the finest picture taken – that of the 'Missing Link' as you style it. I must have caught it at just the right moment for, as you will remember he wasn't very comfortable on that tree. Excepting for some of them being out of focus a bit they are mighty good pictures. I showed them to Dave and Ida and Ida couldn't recognize you at all. However, I think she is just a bit wrong. They look more like you than any of the other snapshots I saw of you.

The story of the dime and pin is a nice one. I haven't heard it for several years now. I guess it takes that time for *chochmes* (wisdom) to reach Newark. That wasn't very nice, was it? Your pardon, Miss.

Sister Miriam is all dated up for the 29th of May to go to Herald Harbor with Aleck. She doesn't know she is to meet us there and thinks that she rides over with us. Well, we shall have to disappoint her a wee bit. It is almost seven PM – eight in your town – and I must hustle home for supper. Olive Oil, Louis

On May 16, 1927, Celia was unhappy to report that she would not accompany her folks to Baltimore. She intended to leave with them Saturday morning but the Chief Clerk refused her request for the morning off, as he did not want her leaving work for a new girl. "The folks intend leaving about seven in the morning and I could hardly be selfish enough to expect them to spend the entire morning waiting for me. I will in all probabilities go directly to Washington.

Ida sent me a wonderful letter, inviting me to spend the week-end at her home. I know I am going to like her because I have pleasant recollections of meeting her at the office a long time ago and will be very glad of the opportunity to see her again.

We did not go to the Delaware Water Gap after all, because on Friday one of my cousins called up and said we were going to have company. All told we had sixteen for dinner Sunday. I was elected chief dish wiper and honestly believe every dish in the house was used. Mother was quite happy fussing over the meal but frankly speaking, I think she would rather have been out riding.

Our bank gave a bridge for the girls and as I explained before I know so little about the game I can't understand how I happened to be the prize winner at our table. I suppose it is beginners luck. The bridge and bowling prizes I fear will go to my head. Nevertheless let them come my way.

Louis replied on May 18, 1927: "Glad to find that your Chief Clerk is a tough baby and insists that you must work while you are working.

"I have made tentative arrangements with my sister and my kid brother to make it a party of six to go out to Herald Harbor for the day, that is Sunday. I certainly hope that the weather will turn warmer and less rainy.

"Glad to read of your prize winning abilities in bridge. You go on and practice up a bit more on the game and when you come here you and I will challenge Kitty and her Al to a hot game of Bridge. Last Saturday night my sister Miriam and I were invited over to Kitty's for supper and after that a little private four handed bridge game. Al and Kitty were partners against Miriam and me. Miriam insisted on playing for something in order to make it the more interesting. We agreed on 15 points for a cent.

"Well, we played until after eleven and during all that time neither Miriam nor I had any bidding hands. All evening Kitty and Al just swamped us. When finally it was time to go home we added up the score and found that they were something over 1,600 points ahead of us. We immediately reneged and refused to pay up claiming a return engagement. The score was thereupon carefully noted down and put aside for future action."

Miriam and Louis were invited back on Monday. "We did fairly well this time and at ten thirty – the time of quitting – we had won back exactly sixty points. This was credited to our account. At this rate, we should be square with them in another two years.

"The United Palestine Appeal drive is in full swing and that means that I am kept busy off and on doing the dirty work.

"Of course you will let me know exactly which train you propose taking – and yes, do be careful. They are very strict about people taking things nowadays. So when you take the train be careful not to get caught at it. I shall be on deck to meet you."

On Monday, May 23, 1927, Celia wrote, "A number of the clerks are getting discouraged and are leaving, some are spending their time vacationing and four are out with the mumps. There is to be a merger of six subsidiary banks and they will have to work until the wee hours of the morning during the consolidation. A few years ago we consolidated with one bank and to get home before two in the morning was considered a miracle. I recall one morning I got home at four and at eight we had to be back in the office again. They were indeed very kind to us, they sent each clerk home in a taxi.

"I don't want you to do any planning or fussing for the time that I am to be in Washington. Let everything take its natural course and it will be apple-pie with me. I do not know as yet what train I will take. Your station is so big that I am wondering if you will be able to find me. I think I better attach a bell to my coat or something. Until Lindbergh goes to Australia, I am, Sincerely, Celia.

"P.S. I am not going to school tonight because an officer just handed me two tickets for a Broadway show."

May 26, 1927, Louis again mentions the Palestine Drive. "The banquet which took place last Monday evening was the driving force and since that is over with there is little incentive left for the workers." Afterwards, the solicitors and others assembled for a buffet supper to report the final returns which that day totaled about four thousand dollars.

"At about 1:00 AM, Miss Rosenfeld, the secretary, thought she heard something moving in the building. We work in the Jewish Community Center building which was supposed to be all empty of occupants with the sole exception of the three of us. We at first pooh-poohed the idea but later we, too, thought we heard something. We were working on the third floor (and) we had four thousand dollars with us, a good bit of which was in cold cash.

"She called up police headquarters and asked for the loan of a cop. In a few minutes we heard the cop knocking at the door downstairs and I, being the bravest in the lot, was elected to go downstairs and let him in. Believe it or not. The cop came up and sat there with us until four o'clock. The boy had a grand time. He smoked cigarettes, which they are not permitted to do during duty hours, and after awhile became a bit restless and I put him to work licking stamps unto envelops. At four we were thru and after taking the others home, I sneaked into my own home and went to bed about 4:30 in the morning. Well, it's all in the game.

"We are all awaiting your arrival on Saturday evening and don't bother about any bells. Just mention the hour your train comes in and then try not to let me find you."

Tuesday, May 31, 1927.
Dear Lou,
Have been very busy at the office all day straightening out the mess the movers made. I was obliged to do what work I could

without a typewriter. At 10:30 o'clock they found the long lost chord and peace and happiness reigned once more.

I think your folks are wonderful. I felt very much at home and credit is due to your whole family for making it so. Your sisters Kitty and Miriam have been underrated by you. It isn't fair that I don't mention the others because they all have been wonderful to me, of course, not forgetting Bobby and Edith (Kitty's children), give them a hug and kisses for me. And, I want to thank you most heartily.

Here is the written invitation I promised you. You are cordially invited to spend as much time as you are able to do so at my home. Just let me know a week or so in advance.

Miriam asked that I mail her a dress or two, so let me know your home address in your next letter. As soon as this letter is sealed I will be on my way to slumber-land because I am oh so tired. I will close with kind regards from everybody at my home to everybody in your home, also Kitty, Al, Dave and Ida. Sincerely, Celia

The dress mentioned would probably come from Little Sam, who worked in the garment industry.

Louis stopped at the Jewish Community Center on his way to work, he next reported, in a letter, dated June 2, 1927. The final auditing of the books for the United Palestine Appeal needed preparation, but after an hour, Louis became restless, made a fancy excuse and left. "I was looking forward to finding a letter in the office from the sweetest little girl in New Jersey. I went there; I found the letter; I read it; I came back to work.

"I want to thank you for many things. First, for coming to Washington, secondly, for saying that you have had a good time (even tho you might not actually have had it), thirdly, for saying those nice things about my folks, my sisters, my partner and his wife.

"Called up Kitty this afternoon to convey your thanks to her and to tell her of the nice things you said about her and she, like the grafter that she is, immediately took advantage of me and sponged upon me for a ride – offering me in exchange, an invitation to supper despite my protestations of lack of time. As usual she won and now – it is exactly 9:34 PM – I have just returned to the office to get this letter off to you.

"It is just lovely of you to have come right back with an invitation to visit you and stay as long as I can. That is just where my troubles always come in. I can never stay as long as I should like to. And when you come here you couldn't stay as long as I should have liked either. Perhaps we can fix that up satisfactorily some day.

"You have certainly left a town full of admirers of you. Everyone who has seen you is talking of the wonderful girl from Newark. Kitty asked me this evening as we were driving to Fort Myer, if I thought it wrong of her to have hugged you and kissed you the moment she saw you at my home Saturday night. I told her that I didn't see anything wrong about it and that I was only sorry that I couldn't do likewise. Well, she told me that someone had remarked that it looked funny the way she did it right off the bat. She didn't know, she said, but it was the only natural thing for her to have done. She saw a very sweet girl sitting right in front of her and there was only one thing to do in such a case and that was just what she did. Nothing could be simpler. Kitty is like that and that is why everyone likes her.

"I was licked at three games of croquet (I think the spelling is approximately correct) this evening by Kitty and I must begin to confess that I can't play that game when I play it with Kitty. She is just naturally better than I am at it."

On Sunday, June 5, Celia wrote Louis:

"We went out for a ride this afternoon and landed in Mountainview." It was an enjoyable trip but they encountered a downpour on the way home. Celia hoped it would clear up, as she wanted to go to a good movie in the neighborhood.

"I want to remind you that you are in for a 'bawling out.' In my last letter I said I had a wonderful time, which I honestly meant. You thanked me for saying that, even though I didn't mean it. Is that nice? I ask you! I want you to assure Kitty that I thought it was right cute of her to have kissed me as she did and I like her heaps for it (I mean this too) I hope she thinks of me as I do of her."

Saturday was a half-day holiday for Celia, so she spent it in New York with Fanny, seeing a movie and having supper there. Afterwards Edith picked her up. Edith and their mother had been at Little Sam's home, setting the date for Edith's marriage. "The date they picked out is September 10th. I think I am more excited than she."

Celia wants Louis to teach her to play tennis on his next visit. "I was called into the main office yesterday and was told my vacation would start the second week of August and not the first as I had selected. There seems to be no choice in the matter so it will have to be the week they selected. Oh well, I hope we have nice weather."

Louis wrote on June 7, 1927, "You may go right ahead and bawl me out any time you so choose. The fact is that it is a pleasure to be bawled out by so charming a bawler. At any rate I am mighty glad to be assured that you really did have a good time. So that's that.

"Yesterday having been a holiday for this office, I put on an old pair of shoes and with golf bag in hand went out for the first time in three years to see if I still knew how to sock the old apple for a row of Russian Kazzatzkies. I discovered that it is possible to get in quite a bit of practice by hiring the services of a gentleman of color to act in the capacity of caddy and just wallop the balls without the walking part that is always so incidental to this great sport of the Scotch." He swung his clubs for an hour and a half and left with aching bones and a blister on his hand.

Louis thanked the "fathers of the American Revolution" for Fourth of July weekend and expected to arrive July 2 to spend his two weeks vacation in Newark, and hoped playing tennis would make it all the more enjoyable. He asked for good weather and that they supply a net, rackets and balls. He also asked if they had a racket for him so he would not have to bring his own. "I quite agree with you that one lesson from so famous a tenniser as I am is all that you will need to make of you a finished player. In the meantime I wish you would spend as much time on the courts as you can as there is no comparison between the fun that may be derived when the players are fairly well matched."

Celia's letter was headed, "This Friday – 4 o'clock," with no date or year but probably June 10, 1927. "I am very glad to hear you are coming here the 2nd of July, the date suits me fine. You know you are welcome to stay at my home. I don't know as yet what we will do (but) we will try and keep you out of mischief.

"Ruth and I have been trying to play tennis this week and as a result I am stiff from shoulders to toes. I intend buying a racket pay-day because my old one has seen its day. I don't think it will be necessary for you to take your racket along because I think we will have enough for a week-end. We have three new balls and a net in very good shape so everything is all set for your coming.

"Yes, as I wrote you before I would be pleased to have you come here in August and help me spend my vacation. It will be something new and different for me. I am tired of the camp and seashore and this idea of yours to come here strikes me as being right nice.

June 13, 1927

Dear Celia,

Once more please accept my thanks for your kind invitation to stay at your home when I come to Newark again. I liked particularly the way you put it: – 'You know you are welcome to stay at my home.' Well, my dear, I'm grateful. However, I will not permit you or your folks to be inconvenienced by me any more than is absolutely necessary. I know that you do not have enough room to accommodate Sammy (Angel) and me at the same time. So, it is once more settled that the Hotel Riviera has a guest during the period of my stay in Newark.

As for the matter of entertainment for me in July and in August, if you are there, I'm entertained to the fullest extent.

By this time you should be in good physical trim as the result of those stiff joints that the tennis practice gave you. Keep right on practicing.

Babe is in the office – it is nearly eight and we are supposed to drive up to Kitty's for a time – and he is sighing away and whistling and in general making a nuisance of himself in order to discourage me from any further writing. It is getting late he hints and time to 'beat it.' With fondest regards, I am, Hurriedly, Louis

June 17, 1927

Dear Lou:

First of all what makes you think that you will inconvenience any one of us here should you stay with us and secondly what makes you think we won't have any room. We have plenty of room. Sammy (Schiff) and you can share a double size bed on the third floor, that is, should you care to stay. You know, I wouldn't want you to be uncomfortable so will let you do as you see fit. But as to this room question, don't let that bother you. Mother is always happy to do what she can for our guests and her children think likewise.

One of the boys in our office is an amateur tennis 'Champ' of Jersey and knows a good racket when he sees one, so I asked him to buy me a good one. He is having it made up for me at the factory. It is setting me back more dollars than I had intended to spend.

Tell Babe not to hurry you when he sees you are so busily engaged as in the case of writing a letter to me.

Louis writes back on June 21, 1927, with: "Have been engaged all day in a charity job to audit the records of the Avukah American Students Zionist Federation. The national president has asked us to do this for him before their annual convention. He is on my neck to finish this job today. How I am to do this is a mystery to me. It is already 6:25 PM and I must attend the Graduation Exercises of Babe's class to-night at about eight when he gets his diploma from High School. Outside of writing this letter and going home for a bite to eat to say nothing of taking unto myself a shave, etc., I have nothing to do between now and eight o'clock but finish the report.

"I don't really know what to tell you now about staying at your home. I should be perfectly happy to do so if I really felt that no one would be inconvenienced. Well, we'll forget it for awhile and we'll see.

"In accordance with your latest suggestion I shall take along only the tennis shoes part of my tennis outfit. At any rate I have a most excellent excuse should it happen that I get myself all beat up in the game. One is not supposed to play his best game with a strange racket."

Celia complained of the heat and rain on June 24, 1927; it kept her and her sister Ruth, from visiting the City park. "Talk about work. I have a split thumb caused by constant typing. I have had twenty letters to transcribe this morning besides my general run of work and the extra amount is being piled on me on account of lack of help. I was graciously informed the other day that beginning July 5th I would have to take short hand notes for six of the consolidating banks regarding all checks that are to be returned to our correspondents for want of official or better endorsements. If the work turns out to be as hard as I think it will, they will be minus a clerk. I am looking forward to next Saturday when you will be in Newark again."

On June 27, 1927, Louis wrote that he hoped she had a good time even though it was too cold for bathing. His luck was better.

"Yesterday I went in bathing for the first time this season." Miriam's boss had a party in honor of his son's Bar Mitzvah. It was held at his fishing clubhouse on the river. At first, he did not want to go but Miriam begged him and to please her he went.

"We really had a great time since everyone was permitted to do just as he or she pleased." His gang started the day by getting into bathing suits and remained that way both in and out of the water. At about three, they dressed and went to a neighboring farmhouse to hire a motorboat. "There were about fifteen persons in our expedition. The seas became a bit rough soon after we started out which of course was the signal for sundry howling and screamings. When we got back and told the others they were quite jealous."

"(Next) we organized a base ball team and talk about candidates! The whole crowd of two hundred or so wanted to play. However, we sifted that down to about twenty eligibles, and you must know that the more anxious one was to play the more eligible he was. One girl on our side knocked a perfect hit but didn't know that it was necessary to run to first base. Despite all the urgings and coachings she stayed there and watched them get the ball. The worst part of the game was that the fellow who owned the ball had to go home while there was still a half hour of daylight. Today I carry with me a nice coat of sunburn for my pleasures of the day before.

"It is now six twenty and I am invited to have dinner with Mr. and Mrs. Leo Freudberg and young daughter, (Grace) – the latter being one of my special sweethearts. I better snap into finishing this as they live about thirty minutes ride from here. I call it 'Hotche plotche.'

"I shall probably come in at the same time as usual next Saturday and I suppose this is the time for me to say whether or not I shall stay with you. The conditions have not changed about the way I feel. However, if you honestly and really believe that Sammy will not mind sharing his bed with me and that all of you won't mind being bothered with me, then, I suppose, I shall stay at your home this time.

"I thank you on behalf of Babe for those nice wishes you transmitted and with happy anticipation of *real* pleasures very soon, I am, Quite as usual, Lou"

July 6, 1927

Dear Ceal,

Tried hard to find a bit of time in which to write you yesterday (but) the gang, headed by Fanny, Annie & Co. walked in on me at the office, and as you may well guess, all was off so far as writing was concerned. I collected my 'How-do-you-do' kiss from Fanny. You know Fanny and I have been on kissing terms for a good many years. She looks exceptionally well. Ida, Annie Glushak and Fanny just left here a few minutes ago with Dave.

After office hours they all went to Ida's for supper. "This high life is ruining me. Couldn't get up this morning and drifted into the office at 9:40. Fared very well on the return trip as I managed to exchange my berth for a lower four instead of the one that I had. I certainly slept like a log. Possibly this time it would have made no difference what berth I had.

"I just had a call from Leo that started out something about Hell and the etc. Seems that he is a mighty hungry man and the house is waiting for me. Isn't really nice at all to make them wait for me, now is it?

"Want to express all the gratitude that I feel for the mighty fine way in which you and the family and your wonderful friends have entertained me but the time is too short and I am too much in a hurry. My warmest regards to all the folks and friends and YOU. Most gratefully, Louis"

July 7, 1927

Dear Lou:

Time flies. It seems as if it was only yesterday that I had received your letter telling me you will arrive at 2 o'clock Saturday. You came and two days later found you bound for Washington. Yes, time flies – we cannot.

Judging from the invites scattered in your direction to dine at 'so and so's home' I am quite positive you will never want for a place to eat. Gee, it must feel great to be popular. We are having some friends for dinner this evening and the only invitation in sight to dine out is for Sunday at my cousin Edith's home. Tell Fanny not to forget she is a married woman, with a husband and kiddies a few hundred miles away.

Since you left Newark we have had a taste of rain each day, I didn't mind it at all this week because my work is keeping me at the office until 8 O'clock and by the time I get home and have my supper I am fit for the hay. The Chief-clerk gave me a very competent girl and the work is getting finished with greater speed than I had anticipated.

July 11, 1927

Dear Ceal,

Just by way of change, the red ribbon was substituted for the black when I started, (so) I shall continue the rest of this in red. 'Tisn't often you get letters in red inked type is it?

Now that Fanny has left these parts things have come back to normalcy. Dave's eyes don't look so sleepy and tired in the morning as they did during the week that she was here. She kept us all on the go until late into the night.

Glad to note that your chief clerk took pity on you and furnished you with an assistant. This merely demonstrates once more the old adage that not half the things you worry about really happen. On the other hand things often happen that you do not anticipate and therefore are unable to worry about.

As an instance there is that little adventure of ours which you will find described in the enclosed clipping out of this morning's paper. Dave and I were busily engaged in some work we had to do yesterday and did not notice that the time had slid right by the closing hour, which on Sundays and Holidays is six o'clock. We wondered at about 6:30 that the janitor did not flash the lights as a signal to us that it is time to shut the building down.

At nights, the place closes at 10:30. We get a flash of the lights just fifteen minutes before that which warns us that time is nearly up. At that we often stay a few minutes past 10:30 and the janitor invariably comes up and knocks on our door. For some reason the janitor failed to warn us yesterday and when we finally closed up shop we discovered that we were very much locked in. There is no fire escape and the first floor is occupied by a bank so that there were no available ground floor windows thru which we might have climbed to get out. Dave then decided to call up the police department and in due time a cop came drifting by on a bicycle. The newspaper account of that part of it is slightly warped, out of true, so to speak.

After a little conversation between the cop and ourselves thru the locked door it was finally decided to call the fire department. By this time, as you might imagine, a crowd was beginning to gather in front of the building. Wishing to avoid as much publicity as possible, I took a cruise around the hallways to see if it were not possible to get out by the back way. (On the second floor, Louis found two occupants, leisurely engaged in conversation, who were very surprised to find that the front door was locked.)

This made us feel much better. Somehow there does exist a good bit of satisfaction in finding that you are not the only one in trouble. When the fire department showed up with a long step-ladder we were all waiting at our office window on the third floor and a considerable crowd had gathered to see the excitement. A fireman climbed up and instructed us in the technique of climbing down a step-ladder, assuring us the while that it was quite safe. Let me say right here, Miss, that it is no little thing to climb down the third floor on a step-ladder especially in full view of several hundred people. However, we mastered the feat one by one.

The whole thing, from the time the cop came until we were down and out, did not really take much time, but the little that it did take was sufficient to bring a reporter and a photographer on the scene. They asked us to pose for the newspapers but I thanked them very kindly for the offer and Dave and I beat it for the car. However, the other two fellows obliged the photographer by climbing up again on the ladder and posing for the picture. The photo that you see on the clipping is thus a posed photo and not the actual and original act.

At any rate we all had a grand time and to-day the whole town seems to know about it. As a precautionary measure we have asked and have been promised a key to the front door. We have long since wanted a key but could not get one owing to the rules of the building. This little escapade has thus been of some value anyway.

July 13, 1927
> Dear Lou:
> I went home this noon for lunch and found your letter (I don't ever recall receiving a letter typed in red ink; I thought it was an SOS.)
> I wonder if it was not a publicity stunt on your part to get in the limelight via step-ladder. Too bad you didn't pose for the photographer because I would have given most anything to see Dave and you descend the ladder of fame.

Celia was finding it difficult to write from the office. After handing a letter to a bookkeeper to mail, he informed the rest of the staff who were now asking her questions. "As I am writing this letter I had to take it out of the machine twice to wait for the disappearance of the clerks. I wrote a letter to our leading newspaper yesterday for their Inquiry Column regarding tennis courts. I even suggested a fee be charged should Clay courts replace the part dirt and grass courts."

Last Saturday Edith planted their net at 11 o'clock at a nearby park and they played until six o'clock. "I was so thrilled with my improvement that I can hardly wait until you come. My father called Edith and myself *mishshuganes* (crazy people) last night because we played for two hours in the heat and came home with a request that a shower must be installed – immediately."

July 16, 1927
> Dear Ceal,
> It is so hot here that it is an effort to move around, to stand still, to sit, to lie, to ride around, and in short to just exist. However, what is is, I was rather surprised that you 'would have given most anything to see Dave and you (me) descend the ladder of fame.' I thot you were a friend of mine. But how could you be and

still express such pleasure at the prospect of seeing me 'descend' the ladder of fame. Funny how the whole town knew about (it). This merely goes to show what power there is in publicity when accompanied by a photograph. Even now, a week after it happened, I am often greeted with, 'Hi, there, fireman!'

So you have become real good as a tenniser? Well, maybe now you won't be afraid to play with me. Dave has been after me to give him a workout but it has been so hot of late. I haven't played with him since 1925 and the Lord only knows how much he may have picked up since then.

I suppose the (Henry) Ford apology (for anti-Semitic remarks) affair has reached as far as Newark by this time. What do you think of it? One of the Rabbis of Washington corralled me as I was coming down to breakfast and asked me to write a letter in his name to the English press expressing his views. I don't like that sort of a commission but when a *Rov* (esteemed Rabbi) asks you, what can you *mach* (do)?

July 20, 1927

Dear Lou:

What publicity seeker wouldn't give a kings ransom to have an audience and a write-up such as you had when you descended the fire-ladder? To some the publicity would spell fame. You admit, that you are often greeted with a 'Hello there, fireman.' It wouldn't have been any fun had you and Dave been obliged to remain in your office until the following morning.

I believe I told you that I had written to the Editor of our leading newspaper regarding the hogging of tennis courts. My letter appeared in yesterday's paper and I am enclosing it for your reading. As yet no articles have appeared for or against.

You asked whether Ford's apology has reached Newark – Well, I declare. I wrote it for him. I personally believe there is a method to his madness. It was just one shock after another. First, his belated apology to the Jews in general and a personal apology to Shapiro. I think it is too good to be true. Lets hope his intentions were for the best and forgive him for his past wrong doings.

May I ask when you are coming out to Newark? I would like to read your article on the Ford subject. Have you it handy? My vacation starts the afternoon of the 6th. I am sure we will have a nice time. Mit fondest regards, Celia

July 23, 1927

Dear Ceal,

Your letter on the subject of the tennis courts reads very nicely and I must commend you upon it. What you should have done was to send that letter on to the Mayor. Maybe that worthy gentleman might be in a position to do something about it.

Talking of tennis, I have just this afternoon come away from watching a mighty fine tennis match for the championship of the District of Columbia. It was played between two young fellows, one the champion of last year and the other a challenger for the title. The loser lost by two games. For some reason the crowd of onlookers was rooting for the fellow who lost. Of course, they didn't know the poor chap was going to lose. As for myself, I am yet to play the first game since I saw you. One day it is very hot and another it isn't hot enough and then it rains and so on ad infinitum.

Your request for a copy of my article to the newspapers in re the Ford matter makes me wonder where you got the idea as to its being an 'Article' sounds kinda high falutin. I merely wrote out in English what the *Rov* asked me to write, his request coming to me in Yiddish. It was short enough to travel almost under the guise of a paragraph.

Have received a letter from a client over in West Point, Virginia, to install a complete system of accounts in their pickle factory. Believe I spoke to you about that there picklery sometime ago. I shall probably go there on Monday morning and the good Lord alone knows how long I shall stay there. I may have to be there as long as two, three, or four days, depending upon the intelligence of their bookkeeper. It seems that they were very much limited in their choice of an office girl on account of the locality of the plant, the theory being, I suppose, that the smart girls don't stay way out there but go to the city for work.

The following is the translated letter to the Editor of *The News*.

Ford and the Jews

With reference to the news item in your paper of June 15, relative to the action of the assembly of less than 100 persons of the Jewish faith in refusing to accept the apology and retraction by Henry Ford of Anti-Jewish statements made in his paper, the Dearborn Independent, I wish to express a thought upon the subject. The Torah and the whole spirit of our Bible teaches us to be tolerant towards all and particularly to accept the penitent into our fold without even a thought as to the possible reasons for his penitence. This is an axiom which the learned Jew has adhered to thruout the ages. We surely can do no less now.

The mere fact that a small group of local Jews have taken an attitude toward the Ford incident that is not in accordance with the Jewish traditions and spirit is in itself very unimportant. I am concerned here only with the possibility that the non-Jew might consider the attitude taken by this small group as representing the stand of all or even the majority of right-thinking Jews in Washington. For my part, and I feel certain that I express the views of the great majority of Washington and world Jewry, I stand ready to apply the teachings of the Jewish faith to this incident and to accept Mr. Ford's retraction without reservation. Rabbi R.M. Barishansky

Celia drew a girl happily swimming in the sea in her letter of July 27:

Yes, this is just what I would like to do today. Judging by the papers the people in Washington and points south must be melting away by degrees. Did you enjoy your trip to Virginia or did you have a pickling good time?

Who said I didn't start something? A letter appeared in the paper by our Park Commissioner, which I am enclosing. We spent an hour trying to locate the courts in question and (learned) that they weren't open yet. Judging by the number of people that were down at the park inquiring about the new courts, I will have to get in line a week in advance.

The reason I didn't want my name published is–The Office Force. Someone would have immediately clipped the news item and tacked it on our Bulletin Board with some wise cracking notation in full view of everyone. In profiting by the experience of others I signed my name 'Optimist.'

The chap that got the racket for me noticed the letter in the paper, clipped it out and gave it to me, saying that it would be a good idea if I would write in. It was all I could do to keep from laughing.

I read the news clipping you sent and think it is exceptionally good. It seems the *Rov* thought as *I did* in the way of forgiving.

What makes you think you are going to have tire and 'what not' trouble? Your mind mustn't run in the direction of mishaps. I would like to know more definitely when you will arrive, that is, the day – not the hour.

July 29, 1927

Dear Ceal,

Just a short time ago returned from my 'pickling' trip to the South and found your letter. Your letter and its contents were very interesting. Now you may expect to have real courts in your town some day. I asked Dave how he came out in the game he had scheduled to play with Babe the days after I left for West Point. He says, among other things (one of which being that day time is no time to be writing love letters), that Babe failed to call him back as per previous arrangement.

I had (hoped) to take a slight swim in West Point (but) such was not the case. That pickly plant turned out to be the workingest place I have ever had the misfortune to drift into. The official working hours (for everyone) begin at seven A M and cease at six P M. The unofficial hours begin at seven P M and cease at eleven to twelve the same night (for) the executives, the auditor, the superintendent, and one or two laborers who have been blessed with the favor of the management. Yet there was no overtime pay for anyone.

I tell you, Celia, I haven't worked so hard as I did these last three days. Seven A M to Eleven thirty P M with two hours out for lunch and supper is, I believe, fourteen and one half hours. I was particularly anxious to get away from there. All of my ammunition was aimed at the poor girl who bore the title of bookkeeper there. This kid knew as much about bookkeeping as I know about fighting rattlesnakes.

THE BOOKKEEPER

A company was looking for a bookkeeper. The President assigned the job of hiring someone to the Vice President. Three girls showed up and the Vice President asked each one, "If a customer has a bill for $40.00 and sends in a check for $400.00, what would you do?" The first girl answered, "I'd send the check back and ask the customer to send in the proper amount." The second girl replied, "I'd deposit the check and deduct the $40.00 and send a refund check for the rest." The third girl answered, "If the customer was so rich and stupid to send $400.00 instead of $40.00, I'd deposit the check and forget about it." When the President asked the Vice President, "John, which girl did you hire?" He said, "The prettiest one."

Celia wrote to Lou on August 1, 1927:

"All my work is finished but I can't go home. " It had been raining very hard and a taxi ordered an hour and a half ago had not arrived. "With no lunch and it looks as if it will be no dinner I am a bit starved. I certainly have been busy. I bet we could match the pickling works and bank and we would about come out even. Too bad you did not have time to take a plunge – the days were quite warm here last week so I can imagine the heat you must have had to contend with down South. Talking about plunges – Saturday afternoon the folks, Ruth, George and myself drove down to the shore but it rained throughout our trip.

"Oh, we had an exciting time Saturday. My father decided to stop the car in the middle of a block but a 'wise guy' that is, a State Traffic Inspector whose car was right behind threatened him with a summons on account of not putting out his hand when stopping." The trouper became angry when Ruth and Celia started laughing because they were not taking him seriously, "so he is reporting us to the Commissioner of Traffic of New Jersey for the violating of a law. In order to right ourselves we have to write him explaining the matter.

"You will stop at our house won't you? Sammy said he would be very pleased to share the bed with you on weekends but he will have to disappoint you during the week on account of his absence."

August 5, 1927

Dear Ceal,

Can't write much now, as the time is late and I have at least six million more things to do to-day. I have tried as much as possible to do work this week so that Dave will not be too much burdened with labors while I am away.

I have little, if any, expectations of getting to Newark any sooner than Monday. I expect to stop over on the way since I prefer to loaf on the road. I have seldom had the occasion to do that. I don't believe in getting up at four to go on vacation.

One thing I am very sorry for. I have not had any chances as yet to do any tennis playing. I am likely to experience some discomfiture after the game in sore muscles. I don't mind it at all as the usual thing when I am at home, but being on vacation makes that an unnecessary hampering of free activity.

Louis charmed not only Celia but her whole family. He always sent thank you notes and small gifts on appropriate occasions, such as this letter of August 22, 1927. Celia, in turn, did the same for Louis' family.

Dear Mrs. Kanster,

I am just exactly one week late in writing this letter. However, I have an excellent excuse. Celia will defend me, I am sure. Excepting for some rather heavy rain we had a very good trip from Newark to Washington. We arrived earlier than I had expected. Please tell Edith that the riding was perfectly safe at all times and even your friend the officer of the law could have found no complaints to make. Ask Celia and then don't believe her.

From the time we arrived here until last night when our guest left us, things moved at such a rapid pace that now I find myself imagining it is August 15th instead of the 22nd. Everybody complains to me (of being) lonesome now that Celia has left us. We are scanning the calendar for red dates when we might have the pleasure of her presence in this beautiful tho lonely town.

This is a rather late date at which to express my appreciation to you and your fine family for the way you made my visit to your city a pleasure. However, I am still a believer in the old and tried adages. 'Better late than never.' Besides I have a very excellent excuse in the person of that charming little daughter of yours, who by the way has turned the heads of every one she met here. I trust that altho belated you will believe my thanks and appreciation to be none the less sincere.

Monday
 Dear Lou,
 I am home but a few minutes and before I do anything this letter is going to be sealed. I have been very busy at the office all day. It looks as if I will be busy for some time to come.

As soon as the train left the station at Washington, I got into my berth – closed my eyes and when I opened them I saw I was in Roselle Park – a distance of ten miles from Newark and believe me I was sorry because I was just getting ready to turn on the other side. I enjoyed the ride home and the sleep as well and should I need the services of a train I would not hesitate in selecting the sleeper.

Lou, I want to tell you that I had a very, very, etc. wonderful time while in the company of your sisters, brothers, relatives and last but not least yourself. I really can't put in writing my appreciation for the part each one had in helping to entertain me and they all have a nice warm spot in my heart. The only thing I am sorry for is that I got back too late to bid your family goodby. (Your fault.) My intentions were good so kindly tell them for me I am sorry. I will write to the girls later.

Ida and Dave are perfect dears and I love them because they are true and sincere friends. Of course Kitty and Al are in the same category. My mother wants me to thank you for her for taking such good care of her daughter and she as well as the rest of the family want to be remembered to you very kindly. So will bid you a fond adieu with personal regards and love to the kiddies. Celia

August No. 24, 1927

Dear Celia,

Once more we renew our paper and type relations which while a mighty poor substitute for the real thing is useful nevertheless. Was glad to get your letter and the sentiments expressed therein. I am sure that I had a wonderful time. You say you enjoyed yourself. Since between the two of us I am the one who has been joking around with the truth, I do not dare question your sincerity. We shall, therefore, let the matter rest.

That morning, Miss Rosenfeld, the Zionist Secretary, called Louis for assistance. Since Miriam also called to be taken with Pauline to Kitty's, Louis picked them all up for the ride. When they arrived, Kitty said, "Do you think I'll permit a bridge game to come in just like that unexpected and then let it get away? Guess again, says she. The upshot of the matter was that the young lady and I retired to the dining room table to read and discuss the mail after which the game began. We spent the evening very pleasantly and at about 10:45 the party broke up.

"This morning, upon coming downstairs, who do you think greets me with a grand smile? My Mamma. She came in very early – about 5:30 AM and not wishing to wake her darling son up out of bed to take her from the station she just wrote nothing, wired nothing, said nothing, and made her own way from the station either by trolley or by taxi, I haven't even had a chance to ask which. She looks well and says that she had a fine time. I hope so. Mother is much impressed with her proposed daughter-in-law and hopes that the colossal *Meshugas* (craziness) of Joe will not work to get him some walking papers. I believe I told you once about his asinine *feribels*.

"Oh yes, I received a formal invitation to the forthcoming wedding (Edith & Sam) which I suppose calls for a formal answer. The trouble with those formalities is that I shall have to look up the correct form of reply and all that means more or less of a bother. So it is quite likely that I will throw formalities to the winds and sit down and write an old fashioned informal letter of acceptance. Worriedly yours, Louis"

Celia's sister Sarah was the first to marry and Edith was the second. Though Celia was the eldest, there was never any jealousy at being the third to go to the altar. She wrote back

Friday at Five o'clock:

'Jugosquaredud Mumorearnuninunjug' or in other words 'Good Morning.' One of the girls in our office came in with the alphabet of the Tut System and we two are going nutty conquering it. Anyway we are having lots of fun. Have you ever heard of it?

You signed your letter 'Worriedly Yours, Louis.' What is the idea, eh, and what possessed you to wind up the letter in that manner? You have me worried now. You gave such valued advice to your sister in Syracuse. I wonder why you didn't keep some of it for yourself.

When you wrote about taking Pauline and Miriam to Kitty's house I felt as if I was a member of the Bridge party. Too bad you all live so far away. Had the distance been shorter I would have persuaded Kitty to teach me the game as it should be played. I am wondering what kind of an instructor you would make.

Mother wants me to thank you for the letter. I also want to thank you for the many nice things you said about me. My mother feared that I might have been a bother but after reading your letter she was satisfied I wasn't. I am glad to hear that your mother had an excellent time while in Florida and I hope that she will take another trip soon, that is, to Joe's wedding. Give her my regards and tell her I was very sorry that I could not see her.

I have made several attempts to call Fannie on the 'phone and have come to the conclusion that she hasn't paid her telephone bill as yet. Edith has been after me all week to get in touch with her. She wants little Earl to be the page at her wedding.

I asked Edith if it would be Okay if you send her an informal acknowledgment of the invitation and after deliberating for several hours she said she would accept. You don't realize how lucky you are. As Edith would say, just fourteen more days and you will be here. Regards to everybody, including Maggie. Less Worriedly yours, Celia

Saturday, August 27, 1927

Daer Ceal,

Looks kinda out of sorts that substitute for 'dear.' Must be a reflection of the way I feel. I am at the time really supposed to be sick. What is more I am beginning to believe that I really am sick. Felt awfully punk last night. This morning I stayed in bed until about eleven trying to make up my mind that I was not feeling well. Was not entirely successful, so I got up; besides, I was really getting quite hungry by that time.

A desire to look at my mail, assisted somewhat by Babe's insistent urgings to take him to the tennis courts, prompted me to come here to the office." Not having been sick for so long, Louis thought he was immune to illness.

Please don't let my apparent frame of mind – so far as worrying is concerned – disturb you. As a general rule I do not permit myself to be worried and so I imagine that this bit of blueness will leave me just as soon as there appears a bit of a rift in the clouds.

Our mutual friend, Babe, is sitting on the chair with the most pins in it judging from the manner in which he displays his impatience. There he goes again, *Cum shoen, nu* (come along already), he sings. Shall I sock him one for you?

While it is but fourteen days as you write 'till I am with you again, I am afraid that that time will seem much longer. It already seems as if you have been away from here for months. Maybe I'll feel better and I shall make certain that no nuisance is in the office at the time.

Monday evening, Late, Aug. 29, 1927

Dear Ceal,

Somehow I have a feeling of owing you part of a letter. The interference handed in by Babe at the writing of my reply to your last letter has made me feel that way.

Happy to report, first, that I am already 75% recovered from my near-cold of last week. Was on the job this morning promptly at nine AM. A most peculiar thing has been occupying my attention all day today. Last Monday morning, first thing, I was called on the telephone at home by the General Manager of the American System Company of Roanoke, VA, whose local agents we are for their Insurance Agency System, and was informed that he is in town and would like to see me. He comes about once in six months and as on previous occasions I was glad to have him come up. We made an appointment for lunch. Paul Taylor, (That's the fellow's name). At evening time I met him and we supped together down town and took in a show. He told me that he would be busy with his patent attorney for most of the next day – that is on Tuesday – and would probably drop in again to see me before he left.

Next day at about three-thirty he came in again to the office and told me that he was leaving on the 7:30 for Boston and asked me to cash him a check for fifty dollars. I thanked him very warmly for the compliment but expressed sorrow at my inability, for cash-ial reasons, to comply with his wishes. However, in gratitude for said compliment, I called up Leo Freudberg and thru him, we secured the money for the gentleman. He told us that he was going to do a few purchasing of gifts for his wife and two kiddies before taking the train to Boston. We shook hands and I promptly forgot about friend Taylor.

Imagine my surprise, upon coming home to find that a message awaited me from Roanoke to the effect that Mr. Taylor had not been heard from since he left Washington Tuesday. I called the local police headquarters and asked for a report of any missing person fitting the description of our man, with no results. I called Roanoke and made my report.

Last night at ten I got another 'phone call, this time from the Raleigh Hotel, Washington, telling me that the assistant manager was here and would I be good enough to see them this morning. Naturally, I said I should be glad to help in any way I can.

This morning I showed up at the hotel and there I met the vice-president of the company, the general manager's first assistant, the Pennsylvania agent, and the lost young chap's brother-in-law. We all started out in my car for a series of calls upon every conceivable person who might have been in a position to tell us something about what happened to Taylor after last Tuesday at four. I was the last person who saw him so far as could be learned. He had wired the Boston agent to be on the lookout for him on Wednesday but he never showed up there.

The funny part about it was that he had been in the habit of writing to his wife every day that he was away from home. He did go to the store here and buy his wife a hat – imagine a man buying his wife a hat in another town – and some toys for his two kids all of which were received by them. All day we searched and we questioned, the radio will or has broadcasted the story today and tonight. All the police departments of all the Eastern cities between here and Boston have been put on the scent. Not one clue could we find of the missing young fellow.

Celia replied on Aug. 30, 1927: "I hope you are well and have long ago forgotten about your so called coming cold. I thought the sign of good health was a good appetite and as you complained about not being able to sleep later than eleven o'clock on account of being hungry I can't seem to figure you out. I suggest that you hire a nurse; (Please place my application on file.); Anyhow you haven't the time to be ill because I expect you here next week. It is so chilly here that I have had to take my winter sport coat out of the camphor bag and put it on yesterday.

"(Back from lunch) On Sunday a friend of ours called for Edith, Sammy and myself and we drove to Cuddlesback, NY, in the Catskill Mountains. In the course of our ride we had to pass a very interesting spot in New Jersey called High Point. It is the highest point in New Jersey being 1,800 feet above sea level. On a clear day one could see 24 counties in three different States. (So the pamphlet read that was distributed to the sightseers). On Account of the fog we couldn't see 24 feet ahead of us. By the time we got home we were chilled through and through, so mother made some hot tea and I immediately took myself to bed. I too, haven't the time to be ill.

"Edith claims she is overworked because she appointed herself Mother's secretary. She is taking care of all acknowledgments of invitations. Oh well, I heard her say this morning just twelve more days. Am looking forward to your coming next week. In the meantime I will try to look up some interesting place we can motor to on next Saturday. Yours for good health. Cel"

Thou Shalt Not Steal

September 1, 1927

    Dear Ceal,

    If my finances just now were in as good a shape as my correspondence stands with you, I should have a nice credit in the bank. However, what is, is.

    Funny how I have begun to be sensitive about the color schemes of my ties, my socks and my complexion to my suits and shirts. Never gave those things a thought before but now even Al talks of clashing colors. By the way, I must report that contrary to my expectations, Kitty's furniture is still in the same state of arrangement as it was when you last saw it. She evidently likes it just the way you arranged it. Maybe there is something to that artistic stuff, after all.

    So far as I know nothing has as yet been heard from my friend Paul R. Taylor. I have discombobulated myself – (Don't try to look that word up in the dictionary. You won't find it there.) – from the hunt for need of making a living. From latest developments it begins to appear that perhaps our friend may have turned somewhat crocked and wants to keep out of the way. He was reported to have been seen at the local Union Station on Wednesday night, a day after he was supposed to have left for Boston. Also when he cashed his check with me he only had five dollars in his account and the check was for fifty and he made no effort to have his family make that check good. The firm paid it when it came in – lucky for us. Furthermore that was the second fifty he cashed that day in this town and he needed no such amount just for his business purposes.

So, all things considered, it looks kinda fishy. I advised his uncle and Vice-president of the company to have an immediate audit of his accounts made. The gentleman thereupon turns to me and says, 'I guess you are right. What would you charge us to go to Roanoke and make the investigation?' What do you think I answered? Well, I told him that I do not believe I would care to tackle that job because I should hate to find anything crooked about his accounts. So that is where the matter was dropped, so far as I was concerned.

Your application for the position of nurse to me has been duly placed on file and in the event I decide to retain you, you will hear from me again. I want to warn you right now, however, that I am a very exacting patient and a source of great worry to any nurse.

Sunday, at home, September 4, 1927

Dear Lou:

Yes I am at home this week end. This morning I got up at 8 o'clock with full intentions of going to the seashore. But the others at home thought otherwise. Today happens to be the first clear Sunday since July 3rd and the first clear day in two weeks. I usually go away over the Labor Day weekend but (since) the weatherman's report was not favorable I did not care to go away. So that's that.

I like mystery stories very much and yours about Taylor was good. Your first chapter was very interesting and it ended in a like manner. I could hardly wait until your next letter arrived to find out what happened to him. To say you are missing your vocation is putting it mildly. Be careful they might lock you up for kidnapping.

Edith is very much excited about her wedding and the fuss is getting her in a nervous state. I persuaded her to have a small affair but she would not listen to me and yesterday she said 'Cel, I think you are right about a big wedding. I hope I will never have another one.'

Don't let the matter of color schemes bother you because you really have excellent taste. I hope I haven't started anything. First it is the furniture and then your tie (I am glad Kitty appreciates my ability as a furniture mover and lets things stand as is.)

This week is going to be a short one. Tomorrow is Monday, a Holiday and it won't be long 'ere you will be here. What time will your train arrive here on Friday? If I am downtown at that time I will be at the station to meet you.

Wednesday, September 7, 1927

Dear Ceal,

Got two letters from you before I have had a chance to answer the first. Thought I was doing pretty well with the credit I had with respect to my letter account with you, but these last two letters have put me behind.

I find that I will not be able to come out to your town on Friday night, but instead will be up on Saturday afternoon as per usual. On account of coming directly to your house from the station, you see I don't even wait for invitations any more, I should be over sooner than usual. Come to think about it, maybe your house will be sort of crowded on those days as the result of the wedding. I cannot imagine that there will not be a gang or two coming out from other cities to attend the wedding.

Now, Ceal, I know exactly how those things are and I shall call you on the phone as soon as my train gets in and ask you about it. If it will put you to any inconvenience whatever, I want you to tell me. I would far rather go to a hotel than let your people be bothered with me at such a time. We'll take up the matter again by telephone. I do hope you don't mind my switching over to Saturday instead of Friday night. Instead I may stay over Sunday night and go to New York on Monday. There are a few things I wish to do in New York on Monday.

Wednesday, Sept. 14th, 1927

Dear Lou:

I left the house this morning without the knowledge that I had but ten cents in my pocketbook. I did not have the occasion to look in my bag for carfare this morning because a chap I know took me down to the office in his car. At lunch time I took a wee glance in my bag and decided then and there to go home for lunch because I haven't as yet found a restaurant that charges ten cents for a meal.

This noon I found your letter requesting me to mail the shaving outfit to you. I am mailing it under separate cover this afternoon.

I was very sleepy while in your company on Sunday but hope I didn't show it. It wasn't the company but the lateness of the hour coupled with the lack of sleep of the previous nights. After you left for your train I immediately took myself to bed. The folks went to New York last night for the remainder of the boxes and when they made their exit I went to bed, that was at 6:30 o'clock and at 7:30 o'clock this morning I got up regretting the fact that I was unable to sleep for a longer period of time.

Sunday we are to have another big affair at Max Berger's expense. I understand there are to be 65 couples in the hall and am sure a good time is in store for all. Will write more about that later. I hope you will pardon the brevity of this letter; I am in a hurry to get home and dress as I have a date for tonight to see *Beau Geste*. I hope I will enjoy the picture as I did the book.

Louis wrote Celia on September 16, 1927:

"Your letter and the package that followed it were both received in good order. My face and I join hands in thanking you muchly for them." Louis also reported how sleepy he was. "I simply could not stay in the office longer than five yesterday. I fell asleep reading something. Can't afford to sleep during office hours.

"I have a date to go over to Dave's tonight and play him some chess. U don't know what a chess expert I am, do you? Years ago he taught me the game and he himself was such an expert that the very first real game we played together I beat him. Then, for a period of many years, say five, he never won a game from me even tho we were fairly well matched at all times. Then, all of a sudden, he started winning from me and now it is a toss up as to who wins. He feels quite well pleased with himself when he plays me to a tie. Of course, we do not play so very often say once in two months."

September 20, 1927

Dear Lou:

Bits of Bits

I am still very tired over the doings of the past week-end and at the rate I am going I will be tired for some days to come. Saturday night I went to Roxy's Theatre for the first time and can say I am very sorry that you didn't get a chance to see the interior of the building. It is simply beautiful. I saw *Seventh Heaven* there and believe me I thought I was in Heaven. There is something about a beautiful theatre and manner in which the prologue is presented that makes the show or picture entertaining. We spent about fifteen minutes looking the place over. One would think I was a hick just coming in from the country.

We had a wonderful time Sunday – Too bad you weren't here. I understand 65 couples were to be there but only 40 couples graced the hall. I don't know why the others didn't come but they sure did miss a good time. If it wasn't for the fact that a dear friend of Max Kane's passed away on Saturday night there is no telling what might have happened. My father and Uncle Lou were sadly disappointed because they were not given a chance to use the ammunition they brought with them.

So you are a chess player too. Say what don't you know how to play. First it is tennis, then bridge, solitaire and now it is chess. Oh me, oh my, you certainly are going strong. Who won the chess game?

Sam heard me speak of the games of Croquet I played at Kitty's place, so one fine day last week he carts home a croquet set. I don't know where we are to play because we surely haven't any room in our back-yard, nevertheless we have an outfit and someday when we get in the mood we will go down to the Park and hammer away, that is, if they let us.

207

At this writing, Edith and Sammy are in Quebec with thoughts of coming home tomorrow. From letters and phone calls received they are having the time of their lives. I understand Sammy has decided to live with us for awhile, that is, until he saves some change to buy a house. I don't fancy the idea very much but what can you do. My mother doesn't say a word, her policy is to help the young folks and to please – and if Edith and Sammy are pleased that is all that counts. Anyway I hope he saves plenty.

You certainly must be popular. First a man does a disappearing act and picks you out as the last person to see him alive and then another man picks out your presence in which to enact a fainting scene. Are you sure this man does not intend borrowing from you – at any rate play safe, do not cash any of his checks.

CONFESSIONS

A Rabbi, a Priest and a Minister met for lunch. It was decided each would confess a sin. The Rabbi said he ate pork when he was away from home. The Priest said he visited a woman in another town for sex. The minister said, "I'm a terrible gossip."

September 24, 1927

Dear Ceal,

Did you win any money on the fight? Did your radio know there was a fight? Did you enjoy the announcements? You don't have to answe (here's your 'r') the above questions if they will embarrass you in any way. For my part I lost one berry and liked it. My sentiments were with Mr. Tunney but my money was on Mr. Dempsey. Moral, always place your money where your sentiment is. All in all she was one great fight. But as Babe puts it, 'There is no show living that is worth my forty dollars.' Guess he has the right idea.

Mr. Dempsey was knocked coockoo by his better and in the same breath that he admits it he also informs the world that he would have been champion had he not had so few brains, and those few very bemuddled at the time it was necessary to step aside and let nature take its course with Mr. Tunney. The eternal alibi.

I am treating myself to a seat at the ball game, it being the last Saturday the team will play at home this year. Babe is to go along. He is due here at three, I told him to stay away from here until time to go to the game because otherwise he wastes me the time he is here. The kid is so restless.

Glad you enjoyed the Roxy theater and whenever the occasion arises I shall be happy to take it in. Our own Fox theater, managed by Roxy, opened up last Monday evening. The place is a dream. And while I did not even attempt to go to see that opening on the first day, I did see it on a few days later. Of course, Roxy is an artist in the entertainment that he specializes in and it must cost plenty dough-dough.

The place here can seat 4,000 people. For our size town, Mr. Roxy is going to have his hands full to keep the place crowded all the time.

Guess by the time you get this letter Rosh Hashono will be pretty nearly upon us. As a matter of fact this is no longer Saturday afternoon. The day has been here and is now went. Ida called me on the phone in the middle of the writing of this yesterday and talked to me all the time until Babe drifted in and then it was time to get to the ball game. As it was, we came in late having missed the first two innings and the 2nd was the best of the game too. That's what a woman can do for you over the phone. As Babe says, I am too damn polite and couldn't cut her off until she was all thru. But then, what's a couple of innings of a ball game, anyway? As it was, the home team won and that was that.

This morning Babe and Miriam and I played tennis for the first time since we played with you, and Miriam seems to have gotten away with the day. She played us both to a standstill. The kid is getting good. I got tired out after the first hour and couldn't sock it very hard. She just kept sending them back and sooner or later the persistent player always wins. After we had played three handed for awhile we decided to play singles, best two out of three. The first games were played by Miriam and me which she won two straight. Then she played Babe and won two out of three. Then I took her on again and beat her two out of three, the third game being a love game. But of course, that was no credit to me since she had played right thru without any rest whereas I rested. Later Babe played her again and won two out of three. All in all, she was a good game of tennis and I am dead tired.

Miriam was two years younger than Pauline and five years younger than Pop. As children, Miriam and Louis did not get along well. Pop said, "As a matter of fact, I hated her guts." Any time he asked her not to do something, she would say, "*Vil Ich nu* (do me something)?"

When Miriam was about 7- or 8-years-old she spent a week in the hospital and when she came home she pretended she had forgotten to speak Yiddish. For years, she failed to say a single word in Yiddish. My father claimed her stubbornness continued into adulthood. She would never admit she was wrong.

If this was true, my mother ignored it and remained very friendly with Miriam all through her life. One thing Mom found annoying in her last years was Miriam's reluctance to buy anything new. Miriam would say, "Maybe I won't live long enough to wear this so why buy it?" She outlived my mother by five years. Fortunately, my mother never paid attention to her age and, if she liked something, she would buy it, not only for herself but for her sisters, my grandchildren and me as well. Aside from the fine jewelry she bought when finances permitted, she also loved costume jewelry. Mother was always beautifully groomed and people assumed the jewelry she wore was the real thing. On her, it looked authentic.

On Friday September 30, 1927, Celia wrote: "I spent some time in *schole* (shul) *Yontif* (holiday), and I intend going there tonight, I liked the sermon the Rabbi made Wednesday and I promised myself then and there that I would go to schole every Friday night thereafter – here is hoping I won't break the promise.

"I just got a call from big Sam to come down to the shop as soon as I get out of the office and finish the typing of the bills as they have to be out by tonight. This means that I will have to work until 7 o'clock and then hurry home, dress and go to Schole by 7:30. I do not mind doing anything now because it makes me forget about my cold. A funny thing about working is since I have started this letter I didn't sneeze and if that is a remedy I am going to continue.

"You wanted to know if I lost any money on the fights – the answer is 'No.' I do not like to bet because I dislike taking the other party's money. To be frank with you I was dozing the time the fight was going on but somehow or other knew enough to get up on the count of 9. I understand that was the most interesting part of the fight so I didn't miss anything by napping.

October No. 2, 1927
    Dear Celia,
    'To horse!' they said in olden cavalier times. Today they don't say that any more. Now it is, 'To pen,' or rather 'To typewriter'! Times do change and with it comes the changeable weather that you complain about so justly. Personally I always liked heat better than cold. I particularly dislike cold shoulder altho I care little for anything cold excepting liquid refreshments on a warm day.
    Just returned from the cemetery where I took mother for her memorial services that all good Jews observe, that is those who have dear ones buried at the cemetery. I stayed there long enough, waiting for mother to get thru with her prayers, to finish a very cute little short story. I took the magazine along on the hunch that the waiting might become weary. It did and I was just about to settle comfortably into the next one when mother decided she had said her say.
    In a scant half hour I am supposed to call for Ida and Doris to wend our way to the Union Station to greet the returning prodigal, one Mr. David Adolph Glushak by name. Which reminds me to say to you that your guess as to his having long since returned was slightly out of true. The gentleman had not returned.
    I trust you have spent the *Rosh Hashing* (*Rosh Hashanah*) holidays in a manner befitting a young lady in your station. It pleased me to find that there are still a few Rabbis in this land of the free who are interesting enough to evoke a resolution from the heart of young Judea to come oftener and to hear more of the words of the Lord. Here, sad to say, there are few such men. Only one is at this time nearly interesting enough to make we wish to hear the finish of his speech. That one is not an English speaking Rabbi and for that reason it is not always easy for me to follow him.
    However, I do have other interests that keep me going to shul – that is my way of spelling it, take your choice. You will

not find it in Webster's dictionary – on Rosh Hashono and Yom Kippur.

And let me say right here that those interests are not the young folks who roam around the vicinity of the Synagogue all the time the services are going on. Rather I like to come to shul on *Yontev* (*Yontif*) and to stay indoors all the time the services are going on. I love Rosh Hashono services and am perfectly content to sit in my seat and *Daven* (pray) and listen to the speeches of the Rabbi, even tho they bore me, until the time to go home to dine.

I was surprised to read of Sarah Henna going to the cemetery. My grandfather always said there was no reason to return there after a burial except to lay the headstone. He believed that after death, there was nothing there to visit. The deceased existed in one's memories and heart and not in the cemetery. While there are yearly memorial services conducted by many synagogues at the cemetery, I do not believe my grandfather ever went. I am not even sure my grandmother had any relatives buried there. Grandpa probably considered this a custom he chose to ignore.

Celia enjoyed Louis' long letter, according to her response on October 4, 1927. She goes on: "I noticed in your letter that you dislike getting the cold shoulder. What do you know about the cold shoulder business; surely you are not talking from experience. I can't imagine you being the recipient of the CS and any one giving it to you.

"I thought the Yontif services beautiful. I can't understand why so many of our Jews will stand in front of the shul and (not) enjoy the services therein. I went to shul on Friday evening and enjoyed a sermon by the Rabbi. The shul was packed to the door and I can see where I will have to get there much earlier in the future if I want to be assured of a seat.

"My father and mother both like to see a Jewish show in preference to any other kind. They expressed a desire that we all go on Saturday evening past and see *God's Gift*. The whole of the family including the dear brothers-in-law went to see the show and I can honestly say that it is one of the best shows I have ever seen and I would never hesitate on going again. They all have the fever at home to see more *Peyahses* (clowns or entertainers). Of course there are good and bad shows in all kinds but that is to be expected." She wrote of playing croquet in the park with her sisters and attracting a crowd of onlookers.

"When you were here last you said you would come out when you saved up some money. I hope you have made plenty by this time and that you will come out soon. Oh what is money anyway – Yes, I suppose it is a convenience."

Louis wrote Celia in October 1927 (Right after Yom Kippur 5688):

"Hope you are all fed up now after the day before, that is if you fasted yesterday. At our home everybody still has the custom and we seem to enjoy the day. I suspect, however, that the enjoyment is really the breaking of the fast at night. Funny, isn't it, how you feel you could eat the whole ice box, and when it is time to eat you lose your appetite. I always eat a very little on the night after the fast. Just a cup of coffee, a piece of tart or pie, and some fruit – grapes and a prune or two, and I am all thru for the day. That is all I had yesterday.

"Went over to Dave's last night to break the fast. It is somewhat of a custom with them to take someone along from shul and feed him. Of course, that someone is I. Last year, however, I broke my fast in Jacksonville, Florida.

"About any possibilities of coming over shortly I am afraid that is out for the present. I have a sister in Syracuse, New York, whose husband – named Harry W. Abrams, has got himself somewhat mixed up in a Foundry." Last month he received a letter from Harry asking for his services in auditing the foundry. He wrote back, "I should be glad to come over provided I get paid for the coming – expenses and remuneration for work done. I quoted him special rates for his benefit. Thereupon I promptly forgot about it. In fact I didn't even tell Dave about the letters since I didn't put any stock in it. Costs about $25 RR fare one way including sleeper and meals on the train."

Then last Monday while at Kitty's with Miriam for supper and bridge, he received a phone call informing him of a wire from Harry asking him to come out immediately. "Since I am not in a habit of rushing out of town in such a hurry, I called him on the long distance and at an expense of five minutes and $1.30 changed the date of my arrival to the coming Sunday evening. However, since this is a trip that will be paid for, I should really not kick. On top of that, I have long since wanted to go to Syracuse, since I have never been there in all the ten or so years that sister Esther has been living there. This, then, gives me an ideal way of paying her and her kiddies a nice visit."

> October 13, 1927, from Syracuse
>
> Dear Ceal,
>
> Have been kept pretty busy here and expect to stay that way till I leave. About all I have time to write you is to state that I may stop in to see you on my way back. Expect to leave here Saturday night and might instead of going home direct, go over to Newark. If I do, and I am not very certain of leaving here Saturday night, I'll get into Newark early Sunday morning and spend the day with you, leaving Newark at the usual hour 12:58 E.S. Time. Don't make any plans for me because I might not be able to make it, but if I can I will.

On his return to Washington, Louis addressed a letter to his sister Esther.

> October after Yontev, 1927
>
> Dear Folks,
>
> It says in the book of good manners, that when one has left the hospitality of another, it is correct to write and thank that other or others for said hospitality. I got back bright and early for the reason that the train crew wouldn't stand for my sleeping much longer after the train got into town than a half hour. Of course the family wanted to know all about Syracuse and its *menchelech* (little people) and would hardly give me the time to tell about one person before asking about another! When I told them that I almost took Ruthie (four years old), along with me they all wanted to know why I didn't. Looks as if we'll have to concoct some sort of scheme for getting the young lady over here.
>
> Eleanor wanted to know if you made ice cream for Friday night and Miriam couldn't believe it that you did that every Friday as Eleanor and I tried to tell her. No kiddin' every Friday night ice cream? I guess they like it. What do you people think? And you

Ruthie? Do you like to eat ice cream every Friday night too? You know, I find myself dreaming that I have Ruthie in my bed with me and when I want to take her around and hug her she isn't there. And I want to say Shush-Shush (Shoshana), come over here but Shush does not make a move.

As for your two *mazikim* (little devils – twins, Yonaton & Yaacov), I am not very much interested in them. For one thing I am still sore. One of them did me dirty right on my new shoes and since I cannot tell them apart, and thus do not know which one it was, I have to be sore at both of them. Sylvia's hefty kiss is good but still burns my *Meile*, fun Esther is *doch shon obgeret* (about Esther I've already told you). She holds down the works to earth and keeps the *scaske drehen sech* (things going on).

October 23, 1927
Dear Celia,

I was called on the phone a few minutes ago and told that Herman Freudberg, my buddy from Philadelphia is coming in with part of his family on the excursion train and I am elected to go and meet them at the station. The sisters (Celie and Dora) of the young man, whom he is visiting, cannot get away from some work they have to do at the store this morning. So I am about to leave here to pinch hit for them.

Dave, Ida, Kitty, and I made it a foursome last week to go see the play *Seventh Heaven* at the Fox Theatre. It was very good indeed. Ida had a wonderful time. She used up two good handkerchiefs. One, her own, went very soon but Dave's being of superior size and saturation qualities, lasted a good bit longer. She was just about to ask me for mine when the picture came to an end. Dave thought the picture was the finest of its kind that he had ever seen. In fact he saw the thing at Roxy's only two weeks before but liked it so well that he thot he would like to see it again.

October, 31, 1927, Monday Morning First Thing
Dear Lou:

It is exactly 8:30 o'clock now and before I do another thing this letter is going to be mailed to you. Last night at eleven I attempted to write you, that is, after the Kane's, Rosenberg's and Shapiro's left. They were with us all day and between the children, radio and bird it sounded like an arsenal.

Last Monday the bank was invaded by the bank examiners and the only evening I had off was Friday because I had to show myself at the Masque party that was given by the Bank Club. I got there at 9:30 and at 10:30 I was on my way home. I had high hopes of resting over the week-end but couldn't on account of the gang coming over. My work this week consisted of typing financial statements, reports and taking notes from the examiners. I have a few more days of it and then I will be through but they will be here for about two more weeks.

How is the Accounting game in your City? I wonder if this information will help you any – if you think it will you are welcome to it. Less than a year ago our bank hired six college graduates and started a New Business Dept. A list is acquired each day from the City Hall of new Companies, Corporations and Partnerships that have been formed and no time is lost in sending our representative there. It is surprising how many new accounts have been acquired all through this system. Would it help you any if you were able to get such a list? They seem to think a lot of it here.

In addition to the normal letterhead of Glushak & Grossberg, Louis' letter of November 7, 1927 also showed branches in New York City and Syracuse, New York.

Don't let the above letterhead scare you. We have not branched out. This is merely one of the last few of this stationery that we have left. We used to have connections with the offices listed above which we have since disconnected or I should rather say discontinued. But you mustn't mind a little thing like that at a time when my fingers are quite cold from having been outside long enough to get them that way.

That is one of the advantages of driving an open automobile in cold weather. You must either wear gloves or get your hands cold since I find it rather advisable to keep at least one hand on the steering wheel most of the time. Having somewhat of a dislike for gloves, I am apt to get my fingers cold.

I want to thank you for your kind suggestions with respect to the 'New Businesses' matter. In fact, as long ago as 1925, that is before I left for Florida, I tried to get hold of current lists of businesses but in this town it cannot be gotten. There are only a very few kinds of businesses that must register and pay a license: cigar stores, junk shops, second-hand stores and one or two other kinds. So you see there is not available here any list of new businesses. That was the reason I gave it up two years ago as a bad job. Now, however, I tried again after having read your letter. I ran up against the same snags with respect to the other kinds of new businesses but the corporations are still available. There are only about four or five a week. However, these are good prospects and I intend to follow them up. At any rate, this office sends its thanks to you.

Yesterday I nearly sold my old wreck of a Cleveland that has been rotting away on Al's lot for these many months. The price at which I shall feel it worthwhile to sever connections with the old faithful has been coming down steadily ever since I wanted to get rid of this piece of junk. Yes, it has come to this.

There was a time when I was proud of its beautiful lines and red disk wheels. 'Tis ever thus. Well, to come back to the story, a friend of mine was purchasing an automobile and he, unlike most people, had no other car to offer in trade. Of course, the automobile people were very much disappointed at that and so, out of the kindness of my heart, I offered to heal the disappointment by sandwiching my own Cleveland into the deal. My friend had no objections. Cleveland's namesake was due to put in its appearance at about 11:30 yesterday. Bright and early, I appeared at Al's and spoke unto my property with kindly words to the tune that it was time to get away from Fort Myer. Something must have been wrong with the hearing apparatus. It gave nary a yip for all the coaxing. Of course, there is a limit to the amount of nonsense I will stand from any car. Did it start? No indeed.

Al was loafing luxuriously on his overstuffed couch when I came in with my complaints. Needless to say he was not very much pleased with my proposal that he come out and see what he knew about the matter. The wind was blowing sixty or sixty-one and it was anything but warm outside. To make a short story long, we took the bus out with a gently pushing from the rear, thinking that the nice behavior of the passing automobiles might set my car a good example. But even that was of no avail. There was nothing left to do but to take the darn thing apart. We did this and in about two hours the damage was repaired and I started off to the appointed place.

Well, as I said before, I almost sold it. The only thing was that the dealer was ungrateful. The man had the nerve to say that he could live pretty well without that car and in order to prove it he announces the value of that Cleveland to him as being exactly $25.00. What happened to the car? If you will take the trouble to look you can find it parked out on Al's lot once more. The thing that makes me sore is that it cost me a whole Sunday. Now I am hoping that spontaneous combustion will help me to sell the machine to the insurance company.

November 16, 1927, six o'clock

Dear Lou:

I am as busy as a paper hanger with one arm. If it isn't the bank examiners it is the fact that I am getting dictation enough for three. I was told that it would not last for more than five days. Where there is life there is hope. The chief clerk said he never heard me complain when there is nothing to do. I think he meant that for a dig.

Please do not think I am too bold in offering suggestions. If you will say that I am not interfering, I will feel lots better. I am enclosing printed copies of letters that our bank sends out to newly organized businesses that they are not able to get in touch with personally. I am just sending them to you to give you an idea what a big company does in the line of soliciting new business. Still if you can give it a trial, I am sure some good will come of it.

Too bad you couldn't sell your Cleveland after all you went thru. It really is a good looking car and it is a shame you can not get a good price for it. I am sure we could get more than $25.00 for our old Dodge were we to trade it in, but then, that is in New Jersey.

I was invited to a bridge party given by a bridge club and won first prize. Big Sam said they gave me the prize because I was one of the guests, but I am differing. Saturday afternoon our bank club is giving a bridge for the employees and their guests at one of our Hotels and I am excited about it. Methinks I am improving.

Our bank club has on its winter program a sight-seeing trip to Washington sometime in December, via Baltimore & Ohio RR Co, but I think it is going to fall thru. In fact I am positive of it because about 75% of the gang were there at one time or another, the other 25% don't count. Some want to take a trip thru the coal regions of Pennsylvania and according to the number of discussions already had, I think they will wind up a few miles from Jersey. I was going to surprise you with a telephone call when I got there but it looks as if that is all off.

Sunday, November 20, 1927
Dear Ceal,
This typewriter has just been decked out with a new silk ribbon. No other will operate on this machine. She is very hi-falutin' is this machine, no kiddin.' And as for me, I'm such a wonderful typist that I must have a machine just exactly to my liking or there is no telling what might ensue. Now Ida, who has been doing some special work for the foim claims that since I have begun to use this machine exclusively she cannot use it. Isn't that something? And then she scoffed at me when I said that I can tell from the feel of my steering wheel when someone other than I has driven my car. So there you are.

Let me say right now and officially that I appreciate your kindness in taking the trouble to make the suggestions anent my business and that you are not interfering at all. This for the purpose of making you feel more at ease. If you would send me just the letter that would exactly suit my needs I would accept it with many thanks and use it. Now do not misunderstand. This is not' an invitation to write such a letter for me.

Your story about the possible trip to Washington is somewhat disappointing. Seems to me you could carry on an active campaign for Washington. I'll give you some pointers on that next week. Why next week? Well, I may be out to pay you a bit of a visit the coming Saturday at the usual time. No, I don't wait for invitations any more. I told you last time I was over that as soon as I accumulate a little wealth I would come out again. The time seems somewhat ripe for Saturday November 28.

Dave doesn't know yet, but he'll find out soon enough. Long ago I promised a cousin of mine that if I could get away from here on Thanksgiving Day, I would make some changes in his books. I believe this time I can get away as promised and I believe I will. However, when one has a partner it becomes just a wee bit awkward to give away your services to a friend. Still, what he does not know will not hurt him. In view of the friendship etc. existing between my cousin and myself I could not think of taking any fee for the little I will be doing for him. Of course you will not mention this in any of your correspondences here, will you? Of course not.

Which leads me to remember that it is positively funny how things get around between the ladies here. There are mighty few things that Ida knows that has any semblance to being a matter of confidence that Kitty does not soon learn from her, in the strictest confidence, of course. The other day I was just a little peeved at Ida although, I did not let on. Dave and I were discussing a matter of business at his house and Ida was present. The matter was somewhat confidential – it had nothing to do with any clients – altho there was nothing said about keeping it to ourselves. I thought that was self-evident. The next day I get a phone call from Kitty wanting to know all about the matter. Ida had told her in confidence and she asked me not to say anything to Ida or Dave that she knew. It turned out to be nothing at all but I was a little sore that day. Are all women like that?

So, since I shall see you in a few days I might as well call this a letter and let it go at that. Incidentally please do not ask me to stay at your house because I know that you are somewhat crowded now that Sammy lives with your folks. I know you will be able to arrange somehow but I will not have it. As a matter of fact my room at the Riviera is already reserved so that is all settled.

November 30, 1927

Dear Ceal,

From the extent of my being busy one might be led to think that I am making money or something to that effect. Don't you believe them. Just now it is about 7 o'clock and I should be at home helping the others to eat. I know I am in for a bawling out since the home staying contingent always complains when I get in late from work.

It develops that I must get up real early to-morrow – as early as 6 AM and catch a bus for Richmond and thence to West Point, Virginia. I may not stay there longer than the rest of the day and then I may stay longer. This trip is to be a total loss since it is merely one to attempt to make a collection for work already done before the birds begin to believe that it is a debt that is not owed. It has been due since July and I have heard nothing from the many requests and letters that have gone out there to attempt to get it. It seems now up to me to do in person what I have not been able to do by mail.

December 6, 1927

Dear Lou:

How did your trip to Virginia turn out? I suppose as soon as the pickle embalmer saw you he immediately made out a check to your order and apologized for keeping you waiting.

Edith has been after me all week to inquire if you still think she is a good driver and if the turning over of the car has influenced you in thinking otherwise. She feels a little hurt to think that an out-of-town visitor had to be in the car when it turned over. When I awoke the Monday after the night before I did so with pains in my shoulder such as one would have after playing tennis for the very first time. Much to my satisfaction it disappeared the next day.

I believe I told you that I was taking part in a minstrel, well, Saturday night was the big night and it took place at the 'Y.' It was a howling success everybody present voted it the best minstrel they (had) ever seen, the participants of the show were invited by the bank officials to be present at a banquet to be given in their honor sometime in January. To encourage clerks to join future minstrels the bank club has a number of surprises in store for those who took part in the past show. I can't imagine what they will be but I am hoping it will be in the form of cash.

I am doing a little reading now and have started a book by Henry Fielding called, *The History of Tom Jones*. A number of people think the book dry – on the contrary, I think it very interesting.

Thanks for saying you had a nice time in spite of the spill.

Louis' letter to Celia on December 11, 1927, outlined the vagaries of the accounting business. It seemed that the work-load was reasonable until one of the partners was away. Then it required super human efforts to keep afloat. Dave had just accepted a job in the New York headquarters of the Zionist Organization for a period of five months ending May 31, 1928. At least it would pay well. Louis said the same thing happened about a lot of work flowing in just when he left for Florida in August of 1925.

Before I left there was not enough work in the office to keep Glushak more than mildly active. A few days after the letter of acceptance went out, we (received) a new case beginning December 15th. This case is expected to take quite some time and is of considerable importance since it means the installation of a system at the offices and plant of the District Grocer's Society, an organization of grocers pooling their bying (here's your 'u'). There are something like 110 grocers in the society and thereby it becomes important. (Then Leo Freudberg called about installing a system in a laundry.) On top of all that it is the close of the year and the books of all our clients must be closed and statements prepared and presented. I am going to have fun.

This is Sunday afternoon at 3:41. Now we are awaiting the arrival of a gentleman who was so smart in his business acumen that he thought he could get away with anything including even the United States Federal Income Tax. The gent managed to forget all about taxes and tax returns from his babyhood days onward. Why file a return and tell your uncle how much money you have made? Why indeed. Everything might have come out O.K. if it were not for the fact that our dear Unc Samuel asked him to be so kind as to state what he did with his 1924 return. This was a question our friend does not like to discuss and he comes running hot-foot to tax experts – the same being us – and asking us how he can lie himself out of it. This, by the way, is one matter that these tax hounds do not care to get mixed up with. It seems that the best thing for us to do is to invite him to go to someone else for advice. Maybe we will. We'll see what he has to say.

I see by your letter that Edith craves my opinion of her capabilities as a driver after the beautiful spill we all enjoyed that Sunday. To ease her mind I hasten to assure her, thru you, that in my opinion, any person, particularly a woman, who has suffered the shock of a spill from a running auto, and who in a very few moments thereafter has the nerve to drive that car away from the scene of the accident without doing anyone any damage is a DAMN GOOD DRIVER – to put it squarely. As for the accident itself, it is likely to happen to the most experienced and practiced of drivers. I hope that she will continue to have as much confidence in herself at the wheel as I have when she is driving.

No I did not get anything for the pains of going to West Point excepting the promise of a note for the amount due. I hope I get that note. I have even wired for it since I left there.

December 15, 1927, Celia congratulated Louis and Dave for grabbing new opportunities even though it meant extra work and a separation of six months: "I certainly feel important today for the simple reason that a buzzer was attached to my desk so that I can get a floor boy without delay. The Chief Clerk seems to think – in fact he said so – that my time was valuable to him and that he had it installed just as a matter of convenience so that I may quickly dispose of finished work or for whatever help he can be to me. This buzzer system is exclusively for the use of Officers and when I think of my name on the board along side of the Officers my chest swells up and maybe my hat won't even fit my head. I guess I feel that way because today is the first day. I'll get over that."

The extra work from The District Grocer's Society was the

beginning of a lifetime association with men who became the back-bone of the accounting practice. This Society, known as the DGS stores, dominated the Washington grocery scene until the advent of supermarket chains spelled the demise of "Mom and Pop" grocery stores. What started out small grew as did their wealth. In time, these men went into real estate and other businesses that prospered in the aftermath of the Second World War. Louis was instrumental in managing their financial affairs and he prospered as well. Most of these men had little if any education but they had "street smarts" and understood the importance of having a professional to counsel their businesses.

Louis writes back on December 19, 1927: "Buzz-z-z-z! Boy, tell the President to come over here at once. Got to see him. Move! Hot Dog! That's the way to learn 'em. So they gave you an instrument of torture with which to harass (Think there is another 'r' in that word, looks weak this way) the poor office boys. I hope they don't waylay you after work some night and make you run around the block just to see how you like it. You are to be congratulated and my recommendation under the circumstances is to ask for a raise. After all, one cannot buy silk hose with a buzzer. Faint heart never won fat paycheck.

"I have been looking with watering mouth upon the red letters on my many calendars. The 26th is useless to me." That day was needed to discuss office policies with Dave prior to his departure. The weekend of January 2, 1928, might be good as it was not a workday. His only problem was with a client leaving for Europe on the third who wanted his annual statement beforehand. Louis hoped to talk him out of it.

"At any rate write me what you have planned for the New Year holidays and let me know if you will have time to bother around with me should it be possible for me to make the bozo satisfied to enjoy his sea trip over there without the report. Who was it said, 'If I had more time I should have written you a shorter letter.' There is real thought in that sentence."

December 23, 1927, Celia encourages Louis to visit: "Let me know if you can get away for the New Year Weekend. Edith and Sammy are planning to go to a Knight banquet and I am sure they would like us to join them. As yet nothing is definite and change of plans are in order. I have been invited to a party and we might wind up there. If you have any plans or suggestions just send them along. Let that 'Bozo' client of yours take to the water without the report – who cares.

"If you can make the trip I would like to have you stay at my house. You will not inconvenience anyone. I am positive so that is settled. With all the work on my desk I didn't have the heart to sit there and type a personal letter. I am sitting at a desk provided only for the use of women depositors."

December 28, 1927
    Dear Ceal,
    This time this IS going to be short. I have a million things to do to-day. Dave is leaving to-morrow which means that if there are any things I wish to have him tell me I better get them to-day or they won't be told me.
    I have managed to fix it up with that 'gazabo' client of mine and that means that the coast is clear for my spending the week-end in Newark. As to where we are to go, I must say what a cop of ours used to tell all who asked him things he didn't know. 'Dam-fino.' Nor, do I care a rap. Any place you elect will be O.K. with me.
    As for staying at your house, I happen to know that there are no vacant places for guests at your home at this time and if there is anything that will make me uncomfortable, it is to cause inconvenience with my presence to anyone. If I stay at your home somebody will have to give up his bed to me which I will not have. However, we'll leave that to talk over some other time.

January 6, 1928
    My dear Ceal,
    You think I got time now to write? No-o-o. Ain't got time but I just got to say to you that I am sorry I'm so busy I can't even do the decent thing and say to you that I appreciate the good time you helped me have while I was in Newark over the *Yontaevim* (the holidays).
    When I got here – it is eight thirty Friday evening – a time never before devoted to labors, I saw a message from this afternoon to call a client immediately on extremely important business about some tax trouble that he is in. Life has been something terrible for me since I came back from Newark. The contrast is killing. Got

a letter from Dave from Rochester which calls for an immediate answer but I have simply not got the time even to dictate the letter into the Dictaphone. Ida comes here and writes my letters for me from the Dictaphone but I can't get it in there.

Everybody wants his statement at the same time and I have to keep stalling them off. We never knew what it was to have so much work to do as not to be interested in new clients. However, that does not keep me from the negotiations that are to take place just three minutes from now.

Wednesday Jan. 11, 1928

Dear Lou:

My you must be very busy especially when you haven't the time to eat. It is a funny thing but your letter had a peculiar swing to it in the sense that when I started to read it I had to do so in a very fast manner. I could feel how busy you were by just reading the letter and in order to accomplish that feeling for the reader, one must be an artist in letter writing.

Celia skipped art class last evening to see a show, having lost interest in the current project. "I have spent three evenings on it with no results. We have to make a sketch expressing a child's dream and it is not to be realistic or futuristic – now go figure that out.

"I went to see George Jessel in the *Jazz Singer* last night and had a crying good time. I think the play beautiful and Jessel's acting was wonderful."

On January 16, 1928, Louis wrote to Dave in New York, using a playful endearment though he was quite annoyed with him:

Dear Darling Dave,

At last a letter. Damn if it ain't a darn. But what can I *mach*? Part of this delay in writing to you is due to Ida. I talked a three quarters full roll of Dictaphone into the machine some time ago. Ida has not typed it and I catch Hell.

First of all let me thank you once more for the beautiful pencil you sent me. It is surely a peach. I am only afraid I might leave it somewhere so I am showing it to everyone so they will know, should I leave it, who belongs to it. I wanted to write a few words to Celia. By the by I don't think Esther knows anything about Celia for the reason that there really is nothing for me to tell her, so you need not say anything. Miriam has gone over to Newark for a week that she had coming to her out of her vacation.

I might say that Ida showed me that lovely letter of yours in which you all but lost your excitement. Just exactly what it was that Ida told you that so burned you up against your inoffensive partner I cannot imagine, for the letter was sure a hot one. Be it to my credit that I never even batted an eye but just wrote it off mentally to a henpecked and irritated husband and not to any partner of mine. At any rate I might say that I put in enough hours every day to satisfy even you.

Sunday, that is yesterday, I had a birthday and to celebrate the same I was at my desk in the office at EIGHT THIRTY AM and outside of going over to the Veg. Cafe for a bite at one I did not leave it until EIGHT TEN PM. This particularly after Kitty had begged me to come over for supper and I promised to be there early and didn't get there until after they had finished. Telling you these things not because I want sympathy (but) only since you saw fit for one reason or another to complain of my incompetence, indulgence, laziness, and what not. It is because they all want their statements at once and each one so far has caused trouble and worry to straighten out after sundry errors particularly by DAG during the year.

But the above sounds a bit harsh I imagine from a guy that is thanking his partner for a nice new gift so we will forget about it. Really I was not sore because I felt that Ida must have gotten under your skin and gave a coupla yanks.

January 17, 1928

Dear Celia,

The #GET OUTA HERE signal has already flashed which gives me just five more minutes to stay here. I know this is no way to start a letter but I do want to thank you and Miriam and the 'gang' for that nice telegram of remembrance on my birthday. I had it all planned to write on Sunday but I did not get thru until after eight and had to beg the elevator man to let me stay after the building's close and lock up. That's a nice way to spend ones birthday, isn't it?

Got a real nice letter, that is I got it as my share of being a member of 'everybody', from Miriam in which she tells us just exactly what I knew was sure to happen – that she is having a swell time and that you as all your folks are, 'the nicest people ever.' Thanks very much for being so nice to my little sister.

Still running around as a chicken in danger of its head but happy to note that some of my heavy work is lessening as it naturally would when one after another of the impatient birds are set at peace with their completed statements. From the losses some of these gents are finding on their statements it would seem that they would not be in such a grand hurry to find out how they fared.

Louis writes Dave, January 22, 1928, about his problems getting a bookkeeper for the Jewish Community Center now that the present woman, Mrs. B., is leaving. A client who was going bankrupt had a girl, Miss T., he could no longer afford who was drawing $30.00, but the Center only wanted to pay $15.

I have just come away from a fuss with M.B., (who) decided that in view of the tightness of money at the center he must economize and wants to pay a girl only $15.00. You can imagine what a steno-bookkeeper you can get for $15.00. I went down there this early afternoon to talk to him about Miss T whom I offered 25 bucks provided M.B. will be satisfied with her non-stenoging. Soon after he came in he called (in) a young lady and says that so far as he is concerned the young lady is hired for $15.00 a week. I asked her about bookkeeping and she says no, she does not pose as a good bookkeeper but that she did study bookkeeping at Tech High School. Of course I was surprised to hear about that subject being taught at Tech and she says, yes, under the hand of household economics and accounts. So there you are.

I said alright let's see if you can answer this question. Suppose we go out to Mr. Griffit and buy, on account, $50.00 worth of supplies how would you record it in a journal entry. She couldn't do it and complained that it was unfair to ask her such a difficult question. So I said that any first grade student in bookkeeping could answer that one and MB says that this merely proved that our accounts are too complicated and must be simplified. He then says to her to step out that he would settle this affair. Can you beat that?

We had a fuss then and I told him that I was willing to train any intelligent girl who knew something of the fundamentals of Bookkeeping but that I would not teach a green girl any bookkeeping. He then tells me that so far, G&G had recommended him two lemons and that now it was his turn to get somebody for the job.

At any rate we compromised the matter by my telling him that I would have a girl in there to see him (who) was highly recommended to me. The Center is *af zores* (in trouble).

As for Babe, I have him hanging around here at a price of five bucks the week and I fully believe that he earns it. He goes all errands to supply houses, gets me insurance and interest data, computes them correctly, computes and checks on inventory data, writes me a letter or two that I can delegate to him and generally takes away from me much of the routine work that has to be done. I wish the kid knew something about bookkeeping. He could be sent around to some of the places to do a little checking as for instance at the DGS. It does not take very long but when I have to do it, it takes nearly as long as it takes him, and at one buck the day I can afford to let him fiddle with it.

Over the many years in which Louis and Dave struggled to make ends meet they always hoped something would turn up to ensure a comfortable livelihood. While they couldn't raise the capital for investing in Florida, a potential new enterprise came along that looked like their salvation. This time, they went after the golden ring.

There is no record of what brought this business deal to their attention. They must have discussed the Argomite Company in personal conversations, rather than by letter. Their involvement in this project was to begin with Dave in New York, who would get things started while Louis would hold down the accounting fort in Washington, DC and handle local transactions. Once it was established to their satisfaction, Louis would close up the accounting office and move to New York.

Louis kept a copy of the License Agreement with his letters, possibly a preliminary offering, as dates suggest the form was used for prior franchisees. It sets out the details of a franchise to sell Argomite Powder and by-products (one of the first detergents) in the Greater New York area and adjoining counties.

> NOW THEREFORE in consideration of the premises, mutual covenants and agreement of the parties hereinafter set forth and the sum of Ten dollars ($10.00) each to the other in hand paid, the receipt of which is hereby acknowledged, the parties hereto covenant and agree as follows.

Dave and Louis, as licensees, will sell bulk and packaged Argomite Powder in the specified New York Counties. For three years (until January 1, 1929 as written in the preliminary offering) they agree to buy a carload (thirty-six thousand pounds) of Argomite Powder every sixty days. Then they will buy a carload every month for another four and a half years, and after that a carload a week for fifteen years. "In the event that the Licensee shall erect and operate a factory the Licensee shall manufacture and pay the Licensor hereinafter stated royalty on not less than the quantities herein provided for as though same were purchased from the Argomite Industries." The licensee may erect a factory after January 1, 1928.

The price is initially set at eight cents per pound, to be kept at two cents over cost of production "but this price shall be proportionately reduced" over time. The licensee and the licensor are given rights to examine cost and manufacturing records and sales contracts, and the licensor promises to protect the rights of the licensee in the case of sales of the company, patents, etc. There are specifications about advertising, trademarks and brand names, not competing within the sales territory and not selling outside of the assigned territory, and the like. In all, there are twenty-seven clauses providing details of the franchise.

Argomite Industries hoped to collect royalties or sales long into the future. Together, Dave and Louis hoped to build the new business into a viable concern, a franchise for the first detergent company. Little did the parties know that around the corner loomed the Great Depression.

January 22, 1928

Dear Dave,

I just received your letter and called up Glover asking him about the answer to (Herman) Barryman's letter (Barryman was the owner of a chain of laundries and became a financial backer of the Argomite franchise). Glover tells me that Dr. Barton was not well and he just replied this morning.

He does tell me that half-cent is an impossibility from the standpoint of the Argomite Industries because the profit on that to the Argomite Industries would be cut down to a negligible extent. He also tells me that while he has been trying to do all he can personally for us he does think that this is an unreasonable request and that getting Argomite for 5 cents a pound should discourage us from worrying about manufacturing, particularly until such time as the business done in New York warrants it.

I am really inclined to agree with him. I believe that Argomite at 5¢ a pound is cheap enough and surely they do not lose money at that figure, so why should Barryman stop at ½ cent if it really means business. I certainly hope that this will not put a crimp in you. I am having Glover up for dinner Thursday night and then we can probably discuss this further. In the meantime I will see him tomorrow.

Louis, in his January 23, 1928 letter, chastises Celia for not writing often enough. He says he writes two letters to her one. Then he writes:

Miriam came home this morning early and she was crying. How come? Oh, just felt blue. Everybody so wonderful to her. She hated to leave. 'Celia such a darling. Big Sam – just the most wonderful fellow. And Sarah- boo-hoo. I'm a damn fool, but I just can't help it. You know they are the finest people, every one. Edith is such a dear and her Angel-Sammy, a real nice chap, you know so likable. Ruthie? I don't see how they grow so good and *zugeton* (attached) to each other. Seems they each live just for one another. Mrs. Kanster is such a lovable woman, so friendly and kind and so much part of the family just a little sister not at all like an older person. I so hated to leave I could just cry and cry they all made me feel so much at home.'

'Mr. Kanster is so full of fun. He makes you feel as if life holds nothing but joy in it, just a lot of fun, that's all. Oh? Georgie? Sure is a nice kid. Good boy. Always willing to do things for everybody. I like him. (George must have been on his good behavior). I tell you I had the most wonderful time. Sarah is just the finest girl, so full of fun and good natured. I'm going to have a miserable time to-day trying to get over my attack of the blues. Etc., Etc.'

You know, Ceal, I believe Miriam likes you and the family Kanster. At least that's what I would gather from the outburst of speech that Miriam permitted to bubble out of her this morning. I had to leave rather early and left Miriam home still tear-eyed. This evening I was detained at the office until about 7:30. I got home after that and there was Miriam, sitting at the table with eyes red from crying. What's the trouble? Oh nothing. Just thinking about how nice everybody was to her. Even Shnubble was friendly. Came in of mornings to wake her up. That, I believe, is going some, from what I know of the friendliness of his royal highness, the Duke of Shnubble. The pup must have caught something of the friendliness that radiated from the Kanster's last week.

My golly, what did you all do to her? From outward appearances one might think that Miriam cried all day long. Of course, she might have stopped a bit during the working hours. I left her crying in the morning and found her crying at night. Well, it was mighty fine of you. Miriam is not given to idle gratitude. But when the mere mention of the names of the various people in your home starts her off on a cry it means that sincerity abounds. I, of course, am mighty thankful to you and to your folks. Newark surely went over big.

What's this I hear about you being able to get away for a time to do a bit of visiting? Honest? That would be lovely. Let me add my voice to Miriam's and urge you to come up, or should I say down? But one thing. If you don't want to bankrupt me wait a little while. I couldn't possibly work evenings with you in town and if I don't do that now they will hang me. I am afraid to answer the phone lest it be another client clamoring for his statement. But a little while later. Then we'll have more time to devote to pleasant matters and then we'll just tell your bank to go hang and to get along without you for a time. How long can you stay, two weeks? Write me about it.

January 23rd 1928, Celia writes on a new Fidelity Union Trust Company letterhead, listing six branches in Newark, New Jersey, with Capital, Surplus and Undivided Profits over $13,000,000. It is Monday Noon. "I believe Miriam told you of the little time I spent in the office. I expected to get a *mof schetil* (probably meaning headache) every day during her stay as my mind was not on the work and it was all I could do to report each morning at the office. Each morning found me getting in late, two hours and a bit for lunch and home before five. I was indeed very sorry that I could not be with her for a longer period of time.

"I am speaking for the whole of the Kanster family. It was a pleasure to have her with us and her company was enjoyed by all. We miss her and hope she will come here again-and-soon. My father said to me this morning, 'You know Cel, I am sorry that Miriam had to leave so soon.' So you see even my father had to say something about her going.

"Two telephone calls have interrupted this letter and they were from friends of mine inquiring if Miriam had really left and I had to sadly inform them that she did. I was sorry to hear that you couldn't find time to celebrate your own birthday and sure do sympathize with you.

"*It is Tuesday the 24th*, now and I am not going to start a new letter because I won't have time to finish it. I am busy as – never mind what. I was excused from school last week so it means that I have to go four nights this week to catch up. Now do you sympathize with me? I hate the thought of going but once I get there I don't mind."

On "Wednesday Nite at 10:30 PM, January 25, 1928," Celia writes from home that she just returned from art school. "I was very glad to hear that Miriam enjoyed her stay. Edith and Sammy Angel are a bit excited they put a deposit on a two family house – about eight minutes ride from our house. The house will be completed in about two weeks and on February 15th they will take title. They saw the house (by candle light) on Monday, decided on Tuesday and signed the contract on Wednesday. It is a very pretty house and I don't think they will be sorry they bought it.

"I want to thank you and Miriam for the very kind invitation. As much as I would like to go to Washington it will be an impossibility for me to get away. And when you said for two weeks why I couldn't get two days off. You see they just can't get along without me in the office. I told Miriam that I might go on a Sunday when the B&O (Baltimore & Ohio Railroad) have an excursion – but I think it will be too much of a trip for one day."

Thursday, January 26, 1928, Louis promises himself his letter will indeed be short. Well, it wasn't quite as short as edited, but the main points are covered. He still wants two letters from Celia for every one of his because he is so busy. "Last night I had the scare of my life. A very important client of ours called me on the phone and said that their bookkeeper had gone home the day before, sick. Since the man's trouble was heart trouble, and he is rather an old man, it seemed serious.

"Well, of all the things that could happen to me that particular bookkeeper's getting sick is among the worst at this time of the year. He does so much that it would take any two normal individuals – good ones – to take his place. This morning I went over there and lo, and behold, the gent is back at his desk and on the job. Something good has to happen sometimes too, doesn't it?"

   Sunday, January 29, 1928
      Dear Lou:
      What are you doing kidding me along, eh! If your idea is to write two letters to one of mine. Okay, but please don't expect me to write two letters to one of yours.

      I am all alone in the house – the radio on and a letter to you in the writing. The folks are all away viewing the house that Sammy bought. On Saturday I went with Edith to do furniture shopping and she put a deposit on dining and bedroom furniture pending the searching and if everything proves satisfactory they will then move in. We are all thrilled at the new step they are stepping and hope they will be very happy in their new home.

Three hours later the gang came home with some friends and between the dog howling and all the noise, she had to finish writing in her room.

"Are you still working hard? Do you find time to answer Dave's letters? How is he making out? I believe you must miss him quite a bit.

"For the next week or so I will have to take care of my correspondence at home as I have a lot of work to do in the office."

Louis wrote to Celia on Friday, February 3, 1928:

"It is just a little before *Lichtbenshen* (candle lighting and blessing, e.g., before sundown for the Sabbath) and it may be that mother has already *benshed her licht* (blessed her candles). I thought I better write." Since Celia did not agree to write two letters to Louis' one, he added, "Your veto is accepted gracefully even tho it be unwelcome.

"So Sammy and Edith have bung themselves a house. Well, well, I certainly wish them all the luck in the world. They are both very nice people and they deserve all they can get out of life. Lord knows it is too often mighty little.

"As to Dave, well, you guessed it. I do miss him and as for that I suppose he misses me too altho the fact that I need him here and he does not need me for his work might tend to make my missing of him be of a stronger caliber of missing than the kind he feels for me. He was here over the week-end just past tho he was too busy with his family to give me the time that I would have wished him to give me. He is apparently happy in his job and I almost don't blame him. The troubles and *Hartzessenes* (heartaches) of this job here often make me feel like running away. Sometimes I forget all about a client. Then he calls up and reads me the riot act and I suddenly remember about him. Then the other guys get left and so it is.

"I must stop to go home. Pa does not like it when I come home late on Friday nights. By the way, did you notice in to-day's papers that Fall River has sustained a mighty heavy fire? You know, Bell Bersh (Rose's sister) lives there now and I wonder if she was affected. Her husband has a little silk mill over there or has an interest in (one).

"The sun has been asleep these thirty minutes or more. I wonder what progress your excursion trip in the making is experiencing. But be sure to let me know a few days in advance so that I may not make any appointments for that day. During the week, these days, I manage to give away the various hours of my Sunday to sundry clients."

It is February 4, 1928, and Dave sends a long handwritten letter from New York. He is happy about the six new cases Louis wrote about and commiserates on the secretarial problem at the Community Center. "To hell with the job and good riddance. For four years all I and you did was to sweat as we couldn't get a bookkeeper who is also a typist who will work Sundays. Mrs. B. was O.K. But to train $15 girls or even $20, to the dozen different things in that place was a job all its own.

"Yes I'll write a letter, but don't forget this Lou, that we got absolutely nothing from the Center. Not one solitary single, miserable, lousy case. There will be no reduction. If the board has no sense of decency then what more can you expect from them?

"So let the other new auditors get and train the new girl to do all of that work. The Center did us no good and they can't do us any harm. Will this other auditor always do it for nothing in the future as well? Why not have that gentleman donate the $500 to the Center?"

Dave complains about his lack of money to cover Ida's hospital bill. "I just got a letter from her telling me that the grocer has finally cut off her credit and that the gas & electric threaten to cut us off. Damn it Louis, I hate like hell to mention this to you but I'm sending Ida on Wednesday every cent I've got, leaving me only a little more than a week's money to live on. She is getting desperate. See if you can't do something for her.

"Your worried partner, Dave"

This was not the first nor the last time Dave needed money or other services that Louis was asked to provide, despite Dave's taking two-thirds of the income from the practice as it was.

February 7, 1928
Dear Lou:
Sammy is an excellent dress buyer but when it comes to furniture we cannot seem to agree. Every time he starts to talk about furniture it winds up in a battle. We argue for about an hour each evening regarding the style and price of the suites and he finishes up by telling me I am right. The next night he starts all over again and the same thing happens. Though Edith has already put a deposit on dining and bedroom furniture, still it does not prevent him from looking elsewhere for a suite that he might like better. I never knew a man to be so fussy and exacting.

I will think about this excursion trip to Washington some other time because my coming will only disturb your peaceful schedule and I wouldn't want to do that.

Sammy bought a very expensive living room set of Italian hand-made furniture for their home. He spent $1,000. When his mother came over and saw the set, she asked how much it cost. When he told her she said, "Wouldn't $500 be good enough for Edith?" Edith and Celia were in the next room at the time and overheard the conversation. Edith then refused to drive his mother to the train station. Since Sammy did not know how to drive, he had to walk his mother over there. Edith used to call her a *Machashafa* (a devil).

Friday at Two, February 10, 1928

Dear Lou:

The excitement has subsided a little at our house and we are beginning to talk and act intelligently. Sam Hamburg is the *bouncing father* of a baby boy. Sam is bubbling over with joy and a sensible word cannot be extracted from him. You could hardly recognize the same big brother-in-law of mine.

Did your ears burn on Friday noon? I'll tell you a secret. If you were at my house this noon you would have heard yourself being lauded sky-high. I can not say any more because I do not want you to go out and buy yourself a new hat.

The cradle filled with flowers that you so kindly sent Sarah via wire was received and enjoyed by all. We all want to thank you most heartily for your thoughtfulness.

I have been entirely forgotten by the household and feel a little envious that a three day old baby has overruled everybody. He already is considered the boss. The younger they are the more power they have.

Monday is considered a legal holiday in Jersey (Lincoln's Birthday) and I am going to use that day recuperating from the thrilling excitement of this week. Oh Boy, it feels great to be An Aunt, Cel

Monday Morning at 1:15 o'clock, February 13, 1928
  Dear Lou:
  The gang of visitors left about twenty minutes ago and as long as I have a little strength left I am going to write you. Talk about visitors, there seems to be no let up. Ruthie and I have been busy washing dishes since Friday. I never saw so many dishes to be washed at one time. You want me to write about our Baby – How can I. I can't find any words in Webster's dictionary to describe him. We feel as if the baby belongs to all of us and not to Sarah and Sam alone.

  Congratulations are due you too. Being an Uncle is not a novelty with you I understand. I hope your sister Esther is getting along very nicely and has long ago forgotten what she has gone through.

  Sam & Edith were to have taken title yesterday but on account of one clause it was postponed until Monday. Edith was handed the bill yesterday and that is causing considerable trouble. Sammy is right there when it comes to over paying. (The bill was $140 for making a title search for their new home. Edith gave a new lawyer the business only to discover that the normal fee was $50 for a first class attorney.) "My cousin Max Kane was here last night and he said if Sammy gave him the fifty dollars he was giving him $10.00 too much. Edith is getting so tired of it all that she wants to give up the whole idea of owning a home.

  Some man was up (at) our house last night and in fooling with the dials he tuned in Pittsburgh, Cincinnati and Chicago and after showing me how to use the dials I got Omaha, Nebraska. It really was thrilling to get these distant stations. Now I will talk about myself. I won first prize in a bowling tournament. It amounted to $7.00. The girls I rolled against were girls twice my age and size. Not so bad, eh?

It was a tradition every weekend for family members to show up to be fed and entertained at the Kanster house. The girls ran errands, cooked and did the dishes after putting in long hours working the rest of the week. Paula Kanster was the perfect hostess and could not say no to relatives. When Sarah and Edith married, the chores were shared between Celia and Ruthie.

The Kane cousins in particular behaved like prima donnas, expecting everyone to wait on them. Finally, one day when Ruthie was ordered to bring Max Kane something, she told him to get it himself. She then went up to her room and refused to come down and do the dishes. That put an end to the "Tradition."

Wednesday, February 15, 1928

Dear Cealia,

See, all free for nothing, you get an extra 'a' in your name. Generous, I am, no? Gosh, I'm tired. I think it's a mistake for a fellow to work from 9 AM to 10:30 PM every night. Last night I attended a meeting at the home of Leo. After the meeting Leo and I played a few rounds of our one-time favorite two handed pinochle at the ante of 25 cents the hand. Time plays a considerable part in this game so we decided on a limit at twelve o'clock. At twelve the games stood five for me and three for Leo. So, the boy being a sport offers to make it one more game for fifty cents so that he will either have to give me a dollar or nothing. We played and this noon I offered to take him out to lunch for part of the dollar he so graciously handed over to me last night. But you never leave Leo's without a discussion of the various affairs of the town, so I left there at 1:30, got home at 1:50 and the phone woke me up this morning at eight. Don't mind me, Celia, I'm kind of in the mood to be babied.

Talking of babies, I, too, have lately become another uncle. I hardly think I changed much myself as the result of this new nephew – yes she is a boy (Hillel). It was somewhat of a surprise to us until we had a hurry call for Eleanor to pack up and take a flying trip to Syracuse for a time long enough to permit Esther to get well.

I suppose you are wondering what if anything has happened to our new pup. Well, for some unaccountable reason that bird is still hanging around altho even Pauline is now threatening to chuck him out. However, he is still here and I do hope mother and the rest leave him stay there. He is right cute and becoming more and more playful. I notice now that his teeth are getting sharper and longer, I tease him and he growls and bites. But last night when I got in at about two and found that the kitchen door was open – we close it so that he will not run all over the house – I lit up the place thinking that possibly he had already been given the walking papers.

I tried the summer kitchen door and sure enough there he was all huddled up in a sweater given him for the purpose and trying to sleep in the cold room. The minute he saw me he started to play and when I tried to put him back in the cold room he whimpered and cried so much that I just did not have the heart to leave him there. I had to let him into the warm kitchen. Something will have to be done with that pup. Talk about my worries!

Louis obviously liked the puppy, which makes me wonder why he never wanted a pet when I was a child. Of course, I was allergic to most of them but even when I had a family of my own and Kenny, our middle child, begged for a dog, Pop tried to discourage us. Mom, however, was all for it. When we did get a puppy, we asked Pop to help name her, in hopes he would enjoy her when he visited. He came up with "Sassy," and so we named our poodle "Sassy Ago-Go of Sassafras," Sassafras being her kennel name. While my father just tolerated Sassy, she adored him. I think he really liked her but would never admit it.

With all the correspondence and visits over a period of one year, it took a box of Valentine's Day candy for Celia to suspect Louis was seriously interested in her. She writes on February 16, 1928:

Do they all come that way in Washington? You have been so very nice and thoughtful in every respect that it almost hurts. The beautiful heart shaped box of candy you sent me, pleased me very much and I want to thank you heaps for it. I feel guilty that you cannot enjoy with me its contents.

The letter you sent written on a Child's (Restaurant) napkin was a riot. You had the paper twisted every which way and even now I am in doubt if I got it all.

Big Sam is very much afraid the Baby will not get the proper sleep on account of the dog so he is already making arrangements whereby the dog shall not reside at 842. Ruthie is quite upset about this affair and she said, 'If Snowball goes I go.' She is very fond of the dog and will not hear of it being sent away. We all have our troubles.

Big Sam's objections to the Kanster's dog were less significant than those of their doctor, who recommended to give it away because of Papa's asthma. So, they gave the dog to their maid, Ruth, who lived ten miles away. Two days after she took the dog, it ran away but the maid was ashamed to tell the family because she knew how much it would upset them. A month or two later, during a heavy snowstorm, the dog showed up at their doorstep, hungry, cold and bedraggled, crying to be let in. Despite Big Sam's objections, the family kept the dog and never figured out where it had been in the meantime.

Here's another joke Pop might have offered about now.

THE DOG

A woman with an animal cage walked up the gangplank of an EL AL airplane headed for Israel. "What do you have in that cage?" asked the steward.

"My dog Fluffy," she replied.

"Sorry," said the man, "the rules of this aircraft are that no animals shall be permitted to ride in the passenger compartment. Animals must ride with the baggage."

"I will not be separated from my Fluffy," she said.

To which the officer replied, "I do not make the rules, I only enforce them. If you wish to ride on this airplane, you cannot take your dog into the cabin."

After a lot of fussing, she finally agreed to allow them to take her dog to the baggage section.

"The president of this airline will hear about this!" she said.

When the plane was within a half hour of reaching its destination,

*an attendant who had witnessed the incident ran up to the pilot and said,
"Something terrible has happened. You heard about the fuss a lady made
about our not permitting her dog to ride with her in the passenger compartment? Well, I was checking in the hold and I saw the dog has died."*

*The pilot's face went white and he said, "Oh my God, that's
terrible."*

*The co-pilot then said, "We may be able to get out of this. There is a
dog kennel next to the airport. Maybe they have a dog that looks the same
and we can switch it so the lady won't know the difference."*

*"O.K.," said the pilot. "You rush out immediately after we land and
see if you can make the substitution. We will keep the lady occupied and
delay her so you will have a little time."*

*The co-pilot successfully found a dog exactly like the woman's Fluffy.
When the lady was finally through with customs and baggage claim, she
was given the cage with the replaced dog.*

"This is not Fluffy. This is not my dog!" she yelled.

"Doesn't she look like your dog?" asked the pilot.

*"Yes," she said, "She is the spitting image of my dog but she is not
Fluffy!"*

"How do you know?"

*"My dog is dead," was the reply. "I was bringing her here for burial
in the Holy land."*

In his letter of February 19, 1928, Louis writes Dave that a revenue agent
did not believe one of his clients owed no taxes. The agent claimed other
individuals in the same business had prospered. Louis had to do a lot
of extra work to convince him and laments, "That was one damn dumb
trick not charging for the tax work." At a Community Center meeting,
only a few people showed up because of a ball game. The Center figured the accounting was not so difficult anymore, and someone else
should take it over since they lacked funds to hire an adequate bookkeeper. Another firm offered to do the work gratis and chip in some
money besides.

"As for money for Ida I'll be damn if I know where I am to get it
for her. Everybody seems broke and there are a few of the large guys
from whom I cannot get any money as yet. I got David H's $100, but
the rest still cannot be collected. I have jotted down the items that you

and I drew since you left here the 29th of December and what has come in since then. It does seem a mystery of what you are doing with all the money you have received. You drew for 1928, $195.15 and in seven weeks time you got from the UPA $700.00, making a total of $895.15. At the same time I have drawn $242.85. And yet you ask me for more money for Ida. With the F…note gone definitely bad, I have already curtailed myself $25.00 and money due for past rent and the Continental note in a wobbly condition I just cannot draw down to the last cent. Today our account shows an overdraft of $150.93 and when you left here and before the drawings, the OD was $1.85. We'll discuss this at a later date.

"I tried to get the asbestos for your furnace yesterday but the stores close here on Saturdays at 1:00 and they were all closed when I got your letter. Will take care of it first thing next week."

After Louis' napkin letter, Celia was not to be outdone. She sent a handwritten puzzle to Louis, Friday, February 24th, 1928. It took several hours to decipher it.

"My mother took in a colored girl on account of the new addition and the extra amount of work." This is the woman, Ruth, who later adopted and lost the dog. There were now 10 people living at 842 Hunterton Street. "A few days ago the phone rang and as Sarah was sleeping and my mother was out the girl answered the phone. My Aunt not recognizing the voice asked who was talking. The girl replied, 'the maid is speaking.' Immediately my Aunt said, 'Wrong number' and hangs up the receiver. A few minutes later she called again and the girl answered in the same manner. My Aunt said are you sure this is Waverly 9694 and if it is let me talk to Mrs. Kanster – just then my mother came in and solved the problem. The same thing happened when a few of our friends called and when getting the same answer (Maid speaking) hung up – thinking they had the wrong number. Many of our friends know that we never use any help other than a woman for washing. We can't seem to high hat anybody.

"Edith & Sammy will probably move into their new home in a week or two. I am going to be very sorry to see them go, but am happy for helping them fix things."

Sunday, February 26, 1928, Dave is pleased that Louis has hired a man. "Of course out loud comes the wail of the $20 per week. There are approximately 254 work days in a year and as we have not that many clients, we can devote almost one full day a month in each place and in some of them two. The main thing then is to look for new work. Now if you replace the three cases on the next three months – alright and if you cannot, then it will be necessary to permit Mr. Segal to depart when I return. Be a good boy, your old partner, Dave"

Louis has had enough of being busy when he writes Celia on Tuesday, February 28, 1928. "I don't know whether you know Kitty's philosophy. It is simply this that when she gets so busy that there is no chance of getting thru with her work she goes to the movies. Sounds kinda inconsistent but there may be something to it.

"Inasmuch as there would be no fun in just going to the movies, I have decided to give that idea a real test and here is what it will be. This here busy gent is just going to pack up a few duds and is going to try a little Newark tonic. How about it? If Newark, Celia, and the Junior member of the Hamburg family have no objections I shall make my appearance as usual and thru the same telephone at the usual hour. Drop us a line omediatle.

"All right, Cap. Coming right down. Gotta say good-by to the sweetest little girl in Newark."

Celia replies immediately, on March 1. "This letter is going to be short. You see I am replying immediately to your short letter that said so much. It will be alright for you to come here. Don't bother going to the Hotel. I think Edith will be in her new home by then.

"I'm sorry to hear that you are working so hard. Maybe there is something in Kitty's philosophy. See you in a coupla days.

"Maybe you can persuade one of the girls to come here."

March 15th used to be the income tax filing deadline, and it was fast approaching. The whole tenor of correspondence heated up after Louis' trip to Newark.

Monday, March 5, 1928, 10:45 by MY – Time
Dearest Celia,
What a colossal darn fool I have been these many months! But, then, I really didn't know what it would be like to kiss you good-by. But I am a plumb liar. The fact is I hadn't the nerve to try it. I told you before I left that I'd think about you before I should fall asleep for about two hours. (Yet) the reflections were so sweet

that I fell asleep. But to-day! I have been thinking of you all day. My experiment is working much too well. I am thinking not at all about my work but entirely about you. That is all right with me, but every now and then March 15 hits me a wallop on the beezer and I wake up out of my trance, and devote a few minutes to work.

I wish I had about three or four hours' time to use up in writing to you. I could write and write to you and feel quite happy doing so. It is the only substitute I have for being with you since I can't do that. I have never written you a really long letter. Nor will I now because it is too late and I must watch my step this last week before the taxes are due.

A client bawled me out the first thing this morning because I have kept him waiting so long for his return. The funny part about it is that I haven't seen a cent from him since November 1926 and at this writing he owes us $175.00. That is just the kind of guys who WOULD bawl out their dreamy accountant. What do I care? Couldn't I just close my eyes and think back to last night and the night before that and the day intervening and imagine myself sitting near my Dearie and then with the use of just a wee bit more imagination feel myself kissing her? He didn't hear me, but believe me, I laughed at him.

Here I am back once more. Miriam wanted to know if I got you to promise to come out here the first chance on an excursion. I told her that we really hardly talked about that. Another bawl out. 'And I wanted so much to tell you to make sure she comes here soon. Heck.' *Nu*, do her something. I told her that for the price of two cents Unc. Samuel will deliver any message she cared to send you. That didn't satisfy her. It was my fault she forgot to impress upon my mind that I must get a promise from you that you will come. I believe the program called for your friend Bert also. But, of course, that end of it doesn't interest me.

It's late and I am here all alone in this twelve story building. No, that is not quite true. I am not alone. You are here too. The only trouble is that I can't touch you. But I need only to close my eyes to see you. How I did hate to go away this time. I wonder if I will hate so much to leave this world when my time comes to go – without packing. Maybe yes, maybe no. But we won't talk about that just now. I have an idea, from what I could gather last night that you don't care very much for that topic of conversation. So we won't say anything more about that.

See, the letter is growing. If I had the time I could tire you out reading. In fact my Miami roommate, Eddy, once told me that he hates to receive long letters and does not write long letters. Since the time of that telling I have sent him a number of three-page (typewritten) letters and his replies to each were about the size of one-half page of mine. But I failed to find very many complaints of the length of my letters. He even objected when I signed it your Ex-Pal and signed his 'Not your ex-pal but your pal.' However, I haven't heard from him for nearly a year.

Yep, it is getting late. I don't know what I can say to you to thank you for the most delightful time I had with you and with your people. After all, a kiss is so expressive. Properly administered, a kiss could tell you just how I feel about it. But here we are again. A great big BUT. With you out of arms reach I must satisfy myself with merely telling you about it. That is why this is so inadequately expressed. My regards to all the family and all my love to you. As always Your Lou

Signing off at exactly 12:12 'My Time.' It is a pure coincidence but it is the same minute as when the train left last night. L.C.G.

Celia is gingerly making her salutations more affectionate.

Wednesday Nite March 7th, 1928
Lou, dear–
Am I bold for addressing you in this manner? I hardly think I am, so (I'm) taking this liberty. Your letter sounded so sincere and true that I can't help thinking about it and because of the happy and pleasant thoughts I am writing immediately upon its receipt.

So you think you have been lacking nerve to kiss me good-bye before this. If you call it lacking nerve it was one of the traits I admired in you. The fact that you did not kiss me during our early friendship some fine points have been stored away in your favor. I, too, have thought a lot about you since you left. Oh, well. After you left it occurred to me that I hadn't suggested any new sights other than the tunnel trip. Will make up for it the next time you come up – with your permission.

I can't seem to find time to answer your letters in the office because there is always someone or other waiting for something and even at home it is hard to find a minute's peace. Right now with Edith and Sammy, Mother and Father in the new house, Ruth visiting a girl friend, George in the movies I am able to sit down and write for a few minutes.

So Miriam bawled you out. Do you think you deserved it? I think not. I have been called away to answer the phone about ten times so far – there it goes again. Wrong number this time. You confessed to me your liking to write long letters, why not practice it on me. Waiting for it, I am, As ever yours, Cel

It is difficult to imagine taking so long to get up the nerve to kiss someone you love. When we consider how rapidly relationships begin today, and how quickly they often dissolve, it does well to ponder the values we have lost over time. While the "old ways" may seem passé, we should not dismiss them out of hand. After all, Louis and Celia managed to maintain a 67-year marriage with great love, respect and devotion.

Friday nite 6:04 PM, March 9, 1928

Dearest,

Funny how Jews always find good out of things normally considered not so good. Here I always considered myself somewhat cowardly and backward about that good-bye kissing matter and now I learn that it was really a great virtue.

This is really no time for writing letters, of love or of any other kind. It is nearly Shabes. That is the reason why this particular letter will be short – don't laugh. I can write a short one. I am writing to-day as against to-morrow or the next day or the next because it is doubtful in my mind whether I shall have the time to do any writing within the next few days. That's how busy I am. Is there money in it? Damfino.

Did you really think I cared a hoot for the sights you could show me in your part of the country? Well, if you did you were wrong. I cared naught for any of them. All I wanted was to be with you and I was. So what more could you give me? As a matter of fact, if you would know, I should not have liked it at all. It would have distracted me from you. So there you are.

Celia was asked to make a design for Louis' office wall. "You could also make me one for my room. I believe I have no decorations on it at all.

"Ida did a little typing for me. I took her home and on the way I asked her if she heard from you. She did and said that you wrote a cute letter. She hasn't had time to answer but she will. I do want you two to be friends. Ida has her peculiarities and her crazinesses altho I suppose she would get sore if she heard me say that of her. She is all right and fine but so darn sensitive. She always imagines that she is being slighted. Still, she is nice and my partner's wife and we have always been the greatest of friends.

"There you are another so called short letter gone to ruin. It has gone and growed. By golly it is late and dark outside and I can see a bawling out in the making. I hate to keep them waiting for me on Friday nights. Papa does not like it and ditto for mother. That in itself is sufficient to makes me try to avoid coming in late. I am a good son, I am. So we shall stop it here. The only thing I have had in my mind since I came back from Newark besides income taxes is your sweet self. Lovingly yours, Louis C"

Monday afternoon, Mar. 12, 1928
My dear Lou:
I know you are very busy so I promise to stay a short while. Thanks. What a mob we had at our house yesterday, about twenty-five guests. Something will have to be done about this entertaining business. (Everyone was coming to see Sarah and the baby.) After all the guests were a long time gone, Ruth and I were still in the kitchen straightening up.

Edith and Sammy have moved in its entirety and are now settled. It has fallen to my father's lot to awaken Sammy each morning by calling him on the 'phone. Not so bad, if the idea only works, but we are trying to find out who will take the responsibility of arousing my father each morning from his peaceful slumber.

Talking about Sammy reminds me that I am to go there this evening. I hope their flattery does not go to my head but it seems as if this is the only conversation at this time. 'Cel, where is a fitting place for this? Does this chair belong here? What would you put in this corner? Get this for me downtown.' And last but not least, 'Listen Cel, If you are not going out this evening or any other evening I would like to have you come up and help me about –'. And that is what I have been doing, every spare evening.

Now that they have moved we won't have any trouble in finding a place for you to sleep, not that we had trouble before but you seemed to think you were always in the way. Even Edith suggested that any company we might get we should send to her. So you see rooms are aplenty. When I came home Saturday afternoon, I found a letter from you, one from Miriam and one from Kitty.

I am glad that you wrote about Ida (I was beginning to wonder if she had received my letter). I suppose she misses Dave very much. You said that you hoped Ida and I will always be friends, I will have you understand that I knew Ida long before I knew you and that I admire her a great deal. Just as you say she has her peculiarities but doesn't that same thing apply to all of us. Even if she is sensitive it does not alter the fact that I like her friendship and the fact that she is your partner's wife makes it all the more interesting. I am, as ever, and ever and ever, Cel

Louis frantically writes Dave on Friday, March 16, 1928. "At last the long grind of the Income Tax work is over and I should certainly take off a few days to rest up. It is no small matter to work from nine until one AM for days on end not excluding even Saturdays and Sundays. The night of March 14th, I did not leave the office until 3:30 AM and last night I filed my last return at 11:45. I am mentally and physically tired. But that is now over.

"You might think that everything here is all right now that the returns have been filed. As a matter of fact it isn't. I am even more crowded for time now than I was before the fifteenth. For the last month I have been telling all our clients that I am too busy with their tax return work to do any of the regular work. The result of this has been a regular deluge of telephone calls all day demanding immediate attention to matters that I have been warding off these last thirty days."

Louis goes into detail about various clients who will go elsewhere if not satisfied. "Each thinks that his is the only important matter for my attention. But I can only do so much and no more." Louis can't delegate enough work to his assistant because the clients won't accept it. Some need new bookkeepers or secretaries and expect Louis to find and train them. "To make things even worse there are some of our clients to whom you gave your personal attention while here who have intimated that they object to your being away from them for this length of time and unless you return soon they may be forced to dispense with our services. I don't care how you arrange it as long as you come back here at once. Please pull the necessary wires for your immediate leave of either permanent or temporary absence from your UPA (United Palestine Appeal) work in New York. Please let me hear from you at once so that I may be able to tell our clients more definitely when to expect something of the service we are paid to render them."

In an earlier letter, Celia relayed that she had a tooth pulled and that Edith had her appendix removed. On Saturday, March 17, 1928, Louis writes Celia.

Dearest,

First my sincere sympathies to both of you poor children. Right tough to lose an appendix and a tooth out of the same family in the short space of one week's time. What I can't figure out is how one with such beautiful teeth as you have could possibly have need for removing one of those molars from its gorgeous neighbors. As for Edith's appendix I can't say the same thing of that. I sincerely hope that by the time you get this she will be spry and chipper as usual and well on the road to health again. It takes a little while to get over the effects of the ether and the soreness of the incisions but what is that to youth? Just a little unpleasant experience, that's all.

I filed my last tax returns at the office of the deputy collector's on the fifteenth at exactly 11:45. Thaink of it, had fifteen minutes to spare! Leo Freudberg was with me. He, too, had to file some last minute returns. He said something that struck me as being quite true. 'Funny,' he says, 'somehow we always manage to get thru in time. No matter how much work there is and how late we work.'

I should have loved to rest up a bit. But that is as far as it got. Sometimes a little extraneous matter in one's anatomy, such as an appendix or two, is a God-send in disguise. Just think how wonderful it would be if I could take off a couple of weeks to sojourn to the hospital for the removal of such cantankerous concomitant. (Watch those remaining teeth). It would be a non-contestable vacation. Dave would rush back to town and I would have the time to dream sweet dreams and think of my own dear Ceal. In the meantime I shall have to continue to work and toil as if there were money in it.

Have an appointment to talk with David A. over the long distance telephone this evening at about nine. It may result in his return to Washington within a week or so.

We were out to Rose Freudberg's this afternoon to take Edith (Al and Kitty's daughter) over there for a visit – the circumstances are not important and while there Rose asked Babe something about a girl of their mutual acquaintance. Babe has no use for that particular girl and he said so to Rose. Thereupon Rose wanted to know what he desired or wanted of that girl. To which he came right back with the statement that all he wanted was less than he was getting.

After commenting on the remaining tasks of the day, including devising some puzzles to send Celia, he goes on. "Just got thru talking over the phone with Al and with Kitty and did I catch Hell from both of them! Why did I take Edith up to Rose's house of all places? Picked out the other end of town at a time when Al was in a hurry and had to keep some sort of engagement. Nu, I'll leave their daughter alone hereafter. With Much love and mental hugs and kisses."

March 21, 1928
"My dear Lou:
"How could you? Your last card puzzle was a wow. I have not as yet been able to fathom it out." Celia says if Louis were there, she would give him a good punishment for sending it. She is happy to report the

missing tooth has been long forgotten and is thankful it is out and Edith is coming along very nicely. She asks if Dave is coming back and if so when and reports it is the first day of spring and how lovely the weather has been. Work is light. "This lunch hour I am going to L. Bamberger & Co., and paint a plaster cast that I bought some time ago. I hope it turns out as nicely as I expect it too. We shall see.

"Now that income tax time is over and all tax returns in, why not rest up a bit but not the method you suggest. Did you think of the hospital as the only escape, all by yourself? 'Fess up now."

March 22, 1928

Lou dear:

I have been elected again to write you upon the receipt of a box of candy for Edith. I saw her last night and she wants me (as she puts it) to thank you from the bottom of her heart and of course I want to thank you too for your kind thoughts of my Sister. She is getting along very nicely and expects to be home Monday. I am going to see her again in about ten minutes.

I painted on a plaster cast a ship and it turned out very pretty. I left it on our radio to dry and along comes our Doctor admiring it to the extent that my mother promised I would paint one for him (and) that is how I am going to spend this coming Sunday. As soon as I find something that I think you will like I will paint one for you. Yes! Big Sam is waiting for me and he said if I don't hurry I will have to take the Bus up. So long mit Love and Regards.

Unfortunately, Celia did not save any of the plaster of Paris paintings she made, and she made them for everyone but herself. On March 24, Louis sent her a couple of mind twisters "inspired by Child's pea soup and other eatments" and promised, "two kisses and one hug."

My dearest dear,

Someone once said that he might just as well be hung for a sheep as for a lamb. So far you have guessed two and failed on one. That makes me owe you. One of these two I am now sending is a rather easy one the other not so very easy. I stand ready to read all the cards I ever sent you and I feel a deep hurt in the regions of my puzzlelaria concoctimis for what you said about those things just merely having been put together without rime or reason.

Spring has been prancing all over to-day and I have been too danged busy to enjoy it. But I really have no kick coming. One trip to Newark is enjoyment enough for me to last me about a month when I can't get any more in between. Watch for me again about the fifteenth of April.

David A. is due here to-morrow night and I have enough nice jobs for him here to keep him busy for a nice little while.

If you knew what is worrying me now you would surely sympathize with me. Such is the penalty of fame that I have been invited to attend a banquet to-morrow nite and to make a speech there. Get that? MAKE A SPEECH. Moly Hoses! I'mmm alll nnerrvousss alllrreaaadddy. One of our new and best clients – the District Grocery Society Stores, Inc. is having its annual banquet. The President (of the DGS has asked me) to make a speech as is befitting the station of auditor of such an organization. Luckily for the guests they won't know what is in store for them until after they will have eaten and will not therefore suffer the loss of appetite that would surely assail them if they heard me first. The funny thing about it is that I have not the slightest idea at this writing what it is I am going to afflict them with. The best bet at such a time I believe is to tell them some jokes but it seems that I can't think of one joke.

I don't know why it is that the good Lord always sends me such nice jobs. To make to-morrow nite complete for disenjoyment I must inform the bookkeeper I have to fire her. Bang! Maybe she'll be able to console herself with the fact that she doesn't care to work for an accountant who makes such a rotten speech anyway.

I may be a hard guy but I do hate to fire people especially young ladies after a banquet. I was trying to tell her this afternoon that she need not come in on Monday but I just couldn't. She had been talking so much about how nice an affair it would be that I couldn't spoil it for her. So I have decided to leave it until after the party. The lady is just no good for that job. If they won't do as I say OUT THEY GO. But really it is a darn shame about that girl. She no more expects to lose that job than she expects to fly under her own power. Wow, I wouldn't like to be her escort home tomorrow nite. Oh, well. Other people have been fired before her and she has hopes of having it happen to her again.

But to talk of *heimlechere sachen* (pleasant things). When may we expect to see you in this beautiful town? But honestly Sweets, you should come and give us a chance to collect or deliver those kisses and the hug. I am sending along now.

The sight for that plaster cast has been carefully selected and all is in readiness to receive and house that piece of art. As for your query, how will you know what I shall like? But then, of course you know, I shall like anything you make.

'Flo was fond of Ebenezer
Eb, for short she called her beau,
Talk of tides of love! Great Caesar!
You should see them, Eb and Flow.'

My love, Lou C. Gee

Louis did not keep a copy of his speech or the joke he chose to tell. Considering the audience were grocers, he might have used this one.

HALF A LETTUCE

A clerk in a grocery store goes over to his supervisor and says, "I have a crazy customer who only wants half a lettuce." Just as he finished saying this, he saw the customer walk up behind him, so he said, "And this fine gentleman here wants the other half."

After the customer left, the super came back to the clerk and said, "That was fast thinking. I have been keeping my eye on you and have decided to make you the manager of our new store in Chicago."

The clerk said, "I ain't going to Chicago."

"Why not?" Asked the super.

"Only fools and football players live in Chicago."

"Take it easy," said the super, "My wife comes from Chicago."

"What football team did she play on?" asked the clerk.

Wednesday, March 28, 1928

My dear Lou:

I have only two minutes to spare so please do not be angry if I write a very short letter. I have been out of the office from 11 o'clock to 3 o'clock for no other reason than to go home and get some sleep. Mother has not been feeling well the past week and we all at home have been quite worried about her. I believe it is just the reaction of the illness of Sarah and the illness of Edith. When mother gets better we are going to persuade her to go to Baltimore to visit her sister and at the same time forget about us at home.

Do try and come here the week-end of the 14th, it will be very nice if you can manage to steal away for that time. When are the Cherry Blossoms due to bloom in their full glory? I hear so much about them that I would like to come out for a day or two during that time, providing of course that it is all right with you, your folks and everybody else.

Lou, I don't mind receiving cards if I can at least read them. Please, I beg, I implore, I beseech you to send me easy cards to read. It seems I haven't the knack to stand on my ear and translate them so am waiting for you to come here the middle of next month and show me how. Did Dave get back? Let me know all about his return.

P.S. I have two plaques finished. When you come you can take your pick.

Friday Eve, March 30, 1928

My dear Lou:

Received your telegrams and liked them better – if I may say so, than the cards. As to the Cherry Blossoms, Lou, I am sorry I will not be able to get away before the 8th of April. How long after the 8th will they be in bloom? Of course you know that is not the reason I would like to visit in Washington. Though I will admit I would like to see them when I come. I think it best to wait until you get here before I decide on the time.

April 2, 1928

Dearest Ceal,

This letter is long overdue. Miriam is here in the office and it is past eight o'clock. She would like to go to Kitty's and play some bridge (so) I thought I'd accommodate her and take her over.

You cannot come over for the eighth? Well, I'm sorry. However, the weather has been rather cool all this time and that means that we shall probably have no Cherry Blossoms this early in the year this season. Possibly there will be an opportunity to see them soon after I return from Newark, on the 22nd perhaps. Yes, I do think I shall be able to get away the week end of the 14th. Glad?

The funniest thing ever happened to me Sunday morning. Dave and I were at work at the office of a client at about 11:00 when I get a phone call from Eleanor saying that she located me thru calling Ida to tell me that I had a guest. Who, says I, Herman from Philly? No, she tells me, it is Celia from Newark.

Immediately I got excited. Where is she? At the station. I'll go right up and call for her. No, Eleanor says, don't do that as she said she would take a taxi. Well, in that case I'm coming right home, says I, quite bubbling over with excitement. Would it inconvenience you very much, she asks. What difference does that make? I'll close the desk and leave right away. No, she says, needn't be in such a hurry – it's April Fool, you know.

Well, I tell you that was put over so well that I took it in – altogether, hook, line, and sinker. Eleanor played the same thing on all of them at the house and also on Kitty (who) took it in real well, too. She was going to prepare a heavy supper and no changes permitted. Can you beat that for a good one?

Rose Freudberg gave birth to a very lovely little 9-pound four baby boy. His *Brit* (religious circumcision) took place yesterday at the hospital and they named him Richard Lee. I was quite busy with various matters connected with the affair one of which was going to see Rose at the hospital with Kitty. My love to you and I wish you and everyone a very happy Pesach.

Friday, April 6th, 1928

My dear Lou:

Oh! What a beautiful day. No work today on account of it being Good Friday. I want you to get this letter before Monday (so) I am going to the down-town post-office and mail it. I wouldn't do that for everybody you know.

I was sorry to learn you were fooled on April 1st and to think I was the innocent cause of it. Had I known they were going to fool you I would have made an appearance and the joke would have been on them. I did get a good laugh out of it and all at your expense. Leave it to Eleanor.

I am just getting over a party I attended a few nights ago. I was given to understand it would wind up as a Bridge party. After arriving in the house I found it to be decorated in the most elegant fashion and the gowns the girls wore were beyond my pocketbook. I knew a few that were there and after being introduced to the rest I realized it was no place for me so I wanted to go home.

They were of the Bohemia type and talk about smoking I thought I was in a Boiler factory. I felt out of place and like a poor hick from a small town on her first visit to New York. My partners were such sharks that I had no show whatsoever. The next time I go to a party I am going to ask if it is going to wind up in bridge and if it is I am staying at home.

I am glad to know that you will be able to make a visit to Newark on the 14th. Let me know details. I will try and be home early.

Louis seems to have proposed during his visit to Newark on the 14th. However, something else happened. He sent this letter dated April 16, 1928, in a very sad frame of mind. Possibly Celia's experience with Bill made her want to be sure.

My Beloved Hard-Hearted Sweetheart,

Just got into the office quite altogether bawled up. I don't know whether I am here or there. Funny how a little girl can mix up such a tough guy as I am. But by golly she did. And there is another thing she can do, no there are two things more. One is to tease a poor fellow to death or near it and the other is to wield a paint brush. Darling, you put it over big with that ocean roamer. Buy yourself a copy of last week's *Collier's* and read a story in it called the *Magic Carpet*. I think your boat – MY boat – will change the looks of the old living room.

I'll get fired for writing this early in the morning of things of love. But how can I help it? You laugh at me when I tell you about it but here I can't hear you. What an unromantic atmosphere an accountant's office lends to the writing of a love letter.

Despite your own feelings in the matter I still love you. And let me say right here, while the saying is good and before David A. drifts in to interrupt the writing of this, that I am much displeased. I am beginning to think that I don't know you after all.

That little question of yours – 'How do you know I care for you' – is something the which I don't know how to take. If I were an experienced love-maker I suppose it would have had some sort of a meaning to me. But being as amateurish as I am I'll be dog-gone if I know what to think of it. So I will do the obvious and not think of it at all.

Since writing the above I have had to take this out of the machine and do a day's work. Right now it is near eight in the evening and I am awaiting the arrival of a client whom I have invited here so that, among other things, we could discuss our fee upon which he has recently begun the propaganda for a reduction of one hundred berries the year. I'll have it out with him. In my mood I could throw him out of the window only for one thing he owes me money and for another there are only three stories to the street from here and that would not be effective enough.

If I lived in New York or in Paterson I would be over tonight and would ask you how you felt about me tonite. I would ask you again to let me buy you a ring to decorate the beautifully tapered finger, which would tell the world that you are mine and I am yours. Oh, sweetheart, why don't you tell me that you love me and that you will marry me?

Dave wanted to know if I am to be congratulated and if not why not. Nu, go tell him that you laughed at me. I told him I would let him know when there was something to tell him. I know he thought I was holding back on him, but he could not consistently press me further. He told me last week that his greatest regret at leaving here is that he would not be able to be present at my wedding. And then he says, 'Say, why don't you get married next month before I leave?' I smiled at that and told him that he must not be in such a rush. I didn't guess, however, that he might leave before even I were engaged. But, no, you wouldn't let that happen, will you? You know, you made me very unhappy, dear.

I do hope that by the time I see you again, your mother will be perfectly well. I am hoping that your frame of mind yesterday and the night before was actuated by worry over your mother's condition.

Speaking of your mother reminds me that Mamma will write a letter to your mother, in Jewish, telling her what is, in her experience, a good remedy for her ailment. You will probably laugh it off and forget it, which I suppose will be all right. However, I have personally observed the healing powers of mother's remedies and they are good. And she offers them in good faith, and in all sincerity.

Please convey my regrets to Edith, Sammy, Sarah, Sam, Ruthie, George, and last but by no means least, your mother, that I was unable to say good bye to them. The circumstances of my inability so to do are well known to you, I think. And by the by, I picked up a taxi on the corner and had ten minutes to spare.

Thank your entire family for having been so nice to me, but in so doing, please exclude yourself. There is only one way in which you can be nice to me and you know what that is. And let me say, Miss, that merely permitting me to kiss you good-bye is not 'being nice' to me. Now, aren't you ashamed? The guy who said, 'You never know women' surely knew whereof he spake. I LOVE YOU. Do You Love Me? In love, but much perturbed, Louis

Celia replies two days later.

Dearest Lou,

Please don't say I am hard-hearted because I never knew I was and not wanting to acquire any more faults I will be patiently waiting until you write and say it was just a slight error on your part.

I hope they all liked the boat. Maybe some day we will be able to take a long trip in it and forget all about my being hard-hearted. Oh! How dem woids do hurt (I mean hoit).

I am going to explain my question 'How do you know I care for you.' You have told me of your love for me but did you ask me at that time whether or not I cared for you? No. So I merely asked how did you know I cared for you. You did ask me some time later but my head was all clogged up on account of Mother's illness that I couldn't think of myself at all. Knowing what every ache and pain in her hand might lead to I was naturally, worried.

Silly, I did not laugh at you. I do care for you else I would not let you come to see me. I did want a little time to think of your love for me because the man I marry must love, love and love me forever. Do you think you are capable of having that much love for me? I am sorry you said I wasn't nice to you. Would you say that now? I don't believe you meant it at all.

Mother is feeling fine now and is on the long road to health. Thanks for your good wishes. She received your Mother's letter and was very happy with it on account of the spirit in which it was sent. Your mother is a perfect dear and for that she will get an extra kiss from me. Tell her just as soon as my mother is able to use her hand she will write her and when she goes to Baltimore a visit to your home will be on the list. By the way, I understand your folks do not approve of anyone riding on Saturday so I don't believe I should consider leaving Newark on a Saturday afternoon to visit you all. As that is the only time I can get away until my vacation, I am going to leave the next move to you. Let me know.

I got a copy of *Collier's* and read the short story you suggested. The story was right nice but too far fetched. Regards to everyone and much love from your soft-hearted sweetheart. Cel

Louis enthusiastically answers the next day.

"Darling Sweetheart,

What a wonderful letter I just received from you! So you really do care for me after all? Such is my love that at the mere doubt of your feelings toward me I became much alarmed. I was afraid that I might lose you even before I had you. Isn't this proof enough that my love is real? And yet, dearest, deep down in my heart I knew that you did care for me even tho I was afraid I might be wrong. Forgive me my fears and my doubts as to the texture of your sweet heart.

I am due elsewhere right now but I could not let time go by without telling you again that I love you with all the love of which I am capable. How much that is, I do not know myself. However, I am ready to match your love for me with my love for you. No wife should want more from her husband, should she? Did you get that, my wife and your husband? Hot Dog!

Talking about ships, do you know what Isabelle (Rose's sister) said to me Sunday night? She said the boat trip from here to Fall River should make us an excellent honeymoon appetizer. After the way I felt from the night before I wasn't so much interested in that. Now honeymoons are subjects of real thought consideration.

This is a very short letter for the reason that I can't think straight. If it were warmer I should seriously consider taking off the day to park myself near where the Cherry Blossoms were and spend the day in day dreaming. I feel like embracing the typewriter but the darn thing is so unsympathetic.

Sweetheart, I'm in love. I'm in Love. I AM IN LOVE. Will write of your coming here in a day or two. With tenderest love, Lou

Love and Kisses, also Hugs

He writes again on April 21, 1928.

Darling Sweetheart,

This is Saturday afternoon or rather nearly evening it being about 5:45. I have many things to do but I can't start any of them until after I have had my few words with you. Somehow, I can't write as easily as I used to anymore. The one thing uppermost in my mind is that I love you, and you – maybe – love me. I say maybe because you have not told me that you do. Your letter, now that I read it again for the ummth time tells me that you care for me.

Now what do you mean, 'care?' Let's see what Mr. Webster has to say about that word:

CARE: A burdensome sense of responsibility; trouble caused by onerous duties; anxiety; concern; solicitude. (Take your pick. Not a good one in the lot. But let us look further)

TO CARE FOR: (a) To have under watchful attention; to take care of. (b) To have regard or affection for; to like or love.

The last of those sounds something like it. There seems to be doubt, however, for, otherwise, why should they put it at the very last? How about it, dearest, do you love me or is it a 'burdensome sense of responsibility' that you have for me? How can a fellow tell when you say 'care' at a time that he craves to hear 'love'? Or can it be that I am an object of 'trouble caused by onerous (oppressive) duties'? No, I won't believe that. It cannot be true because if it were, why did you come downstairs and let me kiss you good-bye?

The fact is that you did not mind my kissing you altho you did nothing to help unless of course you consider it a help that you came downstairs. By gosh, it was a help, now that I think of it for I could not very well have kissed you in the presence of your father under the circumstances of the uncertainty of my position in the affections of my precious Ceal.

On the other hand, your coming downstairs may have had no such motive at all. Perhaps you had me 'under watchful attention' and felt that you would be lax in your duties if you did less than see me to the street door. Oh, sweetheart, what is the matter with me? Why do I think these things? Isn't it enough that you tell me that you care for me? Shouldn't that immediately lead me to the feeling that you love me really and that is all you meant when you said care? Perhaps it should, but love wants to be assured, over and over again. No perhapses and no maybes.

Tell me in your next letter absolutely and with words and in terms that cannot be mistaken. Do you still wonder that I may not be able to love you and love you and love you forever and ever? Well, dear, you shouldn't. I feel that I will always love you and I pray that you may feel the same towards me always. Is that an idle prayer?

TO CARE FOR: To have regard or affection for; to like or *love.* Maybe you do love me after all. Do you think of me sometimes, sweetheart: Why aren't you here, dearest, instead of so far away that I must write instead of tell you how much I love you?

Saturday, you are right. My folks don't like it if any of us ride on *Shabes.* However, what they don't know will not hurt them. I ride always and they don't know about it.

Say next Saturday, get on the train after work and ride over here. That will bring you here about seven or eight o'clock. I will meet you at the station and we will go somewhere. Let me figure that out. Then, at about twelve, we will go home and we will tell the folks that you got on the train at about seven and here you are. Somewhat deceptive, but I would rather have it that way than displease father and mother where you are concerned. So far as that is concerned they will love you anyway, ride or no ride, but I want no reservations to the wholeheartedness of their love for you. You understand, don't you, darling?

I have so many things to talk to you about. It is hard to tell it on paper. And do let me know the very truth about how your mother is getting along. I am old enough to be able to bear whatever truth there is. I told mother what you said about your mother stopping over here when she goes to Baltimore and she was very happy. They should get along wonderfully.

I hate to part with you even when that parting means merely the ceasing to write. What does that indicate? That I am in love with you, of course. Are you glad? I must go now, darling. Your love-saturated sweetheart, Louis

"My Dearest Lou," Wrote Celia on April 23, 1928. "I came into the office a few minutes ago and read your letter for the second time. I couldn't read it with the same feeling at home (with) the whole family being at home for lunch at the same time. Was I glad to receive it! I'll tell the world. You made me very happy saying the nice things you did.

"Talk about defining words, I don't think there is a dictionary in the whole world that can describe accurately the word LOVE. And as for your definition of the word 'care' I don't care for it much. I have a definition that I made up by myself that I like better than your Webster's. Knowing what I know about my definition I will say it again. I do care for you. Now figure that out. But it seems that you are not satisfied with the word 'care.' Why not wait until I see you, then I will be able to say the words you want me to say. I think it would sound nicer were I to tell it to you instead of writing it, don't you think?

"Dear, why do you think of the most unreasonable reasons for my going downstairs and kissing you good-bye? Since you are questioning the kissing episode I will put it to you thusly, telling you the honest to goodness reason. I wanted to be with you a few seconds more. Are you happy now? Please do not doubt me. Let me assure you if I did not want your love I would not permit you to kiss me.

"Your prayer is not an idle one – that I love you as much as you love me. Why not pray together so that we will learn to love each other equally as much. Yes?

"Mother is getting along very nicely. She is still under the Doctor's care and is under a very strict diet. As far as that is concerned I could come out the 28th but it will have to be postponed until the 5th of May. I want to paint a plaque for Kitty and it will take a week to ten days to do it. As long as I intend making it, I better wait until it is finished so I can take it with me when I go. With all the love you expect from me, Celia"

"So you don't know what to put on paper so it will sound like a love letter?" Louis replies the same day. "Does that mean that you want it to sound like one? If I thought that – that is to say if I felt positive of it – I shouldn't mind it if it doesn't sound so love lettery. You see, you won't tell me out and out that you love me just as I tell you. Aren't you certain or what? As it is no girl has ever told me that she loved me for the very obvious reason that I have never told any girl but you that I love her. Which places me in the position of not knowing how it feels to be told such a thing as that. And you, my love, while hinting around it, do not seem to wish or know how to tell me. You surely will have something to make up for when next I see you. Do you think you can do it?

"With me it seems easy and natural to write to you of love. Why? Not that I am practiced. Lord knows I have never written one before some weeks ago. It is just that I put on paper just how I feel. Perhaps I am a good writer, that is provided, of course, that my letters sound like love letters, and therefore am able to put down on paper what is in my heart. I must say that, else I shall have to presume that your heart holds no love for me. See, dear, there is no other way out. You must tell me.

"Hard-hearted? Well, I can't say now either way. I have your word to the contrary but my indictment was the result of your actions or rather inaction and only action can nullify that accusation. All of which means that you shall have to wait until I see you before you will know how I feel about your hard, soft, kind, sweet-heartedness.

"Why not ask Edith for some instructions in love letter writing. She should know being so newly wedded. Or possibly you can get some tips from Sarah; there seems to be little doubt of the quality of her love for Sam the Big. As a last resort you might ask me.

"Dearest, I am really and truly in love with you. I know it because I think of you all the time. I can't even feel any animosity toward the steady downpour of rain that has not halted in its steadiness these last three days. I am happy and at peace with the world. I'm in love and that is all there is to it. I have a feeling of wanting you in my arms of wishing to kiss your eyes, your nose, your lips, your dimply chin, your hair, oh, everything about you. That sounds like love, doesn't it, precious? And you ask if I will be able to love you always. Do you doubt it?

"I must go now, dear. This makes the third letter I have written you in the last few days. I have received but one from you. And that one didn't say I LOVE YOU. But maybe the next one will.

"Plaques? Why certainly Kitty loved that piece of art I brought home. She will be tickled with joy with anything you think will be suitable for her wall. Just send it along and see. In the meantime, to avoid turning the page, I'll stop. As ever your Sweetheart, Lou"

Two days later, Louis replies contentedly. "Dearest Love,

"It is eight fifteen and I have returned to the office for the express purpose of writing to you. Why? Because it is a pleasure and a privilege. A privilege because no other male person in the world has the right to say to you that he loves you and get away with it. This of course excludes fathers and brothers.

"Your letter, received yesterday, was good. The only fault that I could find with it was that, like its predecessors, it stuck to the 'care' and refused to say Love. I certainly have high hopes for your private definition of yon word. It should be even better than the commonly accepted term of the word 'love' to justify your holding out for it in place of any other word. I'm waiting to hear you tell it to me. When it comes to that, tho, no amount of telling can equal one little showing. You could demonstrate your meaning a good bit better with a little action than you could tell about it in a week.

"I hinted around at home that you might come over on the fifth and that settled the matter. You are due here on the fifth of May. We are a selfish gang, however. We are not satisfied with just a day or two. We want more. I have a proposition to make. On the 8th of May, that is on Tuesday night the local United Palestine Appeal comes to an end with a banquet and it costs a minimum of $25.00 per each person or two for $30.00. Of course the money goes for Palestine and we contribute our sixty dollars every year, banquet or no banquet. You are cordially invited to remain over till Tuesday night and be present at the banquet. You should be able to get off for two measly days, now shouldn't you? How about it?

"Miriam was much displeased when I told her that you expect to stay only one day. 'Then we probably won't see her at all,' she says. What makes you so sweet, dearest? Sisters aren't usually crazy about their prospective sisters-in-law. I can only explain it by saying that it is you. This reminds me to tell you that I have not said anything to the folks at home as to status of our relationship. Everybody is curious to know when. I have not said anything because I want to be absolutely certain. Now I think it will be better for both of us to tell them. We'll step up hand in hand to mother and father and tell them that we are engaged to marry each other.

"They used to ask them in the olden days. Now they don't ask any more. They tell them. But I'll leave that to you. I am ignorant of matters of that kind and do not know what is proper to be done so far as announcements are concerned. Possibly it is more fitting to tell your folks first, I don't know. However, I do think that you and I should have that little vocabulary explanation session first before we tell anything to anyone officially.

"I am reminded a bit of the conversation that passed between Fanny and me at the wedding of Edith and Sammy. Fanny and I were dancing and Fanny says to me, 'Louis, I do think that you should tell me about yourself and Celia.' 'Perhaps you are right, Fanny,' said I. 'But don't you think there are at least two others who should know first?' She looked at me kinda funny and laughed. I think she was satisfied that I wasn't holding anything out on her. Isn't life and love just the strangest pair of experiences on earth? They sure is.

"Well, lovely, I guess this will be all for tonite. I am happy to learn that your mother is coming along well. This is no time of the year for anyone to be sick, least of all your dear mother. Kiss her for me and shut your eyes and imagine that I am kissing you good-nite. Your constant love, Lou C.

"I Love You. You Care for Me. God Bless You. Care = great LOVE, Does it?"

April 26, 1928

My Dearest Lou,

I am glad you are taking the right interpretation of the word that has caused a good deal of discussion. Since you know what it means there is no use in keeping it back, so I might just as well say it now. Lou I do love you. I hope you will be able to make me as happy as I hope to make you. Fair! I will honestly admit I didn't realize until your last visit here and your subsequent letters that I was honestly and truly in love with you. See what you made me say. Lest you forget I am timid and shy.

Yes, I do think of you all the time. I can't help it. Your letters and my replies make me think of you all day. I am not complaining, Sir. I didn't expect to say all this until next Saturday evening. Maybe I have some more to say. It is all your fault you made me tell you now.

Thanks for your invitation. I might be able to accept. In order to give the Chief Clerk plenty of time I am going to ask him the first thing tomorrow morning and we shall hear what he has to say. I am going to suggest that he deduct it from my vacation period otherwise I am afraid I will be out-of-luck.

Yes, I am very glad your sisters like me. It will make things more pleasant and agreeable all around. But then why shouldn't they. I like them all immensely and am praying that my feelings are reciprocated.

(I am being called for supper). How about your folks – they hardly know me. I hope they too will *care* (underlined 3 times) for me.

Will I have to take the 9th of May off? I suppose the affair will last too late for train time. You know daylight saving time starts next Sunday. If I do get the days off do you still want me to come in Saturday evening? Let me know.

Lou, dear I feel so happy now that I told you of my love. Do you feel happy too? I don't know as I will be able to eat. There goes Ruth calling me again. Dearest you have all my love now – somehow or other it doesn't seem to belong to me, you must give me all yours in its stead. In Love, Cel

An impatient Louis writes on the same date:

I was expecting a letter from you to-day but it did not show up. How come? You know, dear, I shouldn't write you so often. For one thing you don't seem to be able to keep up with me – this is the third letter you will owe me by to-morrow the mailman will surely begin to complain.

I haven't told Kitty that you are making something for her. I think it will be the more appreciated if it comes in the nature of a surprise. She will surely be tickled with it because, if you make it, it is certain to be great. You see, darling, I have great faith in your ability to do fine things. That is just why I love you – you are so very fine altogether.

Our typewriter is being repaired and this one (is) for our use during the absence of our own. It writes very well. I like the touch and everything. Imagine how much better a machine it will be after it leaves here for having had the honor of delivering messages to you.

Say, dear, why not get away from the office on Friday noon and make the trip here in time for Friday night? That would give you a four days' vacation here – Friday night to Tuesday night, both inclusive. Wouldn't that be just grand!

The office? Oh, heck with them. Tell them to go hang for a few days. To-day was a little warmer and we had a glimpse of what to expect later on in the year. The tree tops are beginning to show green and some of our narrower streets are becoming overhung with the spreading of the leaves from side to side of the street. It will not be long, pretty soon, before spring in all its glory will be among us and what more could I ask than to have you beside me as we walk thru the park telling me what it is that you have in mind when you say 'I do care for you.'

I got ticketed two dollars worth to-day for overtime parking. Do you think I care? Certainly not. Why should I when my own baby in Newark cares? Oh, sweetheart, I'm just nuts over you and if you still have any doubts about it I shall have to say it in red ink. SWEETS I LOVE YOU (in red ink). Do you know, dearest, I like being in love. The only drawback to it is this constant having it in mind. I'm afraid I might run into something all the time thinking about you. But I guess I won't.

Friday, April 27,

My Dearest Lou,

I thought I was doing very good with my correspondence and here you come along and say not so good. I am heartbroken now, you better keep on writing to me else I won't get over it. And don't you worry about our mailman over-working. I'll take care of that. I believe you have received my letter by this time and know that I love you – There I go again. It seems I could go on saying it forever. Yes, sweetheart, I too am in love. Isn't it a grand and glorious feeling?

When I asked the Chief Clerk for a few days off he quickly said 'sure' (here is where the catch comes in) drawback #1 – providing it is deducted from my vacation, Drawback #2 – If work of importance turns up it will be impossible for me to get away. You see, I only heard the word 'sure,' the rest I can't understand. Should he make me stay there will be war in the office. Now that I have set my heart on going nothing will stand in the way. I just can't wait 'till next Saturday night.

I am busy painting the plaque for Kitty. My fingers are covered with paint. What do I care? I am happy because you like my work. Georgie said if I don't hurry he won't wait to mail this letter and as I got a bawling out this letter is going out tonight.

Dear, just keep on thinking of me as I am of you. I don't know what the trouble is but I can't seem to write right. Maybe it is Love. With all my Love, Cel

Louis' letter of April 28, 1928 was written from Potomac Credit Bureau, Clarendon, Virginia:

Darling Sweetheart,

I won't hold out a thing for this letter. The fact is I am over at Kitty's for the first time at this office of hers and I am trying to snatch a chance to write to you. I am afraid, tho, it is too fraught with possibilities of her stealing a glimpse. I put her to work on some of her books but there is no knowing how long she will stay put. She took me to the movies this afternoon and then kidnapped Miriam and me to come up to the house for supper and some bridge. In the writing of this much I have been disturbed only three times so far. This is a devil of a place to write you in reply to that very wonderful letter. You know, dearie, hang it, here she comes again. I am beginning to realize that timid girls aren't in the habit of coming out and saying that they love somebody even if they do. And here I made you say it. I am tremendously glad.

Funny the way Kitty comes up to ask me a question that I cover up the machine roller so she won't be able to read what I am writing, the *gonev* (thief).

Sweetheart. Right now let me say that I and the whole town, are eagerly awaiting your coming next Saturday night. By the way if you can pick up radio station WMAL, a small Washington station on Monday evening, early – the exact time is not yet known to us – you will hear Pauline's concert. Kitty has finished and I have to leave here at once. She has this suggestion for a good-bye line, 'Your candied sweet potato darling,' Louis

Celia writes on April 29 1928: "One cannot concentrate with a baby and radio going at the same time. Lou I am a very poor writer of a love letter. If you can read between the lines I am sure you will be able to understand. The fact that I went out to the corner store to buy a box of writing paper should not pass unnoticed. Also that I try and answer soon after the receipt of a letter from you is another point to remember. When I see you I will try and make up the deficiency in my love letter writing. I wonder if you are writing to me now. I sort of feel it in my bones that you are. Wouldn't it be a coincidence if it were true?

"By the way you didn't say whether or not I am hard-hearted. I wouldn't like it for a row of pins if you still think of me as being hard-hearted. With all my love to you dear, Cel"

April 30, 1928

My Timid Little Lovely,

At last I am alone for a few minutes, at least. I have been trying hard for the last few days to get into a corner alone where I could tell you how happy I am that you have come right out and have said, in so many words, that you love me. I have been walking on air ever since Friday afternoon when I got your letter. And to-day there was another one and that one, too, told me just what I had been praying would happen. This is my lucky month, indeed.

Something else happened to-day which may some day make a lot of difference in our lives – see, dear, from now on it is always our lives – no more your life or my life. It has not quite finished happening or else I should tell you all about it. I hope, by the time you get here Saturday night everything will have finished happening and then I will tell you about it. I know it isn't fair to be half telling you things but I do not consider anything as having turned up worthy of the telling unless it has actually happened.

I really felt a bit guilty about having wrested from your heart its innermost secret. I can imagine how you felt about it, now that you have come out with it. But now I think you are glad that I made you tell.

You don't have to feel your way around when you write to me. You can speak what is in your heart and that, really, makes it much easier to write, doesn't it? You cannot imagine how glad my heart feels when I read that you cannot wait until Saturday night to come to me and that nothing will interfere with that coming. Those, honey, are words of love. That, sweetheart, is what I have been waiting to hear. Life has suddenly become sweeter than I had thought it could be. Love surely gives one a grand and glorious feeling.

Dave and Ida are due here any minute now and by gosh here they are. We are going to celebrate tonite – what it is I'll tell you some other time. Shucks, how can one write of love when there are people on your neck to come on and go, never mind the love letters?

Ida sends her regards and Dave sends his love. Take your choice. As ever your sweetheart, Lou

Louis' "something else happened" is the business deal with Argomite Powder.

May 2, 1928

My dearest Lou,

I, too, have been looking for a few minutes to write you. All my work has to be brought up to date before I dare take any time off. Who cares anyway about work?

I can't imagine what may happen that may make a difference in *our* lives. According to the swing of the letter it sounds pretty good. It also puzzles me to hear that Dave, Ida and yourself are celebrating by way of the movies. You have me guessing now. What can all this be? You will have to tell me just as soon as I see you on Saturday. With much love, Cel

May 3, 1928

My own Darling,

Just a little while ago I got your very welcome letter and to tell you how happy I am that at last I shall be able to see you and in person hear from your own sweet lips the magic words, 'I love you.' Sweetheart, I have been so busy and upset as the result of working on the thing that you don't understand about and which, as I wrote to you before, may have such an effect on our lives. Right now I am worried over the delay that is being caused by people to whom days mean nothing. But, then, you are coming here very soon and that eradicates from my mind all clouds of uneasiness.

I gather from your failure to mention anything about it that you are going to remain here over the banquet, which, of course, makes it real wonderful. I'll be waiting for you at the station and you better be all set to collect and deliver some long past due hugs and kisses. Oh, if the weather that we are now enjoying would only hold out until after you have been here and have gone. What with spring being very much in the air and I being very much in love is it any wonder that I can't get my work done?

I saw Rose Freudberg the other nite and she asked me, point blank, just like that, when I am going to be married. I told her that that was a little ahead of the story but that my sweetheart was coming over on Sunday. So she wanted to know how long you would stay here and says that if you only stay the one day she would not have the nerve to ask me to bring you over but that if you stay till Tuesday she wanted a visit to be paid her. O.K.?

A week later, the engagement apparently formalized, Louis writes:

Sweetheart O'Mine,

Got back into town unexpectedly this afternoon and was disappointed to find a letter from you very conspicuous by its absence. This time I'll forgive you. But you must keep one thing in mind, sweets, according to Dave, who having passed thru all the stages that lead to matrimony should know, an engaged couple must write to each other as often as possible without any regard to replies.

I can't figure out why you, such a wonderful and lovely person should love plain me. I hope I am not cultivating an inferiority complex.

I have lots to do this evening, (but) I positively cannot buckle down to work. I am engaged to marry the finest, nicest, cutest, loveliest, prettiest, darlingest, kissingest, little girl in all creation. Why then shouldn't I feel like I do? But, darling, I must not show it so much. The client yesterday said I'm no longer any good for anybody but my sweetheart. That, dear, is O.K. with me. As long as I am good for my sweetheart I'm satisfied. Last night I was very tired (and) went to bed at 12:00. I put my arms around my pillow and with my thoughts on you I went to sleep. I am terribly in love, dearie.

Heard about mother's suddenly deciding to go to Paterson (due to the death of Louis' Uncle Bersh). I am very glad she did but I certainly could have wished for better circumstances for such a visit. I am glad she will meet your folks. I have long wanted her to.

Yesterday morning mother told me a confidence. She said she felt terribly about it because she liked my Uncle Bersh. She wanted to cry but the tears just would not come because her happiness at hearing about our engagement overshadowed her sorrow and she could not overcome the desire to be happy above everything else. I do hate to see mother unhappy. She looks so fine and is so witty and companionable when she is in good frame of mind and not worried about anything.

I want to thank you and I am mentally squeezing you into a mighty hug for your kindness to take care of mother in a strange land. You see mamma is not acquainted in the wild and woolly vastness of New Jersey. But, of course, it really is not a subject for thanks as I am quite certain you are only too happy to do all you can for any of my folks just as I am to do things for yours. Also from now on there is no such thing as your folks and my folks. They are all *our* folks.

Oh, dearest, I must stop now. Dave has come in and while I no longer have to hide a letter from him lest he espy the Dearest and Sweetheart portions of the letter as he passes I do have to work with him. So I am going to restate my love for you forever and ever. Honey, you are my only love, my first and my last and the Lord only knows how I shall endure all this business of being away from your kisses, few tho they are, your embraces, warm and firm, and mostly YOU. Till death do us part, your sweetheart, LOU

Below was a sketch of a head with xxx's all over it.
    "XXXX=Kisses Celia covered with Kisses"

Celia wrote on the same date as Louis' last letter:

> Dear Sweetheart:
>
> I can't seem to write, read, work or think. Oh yes, I can think, I am quite sure of it because all that I have been doing is thinking of you, and that is from the time you said 'Goodby' until this very minute. I was sorry that you had to rush the way you did to make the train. By the way, did you make it?
>
> Sweetheart, I couldn't wait until I got home to tell the folks with my own lips how Happy I am. They have wished us all the luck and happiness in the world. They all love you very much and are very happy over our engagement. I am sure your folks feel that way too.
>
> I told mother I didn't want a big wedding when the time comes but she said 'nothing doing. You are going to have one like Edith's.' My father also said he would be very disappointed if he couldn't do as much for me as he did for Edith. I personally don't like any fuss whatsoever but what can you do. I don't like to hurt them. Oh well, we shall see later.
>
> I received a long distance call this morning from Eleanor telling me to meet your mother at the station this evening at 7:30 o'clock and after greetings have been exchanged to put her on a train bound for Paterson. The call came as a complete surprise and for a minute I thought someone was fooling me. Eleanor had to do some convincing. I hope it is all true because I am very anxious that the Mothers' meet. I conveyed the message to my mother and told her she will soon meet my sweetheart's mother and by soon I meant tonight. We are anxiously waiting for 7:30, I am sure it will indeed be a pleasure on my Mother's part to meet your Mother. We will try and keep her here a few days.
>
> No doubt you will be very busy now that Dave is contemplating leaving Sunday for New York. I hope it won't be long ere you do likewise. Lots of luck all around.
>
> Dear, I had a wonderful time in the company of your wonderful parents, sisters and brothers, cousins, friends and last but not least yourself. With all my love from your best and only sweetheart, Cel

Argomite is beginning to consume their attention. Two days later, Louis writes: "Leo just got back home and he told me all about the sordid details of the Paterson bereavement. It seems that my aunt took it terribly hard and could not be consoled. I am sorry that mother has to feel all the grief of close contact over there but I am also glad that she will be able to add her presence to make it easier a bit for my poor aunt Sarah.

"Death seems so commonplace on account of its frequency of occurrence and yet we are so shocked when it happens to someone dear and near to us. To avoid having to tell Rose directly Leo came home wearing a black tie and she knew right away what it meant. Life is certainly terrible and its culmination is worse. But then, dearest, you and I should look upon life as something very wonderful and upon death as non-existent.

"One does not write love letters with Leo around. I read mother's letter and I find that you have taken great care of her. Mother can't seem to say enough about what a dear child you are. In Love, Louis"

On May 13, Louis wrote about the Argomite business deal to his brother,

Joe: "You may have heard from someone at the house that Dave and I have taken on the sale of a new product that has come into the market. This product is used for cleansing of all kinds and is called Argomite. It is a wonderful cleaner and is kosher for use by Jews.

"It is a money making possibility and we shall soon need agents of all kinds, sizes and degree of laziness. If you can prove valuable to us you may find in it, in a year or so the answer to your (cash) problem. You may be able to make enough out of it to make a living for yourself and wife. However, our obligations are such as to demand maximum efficiency from our workers and unless you can prove your worth to us we cannot undertake to use you. I haven't the time now to go into detail but I will write you again soon and then I shall tell you more about it. I might state only that our contract gives us the exclusive right to sell this stuff in Greater New York and surrounding territory.

"I am enclosing herewith a little bit of it. You might try it out by first getting your hands good and greasy on the axle of any automobile and working that grease into your hands as if you wanted it to stay there. Then put a little Argomite Powder on your hands and with a little warm or even cold water wash with it as with soap. You will be amazed at its cleaning possibilities. Greasiest dishes can be washed with a mild solution of it in warm or even cold water.

"It washes the finest silk with absolute safety and if you want to try out a little test take a pair of Florence's silk stockings, get them good and greasy with auto grease and then wet them in warm water, sprinkle a bit of Argomite Powder on the wet hose and rub between your hands. As the Argomite gets into the grease you will see the grease melting away. Rinse in clear water and your hose will be clean. You may have to work a little on this sort of a test as usually grease on silk hose spells good-bye hose. Next time I will tell you more about how you can profit by it.

"Dave has left for New York this morning to try to raise about ten thousand dollars we need to put this stuff on the market. We will need many agents and you might as well be one of them if you have the stuff in you. Let me know what you think about this.

"What I shall want you to do is to try your hand at selling it, in the form and at the price I shall let you know of later, and when you have demonstrated to me and to yourself that you can sell it, then we shall talk about your coming to New York and going to work. But I do not want you to go to New York on an experiment. There are plenty guys in New York who are aggressive enough to get and hold these jobs when we are ready for them and since this is going to be a corporation of which I am but one member you will have to produce the goods in order to belong. I might say, however, that producing the goods carries with it a little matter of a living for a fellow. Let me hear what you think of the stuff and whether or not you are interested.

"I have been much longer at it now than I had intended. I suppose you know that I have got myself engaged officially. My girl is a very sweet kid and in general a fine girl. Everybody at home and everywhere likes her. My love to Florence (Joe's fiancé) and give my regards to all."

No one realized the Depression was creeping closer. However, clients failed to pay bills and business prospects were grim as the firm's bills also were not getting paid. Could Argomite be the rainbow on the horizon?

Louis did not keep copies of all the letters he sent Dave, but Dave's responses reflect on much of what Louis had written to him. On the same date as his letter to Joe, Louis wrote Celia. He lowers his estimate of what Dave needs to raise when writing Celia: "Just put my partner on the train for New York where he has gone to start the ball rolling to make us all rich. I most certainly hope, with all the power that is in me that he will succeed in his immediate task, which is to raise five or six thousand dollars. I want this not because I want to be rich. I never cared much about riches. But his success means that you and I, dearest, will be able to get married just that much sooner.

"I can't bear to be away from you for very long and it seems that the only way I can fix that is to marry you and have you with me always. But the economic side of things is very strong in my consciousness. I simply cannot consider getting married before I know, definitely, that I can support you decently. That is why I kept silent on the subject of my love for you when I could not see any immediate solution to the economic problem.

"Then, when Dave had arranged to go to California with the consequent release to me of all the income from this office, I told you of my love. Now all that has undergone another change and I am waiting to see what will happen next. I know we will succeed in this Argomite business. I simply feel that we cannot fail. That prize, darling, is no one else but YOU. It seems that I cannot have you without a lot of struggle.

"Oh, sweetheart, I want you so much! I felt, as I put Dave on the train, that I was sending him away for you. You will probably see him in a day or two and if he has good news for you, you may kiss him with my permission. That, my love, is quite some bit of permission to hand out in a love letter. But his success means so much to both of us, that if he succeeds he deserves even so precious a reward as a kiss from you.

"Last night Dave, Ida, and I went to the movies and when I got back home it was twelve. No one was downstairs but our corner on the divan and my memory of you. I did not dare sit down there. I merely stood in the room, semi-dark the room was, and dreamed that you were there with your arms around me protesting that I was kissing you too much. I could not stand it very long. It hurt too much to find that it was but a dream and that you were miles away from that room.

"Tell mamma – my mamma – that I love her more than ever now that she thinks so well of my *Kalleh* (bride) and her people. Dearest, we shall be very happy. With utmost devotion, Lou C. Gee – Some day it will be your loving Husband"

Celia writes, "Sunday Morn, May 13, 1928.

"After reading your last letter I was positive a letter from you would be in my hands by Saturday, but no (to quote you) it was conspicuous by its absence. Dear, I couldn't possibly have written you any sooner than I did. I will remind you that the train arrived in Newark 10:30 Wednesday evening.

"Big Sam called for me at the station and a short time after I reached home I was in Dreamland dreaming of you. The first chance I had the next day I wrote you.

"There you go again doubting me. Sweetheart, believe me I do love you. I think you know I do but you want me to say it over and over again. I, too, am engaged to marry the finest, cleverest, nicest, kissingest (if there is such a word) etc., etc., etc., in all the world. I do not know what to say to make you believe that I love you truly. I am beginning to think you hardly know me after all. I couldn't possibly write all this and say what I did say if I honestly didn't believe it myself.

"The flowers you sent Mother came a few minutes ago. If you knew how happy you made her feel and what she said about you, you would never forget her. I gave your mother a little gift last night and after re-calling the expression on her face I think it best that we never forget our Mothers on this day (Mother's Day) or any day for that matter. It made them both very happy.

"I want you to thank your father in behalf of your sweetheart for kindnesses done. Do you know he paid for my ticket? He really shouldn't have done that. I appreciate it heaps.

"I haven't announced our engagement to my friends because Edith wants the honor of having several tables of bridge at her home and during the course of the evening announce it. She is going to have it the latter part of next week. One thing I regret is that you will not be here to enjoy it with me.

"How is the new business coming along? I am sorry I am not near you so you could tell me everything. If things don't go as smoothly as they should, don't worry dear, we have each other. Isn't that worth more than money?

"Before I forget, I wonder if you could send a small box of Argomite to my Mother. The size you showed me when I was in your office. After telling her the wonders of Argomite she said she will try it. Regards to all and all my love to you, your only sweetheart, Cel"

She follows with this, written the next day: "I read your wonderful letter with interest. I, too, pray that Dave will be successful in securing funds for the Argomite business. Please, dear, don't let anything worry you, I am yours and to prove it I will wait for you forever. I am indeed sorry that you are so upset about the new business. I am sure everything will come out alright and then – . Please tell me you will not worry. If I have but an inkling that you are worrying I will have to do likewise and do my full share of it because I sort of feel like the guilty party.

"You say you had postponed telling me of your love until Dave had decided to move to Calif. and you would be left with the office. I am sorry for your sake that it has undergone another change but I am glad of the change that made you tell me of your love. I am a firm believer in fate and am sure everything happens for the best. Just wait, we will laugh at the whole world. With all my love, Celia"

That same day, Louis was busy writing to Dave, as well. He enclosed an invoice from Argomite Industries for 14 bags of Argomite Powder "C", 2800 lbs. @ 8 cents a pound for a cost of $224.00. Louis dealt with all the billing, and the merchandise was shipped f.o.b. to Economy Mercantile Corp., 43 East 12th Street, New York, New York, where Dave received it. This detergent product was so new, even the parent company did not know what to do with it. They let their franchisees do all their marketing, research and development for them.

"Your wire received and instructions carried out. Rather surprised that you made such a big sale on the first tryout. I suppose it is Barryman's laundry that bought it. It will be shipped to you first thing in the morning.

"I spoke to Glover (the contact man between the Argomite Company, Louis and Dave) and to Smith and the directions for use in a laundry are given you below. It seems, they are not so very certain as to just what quantities to use. Smith says that every laundry has its own ideas about washing and that your laundry over there will have to experiment to find best results. The following instructions, however, should be a base from which to work.

"They will really have to experiment a bit with this stuff until they learn to use the quantities that will best wash their clothes the cleanest. Glover suggested that they will loan you the services of Edwards (a technician working for Argomite) for a few days if you want him. Of course I don't know on what basis of payment they would send Edwards (so) it may be just as well, until we have a lot of money to get along without that gent.

"I believe that the company expects us to pay for everything we get (as) the steno up there asked me where our office was, she wants to bill us for the boxes of Argomite you took away. I thought it was a present but evidently it isn't. That is O.K. of course, but it means that we shall probably have to pay for all services received.

"Had I.S.T. over to the office this afternoon and told him things about Argomite. Naturally that sort of baby is very willing to buy stuff that is secure and shys at riches where a gamble is involved.

"I opened an account in the bank and deposited Mannie's money. Well, kid, lots of luck to you. I hope you work it so fast that in a short while I may be able to join you. My head is anywhere but on this accounting racket."

Two days later, on the 15th, Louis writes Dave again: "I got your wire and your letter that you sent to Ida. So far as Oakite is concerned you can chuck that stuff out right after the Argomite gets there. Bleach, however, is needed in some cases but in any event it may be cut in half.

"The Argomite, by the way is Argomite C that they shipped you. That is specially prepared for laundries. I think it suds up more than the other and for that reason the stuff they will receive may not be Kosher. I don't know, I haven't asked."

"The Argomite you ordered was shipped early to-day in bags. I spoke to Barton (the inventor of the Argomite detergent) about barrels but he says that the barrels are too expensive. Costs something like 1.50 a piece. Besides the fare adds to the freight cost and therefore is not feasible.

"As for Edwards's time he can't cost us more than about 25 bucks a day and if he is as important as you seem to think why, then, we shall just have to pay that for him. As for Barryman's coming in with us, personally I would not like to have the 51% get out of our hands unless we absolutely must let it go and of course, only to the tune of 50%. I see a great future in it for us and I hate to think of giving up the say in this business just for a few lousy thousands at this time. Don't let your enthusiasm get away with you and don't be too anxious to take in bosses.

"I had a talk with I.S. Turover and if we want complete financing, to the tune of 50% he would be glad to take the matter up with us again."

Edwards made a demonstration in a very large laundry on the Pacific Coast using half the amount of Argomite in a washer in comparison with another washer using soap. They could not tell the difference. With fewer rinses needed, time would be saved and other cleansers such as soda ash would not be needed.

"By the way you surely went and ruined Dora's coat for her. You rubbed out the color with your over zealousness. Now it will be necessary for you to have that garment dyed and us will have to pay for that job. The price I found out is $6.00. I took the coat over to Barton and he says you soaked it too much. Barton says that no matter what is used as a cleaner for such things one must know exactly how to go about it and that that kind of a cleaner is an expert and draws down 100 to 150 a week.

"We must learn not to claim too much for the stuff. I told Dora what the Dr. had said about it and then I suggested she try and have it dry cleaned. She invited me to take it across the street to Lerches and see if they think they can rescue it. I did and then they told me not a chance. So I asked what then, 'Dye it' was the answer. I priced it and he says six berries. So I went back and told Dora that we shall pay for it. She was a bit sore – she paid $65.00 for it last year – and pooh poohed my desire to pay for it. Nevertheless I think we shall do so anyway. So be careful what you demonstrate on. There are enough dishes and floors and dirty hands and laundry and a million other things that Argomite will handle satisfactorily to leave alone the cleaning of garments that the dry cleaners have struggled with for many years.

"This will be about all. I should breathe a whole lot easier if you would wire me that you have secured 10 grand and are ready for your first retail car. In the meantime I am waiting with great impatience."

Louis also writes Celia on the 15th: "This is an outrageous hour to be writing love letters. But at the same time when that guy's mind is on that same sweet sweetheart of his, how can he work? The answer is that he can't and thus he sits down to the typewriter and tells her of his love so that he may be able to go about his business. The first mail did not bring any letters from you, dear, and I can only hope that the next one will.

"Sweetheart the last letter you wrote was the finest I ever received from you in which you assured me I was all wrong in believing you didn't care for me. This last one seemed to come from your heart and that, dearest, is just the kind of letters I want to get from you. So you really do love me? Isn't that just wonderful! I think that I am slowly beginning to know you and to understand you, honey. You are a very reserved sort of person with very – just now the mailman came in with just one letter. That one, darling, is from you. Wait, I'll read it. Oh, shucks, just one page. But what a page! Would you, really dear, wait for me forever? I don't believe it. Do you know why? Because I won't let you.

"Somehow this will all come out right and that very soon, because I can't wait forever, even tho you, my love, seem willing to wait patiently until I can claim you for my own. This business of being in love is so wonderful and yet so terrible. I can't work, I can't sleep, I can't think of anything but you for a longer period than three minutes.

"Ida has encouraging news from Dave. Seems that he is working over there. He has ordered 2800 lbs. of it for trial in Mr. Barryman's chain of laundries and he now writes Ida that if we can convince him by demonstration that this Argomite of ours is the more economical and effective method of washing (he) will be able to use more than our total requirement right off the bat. Maybe everything will be O.K. after all.

"Lovey, we'll laugh at the world yet, as you say. Wouldn't it be just glorious to enter a nice business and be married at the same time? I always did wish to get out of the professional game and go into business. And now, to be married also and to the finest girl in the world! Sweetheart, God is good to me. But don't you worry, dearest. I am capable of carrying all the burdens of this family all by myself. However, the joys I insist on sharing with you. Now, sweetheart, I must leave you. I have just talked to Dr. Barton, who as you will recall is Mr. Argomite himself and I have a date with him for at once."

Louis writes Celia again on May 16: "I have so many things to do right away that I thought I might just as well do the most pleasant thing, and that, of course, is to write to my fiancée. That's what you are, sweetie, my FIANCEE. Am just now awaiting the second morning's mail which is due here any minute. Maybe there will be one from you altho I know I don't deserve one since I didn't write to you the day before yesterday.

"What do you think I did last nite? Bet you couldn't guess in twenty-five guesses. I came back to the office last nite to do some work that has piled up and before getting down to work I thought I'd re-read your last letter. It sounded so good that I read one letter after letter. You know, dear, I have a copy of every letter I wrote you on the typewriter since that first one in February 1927 and, of course, every one you wrote me since the first one.

"I read thru your letters and my replies from the first to about July and that took most of the evening. It was very entertaining, indeed. The funny part is that as early as the second letter I wrote you, I injected a note of yearning for you. Isn't that strange? Love at first sight? Well, maybe. The talk was about Washington's Birthday, February 22, and I was saying that once upon a time it meant a holiday for me but that now it was just another opportunity to do some extra work in the office. Then I added, 'But with you in Newark, I might as well work.' Now, wasn't that nice as long ago as one year & three months?

"I suppose by this time Dave will have made some sort of an appearance up your way. He is engaged in big plans and is trying to sell Mr. Barryman all the washing material they need in their chain of laundries. If he succeeds, and I have high hopes, then, sweetheart, you might as well begin to consider yourself seven tenths married. Honey, it won't take very much longer now. Our love would make sales even if the product weren't any good.

"Imagine what can be done with the combination of a good product and our love! Things are so up in the air that I have no heart for my clients or their record troubles. It wouldn't be so bad if Dave were all settled and working on Argomite sales. Then I could sit back and watch him toil the while I attended to my own business.

"The above paragraph has really no place in a love letter. I should not worry you with my troubles. I hope not to worry you with them when we are married and certainly I should not bother you about them now. Ida just called up. She is coming to see me in re a letter that Dave wrote her. In the meantime, my love, I shall console myself with the knowledge that you are keeping me in your thots always. Forever your beloved, Lou"

On May 16, 1928, Ida wrote to Dave. Louis added his own P.S. on the back.

"Dearest,

"Brought Louis your letter of the 15th and am using the time to write you a real letter. This machine has begun to bunch up the letters again, due undoubtedly to Louis' aggressive masculine touch.

"Received a lovely letter from Celia, in which she says she is sending the children the ice-box to match the kitchen cabinet." This was a metal replica made by the Kanster/Hamburg Company.

Ida suggested that since Barryman was so interested in Argomite, it might help them financially if he became a partner. "One percent is already gone to Manny, which leaves 99%. Louis agrees with me that he would be willing to divide the business into three equal shares. 33% for you, 33% for him and 33% for Mr. Barryman. Then you could talk turkey with Mr. Barryman, and one thing sure, I think you three could trust each other absolutely which you know from experience is a tremendous thing in a partnership.

"I think Mr. Barryman is treating you marvelously, when he says that from a friendship basis there is no question of his lending you $2,000. I am afraid I know very few others who would. However his idea of selling about 20,000 pounds a month does not seem so good to me. Unless this 20,000 pounds is aside from the carload which he himself might be able to use. Which means that besides our living you would have $800 a month.

"I read with interest Leo's (her brother-in-law's) contribution to our success, and your success in interesting the superintendent and the others in the hospital.

"It is a curious thing that Manny invested with you, a sum which to him must be very great, while Al does not think enough to even lend you that sum without a lot of talk, and then probably not at all. One thing is sure, Barton gave you the contract but he has no intention of giving you anything else. I was very much surprised to learn that he charged you for the samples of Argomite which you took with you. Well, he's in for the money.

"Louis is wondering just how long the laundries Mr. Barryman mentions would take before sending payment. 60 days delay would stick you good and plenty.

"All kinds of love, darling, Yours, Ida"

"P.S. (from Louis) I was just talking it over with Ida about her suggestion to you anent the three ways partnership." Louis was certain that Barryman would only agree to a 50–50 split.

"Even if only 60,000 pounds were used there instead of the 72,000 for 2 cars that would be $2,400 profit a month. Then, with the little money we can scrape up, that is the Mannie thousand, the Barryman two thou, the Judea stock money, my insurance money and a possible thou from Celia, to say nothing of some money I might be able to get from Paterson, that would be all we want to go right ahead, without bosses or side partners. I am all for working it ourselves if at all possible. There is plenty of time to split it up on a fifty-fifty basis.

"I don't know what else I can add to your questions about the laundry wash. I told you before that Barton and his gang knows not so very much about it specifically. I have tried to find out how much they will want for Edwards. They have shipped the stuff to NY under date of May 15 and I am to get the B/L tomorrow and also the bill. I suppose I shall have to give them the check for the stuff very soon. So you better collect from Barryman as soon as you can. So long and don't get fidgety about my not sending you all the details. It will probably pay us to have Edwards go out there as soon as the stuff gets there. So long, son. We are all pulling for you, Louis"

On the same day, Celia wrote: "Edith is to call for me within ten minutes to drive me to Paterson to see your Mother and perhaps bring her back. We received a letter from her this morning stating that she will probably go to New York to visit friends and relatives at the request of your brother. We are hoping she will stay with us a few days at least.

"I have not as yet heard from Dave. I suppose he is waiting until he has a great deal of good news to tell me (about) this Argomite business. I hope he will have little trouble convincing Mr. Barryman of the merits of Argomite.

"I had an appointment with Dr. Perlman for this past Monday and thinking my appointment was for last night I called to verify my hour. This is what he said. 'Cel, I believe you are very much in love and not only do I believe it, I am positive of it. Just to get you out of a trance, your appointment was for last night and if you don't wake up you will miss the Friday appointment!'

"This is just one case. I will mention another. Our Chief Clerk asked me why I didn't answer him when he asked me a question the other morning and not waiting for an answer from me he said, 'Oh, I know you are in love. I hope you are not keeping anything from us Miss Kanster.' I just laughed it off saying maybe you are right. I haven't said anything in the office so they don't know a thing.

The next day, May 17, Louis replied that he had received her letter in the morning mail: "It was really the only reason for my coming to the office this morning as I had everything all ready to attend to a client directly from the house. However, you know I couldn't work anywhere with the feeling in my bones that a letter from you awaits. So, I went to the office and found a letter from you and Dave and also a message from Ida to the effect that Dave had wired he was on his way back.

"Seems that he thought the tests to be conducted by Mr. Barryman when the Argomite gets there are so important that he wanted to find out all he could from the head office here before attempting to demonstrate. Just as soon as the Argomite reaches New York, Barryman will wire us and then Dave, together with a local expert from the plant, will go over there and do their joint stuff. You might pray for the success of the tests, as they will just about mean the difference between smooth sailing and rough *hartzesseness*.

"Now I know you love me. At least the signs are cropping out. Do you know that you actually used the same expression in the finish of your letter to-day that Ida used in a letter she wrote to Dave yesterday? She, too, asked her sweetheart to take care of himself. That is an admonition that is prompted only by love. I am glad. After a time I think I will be fully convinced that you really and truly love me. You see, dear, I have loved you for a long time and when finally the time came to come out with it, it was oh, so easy to say it. In your case, well, you are just learning to love me. Am I right or wrong?

"Theresa Shefferman tells me that you have the cutest smile and Sylvia Rosenfeld insists that you are just altogether the most adorable girl she has ever, ever, met. And then she turns around and says to another girl in the room – 'and I used to think I have some sort of a chance with him.' What do you think of that for frankness? Well, I might have told her that she didn't particularly since one certain Sunday afternoon or rather evening about February 13, 1927. Well, life is like that. But what I want to know is why don't you love me in the day time same as you do in the evening?

"I can remember having read just a few days ago something that has the sound of love. It was your own letter, now that I come to think of it. It said, 'Don't worry, we have each other and that is much more than any money.' Sounds like love. But then, why won't you love me in the daytime –

"I came here to do some very important work (but) decided that a letter to my sister Esther in Syracuse was absolutely essential. Not having written to her since about last November, I tried to get a lot in and it took three and a half full pages of this type. I told her about you and about Argomite. It seems horrible and sacrilegious to mention you and Argomite in the same breath, yet since I must have Argomite to get you, I suppose I may be forgiven. I recalled what I had said in a letter to her some time ago that possibly I might find me a nice little wife who would have as one of her special duties the maintenance of my private correspondence. Is that all right with you, sweetheart? Will you take over the business of writing my personal letters?

"Just one more word. I have ordered some packages of Argomite, one of which will go forward to your mother. I want to send her a five-pound bag, which will keep her supplied until our New York warehouse will be able to supply her.

"I leave you here, my love. Your sweetheart alone, Lou

"P.S. By the way. Should mother stay over with you Friday nite and Saturday, please don't ask her to go out riding. She is very religious and it would hurt her if you did things that were grossly against the law while she is around. Love again and always, L.C.G. The famous initials"

That same day, Celia wrote:

MY FIANCE,

I have just time to say Hello, dear, how are you. I am very sorry your mother spent so little time with us. She left this morning for New York with your brother Will, to visit friends and relatives. I believe she will leave for home tomorrow.

So, you have made carbon copies of all the letters you sent me. Keep it up I will want to read them all over again. I usually keep the letters I receive, consequently I have them from the year one. I have a good many of yours in my drawer especially *the later ones*. I envy your wonderful gift of letter writing. Everything that you manage to write about is interesting news, whereas everything I don't write about is news.

Dear, I will be very glad when you will get a call from Dave to come to New York. When you do, it will mean that the wind is blowing in the right direction. Did you hear from him directly? Did Ida have good news for you from Dave?

Lou, I did not dare put a letter-head in the machine for fear one hundred eyes would see what I was writing. Thinking of you always and with all my love, yours, Cel

May 18, 1928

Dearest girl,

Got your peck of a note and am grateful for it even tho it is only like some of those earlier kisses of yours – just the suggestion of one. David sits within touching distance of me and labors. It is 5:50 in the afternoon and the rain has just finished shedding its summery showers. I am surprised that I am not afraid he will look. What do I care if he does? The whole world may look and see that I am in love with the dearest girl in the country and let them be jealous.

Mother just came back this morning on a sleeper and she cannot find words to describe the feelings she has for everyone in Newark. She raves about this one and that one and all the time she speaks of Celia. Say, who is this Celia, anyway. I haven't thought to ask her. Must be quite some wonderful person. It certainly was mighty sweet of all of you to be so nice to my mamma.

Big Sam won himself a warm spot in mother's heart. She thinks he is just the most wonderful fellow, (Outside of her own son Louis–sh, don't tell anyone) to be so pleasant and nice to a stranger, comparatively speaking. And your father and mother and all your sisters and even the baby are just dears. So what more do you want?

Dave just tells me that you called up Fanny and Mrs. Glushak and Rabbi Glushak and told them all about our engagement. What did each of them have to say? I got a letter from Joe, the Floridian this morning and he is loud in his praises for his brother. Can you beat that? He says he doesn't know the girl I am engaged to but he feels certain that she must be the right one. One thing he does know and that is that the girl's fiancée is the – etc. of a fellow in the world. I'll have to send him a quarter for that. Yes, it was very complimentary. But maybe he is working me for a touch. Yes, that must be it.

I don't see why you should envy me my what you call 'wonderful gift of letter writing.' Isn't mine yours and yours mine? I am perfectly satisfied with your letters. The way you write them suits me just fine. The only fault if there is one is their usual brevity, altho, I must say that occasionally you do uncork a nice lengthy one. But why worry about people seeing you write? Personally I don't care any more who sees or who envies.

David has gone home and I am here alone with you. Oh, if it were only in the flesh! But no, you are here only in my thoughts. To appreciate you, to hug you, to kiss you, to whisper to you, to look into your beautiful eyes, I must have you here in the flesh. And I can't have you thus, it seems, until later. Maybe things will turn out so that it won't be so much later after all. I don't know.

So many things depend upon so many other things and people who have money are only ready to invest it in good things when those good things are not any longer available to them. But, who knows? I am beginning to believe more and more in fate myself. Perhaps all this is for the best after all. The less money is invested with us the more will be our share of the ultimate profits.

Sweetness, I am in love with you and that is all there is to it. Whenever I feel a bit blue I turn to the file that has no label on it and is placed among the Ks and read a few of the letters in which you tell me that you love me even tho I might be inclined, for one fool reason or another, to doubt it a bit. This consoles me wonderfully and everything begins to look brighter. I LOVE YOU, DARLING, Louis

May 18, 1928, Celia sends Louis a poem she cut out of the newspaper changing the last four lines to read:

> 'Since you know what I think of you,
> Will you always be good and true?
> I am sure we will get along,
> Like peaceful doves, Cel and Lou.'

Don't be too critical re this. C
With all my love, Cel

Saturday May 19, 1928

My own Lovely Poetess,

What do you think of that? My sweetheart is actually a poet. See, I thought I didn't know you. Here all of a sudden I discover, after so many months, that my baby can write poetry with meters, feet, 'neverything. What next, I wonder. I am looking forward with real anticipation to learning all about you in the many years that are to follow that happiest of all events of my life when I shall bestow upon you the name Mrs. Louis C. Grossberg. I am very sorry that I cannot reply to you in kind. In past years I have come to the gatepost of the poets with some school work on limericks. But poetry? God forbid.

This is Saturday afternoon and Babe is here waiting to go somewhere with me. Certainly a very poor substitute for my darling Celia. It is perfectly wonderful outside and if this letter turns out to be shorter than the usual Lou letter, please blame it on Babe and the weather. For some unaccountable reason Kitty has not called me up this morning and I am, therefore, outside of having Babe on my hands, a more or less free agent.

It seems that my folks are all *farsorgt* (concerned). One of the Kitay cousins of father has put in a reservation that my folks stay over with them on Friday nite and Saturday should the wedding be on Sunday and should they wish to come down on Friday. Can you beat that? Didn't know we were so popular with the Kitays there. I never visit them when I go to Paterson and thus they don't know me. Well, maybe, when I come out to see you, we might make a few visits there and see what it is all about.

So far as our wedding is concerned, I haven't even bought you an engagement ring. Heavens, can you imagine that. I have just got to get that ring for you. I wish, when you have a chance, you would go around window shopping and make up your mind what sort of a setting or mounting you would like to have for an engagement ring. Then, the first chance, you and I will take a little run out to Philly and buy just that sort of ring thru Herman. This reminds me I haven't written to that boy of the glad news.

Long ago, when first I told him about you – 'way long before anyone else knew – he shook hands with me and told me that he just knew you must be the right girl if I wanted you for my wife. I assured him that you were and now everybody knows that you are. Sweetie, he will certainly be happy when he sees you because he and I were buddies from 'way back when he and I were pups. So make up your mind what you would like to have and if Philly has it and it is this side of five thousand dollars – I ain't saying how far this side – you shall have it. It is time to leave. Sweetheart, are you still thinking of me all the time and would you kiss me now if I were near even tho it is daytime? Hah? Your dreamy Only Lou

My English seems to suffer when Babe is around. He worries me with his nervous impatience.

Celia writes on that Sunday: "Did you like the poem? Little do you know that you are going to marry a poetess – and what a poetess. The poem attracted me because my sentiments were reflected therein.

"I have made several attempts to locate Fanny on the phone but to no avail. I am going to write her a letter in a day or so and tell her the wonderful news. I am sure she knows about it thru the Glushaks and is quite happy over it. Fanny was always interested in my happiness and has been a wonderful friend to me. I did call the Glushaks' home and I spoke to Mrs. Glushak. (Just a specimen of our conversation)

"'Hello Mrs. G. this is Celia of Newark.'

"'Congratulations, I wish you all the luck that you could possibly wish for yourself.'

"'Thank you,' I said, but wait a minute, how did you know?

"She said, 'You know Celia, I knew it all along, something in me just told me so, in fact Rabbi said it was inevitable.' I asked her why she didn't let me in on the secret; it might have interested me a great deal. You know I stand Ace High with the Rabbi. I expect to be in New York soon and intend to visit them. In your letter of the 17th you asked me several questions. Here are the answers.

"(1) Yes, Sweetheart, I started the game of loving you some six weeks ago and honestly believe I have progressed rapidly. Now to come back and ask you one. Have I got very much more to learn? If I have it is up to you dear, you know the work of a good teacher is reflected in his pupil.

"(2) Yes for the nth time I love you in the daytime as much as I do in the evening. What makes you say I don't?

"(3) Yes, dear I will relieve you of all personal correspondence. Just let me know when."

Louis writes on the next day, May 21: "For once this is going to be short. Dave is leaving for New York again to-morrow morning early and I was busy with him all afternoon and will be with him again this evening. It is past six and he is my transportation. I have just finished addressing two five-pound bags of Argomite to your mother and to your sister Edith. The little booklets are instructions that are to guide them in the use of this powder.

"As yesterday was Sunday, I spent the evening at Kitty's and we played a bit of bridge – Al, Kitty, Pauline, and I. Al and I were partners and we got swamped by the women. Kitty made a three club bid and Al doubled her. She came right back with a redouble and made a small slam. Wow, was we hurt? I'll say we *were*. After that sickening game I lost interest and when it was my turn to act dummy I lay down on the couch and imagined myself lying there during your recent visit – and you and Kitty busy in the kitchen making supper. Then I called you to me. You came over to the couch and looked at me as if to say, 'What can I do for you?' 'I must have a kiss at once. All day you haven't kissed me.' I thought myself saying to you. And you came over or rather bent over and kissed me. Oh, yes, it was much better than the way it actually worked out on that evening. That time, you didn't kiss me. I kissed you. You merely loaned me the use of your lips. But last night! I certainly have a wonderful imagination."

Dave's demonstration in New York was delayed until Thursday but he was leaving anyway to open an office and try to raise money.

"If Barryman does not himself care to invest he has signified his willingness to loan Dave a couple of thousand dollars and with the few thousands we can borrow here on some stock we hold and some insurance, we shall go ahead without investors and will, no doubt, be much better off for it.

"To-day Dave had a talk with the local distributor and he tells him that all the local street cars and big jitney busses are now using Argomite to clean the outside. They only dust the inside and I suppose as soon as they need to really clean the inside they'll use it for that, too. Can you imagine how much Argomite New York's street cars and subways and other trains would use if they all started to clean it with our treasure! Hot dog, that would be something real.

"While speaking of dogs, the maid at Ida's washes Snowball, their dog, in a weak solution of Argomite. Try it on your Schnubby. Take about a tablespoonful to about a gallon and a half of warm water, dissolve thoroughly. It will clean the dog thoroughly and will also kill the fleas, if he has any. Rinse him off with clear water after the bath. It will not hurt him if he licks some of the dissolved Argomite. Dave tells me that their Snowball likes it and licks it after or during the bath. We are going to try to sell it to the kennels in New York at a fancy price. They wouldn't buy anything that is cheap…"

Dave wrote to his uncle on May 21, 1928, telling him of the wonderful product he and his partner Louis were trying to promote. "I am taking this belated opportunity of answering your last letter. I don't know whether I had ever written to you before that the accounting business was pretty rotten. We sent out $1,600 of bills for work past due and of that amount less than $250 has come in. Last October I suddenly discovered that a certain new powder for cleaning purposes was being manufactured in Washington and was being sold in bulk only to several large users. It appeared to me to be a marvelous product, so much so that I tried to find out all about its distribution. I discovered that the whole country was taken…"

Dave explained that it cleaned everything from silks to carpets, walls, grease stains, iodine, blood and medicine stains, pots and pans. Clothing came out looking like new and he got a local Rabbi to give a *Hechsher*, an authorization as to its being Kosher. Dave had already left for New York to work with the Zionist Organization but received word from Ida that the territory for New York became available and Mr. Barton, president of the company, was offering it to Dave in gratitude for the Hechsher.

"This was an opportunity that I had always dreamed about. So about two weeks ago he gave us, that is my partner and me, a contract to sell Argomite in Greater New York, Long Island and Westchester County for twenty years. I am trying to raise some money and so far have not had much luck." He said Mr. Barryman gave a big order for his laundries and offered to invest a couple thousand dollars. Dave could not borrow on his house and needed $6,000 or $7,000 to get started. His brother's hospital was ready to place an order but he had none to deliver yet, as he needed an office, salesmen and capital. Offers had been made to invest $20,000 for one half interest in the business but he preferred to get money from family and friends.

"I am wondering, uncle, if you would be in a position to invest with me one or two thousand dollars, or whether you would be willing to lend it to me personally, giving you my personal note for the use of the money. In the meanwhile, I will try and get my family to let me have a couple of thousand dollars. But with a father who is only a *chazan* and a brother who has just gotten established in New York, it is not going to be an easy matter.

"While writing to you I got a call from Ida and she told me that she just got a lovely letter from you in which you sent us a check for $100 for the baby. You can hardly understand how much we appreciate it. Doris was a very sick little baby. Your gift really came in like a Godsend to us, for living as we are from hand to mouth, it is a very difficult matter indeed to be able to save even the amount that was necessary for the hospital bills. I only hope and pray that I will be able to pull myself out of my present financial predicament in the very near future..."

Celia sends more poetry on May 22:

> *Write and tell me all the news,*
> *If your Argomite cleans old shoes,*
> *Have you tried it on your hat?*
> *Even write and tell me that.*
> *Write me anything you choose,*
> *Anything from you is welcome news.*

You didn't know that I could write poetry. Well neither did I. This just goes to prove that we better stick around each other and we will both learn a thing or two.

Sweetheart, be frank with me. Are you sure you do not need the money you will spend for the ring for other purposes? As much as I would like to receive a ring from you, I do not want to see you inconvenienced in any way.

I am thanking you in advance of the arrival of the Argomite. It certainly is sweet of you to send as much as you did to Edith and Mother. So Dave is in New York now. I hope and pray the test proves successful and that Dave will have little trouble securing the necessary dough-dough (your patent). Keep me in touch with the outcome of the demonstration. The first hundred years are the hardest they say. So don't worry if the Barrymans don't come your way. If they don't like it, there are others who do. For instance, Dave, Ida, Ceal and Lou. There I go again, dreaming and talking Argomite.

Louis replies the next day: "If I had plenty of time, say a month, I could figure you out an answer to your last letter in rhyme. Does Argomite clean shoes? I don't know. Don't try it on a new pair. Besides, the poor bootblacks have to make a living, don't they?

"What chances are there for your coming along with your father and folks when they go to Baltimore next week? As for myself, I should very much like to come out soon. The better the sooner, the sooner the *schneller* (faster), the quicker the hastier. Now, what can be done about it? Of course, I *could* take an aero plane. Guess I better not. But when, when? Next Friday, well, maybe. I'll have to see how big the bank account will be, David being away makes it again hard. Then, again, it may be that I shall have to go out there to see what I can do about getting some money from my friends and relatives in Paterson.

"As I told Dave, I should much prefer to raise what little money we need from different sources among our several friends and relatives rather than from one man. One man investments are bad from the standpoint of the share of say that he has in the running of the business. If he would only get going to draw a living wage out of Argomite for his family I should be in better position to begin planning the business of marriage to my little sweetheart over in Newark.

"The business of putting an organization such as we need across with the handicap of no money is no small task. But my partner has broad shoulders and my advice to him is free. Maybe money does not mean anything, but you cannot convince me of that for I need it. In something like a hundred years it will all make no never mind whatever.

"About the ring? Of course I can use the money. But what can be more important a use for money right now (outside of Argomite) than to buy a ring for my only sweetheart. The answer is there isn't any such. It may be necessary to exchange that ring for a real one some two or three years hence when such small money as fifteen, twenty thousand dollars will mean nothing to an Argomite executive (That's I am). So we shall see what there is to be bought by way of an engagement ring for the future Mrs. Louis C. Grossberg. And by the way you might as well begin to learn that your future middle initial will be C and not G. Can you beat that? Here is a young lady engaged to marry a gent and doesn't even know that male's correct name. I'm horrified. Several of your letters were addressed Louis G. Grossberg.

"Your ever wondering beau, Louis

I dream of you by Day,
I dream of you by Night;
When will you come and stay
That I may hold you tight?

"Ahala! Poetry. Maybe it's my empty stomach. LOVE, Lou"

Celia was busy writing the same day: "We received the Argomite this morning and I already witnessed a bit of the results this noon. Mother washed an oil mop that did not see water in eight years. Well, you should see the mop now. As good as the day we bought it.

"Mother said Argomite will always find a place on our pantry shelf. No other article in our house had as much oil and dirt as this mop. She said if it will clean this mop it will clean anything. So there you are. My father is going to try it on the car this afternoon. If it takes off the paint from the car, prepare yourself with the idea of buying him a new one. I will let you know the results later.

"My mother, father, George and Ruth are leaving for Baltimore and points south this coming Monday or Tuesday morning. Dear, I wish I was going with them. Mother wants me to go, I told her not to worry that after being in your house just ten minutes she will feel as if she was born and bred in Washington.

"How do you like this for smartness. My side partner said, 'Miss Kanster, why do Electricians, carpenters, printers, etc., call themselves by the title "Doctor." In fact on nearly every bill that I have had so far the "Dr." appears after the name.' Nu, go tell her the truth. (Dr. means debtor). She said she honestly believed that they were specialists in their particular line of business having acquired the right to the title 'Doctor.'

"How is little Doris? I wrote to Ida some time ago and have not as yet received a reply. I have been a little worried. Your best and only sweetheart, Cel"

On May 23, 1928, Dave writes to Ida and Lou from New York.

"I got into Philadelphia and I got over to Murray's office in short order." He learned that a crew was out doing house-to-house canvassing and vacuum cleaner salesmen were starting on the job. Murray told him a salesman was working on a chain of 65 lunch rooms to use it for dishwashing and the Curtis Publishing Company to remove ink from their pans. If successful, it cuts the cost of washing down to less than 2 cents per pound. He expects to sell them 300,000 pounds of Argomite a year at 12 cents.

"I got into New York near 4. I think that I will get the $1,000 from (my brother) Al. We figured that I would need $9,000.00 to work this game on the wholesale basis for four months if I did not make a single sale. That would include the salaries of three salesmen as well, and if in that time I sell my quota of two carloads, I will have at least covered my entire expense."

Dave saw Mr. Barryman who said he sent down two bags to the laundry to try it out tomorrow. Dave said he was nervous as a cat about the test. Next was to find office space.

"I did not want to go over $60, but those at that price are not so exciting. Finally I saw an ad in the Times and I visited a new office building 55 W 42 St. and on the 24th floor a certain company had rented the whole floor and they in turn sub-rented each room either furnished or unfurnished. There was an operator always on hand to take all incoming messages, and one could hire a steno for 75 cents per hour. I can get a small furnished room for $65.00 and a larger one for $75.00. If it is necessary to move into larger quarters we can do so in the same building without any change in the address or phone number.

"Now I wish Lou would do something for me. Ask Glover for the name of the warehouseman who charges 5 cents for handling and 10 cents for delivery. Also get Seager (a worker for Argomite) to give me a copy of the instructions for laundries (and) to take you through the dishwashing establishment of the Press Club, and try to get a letter from them. Tomorrow I intend to pump Mr. Edwards dry (re) Argomite. So here's hoping that you both pray and if possible say a few *capitlach* of *Tillim* (lines of prayer) that the test be O.K."

Louis wrote to Celia on May 24: "Before anything else let me yell out to your father, thru you, NOT to do it. Who ever said Argomite is good for washing Dodges? It will take the paint off if you don't use it in the proper solution. All paints have an oil substance in them and Argomite dissolves oil. Hence and therefore don't do it. Of course, where the paint has become long since hardened a weak solution of Argomite is not going to hurt the car or any other paint. The solution, however, must be weak. And if you don't know how to make the proper solution, the paint is apt to walk off with the washing especially where one gets extravagant and uses the raw powder right on the body.

"I washed my car in it last Sunday and no paint came off but I did it by first, the night before preparing a jelly of it by dissolving one pound of Argomite in a gallon of water and bringing the solution to a warmth of about 160 degrees F. This I left stay in the container until next morning when the solution had solidified into a jelly or soft mass of Argomite. In the morning I took a half bucket of water and dumped a handful or two of this jelly into it and dissolved the same into the water. This, then, made a properly weak solution for the car. The result was a pretty clean car and no paint gone. However, the jelly put on as is to the running board and the hub caps and the running gear and floors and windows does wonders.

"The aluminum on my car was never so bright and shiny as it was after I put a little of the jelly on it and scrubbed a bit with an ordinary kitchen brush. The running board, too, that is the linoleum, washed out beautifully clean.

"So you would like to come along to see me. I wonder why. If you come here and stay till Friday I'll go back with you to Newark. As for the rest of the folks, I might perhaps meet them somewhere or even maybe in Baltimore and show them the way over.

"So your mamma likes the Argomite we are selling. That's fine. I just knew she would. And what about Edith? I suppose she doesn't know what to do with it. Tell her to put a little of it in some water in the pan – when she burns the cooking – and boil awhile. Oh, she doesn't burn any meals? Excuse please.

"To-day was the big test over at the Barryman hang-out and I am rather fearful, because, if he had chalked up a huge success Dave would have wired me of the results. No wire having come, I am afraid that nothing happened. I must leave you now, dearest, Always your devoted, sweetheart, beau, Chosen, fiancée, and what not."

That same day, Celia was writing Louis: "I am angry, angry, etc. This is not the way to start off a love letter but I asked for three days off, of course deducting it from my vacation, but the Chief Clerk said 'Nothing doing.' He (said) that I wasn't the only peble (sic) on the beach and if he allowed me the privilege then he would have to extend the courtesy to the others. If I can't get the time off I will have to console myself thinking of *You*.

"Tonight is Yontif and I have been called several times to help with the supper.

"By the way Mother wants to know if you and your family would like to send announcements of our engagement to your relatives and friends…"

And in another letter on the same date, she writes: "We are all very strong for Argomite and to prove it I am going to state a few instances. Sarah has a silk blouse that she can't wear on account of several stains on the sleeve." She dipped the sleeve in diluted Argomite and the stain disappeared. George's greasy hands were transformed after washing them with Argomite. "My mother said if she did not see George she wouldn't believe they were his hands. My father also tried it on his hands and said, 'There is nothing like it in the world.'

"I bet you haven't thought of this one. My father has so much confidence in it that he even washed his teeth with it and said it never felt so clean in his life. Yes? Edith has not as yet tried it but will open the bag today.

"I have been thinking all morning of you and Dave and how he is making out in New York. I understand they are going to use it in their wash today. Talk about washing clothes. My father was painting the swing the other day and before applying the paint he wiped the framework with a cloth. Mother found out it was a new handkerchief and by the time she spied it, it was black as coal. She put it in the washing machine and after they had been washed she couldn't find it because all the 'kerchiefs were as white as could be. The same applies to several soiled collars.

"This letter is getting to be kind of washy-wishy but you don't mind, dear, because it is all good news and it is the kind you want to hear. Sweetheart this all goes to prove that it has excellent merits and it just has to go. By the time you get this letter I hope that you have heard from Dave as to the success of the test."

In his letter to Dave, also written on the 24th, Louis says he will see Glover and Seager the following afternoon. "The thing that puzzles me about your letter is the office part. How come you are looking for an office so far uptown as the heart of the theater district? I should think that you would look for a place somewhere more towards the industrial section of town. How are you going to get 200 lb. bags of Argomite up to the 23rd floor of a new office building? I hope you know what you are about.

"All day today I expected and awaited a wire from you since I rather thought you'd send one if the demonstration was satisfactory. Not having received any I am inclined to believe that your test did not come out so hot…I had Fred B. here the other evening with the view to getting him to sell it for Seager. He was much interested and promised to go to see Seager on the morrow. The next news is due from you. Love and high hopes, Lou"

"May 25, some hours later (1928)," Celia writes. "For the want of something to do I am writing to you again. It seems when a person is in love they are not responsible for what they say or do. Why, I didn't even spell pebble correctly in my last letter. I have it right here but I am not going to open it because I might find more errors. If that is what love does then I don't mind.

"I am leaving for the drugstore in less than two minutes. I want you to get the letters tomorrow. Good night and God bless you, Cel"

"My most Adorable," Louis replies the next day. "This is Friday evening. I have been trying to warm myself up by thinking that your arms are around me and mine around you. It surely is chilly here to-day.

"Your Argomite experiences and record of tests were very interesting. As to your father's idea of brushing his teeth with it, I washed my own teeth in it one day last week. The trouble about that is that they forgot to scent the stuff or sweeten it. It tastes as rotten as it cleans well. No, thank you. I prefer my Colgates. What's the idea of letting that stuff take up nine tenths of the letter? You devoted the teeniest little bit of the letter to me and the rest of it all to Argomite. I am jealous."

Dave's letter today says the Argomite test "came out fairly all right." The trouble was the people in the plant did not like changing their methods of washing. Dave offered Barryman a very attractive price provided he buys it by the carload. The laundry could then cut its bleach by 50%. "I, Personally, do not care whether Barryman buys or not."

Louis' immediate interest was to sell their required quota and thus earn enough profit to provide Dave with a living, "so that I may be able to figure on marriage within some definite time. The only trouble with us is that we have no money. If we had about ten thousand dollars, I would look around at once to getting rid of this practice and go over to New York and work right along with Dave. It takes a bit of time to introduce a new product and we haven't the time to give it and want a success from the start. But I still refuse to worry.

"I am so lonesome for you, honey. Our couch has no interest for me at all with you in Newark. How wonderful it will be when you and I will be married and I will come home from the office, whether here or in New York, and find my sweetheart setting the table for my supper. I won't have to be lonesome then. If necessary I could get away in the middle of the day and go see my wifie. But all these things seem so far away.

"Let's see. This is practically June 1. June, July, August, September. How would sometime in September be? Well, maybe. If everything goes half-way good we might make it then. How about it, dear?

"To-day is *Schwuoth* (*Shavuot*, a Jewish Holiday in the spring) and

I have to go to shul. It is almost time for that. Yontev in our home is very enjoyable. The atmosphere is right and everything is fine.

"I feel as if I can no longer express my love for you, sweetheart, by correspondence. I have to take you around and show you just how much I do love you. And, by golly, you just wait. I will, too. Your own love, Louis"

"By gosh, darn if I didn't get two letters from my honey," Louis writes Celia on May 26, 1928. "Don't be angry, dear. It only serves to make lines on that beautiful forehead of yours. Never mind, dear, I'll be coming over very soon now. Most likely next Friday. So just laugh at that fussy old chief clerk and tell him that soon your sweetheart will take you away from him altogether.

"They are all excited at the house at the prospect of seeing your folks Wednesday morning. We'll all be waiting for them. This is such a wonderful afternoon! But what good is it to me when my thoughts are so far from here. I have to write a very important tax brief for an appeal to the Board of Tax Appeals and I just can't bring myself to start it.

"As to the matter of announcements of our engagement, I care nothing either way. I am expected at Kitty's this evening where I am going with Miriam and Pauline and there the ideas of the family will be aired. I'm all for no fuss of any kind for anything. But if you or your folks have any desires on the subject either way, I am satisfied. But more of that shortly.

"Ida called me on the phone to-day and told me of her letter from Dave. It seems that he is going to have a confab with Barryman this evening and then we shall know more about the results of the demonstration from a monetary point of view.

"I had a phone call from Mr. Edwards the local expert who was with Dave on his tests at Barryman's. He (said) the tests were highly successful. He tells me also that he took the opportunity to utilize an extra day to get Dave accounts there. They are some large steamship companies, hotels, and industrial plants. He merely paved the way for him.

"Personally, dear, I have no doubt of the final success of the venture. The early stages are, of course, the hard ones. One just has to have the heart and the staying powers, If Dave doesn't have it I may decide to send him back here and take over the New York Job myself. Which reminds me, honey. Love does more than encourage making mistakes. It also overlooks them. The fact is that I never noticed that you had misspelled the word 'pebble' until you mentioned it in your second letter. What I did notice was words such as these: All my love' etc. So why worry about little things like pebbles?

"I'm so impatient I can hardly sit here and write. I feel like doing something that will let me forget that you are not here and that I cannot kiss that darling little chin of yours. And what is even more peculiar I am beginning actually to believe that you really love me after all. It seemed so hard to believe that in the beginning. I just felt that you were uncertain. But now, sweetheart, I am beginning to think that I was all wrong – at least that if you did not altogether love me before that you have changed in that regard.

"Oh, dearest, I am so glad! I could not possibly stay in love with you for ever if I thought that you did not love me. You know, dear, I am actually physically uncomfortable because you aren't here. It seems that even my bones are in love with you. But I must get busy with my brief writing. So may the Lord speed our permanent union so that we may both be the happiest kids in the world, Forever my love, Lou"

"This is once more a combination letter," to Ida and Louis, Dave writes on his father's letterhead, May 27th. "Today is now Sunday and the Holidays are over." Dave assumed Louis had heard from Edwards and learned about the laundry test. He was now awaiting the letters of introduction Edwards promised. "At this time Louis darling, you may order 20 bags, empty ones that contain 25 pounds for sample deliveries."

His brother Leo doubted that even $1,500 would do them much good and would be difficult to advance anyway. However, if he needed money to live, he would give him $1,000 without question. He wanted nothing to do with the business for himself.

Barryman offered the use of his floor as an office without rent for a couple of months. It was spacious enough but he would have to buy a desk for $25.00. "I did not ask him for any money at this time, for I felt that he was not so interested. I am beginning to get shy as the very devil. I feel like a *schnorrer* (beggar) and the people that I have asked for money seem to think likewise.

"If we had started out to form a corporation of 100,000 and sold some real stock, it might have been a different story, but the way it is now, just piddling along this way, I am afraid we can't get anywhere. For a fifty share in the business it is necessary that somebody put up 20 or 25,000 dollars." Dave felt it imperative to get from three to twenty salesmen who knew the city well, and that required capital.

"Our figures, Lou were O.K., but we can't play on nothing. I think that we will be able to get some large orders from Barryman and from him I will be able to get to the other laundries, but it will take several months yet before it materializes."

Dave planned to revisit the hospital and would probably get an order but it would take time. "So unless you can see your way clear to raising some money on your side of the fence, old chap, I think that we stop monkeying around and get down to real business. In my opinion, even one half is better than nothing.

"You may therefore order me 10 sacks at 200 and express me one 100-pound bag care of the Economy Mercantile 43 E 12 St. Also send out 100 lb. of Argomite Blue for sample purposes. It is really a devil of a note. Here I am trying to do things on a decent scale, to put across a real business and I am stuck from the very beginning. I really mean this tho, that we stop monkeying and see if we can't get somebody to take over the real financing of the whole matter."

"My one and only Sweetheart," Celia writes the same day. "Why is it I feel more lonely on a Sunday than during any other part of the week? I suppose it is because I have more time to think of you. Something will have to be done about this. The Chief Clerk wouldn't give me a satisfactory answer on Saturday so am in doubt if I will be able to go. He said just what I expected him to say. 'Too much work during that part of the month for Gladys to do by herself and I have no one I can spare to help her'.

"I didn't say a word to him but walked out. I felt like telling him, when I leave he will be lucky if he gets two weeks notice.

"Dear, you haven't told me if you are coming here on Friday. You see, if you could come here then, I wouldn't feel badly about not being able to visit you. September is an ideal month for a wedding and what not. The first reason is this; my birthday is during that month. In the 2nd place, Edith and Sarah were married during that month. Sept. is a lucky month my sisters say and they ought to know.

"I was just interrupted to answer the phone – guess who it is. Your

brother Willy telling me he will be right up with the Naiman brothers. I believe he said they were from Allentown. When I heard Willy's
voice I thought it was yours. It just proves to you in what direction my
brains are working…"

"Please forgive me for this seeming neglect," Louis' sister Esther
wrote, also on May 27, 1928, "but you know that my heart and thoughts
were with you when ever Shoshana was feeling a little better. My hearti-
est congratulations my dear to you. I am so happy to think that you have
found someone that you can love. I wish you the very best in this world.
Oh how anxious am I to be able to see your beloved for I am sure that
I'll like her. She must be a very nice girl if you have selected her as your
life's partner. May you both live to see your great grand children and
warm your old dear selves in the sunlight of their youth. That's rather
a funny wish to a young man but my dearest, I know that when you'll
reach that age this will be one of your highest blessings.

"I also feel and know my dear no matter what stands before you in
the long years of life to come, may it be nothing but happiness to you,
but one can stand it so much better no matter what it is if two people
have full faith in each other and keep the love fires burning, because
there surly are times when one needs them badly. I am afraid this is
becoming a real Sermon, but I do wish you both all the happiness in
the world."

She asks for a photo of Celia if Louis can spare it, and chides him
for not calling her with the news. "Next time do not deprive me of a
little joy, I need it.

"Now my dear lets go to the other story you were so good to tell me.
I am very glad for you if you think that the soap business will make you
rich? May G. be with you, but what about Dave's position in Rochester?
We haven't heard from him since he left Syracuse. As for the soap, I received it yesterday and if you will send me the bill I'll be glad to send
you the check for same. I shall try its ability tomorrow. I am sorry that
we are always so tight about funds.

"Harry is worried dreadfully we have very large payments to make
this coming first and no money to do it with. If times were different I
am sure he would have come to your aid, but I need not tell you for you
know better his circumstances than I do."

"Dear Ida and Louis," writes Dave from New York on May 28. He had spent the day trying to get a room at the YMHA. Though only $5 per week, "they were so rotten that I could not even force myself to think of them. I saw ads in the papers for nicer rooms at $8 to $10 per week and I thought that I would be able to get a room at the YMHA but the one I applied to downtown won't have me as I am too old. I swear I can't live like a pig during the hot weather in New York even to save the much needed dollars. Auntie wants me to come to supper every day and I might take her up on that.

"I have finally made arrangements with the Bush Terminal Company to handle all of our stuff for 10 cents each way per bag and 10 per month storage. They also make daily deliveries (and) we can rent a space 550 square feet for $45 a month in which we can do all of our own packing and rehandling. Here are the instructions for all future transactions:

> Consign to: The Argomite Co. of NY or John Doe, Care of Bush Terminal Company,
> Distribution Division, Building #26, Bush Docks Station, Brooklyn, NY.
> Forward delivery orders, manifests and bills of lading to:
> Bush Terminal Company, Distribution Division, 4206 First Ave., Brooklyn, NY.
> I saw a lovely large office in the same building down on 53 Park Place, which would not be over 10 minutes from the Brooklyn terminal for $85 per month. It is an office 13x30 and has facilities for carrying quite a few samples in the office. It would be right down town and would be ideally located for us.

Dave said, as a money raiser, he had been a miserable flop. Al was not interested in investing and he had gotten nothing from Barryman and won't ask for it any more. At the laundry, the washer and chief said Argomite was all right, but it would take time to be accepted by the rest of the workers.

> I really believe that Barryman is waiting for a couple of months to see what happens. Of course that means darn little to me at this time. It is necessary to have a force of salesmen both in the

wholesale and in the retail, and that means some money to start on. I don't know how much I can sell by myself, for all I want to do is to go after extra large accounts.

I just drew a check for $50 from our account G&G as I have to buy a desk. Also when do I or don't I begin to draw a salary, and if I do from where is it coming. I would suggest that we try to get together some real money on a 50–50 basis. This real money might be more than 25,000 if possible. I feel like the very devil working here on Manny's measly $1,000, without which however we would have been in a devil of a pickle. I am now going to try and sell it to diversified users, the automobile, the lunch rooms, the hospitals and etc. I am awaiting Edwards' letters as I would certainly like to get hold of the Standard Oil company work.

Here I have been hoping that I might be able to make the trip but Edith with no thought in the world of going calls Mother and tells her she would like to be the fifth party of the gang.

Celia writes, also on the 28th. "Not that I begrudge Edith the trip but wouldn't a thing like that make you good and angry. I wanted to, but can't, she didn't, but is. Get that! Mr. Whitman has been trying to get on the good side of me but it is no use. He has been telling me how unreasonable I am. I admit they are short of help but what has that got to do with my going. None whatsoever!

"I can't say anymore about my love than what I have said in my previous letters so if you want to know what I think of you just take an old letter out of your file and read it again. Come to think of it, it isn't fair and I wouldn't want you to tell me to do that. Yes, I take that statement back and will tell you over again that I love you, etc. etc., So will close this epistle with all my love to you. Cel

"P.S. I am going to try and remember that your middle initial is *C* see like *Celia*. C"

"Dearest Sweetheart," writes Louis the next day, May 29. He wanted to visit Celia the next weekend and buy her a ring in Philadelphia but Ida tells him he should go to New York to put some pep into Dave who has gotten discouraged at his failure to raise money. "So what would you advise your husband to do, if you had a husband?

"We are all still as excited as before about your folk's coming on Wednesday. I am keeping the day as clear as possible so I can spend it all with them. Of course, it is merely so much wasted longing to long for your being here too.

"So you, too, think that September would be the right month for us to get married? Well, sweetie, I'll tell you something even better than that. I think June would even be better if – . That is just the trouble there is always some sort of an if to butt in and spoil the joys of life.

"If things of Argomite would only open up a little and we could see daylight, I might be in a position to really talk definite time. Of course, Dave hasn't really started. We must give him a chance to do something before we begin to lose heart. I wrote him a scorching letter last night telling him what I thought of his pessimism. Maybe, if I go over there, and instill a little enthusiasm in him he will become more perked up, as they say. We'll see.

"Now, dearest, I am awfully sorry that you are so lonesome, but also I am, oh, so glad. Your only true love, Louis"

"Time seems to heal all pains and so mine too has been healed," writes Louis in a second letter dated May 29. "I am alluding to the disappointment of not being able to expect you on the morrow. I shall begin to look forward to seeing you anyway despite that chief hokum of yours.

"Well, dearest, what now? I am honestly getting to dislike the poor substitute of letter writing and receiving to talking to you and seeing and kissing and hugging you. Oh, how I should love to have you with me now instead of in the future. Seems as if everything I want is in the future. I shouldn't kick, tho. Look at the difference this year had for me over the year before. Now I *can* kiss you and love you and have you. Last year at this time I had none of these and the prospects even very remote. Guess I'm ungrateful. I'll try not to fret any more for a time. This kind of a mood invariably makes me feel sorry for my self – a bad sign.

"Got a lovely letter from my sister Esther and my brother-in-law. I had written them a letter and told them about *you*, that is not really much about you but about my love and our engagement. I am enclosing their letters so you can see for yourself. Now that I read it over seems that I, and not you, are getting all the tributes. However, don't mind them. They don't know me any more. Esther and Harry are nice and

I'm sure you'll like them both. It is a pity that they are so far from here otherwise we should surely run up there and see them.

"I was very happy to read that Edith has decided to come along. I am only sorry that the two Sams and Sarah could not have come too so that the two families could have got acquainted in toto. I can see lots of kisses in store for me tomorrow. Hot dog!

"By the way, now that the subject has come up, Is it all right and proper to kiss all the women folks in your house (excluding non-Kansters) whenever I come and when I leave? You see, not having ever been a prospective son and brother-in-law I don't know the ropes. I'm really not kidding, sweets, I'd like to know. Please don't tell anybody I asked. They'll probably laugh at me. Just you tell me yourself.

"If I come up this weekend I shall want to go to New York and see Dave. In fact I shall not only want but I shall have to do it. Ida expects to go up on the excursion. She suggests that I see Dave on Saturday and get over our business so that she will be able to enjoy the day with him. Maybe I can get Dave to come over to Newark and see me there. That boy needs some encouragement. He has dropped low in his heart on account of the failure he has encountered to raise the money he expected New York to throw into his lap.

"I tell him to forget raising money and get busy selling Argomite. After sales have been made the money will take care of itself. I've turned over some stock I have to Leo (Freudberg) to try and borrow on it. I am not so much perturbed about the money. As soon as sales are made and profits are shown they'll be asking us to let them come in. But why worry you about it?

"My love, sweets, is everlasting and it all belongs to you, even tho if you were to look at a letter that I write to Dave sometimes you'd find it end 'Lovingly.' But that is different kind of love. The love I have for you is like Niagara. It keeps pouring out but never lessens."

Celia was also writing on the 29th. "I have less than two seconds to spare. By all means come out here this Friday. The ring can wait but Argomite cannot. I hope your appearance here will help Dave in every possible way. Let me know when I may expect you.

"I am glad my folks are going to meet yours tomorrow and sincerely hope there will be a mutual feeling all around. Give my love to everyone in your house. Tell them I am sorry I cannot be there."

"Glover tells me that the Bush is a good terminal and another one was the Hudson Terminal," Louis writes to Dave, also on the 29th. "Barton said it was O.K. for you to sell in Paterson and in New Jersey and that he would send you a letter to that effect.

"I guess Ida must have told you all about Mannie's offer to go to New York and spend a month there at your command. He feels that Argomite has enough future for even him there as a salesman and he is willing to invest a month on commission only to see what he can do with it. So I told him right off 'You're elected.' I shouldn't want him to go just yet until after you have become a bit established. He is ready to leave within a couple of weeks.

"In the meantime I have made my application for $475 loan on my insurance and Leo has also taken the stock and promises to get us one thousand dollars. When we get that, we'll have $2,500. Enough, I say, to stop worrying and going ahead selling Argomite–not stock. If Korvin here can make his sixty dollars a week you should at least be able to do likewise–on a small scale. We have three months more before we need worry about our carload. And let me tell you, sonny, that in any event you will have a hell-of a-time getting any kind of decent capital without in the first place having made some sales and showing the prospective capitalists that Argomite is commercially salable. So I say once more, FOR HEAVENS SAKE STOP WORRYING ABOUT CAPITAL AND GO TO WORK.

"Show me accounts receivable in the amount of about $2,000 which should be possible with our capital of $2,500 and then holler about money. But as long as you keep crying with the original $1,000 still untouched, I'll be damned if it doesn't sound like chicken heartedness.

"Them, son, is hard woids, but you need to be jolted out of your apparent lethargy. Don't ask anybody for more advice and go ahead and peddle your Argomite. In the meantime you might hint to Barryman that the trial shipment should be paid for..."

"I was rather interested in the two sour letters I received from both of you," Dave writes to Ida and Louis, "in which you tell me to buck up my courage and to be a man and not feel downhearted or etc.

"I do not think that my asking for a 50–50 basis of financing is a concession of failure except in a failure of getting money. (Do) you realize that I have two things to do, first make enough sales to sell my quota and then incidentally to make a living but did you ever try to think that a carload is a lot of Argomite and that unless I can get some very large users, I won't be able to cover my quota. Of course if Barryman comes in as a real purchaser, that will just about settle the whole problem, but he is not doing that thing yet. So in the meanwhile I can only go as far as one man and a not too experienced salesman can go.

"I am at present only going after very large prospective customers but to sell a big user takes a lot of time and patience. I have already found that out with this laundry."

Mr. Sheehan of the Norton Company asked for samples for his floors. Sheehan claimed that at least 100,000 pounds of cleaning compound were used daily in that part of the city alone. The hospital was interested but the Federation of Jewish Charities would have to pass on it first. As for building superintendents, he first needed to show each one how to use it.

"So you see what rigmarole it is necessary to go through before landing a real order. If I can get Argomite on the Federation schedule why can't you see what it will mean, but just the same it is not being done overnight. That is why I need money…"

Dave listed his needs: printing circulars, stationery, an order book and several hundred dollars for miscellaneous. Since he had to leave the office at 5:30, he needed a girl to write letters as he was a "rotten typeset," or get another machine and do it at home without his files. He also needed at least one salesman to handle the Kosher restaurant business.

"So don't get so darn scared and shudder and think that I am blue etc., just because I am beginning to realize that it does take capital to run a business. Just the same, at this time I will let you play the financial wizard. I will try and sell Argomite and stop bothering you with the pesky details of finances. I think that you should have sent me the 100 pounds by express and the 10 bags to the Bush Terminal, (and) let me have some money to pay for the freight on the stuff as it comes in.

"I just bought a piece of junk desk and a new chair for $27 and I ordered some cards for $3.00. But I have to get other stuff as well, such as small boxes, and the etceteras. Now while you are resting, order me 100 small five-pound bags and about 25 25-pound bags. Now please Louis, please send me or bring with you when you come here at the end of the week, the following: the hand punch, my personal cards with just my name on them, and the empty fillers for my pocket note book. Also order me a 200-pound bag of Argomite Blue to be delivered to Barryman, as I want to have samples made of that for talking to dairies. At present I can't do a thing as I have nothing with me for samples. Get the Royal (typewriter) fixed up – and let me have it"

The Argomite Industries monthly statement dated May 31, 1928, contained an item from May 18 for $413.68, which was paid in cash.

The same date as the Argomite statement, David wrote Ida and Louis. "I received three (letters) from Ida and one from Louis. Alright old socks we will attend strictly to business and no more to the worry of financing. However today I am left in the lurch so-called. I had asked you to order me 100 pounds of Argomite sent by express and I have not gotten it yet. I have used up my last sample and there ain't no more. It is of no value for me to go trying to sell my wares unless I can give or show a sample. I thought that express meant something. At any rate today I saw a certain Dr. Kalen and he is the purchasing agent of 16 to 18 drug stores and he is also a friend of Leo's who might be interested in the stuff. So I left him my last bag and a leaflet of instructions. He promised to put it to every test and told me to return next week. I think that Manny is a prince. I hope to have some real work for the boychick as soon as he comes in, and two weeks from now should be fine. I will put him on to the office buildings, and that is field enough for any man.

"In re the Paterson stuff in the silk mills, it will most decidedly be worth plenty as they can use lots of Argomite in their silk dyeries. I have the names of two of the largest in the country with letters of introduction to each.

"Yesterday being Memorial Day, I spent the day at Leo's. I certainly sold the stuff to the maid, and she is going to tell it to her friends who are also maids and I told her that I would send it to them by mail at $1.50 per bag. She certainly was enthusiastic.

"This part, Louis is for your ears only and is in singlicate. If you can spare some change to the old lady it will be greatly appreciated. So far this month I think that I drew about $140. It will be another week or two till I can start earnings, and you will have to pitch in from your end to help pay bills."

Celia wrote on the same day to, "My only Sweetheart. The special delivery letter came a few minutes ago and I was happy because you wanted me to receive it *today*. The letter was the next best thing in your stead.

"I was very happy to read the letters of Esther and her better half. I know I am going to like them, why, because they are members of your family and the same applies to your relatives. I hope you will feel the same about mine.

"Dearest, it will make me very happy if you will kiss Mother when you come and go – as for my sisters, they won't need any coaxing as you can guess by the actions of Edith. I have never read a rule or a book on the subject but what I do know is it will please my mother and what pleases her in this matter will also please me. I do want Mother and my sisters to love my husband-to-be."

"Dear Gang," David wrote the next day. "Today everybody must have gone on strike as I got no letter from anybody. I have not yet gotten the stuff here and therefore am very much stuck. I am sitting on pins and needles. I wanted to see some people and make some demonstrations and try to land some actual orders. I can't understand how it is possible for the express company to lose so much time making deliveries.

"A young fellow that Mr. Barryman sent might start to sell Argomite for me on a commission basis, with possibly a small drawing account of about $25.00 a week. He knows the superintendents of several large office buildings (and) knows the manager of the Long Island territory of the Eureka Vacuum Cleaner Company and he tells me that in that territory alone he has a crew of 180 men selling cleaners from house to house. Those fellows are making money. Do you realize what the field is now in the retail game?

"In Paterson, NJ, practically all of the silk of the country is dyed there and a great deal of soap is used. If I get one of those dyers, that is a quantity outlet.

"The Argomite Company of New York, by David A. Glushak, President"

"So here I am once more thru the mails," Louis writes to Celia on June 4. "How inadequate mail can be in competition with the real thing. And what a *real* thing you are, Sweetheart! I have been going around as in a trance all day. Dearest, this was the most wonderful visit I ever made anywhere at any time. It was just perfect, except for the one lost hour I missed because I anticipated gaining it thru daylight saving.

"I am beginning, also, to believe more and more that you love me. It is gaining momentum anyway and I have hopes that some day you will love me sufficiently to satisfy even my ravenous hunger for your love. Did you get that? Your *love*. YOURS.

"Ruth was given the gate to-day and I had the pleasure to assist in getting her out of town. She made a hit here. She seems to have become very popular with papa. And by the way she was responsible for starting quite a fuss in the house. It seems that in all the excitement mother forgot to give her some things to eat on the way.

"When we came home after taking her to the station father wanted to know did we give her something along for the ride – something to chew on. Mother gave out an *Oh-ich hob fargessen* (oh, I have forgotten), and father hasn't been able to forget it all afternoon. You'd think that he let her go away without anything to eat for a two days' trip. As late as seven o'clock this evening – long after she should have been home, father was still worrying about it. *Es ken mir emes ergeren* (how could it be worse), he said.

"I hear that Ruthie made quite a hit with Babe. Mother says that all of you seem to make just one harmonious person. I gorra go sweets."

On June 4, 1928, Dave writes Louis and Ida that the Argomite still had not arrived, but a call to the Bush Terminal said it would be delivered tomorrow. Another wasted day. However, Dave hired two salesmen who appeared rather bright. "Without seeing a drop of the stuff and no tests they were already excited about it. The fellow Grossberger (no relation) who was here before, has some darn good leads and he is only waiting for the stuff so that we can make samples of it and make tests. I spent the whole afternoon lecturing to the men. I believe that they will remain with this organization for some time and the real secret of this job is getting salesmen."

"Another day has went by," Dave writes them again on June 6. "Yesterday I spent a half a day getting my samples in and explaining the stuff to my two salesmen. I gave each a bag and told them to go home and play with the stuff, and after they have sold themselves, to go out and sell it for me."

His new salesman, Grossberger, showed it to a superintendent of a large building and left a sample. He also left a sample with the super of the Equitable Life Insurance Building and gave a demonstration at the Hebrew Home. He left a sample with the super of Cooper Union and met with a Captain Bastian of Standard Oil Co., who needed a product to clean out his tanks. He hoped to meet someone from the regular Standard Oil Company soon. His other salesman did not show up.

"So far gang, no orders yet. I can't afford to start working on small orders. Mr. Barryman says, go after one client at a time, and either land him or chuck him. So far I have gone after only the larger fellows, and I am not thru yet. But I am still hoping. I found that I have no trouble at all in getting an audience and people are really interested in the stuff. It is just a question of patience for a little while. Find out from Korvin if the Union Station is using the stuff. Thanks for the check. It has already been deposited.

"Ask Barton if there is any chemical test that a salesman can show that the stuff is not harmful to marble, and that there is no free caustic. So here's to luck to ourselves."

Dear Lou,

Just a postscript to ask you to let the Mrs. have some loose change yet for last month. I am hoping darn hard that it won't be long before that will be ended, as the checks will flood in from here. Dave

"I LOVE YOU AND ONLY YOU" was handwritten in large letters across the page of Louis' letter, June 6, 1928, 12:30 PM where he writes, among other things: "Your picture – the one that is so terrible – has been taken out of the middle drawer of the desk and is now leaning against the telephone. It smiles. It may be a poor likeness but, Honey, it is the best I have here. If you want it back you better hurry up and let me have a better one or you won't get it back even then.

"You are a wonderful little sweetheart even if you don't know how to love me so that I will be satisfied. Your dear, Louis, Sealed with a kiss"

"Got your letter and the sincerity of it just gushed out in a way to make me, too, feel that you do 'care for me,'" Louis wrote in another letter, also dated June 6. "How wonderful it is to feel that so exquisite a person as you are loves me. Your letters lately, that is the one I just received, rings so true that I know your heart wrote it for otherwise you could never have but down on paper the things you said. Even I can now be satisfied with the word care. It means to me the same that it means to you and maybe now it means more to you than it meant in the beginning of things. This reminds me that I now am figuring the beginning of things from the date of our engagement. It feels even wonderful just to be alive.

"Sweetheart, please don't ask me to return that picture of yours until after I have received one of your new ones. There is no one in the office but you and I. You are leaning against the calculating machine smiling down at me trying to make you think I am really a typist with the two fingers that dance all over the keys in an attempt to beg you to leave you stay here. Honest I won't show it to a soul. Not even to the washer lady who comes here to tidy up every night.

"I certainly am happy that Ruthie feels that she had a good time. Babe is tremendously impressed with her niceness. Nice little kid, she is, he keeps saying. The funny part about her is that she feels freer about giving her brother-in-law a hug and a kiss while everybody is looking on than you do your husband. Aren't you ashamed?

"Ask Ruthie how to snuggle up to a sweetheart. But she did tell me something out of school – at least she told it to someone in the house. It seems that your love affair is no secret to the Kansters. They all know about it and they say that you are quite a whole lot in love with that guy over in Washington.

"There is little news coming forward from Dave this week. He did say that he has interested a couple of likely looking salesmen to work with him. It is, of course, a slow process the way we have to work and it will take patience. All I want of him just now is that he hurry up and make his own living out of it and sell enough to safeguard our contract.

"That program up top will just about mean that you and I may talk seriously of the exact date when you and I will become one; when I will have the right to call you wife and you to call me husband; when I will close up shop; to come home to my own home and mayhap to bring home a guest to meet the wife and have dinner with us; when I may

317

have the pleasure to see my home grow in beauty with the creations of my own wife; when the distance of the local phone call will separate us at any time during the working day; when nothing will separate us during the night; when by and by I'll become the proud papa – this better cease right here. David has a nice holy job on his hands. May the good Lord guide him alright to fulfill his task with speed and with precision. Amen! The proudest Chosen in town.

"Have just put your picture back to bed. She sends her regards and she does not want to leave me unless thru substitution by a suitable representative. Good luck. Love, Love, Love, Lou"

Celia must have been thinking along the same lines, because she sent another picture in her letter of June 7. "Take a peek at the enclosed picture. I think it is pretty good. We sure do look happy don't you think! I am going out and catch a breath of fresh air – it is too nice out to stay in. I think I will take you along with me while I walk."

"I have been busy all morning," Celia explains, "reading and answering the correspondence for the radium victim employed in our bank. The letter that I have just finished is to Judge Conner of this City thanking him for his cooperation in the case. He merely acted as a citizen and has personally guaranteed the girls $10,000 each out of his own funds should the case be lost in court. Grace Farley is a very pathetic figure and I am only sorry I cannot help in any other way.

"I must look up the words coincident and coincidence. Now–how did I use the word coincident? I said something to the effect that it was a coincident I was in New York at that time. Let me see what *Funk & Wagnalls* have to say about it. Just one minute please.

"Coincidence-Agreement; a circumstance agreeing with one another; often implying accident.

"Coincident-Agreeing, as in position, extent, time, concurring or corresponding.

"After reading the definitions I still think I am right. I would say – It was a coincidence that she wasn't hurt. I don't mind being corrected so if I am wrong do not hesitate in telling me where and why.

"Have you heard from Dave? I hope he is not losing heart but instead gaining Argomite users. I think Sarah told you about a silk shirt that had a stain that could not be removed, well, last night she applied a pinch of Argomite to the spot and as Dave would say, 'The darn thing disappeared.'

"Edith said Argomite is doing wonders to her woodwork. Honestly, if everybody would like Argomite half as much as we like it, your troubles would be over."

"Dearest Celia," writes Louis on the same day, commenting on his lack of mail from her today. "I have already had my morning's glimpse of your sweet face but, in accordance with my promise of yesterday, I have put it back where no one will see it. Ida is coming in this morning to do a little typing for me. You may rest assured, sweetheart, that I shall not say a thing to her about the picture. So far as anyone is concerned that ain't any such.

"Dave is due to come in on the excursion Saturday nite to Sunday evening. At some future date I'll try it out myself going your way. If I like it I'll get a reservation for the season."

Dave's letters complain that large users are reluctant to buy Argomite without a thorough test first. "If those large users only knew what is dependent upon their purchases they would surely hurry up and leave their tests for later. Maybe it would be a good plan to print a little circular to go with each sample in which the story of our love is told. And then, I'm sure the buyers would just flock in for their orders.

"When may I call on you, my love? If it isn't money that holds me back it is time. This week. I couldn't go for lack of time. The money part, then, does not matter.

"Your niece Edith (Cohen) and your adopted nieces Reeva and Gracie performed on the stage the night before last and the performance was just what I had anticipated. They cavorted around and everybody who had children there had a nice time. The uncles didn't enjoy it so much. But I suppose it is all right. Kitty figured out just how much the various dances Edith did cost. It was really funny.

"So sweetie, what? I have an ache in my heart that I can only diagnose as lonesomeness for you. I believe I would be the happiest man this side of Eden if I were fortunate enough to have met and conquered the lady of (my) dreams and married her. And it all seems right up to Argomite. Isn't it strange tho, come to think of it? The whole story of our meeting and the things that followed and the Argomite and Dave going out to wash New York for us so that it may be clean enough for us when we get there, all this is certainly an excellent theme for a 'best seller.' Maybe you and I will write it some day, huh?

"I'm going dear. Your impatient husband-to-be to be your husband. LOVE ME? Yours forever, Lou"

"Dear Ida and Louis," writes an excited Dave on June 8. "My star and only salesman came in with the first order for 100-pounds of Argomite. A sale has been made and an order taken. He has been doing some real missionary work and has seen some nice people.

"Tomorrow is Saturday and I should not ask this of you, but get me some 100-pound bags of Argomite. Ship out 10 in 100-pound bags tomorrow, as I have not got facilities here for filling one hundred pounds full. Please ask them to get them out tomorrow to the Bush Terminal. I did not get the Blue yet..." He also wanted some Blue books from Edwards. "I had an interview with the purchasing agent of the Standard Oil Company of New Jersey." If Ida would type up a detailed report about Argomite, he would submit it to the engineering staff of Standard Oil for their entire organization. "I don't know yet what will be the result of the test on board ships but it is to be given a fair test."

"Sweetheart Mine," writes Celia on June 8. She is rushing to the photographer's to sit for a portrait and promises to send the new one after receiving the old one back. "Ruthie hasn't stopped talking about your family and of course 'Babe.' She sure was sorry to come home. I cannot blame her a bit for that because I felt the same way when I visited your home. As for the sandwiches, tell your Mother not to worry because Ruthie tells me she had little time to eat because all her time was taken up thinking of the wonderful time she had.

"I was very sorry to see you go dear and am now hoping your next visit will be a longer one. I am beginning to think that I do *Care* for you.

"Beau Night, Friday, June 8 1928," She writes in the next letter. "I went to bed early because I was tired and sleepy. Did I sleep? I should say not. Yes, I think I am in LOVE."

"I am glad Sylvia likes me, etc.," she writes in response to something Louis wrote earlier about a Federation worker. "I think it right nice of her to say nice things about me. But why should she say you *have become quite fresh*. Does she know something about *yourself* that

I am ignorant of? And since when has an engaged male acquired the authority to call whom he pleases 'Darling.' 'Tis true they say everybody loves a lover but I have never heard anybody say a lover loves everybody. To set you right, this is to inform you I am the only privileged character who may accept your love. You know dear, I thought I was the only one you called 'Darling' – now I see I am one of the many. Booh! Booh! And a few more.

"I went to the photographer's last night and as soon as the picture is finished I will send it on to you via Air Mail. All because I am anxious to get the old one back. Sealed with two kisses."

"Have been duly bawled out for being so free with something that belongs exclusively to you." Louis replies. "Anyway, you are my 'Dearest' darling and that should make it up to you for my calling others darling – sometimes. However, I must insist that I still retain the right to call Dave darling whenever the occasion demands. All right?

"No, I'm sorry to say that Sylvia really knows nothing about me that you could not know. I have at all times been more or less of a good boy and there seems to be no one, at this writing, who could give me away. But Sylvia did say at one time during our work that despite my being engaged I have not lost the knack of blushing. I don't remember now what caused me to blush the other day. I think Rabbi Schwefel said something.

"I certainly hope the picture that is being manufactured is a good one. The little snapshot of you and me certainly wasn't good. I don't see where you get the idea that we look happy. I know I was happy and I think you, too, were happy but we certainly look mighty glum on the snapshot."

"If anybody had looked over my shoulder while I was reading your very wonderful letters," Celia writes, "I am sure there would have been no doubt in their mind as to our marriage. And do you honestly think I am still backward and shy? If I am I can't help it – I will try and overcome it.

"Did you get the letter with the two kisses? I can see right now that I am more liberal than you are. All this because you sent me only one. You will have to do better than that.

"I will call for the proofs this evening and praying that there will be a resemblance. Everyone says I am better looking than the pictures

I take. And as I consider some of the snap shots good, well you can guess the rest. No, I am not getting swell-headed. But really I cannot for the life of me understand what is expected of me in a picture. For your sake I hope they come out good. Yes, talking about pictures I haven't a right nice one of you. Have you a good picture at home that you could let me have?"

"Dear Heart," Louis replies on June 9. "Just tore out the first letter I started to write. The first sentence started off poorly and I continually made it worse by trying to patch it up. It had something to do with the two kisses with which you sealed the letter of several days ago. You know, dearest, a kiss in the flesh is worth a dozen on paper.

"This is Saturday afternoon and I am not working to-day. The day is just one of those dreamily gorgeous ones that one usually expects once or twice during the month of May. I am restless and cannot seem to find me a place to sit or to stand. Love makes me feel so blue at times. The fact is that I am so dissatisfied with everything around here. The sound of the telephone bell annoys me. My moods are so changeable. I don't know what I want. I am plumb restless. I may decide to take my golf bag and go play myself a little golf. It might relieve me of some of that restlessness that is upon me to-day. The very shoes on my feet irk me. If I had a race track at hand with a racing auto I believe I could run up a speed of 100 miles per hour. I know tho, that your lovely little hand placed upon my restless head would quiet me at once. What a glorious being the good Lord has made so that I may enjoy life. But the fact that he has placed her so much out of my reach must be a punishment for some sins that I have at some time committed.

"I really shouldn't write this to you. Why should I burden my beloved with my moods of loneliness? What can she do to help me? I don't want you to feel sorry for me, as it will only make me feel blue. And it is my business in life to make you happy at all times.

"About a picture of myself, I really haven't any. I have never had a photograph taken of myself. I don't even know what I look like. I may infer from your letter that your picture should be nearly ready. Wait a minute, honey, I am going to take out your picture and for the second time this afternoon – here it is – gaze upon it with awe and wonder that so exquisite a little human should write to me every day and insist that she loves me and only me.

"Darling of mine, sometimes when the present mood assails me and I feel so unhappy that you are not here I am almost afraid that it is wrong of me to love you so much. Sounds very strange such a thought but I can't help it.

"What makes you say this picture of you is so terrible? The more I look at it the better I like it and the more I love you if that is possible. Please don't worry about me, darling. I know it will pass over. I love you dearest as I never loved anyone before in all my life – not even excluding the puppy loves, which no doubt I experienced in my younger days. Louis"

"In your letter," comes Celia's reply on June 10, "you stated if a fellow really loves a girl he wants to see her happy and whatever she thinks necessary to make her happy he wants her to have. Well, dear I would like to have you come out and since the feeling is mutual how about this coming week-end. I wonder if you would make it for a Thursday night.

"I have the proofs here and the results are not so good. The photographer invited me to visit his studio for another sitting. Sweetheart I will have to get used to the idea that a homely girl can't expect to take a good picture. Oh well, we shall see what the others look like. Every time he snapped I thought of you so I have every reason to believe the result will be marvelous.

"Lou, I didn't bawl you out in reference to the 'Darling' episode but since you considered yourself bawled out – well and good. I *do* want to be the only one, dear."

"This is Sunday late in the evening," Louis writes on the same date. "Dave was here and has left. That is the tough part of these pesky excursions. You barely get in when you have to leave. Of course, the time it takes is practically none and the capital ditto. I might drift over next week. Don't depend on it yet as it is highly problematical. You may think about my idea of getting in late Thursday nite and tell me how to work it so I don't wake up your folks when I get in and so you get at least three hours sleep – from 10 PM to 1:00 AM. Unless you can promise me these two things I am not coming until Friday nite.

"Beyond the fact that Dave is getting himself a wider range of possibilities there is little to report. Should one of them break our way we'll rush off and get married and I'll keep my lovely little sweetheart all for myself and no separations of a month or so will be allowed. Dave is working on Standard Oil Company business and of course it takes time and should they adopt its use for their tank car cleaning then – well, dearest, I really don't expect that they will because so much good luck has not happened to me since I met a certain little lady over in New York some sixteen months ago. I shall be well pleased if he covers our quota and makes himself a living in the next half year.

"I came here to work but I think that I need to see you every little while to recharge my longing for you. If I didn't the shock of seeing you again after a long absence might be too great for my nerves.

"I am anxiously awaiting the arrival by air mail of the new pictures. But maybe it would be less foolish to send it by regular mail as it would probably get here in the same time and would cost much less money. Dave would like to see the pictures that were taken on Sunday with his camera. He took some pictures of me to-day and if they look good I'll send you some.

"By the way, when you see Dave next, just shoot him, will you. I told him that you were having some pictures made by a regular photographer and that bird had the nerve to ask me whom you are going to get to pose for you. I was for killing him right then and there but Ida suggested that you are the logical person to murder him for that wise crack. He, however, insisted that you yourself always claimed that you did not take a good picture. At any rate use your own judgment.

"Ida asked him about next week and he said no, he couldn't come home then as he is planning to visit our sweetheart next week. I gave him one black look and told him to stay away next week as I am planning on that date myself. He insists that you are neutral in the matter and that you would as soon have him visit you as me. How about that, huh?

"Your letter just in and dear, it was just wonderful. You are beginning to get the knack of writing love letters. Maybe I taught you by good example."

"No privacy whatsoever in this office and if I write to you when I am at home, you do not get the letter in the morning mail." Celia complains on June 11. "And to think you said I do not know how to love you. Dear, I love you as I have never loved anyone else in my life, yes, even my puppy love affairs. Never in all my life did I for a minute ever think I would ever *say* it or *write it* or even *confess to myself* that I loved anyone and to think it all comes too easy to tell you what my feelings are.

"I know there is such a terrible thing as money standing in our way but really dear, if you will stop and consider how much money you will save on railroad fare after we are married, you won't mind the expense now.

"You say you are afraid our honeymoon will last only a week. Let me correct you *here* and *now*. Our honeymoon is going to last forever and a day. The few days or maybe a week that we will use to go away is just sort of a vacation. Our real honeymoon is yet to come. I personally don't think it necessary to go away for a longer period of time as long as we are together. If my guess is right we are going to be a long long way from earth, even heaven will be too near.

"You want to know again if I think it is wrong for you to love me as much as you do. Sweetheart I don't think you will ever love me as much as I would want you to. So don't ever say it again about this loving me too much business.

"Try and make it for this Thursday night. I do promise to take a nap before you get here. Forever yours – Amen, Cel"

June 11, 1928, Dave writes, "Hello Gang, I did not get the letter from Louis that I was expecting. I absolutely must get the signatures of Rabbi B as I am going to need it darn soon. Today I went down to the Home and demonstrated at the laundry. The work was satisfactory and I got an order for 200 lbs. for the laundry and 200 for the kitchen. However, just to show you what the stuff actually does, last Sunday they had a banquet there and the caterer almost had a fit to wash his dishes clean, and he had tons of silver and his waiters deserted him. What happened was funny when the superintendent, the goy, told him to try a little of the powder that the Rabbi's son was selling and upon the trial he was sold on the stuff.

"Tomorrow I have to meet the distributor of the Anso, and I made a test to show him. I found out the Argomite will go further than their coconut soap. It sure cleans out iodine and automobile grease.

"Did you order me the ten bags in 100 pounds? I need it. Get the name and address of the Erie Pa. man P L E A S E. Otherwise no news. Leo wants the stuff for his instruments and I expect to meet Dr. Tunic, the foot doctor and let him try it on feet."

"It's very late and I have been typing all afternoon," Dave writes in a letter with only June, 1928 as the date. "I prepared a bunch of dope for the Sheffield Dairy Farms Company. I am afraid that I will have to get me a young lady darn soon, as I can't afford to sit in the house and type reports and instructions.

"Ask the Argomite Company for a lot of copies of the Bacteriological test. If necessary pay for them. I can use at least 100 sheets of them. Then get a few more copies of the letter from the Minerva Company and from the Evans Bldg.

"I have yet to write an ad in the Times for salesmen and I will have to do that tomorrow. Must be in a laundry tomorrow at 7:30 to see what Argomite C will do. Got no other news. Lots of work to do, but no more sales yet.

Louis answers on June 12. "Have attended to the various things you wanted me to get for you at the plant. They haven't got a hundred copies of the Bacteriological test but they gave me about twenty copies. If that is not sufficient, I'll have to have it run off for you." He then gives names and addresses Dave requested of Argomite distributors in Erie and Chicago.

"The guy who handles the Anso up your way must be mighty wet according to what I hear from Glover. It seems that Phipps and Bird, Inc. 207 East Main Street, Richmond, Va. who handles Anso for them over there has bought 3,550 lbs. of the stuff at .15 since March 23rd. I saw the sales copies. That means that he must sell it at least for 20 cents to come out. This Phipps guy certainly is selling it in Richmond." Louis offered to write to each of them to save Dave the trouble.

"I am shipping you some Argomite jelly I made with two parts water and one part Argomite, by measure – not by weight. It comes out mighty thick and may be useful to fight cheap competition. See what you think of it.

"Barton insists that your best bet is the five pound package. The big stuff will come easier when you have the retail going. Miss Crowlin (an Argomite Company stockholder) tells me that her friend over in New Jersey is doing very well with the five pound bags. I too think it will be easier to sell.

"You might shoo that good salesman of yours over to the bakers.

Glover tells me that the only thing they sell to them is the fifty pound bag.

> June 12, 1928, letter from Louis to Argomite-Erie Co., 12th Street, Erie, Penn.
>
>   Attention Mr. Salisbury
>   Gentlemen:
>   We have recently contracted with the Argomite Industries Corporation of this city to market Argomite powder and all by-products in New York City and surroundings. Our Mr. David A. Glushak is now in New York organizing our company which is to be named THE ARGOMITE CO. OF NEW YORK. He is contemplating the sale of Argomite in the five-pound package to be sold thru house-to-house canvassers for the retail price of $1.50. (Glover had suggested that there be an interchange of ideas between various distributors. Apparently this Erie distributor was having success and Louis requested information along this line.)
>   We understand from the local distributor that he is having difficulty in getting the housewife to spend as much as $1.50 for a cleanser when all sorts of cleaners are obtainable in the stores in ten cent sizes.

Louis raises a number of questions in this letter: Was Erie having difficulty securing salesmen? Were men or women canvassing houses and who was doing it better? Were they demonstrating in department stores and with what success? Were they selling five-pound boxes or using Argomite Industries bags and how many were sold a day? Were they selling smaller packages? What advertising were they doing? How were instructions attached? Were samples distributed? And lastly, he said that copies of advertising literature would be appreciated.

"You may be quite certain that we shall appreciate your kindness and will be only too glad to reciprocate. Our Mr. Glushak has made experiments and has discovered that Argomite is of great value to physicians and surgeons in their sterilization of their instruments. It will ABSOLUTELY PREVENT CORROSION.

"The Argomite Company of New York, By Louis C. Grossberg"

"Dearest Sweetheart," Louis also wrote to Celia on the 12th. "Your most wonderful letter re-read for the 3rd time. To think that my shy little darling should come out even now and say all those love things and to say them all to me! Verily I have taught you well. Now we'll see how you will behave on our private love couch – soon.

"Righto, dear, I shall see what can be done about making that trip this very Thursday. I have so many things to do to make up for the absence that is to be Friday, Saturday and Sunday. While I seldom work on Saturday, I do go to the office Saturday nite. I have yet to write to three people for Dave's Argomite matters, and to finish the Avukah Zionist Student Federation report which is an annual job of ours – gratis, thank you.

"I'll hold you to your promise to take the nap Thursday evening because I do not expect to get in before about 1:30 your time. You should go to bed the same as usual – only earlier. And I should certainly like to be able to get in without having to ring the bell and wake your mother and father up out of bed.

"Can you leave the door open just before you go to bed and I will lock it when I come in? And tell me what room you will sleep in so I can wake you up without drifting into your mother's room.

"You know, sweetheart, I haven't spent one waking hour in which you were not in my thoughts. But we'll be together again very soon, dear. But the way, I wish you would find out where and when on Friday I can take the examination for a driver's license. I may wish to run over to see Dave Friday too, and be back in time to meet you from the office."

Celia replies on the same day, June 12, 1928:

"Then I am to expect you on Thursday; that is wonderful. I promise to take a nap before you get here so don't worry about me being tired. Of course I won't promise that I will be fully awake until three but I will try my darndest. I am sure the folks will be asleep so you need not worry about disturbing anyone, dear. I will leave the front door unlocked and yours truly will be waiting."

As punishment to Dave for his remarks, Celia said, "I don't think I will let him take a peek at my photo when I get it. I was only joshing when I said I would send the photo out by air mail. I intended to keep it here until you came out on one of your visits. While you are here we will mail one out to Esther.

"The assistant chief clerk passed several times and each time nodded his head. The last time he passed me he asked me if I am taking a correspondence course because every time he passes my desk I am busily engaged in typing. I said, 'oh yes, I am engaged.' I smiled and kept on typing. Little did he know what I was referring to. Lovingly, yours, Cel"

"June 13, 1928, Sixteen Months Later," notes Louis. "Do you know that this is exactly sixteen months since I know you? Well, it is. Of course, by this time – if I had my way – I should have been married at least fifteen months and perhaps have had four or five kids or something. But, where am I? Still only engaged. However, it might have been worse. Two months ago I wasn't even engaged so I suppose I have to be thankful for that.

"It begins to look as if I am going to be with you to-morrow night. The door open is just the thing. I don't want to wake anybody up at 1:30 or so. I'll admit it is an outrageous hour for a guy to drift in. I should never have thought of doing anything like that some months ago. But then, what good is being engaged if a fellow can't have some privileges and can't display some sort of *chutzpah*.

"I have had no opportunity today to take the customary eyeful of the little sweetheart's picture so cruelly hidden away in the drawer of the desk. It's really a fine picture even if it does not look like you. It had that wonderful smile of yours with those laughing eyes. I love you, darling, Louis"

"Another day has went by," Dave writes Louis and Ida, June 13, 1928. "And my man brought one order for 200 for a garage, and he took 200 for himself to sell in five's. His neighbors have been asking him for it. But so far I can't afford to start printing either literature or labels or anything like that. I went to see the Sooper Union man and he was absolutely satisfied, and by the end of the month he would order the first bag. In the hospital they have not yet given it a trial, but they expect to start tomorrow.

"In re your coming here on Friday, O.K. for me, but don't come in here before around four o'clock and then we can spend the evening together.

"I have already written to Erie, and tomorrow morning early I will write to Chicago, and to the rest of the gang. What part of New Jersey is Miss Crowlin's friend working it?

"Only at this time the retail stuff is entirely out of the question, as I have no funds for no such monkey business."

"Want to ask you to do several things for this corporation after talking to Mr. Barryman," Dave wrote four days later. "There is a beautiful loft across the street from this place here about the same size as the Economy, which the agent wants to rent for $3,000 per year. Mr. B. offered $2500 and the agent is coming over this afternoon to talk like a turkey."

Dave wanted Louis to ask Dr. Barton the cost of having Argomite delivered in 100-pound barrels and for prices on 100-, 50-, 25- and 10-pound bags with round bottoms. Round bottoms were necessary as 100-pound bags would not stand up.

"All of the other cleaners on the New York market are delivered in barrels, or small kegs, and in as much as we are introducing an expensive product, it is certainly to its disadvantage if it comes in an unwieldy container. I just noticed that the flour containers for 5 pounds of flour, paper bags double, are made with round bottoms. Also tell them that we are expecting to send in our order for the first carload within the next few days.

"The two fellows who started to sell in Brooklyn, gave me two orders from drug stores, and told me that they intend to sell 5,000 pounds this week, they were so insistent on that that they made me give them an agreement that if they make real orders and I can't make immediate deliveries, that I should pay them their commission anyway. Well, they need the money, are getting no drawing account and if that is the case, I told them to bring in the orders, I'll worry about the deliveries.

"I started my other new man out today and told him to work only garages. He told me that he thinks the price too low and that in the light of what the other soaps are selling for, he feels that he can get considerably more for it than what I am asking. I told him then to experiment (and) we will go 50–50 with him on anything above the quoted price."

The man in Chicago expects to sell 50 tons a month. "Not so bad for a starter I am sending you back the last ARGOMITE bill and get it adjusted."

"Dear Mr. Grossberg (and Mrs. Glushak Assistant)," writes Dave, June 18, 1928. He is ecstatic about new developments. Tomorrow, a gentleman will bring him a lease for 19 months on a loft two doors down the street with almost as much space as Barryman's, for only $1,800 a year for the first seven months, and $2,000 for the balance of the twelve months.

"The space is ample and there are about $200 worth of fixtures that we won't have to buy. Mr. Barryman is apparently in this with a vengeance. From now on we act like human beings. We are to get occupation before July first and the place will be dolled up something awful. Two elevators, two toilets, and all modern inconveniences. Mr. B. was kind of worried about tying ourselves up for such a length of time because if we outgrew it, what will we do. I told him in that case we should worry.

"Now for dope. My new man sent me his first day's report with an order for 50 pounds. He saw eleven garages and every one of them is going to become customers just as soon as they get thru with the stuff they have on hand. Go to the A Co. and get ten or fifteen each bags of 25 and 50 pounds and mail it to me parcel post special handling. Don't forget the wires. Do this at once.

"I hope that you found out about the round bottom bags for me. Also ask Glover the name of the paper box concern that is making the boxes for Murray of Philadelphia. The price in this town from the American Can Co. is too high."

Dave was glad Louis was coming this weekend since he was working on plans for the layout of a shop. He also wanted to ask Mr. Kanster to help him design a filling hopper which would be less expensive than if made in New York. "When you go down to the Argomite plant, ask Hellert to show the spout through which they fill the bags. Didn't you get E in mechanical drawing? I want to make something like that here, so that we can empty five or six 200-pound bags into the hopper and then fill the small bags from that. It would only increase production by about 1,000% over scooping it out of bags or bins.

"Mr. B. wants the place close at hand, I am getting afraid that he is becoming an ARGOMITE nut. His wife raves about it and the girls in the office are already talking about cleaning kids' knees. I think that we will order a carload within the next few days."

"Seems as if I can go right on doing things and losing sleep while in your company without the least strain," Louis writes in his June 18 letter to Celia, "but as soon as I go away from you. I feel like a man knocked out. You surely are the finest little sweetheart a fellow ever had.

"I can't begin to tell you how much I am in love with you, dear, and how horrid it is for me to leave you. I have had a wonderful time, dearest. There was just a little too much visiting and railroad time-wasting to suit me. I would give quite something if I had some way of finding out positively whether or not you really like to be kissed and hugged by your sweetheart out of love for me or whether you are making it appear, out of love for me again, that you like it so as to please me.

"Because of the nature of the question I am almost certain that I could not believe you no matter what your answer. I don't mean to imply in any sense of the word that you don't love me because I am convinced that you do love me. You might comment upon this question of mine – You see, sweetheart, actions speak louder than words and a reputation once established is hard to live down and never leave anything till to-morrow what you can just as comfortably do next month and a rolling stone gathers no molasses and if I had time I would look you up many more sayings but you probably aren't interested in them.

"So dear, you may give my love and kisses to the entire family and thank them for being so nice to your sweetheart. No matter what, darling, I LOVE YOU."

"It is pouring outside and every flash of lightning makes me two degrees paler" observes Celia on June 19. "If it keeps up they will think I am a ghost in disguise. I get so frightened that most times I lock myself up in a closet until it is all over. I suppose the lights will go out any minute now. But if you were beside me how brave I would be.

"Ma told me to send you a check for ten dollars but I told her my sweetheart wouldn't accept that much so we compromised and nine dollars was agreed upon. I hope all Argomite users will like it as much as we do *and if they do* – oh! I just hate to think about it.

"Let me know in your letter how many we may expect from your house for this Sunday. The more the merrier.

"I went to bed at 8:30 and at 7:30 this morning I was still in dream-land. I understand my father was trying for fifteen minutes to make me realize it was time to get up. At 7:50 I agreed, hurried out of bed, no breakfast, and got downtown on time. Wow, what a dream I had. Yes, it was about you. No, I am not going to tell you.

"I looked at the pictures again and I found fault with the collar on my dress. " Mr. Steinberg said to bring them back and agreed the fault was his. He would make new ones without charge. "Not only is he making them over but he is fixing the negatives of the other two and will give me two pictures free of charge. I think I must have hypnotized him.

"Since you always try to tell me that you think I do not love you, you will have me believing there is something in it after all. Dear, I don't want you to mention it again because it hurts me when you say it. I love you and only you. Kisses or no kisses, hugs or no hugs. It seems every time you go back home you doubt the sincerity of my hugs and kisses. Dearest is that nice, I ask you? Good-bye Sweetheart, Forever yours, Celia"

June 19, 1928

Darling Ceal,

It is really wrong of me to get you so tired out when I come. But, dear, I can't help it. Your only consolation is that I won't be around again – excepting possibly on the excursion next Sunday – for at least three weeks from now. So that ought to give you plenty time to rest up for the next ordeal. Was that a black look, sweets? Excuse me, dear,

Ordered for you the hundred pound ARGOMITE. As soon as I get the B/L and the invoice I'll send both to you. Sam can get it from the RR freight office.

Today I had lunch at Ida's (on) account of having to take a part of her washing machine over to a welding place for repairs. She tried to get them to come out for it but they promised and didn't come. She tells me that Dave was very happy with the results of our Saturday evening conference over at Barryman's and has taken a new lease on life. She tells me he got quite a kick out of introducing you as 'Our Sweetheart.'

Ida tells me that she told little Doris that her Uncle Louis was going to be married. 'Oh, I know,' she answered quickly, 'and I know to whom, too, to Celia.' Then after awhile she says, 'Then she'll be Aunt Celia, won't she? Gee, I'm glad, 'cause I like her. I think of her all night.' That makes two in this town who think of you all nite.

Ida just came in to write a letter for me that I talked into the Dictaphone to Dave. It is much more convenient and faster that way. What a wonderful little sweetheart you are! But you are like a fresh breeze on a hot summer's day. You blow away after a little while and then I have to go looking for you again. But some day I'll catch that breeze and bottle it and keep it from blowing away. Then what will you do? Can't write love letters with others around. But I love you just the same. Your dearest beau, Louis

"Wednesday, June 20, 1928," Celia writes before going to the movies. "Whether in the home, office, street or highway you are always before me. It seems lately I have to watch my step as never before while crossing the street. I had a narrow escape yesterday – but – never mind; they say a miss is as good as a mile. Really my thoughts are miles away. You see even though you are actually not here you are here. And then you ask whether I really love you. How could you?

"I hope you will be able to come here Sunday – I will give you an extra hug and kiss when you come up and I won't care who will see.

"If Dave isn't going home Sunday you could invite him over to my house for dinner. You will probably want to hear how Argomite is getting along. Sweetheart, I have to go. Dearest, do you know I am yours for keeps? I could go on writing love phrases but Bert is after me to start. What does she know about love?"

"I apologize most humbly," Louis replies on the same date. "I shall take you at your word and believe that you love me as wholeheartedly as I myself could wish for and try to forgive you whenever it appears that you are somewhat lagging in the ardency of your love making. If worse comes to worst I can always complain to my friend Edith and then, I am sure, you'll get good again.

"Your letter was real nice, too. It sounds so even and free – much different from the sounds of those earlier and less lovey letters of yours. When I think of what I lost by not telling you of my love and asking you for yours and springing the 'wilt thou' act much sooner, I feel genuinely sorry for myself. But somehow it could not be before.

"As for Sunday, well, it seems that only Miriam and Babe will be able to come along. But that should be sufficient from one family for one time. Babe has already served notice upon Al (Cohen) and Solly (Grossberg) that he is off next Sunday and that's all there is to it. To insure having the necessary wherewithal he has placed in my care a nice full size ten spotter. What misplaced trust! Little does he know that before the week is out there will be little trace left of that particular tenner. However, I admire his confidence in his big brother. Babe, by the way, is working for the Dixie Argomite Co., the local distributor of Argomite, on his off mornings in order to gain experience for his bigger and better job with the Argomite Co., of New York. You see we are training them young.

"Got a letter from Rose Naiman, the girl we met in Philly last Sunday to convey her regards to my sweetheart and to tell me how wonderful a girl I picked out to wear the name of Mrs. Louis C. Grossberg. Another score for you, dear heart. It must be the truth.

"Your check, by the way is returned to you on account of incorrect amount. I will not have any profits on *your* folks' purchases and therefore, I want no pay. I shall let you know as soon as I find out how much to send me.

"Dave feels all buoyed up with high hopes and I might say that I feel just as he does. Right now I have to go over to the Argomite Company. I love you as always and ever and forever, and without a stop, or a halt, or a pause, and oh,

"LOVE ME AS I LOVE YOU ALWAYS, Louis C. Gee"

Louis also wrote to Dave on the 20th. "This Argomite business seems to raise the very devil with my time. It ruined me the afternoon yesterday and ditto to-day. This is not my way of complaint but I do wish you would think up more or less at once what you want there so I can go down once or twice a week and take care of things.

"Barton and Glover are still out of town. Have gotten the bags for you and also ordered – without your request – 100 each of 25s, 50s, and the wires. What's the use wasting time and postage money for new containers every little while. I hope I haven't over ordered, but you should be able to get rid of that many of those sizes very shortly.

"Have inquired as to the filling machine and it develops that theirs is a special machine made by the J.H. Day Company, Cincinnati, Ohio. It seems that the gravity action is insufficient to make it feed, inasmuch as it clogs. They have to use a machine that has a worm inside to keep making the powder flow thru. The worm is machine driven. They picked it up second-hand and at that it is not inexpensive. You might look around there and see if you can pick one up that will do.

"I'm afraid that Mr. Kanster will not be able to help you much as I don't think he is so much the mechanical motor driven expert as he is the designer of things inanimate. If you are not coming home for that day, you can meet me at the Kansters' Sunday and we will go over all things including the filler with Mr. Kanster. Maybe I can go right on to New York on the excursion and visit the new plant and spend an hour with you and then you and I go on to Newark. Write me at once, as time is getting short.

"Referring once more to the J.G. Day hopper, the one they are using at the Argomite plant is not entirely satisfactory on account of their having two hoppers. The upper one is the large one and feeds the lower one. The upper hopper seems to be geared somewhat too slow feeding and the lower hopper has to wait for the upper one. The gear ratio of the upper one should be made to feed faster.

"By the way Edwards' bill for his trip to NY is $37.13. It is enclosed herewith. I hear from Edwards that he will probably no longer be connected with the company after next week. It seems they have decided his services are not needed. That will sort of put our Standard Oil experiment in the air. I'll talk to Barton about it when he gets back. We may have to do the experimenting ourselves on that.

"Mighty happy to read your letters that now come floating over the mails these days. The tone of voice is much improved over the hoarse croakings of the early stages of the game

"The partner, and Vice-President, The Argomite Co. of New York, (Louis)"

"I expect to sign the lease tomorrow as president," Dave writes to Ida and Louis the next day. "Louis is to be secy. and Barryman, Treasurer. I have ordered the telephone, French by the way, and the place is being dolled up to beat the band. It has not yet got a partition for an office, but I might either build it myself sometime later on, or have it done."

While investigating boxes, one of the men asked if Argomite could be put into small packages to sell for 10 cents. Dave said absolutely yes. If so, he would guarantee to sell all the chain stores through their ad agency, as he knew all the buyers intimately. "My two Brooklyn men have been turning in a few small orders. I think tho that the man that Louis saw is turning out to be the real thing. He has seen so far at least 30 garages, and everyone of them told him to come back in a week or so. He has been selling samples of 50 pounds at about 3 each day and so far has sold small samples of 10 pounds to eight people. I can expect a repeat of 200 and so far everything is cash.

"I gave a wonderful demonstration in the kitchen of the Hospital today and they went wild over it. I am expecting to get a letter of recommendation (for) the Federation (UJA). If they do that then it means that we have about every hospital in town tied up and every other large institution. I am very sorry indeed to hear that Edwards is leaving. I wonder why. Please find out why. It worries me more than you can actually know. He has been with Barton almost from the very beginning and has developed most of the stuff anyhow."

"This is to inform you that we shall expect Miriam, Babe and you for breakfast on Sunday morning," Celia writes Louis, also on the 21st of June. "Don't waste any time downtown. We shall all be up bright and early celebrating your coming. I'll see what we can do about a band."

Celia didn't like the film *Street of Sin* and tells Louis not to waste time seeing it. She wants to find a good art teacher, preferably a woman. "Now that school is closed and my old boy friends crossed off my list, I have time on my hands. During one of the evenings of this week, I rid my dresser drawer of all old correspondence. Yours I have kept. I am surprised at the number of letters I have saved that you have written to me. I did find enjoyment reading them over again. Just keep it up dearest, honey and my only, Sweetheart, Cel"

Louis' letter on the 21st provided details of who would be coming to see Celia's family: Babe for certain, possibly Miriam, but not Pauline and Eleanor, who thanked Celia for the invitation but extended their regrets. "Friday, June 22, 1928" Celia wrote back on Sam Hamburg's stationery. "By all means tell Miriam to come this Sunday and about her other visits – just let me take care of that. I am sorry that more Grossbergs are not coming – maybe some other Sunday, yes? I am glad Sunday is not far away. I don't mind waiting for bills, thunder showers and what not but waiting for you – Oh! That is a different question."

"The brass band is O.K. but who needs it?" Louis replies

on June 22. "As for me, give me that little corner of ours and Celia S.H.D.S.D*H.K – r, and privacy and that is all I want. In a pinch I'll even forego the privacy.

"Have written to Dave and have suggested to him that he come out to your house and partake of that wonderful dinner that was being prepared for the Washingtonians. I am not so very certain that he will accept but you might as well put in an extra potato for him."

Louis writes after the Sunday dinner visit, on June 25. "Once again I am back in the dreary, drab, Celia-less place where I must await that happiest of all the happy days of my life when I may point with pride to a little woman and introduce her as my WIFE. Here I am once again communicating with my dearest sweetheart thru the medium of Uncle Samuel's mails. But thank God for that privilege.

"I have not yet made up my mind as to whether this experiment of visits by excursion is successful. As Dave puts it, 'The trouble with them is that before you know what has happened you are back home.' The trip back home was not so bad. Got home in time to get a good night's sleep. If I ran a railroad I'd have a special train for tired and sleepy gentlemen sweethearts. I would have absolute quiet aboard that train and no porters and no time limit as to when a lover must leave the train. I'll have to speak to Mr. Pullman about this.

"I wonder, dear, why it is that I should love you so. We aren't related to each other in any way and a few years ago I didn't even know you. Yet, to-day, I feel that you are as much part of my life as is my arm or my eye. In fact more so, because I never think of either of those two members of my anatomy unless they pain me. No, I can't say it is because you pain me. Sometimes you do pain me and at those times the pain seems to be in my heart and you are generally nowhere to be seen at those times. Maybe absence does make the heart grow fonder. In my experience, where you are concerned, absence makes the heart painful.

"Of course it is needless for me to say to you that I am much grateful to you and your folks for everything. It seems now so strange for me to thank you for being nice to me – as if I were thanking my mother for being good to me. She is that way and it is taken as a matter of course. Dearest I hope to love you always no less than I love you now. I cannot speak for more, as I do not think that is possible. But I can speak for no less. My constant love, Lou."

"Were you really here yesterday or was it your shadow?" Celia writes that same Monday. "You were gone before we realized you were here. Did you find a comfortable seat? Let me know about this trip.

"Dave came back to Newark with us because he had nothing to do in New York. The only topic of conversation was Argomite – and that reminds me that Argomite and I will be enemies if it is not already at 842 as I have plenty of washing to do this evening. We stopped in an ice cream parlor and had drinks and all had a very enjoyable evening – no I am not *spaking* the truth. I disliked very much that you were bound for Washington. One of these fine days I will come on an excursion and that will be giving you a dose of your own medicine."

Louis' second letter of June 25, 1928 was written on stationery of the United Palestine Appeal. "I am stealing a bit of time away from work here which is to make the final check-up of the various funds over which Sylvia (Rosenfeld) has charge before she leaves for her summer vacation – without pay by the way. I might say to you that both Sylvia's vacation and my work are without pay.

"The pictures, darling, are just fine. Everybody just loves that picture and mother says she would love to see you. I might add that there is at least one other person at 505 who should love to see you. The person is an accountant and does a good bit of charitable auditing work, which may be one of the reasons that he can't support a wife.

"It wasn't much of a visit I had with you this time but it gave me the opportunity to see you and hold you in my arms. We got into the train on the way back not one second too soon. The train filled up just as the gates opened and everybody made a scramble for the seats. We got us a good seat tho and had a fairly pleasant trip back.

"Was much too busy to go out and look me up a frame for my sweetheart's picture. But I have the picture in the office and that is quite a step forward. The first visitor, and the only one of the day – I am never in long enough to have any visitors – wanted to know who is this beautiful young lady. I told him and he pronto extended his congratulation. He is the National Chairman of the AVUKAH, The Students Zionist Federation which functions in the universities of the country. He is a very critical young man but you looked good to him. Well, sweets, I might say to you that you look good to me too.

"Every now and then, I close my eyes and imagine myself riding in your car to New York with you on my lap and in my arms. I still have both considerations to overcome – time and *mazuma* (money). Once there was another consideration – 'How does it look?' I did not always feel free to come up whenever I wanted to or could afford to. I had to consider the expediency, the appearance, the look of it, the bother to you and to your folks, and oh, the possibility of murdering my welcome."

"I am afraid you didn't get my yesterday's letter." Louis wrote the next day. "I was simply too tired and sleepy to go on to the post office so took a chance (on) the mail box across the street.

"So far there seems to be no letter from David. In fact the mailman has not made his second trip hereward. Sweetheart, you are sitting or standing right over my right shoulder and smiling down at me. How lovely you are! The finest flower of that magnificent garden. They do say that true love never runs smoothly. In our case love does run smoothly but the affair is plenty ragged. If I had the wherewithal, the dough-dough, the cash, the mazuma, oh, the coin of the realm, I surely wouldn't have to get just a glimpse of you every now and then. I have to sit here and wait. Oh, damn! Excuse please, darling. Shouldn't swear in a love letter.

"So you took Dave out to show him Newark. I hope he liked it especially the ice cream. He is a good boy and I do hope he hurries up and makes some jack or something – But why keep worrying you about it? Dear heart, you are the finest little sweetheart anyone ever had. Even Miriam likes you, no loves you."

Despite Louis' concern, Celia did receive at least one of his June 25 letters. "I don't suppose I will receive a letter from you today as the one you intended that I receive today was delivered in yesterday's mail. You no doubt mailed it very early yesterday morning as it was received in our afternoon mail. That is what I call speed.

"I went to Edith's house last night and played bridge. What would you say if I told you I made a grand slam? And without the slightest effort on my part but the players were so unappreciative that it took all the joy out of it. In fact I do not think they even knew what I made.

"I suppose I can account for the dullness of the game to the fact that Edith and Sammy were almost the owners of a second hand Cadillac, year 1922, open air design, brand new paint job, two very good tires, three fairly good ones, privileged to have (their) own mechanic look over the car, and altogether right good looking, for the sum of $450.00.

"Sammy said if they come down to $300.00 he might consider it a good buy. Not that it isn't worth more in his estimation but being a first class dress buyer at heart he knows that he must bargain. I doubt very much if they will leave it go for $300.00. In fact I am quite sure they won't. If you were in Sammy's place would you consider buying a second hand car of a good make in preference to a new car of a cheaper make?

"Dear, your last letter was so sweet that I could love you all over again for it. It is what you say and how you say it that makes me believe you do love me.

"Edith used to say 'You know Cel, I don't believe there is another couple in the universe that can compare their happiness with ours.' And I used to think maybe there was something in what she said but now *I am sure* there is not another couple in the universe that can compare their happiness with ours. I am not telling Edith how utterly wrong she is but what she does not know will not hurt her. First of all, in order to insure happiness we must respect each other's ideas and methods and in respect there is love. Love me as I love you and it will be EVERLASTING."

Dave's letter of June 27 begins: "I am enclosing herewith a copy of option that Mr. Barryman is to get and for your signature. Sign on the bottom line and return to me immediately. I wish you would at this time get our set of books working or at least send me some loose sheets to start out with. We will need books as follows: a Sales book to take care of distribution of 5–25–50–100 and 200 pounds. The kosher ones we will mark K. I just hired a young girl to take care of our work here and she has started in order to get out a number of letters.

"I made a demonstration in Borden Laundry and they promised me an initial order. I hope you have taken care of the order for the half car as I am practically out of stock now. I have a new salesman working on Garages, on straight commission, and a sales organization wants to get hold of our product for distribution. All things for the future.

"I bought some lovely furniture, which by the way, my desk does not match, but it will have to do for the next few months. By the way, have you done anything on the other File Cabinet yet through Rand Kardex?

"Louis, Endorse the note on the back, the balance of the $3,000 will be forthcoming shortly. Mr. B. is a little tight for cash today."

"If my imagination were only a bit stronger I could imagine that you are actually sitting upon the cabinet and smiling down upon me. But you are only a picture here," Louis writes to Celia on the same day. "And your image and not you is looking down upon me. I want you more and more, dearest, and I wish that you were here instead of your picture. Understand me now, dear, I even love your picture but how compare that with the gorgeous original?

"So the postal service on my letter which you received on Monday was good. Well, it must have been darn good if you received it by the last mail since I didn't write it until the afternoon. Every now and then you, too, uncork a real sweet letter. And then, honey, I feel so happy and every bone in my body cries out for want of you but it is a great pity to deny one's bones anything.

"Edith was surely right but she is wrong just the same. To her way of thinking there never could be any other couple so happy as they are and to our way of thinking there never, never can be a couple so happy together as you and I. So what is the answer? There is no answer to love. Love continues to be the greatest discovery of the ages and if I had the exclusive right to its sale in any territory, no matter how small, I should be a millionaire or at least wealthy enough to be able to support a little wife for my very own. There would be buyers in every village, town, and hamlet and the price would be reasonable no matter how much I charged."

"I received two of your letters this noon and they served not only as an appetizer but practically the whole noon day lunch," writes Celia. "After reading the letters I had little room left for food. My meal consisted of two wonderful letters from some chap in Washington by the name of Louis, and one half cantaloupe – the latter unnecessary.

"Now that my new photo is settled in your office I wonder if you will part with the old one. The old photo exaggerates my weight to such an extent that if shown to a person who did not know me they would think you were engaged to some fat person and far be it for me to have anybody think that I am fat…"

Louis replies the next day. "I love you so, dear, my arms hurt for want of taking you around; my lips are sore for want of kissing you; my eyes are smarty for want of seeing you; my voice is hoarse for want of talking to you; my ears are wobbly for want of hearing you talk; my heart is affected for want of having you near; and altogether I'm a mighty sick guy for want of YOU. How can you do it?

"I'm not so certain whether to be glad or sad at your last letter. You tell me that you got two letters from me and that you didn't eat any lunch on account of it. One really in love cannot sleep, cannot work and cannot EAT. That was it – wasn't it?

"I see that you do not care to have anyone think that you are a fat lady. I wonder why. It seems that Mr. Barnum pays heavy dough-dough to ladies who are sufficiently fat to attract him. And yet you object to being fat. There seems to be no satisfying these ladies of to-day. But never mind, honey, don't let them fool you. Your sweetheart is in perfect accord with you. He doesn't like fat ladies either. Of course, he would love her just the same no matter how fat she got, but deep down in his heart he wouldn't like it near so well as when she retained that neat, trim little figure which is hers right now – or was the last time he saw her.

"So, if you really want that picture back, you shall have it the next time I go to Newark. It may be for the fourth but I am very much in doubt of that. If the Schiff's decide to come, I don't want to be away from here. But please don't say that to Edith or to Sammy it would be the height of selfishness on our part to sacrifice hospitality for personal gain…"

"I am enclosing a copy of a letter I am sending to garages," writes Dave on June 28th. "I have sent out about twenty of them, and using that as a basis, you can send me a corrected version.

"I am still working on boxes of different sizes and I am expecting to be at Newman Brown this afternoon for their advertising program. In re of kosher boxes I think we will really go into that on the basis of 20 cent a package. I am developing a kosher box of that type and will try to get it into Jewish stores by salesmen, giving the storekeeper a large commission on his first sales." The kosher trade is unlikely to buy five pounds but will pay 20 cents for a kosher label. "The only thing in the market to-day is Rokeach round can and the cake soap, so probably a beautiful blue and white box well designed might in itself have an attraction to that class of trade."

He picked out seven counties in New Jersey for Barryman's son to incorporate. "I hope they have already shipped the stuff to us as I am practically through. To-day I received 3–25 lb. sample orders for

Argomite Blue. The sample that the salesman used was Argomite Tex and they were so amazed. I wonder what they will say of the can of the Blue?"

> June 28, 1928, New Roslyn Garage, Bronx, NY.
> Gentlemen:
> We thank you for your valued order for ARGOMITE, which we hope, will be the first of a series of orders. You will find AR-GOMITE to be without equal for all cleaning purposes around the garage.
> We are enclosing herewith for your information some general instructions and recommendations as to the best uses of AR-GOMITE. You will find ARGOMITE absolutely indispensable to you in the garage after a few days use of it and it will affect great economies in the maintenance of your organization. Note particularly the practical cessation of plumbing bills.
> Again thanking you for your valued patronage, and hoping to have your continued business, we are,
> Very truly yours, THE ARGOMITE COMPANY OF NEW YORK, By David A. Glushak

Celia writes on the 28th, asking if Louis will visit on July 4. It is payday and the bank employees left early to go shopping and she is worried about locking up the office on her own.

Thou Shalt Not Covet

"Don't think you are the only one who can gaze upon the face of a loved one," Louis read in Celia's letter of June 29. "I, too, have a picture to be proud of and that is a snap-shot of you dear taken in Washington a few weeks ago. There isn't a day that goes by that I don't tell someone about my sweetheart and if the party is particularly nice I let them take a peek.

"Sweetheart, your advice was accepted (regarding a used car that Edith and Sam were considering purchasing). The Cadillac car is out of the question for reasons outlined in your letter. You see the Cadillac was the first car they looked at. Edith has since been looking around and has gotten a little car knowledge. This evening a demonstrator is coming to show them how his car can travel. (It's a) Studebaker, year 1927, Coupe, 5,000 mileage, excellent tires and the price will probably be $950. Sammy dislikes using the trolleys and buses traveling to and from the station and wants to buy a car. Good luck to him."

Edith's Sammy did not learn to drive until well after Edith was the family chauffeur. He did not know how, at the time this letter was written. He was the world's worst driver, once he learned. I remember riding in the back seat, holding my breath until we arrived at our destination. He paid no attention to the road, only to everyone in the car. All through the ride he kept up a running conversation on the fashion industry, pointing out various dress shops and telling us about their

345

show windows and merchandise. This conversation was punctuated with constant turning of his head to the rear to make sure we grasped everything he said and had not disappeared out the back window. Believe me, I wish we had!

While it might be charitable to attribute Sammy's lack of driving skills to the lateness of his introduction to the wheel, that would be unfair to all new drivers. Sammy never improved and I can only wonder who allowed him to pass his driving test in the first place. Of course, he was from New Jersey. That must explain it.

Celia's June 29 letter continued by recounting a drama from work. Mr. Kramer had been their Chief Clerk, was well liked, and at 32 years of age about to become an officer, but did a foolish thing. "He gave an old depositor (who thought he didn't own a cent in the world) blank checks to sign and after cashing the checks would divide the cash. The depositor was an old man having lost his mind some years before, didn't know that all the money was rightfully his. Mr. Kramer was caught and before being released from jail had to give his share back. He is now selling cars for a living. The old man died soon after Kramer's arrest never having pleasure or comfort from his money." It looks more likely to Celia that Louis will visit on the 4th.

"I must write a letter to a young lady and ask her would she please come here and see me as soon as possible," Louis wrote in his June 29 letter. "No, dear, don't get jealous. I'll admit the lady is rather pretty and at one time was the cause of getting me pinched for speeding. The young lady is an ex-bookkeeper of ours and has recently left this city for Pittsburgh from where she wrote me she would like to come back here whenever we have something good to offer her. She is a good worker and a crackerjack bookkeeper and I have need of her."

"I will have an uninterrupted week-end to think of you and dream of you. That is all I seem to be doing. Even to-day a client asked me when I am going to be married and advised me very seriously to hurry and 'Marry the girl' so that I may be the old alert, snappy Grossberg as of yore. Nu, go tell him I can't afford it. They try to tell me how much nicer it is to get married. As if I don't know.

"About the fourth? Well, I need no coaxing. I want to come. But why should you feel hurt if I cannot come up on account of money?

After all, isn't it just a matter of money that you and I are not married right now?"

Saturday Evening, after the 'Childs' Supper, June 30, 1928:

My Darling Little Wife-to-be,

For some unaccountable reason the printer left off the seal from this sheet of stationery. That was a wonderful letter you wrote me yesterday! You know, dear, I should encourage you to write at home rather than at the office because all the finest letters you ever wrote me were written at home. I do believe you are in constant fear that someone at the office may see you writing to your sweetheart. I'm going to buy you a nice box of stationery so that you will feel an urge to write to me from home now and then.

(Though he is glad Edith is postponing her visit, he is also sorry they are not coming. He is almost ashamed to tell Dave he is contemplating a visit to Newark from Wednesday to Monday.) "I said 'contemplating' advisedly as at the present time I see neither time nor the *fuhr gelt* (travel money) for that joyous-even in thought-trip. But if it can possibly be arranged I shall be over on the evening of the fourth.

I really should make you a picture for that space on your dresser. I can't see what you like in that snapshot of me that you have. I presume it is that one which Dave took in which I have one foot on the bench and a hand in my pocket. The thing I don't like in that snapshot is the hand in the pocket. If you are showing that picture around to people I may get like you and want you to have another one so I can take that one away from you. I have never taken a picture other than a snapshot and it seems strange to me to take one. Of course, I have never been in love before either and now it certainly seems anything but strange.

In the June 30, 1928, monthly statement from Argomite Industries, as sold to the Argomite Company of New York, the balance came to $1,760.88, after payments on an original bill of $2,093.36. This included charges for the Argomite powder, bags, wires, filling of bags, twenty testimonial letters and parcel post. Empty bags of 5 lbs. to 50 lbs. cost between 6¢ and 38¢ a bag. Regular, Argomite Blue, and Argomite Tex – cost 8¢ a pound. The services of Mr. Edwards for two days were charged at $37.13.

"Sweetheart O'Mine," begins Celia's letter of July 1. "I am not going to be with you long in writing this afternoon –

"It has become a habit of mine to sew, wash, mend and get things in general together on Sunday for the coming week. I have washed several things in Argomite and dear, that stuff is great. One would think our house was a laundry to see the personals on the line."

"This is Sunday evening nearly eight and I have just a little while ago returned to the office from the station and home," Louis writes to Celia, July 1–2, 1928. "I had Dave and Herman (Freudberg) for visitors here to-day on excursions." He was able to see Dave about Argomite and then went to visit with Herman, who came to see his father in the hospital. "He has had an operation for some bladder trouble and is a very sick man indeed." Herman's train left at seven. "I seldom come here after six on a Sunday night (as) this building shuts down at six on Sundays and I have to use my private key to get in.

"Herman wanted to know when we are coming up for that ring. He says it will be all finished by next Sunday. I'll have to consult you, I told him, But we'll talk about that when I see you, precious sweetheart.

"Dave has already had the pleasure of filling a few re-orders which, of course, is a real sign of good times. He is doing all he can do to make a quick job of succeeding for 'our sweetheart.'

"Sweetheart, don't you ever get tired reading my letters of love? They are all more or less of the same tune and they all tell you over and over again what you must surely know by this time – that I love you so dearly that I cannot live very long without you. How long I can live with you, I don't know. I do know, however, that no matter how long I live with you it will seem as one day compared to the time I have lived without you.

"I feel quite happy to-day and life would seem exquisite if only you were here with me. I believe I better get busy and start some of that work that MAY permit me to take that wonderful vacation I am planning or else I shall be lonesome for a longer period than I am bargaining for."

And to think, all this agony began when Louis sent Celia a 5-pound box of Valetes Candies in a heart shaped box on Valentines Day. That is what convinced her he was serious. On the 2nd, Celia's response includes this: "I believe I am very selfish for asking you to come out on the 4th. If you cannot make it, come Thursday evening instead of Wednesday."

"Just a few words," Dave writes Louis and Ida on the 2nd. "We have already moved in and I am expecting the stuff in to-morrow. The furniture is in and looks fine. One of my best salesmen brought in four orders amounting to 700 lbs. at a price sufficient to make him about $17 commission.

"Today was wasted, but tomorrow I have two important appointments and hope to have some good news for you. On Wednesday, I am going room hunting and will bring Ida over here at the very earliest opportunity. Mr. Barryman saved me four rooms in one of his buildings for $66 but I am going to look over Mt. Vernon first…"

A July 3, 1928, invoice of $80.00 was for 1,000 lbs of Argomite "C" in 200-lb. bags.

On July 7, 1928, Esther writes from Syracuse, NY. "Words are not at my command to be able to express how happy you made me by sending me this beautiful picture of your future bride. I thank you a thousand times. To tell you that I have been looking at your sweetheart every minute I got a chance. You perhaps may doubt me but it's nevertheless the truth. I feel safe in my innermost heart that she'll make you a good wife, her smiling face shows innocence and a sweet character. I am so glad for you my dear brother. I hope both of you are going to be very happy. I could just kiss that dimple in her chin and have fallen head over heels in love with her myself, before I thought myself to be happy if I could see her even in a photo now my arms ache for want of embracing and taking her to my heart. I am just wondering if she will like me as I like her?

"Now please my dear I shall be bold enough to ask you for your picture, I promise it will have the honor place in my home. My favorite brother and his bride, *think of it*!

"I haven't heard from you on my last letter, please don't let me wait to long. When do you expect to be married? Do you expect to have a big Wedding? I wish you would tell me all about her, I would be so glad to know it all. How is business?"

July 9, 1928, after Louis' July 4 visit to see Celia, he writes: "As you might guess from this letter I am back once more. At any rate, if I were not so warm – and this town is hotter'n Hell – I'd be quite comfortable. It was hot before we started but as soon as the train began to 'percolate' it breezed out all the heat and the result was a nice cool night. The daylight saving hour came in very handy, too.

"Dearest, I have, of course, had a splendid time. All I know is that I am madly in love with you and I care not who knows about it. Everyone at home thanks you for your regards and are all impatient for next Sunday when you will be here in you own sweet person. Please let me know by Friday or Saturday if Edith and Sammy are coming along. Mother also wants to know what the name of that salt fish is so she can try to get it here. Please find out and let me know.

"No one can say anything about your being cold any more. You have certainly improved wonderfully in the last month and the improvement over last year is simply amazing. Your kisses of 1927 were so informal, so impersonal, I never knew whether it was you kissing me or Miriam. There was no flavor to them. But now! *Ober yetzt* (but now). I am already crying for more.

"Got a wonderful letter from Esther this afternoon and I am really ashamed of myself for not having answered her letter of congratulations and that of her husband. Let me read to you the interesting parts of that letter."

Louis quotes from Esther's letter adding: "Funny how near she comes here to my own sentiments and how closely she follows my own expressions of a letter I wrote you recently. THINK OF IT!

"Now, wasn't that just too sweet of her? For the first time one who knows you not has showered compliments upon you instead of telling me how nice etc. I am. And all she had to have to know all those nice things about my darling was her picture. I must write her a few words of thanks for all the nice things she has said."

True to his word, Louis writes Esther that same day. "I am really ashamed of myself for not having answered your and Harry's lovely letters. I had an excuse. I thought I could kill two stones with the same bird by thanking you for your kind sentiments and wishes and sending you the picture all at the same time. However, the picture came and I sent it but still no letter went with it. I have been right busy. I know that no excuse can possibly be a good one so I hope you will forgive me anyway.

"I am so glad that you like my sweetheart. You really cannot help it when you see her. She is such a sweet girl that everyone who sees her likes her right off. She comes of a very nice family all of whom are very friendly people. They are not exactly *frum* but their house is Kosher and they are good Jews. You wanted me to tell you all about her.

"She is a very lovely girl, short, a bit shorter than Miriam and is well proportioned. Her hair is black and she has the dark Grossberg sort of eyes which always seem to laugh." Love is certainly blind. Her eyes were hazel. "She is very good natured and kind and is extremely efficient in whatever she does. Her taste is excellent – she is at heart an artist.

"Perhaps I can best describe that part of her by an example. At Kitty's last Summer she looked around the room and, after having been asked for her opinion on the subject suggested changes in the layout of the living room furniture which still stands as placed.

"The same thing is true of our own living room. We were moving the room all around and were not satisfied. Then she came, and in a few minutes fixed things up so that everybody was pleased and so it stands. Whenever they want to buy something important over there – any of the sisters, two are married, they always consult Celia and abide by her advice. Her sense of colorings is very good. You probably have heard about the plaque she painted for us and which is hung up on the wall in our living room. In line with this talent she dresses very becomingly and can wear clothes that cost very little and appear to be well dressed.

"Celia works at the Fidelity Union Trust Company which is the largest bank in New Jersey. She is the only Jewish person there, as they won't employ Jews there. I don't just know how she got to work there in the first place but I think it was on a temporary job and then they liked her so much they kept her. Fanny Glushak was the other Jewish girl working there before she was married. That is how I came to have met Celia. But that is another story and maybe some day I'll tell you that one too.

"To-day my sweetheart occupies a very important job there and she draws a handsome salary. She is officially a mail receiving teller, which means that all deposits that come in thru the mails pass thru her hands. She has accounts from people as far up North as Canada and West as California. I understand she handles about a million dollars a day. Officially she knows most of the things that go on in the bank. She has worked in many of the departments and at one time was what they call a 'floater'.

"A floater is a person who can substitute for anyone whenever that one is away. She used to be a chief bookkeeper at one time there so that when any of the bookkeepers could not balance out his or her cash for the day Celia was called in to find the error. In this way she has become familiar with the various things that go on in the bank. In short my little sweetheart is a very smart little girl.

"When they found out that she was engaged to be married the head bozo over there wished her lots of luck and so on and said he will be willing to let her get away from him only if she gives him one year's notice.

"Which reminds me that you asked me when I intend to get married. To tell you the truth I don't know myself. I want to get married as soon as possible but I must wait a little while longer until Dave makes some progress in New York with his Argomite sales. He is coming along as well as could be expected for a new enterprise but not fast enough to make a living for himself from that source as yet. I have to help out from this end. But it will not take much longer now.

"I was in New York yesterday and saw Dave and he tells me that in two or three months I can get married and live on the income of this office. We plan to have him work things up, over there until there is enough income there for both of us at a decent salary and in the meantime I am going to continue to run this office. There is enough here for one comfortable living but not for two. So it seems that it will take about three or four months before we can begin to set a definite date.

"I want and hope to be married before the end of this year anyway. As to the size of the wedding we don't know yet. The chances are that we may have just an immediate family wedding with only brothers and sisters and their husbands, if any, and no cousins or uncles. I'll write about that later. In the meantime you might as well begin to plan for a trip to this part of the country in about four months, as you and Harry will, of course, be at the wedding.

"So please thank Harry for his kind wishes and believe me when I say that both Celia and I thank you with all our hearts for your lovely letters of congratulation..."

"The day after the night before, July 9, 1928," writes Celia. "Where are you? I came home a few minutes ago expecting to find you waiting for me but here I am lonesome, blue and disappointed. I can't believe you have gone back to Washington – but alas 'tis true. I had a wonderful feeling all afternoon that as soon as I would step into the house I would walk into your arms and be greeted with a kiss from you. But dear, you were nowhere in sight. Didn't we spend a glorious few days in each others company?"

"Well, dear, you are lonesome for me aren't you?" replies Louis on the 10th. "I am so glad. Sorry that you lost so much sleep but no time is wasted that you think of me. It does seem that I am your original sleep loser. You can't sleep when I am around and now it appears that you can't sleep even when I am not around. God bless you, my sweetheart. No wonder Esther's arms ache for want of taking you to her heart. My whole body aches for similar wants. You look so sweet here smiling down upon me from the wall.

"Kitty wanted to know when you and I are going to be married. She let loose a great big shout of joy when I told her that it seems now that we might spend some time in Washington before we move out to New York."

"Edith took my picture to the news office," Celia wrote, also on the 10th. "But from what I can gather the reporter changed everything around.

"At the office this afternoon I was besieged with copies of my picture. Across the top of the picture it said, 'Newarker engaged to Washingtonian.' A few have already told me that at the mere mention of your name my eyes brighten. See what love does! I don't care, I want the whole world to know.

"The name of the fish you asked me about is called salted-dry cod fish. I am going to take a pound or two along with me on Sunday. I will also take a few of Ma's famous recipes and by the way tell your mother to practice the art of cooking cod-fish because when I go to Washington to live I would like to taste a dish commonly prepared at our house.

"Sweetheart, I enjoyed the excerpts from Esther's letter. If you were watching me you would have seen me wipe away a few happy tears. It was mighty wonderful of her to write the things she did about me – yes, and not knowing me at that, I feel as if I know her already.

"I can see the resemblance in character and disposition and I am loving her for it. Give Esther my thanks. Tell her I too, am glad you found me, or is it, we found each other, and that my life's job will be to make her brother happy. (My task will be a cinch.) I love her. And of course, I love you."

Celia's photo was attached to this newspaper clipping. And now the news was out.

Miss Celia Kanster

An attractive engaged girl is Celia Kanster, daughter of Mr. and Mrs. Jacob Kanster…Announcement of her engagement to Louis Grossberg of Washington, DC, was made Sunday evening at a dinner party at the Kanster home. No date has been set for the wedding. Mr. Grossberg is a member of the accounting firm of Glushak & Grossberg. Washington.

"Isador Freudberg was in to see me this morning," Louis wrote Dave on the 10th. "He tells me that Seager is running his business cockeyed. He says he had three orders of apartment house owners who wanted to use it and who wanted to buy 25 lbs. as samples at a price of fifteen cents. Seager tore up the orders, as he wouldn't deliver unless they paid the 25-lb. rate. Babe, too, tells me that Seager will not deliver a five-pound package to a garage under the $1.50. This is true of the 20 cent package too. I am beginning to believe that our Washington people are cheap. I'd like to see you let some men loose on the bakers like that Chicago baby is doing.

"Paid your house interest in full out of the Argomite a/c. I can't see any sense to trying to stave it off part way to next month by note, as we won't have any more money here next month…"

"In connection with Isador," Dave writes to Louis and Ida on July 11, "I think that Seager is cock-eyed. I have found it absolutely necessary to sell 5- and 10-lb. samples at 100-lb. rates, and these samples are bringing results. It is not possible to sell hundred and two hundred lots right off the reel. Mr. B. never pays for a new product. He (takes it) on approval, if satisfactory, it is paid for; if not satisfactory, there is no charge.

"I am having 50,000 labels printed for my 3½ lbs. boxes. I can get it for 1.1 cents a label, as against 2.3 in lots of 10,000. I may sell this same label to Murray and the Chicago man and maybe Seager. As soon as I get the original drawing, I will rush it to you and I want you to get it copyrighted immediately so that if these other agents want to use it they will have to pay me for my artist work on it, which by the way, thru Neuman Brown, I am getting darn cheap. It will cost me $215. Mr. B. is taking a more active interest in this place and we will probably put on a number of salaried salesmen mighty soon."

"I started to write you at home but the gang would not wait so I had to take a sheet of paper along," begins a letter from Celia, July 11. "I am sitting in the car while writing and will say that position is everything in life. My father had to deliver an order and I went along. It just started to rain, in fact it is already pouring and one can see flashes in the distance. Why aren't you here, Dear?

"Everybody who looks at the rings want to know what the attraction was in falling in love with a Washingtonian – *Nu*, go tell them..."

Louis also wrote on the 11th. "This is exactly 8:30 PM and I have not eaten supper. This morning I was informed that the Nabins are coming over at noon and that I was expected to come over for lunch. The Nabins as you may not know are Joe's prospective in-laws from Florida. Well, dear, they came. Altogether a party of six and a child. I knew the Nabins but didn't know the others.

"We got acquainted very soon and as they were so loud in their compliments for my own little sweetheart, I thought I have to be double nice to them. Therefore, and upon request by them, I piled in Eleanor, Pauline, Mother, and Babe in my car and the two cars went out sightseeing. We just got back at eight and now they are preparing supper. I didn't want to miss writing to my darling and I wouldn't let anybody's in-laws, prospective or otherwise, interfere with that pleasant task.

"Honey, that clipping was nice, Thanks for the name of the fish. I shall tell it to mother and I am sure she will love to have a pound or two from Newark if it isn't any trouble for you to get it.

"Miriam just called me on the phone to hurry up and come on

home as it is getting late. Just another word to tell you of my increasing love for you, dearest, Once more I shall experience the sublime thrill of holding my own darling in my arms and kissing her gorgeous lips, her sparkling eyes, her shapely nose, her slender fingers, her dimply chin, and her beautiful face. Dear, I'm more in love with you now than I have ever been before and that is saying quite a whole lot."

"After Supper, July 12, 1928." For a change, Celia had time on her hands at the bank and used it to demonstrate Argomite. She had given a little to one of the girls who couldn't stop raving about it. Other girls then begged for some, too. "So this noon I brought some down with me and the first test was made washing rings and trinkets. The result was wonderful. I then suggested that we wash the rubber keys and twillers of our typewriters in Argomite. The quickness of the cleansing powers of the Argomite powder surprised all. If you have rubber keys that need cleaning try *Argomite*.

"Mother made a complaint to the Penn. RR that a 100-lb bag of Argomite was torn and contents lost. They would like to have a bill from the Argomite Co., for the 100 lbs, so if you could send us one, we will in turn make demands for about 50 lbs. Many thanks.

"I am writing to Dave this evening. Only a few more days now and I will be with you again. Don't get up to meet us. I will go in your room – kiss you good morning and presto in your arms. There goes a flash and now it is thundering. Oh dear, where are you?"

On July 12, Louis wrote more about the visit of the Nabin family. He stayed overnight at Kitty's and his siblings vacated their rooms too, so the Nabins could sleep over.

I fixed up my wall so that you alone occupy the whole wall above my desk. And what a decoration you are to that wall! Your lovely picture makes the whole office bright. Yesterday as I looked at your picture, I became conscious of the outlandish contrast between the neatness of your appearance and the sloppy condition of my desk. So, I pulled myself together and cleaned up. Now everything is neat above and below the desk – I mean the desk top level.

I hear that Dave rented an apartment on Brighton Beach and may take his family out there this Sunday or Monday. Ida says that Dave is real well pleased with the apartment. It is just three blocks from the water and near schools and Hebrew schools and everything just Jake. It did take him fifty minutes to make the trip but he says that is an inconvenience he will have to stand until his finances are in a more staple (sic) condition.

If business only picks up, you and I, sweetheart, will be able to begin our little adventure and show the world how married life can be made happy. And that, dearest, should not be hard as long as I love YOU and YOU love LOU.

Later that night, Louis writes another letter from the office where he is working late. It is 10:30 PM and the building is closed. He reminisces. "I wrote you over a year ago (when) I said something, which now seems rather funny. Wait, I'll try to find it. Here it is. Just listen. Date: 'Washington's Birthday, 1927.' That makes it just ten days after I had that most wonderful of all pleasures – as it has turned out – that is to have met you, THE GIRL. This letter is apropos my prejudice towards the disability of women to drive automobiles.

"'I am afraid that my prejudice was born some six or more years ago when I saw a woman drive her car into a lamppost. Maybe she was in love and couldn't keep her mind on her job – I don't know. Of course, such a thing could never happen to you. I can't conceive of your becoming so engrossed in anything, even love, to the exclusion of the immediate work at hand. A level headed person never does.'

"Wow, what a change has come over you and me since the writing of that little paragraph. Will you kindly notice that the change is not only in you but in me, too. And what an indictment! According to that I must be cock-eyed. I merely remembered about my reference to your immunity from permitting anything to get you to lose your head, even love.

"As it stands, the case against myself is pretty strong. Oh, well, I was inexperienced then and didn't know whereof I spake. How could I be expected to know what love could do to a person since at that time I had never been in love. I wonder now what prompted me to make that observation about you. I must have noticed that you were very efficient and guessed that you were rather aloof and cold-like. Now I can really understand what they mean at your house when they say that you have changed so much.

"Some day, honey, when you and I will be living here together and there is rain or snow outside and no one around we shall take out my file of our old letters and re-read them all and laugh over our formal manner of address and over the way we thought we knew what we were talking about. It even gives me pleasure to be thinking about the time when we will be Mr. and Mrs. together. Oh, when, dearest, when? Impatiently your intended husband, Louis"

On July 12, 1928, Louis also received two letters from Dave requesting more supplies and saying that the Argomite trade mark needed to be shown on the front of the #5 bags. Dave also asked for a letter from Barton giving permission for sales to outside stores since Neuman Brown knew 300 buyers of the largest department stores in the country. He was pleased with his new $15 bookkeeper, secretary and office manager and discovered that the repaired mimeograph machine was useable after all, despite being told it was a piece of junk.

The next day, Celia asks Louis not to arrive at the end of July, due to work. "As for Kitty and Al, it will be all right for them to come the 27th, as there are others at home to entertain them. I will do my share but I have been instructed by the gang to keep my distance and leave Kitty and Al to the married folks. When you are here I want to think less of my office duties and more of you…"

"While this message of love and adoration will be speeding towards you," comes Louis' reply on the 14th, "YOU, my dear, will be speeding towards me and my waiting arms. I am expecting you to wake me up so that when I go to bed tonite it will mean that the next conscious moment you shall be in my arms. But always there seems to be something to interfere. By the time you will read this you will have been here and gone.

"You remember I wrote you the other day that there was a two year old child in the Florida party. When it got late I carried his sleeping form into Kitty's and out, and into the house again later. As I was holding the baby in my arms one of the visitors told me that it was very becoming to me. Do I look domesticated, dear, or what?

"Later, on a similar trip, another of the ladies said the same thing altho she had not heard what the other lady said. They all told me that I will make an ideal papa. What do you think, sweetheart? Yesterday

Pauline tells me that the kid woke up at about four thirty in the morning and yelled 'I want my Unkie Oooo.' That's me, his Unkie Oooo.

"I can't write any more now, sweets, In the meantime I want you to know that I am mighty sorry you have gone back home and I hope you had a good time. I Know I Will Have Did. I love you, Papa, Louis"

Monday, July 16, 1928. Celia's letter begins, "My only, dearest, best Sweetheart. How I did hate to leave you behind. You know, dear, we were quite fortunate in securing seats together on the trip home." The train was very crowded but Dave asked the conductor if another section was leaving and when the conductor said, "Yes", the group ran to the next train and found it all to themselves, until the word got out.

"I wrote you a few days ago that I gave my assistant a little bit of Argomite. Well, this morning she asked me if I couldn't get her 5 lbs of Argomite. Of the little that I gave her she gave some to her Sister-in-law to try on silverware and dishes." After that, three more people wanted 5 lbs each. " I had to send Dave another letter."

The same day, Louis writes her. "All day to-day I have been happy in the remembrance of your visit here and I do hope that your return trip was an easy and pleasant one. And it was me you visited and not Miriam wasn't it, despite your story about having come merely because Miriam asked you to and not because you wanted to come and see your sweetheart?

"I am beginning to believe that you are right. I have decided not to come on the 27th whether Kitty and Al go then or not. HOWEVER, In view of the fact that I am after all your sweetheart and you, to quote Shoshana (Esther's daughter), are after all 'my friend,' and furthermore, inasmuch as Dave has suggested that I drive his car over the next time I go to Newark, BE it RESOLVED then, that if I can get away, I am really coming out to see Georgie and not you, Friday July number 20, this year.

"The ride may not be such a wonderful one since to my mind, as pieces of junk, Dave's car runs a close second to a certain other car that I have in mind. But that furnishes me with the excuse to be with you (I mean Georgie) as soon as possible. So, even tho I am coming over just to see George, you might grab off a kiss from me while he is not looking."

"Was very much surprised," Louis wrote Dave, also on the 16th, "when Glover called me up today to tell me that you wired him to cancel that order for the half car of Argomite. To me, who is not used to good news happening just for nothing, this sounds not good at all. Of course, I can only guess at the reason. Either you can't get the money just now to pay for it or that those 4,800 lbs. of orders were fakes and that you got yourself done. At any rate I am far from pleased and all I can do is hope for good news as to why…"

On July 17, 1928, Dave writes, "I got your letter after I got back from the Jerseys where I have been trying to straighten out one hell of a mess that two damn bxxxxxds got me into. Every one of the orders those lice sent in were fakes and I have been getting letters from the parties that no orders were made and therefore no stuff was requested. However I have a hunch that this will prove to be a boomerang. I have followed every one of the orders so far and in every case they all want trial samples. I had sent out letters of acknowledgment to the various places and I made my mistake by having the stuff shipped for Monday. This is the first time that the Bush terminal worked so darn quickly and got the stuff out on the road before I got a chance to recall it. Boy did it make me feel sick. But I'll be hanged if I had suspected such a low down dirty trick. I sent a letter to the salesman and his letter came back unclaimed. Just what he got out of it I don't know either. I had given them a little advance, but I stopped those checks in time. A bitter lesson my dear sir, a bitter pill to swallow."

"Of course I came to see you," Celia responded. "While I said it was Miriam's letter that decided my going I also said that you were my main reason. If you didn't hear me it was your own fault, anyway you should have known as much.

"I am so glad you are coming to see Georgie. Whilst thou my Lord condescend to kiss a maiden. Maybe I will be fortunate in escaping with a kiss or two. Being the devoted sister that I am, I am going to plead with my dear brother to permit me to substitute in his stead during your visit.

"By the way have you forgotten about the Argomite bill I asked you to send us? Mother wanted to know if I asked for it."

"Dearest, I think of you so much that I can't get my work done," Louis writes the same day. "I see you with my eyes open and I see you when I close my eyes. At times I see you even when I don't want to see you. Yes, there are such times. One such was this morning when a client was trying to explain something to me and I was trying hard to understand. It wasn't very clear and then I saw you and I lost him altogether. I was almost embarrassed – only he explained it over again in other words and this time I managed to keep you out of it. It was mighty hard too.

"I am still working on the hope and the expectation of being over this Friday evening. At this writing I don't even have the money to go since I shall have to hustle around and get extra dough-dough for the special needs of Dave's moving. Ain't love grand and poverty Hell! But we shall worry about that, too, some other time.

"Yes, dear, I must admit that kiddies seem to like you, too. This morning Shoshanna asked me why I didn't give you my 'marriage ring' and marry you. Can you tell her, dearest?"

> July 18, 1928
> Darling Ceal,
> It does appear to look as if I may be with you after all, this coming Friday night. I hope that old tub of Dave's will stand the trip. I should just hate to have to abandon it on the way and walk fifty miles to a railroad station.
> Yes, my Lady, your Lord will condescend to kiss a maiden if your Ladyship will kindly furnish the maiden and the same is sufficiently attractive to your Lord to tempt him.

July 23, after Louis returned from visiting Celia, he wrote: "Rolled into town bright and early and the first thing that greeted me as I entered the house was your sweet smiling picture. The frame must have arrived for else how would it have been hugging you, dear. This reminds me also that I am, oh, so jealous of the frame.

"My aunt thinks you are wonderful and that we are a heavenly mated couple," Celia writes, July 23. "She said she hoped the wedding would take place near enough to her home so that she could be present. Mother and she are very much attached to each other so I hope some arrangement can be made whereby my aunt will be present. She discouraged my mother in having the type of a wedding I suggested that is; sisters and brother, aunts and uncles and half convinced my mother to have one like Edith's or a strictly private one. Since I disapprove of an over-stuffed wedding I will have to get your mother's and father's views. I am beginning to think as you do and that is to have only the parents present. I can't believe I am writing about our wedding but then again it seems so natural.

"Whitman is back from his vacation and came in my office a few minutes ago to say 'Hello.' I asked him how many weeks he would want as notice for leaving. He was so stunned he couldn't answer me for a minute and then said, 'NO, Miss Kanster, you don't mean it, I can't let you go.' I told him that since I had a sweetheart he had first choice and the Fidelity Un will have to be pleased with two weeks notice. I felt as if I had to give him some sort of a hint since he is talking about wanting six months notice…"

"I feel like the last rose of Summer left blooming alone," Louis writes the next day. "Just got here, too." He has been home sick all morning, and only came in to get her letter and thank her aunt "for them kind woids."

"Verily, my dear, you are learning. You even find it easy to write about your wedding. After awhile maybe you will even be able to talk of our children without blushing. But, yes, the wedding. I have never discussed it with my folks. Of course, there is really only one thing to it and that is how you and I and your parents and my parents feel about it. I'll talk it over with mother and the girls. And then, maybe we'll do what we please about it anyway. The real trouble is that we don't know what we please…"

Over the next couple of days they exchange letters about his illness and recovery, spiced with a brief and humorous dispute about the different definitions of "excuse" and "pardon" and the relative merits of their respective dictionaries.

"Things here are relatively up in the air," Dave writes on July 26, 1928. "I can't get salesmen. The cheap kind cost me money and are not worth a damn, and the good kind don't want to come in on straight commission. So I am now trying to (show) Argomite to prospective large users. I must get one of them to use the stuff in quantity, then hire a salesman on straight salary and have him sell that trade on the basis of the one user. That seems to me the only thing to do."

Dave sent a trial order of 200 lbs to the Borden laundry but learned that one of Mr. Barryman's laundries doesn't want it. A 10-lb sample was sent to the Yellow Taxi Company and 200-lb to the largest wool washer and dyer in Brooklyn, but he needed wool washing instructions. After feeling blue last week, he has high hopes for the retail market as the five-pound bag sells well. The labels and boxes are almost ready and his car is a lifesaver, allowing him to do about 50 miles a day.

"P.S. Call up the Federal Sec. & Mtg. Co. about our house and tell them that it is for sale and that it will probably be sold within a few weeks. If you can beg off the payment on the principal do so and just pay the interest which amounts to about $10. The June rent has not yet been paid. I hope the damn thing will be sold soon otherwise I'll have to try & rent it for whatever I can get out of it."

"July, 1928," Dave writes, apparently in response to a letter from Louis. "Your sorrowful letter to hand, and the bawling out is accepted at face value. One mill to whom we sent a sample came back with a darn favorable letter and asked for more dope. I have several such irons in the fire and my 10 cent store man is getting himself all het up in anticipation. I gave him a 5lb sample to take home and sure enough he sold himself on it good and proper. Next week we will try and get up some special dope for the chain store men and they'll try to land them, and oh boy, should that terrible thing happen, it will positively break my heart. I have a hunch, big boy, that there is going to be something doing pretty soon…"

In his next two letters, Louis writes of the Tuney-Heeney fight he heard on the radio at Leo's place. "I gather that our friend Mr. Heeney has a very sick nose and an optic or two. However, with a check for 100,000 live smackers to act as salve, to quote Rose, it should not be as painful as it might otherwise be."

Then he turns to the subject of their wedding. "Had a bit of conversation with mother and the girls and mother is against a large wedding and the girls are objecting strenuously to a mother-and-father-bride-and-groom affair. They say they waited all this time to see a brother married and now to be cheated out of seeing it! Nothing doing. So it puts the thing back to the sort of wedding you and I prefer. However, there is a new trouble.

"It seems that when mother was over to one of our Kitay cousins, this cousin made a reservation to have the Grossberg family stay over with them Friday and Saturday before the wedding, in the event the wedding takes place on a Sunday. Mother agreed to that and now that cousins are taboo mama feels a bit funny about it and can't see how she can fail to have them come. Of course, I said nothing doing. When cousins are taboo these cousins are no better than your cousins. So it was left there. I suppose this about clinches the matter of the medium sized wedding. I certainly wish I could announce to you the date. No, darling, you don't count in this. So when your lord and master says you shall be married on such and such a day that settles it."

"Darling Fiancée," writes Louis, July 27. "Got a letter from Esther this afternoon telling me that she had received a letter from her oldest daughter, Sylvia, in which said daughter tells of having met my sweetheart and expresses the opinion that said sweetheart is the sweetest and prettiest lady she has ever met. I second the motion and the AYES have it by a large majority. What am I to do about it when I want so much to kiss you and to hug you and to talk to you and to look at you and to ruffle your hair and to pinch you and to love you, and you are not here?

"Why didn't you tell me long ago that you always liked my company? I should have been happy to send you the whole company long ago as it isn't much good to me. Anyway, dearest, don't mind my prattling.

"September 1, 2, and 3 are natural holidays. This means that you may expect your dear to show up, provided he has the necessary dough-dough to swing the deal.

"Was very much interested in your letter detailing your visit with Fanny and her hubby…" Especially the tidbit about meeting Fannie for lunch at the Astor Hotel and noticing Georgie Jessel sitting two tables away. Louis wrote in response to another of Celia's letters, July 30, 1928. "I shall be very happy to join you in paying them a visit. I have something of a brotherly feeling for Fanny and now that she assisted so ably in acquainting the latest love birds with each other I am particularly kindly disposed towards her. I don't expect to be in Newark until September first." Louis wonders if Fanny could put them up for the night but says Ida would be sore as they owe her a long visit. "Well, let's worry about that some other time."

Dave and Ida were well aware of the monetary constraints on Louis. Since he had been providing the bulk of his income for his partner, it was necessary to settle accounts before setting a wedding date. Ida quotes from one of Louis' letters when she writes on July 30 "'I cannot even begin to think of getting married until the bills are paid.' Since only these bills stand between you and matrimony, take them – and with my blessing!" Ida reports on how busy Dave is.

"He has been working on leads to the Yellow Taxi, Bordens Dairies, and a number of big concerns. Dave feels it is better getting repeat sales than in adding to a list of small unconvinced purchasers. As for the two salesmen who swindled the concern, he says the introduction which their action furnished was worth much more than the amount of money they got. By the way, while hanging clothes on the roof here, I sold the Supt. of the Bldg. on Argomite. Dave finished the transaction."

"July 'Last' 1928," Louis writes to Celia. "One of these fine days I may get good and sore and come flying over to Newark, grab my sweetheart, and fly off with her. Would you be real sore if I did that? Or deep down in your heart would you wish me to do that to you?

"Your picture sits here and smiles down upon me as if to say, 'Can that chatter. You know full well that you haven't the nerve to do such a thing and even if you had you would never run away like that. You couldn't do it to your folks and to your folks-in-law and I must bow my head and sorrowfully admit that you are right.'

"I owe you seven more letters before you come here. Someone figured out how many months of the year one used up in working, in sleeping, in eating, in playing. I wonder how many months you and I use up in writing love letters to each other. I love you, I love you, I love ONLY YOU, DEAR…"

While Louis and Celia continue to exchange words of love, Dave writes to Louis of business on July 31. "My poor forlorn & forsaken Darlint. Business in this town in as far as Argomite is concerned can't be said to be bad (and certainly can't be said to be good)." That is because orders have not started coming in yet but prospects are good, especially in the small wholesale field. He spent a long time demonstrating at Mt. Sinai Hospital and they ordered two-hundred pounds for a trial. If satisfied, they will use six to eight bags a month. One pail of Argomite water replaces three pails of soapy water.

"It's late again now, so I'll kiss you bye-bye and am enclosing a good check for $3.25. The fives I'll pay for in installments in two weeks but oh boy, they are certainly helping me to sell Argomite. So we'll call it a day my darling and here's hoping we'll have you here darn soon making a decent living without the worry of a set of miserable clients."

Kitty is in Louis' office and writes to Dave, August 1, 1928. "First of all, I hope that you and your family are quite well, and that you are also very happy now that you are at last together. Poor Ida, she sure missed you, though I never could see just why.

"You may tell her for me that I hope she will have you for the usual Jewish 120 years. In *shimches* (*simchas*, joyous occasions), in fusses, in everything. I wish you most of all that the Argomite shall become the most desirable article on the New York market and that the supply should not quite equal the demand. Louis is already yelling for me to hurry up and tell you that Mrs. A., *soll sie gesund sein* (that she should be well), pounced on him the other Monday at her place of business, because meat isn't selling.

"News item #2. The Security Co. is not willing to forego the principal for three months, but that they accepted the interest for just two months. In the meantime he paid them $13.40 interest for those two months."

As Louis commiserates about his financial condition, he finds consolation in small signs that things will work out. This was the year before Black Thursday, the 24th of October 1929, when the stock market crash ushered in The Great Depression. In 1928, no one suspected what was in store, since it was preceded by a short boom economy. Things were actually looking up and Louis was encouraged by his prospects.

"One week from Tonite, August 1, 1928," Louis answers one of Celia's letters. "Honey, I have been figuring and I am beginning to believe that we shall be all set for your wedding day about the latter part of October. By then I expect to have Dave's bills all paid up and a bank balance in my favor of about three to five hundred caplunks. Besides that I expect to have a regular income of something like three hundred dollars a month net – if too many gents don't drop away from me – which, according to your own guess is sufficient to support you and your children for the first year at least. My income now is really greater than that but some of it I cannot figure because I can't get it regularly. They keep piling up until a big bill accumulates and then, if I'm lucky, I get a note to discount.

"Does the latter part of October suit you and would you take a chance of embarking upon the ship of matrimony with me and with my prospects? Tell me, dearest. Maybe, if a good stroke of fortune socks me a sook, I might be ready to start life sooner. And don't you think there aren't strokes of fortune awaiting me? For instance there is one in the form of the collection of even 75% of the amount of the bills that I sent out yesterday. I mailed bills in the sum of exactly $1,982.50! 75% of this amount is approximately $1,486.88. Golly Moses, if I had that money. Out of all this I am figuring on collecting just about five hundred dollars this month. The trouble is that they are broke and that is why I must wait until I make it anew and save up. If any of this weak stuff comes in it will probably come in handy but just now I cannot pay bills with it.

"All this, of course, does not take David into account at all (except) the need of paying off his local obligations, which I am giving preference over everything else. Anyway, dear, there is a consolation for this waiting. It gives you an opportunity to make those underwears that you were telling me about. But I say, Darn the underwear!

"If only I could find somebody who would pay them just as easily as I got them everything would be O.K. To tell you the truth things look much better to me than they looked two months ago and very much better than they have looked for these last four years…"

"What makes you think I will be taking a chance when I marry you?" Celia asks in her August 2 response. "Your prospects don't interest me in the least – it is you and not your prospects that I love. Dear, I believe we could live comfortably on most any amount. Just as long as we are together. I suggest you give me a few months notice. That's all.

"I can't visualize our wedded life. What I can see is a boy and a girl deeply in love. They are bound to be happy because he loves her and she loves him. What else matters?"

August 2, Louis tells Celia, that for her upcoming visit, Kitty insists that they stay with her instead of at their parent's house. "Personally I am in agreement with her. It is so much cooler over there and besides we shall have all the privacy we want which is a mighty strong item.

"With Eleanor and Miriam each more or less entertaining gentlemen friends it is rather inconvenient to either hog the front room or share it with others. Particularly that is true with the kind of shy and bashful sweetheart that I have. Besides, so far as I know, neither of the other two couples are on kissing terms and that makes it the more awkward."

Then Dave addresses a business letter to Louis, August 3. "Got Kitty's letter and your addenda attached. A few comments on my part. Business this week was fair – results are rotten but prospects are very good.

"I have gotten the 10 cent store man in this business and he is going to get me into some other large places. He is sold head over heels on this product. The story is that he is giving out samples to a half dozen of the largest buyers for them to use at home, not mentioning the sale end of it. He will head for that in a few days and wants to be prepared.

"He wants some information of some of the retail business from Washington. I want you to get me several copies of the half-page ad that was in the *Star*, Thurs. June 14, showing that the largest stores in Washington are using it. I wish you would tell Seager to get me a letter through Lunn & Martin about its salability."

In an August 4 letter to Celia, Louis starts out: "Saturday Nite Before Supper, Just Four Days And 30 Minutes More to Wait." After telling her details of his day, he speaks of their marriage again. "So you don't give a rap for my prospects? Well, well! And while I really haven't anything as yet, I know that it would make little difference to you, except as it would please you for both our comforts, if I were worth a fortune. I don't know why you should, but I do know that you love me for myself and for nothing else. And I am infinitely grateful and happy. Thank you, my beloved. Awaiting your arrival, Your betrothed, Louis"

> August 6, 1928
> Darling Dave,
> Saw Seager this morning and he is selling quite a good bit of the retail stuff particularly his 20 package. He insists that the 1.50 package is more or less a flop…
> Seager is confining his activities to the Department Store Chains, The United Grocers Society, and other chains. His sales and advertising program is all ready and hinted that others chip in if interested. Seager held drives at the Peoples Drug Stores with posters, did newspaper advertising in *The Star*, *The Times* and *The*

News for $175 and offered salespeople prizes. This produced $350 and he was very pleased. He discontinued house-to-house sales as most housewives bought cleaning products at the grocery store and he was selling the small size for $6.20 a case of 48. Seager was happy with his packaging and suggested everyone standardize, naturally using his boxes.

Celia comes here Wednesday nite to spend her vacation of ten days and I am trying to get as much done as possible before she comes.

"Got your nice letter today and upon reading it felt rather encouraged," Dave replied on August 6, 1928. "I am glad that Seager is starting to do business. I noted on that report of his that he is selling or anticipating a 98 cent box. What about it? I believe that the flop of the 5-lb box is for two reasons. First the box looks like hell, is very unhandy and bulky and second the 1.50. I think that extra .50 makes the difference. In re the boxes as soon as I send you the label get it copyrighted at once and start to get a patent of it as I want the words 'Reg USPA Off' on the box.

"With regards to the bulk sales, I wish you would get in touch with Glover and get a list of real bulk users who are using Argomite. Is it true that Westinghouse is using A blue for their metal cleaning and if they are what is the price they are buying it for? My real competition in the industrial line is Oakite and I frankly don't know enough of the action of our blue to know whether it is as good, pound for pound as Oakite. Ask Barton that also.

"In the meanwhile things are slowly developing. I am not a bit discouraged but I do wish Barryman would come in whole heartedly instead of hanging around on the outside.

"With regards my house, please do this for me, Louis, old scout. Get in touch with Cafritz & Shannon & Luchs (Realtors), and ask them to try and rent it for me for $50 per if they can't sell it. They might have to repaper the place and if so let them do so and I'll pay it by a note...

Louis and Celia anticipate her arrival in Washington in their letters of the next couple of days. Dave writes from New York on August 7. "I have been out today trying to dispose of Argomite to some carpet men. Just how our product competes with soap on carpet cleaning I don't know. The fellow was very much interested and bought 10 lbs. in a hurry and even called for it…"

Dave asks for more information on the Rayon boil off. A Rayon Mill has been using soap to boil off the oil and tried Argomite but was dissatisfied. He wants to know from Dr. Barton, how to use Argomite to remove the oil.

"Please Lou, make it a point to get me a list of big users today. I want to know why any have dropped out if they have. Please get me also the following info. For carpets, is A 'C' as good or better than the straight Tex?

"So darling, we'll close this love letter, oh yes, I believe I have got a nice Surgical Instrument store to handle our boxes as soon as they are ready for the medical trade. They will send out their men to demonstrate it and then to spread the gospel. So long and loads of good luck both ways, Dave

"P.S. Please send me my check book from Rochester. I forgot the name and the bank acct."

August 10, 1928
Dear David,
Am just got here after taking Celia over here to visit Kitty. Have just awhile ago left Doc Barton after quite a conference with him. (Louis recounts business with the realtors.)
Now as to Argomite.
1) Talked to Sargent to-day and he says that he personally knows that the word Argomite is registered. As regards the label he says that you must have the words Copyright, 1928, by Argomite Corporation of New York on the label before you can get it copyrighted. This is just the reverse where the patent must first be gotten and then the words 'Patented' stuck on He gave price of $20.00 for the job, which includes a Gov. fee of $6.00. If you have already got your printing done you are out of luck for a registration unless you want to rubber stamp the words over all the labels.
2) Westinghouse is using the blue for their metal cleaning… (They used Oakite before but Argomite is more efficient.)

3) As to the rayon boil business, Barton says do not boil rayon as it injures and weakens it. To know when there is no more oil you have to feel with your hands on the rayon.

4) Some people came to Dulin and Martin and called for Argomite because of some broadcasting that was done when a woman told of how to keep house and mentioned the use of Argomite. Barton thought you might have bought that ad.

5) For carpets 'C' is as good as 'tex.' (Louis continues with the instructions for its proper use on carpets.)

August 12, 1928

Dear Lou,

Got your letter this morning and much obliged for some of the information and thanks for the things you did for me. Let me get my personal stuff off first. Sell my house for whatever it will bring. I will be willing to take back a third trust payable as low as $5 or $10 a month plus interest for the rest of my equity. If that don't go, then ask them to rent the house after it is fixed up.

Dave learned that the largest silk dye works could not use Argomite and wanted to know what silk mill was using it. It was good that the Westinghouse Company was using Argomite with Oakite selling for 12 cents a pound.

Please ask Dr. Barton to let me have a few pounds of Argomite in the solid form for the automobile game. (The powder was being wasted by the help but if a cake could be put into a bucket of water like they now do with soap, it would last all day.)

With regards our labels, I want you to see Barton at once and ask him if he will take over our slogan. (If) not then we will register it ourselves. I don't think we should share our particular work with everybody especially when the cost is several hundred dollars.

A new sales executive, Deutch, was interested in coming in with them but wanted a contract for the first year of $6,000 with assurances of getting a piece of the action afterwards. Dave was amenable if terms could be met. The man remembered a chap who started with the Brillo Company and later became vice president.

I hope that the sweetheart is being entertained in the correct manner as is befitting a sweetheart of Glushak and Grossberg. I also would be interested in knowing what is happening in Washington. How is the work being attended and what is going on in the general scandal of the *shuhl* (shul) business?

August 14, 1928
Dear David,

I'm sorry that I am being kept on a continual go this week on account of the little sweetheart. She is due with Kitty at any moment now.

Saw Barton yesterday and he gave me a sample of the hard Argomite and also said that he had never tried it in the cake form but does not think it will work. You may go ahead and experiment on it. The stuff I am sending you is the Tex.

I am interested in your negotiations with that fellow Deutch. We are hardly in a position just now to tie our selves up at such a fancy price as 6 grand per. Of course, he may be worth that and more but where is the money to pay him? Also it is a good idea to find out what he has done that warrants his claims to such great ability. Since Heckman got himself all burned up with his expert I am a bit leery about the worth of these so called wonders. What is he doing now and if he is out of a job, that in itself spells something not good. I suppose you and Barryman are aware of these things and have your eyes and ears wide open.

Barton is asking about the Kosher packages. He wants to see them on the market. Incidentally, talking about Barton you asked for a ten day credit and when he extended it you neglected to make good within the specified time. I should think you would watch that very carefully as he will surely shut off your credit if you don't pay up on time and I should not blame him for it. Sending along the hard stuff by PP today...

August 16, 1928

Dear Louis,

I received nothing from you today – probably because you did not write. I want some specific news from you and get it out as soon as possible.

At the DGS find out the cost of every single kind of soap and cleaning powder that they have, such as, Lux, Rinso, Chipso, etc. That's all the news you get today. Loads of love to the sweetheart, and regards only to you. Dave

August 17, 1928

Dear Louis, and etc.,

A few woids...Ask Seager or if possible ask Needle of the Vogue Cleaners, just how he uses Argomite in his plant. Jack up Barton on the questions I asked him, such as the name of a carpet cleaner who has used it on Oriental rugs. I have the largest rug man in town waiting for the list before he orders; otherwise he would not even try it. He won't take a chance on a $2,000 rug.

Grossberger has just landed two large real estate foims and they have each ordered 100-pound samples of the stuff for trial. The third hospital that I worked on ordered some on the phone after a competitive test with some other product. So that is the story to date. Tell me what you have done about the labels and if you have registered the slogan and the trade mark for us.

Listen, Louis, let me ask you a poisonal favor. See if you can't follow up the dope on my house. I swear I can't afford this month to meet the $43.75 on it and see if you can't push the renting and sale of the damn thing. I hate to walk out of a $2,000 equity just like that. If I could get $600 or $700 cash out of the darn thing I would be satisfied.

I am trying out the hard soap idea and I got a hunch that it will do the trick. If it does, the Washington gang will have to get busy and make it up for me. Seager is satisfied with the progress that he is making in the package business in Washington and says that he is showing a black balance...

The love letters begin again after Celia returned home from her vacation, mostly about the wonderful time they had, missing each other, and how tired she was. Miriam had accompanied Celia for a return visit. In a letter on August 20, Celia talks about the office. Her boss, Mr. Whitman, had been looking for her. "I went downstairs to take a nap and must have fallen asleep. When I met hizzoner, he asked me if I intended to start work. He said, 'really, Miss Kanster I had no idea you had the morning off.' Of course, everything was said in fun."

The next day Celia wrote that Miriam was in the office waiting for Sarah to go to lunch. "Mr. Whitman was in to see me this afternoon about my work. He wants to know if I can manage to stay there until the first of next year. He said he didn't want me to get 'in wrong' with my sweetheart on his account but if it could be arranged he would appreciate it. He claims he will need all that time to break in Miss Gladys to take my place. I told him plans have not been made but if my Sweetheart consents I will be happy to stay. It made me feel good to hear the Chief Clerk talk as he did. Loads and Loads of Love, Cel"

"You didn't get a letter from me today and I didn't get one from you so we are even," Louis complains to David, also on August 21. "Called Seager on the phone and he told me he wanted to see me. First off, your dope as to the Vogue using Argomite is cockeyed they haven't bought any for six months." It seems Barton is selling Anso to someone in Richmond for 15 cents.

Seager had a lot to say. He thinks the only way to market Argomite is to organize the whole country to do national advertising on a big scale and talks of a $1,000,000 stock offering. The problem with this idea is the different holdings of territory of the various agents.

"He says that the Board of Health here has got after him on the germicidal qualities of Argomite. The certificate from the University of George Washington is not bona fide. It seems that the University never heard of this analysis but that it was prepared by someone working in the University laboratory and without the knowledge of the powers that be," Louis tells Dave. "Barton says that the burden of proof is upon the Board of Health to prove that it isn't a germicide but you know that is baloney. If your brother knows how to make a test for germicidalitis and this does not cost the Argomite Corp. any money it would be a good idea to have the same tested in your town."

Seager said success could only be achieved with a chain of grocers or large jobbers through adequate advertising, either by themselves or by giving an advertising allowance. He had already wasted $1,400 on streetcar advertising. He also fired Korvin.

Edwards worked for Seager when he finished with Barton and told Korvin the stuff was not worth more than 15 cents in any fashion. Korvin's sales fell off right away.

Seager said to watch out for the Argomite 'S' which is a product that Hellert tries to pan off on agents whenever he can. It is slightly different in color from the Tex and he personally checks every bag. "So when next you order, be sure to specify Tex and watch to see what you are getting."

A man in town is trying to sell to the A&P and was referred to New York. "I asked him how come he is to drift into our territory and he says that he does it just the same way that you will sell to them for distribution in his territory. So there you are. I suppose it will be time enough to holler when he makes some sales there and they begin to worry you.

"How do you propose to go about selling your package wares? You should have some sort of plan worked out, don't you think? The only thing that is certain here is that money is scarce. I have hardly begun to pay on your bills and they worry me."

August 22, 1928

Dear Louis,

First let me ask you to see to it that the slogan of Argomite is protected in some fashion. I thought I told you I wanted the slogan patented, that is Registered. I don't care how when or where, but in order to safeguard our name I must have it patented. That is plain enough even for a partner. (Louis and Celia are invited to spend their time at Dave's.)

In re the Seager matter, I think that he has the right dope on a national organization. I want you to go to the Barry Laundry Company and also to the Ambassador and find out why they stopped using Argomite. Ask Barton if he would consider putting in an ad in the *Laundryman's Age* for a year. A half page only costs $50 a month by the year and I would be willing to pay half. Tell Barton that to Laundries I can afford to sell it at $.10 fob Washington. I am having Barryman have the National laundry association analyze the stuff to determine if it will do what is claimed for it.

It is certainly funny that Seager should say that the Vogue is not using it, when a perfect stranger visiting Washington found it out and stated that they were tickled pink with it. I am going to write to that fellow in Richmond and find out about the Anso thing.

What is Edmunston doing now and how is it that Korvin is out? What the devil has struck the place? What is this Argomite S? It will be a fine howdoyodo if we can't depend on the stuff once we actually order it. I think that Seager is considerably wet if he thinks that he can sell Argomite thru New York City direct without me knowing it. Altho I would be satisfied if he did. It should not be bad advertising.

Aug. 22, 1928

Dear Darlint,

Another letter tonight even after I sent you one from the office. First in re my house… (Dave is desperate to sell it and hopes he can transfer title to someone who buys property.) The only other thing is as follows: Repairs $121, Taxes $60, Interest $200. If the house is rented for $50, that takes care of my second trust and the agents fee only. That means then that I will have to spend about $400 each year for another 5 years in order to save my property, and I wonder whether it will ever sell for that price. I would however like to get my original payment of $600 out of it. Maybe some of my clients who make RE deals would accommodate me, for the darn house will actually bring $6,650.

Now, in re Argomite. Why did Seager let Korvin go and where is he and what is Edwards doing? It's funny how the few hospitals I started in it, like it. It will become a universal powder used by doctors throughout the country.

(Dave wants to know from Glover or Barton, what is wrong with the laundry business.) The laundry assoc. is having its annual convention, Hotel Statler, Boston, Mass., Oct. 15–19 and I think that Barton should have an exhibit there. It would even then pay for itself in the publicity and should be worth everything to them.

Find out why he won't – if he won't. Well, darlint, *Kol Hascholos Koshos* (all beginnings are difficult).

August 22, 1928

    My Little B.&O. Sweetheart,

    You are wrong, dear, it wasn't the work which made me so tired but the realization that you, my 78% wife, have gone away and left me high and dry in lonesome old Washington. Now to try and settle another matter. The matter herein referred to is that of most vital concern to me and of but mild interest to you. I refer to our coming marriage. That's just what is wrong with it – it is forever coming. The first reaction I experienced to your proposition – and I must call it yours because of the statement you make that if I agree you would be HAPPY to consent – to wait until the first of the year was an emphatic NO. What, I wait four and one quarter more months? I should say *not*. But I got to thinking. How would it be to make a proposition with Whitman, for you to get two or three weeks off in the not far distant future in which to get yourself all securely married? Then to come back and work until the end of the year at which time you would begin life as a regular wife in the home town of your husband. During this time you would live at home in Newark and your husband would live in Washington. Of course, he wouldn't be living but just existing. But why worry about the husband? Friend husband could drop over to visit the wife occasionally on a week-end and the time would pass until the end of the year.

    Personally I don't like the idea worth a continental gol dern. But your apparent willingness to postpone the wedding stirs compromise ideas in my mind. Is it because you feel a loyalty to the Bank and want to help them out, or because you figure that the extra money you could make would come in handy for sundry bargains that occasionally strike your eye, or because you are plumb 'frightened' at the marriage thing?

    You see, dearest, your sweetheart wants to get married right away and I do not wish to wait any longer than I have to, not considering the bank or your money at all, – I want my wife 100% and not 1/100,000,000 percent less. Then, again, I am not at all in favor of my wife working for anyone excepting me. So you see, honey, it is all settled and we do NOT wait until January and the bank and Whitman and the money be damned. So there!

My arms are beginning to itch for want of being around that sweet little lady with whom they became so well acquainted recently. I must keep my mind off you during the working hours of the day or I cannot give my clients the service for which they are supposed to be paying me. Your befuddled lover, Louis Castleton Grossberg

"Sweetheart Mine," starts Celia on the same date. She has decided to devote the time from 1:30 to 2:00 o'clock each day to writing to Louis. Mr. Whitman disturbed her the first time but she plans to try this from now on.

"As per usual it is raining. If tomorrow is a nice day the folks are going to the shore and poor me will have to stay put in the office. I don't mind staying home when I think of the wonderful time we spent together – 11 days in Washington, 264 hours as it were. 15,840 minutes without a doubt and 950,400 seconds without figuring. Don't prove it dear, it is bad enough I think it is so. An ocean liner full of love, Cel"

August 23, 1928

Sweetheart Dear,

I like the idea of your setting aside 1:30 to 2:00 every day as my half-hour. In fact I like it so well that I shall try to do likewise and if I cannot write at that time I shall think of you then, more than I do the rest of the day. That will make it my time 12:30 to 1:00.

Just thinking what a lovely sweet bright smart nice pretty gorgeous little sweetheart the good Lord picked out for me and how lucky a fellow I am to have been around when He decided to give you away. You were here, by your own count, – which by the way was off just exactly 17,400 seconds since you were here 11 days 4 hours and 50 minutes and not just eleven days as you have it – nearly one million seconds and never did so many seconds seem so short and the neighboring seconds – before and after that million – so long.

Just one week from now I shall be getting on the train to come to you, dear heart, and then we shall catch up on lost kisses, hugs, and embraces. I can't send an ocean liner of love since mine goes by rail. A whole train load of LOVE, To My Dolly, Louis C

August 23, 1928

Dearest Lou,

It is exactly 1:30 now. I was able to arrange my work this morning to spend at least one hour with you. Here goes, Sweetheart.

Miriam tells me that you have paid my fare home – consequently she won't take any money from me. Dearie, you shouldn't have done that. Later on when we are married I won't object, but now it is different. I told mother about it but she said, '*Narishe kind* (nonsense), what is yours belongs to him and what belongs to him is yours.'

I know you won't take the money now so I have gone to Bambergers' store and bought you a very neat dressing robe. I intended buying you something anyway. I will give it to you on your next visit here so in case you don't like it, it won't be any trouble returning it and selecting another one instead.

Thursday, August 23, 1928

Dear Dave,

Your long letter received but there seems to have been practically no news in it. I am also interested in your experiments with the solid Argomite. I have a little piece here and I use it occasionally to wash my hands with. It does not suds up as quickly as soap but you can take off the dirt.

Barton was out of town today and will be back to-morrow. I'll see him then re the patenting of the slogan and the insertion of the ad in the laundrymen's paper.

Saw Needle of the Vogue and he tells me that Seager never tried to sell him any Argomite but that many months ago someone came to him and asked him to try it out in the gasoline. He did, and he was satisfied with it for a time. Then they switched the color of Argomite – possibly gave him another kind – and it didn't act so well. So they stopped using it. He hasn't had it in his place for about eight months.

At the Barry laundry they used it many months ago and stopped because it would not stand up under high temperatures. Just what that means I can't tell you. Couldn't get to the Ambassador laundry to-day.

Your invite to stay with you the whole time I am in your neighborhood is very sweet and partner like. However, it pains me to find that so young a fellow as you are have already forgotten the ecstasies of the 'engaged to be married' state, for otherwise how could you suggest such a thing to a guy who goes to visit his more or less brand new *Kalleh*.

You better just figure me for the better part of Friday and the sweetheart for the late afternoon and evening.

P.S. Miss Crowlin keeps asking me what about that carload of Argomite for you. Don't you think it would be a good idea to purchase the difference on that first car so as to be on the safe side?

On August 24, Louis tells Dave of his long talk with Barton and Glover. Barton liked the label with a few small criticisms and promised to have the slogan registered at his own expense. He was not interested in taking an ad in the *Laundryman's Age* after being disappointed from an ad in a Paper Mill Magazine that brought no inquiries in a considerable length of time. Louis was inclined to believe him.

Glover confidentially advised me to stay away from Seager and his schemes for a national organization. It seems that Seager is a rather tricky and selfish individual. Glover wrote to every distributor the same as to you and asked what you thought of the sale to any chain for delivery and resale in some other agent's territory. You said you are willing to let the man doing the selling get the cake. Seager was absolutely opposed.

Then, a few days ago he started dickering with the New York Liggets and I understand now that he received a wire from his man that he had sold Liggets. Now, of course, Seager is quite willing to have the cake when he sells to outside of his territory himself. Glover asked him what caused his change of heart? So Seager says he wants to take advantage of his own sales but does not want the other fellow to have anything out of his own territory. This was said in jest but it was meant in truth.

Glover and Seager do not seem to have any too much love for each other. So now Glover suggests that you write a letter to Barton and say that you have reconsidered your previous agreement to permit another to sell in your territory. Later there may be a precedent set...

August 24, 1928

Dear Lou,

Got your letter and want to write to you several things. I want you to make out a note for $3,000 to Barryman and either sign or endorse it and shoot it over to me. I need the dough and Mr. B. will let me have your receipt of the note. Note is for 1 year no interest.

On August 24, Louis confesses to Celia:

I am awfully sorry but I was unable to be with you to-day at the appointed hour. I was busy at the office of a client. (And) a cop sneaked up on me and planted a ticket in my car for over parking. It was really a fine for when I should have been in communion with my dearie. I paid my $2.00 and I hope I am forgiven.

First of all I want to accept the bawling out that you gave me for paying for your return ticket. Of course you understand just why I bought that ticket. Well it was because I was so anxious to have you go away that I even bought you a ticket to get rid of you. What do you think of that?

I guess you'll be returning the dressing robe now. But don't do it, dearest. I think I shall like it. As a matter of fact, I was looking at one the other day and might have bought one myself if you hadn't said anything about it. I appreciate it and I know there is just a bit of pleasure in it for you. Have Miriam kiss you for me, will you, dear? Of course I don't expect you to find any satisfaction in such substitute kisses, but it does come from Washington and that is something.

August 24, 1928

Dearest Sweetheart,

You are the dearest sweetheart a girl ever had. What a wonderful letter you sent me! Dear, I will (be) *more than happy* to work for you. If I can be in the least way helpful to you in your work it will be my greatest pleasure. I can't compare the feeling I would have working for you to that of working for Whitman.

I told Whitman I would be 'happy' to stay because I had no other alternative. It was my place to say it. Dear, it isn't that I feel a loyalty to the bank or because I am plumb 'frightened' at the coming marriage. No indeed. When he was talking about my staying until the first of the year I was only thinking about the money I would be earning. So please forgive me, dear.

All my difficulties would be overcome if I would only call the Citizens Branch on the phone and tell them to credit my account with $200.00. I have enough collateral on hand so won't have to worry about that. I can use the money buying a few things that will come in handy after our marriage; such as a coat, shoes, a few dresses, etc.

Let me tell you why I will be perfectly in the right to make a loan. There is a rumor going around the bank that the stock I own is going up because of an increase in capital that will undoubtedly become effective the first of the year. It sounds too good to be true. I owe the Citizens Branch $1,250.00 so if the rumor is correct (which I doubt) I can pay off my loan outright and have 200 shares free and clear in the bargain.

If I thought there was some truth to it I would hand in my resignation today and take things easy for awhile. (I wouldn't have to leave Miriam at home while I went to the office.) I would be happy to inform Mr. Whitman that Yours Truly had a sudden change of heart and desires to leave and I wouldn't give a darn whether or not he like it.

The compromise you have in mind will not work because it is the rule of the bank that all girls entering the field of matrimony must resign. We have a few married women in the employ of the bank but they have been here a long time, long before the rule had been enforced. I don't think it is a good idea because I would be very lonesome. I surely wouldn't want you to leave me here or I leave you in Washington after we are married...

I am certainly glad that you are in accord with me on the subject of getting married as soon as possible (Louis continues.) about your borrowing the two hundred, it is right funny. Why should you ask me about it? The money and the collateral are yours and the need for the money is probably also yours. So, if you think you should borrow the money, why your sweetie is satisfied and that's all there is to it. The old man might kick later when it comes time to pay off on the loan but why worry about that now.

I am so sorry that I cannot go to the file now and get out your letter as there is something in it that I wanted to comment upon. Kitty is just itching to find out where I keep my love-letter file. But she don't know where they are. Right now she is examining the file and has picked out a folder of personal correspondence. They are the pre-love letters and here it comes, 'Why that's terrible, they are too old.' I thought so, that is why I let her take them. I better stop now before she really does find them.

Mom said Ida tried to break up the impending marriage a month or so before the wedding. Since Ida was accustomed to Louis paying their bills over the years, his marriage would put an end to that. Mom remembered the four of them on the way to shul one evening. Louis and Dave were walking ahead of the ladies. When Ida had Celia's ear, she told her how her life would change after she married Louis. She would be marrying into a very religious family and be expected to keep a strictly Kosher house, have lots of children and wear a *sheitel* – a wig worn by ultra-orthodox married women to hid their hair. Keeping a Kosher house was no problem since Celia had been raised that way, but the other two requirements were a blow. She loved her in-laws dearly but would not agree to live up to those expectations. When Celia confessed to her parents she might have to break off her engagement, they cautioned her to speak to Louis first. Celia was reluctant to do that in a letter so they suggested she confide in Kitty. Celia then went on a day excursion to see Kitty in secret.

Kitty was furious to hear what Ida had said. "How dare Ida say such a thing! Look at me. I don't keep a Kosher house and I only have two children. Do I wear a sheitel? My mother never wore a sheitel!"

Later, when Celia told Louis about this, he was very upset with Ida. He claimed she was always peculiar and probably said this out of jealousy, but they would show her and be happily married forever.

"The rumor about which I wrote to you the other day was somewhat inflated," Celia confides. "I had an idea it sounded too good to be true. The information I have now, though not authentic sounds logical. For every two shares I own I get a 'Right' worth a little more than $4.00 or $400 in cash should I desire to sell. I was advised by the head man of our Securities Dept. to use my 'Rights' towards the purchase of 100 shares for $1,250. He said the Citizens Branch will buy it for me and keep it as collateral. Not so bad that way either when you consider that I won't have to lay out any cash myself. I can get 100 sh by just signing my name to a note for $1,250, same being worth $2,475. I'll want my husband's advice on this matter so we will talk more about it when you get in town..."

August 26, 1928

Lovely Sweetheart,

I am beginning to worry about my coming trip (and) the leaving of this burg and the office for four days. Then, why shouldn't I take off time from my labors, which are usually not paid for anyway?

(Louis spent two hours at the office re-reading love letters.) Sometimes I wonder how I am going to stand all this waiting, dear. Every day is like a year and every week like a generation. And our wedding day still over two months off – if not more.

You know, sweets, I have come to think of our wedding day in terms of November 11th. I looked over some of my debts to-day and also the money that will probably come in to my coffers in the next month or two and it seems enough to pay those debts and leave a little bit for spending money change. That's the trouble, honey, it is only change.

Kitty and I had quite a *schmues* (schmooze) Saturday afternoon. We figured how much money it will take us a month to live and if she is (correct), I should be able to take the role of provider and stay that way. Somehow we shall get along anyway. But then I stop and do a wee bit of thinking and decide that it would not do to start life with a wife when in debt. Which all means that we just have to wait. Isn't life tough, honey?

Louis decided to take in a movie and found to his surprise, that the kisses on screen did not compare to those they shared.

August 26, 1928

Dear Lou,

Got your letter in re Barton and Seager. In the first place what do you mean that Barton will register the trade mark for me? I am not interested in just saving the registration price. I want him to pay for the drawing and the plates. I am satisfied to buy my own labels, but he will have to pay for the original expenses, and in as much as I owe him some money already I will hold off paying it until we settle on the rest of it. This is important.

Dave says Seager can't get away with selling Liggets drug stores thru New York City. He has a letter from Barton to that effect. He is willing to spend $20 to come to Washington if the men from Chicago, Philly and the locals come to discuss Argomite. Business is slow and he blames the home office for not cooperating. They should have spent a lot of money testing the product and advertising to laundries where the potential was enormous. Dave decides to go after specialized lines like doctors, dentists and hospitals. Then it will find its way into their households at $1.00 a box.

He tried silk mills and rayon mills but got no cooperation from Washington. "In other words they don't know what it is all about and I can't afford an experimental technical laboratory yet. I did manage to sell a few Dry cleaners but I have absolutely no information to go by. If Barton is telling me the truth about selling 10,000 lbs. of Anso a month in Philadelphia, why does he not tell me how to use it? Please tho Louis, follow up the two laundries and find out why they cut it out. I want the real reason. This applesauce about it breaking down at high temperatures is rubbish. It stands up better under boiling water than it does even in cold.

I am certainly looking forward to seeing you again to have a long schmues. If it is necessary to visit a *Kalleh* then it is not especially necessary to visit her family, and the *Kalleh* can spend the day Sunday and Monday here in Brighton.

August 27, 1928

Dear Dave,

I saw the Bay laundry owner and he tells me that the reason he stopped using it is because it would not stand up at high temperatures. (Louis asked, why then did he write a letter of recommendation? He said it was fine in the beginning, but after the same clothes came back week after week, eventually they turned yellow. So they stopped using it.)

The Ambassador tells me, however, that he was quite well pleased with it at the beginning in quality and price but that after a time they boosted the price on them and it became unprofitable. He knew nothing of any failure to stand up in high temperatures. I would not worry too much about the home office. You might just as well make up your mind that you won't get very much cooperation from them and forget about wanting it. They don't know and they will not spend any money to find out.

About our spending Sunday and Monday with you I still can't see it. Celia does not like to go bathing. We went bathing here the other day and I know she had a miserable time all the time we were in the water. It seems that the water gags her. Somebody dunked her here and it took her half an hour to come to herself. So your beach is a very little inducement. I think they have arranged something for the four of us, Sammy and Edith, Ceal and I.

As a Chosen, what interests me particularly is a maximum amount of privacy especially when it gets kinda late in the evening. I frankly can't see where you will be able to supply us with a nice private spooning sofa after the old folks' bed time. Besides, where will we sleep without causing considerable and unnecessary inconvenience?

We, that is Ida, you, and us could maybe meet in New York and see a show and then go home with you and spend the evening. That should give us time enough. When I am with Sammy and Edith it is equivalent to being alone as they are at all times just as busy with each other as Celia and I are. With you and Ida around it would be a crowd. You have grown old, kid, and you don't remember.

At the Kansters, it has been mighty fine that way. Everybody – by common consent – goes to bed or gets out of the front room into the kitchen no later than about eleven and we have the parlor, its furniture, and the night to ourselves. However, visselsee.

About your house, I would suggest that you send them a check for $9.20 saying you cannot pay more at this time and being offered for sale at a great bargain and is sure to go very soon. That will keep them off you for a little while anyway…

Dave complains to Louis on August 27. "Just a few words. I was thinking over very seriously the labels for our boxes and I hope you haven't acted like a sap and given it away to Barton. I have spent a lot of time as well as money on the labels and attached dope and if anybody wants to use it they'll have to share the expense with me. I absolutely won't give up the labels for less than $4–500 and that is what it actually cost me in time and money.

"I will be waiting to hear from you when the Chicago fellow intends to visit Wash. as I want to be there. See if you can locate Korvin, and if you do, see what's what. I hope you have already sent me the note, as I need the money. Things are particularly slow this weekend and will remain this way until after Saturday…"

Celia wrote about missing Miriam and looking forward to Louis arriving in the next few days. Louis replied on August 28 that "I am afraid our lives will pass too quickly and before we know it we shall be dead of old age. If the speed with which time has heretofore passed for me in your company is any criterion, it shouldn't take long before you and I will be quite old folks. But we shouldn't think of those things, dear. Right now there lies before us the most wonderful thing in our lives. The day I have been waiting for since I laid eyes upon you is almost within reach of my fingers. For my part, honey, I am simply thrilled with the mere thought of it and at this time it seems quite beyond my comprehension how it could be possible for us to be anything but extremely happy.

"Yes, dear, I am to be expected in your town shortly. But don't wait up for me. Just leave the doors open as you did the time before this one and go to bed. You should be able to snatch from two to four hours sleep before I come. My brother Joe, the Floridian, has returned and we are busy talking things over. Yesterday was some day for the return of travelers. First, Miriam came home. Then Joe showed up. Mother came in from Atlantic City at about five and at seven Sholem (Sol) returned from a two weeks trip to New York."

> August 28, 1928
>> Dear Lou,
>>
>> I got your two letters and thanks for the info in re the laundries. I am getting about fed up with refusals. I will tell you a lot of dope that I did not know when I started this racket. I am beginning to get afraid of this wholesale stuff…

Dave fears Argomite is not commercially feasible. In the real estate business, Argomite cannot compete at 12 to 15 cents against other powders for 3 to 6 cents. One of Barryman's laundries used 2,000 pounds and now does not want it even at 10 cents. They are using Soap and Oakite. Another one also said it was no good.

A Rayon mill tried it three times and stopped. The Ipswich Mills in Massachusetts found Olive Oil Soap to be better. A wool washer tried it to replace soap and soda but it did not work. In New Jersey, Fuller Woolens reported it would not do. And the National Silk Dye Mills gave a negative reaction.

Carpets are cleaned in several ways. Some make a firm jelly of 7 pounds of soap in 50 gallons of water. They pour it on the rug and scour it with an electric brush. This prevents it from getting too wet or else it takes too long to dry. Argomite won't thicken up unless 15 to 20 pounds are used. Other rug cleaners use a thin solution in a hose with a brush.

> Now how am I going to sell to carpet cleaners when I don't know how in the blazes it works or is supposed (to) and Washington tells me nothing for they don't know it themselves.
>> With the blue I don't know yet what it will do. The only field in which it is perfect is the retail field. At home the stuff is marvelous.

I was in a large mill today. He asked me how to use it and altho I know the general formulas, he tells me he could not afford to use a chemical, costing 11 cents a pound to replace two products, one costing 8 and the other 1½. He asked me how much to use and altho I gave him figures he laughed at me.

Take this letter over to Glover. Let him show you who are using the stuff. To whom is the Argomite Industries selling, and for what purposes? How is it used and what does it replace? It is one thing to be sold on Argomite for general cleaning, and altogether another thing for selling Argomite to highly technical industries using complicated methods and procedures.

I am therefore very anxious to meet the Chicago fellow and also Murray of Phila. and Seager and actually find out what wholesale stuff is being sold and to whom.

Barryman has written to the Mellon Inst. for a report of Argomite and will let you know as soon as he gets an answer…

Barton wrote to Louis on August 29. "Mr. Glover is in my office and has explained to me a conversation he had with you yesterday afternoon, pertaining to the conversation between yourself and Mr. Seager of Dixie Argomite Company." Barton confirmed Dave's and Louis' exclusive rights to their territory and said any infringements by Seager or others would not be tolerated. As for the packaging, he claimed they were hoping to standardize it, "using the Dixie 8-oz. package if practicable. Inasmuch as you people did not understand this and have already gone ahead and spent considerable time and money, we deem it only fair that we allow you to use the package. To our mind, it is a very good package (and) has beautiful art work.

"We do wish, however, that if, at some later date, all distributors should adopt one certain package that you will fall in line with them so we could have universal style of advertising as outlined in all contracts. We want to do everything to assist you people to do profitable business. We do, however, want and must insist that you, in turn, comply with your contract in the quota agreed upon for that territory.

"If the quota is too large, you should relinquish some of your territory. We believe that if you would have abandoned attempting to sell rayon plants and some other so-called large users and devote the major part of your efforts to your small package business, you would have gone beyond your quota. These large users, as much as we would like to have them, require considerable time before they are landed, so to our mind it is not wise to let the small fellow go and play a waiting game for the large ones."

Louis writes of playing golf and looking forward to visiting Celia. Celia writes back after his trip. "How I worked this morning is beyond me. My eyes kept closing all the time, Sammy called the house last night to say good-bye to you but you had left less than five minutes before."

Celia called the Citizens Bank and requested a loan for $500.00. "I am going to use only $200.00 for myself. Should your clients fail in their payments we can use *that* and when they pay you we can pay back the loan. By *that* I mean $300.00. If we don't need the $300.00 I can at any time give it back to them. I have to go sweetheart. You have my love wrapped around you."

"It does seem as if I am back home again," Louis pens, also on the 4th, "even tho my heart remained in Newark. Right now I rushed back to the office after (a) ball game and schmues afterwards, with the sales manager of the Argomite Industries here. The ball game was to me a waste of time to say nothing of the cost but I had to do it for the sake of Argomite."

"Sweetheart Mine," writes Celia, September 5. She had mailed Louis the shortened dressing gown but the tailor forgot to include the cut off hem. She would send it later. "I should like our Wedding Day to be the 4th of November, but-if-Kitty or any one member of your family find it inconvenient to get away and if you find it difficult to take that part of the month off it will be all right to have it on the 11th of November. I want to please everybody.

"Ma wants to know if she may have 100 lbs. of Argomite. Can you send it or shall I write to Dave? Thanks, dear."

"Sweetheart," replies Louis. "I want you here in the flesh so that I may hug and kiss you, and you of course to hug and kiss me. Do you know that you have become the most important part of my life, dear? I love you. What did you do to me sweetheart?"

"I suppose you will miss your old life when you come here to live the new one," Louis offers on the same date. "I will not blame you for that, as now you do just as you please barring the conventions which, it is true, bother you more than they do many other girls – the lady of the hoseless legs of the subway, as an instance.

"When you are my wife you will not be able to go to work at the bank. You may work in some other manner but it will be different. You will have to learn to darn socks and sew on buttons. Picking out your husband's neckwear and shirts will become one of your indoor sports. And above all you will have to baby your husband – at least until another baby smaller and more helpless than he, if such be possible, shows up on the horizon. I wouldn't be surprised to learn that you are nearly as anxious to begin The Life as I am. I said nearly because I am sure you couldn't be AS anxious as I am. Every day that you are not my wife is a torture to me...I even visualized a beautiful apartment for two. But about that three hundred, you are the perfect sweetheart to have asked the bank for it, but I hope not to need it.

"When I came home Tuesday morning somewhat perturbed over the smallness of the bank balance, which the monthly statement indicated to be just $64.09, what do you think my mail had for me? I'll tell you. Checks totaling exactly $216.18. Right off the bat I got visions of an early marriage. Of course $216.18 isn't such a much at all, when one needs as much money as I need. But it does represent nearly half the money that I owe to-day and it heartened me considerably. With a little luck I should collect enough money this month to pay off all I owe for Dave's account and then I shall have a bit for ourselves that may be expected to come in October, and the four days of November.

"So, honey, darling, since it does cost $1.50 a month to keep the $300, I might suggest that you return it right now, and then in November, if we cannot get along without it, you can get it back.

"Leo was up last nite and he saw your picture. Can you imagine what he said to your sweetheart? He says he can readily understand why I would go to Newark to get a girl like you but he'll be hanged if he can figure out why such a nice girl like you would come to Washington to get a fellow of the likes of me. Isn't that just terrible talk! You think I'm a pretty nice fellow don't you, dearie? All of my love you already have. This is just enough more to refill what might have spilled out in your travels from place to place. Your worshipful devoted Love, Louis"

September 6, 1928

My Sweetheart,

You tell Leo that he doesn't know what he is talking about. Anyway thank him for saying nice things about me.

I had a heart to heart talk with mother (and) it will please her if we invited Aunts and Uncles to our Wedding. She said your mother and father would also like to invite the Aunts and Uncles. Since there is only a difference of ten couples or so the added cost won't amount to very much. I understand that you have to start looking for a place at least six weeks in advance because October, November and December are very busy months. If we cannot get a place suitable for our needs in Newark would you like it if we had to go to New York? I get all excited when I think of it...

"My Darling Sweetie," wrote Louis on September 6, 1928. "You surely wrote me a wonderful letter, dear. About the Argomite. I wonder what your mother wants with another hundred pounds just now. Are you going in the business or what? Of course, I shall send along the 100 pounds as soon as I go down to the Argomite plant, which may be in a day or two.

"I note what you say about the date of our wedding and I am now inclined to think that we better leave the matter rest until you get here next week. We might as well talk it over as write it out."

In her reply the next day, Celia writes of being love sick and adds: "Mama tells me the reason she spoke to me about the Argomite at this time is due to the order Edith placed with her. Another reason may be that she didn't want to find herself without Argomite in the house and to avoid a recurrence of a delay in shipment. And that reminds me, anything encouraging about Argomite? I have a reorder for 5 lbs. that I turned over to Dave and just as soon as my other customer hears from her friends, I expect a few more orders. Long live Argomite."

"The robe came to-day and it was admired by all and sundry. My brother Joe, who knows the values of clothes since he sold men's furnishings in Florida," Louis reported to Celia on September 7, "offered to trade at once. He says it is an expensive piece of machinery and he approves your taste perfectly. I think it was wonderful of you dear to have given me that robe and I won't use it until after you and I will lounge around together in our own home. Can you imagine it, darling, you and I will soon have our 'OWN HOME.' It thrills me just to think of it.

"About the inclusion of Uncs and Aunts at our wedding, if your mother really thinks that she would prefer to have those others then there is nothing more to be said about it. We better leave all that to talk over next week when you will be here."

"I am all mixed up today," Louis confides to Celia on September 8. "Babe has put a bug in my ear to the effect that in view of the fact that this Sunday is the last excursion out of here to you I should take advantage of it and go see you. His own interest in the matter is to pay a visit to his lady friend Ruthie. This is the last day of his vacation which he has spent entirely at home.

"At first I pooh-poohed the idea. I am not supposed to be interested in excursions anyway so why care about this one. Then, again, I don't know just whether it is the right thing to do so, to bother your folks with my visits every week. Then again I have an important piece of work to get out for presentation Monday, and Esther and family are here. All in all never has there been a contemplated visit with so many reasons for not going.

"Pa thought it was very foolish of me to go again when I was with you just a week ago and when you are coming here in a week from now. Well, dearest, shall I go? Would you go, was you I?

"Have been at work here in the office all afternoon. In order to help the cause along Babe donated the afternoon to me. And still I don't know what to do. Do your father and mother mind? Does Sarah mind? Does Ruthie mind? Does Georgie mind? Does the baby mind? And how about Sam? Please ask Shnubble (the dog) if he cares if I come up oftener than heretofore.

"Your gifts for the kids came and will be distributed tonite. They are expecting to leave here to-morrow morning. Your lonesome and lovesick, Louis C"

Louis apparently did go, as Celia sends this card the next night: "I had a very, very enjoyable day and am happy that you came over so unexpectedly. It proves in every way your love for me and because I enjoyed your visit proves in every way my love for you. What could be sweeter? I hope you had a restful return trip. Goodnight and God Bless You. Always and Ever your Sweetheart, Cel"

"Talking of letters," Louis letter asks the next day, "were you surprised to get one from me today? I know you didn't expect any as I wanted to surprise you, dear. I am always wanting to surprise you with nice things. Yesterday I brought you me and today I send you me again in script." Louis promises to bring her more than himself in the future, like candy, flowers and other unsuspected delights.

"And just think, it will be a full seven or eight weeks before you and I will be living in the same town for good. But when that time comes, we shall not only be living in the same town but on the same street, on the same floor, in the same apartment and as if that in itself were not bliss enough it shall be in the same room and even in the same – oh, honey love, why do you torture me thus!"

> 1:30 PM, Monday, September 10, 1928
> Dear Sweetheart,
> I felt a little guilty sending you a card instead of writing you a letter, so last night after I had sent Georgie out to mail the card I sat down to write you a letter.
> It was very nice of you to come out at a time when you had your sister and brother-in-law from Syracuse visiting you. By the way, I must not forget to tell you to bawl your father out for trying to dissuade you from coming to Newark to visit your Sweetheart. The idea!
> I am due for dictation any minute now. If I have time I will type on this sheet a poem that I read this noon. Affectionately Yours, Cel

"How do you like the picture I am enclosing with this letter?" Celia writes the next day. "I think it is exceptionally good. I took it down to the office and showed it to different ones and you should have heard the remarks passed. 'Wonderful couple.' 'They sure are in love.' 'Look at the dimples, etc.' I agreed to everything that was said and some more. I sneaked this snap shot from Edith to send to you. I didn't dare take any others for fear she would miss them. She always insists that Sammy look at them before they are distributed. Edith sent three packs of films to the corner drugstore and received only one dozen in return. The other two packs were not focused properly. The only ones that did come out were those taken at the Delaware Water Gap. I am having a set made for OUR ALBUM…"

September 11, 1928
Dearest Honey,

For once my threat will be carried out. This will be the shortest letter you ever got from me, the reason being that I must catch my train for Baltimore and the boat to West Point right away. I have fifteen minutes in which to park my car and get to the station. I'll write again to-day on the boat and I want you to keep writing every day, as I may be back here to-morrow nite. I love you as always, Louis, Enclosing CK for 2 dresses $25.00.

On Board Ship, The ss City of Richmond, September 11, 1928
My Darling Sweetheart,

I don't know just when you will get this letter because mail out of West Point is not as frequent as it is out of the more civilized cities and counties. For some reason the U.S. Post Office Department has neglected to put up mail boxes on the Bay corners.

I'm going out of here as it isn't the last word in comfort to write from here. This is the lounge, I suppose, and I find that altho the seat and table are more comfortable there is quite a bit of vibration here from the engines and I will probably have to move again (Louis recounts his search for a suitable place to write). So far this letter hasn't said anything. Shucks, this would be a good opportunity to tell you something I have never said to you before and that is that I am quite some in love with you – but I have no place from which to write and so can't tell you.

How nice it would be if you were here with me and as my wife. The seas are so nice and calm and the vibration of the engines – except for writing purposes – are very restful and soothing. The stars are out and the night is dark. Now and then a boat passes. There is surely ample room here for romance. All I need is you in my arms and the night would be complete.

This morning Babe (18), Joe, and I got into sort of a discussion on the subject of love letter writing. Babe couldn't see how anyone could have so much to say to another that a letter a day couldn't soon exhaust the stock of things to say. The only salvation he could find was that he must write the same letters over and over again. Of course, I told him the truth – that when he grows up and finds the only girl for him the wonder of it will be so great that he will be quite unable to exhaust the subject. From this it must follow that the greater the wonder the slower the point of exhaustion and conversely, the faster the point of exhaustion the less the love. Remember this – sweetie of mine.

Your letter to-day was grand and the attached poetry right good. It does seem from that that I shall have to teach you to drive very soon. Otherwise, as the wife, you may not be able to stomach the abuse. Do you think I shall ever be like that to my wife? I hope not.

Celia and Louis continue writing while he is in West Point, working with the pickle company. Dave writes him on September 14. "Before I forget, the small towels that you want are only $2 a dozen but they are not of the same quality as the large ones. Mr. B. hasn't got the same quality in the small towel so before I shipped them to you I thought I would tell you.

"I received the *tolis* (*tallis*, prayer shawl) for which I thank you. It shows that even a partner is a *mench*, though a late one."

Dave entertained Glover when he was there and said to forget Seager. He liked the consolidation idea and said he would advise other agents to adopt their label by paying $100 for the original royalty. The Sheffield laundry test did not go well and it was good that Glover was there to see it. Now he knows what they are up against.

"Grossberger finally landed one very sweet account. It was that of a packer, and after a sample order of 200 lb., this wonderful gentleman ordered a whole ton at 14 cents. *Zol is nor zein mit mazel* (should only be with good luck).

"They tell me it is going to be New Year (Jewish New Year) in Washington also, like here in New York. Permit me therefore to wish you a very happy New Year, one that is full of good health, joy and prosperity. May this year prove to be a turning point in our lives…"

"I am so tired and sleepy," Celia writes after her visit to Washington. "To make matters worse I not only had today's work to do but Gladys left a portion of Saturday's for me to finish today. I bundled my things together, got dressed, changed trains at Manhattan Transfer, walked to the office, parked my valise, and went out for buttered toast and coffee. A few business letters are waiting to be answered. I am even too sleepy to attend to that, but what can you *mach*. Goodbye Sweetheart, Cel"

It was over this weekend visit that Celia and Louis decided October 28, 1928 would be the date for their wedding. The choice of this date meant a big financial loss for Celia, since she would have earned a $360.00 bonus, 10% of her annual salary, had she worked to the end of the year. But Louis couldn't wait.

"My Dearest Little 94% Wife," Louis writes on the same date. "The day is practically gone and it means that one day has been chopped off the six weeks I must wait before my darling little girl comes to me again. I'll wait, dear, but with mighty poor grace.

"For the first time since I can remember, I was so sleepy after you left, that while reading a short chapter of a story in *Liberty* I fell asleep and left the light burning all nite. I woke up this morning at about seven to find the book near my hand and the light going full blast.

"Do you know that our wedding day is set, dearest? I can hardly endure to think that it will be so long yet to wait for THE day. The public is beginning to ask me when I am to be married and now for the first time I can tell them. It is a puzzle to me to figure out (to) whom I should not send announcements.

"I have my clients here, many quite friendly. However, I never mixed with them socially. Would you say that I should or should not send them announcements? First of all I wish to avoid making it appear that I am in any way angling for a present and secondly I don't wish to have them become intimate to the point of visiting me at home. I don't think it is good business for me to mix socially with my clients. Remember that some of these men and women know me fairly well and call me by my first name.

"I love you so much it hurts me. Your sleepy but blessed husband-to-be, Louis, Esquire"

Tuesday, September No. 18, 1928

Dearest Wonder Girl,

It gives me great delight to present to you one more day of the remaining days before our wedding. I go to bed with alacrity and enthusiasm these nights, well pleased with the knowledge that one more of those pesky days has been put behind me. So honey dear, another day has flewn by and I have high hopes that October 28th will come a bit earlier this year than it has heretofore. Your true love, Louis

"Sara, Sam, Ma and I went to look at a hall in Newark last night," Celia reports, also on the 18th. "They told us they were very sorry but that date was taken six months ago. Big Sam then suggested the Avon Mansion, a new place opened one year. We rushed up there and the only thing he had was the afternoon of the 28th. The place is very beautiful. Our next worry was if he would give it to us for 20 couples. After deliberating for some time he consented and before he could change his mind we gave him a $28 deposit. I am sure you all will think the place beautiful. It is a strictly Kosher place (and) the Rabbi must bring his own canopy.

"We picked out the menu and it is up to us to have it printed now. We can enter the hall at 12:00 but we must leave at 6:00. Dinner will be served at 3:30, possibly at 4:00. Sweetheart, I wish you were here to enjoy with me the selecting of this and that. When you come up here next I will take you there to look the place over.

"I feel had we waited another week we would not have been able to get a place. I am all excited Sweetheart."

"Yontev I *davened* (prayed) in the shuhl round the corner," Dave writes on the 18th, "and for the first time in my memory, got out of *shuhl* at 3:15. The *Chazan* was terrible and choir, agony personified. How that combination could have received $3,000 bucks for their services is more than my small mind can grasp. But such are the cases boy. It was awful and more so.

"We had a lovely time at home. How did you spend the holidays? What did the Chazan do? How were the crowds and in short, what is the latest dirt?

"In re – me. We got our boxes and I got the machine working and I am waiting to start packing the boxes. Mr. B. got a darn good man to start out after superintendents. In the meantime we tried out two more laundries and the first results look good.

"Grossberger went after another meat packer today and got a nice size sample order and got him wild over the stuff. So here's hoping. Another of B.'s laundries is taking a ton of Argomite to try regularly…"

Louis replies to Celia on the 19th of September. "Much interested in your search for a hall and gratified that you located something that you like. I am only wondering why it takes a hall to marry us when I should be perfectly happy to be married to YOU even in a telephone booth – just so long as we are married. However, if you must have a hall all right, but I really do think that a telephone booth could be procured for so much less money and no reservations need be made in advance.

"I, too, dearest, was busy last night. I took me down to the AAA and made inquiries as to the best places to travel on a honeymoon considering the time of year, the time at our disposal, and my natural desires. One thing I may say and that is that we start from Newark and we end off at Washington at the tail-end of the honeymoon.

"It has been raining and blowing all day. I understand that we are enjoying the fringe of the Florida storm, but like most fringes, this one is harmless. I love you as usual. Forever Yours, Louis"

On the same day, Celia writes. "A storm is brewing and the papers have warned the inhabitants of Jersey to expect a 'nasty storm' late to-night. This morning the wind was the cause of trolley wires causing a tie-up of traffic lasting one hour. (I gave) the five blocks I had to walk (as) the excuse for my lateness. The truth is, I would have been late anyway.

"Sweetheart, I am frightened. I am sitting upstairs writing this letter to you and the noise that the wind makes startles me every minute. The rain is coming down in bucketsful and the big tree outside of the house is rocking to and fro and every now and then the branches slam against the window. The electric street lights are out of commission.

"Dear, I have asked different ones whether or not it is the proper thing to send announcements to business associates and everyone said, 'Yes.' I personally see no harm in sending your clients A'ments. But if you find out to the contrary you may do as you please. In the meantime you may start making a list of the names and addresses of your relatives, friends, clients and bill collectors. I am going to start on mine in a day or so, as I want to get a general idea of the number I am to order.

"Now, about the hall. I can't wait until you see it. I left it to Edith to take care of the Music. She has more time than I have. In the meantime your mother may invite the Aunts and Uncles. I think it is fitting and proper that she send each one a letter telling them to meet at our house between 12:30 and 1:00 Sunday afternoon.

"I didn't hand in my letter of resignation as yet but I told Whitman I was going to leave on the 15th. He said I was some fine person to put him in a hole like that and after inquiring as to the date of our marriage he wanted to know if I wouldn't stay until the 20th. I told him I would if he really wants me to. He gave me to understand that when a person leaves he must do so the 15th or 30th of the month and that I should appreciate the request he has made.

"Sweetheart, I too am counting the days. We are truly both in love. Thank Heavens one more day is over. I love you always, Cel"

"I'm so sorry I could not accommodate you yesterday with the presence of my manly bosom wherein you could have snuggled to keep away from the windy noises of the storm," Louis replies the next day. "I think this desire to protect is an instinctive one. You become even more gorgeous and sweet when you are frightened and that I must tell you is quite some dish.

"I remember years ago, when Fanny was in Washington living with her stepmother, she and I wound up on one of the benches of the Carnegie Library Park right near us. We sat down and she started to pour out her troubles to me when she started to cry. I don't remember whether or not I kissed her then, I think I didn't, because in those days we were not on kissing terms, but if I did not, it was only because of a superior brand of will power for she was certainly alluring and sweet looking. I remember distinctly that she looked so much finer with tears in her eyes. It is quite some years ago, but I remember it as if it were last year.

"I might as well confess it, honey. I longed – in those pre-sweetheart days – to see you cry when I alone was around. It offers, besides the spectacle of something wonderful becoming more so, the opportunity to console and to caress. And in those days, dear, I so wanted to caress you. Now, of course, I have the privilege and pleasure of caressing you and it is not necessary to have you cry.

"I am trying to kid myself into thinking that five weeks and two days are not such a long time to wait. However, if one awaits electrocution that length of time is like a few hours but when a wedding to the dearest girl in all the world awaits one, so long a time is as five years and two months. But I suppose we cannot very well hasten the ceremony in view of the deposit placed upon the hall.

"The arrangements for the wedding are in mighty capable hands. I should prefer to give you a blank signature, which you may use to indicate my approval of everything you do. (But don't use it to sign checks.)" Louis admitted he had not yet started on the list but promised to do so soon. Since an address would be needed for the At Home card, he would need to get busy on it for the printer. He estimated he would need 100 cards for announcements.

"I hardly think, tho, that it is feasible to rent an apartment much more than two or three weeks ahead of the date we are expected to move in. It will therefore, be necessary for the printer or engraver to get the job done in a hurry. Tell the engraver that you cannot give him the entire spiel until about October 15th but that he may let you have the envelopes to address before then. By-by, sweetness. Your almost contented husband-to-be, Louis

"P.S. I told the girls of the renting of the Hall for an afternoon wedding to vacate @ 6. They were a bit sorry (because) of its breaking up the day. What to do with the evening after six? But that can't be helped, so they'll have to make the best of it.

"P.P.#2. Please let me know at what hour you think the ceremony will take place. I want to tell Rabbi Glushak."

Of course, Celia was also busy writing on the 20th. "The enclosed clipping will give you an idea of the scare we got yesterday (from the storm). Pa had us all worried, he didn't want Sam to take the baby upstairs and he didn't want me to sleep alone. We promised him that we could come down just as soon as we thought it necessary and that we wouldn't need a second calling.

"Edith called the Musicians Union and made inquiries about a violinist and pianist. They suggest a cellist to complete the program so we shall have a three piece outfit.

"I am handing in my resignation today as I have been advised to by Mr. Whitman."

Celia included a draft of her resignation letter to the President of the bank: "As I am to be married the latter part of October, I must terminate my relations with the Fidelity Union Trust Company on October 20, 1928, and I therefore resign my position to take effect as of that date.

"It is with deep regret that I tender my resignation and I feel that I cannot part, after ten years of very happy service, without saying that the treatment which has been accorded to me by all has been kind and considerate and that, therefore, my associations have at all times been very agreeable. I am sure I will always have a tender feeling in my heart for the Fidelity Union Trust Company, its officers and employees, Respectfully yours,"

"I am not at all in the mood of writing to you just now," Louis' September 20th letter to Dave opens. The wedding and the recent Jewish holy days are more on his mind than Argomite at this time. "I can no longer, as in those Florida days, tell you that I love you. As witness I would refer you to the love letter file of yours truly. But to a second-fiddler, what is there left to say? Damfino."

Louis was happy to hear of the Sheffield test, the packing house order and that Mr. B. is actively involved. Maybe, "sitting thru a Rosh Hashone *davening* until three-thirty is enough cause for a prosperous New Year.

"In our town Mr. Novick (the cantor) really did himself proud. We had the same expert *bal shofernick* (rams horn blower) and of course, he won the day. All in all the services would have been quite enjoyable were it not for the annoying interruption of Rabbi Schwefel with his thirty minutes of preaching and blabbing. Particularly was the Yontev, a lovely one on account of the presence in town of my little sweetie. Incidentally she thanks you for the Argomite, and she has deposited with me one check for $8.50, which I (am) sending to you.

"By the way, the official date of wedding is Sunday afternoon October 28th at Newark. I guess I shall have to let your dad know so as to reserve the date. Money is coming in very slowly and consequently your friends the creditors are getting theirs in similar lackment of speed. In the meantime, should you be considering the purchase of a new car you better make it in time to let me have it before the 28th of October.

"Incidentally, I want to reserve your Gladstone bag for my honeymoon. My own hand bag is much too cumbersome. Figure out how you can get it to me between now and Friday morning, October 26 early..."

Celia sends two letters on the 21st, one written at "Our Time," when she discusses some extra work she's doing, and some shoe purchases she's recently made and a pair she's contemplating buying for the wedding. She wonders about moving her belongings to Washington. In the second letter, written late in the evening, she mentions some more wedding details in response to Louis' inquiries:

"As to the time the ceremony will take place I should say about 2 o'clock. Tell the girls I am very sorry about having the wedding take place in the afternoon. I had an idea that they would rather like it on account of their not wearing evening gowns. Etiquette tells us evening gowns are for evening wear only and as I didn't want the girls to go to any expense I was rather pleased with the arrangement. After the ceremony they will serve dinner and after that they will all go to my house."

"I have been thinking about our wedding day," Louis tells Celia, also writing on the 21st, "and it is not a very good thing to be doing if one wants some work done. I have been budgetizing between now and October 26 and I cannot exactly say that the prospects are so very wonderful. There are, of course, two big debtors of mine either one of whom could fix things all up for me but I cannot even expect anything from either. The only thing may be that I shall have to ask one of those clients to give me his note and then I'll try to discount it at my bank. The amount of one of them is $425.00. This sum, if collected in cash would put me on easy street."

Doyle, Louis' printer, said it would pay to get the announcements through him at fifty per cent off. The latest style is full size, not folded, with a small attached AT HOME card. Celia should get a quote from Edith's printer. Tomorrow Louis was going with Kitty and Miriam to look at furnished apartments.

"Your letter of resignation reads very nicely and I hope that they recognize their indebtedness to you for your past splendid record and give you as a wedding present a little block of 500 shares of the stock of the bank. Yes?"

"Imagine it, dear," begins Louis' letter to Celia on the 22nd, "five long weeks more and you wanted to wait until after January 1st! I just couldn't have stood it that long, that's all. However, let us not lose our sense of proportion. Had we been married a month ago you would not have had the white and gray slippers you tell me you bought the other day.

"Kitty and Miriam are due here pretty soon to see what the town has to offer as a place in which you are to cook my first breakfast for me. Can you imagine that? Our (maid) was saying to one of the girls this morning that from all the talk, this wedding of ours should be the finest in New York this year. Can you blame her?

"There is a weekly paper by one of the stationery houses with which we deal, a Chicago firm Tallman, Robbins, & Co. by name. The other day I wrote them a business letter to compliment them first upon the marketing of a very excellent card file and secondly for some excellent service they rendered me in expediting the shipment of an order. In to-day's issue of *Tarco Talks*, I find both of my paragraphs copied verbatim as coming from one of their Washington, DC customers. I recognized the wording at once. They must have liked my letter to pick two paragraphs out of it for quotations.

"This is a most beautiful day and reminds me that I better begin getting busy with the tour book and some paper to map out just where we are to go on our honeymoon. From present indications it would seem that we keep going until our money gives out and then we shall trundle ourselves home. Kitty suggests that we rent our apartment as from November 1, so she will have the opportunity to fix it up a bit for us so we will be ready to move right in when we get back. Nice of her, isn't it, dear?

"I have just gotten wind of the fact that they are planning to out-Cohen the Kansters and the Bergers in worrying us after the wedding. I told them they are welcome to it if they can find us as I have plans all my own to fool them. I am considering writing there for reservations. Then, after we leave Newark we beat it for New York in the car and if they follow us O.K. We park in some garage and take a taxi to some other hotel and in the middle of Broadway traffic get out of that taxi and enter another one going the opposite direction. They will hardly find us, I think. We'll talk it over when I see you months from now."

Louis writes Celia a second letter on the 22nd, about apartment hunting with Kitty and Miriam. "I saw a rather large 2 room kitchen bath apartment – unfurnished – for $62.50, furnished $85. The place is nice but I think rather seedy looking and of course, $85.00 is quite some dough but I wouldn't mind that if I really liked the place. So, it appears that I have a nice job on my hands if I am to get us an apartment suitable and reasonable before the time for the wedding.

"Quite a lot of trouble to marriage isn't there, honey? But look at the rewards after all the troubles have been overcome.

"I am getting more and more impatient. I feel often like – I don't know what. I could just crush things and kill things. You ought to be afraid to marry me honey. I am that fierce. But 'music hath the power to charm beasts' and you, dear, are music to my eyes. So you really have naught to fear from me.

"It is just five weeks more such a long time. Still these letters of ours do help to break the monotony. Your fondest love, Louis"

Dave writes "Darlint Lou," on the 23rd. "Just a few woids before Yom Kippur to let you know that we are still alive and barely struggling. The hopes and the aspirations of the foim will start on Tuesday morning. On that day we are hoping to let several salesmen try and dispose of as many packages of Argomite as it will be possible. The only things missing are the customers.

"Was particularly tickled to hear of the date October 28. Well God bless you both and may you be everlastingly happy, and now that a new year is on the immediate offing, may it bring the change in our fortunes that we have been looking forward to. So wishing you a *Chsimoh Tovoh* (to be sealed in the good book), Your darling and loving podner Dave"

"Saturday morning," Celia writes Louis on Sunday, September 23, 1928. "Mr. Neville, Assistant Vice President of our Bank called me in his office and wanted to know the exact date of my leaving. I told him I was leaving on the 20th of October. He just nodded his head and I could see him jot down the date on his memo book. It might have some meaning but I am not going to count the chickens until they are hatched. If you ever meet him after we are married you will hear your wife being lauded sky-high. It does me good to hear him talk. Now that all is said and done if he doesn't come across with a gift I am going to discount everything he said…"

Celia overheard some of the office girls whispering about her. She suspects they are planning a surprise for her.

"I like the idea of separate 'At Home' cards, as it is very simple to save the card for future reference. I went to the printers and gave my order for fifty menus. Most of them have it this way: Mr. and Mrs. L.C. Grossberg, on account of not being able to get the full name on the line.

K–G Wedding Reception
in honor of
Mr. and Mrs. L.C. Grossberg
October 28, 1928

"I think I am going to have him abbreviate the and, and write out the name Louis. (Sh! I love it.) Wait another minute, dear. The violinist is here with the contract. Excuse please. I signed the contract, dear. I think I am very fortunate in getting three excellent players from the Schubert Theatre staff. They may play a few jazz numbers but their time will be taken up playing classical numbers while we eat. Edith rushed in and gave me the best address that she has for the engravers. I love you, I love you, I love you, Cel"

"I have been amusing myself with pouring over maps and schedules and rates of hotels etc. for a certain little trip that I and the most wonderful girl are going to take commencing about October 28th PM." Louis reports, also on that Sunday. The man from the AAA talked him out of driving to Chicago with only a week's time. Another plan covered 1,700 miles but meant traveling two hundred miles a day and was discarded. "I don't want to be chasing myself all over just to make distance. So I have been cutting that down (to) about 1,250 miles. I'll figure out just where we shall stop in each place that is designated as a stop. I even have a book of rates of each of the places that is recommended by the AAA. I only wish we had about two months' time and plenty of money and a nice car, say a little Stutz Roadster, for the honeymoon trip. Who knows but what our third anniversary we shall have all of that. But then we are sure also to have a little family and that is more or less a drawback to honeymoons. Still, we should not really complain. More young married couples have less to plan a trip with than we have. A nice six-year-old Stearns-Knight open automobile with about ten days time and a couple hundred dollars road money and the finest girl in all the world – what more can anyone wish?

"Pretty soon it will be necessary to sit down to a meal of *farfasten* (pre-fasting). Good-bye, darling and may this be the last *erev* Yom Kippur that you and I are separated for the next 100 years. God Bless You, my Dear. Your 95% husband, Louis"

Monday Nite, September 24, 1928
Sweetheart,
I just finished my first meal of today and didn't mind the fast one bit. My father and Mother were in shul all day but Ruthie and I went there at 2:00 o'clock and stayed until it was all over.

Have you done anything about inviting the Aunts and Uncles? Ma called several and they all said they will be on hand. Edith Kane called us on the phone to wish us a Happy New Year and Ma told her of the coming wedding. Ma told her she intended to have a party for the young folks when we return from our Honeymoon. I think we will have to plan our trip so that we will be in Newark over a week-end. What do you think of it, dear?

Only this morning I took some of your March and April letters and read and re-read every one of them. Now I can say I am sorry I had laughed when you told me of your love and I don't blame you one bit for calling me hard-hearted. We are now engaged to be married the 28th of October when a new chapter in our lives will begin. I hope and pray that it will be a true love story all the way through and that we will live happily ever after. Your Sweetheart, Cel

Celia wrote on the 25th that she ate too much after the fast but is feeling better now. A call to the Marriage License Bureau informed her that 72 hours must elapse before the license is legal. "In that case I think it will be best to get the license when you come here next.

"I am happy to hear that you are having lots of fun planning our honeymoon. If it is going to be cold around that time I will be content staying in some hotel nearby, say 500 miles or so and you near me. It is not necessary that we go any distance just for the sake of traveling. I will close this letter with all my love to you. Your 95% Wife, Cel"

Tuesday, September 25, 1928

Dearest Wife-to-be,

How lovely it was of you to call me on the Phone last nite! I wanted to tell you that I love you and that you are the finest sweetheart any fellow ever had but unfortunately I had a particularly large audience and could not say those things. Aaron Freudberg was there and Alec Freedman and a friend of Babe's and mother and Joe and the girls and all standing around the phone listening in. I can readily see why you went to a booth and believe me, honey, I should have liked to put a booth around me, too. Hereafter, go to a phone booth and call me at the office. That will assure us both the privacy we want. All this with one proviso and that is that you must reverse the charges to me.

Talking of honeymoons, dearest, I don't feel that I can afford to stay away two weeks, both from the point of time away from the office and from the money part of it. I am planning to be back in town on the night of the seventh so that I shall have Thursday and Friday to be in the office. Leaving on the 26th of October and returning on the 7th of November means being away from the city just thirteen days. While I have no objections to the young folks having a good time, I am not so anxious for another fussy party so soon after our wedding. Why must it be a week-end? We might manage to be home on the night of the sixth which is Election Day and I presume a holiday in your part of the country.

I am going now, sweetheart. No doubt you have paid out plenty in your time for wedding gifts to employees of the bank. I know if I were working in the Bureau now I should be a candidate for some nice gift from the gang. But as it is I am only a giver of gifts. Not a receiver. But I am satisfied. The finest gift of God comes to me, so why be dissatisfied with the possible failure to receive mere trinkets. Your own sweetheart, Louis

Mr. & Mrs. Louis C. Grossberg. I, too, love it.

Louis writes of apartments again on the 26th. "I am afraid that we shall have to rent a really expensive apartment for the first month as it will be nearly impossible to rent anything really nice furnished for less than

$100. I hate to part with all that money just for a month's rent. Kitty, on the other hand thinks it a bad policy to live in a very nice place for one month and then to move into something not so nice. Incidentally, do you realize that the three weeks have nearly gone and that in one week from to-morrow nite, I shall be with you again?"

Louis gave orders to his family to draw up a wedding list so no one would be slighted. As for the honeymoon trip, maybe Celia was right. They would discuss it on his upcoming visit.

That same day, Celia notes that letters written from her office have a different quality. "So you like the letters I write at home, well, here is another one. I can't wait until you get here Sweetheart as there are so many things we will need to talk over, yes, even to a bawling out that is due you. Since I have mentioned it I will tell you that I was a little displeased over the telephone episode. Dear, do you know that you said good-bye to me first when I called up the other night? Since I was the one who was doing the calling I believe it was my place to say 'Good-bye first.' Don't you think so, dear? I was a little hurt but I feel better now since I told you.

"It is too bad we cannot plan our honeymoon together. I will be happy to go wherever you take me. I don't seem to be the least bit frightened, dear. (Sh, I am getting recipes together.) I am your 96 1/8% Wife."

"You are mighty lucky that you were not here this morning when I read your letter," Louis scolds Celia the next day. "If you were, you would surely have been a party to an old-fashioned spanking. I hardly have to elaborate on the reasons for my ire. To think that you could even consider being hurt by something that I do to you under such circumstances is enough to make me sore.

"Up to the time I read about it I didn't even know that I was the one to tell you good-bye first. And what if I did? Does that immediately mean to you that I intended to cut you off or to slight you or to hurt you? You must not be so sensitive, honey, where I am concerned. You should be a little willing to give your sweetheart the benefit of the doubt. And to think that you carried the grouch all this time until yesterday before telling me! Now, tell me dearest, don't you deserve a spanking? As a matter of fact there was so much noise in the hall what with Aaron and Babe's friend coming in just as you called and everyone around the phone and myself so excited that my sweetheart was calling it is quite possible that I did say good-bye first thinking that your call would run into extra time. But to twist that into a cause for feeling hurt! Shame on you, dear..." He goes on to discuss some details of the wedding arrangements.

"I am certainly pleased to note that your old fright has apparently left you. After all a little girl who was so frightened heretofore has certainly got a right to fiddle with the truth now and then. But then, no one really can tell, certainly not a man, what a girl of your admitted timidity and shyness thinks or how she feels a month before her wedding day. So I'll take it at face value and believe you when you say you are impatient for the day when you and I will be MAN and WIFE. Oh, darling mine, how wonderful that will be!

"I wonder why you say that we cannot plan our honeymoon together. Is it customary for the gentleman to do all the planning of that by himself? We can plan it together anyway or else you will just have to go where I take you. In any event I thank you mightily for your offer to trust the matter entirely in my hands and go with me wither away I might wish to lead. I might mention in passing that this is the first time any lady ever made the proposal to me to go with me wherever I wish to take her. Thanx. I love you much and with great tenderness and zeal. Forever your sweetheart, Louis"

> September 27, 1928
>
> My Dearest,
>
> We have a colored man working in our bank who is a mail clerk by day and a Baptist Minister by night. He is a graduate of the NYU, and all told well liked by all. He very seldom speaks to me but late yesterday he came up to me and wanted to know when I was leaving, as he didn't want me to leave without his good wishes. He told me of his love affair and how his wife lived in NC and he in Newark. He hopes our love for each other will be as strong as his love is for his wife. Of course I thanked him. Even (he) knew I was in love. He said he could tell by the sparkle in my eyes. I bumped into two friends of mine. Immediately they said, 'Cel, you can't hide the fact that you are in love, one only has to look at your face

to tell.' Dr. & Mrs. Perlman said the same thing to me last night. I wonder what it is they see on my face.

I received a wonderful reply from the president of our bank in answer to my letter. I'll show it to you when you get here.

About the apartment. I think $100 is quite a sum to put down for one month's rent. It doesn't have to be classy – after all we are only renting the place not buying it. I believe $75 should be our limit – even that is too high…

The next day Louis writes: "Do you realize that this is just exactly one calendar month from our wedding day? The contrast between the letters I used to get – even after our engagement – and the letters I am receiving now is so great that my only hope and prayers are that we shall always keep loving each other and intensifying the quality of it as we travel along on the journey of life.

"You are a marvelous influence in the life of a poor lovesick Romeo. I am surprised that you should find it a mystery, what it is the public notices in your face that tells them that you are in love. And by the same token there must be something similar in my face. You cannot hide it and I am glad to note that you don't wish to hide it.

"Every stranger who walks into this office wants to know who the wonderful looking person whose likeness hangs on my wall is. Just this afternoon the Revenue Agent asked about it. Pretty soon now I shall be able to tell them this little lady is MY WIFE. Won't that be just great!"

September 28, 1928

Dearest Sweetheart,

I wish I were in your office yesterday to receive the spanking that you think I deserved. Dear, I know I am a little sensitive so you must bear with me. If a stranger acts in a way not to my liking I never pay any attention but if a dear friend especially a wonderful sweetheart acts that way – well, that's different. Think I like this sensitiveness of mine? No! Not one bit.

She reports that her invitation list is nearly complete and missing only three addresses.

The reason I said I am sorry we cannot plan our honeymoon together is because you are in Washington and I am in Newark. I know of no law or code to prevent our planning it together. So bring all your paraphernalia along with you and together we will come to some sort of arrangement.

I suppose you are tired hearing me say how I miss you. Little did I dream that you could make such a decided change in a shy-timid-little girl from Jersey. By the way, do you know if the Argomite has been shipped out? If the delay is due to the RR we will have to look into it.

Louis responds on September 29:

What a gorgeously wonderful sweetheart I have for a wife-to-be! Imagine any girl answering a bawling out the way you did. God, how I love you, sweetheart. My only concern is to be able to provide for you always and to keep you loving and lovely all the rest of our days.

The clock says exactly 8:30 and this means that you are getting ready to make the call. There, we talked and it seems that I was right. Telephoning is such a poor substitute for the real contact method of loving you. It is so inadequate and unsatisfying. But thank God we'll have the real thing next Saturday night. And it strikes me now that I once more said the good-bye first. Yet I still think there is nothing wrong in that. I heard the operator tell you that time is up and I didn't want you to run up more charges and I'm afraid you cannot be trusted to keep a bargain. I asked that those charges be reversed but you don't seem to fall in with that idea at all. I should certainly wish to keep up this telephoning as advertised, once a week on Saturday night. This is about enough for an extra Sunday letter. You must not be spoiled. My love is boiling over. Is yours for, Louis?

Sunday Morn, September 30, 1928

   Dearest Sweetheart,

   I have been busy all morning getting my things in shape. Do you think we will be able to take anything back with us on the way to Washington? I am afraid to trust it with the express people.

   I feel very very happy that I am going to live with you and at the same time I feel very blue when I think of leaving my family and friends behind. I try not to think of it but every time marriage is mentioned to a friend or relative they tell me that I will miss my family very much and that it will take time to get used to it. I know that you will do everything to prevent my getting lonesome, won't you dear?

Celia quotes engraving prices from Hausler & Company, figuring she will need 50 announcements.

   Celia called Rabbi Glushak to reserve the afternoon of the 28th for the wedding. She thought Louis had done it. The Rabbi was pleased it was to be in the afternoon as that evening was already reserved. If a second rabbi would officiate, Louis should write him himself.

   Sweetheart, I am getting quite a bit of help and advice from the old married folks, such as cooking, hints, recipes, etc. It sure is some help.

She writes again that evening. "I have been busy all day, sewing, pressing and even packing. I caught my mother crying and when I asked her to tell me the reason she wouldn't tell me. My father tells me it is because I am going away. She then told me to write to her every day and call her up at least once a week and to come out as often as I am able to. I have had to make promises of all sorts.

   Dear, when you come out I want you to have a good talk with her. I am sure she would feel better if she hears that you love me and I love you. Of course she knows it but I am sure she would like to hear it from you. I am sure you can appreciate her feelings. Mothers are so wonderful that we must not do anything to hurt them…

On further apartment hunting, Louis says that vacancies last only a couple of weeks so they better wait. If necessary, they could take an apartment hotel temporarily, until the right place is found. He suggests that "At Home" cards be printed without a date, just, "After November Tenth."

Back to business, Louis receives mail from Dave, September 30. "This is a letter I have been owing you for quite some time now. Last week Grossberger sold another packer a half ton (of) Argomite and got three more packers interested. In B.'s laundry where we sold them a ton of the stuff the results were O.K. (It's) a specialized laundry where they wash barber towels and a lot of soap suds are necessary to get rid of the hair. But they worked out a formula that seems to be doing a good job."

As for the boxes, a salesman placed 21 cases with superintendents of apartments to resell to tenants and Dave sold a case to a surgical house. He planned to visit several department stores next week.

> Today I met Major Goodwin of Chicago and he seems to be a wonderful sort of a chap. Has dough, and knows what to do with it. He told me some very disquieting news about the Wash. office in particular. This stuff is confidential. It seems that Barton, Glover and Green are to meet Goodwin in Chicago next Wednesday to discuss a consolidation and he wanted to find out where I stood on the deal and kind of hinted around that if Washington got mean our contract is worth damn little. However he told me he'll keep in touch with me. There is so much dirt involved that I never could get it over to you in a letter.

On the first of October, Celia's letter is taken up with details of where out-of-town visitors will stay, and names Ruthie to be maid-of-honor. She asks if Louis wants Joe or Babe to be best man. "My mother is busy baking *Taglachs* for the guests. She finds a lot of pleasure baking for a pair of lovesick doves. Oh, sweetheart ain't love grand? I know I will be happy after all the excitement is over. I know now that I would not have liked a big affair and believe I have acted wisely in making this a family affair. I think you like a small affair, don't you?"

"My dear 96% Wife," begins Louis' October 1, 1928, letter. So far he has compiled the names of sixty-five invitees with a possible fifty more and worries that sending announcements might obligate them to send gifts. "Take the Gundresheimer Bakery as an instance. There are three members of (the) family. Would it be proper for me to write one announcement to the office or one each to the homes of these three?"

Louis noted a ring of unhappiness in her Sunday letter and realized, "some friends and busybodies have been filling you full of pessimistic stuff about being lonesome for your family when you leave Newark. I suppose you will miss them a bit but our love should more than make up for anything of a vacuum that your heart will feel as the result of leaving your friends behind. After all, honey, we are only five hours away from Newark and who knows but that before very long we shall be living very very much closer, if Argomite does well in New York. If you find that you must have a family I shall see what can be done about getting you a little starter for a family of your own."

Louis decided Rabbi Glushak would be the only rabbi and is happy Celia reserved the date. "We'll call him up again when we go to visit Dave which I suppose will be Sunday.

"My everlasting devotion and love" and below in a squirrelly script, "Hindu Love Signs, you see dear I love in other languages too."

Thou Shalt Not Murder

When Louis wrote Dave on October 1, 1928, he could not foresee the Pandora's box that was about to open, and it had nothing to do with trousers. "You Blankety-Blank-Blank Hussy, You! How come you got so dumbstruck of late as not ever to write your once upon a time inseparable partner, a line telling him to go to Hell. Here I burn up with curiosity to know just how much of a flop your package game has suffered to date and I can't even get so much as a yip out of you. If you only saw the murder in my eye every morning that I don't find a letter from you I'm sure you would hasten to ward off the *aiin hora* (evil eye).

"The other day I looked over my account at Wilner's and rejoiced that I have a credit of $50 with which I could purchase some much needed cloth goods. But our friend Mrs. Thomas informed me, your account shows a balance of $45.00 which virtually murdered the balance all in one fell stroke, Although you failed to list it, I suppose I have to swallow this red pepper.

"The worst of it all is that my Tux is somewhat out of date. I took them over to be widened and the answer was a decided negative. So it became necessary to match me a pair of pants. The weave, I am told is the same and the color, too, but the shade is different. The theory is that Tuxedos, being worn in the dark anyway, never disclose any variations in the shade between the coat and the vest. (So) I gave the signal to proceed. It wasn't until last night, as I was wending my way wearily thru the alley from my garage, unpaid for as to rent, by the way, that it suddenly occurred to me that the wedding is scheduled to take place at two or so o'clock. Now what? Damfino. Looks as if I shall either have to buy the rest of the suit or else make a purchase of a coat that will match the pair of pants.

"I Expect to be in Newark all day Friday. I am anxious to see your machine and the way in which retail boxes are put up by the Argomite Corp. of New York. So you might as well expect me both days, that is, the one at the office and the other at the house with the little sweetheart. Incidentally, you might answer this at once and for Krist sakes RITE. Louis"

> Tuesday October 2, 1928
>
> My dearest Sweetheart,
>
> Dave was in to see me and (says you) sent him a very hot letter. He wants me to tell you that he couldn't find the time to write. He received a nice size order and seemed elated over its prospects.
>
> Of all the places Edith has received estimates for engraving – none compared in quality and price with Hausler's. It will not hurt to send the announcements to the individuals. It adds a personal touch.
>
> I bought a very nice set of dinner dishes that will be delivered tomorrow. I love to buy things for our home and get quite a kick out of shopping. I don't know how I will be able to pay for everything but I am not going to worry about it now because everything will turn out all right. Pa is rich and Ma don't care.
>
> Dave asked me whether he could take his children along to our wedding and I told him it wouldn't be a good idea because none of my kid cousins would be there. Just one more thing. I handed my work over to Gladys yesterday and she certainly bawled things up. I have had to trace every error that she made. Whitman does not want me to help her; he wants to see how she will handle the work herself over the heavy part of the month. Goodbye Love – it's all yours, Cel

Tuesday, October 2, 1928

Darling Dear,

It is nearly 6:08 PM I must get rid of those birds whose work must be done. Next month these gents will just have to wait for it until I get back from the most pleasant days of my life – so far. I don't know, of course, what is to follow in the course of a whole life with you. There may come a time in our wedded life, honey, when you and I will spend a happier ten days (though) I hardly think so as I cannot conceive of anything more pleasurable than a honeymoon trip with the sweetest of all girls in all the world.

I saw the samples of the cards that Hausler sent you. I shall take the samples over to Doyle and see what he has to say about the cost of duplicating that particular quality and style. I personally believe that an announcement card should not be cheap as it reflects the station in life of the sender.

About my best man, In view of the fact that Ruthie is your maid of honor I suppose it would tickle Babe if he were designated the best man. If they have anything to do in the way of duties they will like to cooperate and work together – at least much better than you and Sammy's best man coordinated.

So, you better let me know what the best man is supposed to do before I name him for you. And also is it necessary for that man to wear a tux or is it O.K. if only the groom is bedecked in a soup and fish. All these are matters of grave import. Your Sweetheart, Louis C

Wednesday, October 3, 1928

My dearest Sweetheart,

About a best man – I think he will have to wear a tux because Ruth is going to wear an evening gown. One of the duties of the best man is to take charge of the wedding band so use your own judgment about selecting a body-guard.

Sweetheart, this letter will be short, after all, tomorrow you will be here and together we will be in Heaven. I am waiting for you, sweetheart, just waiting, Love, Cel

October 3, 1928

My dear Mrs. Grossberg (to be),

Have you thought much about how you will like to be called Mrs. Grossberg? It should be a novelty to say the least. It won't be so very long now, dearest, but to me it still seems like a million years off. I love you too much for one fellow. Better look me over to see that I am not twins.

By the time you get this, honey, it will be very close to Thursday night at 11:30 or thereabouts and your sweetheart will be with you in spirit and in body. We have just got to make the most of this visit of mine as we shall have to wait three long weeks before you and I will see each other again. You are the only person I have ever loved. And the thing that I cannot get over is that YOU will be MY wife in just 25 days from now. The strain of waiting is beginning to tell on me.

Dave writes again on October 3. "You will get this letter whether you are deserving of it or not." Wanamaker Department Stores is allowing Dave to sell Argomite there. He is getting a demonstrator and wants Louis to visit Seager and the various stores he demonstrated in and find out how he did it. He has also ordered another half carload of Argomite.

"I told Celia that I sold Lewis & Conger six cases as a starter. They are the best houses of its kind, having a large mailing list. Grossberger is still working on the meat packers and I think we are getting into the laundry game. The Sheffield dairy has not worked out at all as it did not improve upon the stuff they are using now, and certainly the Argomite costs more.

"I want you to take it up with the Baltimore Sales Co. Three months after giving our order, we received our order books, and then we found they were not numbered correctly..."

"I got back from New York a few minutes ago," Celia informs Louis on October 8. "Sweetheart, I bought a radio. Dave said it was wonderful all around and that we couldn't duplicate it anyplace. The regular price is $325. It is very plain and neat. You see I know very little about radios so I left it entirely to Dave. They had only one model and one price $149.50. The carrying charge is $3.00. The first payment (was) $49.50. The monthly installment amounts to $17.17. I had a hard job with the credit-man. He wanted cash for the reason that it was to go out-of-town. I am enclosing a picture. Let me know if you are happy about the idea.

"I got a position for Ruthie at one of our Branch Banks this afternoon. She starts Monday. The kid is too excited to talk. Dave tells me that Mr. Barryman and he are likely to be in Washington, Friday of this week, regarding the Manufacturing of Argomite. I don't know if he told you (but the) half carload of Argomite amounts to $1,500.

"Sweetheart, I was very sorry to see you go last night. Goodbye dear, honey, sweetheart, darling…"

"I love you. I love you. I love you, 20 more Long Days!" Louis writes on the same day. The wonderful visit was too short. "I should have gladly given the (train) porter at least 12 cents had he left me alone. I was that sleepy." But he got up, dressed and went home, leaving his suitcase locked in Joe's trunk.

"Had lunch with Leo Freudberg and talked about weddings, honeymoons, apartments, and the like. The result may be of some assistance to me as he put me in touch with a friend of his who is in charge of a certain group of buildings in which there may be an apartment suitable for me and for you. Leo has a Grebe radio and when I told him about the Gimbel sale he said don't wait a minute, but buy it.

"Now that we have decided to meet this coming week-end, I can just picture myself in the arms of my cute little *sweetskele* (little sweetie) with my lips in a love kiss with hers and the sensation is fearfully and painfully wonderful. And for all that, I love you, I love you, I love you, Ever Yours, Louis"

"First of all I am happy to hear Leo's advice regarding the Grebe radio," Celia replies the next day. "I am sure we made an excellent buy. I am to let them know within three weeks the address for shipment. If I do not know the address of our apartment I will give them your home address. The radio has everything that we would want in any $350.00 set."

The families Kane and Berger, cousins of Celia, had informed Celia's mother that they intended to come to the wedding, invited or not. "I do not want to get in the wrong side of the Kane's and Berger's so since they insist on crashing the gate, we might just as well act like *menshen* (good people) and give them a place at the table. Kane said, 'what, Celia going to get married and I won't be there: I should say not and because of my feelings in the matter we all are coming anyway.' Since they do not stand on ceremony we might just as well have them. When I see you Saturday I will take along the table chart and together we will work on it."

Louis is happy about the radio as it will afford them entertainment for quite some time. He then turns to the question of best man on October 9. "If worst comes to bad and Babe can't get himself an outfit as best man and ditto for Joe, do you think it would be much inappropriate for me to name Dave? He has an outfit and the only thing against him is that he is a married man. Ruthie wanted a tall big fellow anyway and he would seem to cover those requirements. I know they neither of them have any money and the cost of traveling alone will eat into their finances plenty. If the crime of having Dave is not so very great it might solve the problem at no cost."

"Dear David," wrote Louis, also on the 9th. He had been too busy to see Barton or Glover but expected to do so the next day. Was Mr. Barryman coming to Washington on Friday to see Barton about manufacturing Argomite? This would mess up Louis' plans to meet Celia in Philadelphia Saturday afternoon to pick out a wedding ring and spend time with cousin Herman Freudberg. Celia also wanted to bring things for Louis to take back to Washington.

"So, if you have the info it will be a real brotherly act on your part to come thru with it. Otherwise you may be cheating yourself out of my entertaining company. Incidentally, if you plan to see Barton Saturday morning I wouldn't be able to join you anyway as I have a conference before the Bureau (of Internal Revenue) at 10:30 A.M. Love to all, Louis"

On the 10th Celia hopes Louis will have luck finding an apartment. "It is not necessary to include the ('At Home') cards unless the newly married couple intend living there for six months. I personally think it is all a matter of taste, so if we have an address we will have cards engraved, if not, we will have to let it go." Celia felt, that if she received the invitations by the 20th, she would have plenty of time to send them out.

"Now that the Berger's and Kane's are coming I am glad. Kane said to Mother the other day, 'Just to prove to you that I am not a selfish cousin I am seriously thinking of taking the newly wedded couple away after the wedding and treat them to a time that they never had in their lives.' I didn't realize they would feel that way about it. As far as gifts are concerned we will not be sorry they are coming. In due fairness to your family, Mother suggests that you invite some cousins that you would like to be there. Your sister said something about wanting Minna Kitay.

"Sweetheart, it is your privilege to invite whom you please to act as your best man. It would be fitting if the best man had a Tux, but, if you want Joe or Babe and if he hasn't got one it will be perfectly all right with me. I have never heard of a married man being a best man but if you want Dave invite him to act as your best man. We do not have to stand on ceremony since we are all *hameishe menshen* (very warm people)."

"October 10, 1928" writes Louis, "I was certainly glad that the gang is intending to do some crashing. I really did want some of that outfit at our wedding as they will liven things up. Incidentally it makes me free to ask a few of the friends I wanted to invite from our side, such as Leo and Rose, Herman and Rose, and Celie and maybe Dora Freudberg. Perhaps there are one or two others (like) Minna Kitay but then there are another few in the same family with whom I might get in Dutch. Maybe will write her a letter in strictest confidence and tell her.

"Talked to Leo this noon regarding this crashing business and he now tells me that originally it was their intention to crash anyway but that since Rose's mother was over and expressed the idea that on account of their bereavement they should not go to any parties but now that there is more or less of an invitation he doesn't know what they will do.

"As to the threats of initiations and the etc. well, I'm not worrying about that just yet. If we get it, we get it, that's all. So far (as) I can see that all those who suffered from the initiation exercises got over it. And in so far as losing a night's sleep goes, in case that is what we are in for, I hardly think I need to worry much about that as I might as well sit up all night as lie up. But joking aside, honey, it should make the wedding more like a Kanster – Berger affair and that means there should be something to talk about afterwards.

"I am certainly glad now that I can invite Herman. He is a real buddy of mine, one from the olden golden boyhood days and if he had a shirt I could get it from him."

Louis saw a client who could get them furniture wholesale plus 5% to 10% if they went to Philadelphia or Baltimore but it had to be in cash.

"I am glad you are in accord with this crashing business. I am only worried about the place being too small," comes Celia's response. "Had I known this was going to happen we would have gotten a bigger place. I feel highly honored that my relatives and yours are interested in Our Wedding. When you invite your cousins tell them to say they are crashing in.

"The charwoman of our bank called me aside and handed me a neatly wrapped package. When I opened it I found a bottle of perfume, toilet water, mirror and a glass powder jar. I thought it was mighty wonderful of her.

"I am glad you are getting some ideas regarding the furniture. If we could get furniture at wholesale prices. I am sure it would pay to put up collateral and secure the money from the bank. I hope you will be able to arrange your affairs with Dave on Friday and Saturday so that you will be able to take a late train out to meet me in Philly." Celia said she was so engrossed in wedding thoughts, she missed her trolley stop and had to walk back seven blocks.

On Thursday, October 11, 1928 Louis thinks 'The Kane talk' is just so much talk. "I am not figuring on anything to happen to us beyond possibly the detention for some hours. After that they will probably let us go the same way they let Sammy and Edith go. However, I am not averse to enjoying myself at Kane's expense, and if he has any real good propositions to make us, we shall certainly be there to give it our most serious consideration."

As for Saturday night, "Quite ala Dave, he has as yet said nothing to me." As soon as he knows he will wire her what train to take and where to get off. "I shall be there waiting for you" but if not, "look in the phone book and find Herman Freudberg there at 2650 North 30th Street.

"Will see about the best man. Babe has been designated such so far and he says that he will have a Tux. My worry right now is that I should have one as I have to see my tailor and I haven't the time to take it over there.

"16 DAYS FROM NOW. Forever and ever your, Dearest sweetheart, Louis"

Oct. 12, 1928, 2:49 A M, (Western Union telegram to Louis)
"EXPECT TO ARRIVE AT UNION STATION SATURDAY MORN-
ING AT SEVEN MEET U.S. AT UNION STATION CAFE AT SEVEN
THIRTY STOP MAY LEAVE SATURDAY NIGHT OR GO WITH YOU
TO PHILADELPHIA DAVE"

On Friday, October 12, 1928, Louis reports to his "Dearest" on the telegram and the meeting at 7:30. "This is an outrageous hour to meet any
one on a Saturday morning." Celia is to meet him in North Philly, Saturday evening and he tells her which train to take. They will have dinner
with Herman and Rose. Celia replies the same day that she understands
his instructions and will meet him in Philadelphia.

On Monday, October 15, 1928, Louis writes to his "Dearest Wife-to-be,
Alias my 98% Wife."

"I do hope you got home in good time and early enough to get for
yourself a real good night's sleep. Personally I got neither.

"This reminds me that our friend the Graf Zepp was in town this
morning at about 12:30 and just as someone was asking me what had
been heard of it, we heard the roar of the big ship and the blowing of
whistles and ran out to see the beauty. She was certainly pretty gliding
there in the clouds.

"I have just returned after seeing Kitty and Al. Kitty means apartments, so she and I went over to see a place that she told me was nice."
It cost $67.50 but it was in a court facing other apartments and the bath-
room opened from the entrance hall. "Another of the faults is that the
kitchen cannot be reached excepting thru the living room. Otherwise
the place is a dream. The kitchen is large with plenty of space for eating. There is as yet no Frigidaire but they expect to put them in at about
three bucks for service charge.

"Another apartment faced the street but cost $82.50. I offered him
$75 and he came down to $80. So I and he are both to think it over. What
do you think? How about the inside one? May get it for $65. He offered
to hold until Nov. 15."

Pauline wanted to know if the musicians could accompany her to
the *Caro Nome* song from *Rigoletto*, Mr. Verdi's lullaby, and *O Promise*

Me. "Looks now as if Celie and Dora, after all our seating work, may not come anyway."

This October 15, 1928, Louis writes to Minna Kitay.

> Dear Minna,
> Don't faint. I know that it is quite a shock to you to receive a letter from your cousin, but it is really quite a shocking matter that I am going to propose to you which makes it rather appropriate that you should get a foretaste of what is to come.

Louis explains that he and Celia arranged for a small intimate wedding with just brothers, sisters, in-laws, parents, uncles and aunts invited – a total of about twenty couples. They just learned that some of Celia's cousins intended to crash the party whether invited or not. This was customary behavior from the clique of eight and accepted with humor from the rest of her family. Under these circumstances, it was only fair that he, Louis, invite a few cousins or friends he would otherwise not have been able to include. However, this had to be done in the strictest of confidence, so as not to create family *feribels*. Instructions were given as to where and when to meet.

> Now please, dear, remember that I am entrusting you with a delicate matter. I do not have to explain to you just what it would mean to us, unto the third generation, if it leaked out that you were invited but that my cousin George from New York, whose father will be present was not invited; or that none of my other Paterson cousins were invited, and whatever you do please let me know at once that you are coming as we must make arrangements with the caterer.
> This is quite a *megilla* to write to a gate crasher but for heaven's sake and for the sake of family peace keep this quiet and remember that officially you are a GATE CRASHER.

A very similar letter was sent to Louis' cousins, Belle & Billy Abrash. Louis had just learned Leo and Rose Freudberg intended to crash on their own also. He probably hoped Belle would come if she knew her sister Rose was crashing.

> As you well know, Belle, in our *mishpocho* (family) if this ever got out, that I invited you and did not invite some other cousin, this would be enough cause to shun me, my wife, and children unto the third generation. I am leaving it to you to tell no one that you are invited or that you will attend the wedding. With much love and anticipation of sweet wedding kisses, I am, Your befuddled cousin, Louis

Celia wrote of a crowded and unpleasant ride home on the train on October 15.

> Just as I was comfortably seated alongside a girl – a seat meant for two – a portly woman squeezed herself into about ten inches of space and this other girl and myself were nearly thrown out of our seats. Poor me was in the middle.
>
> Herman and Mrs. Herman are very nice congenial folks and I am glad they are coming to our wedding. I had lunch with Bert Fried this noon and she tells me if she had more nerve she would do some crashing herself. Sweetheart, I made a mess of things. Why didn't we have a big wedding! I am going to coax her to come. Dearie, it is just 13 days and together we will be one. Ma expected me to tell her how many from your house were coming over for the week-end. I wish you would let me know, dear. With all the love of a wife-to-be, Cel
>
> P.S. Do you think we should invite Fanny and Al under the circumstances? I am afraid her father and Dave will queer things. Somehow, I think we owe it to ourselves to invite them. After all if it wasn't for Fanny I wouldn't know you. Let me know what you think about it.

"It is just right to invite Bert and so far as Al and Fanny are concerned I am ashamed, that it never occurred to me," replies Louis the next day. "Just as you said, if it were not for Fanny you and I would never have

427

had ourselves. So, by all means, dearest, explain the fact that at last you can invite whom you want, (and) will feel that they are angry if they do not attend.

"For my part, I am beginning to feel that this is getting away from us and that we are likely to look like saps trying to make anyone believe that all these others are gate crashers. The only thing to have done was either only immediate family or else a large wedding." Louis rented an apartment for the 15th of November, but furniture could not arrive before the 20th. He favors renting a place for a week before the apartment is ready for them to move in.

"I have loads of work to do. To top it off I think I have the makings of a sore throat. It would certainly be something by way of punishment to us for all the trickery we are perpetrating if the groom were to show up absent at the wedding (on) account of sore throat, cold, and general disability. But don't you worry, honey, I'll be there, sore throat or no sore throat.

"In one week from this coming Friday I should be with you again and this time to stay with you for life. Hurray, Hurray! I'm happy, dearest.

"Better begin to think seriously about furniture and I might suggest that you see Mr. Barryman and get an idea of what you can buy from him. The rooms are very spacious and I think it is almost as large, that is the bed room, as Edith's living room and the living room is a little larger than hers. The kitchen is partitioned off into a dinette and a kitchen and the dinette is just large enough for a kitchen table and some chairs. Your happy lover, Louis"

October 16, 1928

Dearest Bestest Sweetheart,

Mr. Neville, Vice President of our bank sent for me a short while ago. He is the officer who has taken quite an interest in me and who has given me valuable advice from time to time. He wanted to know if I had any money. I asked him why he wanted to know, and he said you know our Securities Department does all the buying of stock and bonds for its customers and for the company as well, and the Public Service is the largest Corporation in the State of New Jersey and one of the largest in the Country.

No stock is available to outsiders. Only stockholders and officers of both institutions (can) subscribe. A number of blanks have been secured by the officers for their use. That is how Mr. Neville happened to suggest that I take as many shares as I can afford. He said it will go up at least ten points next month.

I subscribed for five shares totaling $250.00, the price per share is $50.00. I sent in a check for $25 accompanying the subscription and if I am allotted the whole five shares the balance must be paid by the 30th of November. He said it is subscribed a few times over. Mr. Neville knows the exact condition of my finances and regardless of the money I owe suggested that I put my order in.

I think this is a wonderful opportunity and am glad that I didn't turn my $300.00 back to the Citizens branch. We can borrow and use the stock as collateral. Mr. Whitman, the chief clerk suggests that if I am ordering more than five to order it in another name. I wonder if someone in your family could use the blank…

In a second letter that day she writes, "Pa wants me to get 2 shares for Georgie as he has $100 saved up and one share for $50.00…" She can't wait to help Louis in Washington.

On the 17th, Louis writes, "Of all the things I have to do this was altogether unexpected. Yes, dear, your sweetie had no more sense this morning than to get up with a sore throat, a fever, and a cold! I was all for going to work anyway but mother laughed it off and here I am sitting up in bed writing you. This is the first time I can remember having spent a day in bed for about three years. Of course, if it is a substitute for being sick during our honeymoon I'm glad I'm sick.

"The purchase you made is O.K. Dearest. I think we should buy another five shares but I am not a stockholder nor an officer? Also if they don't want outside stockholders how am I to attach a Washington check? Tell you what, dear. Will return the blank and you buy five for us in Sam's name. I'll mail you the $25. If only you were here to put your little cool palm on my forehead, all the fever would leave at once…"

"Ma is going to buy me a pair of candlesticks," Celia writes on the same day, "and she wants me to go with her to select them; also I intend stopping at a furniture store to get an idea on prices.

"I am exceedingly happy that you have at last found an apartment. I am sure I will like it. I think if we buy the furniture in one place the payment per month would be less than if we bought it in several places. How much we should spend for furniture? If I knew how much we could afford for the monthly payments I could tell just what price and quality to look at.

"Rabbi Glushak was in to see me. Incidentally I told him about FUS & Bond Co. and sent him over to one of our officers. He was advised to buy as many as he could afford and to do so as quickly as possible. He put an order in for 10 shs. I am putting an order in for 10 shs. for Sammy. I will be able to borrow as much as we have paid for it…"

In a second letter on the 17th, she continues. "We just got back minus the candlesticks. I saw nothing that I liked. We stopped in Roessler's furniture store and saw a very beautiful bedroom set on display – 4 pieces for $269. The man showed us the original tag and as soon as it is taken out of the window it goes back to its original price of $475. Each week they mark down a set for display purposes. If we buy any furniture from Barryman's friend I would like to have Ma come along because she has a wonderful knowledge of quality, style and price. I will call Dave in the morning.

"I am picturing the apartment all fixed up, you are sitting in a cozy chair and I am sitting on your lap and hugging and kissing you. Oh sweetheart, just wait until the excitement is all over. I will be able to think more clearly. Goodnite, dear, Cel"

Thursday October 18, 1928
Dearest of all My Dear Sweethearts,
No, I'm not exactly back on the job but I am playing at it this afternoon. I compromised with mother by offering to loaf at the office the same as I might have loafed at home. I took a taxi here and will taxi back so as to get a minimum amount of air. Seems that one in my state of disrepair must get as little fresh air as possible. I came here at 12:30 and I feel much better and (my) thermometer reads normal. I feel a little not so peppy and my tongue is quite a bit coated, but I think I shall be all well again by the time our wedding day rolls around. How lovely that sounds, our Wedding Day!

As for your inquiry as to how much I think we can afford
to spend for furniture every month I really must admit to gross
ignorance. I'll tell you how things stand and you may make your
own guesses.

Louis listed his expenses and the reliable income to date. "Figure out
just how much we can afford to put aside for furniture every month. My
tastes run towards either good or none at all – as witness my choosing
of a wife. I waited all this time to get a good one.

"There is always the danger of getting a new client with the corresponding fear of greater income. But I always like to count my chickens when they are running around the yard and not when I merely
hear their yip-yip. Incidentally, a fellow just came in here and after a
little talk extracted from your sweetheart ten iron men to help swell the
Washington income of the HIAS drive, an institution that does wonderful relief work among Jewish Immigrants. This gentleman stayed over
half an hour, not trying to sell me the donation, for I paid that over in
the first five minutes, but telling me about the work of the HIAS and
the suffering of our peoples all over the world. I saw a check of $1,000
that Bamburger of Newark (department store) gave them for a drive of
$500,000. I told him that if Bamburger gives $1,000, I should give thirty
cents. However, we settled for $10.00.

"I see where there is apt to be war unless I get busy with my address list at once. But about that furniture. It seems that you are right
about buying everything in the same store. At the same time, if we find
a bargain somewhere else there is no reason to sacrifice real value just
on account of the lack of cash. I find nothing in my book of scruples
that prevents me from using some of your securities to hock as collateral for a loan at my own bank. We can pay the bank just as easily as
the furniture Co. and save money. Our apartment is a really nice one
and it will take artistic and good house furnishing (on 0 money) to do it
justice. I know that with your wonderful artistic ability we shall have an
apartment that we will be proud to exhibit to our friends. So you just go
ahead and do all the buying you think you should." Louis then tells her
who has responded to the invitation and who has yet to answer. Among
his siblings, only Esther and Harry said they could not come.

"The eventful day is nearing and my only concern is that I should be able to get thru with all my work here. The little incidentals of married life are mere nothings. I know that I will feel at home after a day or two. It will seem strange only the first 3 or 4 days of the honeymoon but after that it will seem quite the ordinary thing."

In the next couple of letters, Celia is happy to learn that Louis is feeling better. They discuss details of the wedding, guests, and the music. Celia asks, "Sweetheart, I wonder if you could fix the seating chart. I have to make cards with numbers. I also have to let the caterer know how many more to expect.

"I called Fanny and she felt much hurt to think that we did not invite her. In fact, she cried. She said she would rather go to my wedding than to one in her immediate family. She promised to come." Louis is happy she accepted the invitation and says he is sorry not to have returned the seating chart as it would need to be changed again anyway. He ends with, "Your $98\,5/7\%$ husband will be in your arms in less than one whole week."

On the 19th, Celia catches Louis up some more. "The Auditor of our bank told me a few minutes ago that when the stock comes out on the open market it will be at least 15 to 20 points higher on account of the demand. Dear, I am very glad that you approved of the buy and I am sure we will not be sorry. I have made some sort of a budget and in that way we will know where we stand."

Monthly expenses are: "Rent $75; Gas & Elec. $5; Insurance $17; Car $30; B&L Ass'n Savings $10; Office $100; Radio $17; Household $60 and Incidentals $6, for a total of $320. With Income of $420, if you subtracted the Expenses of $320, that leaves a balance of $100 a month. I believe with $100.00 left we can afford to pay $50.00 to $65.00 a month for furniture to be paid out in ten or twelve months. And we can buy very good furniture. I am not going to do any buying unless I see an exceptional good buy otherwise we will do our buying in Washington.

"If we spend $350.00 for a bedroom set, $300.00 for a living room set, and $50.00 for a kitchen outfit; it totals $700.00 and divide that in twelve months makes a payment come out to $58.00 per month. The first year will be the hardest but then we will have furniture that we can be proud of. I think if we buy at around that price we will have a very beautiful home.

"Let me know how many windows the bedroom has. I have a

bedroom outfit of coverings and curtains and if we have more than two windows that means another pair of curtains. I hope not.

"Tomorrow is my last day at the office. I am having Ma bake a cake or two as I expect to take it to the office as well as a bottle of wine and *taglachs*. I am all excited. They just won't let me work. Every minute I hear some one say, 'Tomorrow is the last day.'

"Wow! I never thought we would be able to pay $75.00 per month. The place must be a beauty. With beautiful furniture – what could be sweeter? Should we need collateral I have 100 shares of Bankers worth $2,400 and 5 shares of B&L that is worth about $400.00. My remaining collateral is held at the Citizens Branch against loan.

"Don't forget to remind Dave to loan us the camera. I am sure he won't mind. Sweetheart, the excitement is too much for me. I will be glad when it is all over.

In a second letter that day, Celia conveys a message from Dave.

> (1) A jobber is trying to handle Argomite and that he ordered two tons.
> (2) The meat packers have ordered two tons.
> (3) The laundries are using it and last but not least they start demonstrating in Gimbles next week. Isn't that wonderful? He said he is too busy to write you. I invited him out for the week-end but he said he was too busy to accept.
>
> I spoke 2 Barryman, in fact he kidded me along thinking I was Fanny. I am to be at his home Monday evening at 8:00 and he will take me to the place. I am going to take Ma along. I hope we will be able to make a wonderful buy at Barryman's...

Louis writes "Just 8 More Days, Saturday, October 20, 1928":

> I was out shopping for a few things that I think I need and before I saw what happened I had spent $33.05 and there wasn't a thing to see. My tastes are too expensive, darling. I think you will have to tone them down a little bit (or) make more money.
>
> I think I shall go down to my tailor and be measured for a suit of blue -just to please my darling. To do the same I bought

me three new white shirts. See, the little wife-to-be is already influencing me in the things that I am going to wear. Just one more minute to the half hour, dear, and if you are on time you should be saying hello to me. There is so little satisfaction in the long distance phone calls. There goes the bell but the connection was no good. Couldn't hear a word you said. At least I guess it was you. There we have talked and it wasn't at all as bad as I thought it would be. I am checking up on you, honey, finding out if you really transferred the additional charges to me.

I am very glad about Dave and the Argomite. We surely need some good luck now. We need health and happiness and a sufficient amount of *mazuma* to cover the needs of not only you and me but also of your folks and mine. That, dearest, is one of my ambitions; to be able to provide for our folks if their own circumstances are such that they can be made more comfortable with greater amounts of income. But, God willing, we shall some day have enough for all and then, maybe, I shall be able to do the generous charitable giving that I have always wished to do and couldn't.

Louis lists "a total of fifty-five souls that apparently can be expected, plus 16 who have still not responded. Looks like our wedding has already crept out of the private class and is a full grown grandmother. Gosh, now the arrangement of the dining room is almost not any good any more. We almost made a mess of things, honey, And yet, dear, I am not sorry. Almost all of those who are coming are guests and friends we want to have there. Well, at the most, it means that it will just cost a bit more and be a little less cozy but a lot more lively and the possibilities of feribels are plenty and considerable, If we are poor we will live right here away from all that gang and if we live in your neighborhood it means that we shall maybe have wealth and then they will all be glad to forget all about the feribels and will be quite friendly. So, we should worry.

"There are so many things to be done and my collections are not coming thru as I had anticipated. I am still as madly as ever in love with my sweetheart and almost 99% wife."

"What a day!" Celia's letter proclaims on the 20th. "The first thing this morning I was called in the office by the VP. Mr. Arnold and was handed a fifty dollar bill. When I got back to my desk I was handed a very beautiful bouquet of flowers with a card attached which read 'From your Friends of the Fidelity Union Trust Co.' After that I couldn't do any more work so I started on my last tour of the bank and said Good-bye to all the men. The girls were all invited by me to partake in the eating of sweets. We had a wonderful crying good time. Gladys cried like a baby.

"The only kiss I received from a man was from Mr. Arnold the V P. He was dared by the other officers and not wanting to be a coward – so he said – he needed very little coaxing. Before it was time to leave I was covered from head to foot with confetti. I felt like a real bride. Each girl was kissed by me.

"Just one more week, dear, do you realize it? Love to you always, Cel"

On October 21, Dave's letter brims with optimism. "First, this last week, we have actually gotten into a business basis with Argomite, and if things continue, we can look forward to an increase in business. I was reading some statistics the other day and Uncle Sam said there are 40,000 millionaires in America, and I want to join that club some day.

"Already one of Mr. Barryman's laundries is sold on Argomite. A jobber who sells to janitors, was quoted 10 and a half cents in carload lots, said he could not handle a new product over 10 cents. Later he ordered two tons, paid C O D and ordered another ton, leaving a nice margin of profit."

Fortunately, Grossberger got into the meat industry where a jobber sells 2,500 barrels of Wyandotte a year that Argomite will soon replace. While there is not much profit, it leads to a quicker disposition of the Argomite, and a speedier acquisition of a factory.

"We have disposed of boxes of Argomite but the money has been slow in coming in. Some of the superintendents have done very well, others have not." Dave easily sold four dozen in the store of his apart-ment and a new man selling to grocery stores will demonstrate in the Food Show in Flushing.

"At Wanamaker's, our demonstrator has not made an overwhelm-ing success yet. However, we must have patience. The buyer for the larg-est department store in Pittsburgh, Boggs & Buhl, is interested in buying it for the Pittsburgh store. I just received permission from Glover and

Barton that if I can sell them, it is O.K. The one-half carload that I just ordered is practically gone by now.

"I understand from rumors that there is going to be next Sunday a wedding at which I am looking forward to create as much disturbance and discomfort to parties involved as I can. Biting, hitting low, and hitting in the clinches will be permissible…"

"Darlint Dave," Louis replies the same day. "Before I can check out of here for a coupla weeks, there are a few things I want to say. One of those is that you are requested to let me have along on my trip your little German Camera. It would be just the thing for a guy who knows not much about cameras and also it is small and anything we want enlarged should come out fairly O.K. Then again the films are small and ditto the cost thereof. So take it along when you show up Sunday, please.

"Next I wonder if it might not be an occasion during the festivities for you to deliver your famous German speech. So I would suggest that you go over the thing once or twice so you could recite it in case it should prove to be appropriate. In a great hurry and busy as hell. Regards to the good wife. So long, Your almost married buddy, Louis"

> Sunday, October 21, 1928
> My beloved 99% Wife,
> I am glad the employees of your bank were so noble to my sweetheart and I hope that Mr. Nolan appreciated the honor that was his – to be permitted to kiss you. Of course, that old coward gag is stale and we do not have to believe him.
> Your ring came yesterday and it is really a dandy. I think it is just what you will like.
> Leo asked to place an order for 10 shares and Babe wants 5 shares of the bank securities. Louis would order more but needs to conserve his cash.

Some of the DGS members said they might come to the wedding. "They are the leaders of the organization and are probably worth about $500,000 between them. This, of course, means nothing to us but they are nice people. The DGS is my best and most important client, adding just the price of our monthly rent to our income, in other words,

$75.00 a month. We may not know until Thursday whether or not that bunch is coming.

"I have you in my thought so much that I can't work. Still, a fellow can't be *chazer* (piggish). He can't have you all the time. But, soon, dearest, soon, Love, Louis"

(Written on the back:) "Sweets, A Postscript, honey. Just came back from the apartment and I find that it has shrunk a bit on me. All those I saw that day were so small that this one seemed quite large by comparison." He then gives Celia the rooms' size dimensions and sizes of the windows for curtains.

Celia writes on the 21st and the 22nd, of more preparations. "Our talk last night was most enjoyable. About the pillows – I'll say your prices are too high. Ma bought the finest quality in a factory where they make them while you wait. So you actually see what goes in them. She paid $14 a pair. I think we better keep them."

In New York she was to meet Mr. Barryman about getting furniture wholesale, and had already packed a barrel of dishes for shipment. Glasses she received from the bank were also to be shipped. "Edith is taking me to a wholesale house to pick out the silverware. I hope we get something nice and reasonable."

"This had been a day of fast and furious work with really satisfactory results," writes Louis "I collected $230.00, no it was $255.00. I have still some little to go to cover the budget I set myself at the beginning of the month but the crisis has been passed.

"Babe got himself all fixed up with his Tux and I have lost my Tux shirts. Looked high and low. Mother is already wondering if the (maid) we had hasn't done away with them. I hope they show up sometimes to-morrow. I'd hate to have to buy a new shirt. By the way, Willie has reported that he cannot be present on account of not being able to get away from work. Oh, darling, can you picture yourself honey-mooning with the best husband you ever had. I was about to say sweetheart, but we shall be more than sweethearts.

"Please, dearest, let me know how much the flowers are and whatever else there is for me to pay for. If it doesn't come to over $3,000. I may be able to pay for it. Beyond that I'm sure there is no use to look."

Shortly after Celia and her mother arrived at Barryman's home, he had to leave. But beforehand he called his former landlord about the furniture. It seems when Barryman moved, they became very unfriendly and the man refused to talk to him. Mrs. B. then said when their son was married they ordered furniture from this man through a catalog and were very dissatisfied and sold it for a loss. She recommended they buy from a department store. "Had I known (this) I would not have gone in the first place. I like to see what I buy."

"I am going to meet Fanny at the Waldorf this afternoon. I spoke to her this morning and we are sure to have a nice chat.

"I received the announcements and cards this morning. Do not forget to bring your list of relatives with you. Have you made reservations at a hotel in NYC? Did you write to Dave about the camera?

"I think of you always, dear, I love you. The flowers will cost $17. I went to another florist to get prices and I find the store you and I were in was $10 cheaper so that is where I placed the order.

"Sometime later. Is your shed large enough to hold a barrel of dishes? Let me know the name of the express man who makes deliveries in Washington. Good afternoon Sweetie, 5 More days – Cel, This letter sounds more like a telegram."

"I received your letter and am answering you on it at once," Dave replies on the 23rd. "The main thing seems to be the camera. Well you know old scout that you can have it. However it is the hardest kind of camera to operate and I will have to show you how to use it. It will be no use to you otherwise..."

While the wedding plans have gone ahead blissfully, trouble is brewing. "I have a very serious thing to discuss with you at this time and believe me I wish I could have postponed the whole matter. The enclosed letter copy that I sent to Barton will tell you everything.

"Here things were just beginning to come along and suddenly this thing blew in on us. Ida told me that Barton told her, he had something to do with a plant in Penn some place and she thinks it is Apollo. I think that Glover told me that Barton was once connected with the industrial chemical company.

"Now if the stuff is patented who in the devil has the patent? If we are O.K. then how about the price? See Barton as soon as you get this letter and he will have the package at the same time as it is being sent to him special handling.

"Find out what the dope is, for we have just discovered that Argomite is great in laundries. One laundry already told me he wants 15 bags a week. So do your darndest.

"Loads of love. Tell me when we can expect you. We are expecting your dad and mother for Friday. Lovingly yours, Dave"

"Dear Dr. Barton," Dave wrote on October 23. "We received a most unpleasant surprise the other day. Mr. Chandler called us up and told Mr. Barryman that the Industrial Chemical Company of Apollo, Pennsylvania had sent him a sample of a product called Launola for laundry use that he says is the same thing as Argomite. Mr. Barryman thereupon sent for a sample and he received it yesterday. I am sending you a sample of the stuff under separate cover. This stuff has certainly gotten me and Mr. Barryman decidedly worried. These people have offered it to Chandler at the following prices:

"5-lb. bags 6 and three-quarter cents.

"50-lb bags 6 and one-quarter cents

"100-lb bags 6 and three-eights cents

"200-lb bags 6 cents in lots of five bags and over.

"We made some preliminary tests of the stuff and it seems to do the same work as Argomite. I have not tried to make any jelly with it. Mr. Chandler wrote to them and asked them if they knew about Argomite and the reply was that while they did not know much about it, their product was far superior.

"In the letter they sent to Mr. Barryman they gave some instructions for laundries and I could tell that they knew mighty little about the laundry business. Yet this is the description they gave. It is a colloidal substance made of carbonated alkalis and dehydrated cotton cellulose.

"Is Argomite patented and have they discovered how to make it and if they have, what can be done about it? Also how in the blazes can they sell it at such a ridiculous figure? Of course they state that it should sell to the laundries at not less than ten cents.

"Please examine the stuff at once and notify us of your findings. In the meanwhile one of Mr. Barryman's laundries is very much pleased and is going to use about 15 bags per week. But this has sort of taken a lot of pep out of me. If any Tom Dick and Harry can actually make our product or a similar one so easily, what are we going to get out of selling and introducing and advertising our stuff?

"We certainly will appreciate an immediate reply…"

October 23, 1928

Dear Lou,

I felt I just had to write to you again on top of the letter I already sent you. I was testing some of this Launola and I believe that it has some caustic as it does have a sting to it. I also believe that Barton either still is, or was connected with an Industrial Chemical Corporation and I know it's in Pennsylvania. So, are these connected in some way and if so what is the proposition? The whole thing has decidedly upset me as it most certainly did Barryman. We are now beginning to worry about what we have got or have not got.

You see Louis, I'll write to Chicago and K.C. as well and tell them about this new stuff and we might have to get together and kill the damn stuff or we'll be wiped out just as soon as we have spent our energies to develop a business. This is more serious every time I think of it. Pump Glover as well as Barton for all you got. This is a damn important matter.

It is a hell of a time to have to worry about things like this just before a guy is getting married, but believe me Lou, I wish the damn thing never happened. Well old scout do your damndest anyway, Yours, Dave

Despite Dave's concerns, Louis' October 23 letter to Celia remains upbeat. "It seems that things are shaping up and if it were not for the fact that I am still quite a bit behind with my collections, everything would be quite excellent. Still, there are a couple of days more left. And if not, well, we won't worry at this time.

"I received a letter from Mr. Snyder, you know the old blacksmith who comes around every now and then. Attached was a check for $25.00 and the enclosed was a letter. Don't you think that was really wonderful of him? I didn't ask him to come to our wedding either, and he didn't have to do more than shake my hand and wish me well."

Louis immediately writes Mr. Snyder a thank-you note. "I hardly know how to express to you what is in my heart. It seems so commonplace a thing just to thank you for that lovely gift and those real wishes for our happiness, my sweetheart's and mine. You are a real friend, Mr. Snyder, and the way in which you expressed your congratulations proves that your heart is still young and beating to the tune of romance.

"I have forwarded your letter to my sweetheart with instructions to keep it among her many love letters yes, she has quite a few. I know that she will join me in thanking you for your kindness and for your warm-hearted congratulations and wishes."

"Dearest Little Almost-Wife," Louis opens his October 24 letter to Celia. There is still no sign of worry over Dave's recent correspondence. "Gee, today I am really tired. I worked at top speed all day and can already begin to see daylight and there is hope that before long I shall have everything done and finished." He tells her "that express man of mine" has offered to deliver "whatever we have at the right place," and gives details of some people who won't be able to make the wedding.

"As a substitute there is now likely to be one young fellow whose thousand dollars started us on the road to Argomite and its troubles. He expects to attend a foot ball game in New York Saturday and asked me if it would be O.K. for him to come and see the good words spilled all over us. I invited him to the affair as an invited gate crasher. He may be there." and adds, "Sorry you couldn't get anything nice in the way of furniture, but we'll get it. I love you dear."

"Do you know that tomorrow I will write my last courtship letter to you?" Celia asks Louis on the 24th. "Did you stop to think about it? I did. After I gave it some thought, a peculiar tingle ran up and down my spine." She updates details of expected guests and ends with, "Edith and I are going to see the show *Hit the Deck*. I heard it was very good and being from Missouri I want to be shown. Take good care of yourself dear and don't work too late, and when you drive up be very careful."

Four days before the wedding, Dave writes Louis again. "Have been worrying like hell on the latest developments here and can hardly wait till tomorrow when I expect a letter from you. Do you realize, Lou, that if those suckers in Appollo are not stopped, our contract is not worth a nickel? While it is fine to be sales representatives of Argomite, where can we get off at if this other company comes in and sells it to any jobber at 6 cents? If Mr. B. wants to quit at this time, fine, I can try to get somebody else to put up the money and continue in business. But the laundry business would then be closed to us entirely. For after all why should he buy from me when he can get it for his own laundries at 6 cents, from this other place.

"This knocks the whole scheme in the head. Money on the other hand won't come in unless it can get the whole country. The question is then, how securely is the stuff patented, for if a little chemical shop in Penn. was able to make it, then we have nothing at all except a beautiful debt facing us.

"The whole thing is almost driving me crazy. If you have not already written, for christ sake wire and tell me what you found out. I do believe that our stuff is better. This stuff has a bite to it, and the jelly looks like a mud pie, but what the hell as long as it does the work. It has not yet been used in the laundries, but the preliminary tests prove it to be the same stuff or near enough alike to pass muster, and look at the price.

"Sorry as hell old man for having had to so bother you and that just before your wedding, but I don't see how I could have postponed it at all."

Telegrams crossed that day, one from Ida: "SUGGEST WIRE DAVE IF BARTON INTERVIEW REASSURING DAVE TERRIBLY UPSET"

And a handwritten draft on the opposite side indicating Louis' reply: "Don't worry, Product inferior. Analysis tomorrow prosecution promised if infringed."

The next day, Ida sent another telegram. "TELEGRAM DISTURBING CONVINCED PRODUCT MAINLY ARGOMITE GLOVER MENTIONED PENNSYLVANIA LABORATORY"

"Dear Upset Partner of Mine," Louis writes in an optimistic letter right after Ida's second telegram. "I was out all morning getting various things ready and making a few last minute calls on clients who have promised me checks and half gave and the other half did not give. However, all this seems now to you so trivial, that it does not matter."

Barton is not alarmed and says this guy has nothing but a cheap soap that will ruin clothes. No infringement exists. He is fully protected and if anyone tried, he would stop them immediately.

"He read me part of your letter telling about the trick that jobber did you and he says you can feel mighty certain that he will not buy any Argomite if Barton knows anything about it. Of course, Dave, one in the game of trying to become rich must of necessity go thru all sorts of grief. Whatever you do don't lose your grip on yourself. After all even tho another product as good does come out it does not detract from the goodness of Argomite. True it means competition but I hardly believe it means that we must lay down and die.

"So far as connection with Pennsylvania is concerned I don't think there is anything to it. He did say that he worked there long ago and knows them all very well. The man who runs the place was in to see him last week and doesn't know how to make Argomite and if he did, Barton would stop him.

"Barton said that he believes Chandler is stringing you and playing you for a better price. At any rate, go about your business as best you can without blowing away your nerve. I'm leaving for parts North very early in the morning and will probably get in touch with you Friday night by phone. Sorry all this has happened but it will just make ultimate success that much the sweeter."

Louis' thoughts are understandably elsewhere. He wrote Celia on the same day. "Just got your very short note and I am commencing to shoot a similarly short one to you. I think I am about thru with things here and most of the money I can expect to get has come in and in fact the bank is closed. I bought some ABA traveling checks which I prefer to carry along rather than cash.

"Yes, sweetskele, this is the last of the courtship letters and I am wondering what you meant when you said that to-day you are to write the last of them to me. If you write to-day I won't be here to get it to-morrow as I expect to leave here very early in the morning. But what do I care for a letter when the sweet little person who wrote it will be in my arms to-morrow night? Do you realize that in just three days from this very hour you will be my WIFE?"

After the honeymoon the newlyweds lived in the Cavalier Hotel apartment house on 14th Street near Park Road. Only two pictures taken on the honeymoon survived and were preserved in the albums Celia so carefully organized. Mom said she went down to the grocery store every morning to buy 3 eggs so they would be fresh for breakfast. Two for Louis and one for her. She said the grocery man thought she was nuts. They worked together in the office, saved every penny and bought wisely.

Louis and Celia continued to write each other whenever they were apart. Some of these letters were undated. Celia visited Newark alone a number of times due to her mother's ill health. Her diabetes in those days was little understood and treatment was mostly of a dietary nature. Mom thought her mother died of starvation.

Celia's first visit was probably March 10–18, 1929. Another was about September 29 to early October, 1929. Pauline Kanster died in December of 1930 and I was named after her.

In fact after she died, all four Kanster daughters named a child after her. Sarah named a son Perry, Edith named a daughter Paula, Ruthie named a son Paul and of course, Celia named me.

Letters continued regularly between Louis and Dave, mostly about Argomite. Over the next two months, these revealed an apparent bit of chicanery among the principles in the Argomite business, as knock-off products continued on the market and different formulations of Argomite were sent to New York.

"Just a few words to let you know that I am still alive," Dave wrote Louis on November 9, a couple of weeks after the wedding. Barryman met with a young man who might be able to sell stock and raise $100,000 for them on a 50–50 basis and a jobber would sell Argomite jelly if it could be made an amber color. Barton had not responded to that request.

"I got a letter from a Mr. Richards in Chicago with regards a survey of the Argomite Industries of Wash. I wonder if that has something to do with the possible merger. I found several other things that I frankly don't like, and that is that the Argomite does not run uniform. Tell Barton about it and it is indeed a serious matter.

"For example Ida washed some of my silk things in Argomite, my silk scarf that was washed in Argomite already four or five times and it spotted it. I can't figure out where the spots came from and besides Ida complained that it stung her hands. Now that is a serious thing and for that reason I must figure on getting a factory, and that darn quick. I talked to Mrs. Kanster the other day and she was kind of lonesome for her darlings and I pooh poohed her out of it.

"Alright then me loves. I'll close now with the best of loves to the darling wife and also to the husband pardner from the boy friend."

November 11, 1928

I am enclosing a copy of a letter I sent to Dr. Barton. That will tell you lots. In the meanwhile another fellow will arrange to have me meet his father who is the gentleman with the dough. He himself has been a soap and detergent salesman (to) some of the biggest companies, and (would) try it out in several large places. AT A PRICE.

Lou old chap have a talk with old man Grant of the District National Bank. I believe he is one of the main stockholders of the Argomite Industries and advise him of Launola and find out what the Hell is going on in Washington. I heard that Glover has just gone to Kansas City and I also have no reply at all from Major Goodwin of Chicago, and I am beginning to wonder if the whole works is beginning to disintegrate or not. What the devil is doing throughout the country? Is Washington still alive and selling Argomite in the stores?

November 11, 1928

Dear Doctor Barton:

We had a conference with Mr. Chandler of the Carmen Supply Company on Friday afternoon with regards putting up a factory for the production of Argomite in this territory for Mr. Chandler to sell his Argomite mixture to laundries. The conference broke up (because) Launola has proved its ability to take the place of Argomite C and he gets Launola for a little over 5 cents per pound.

Now Doctor, we are beginning to wonder whether Argomite powder is protected by patent pending or whether it is only the name that is registered. We have tested Launola and have absolutely proved to our satisfaction that it does everything that our straight Argomite does. It is not a soap, for all soaps, whether good or bad, form thick leathery jellies that are not soluble in water. The additional fact that the two companies are rather intimately bound together leads one to think that one has gotten some of the basic products from the other.

How long will it take the Launola people to displace us? We have slowly started to develop and will discover ourselves out

445

through an undercutting of the price below what we can purchase it for.

After all, Doctor, you never did reply to me with regards Launola that the two products are not the same and that there is no infringements of one upon the other.

But can you advise me, Doctor, what selling talk I can have when I sell Argomite to a company and they show me a product that looks like Argomite, and ACTS just like Argomite with the same quality and sells from one to three cents lower than our price?

Dave compared using Oakite and soap, in laundries with or without bleach, to that of using the various types of Argomite, and claims there are other products equally effective and less expensive.

We know that Oakite is mostly trisodium, yet Mr. Barryman told us that to use straight trisodium they never got any decent results. So there must be some addition with the trisodium that Oakite have developed that makes it effective.

We received a letter from Mr. Richards in Chicago, requesting information (re) a survey for the Argomite Industries in Washington. I was just wondering what this survey was for?

We are awaiting a reply to this letter, advising us specifically why Launola can't be stopped, and if it can't be stopped, then why we can't get Argomite, at the same price that the local jobber can get Launola?

On November 13, 1928 Dave wrote Louis:

"I have a little dope for you. Business is rotten for I am hampered with the lack of initiative and capital and I can't do a thing about it."

The president of the Dold Products Corporation called Dave to see if the Argomite company could be bought, patents and all. He would raise $500,000 to put it over and asked if the slogan was registered. Dave said yes. This man also knew Burrows in Chicago and said he could not live up to his contract.

"In the meanwhile Glover went to Kansas City knowing that we had just shipped a carload to Carman (and) called us to find out how much we charged them for it. We of course told them our price. Yesterday Mr. Barryman told me that I should write to Glover and generally ask him what happened in K.C., for Chandler told him that Glover is trying to double-cross us with the Carman Supply Company both directly and thru this damn Launola stuff.

"Talk with Barton and find out if the Argomite Patents and the company are for sale. Mr. B. (thinks) there are no patents, but that he and the Launola people are making the stuff on a secret mixture…I got a hunch…that something is going to happen soon. But in the meantime I am having a lot of fun. It seems that a little more of it and I won't be here to enjoy it. It is sometimes a wonder to me whether it pays to become a millionaire or not.

"Alright, boy, scout around and find out what is the lay of the land. I hate to think that we are being double crossed, but circumstantial evidence points mighty that way…"

> Sunday, November 18, 1928
>> Dear Lou & Cel,
>> I hate like the very devil to write to you of my worries but there's nothing I can do about it now, so I might as well let you have the works without any further delay. Washington has completely double-crossed us so much so that the whole game was almost up in smoke on Friday and the death has been postponed now for a few more days to await developments. There is no wholesale market for Argomite at all.

Dave says they are getting no repeat orders despite initial successes. Workmen who were warned to economize became lax, the Argomite was used up, and the cost became too high. Even in the meat packing industries where it was marvelous, the repeats were nil. In order to work in laundries, a great deal of experimentation was needed which left retail as the only game in town.

"We tried selling the stuff to superintendents for resale to their tenants. Well, after a month and the expenditure of 200 or so we discovered

447

that there is no lazier class living than the superintendents of NY apartments. In other words it was a flop." A demonstrator visited a store for two days but would need about $50,000 to put it over.

Dave said Barton finally conceded, that Industrial Chemical was a subsidiary of Argomite Industries. While he said that Launola was not Argomite, Dave claimed that it was. Barton offered to 'graciously withdraw' from selling to the Carman Supply Company.

> Then Glover goes to Kansas City (so) Carmen Supply Company can manufacture Argomite after we had already almost arrived at an agreement to let Carmen in with us (to) manufacture Argomite in this territory.

Mr. Barryman has now decided the Washington gang are crooks. If Chandler had put up a factory for them in Washington, they could have manufactured Argomite for 5 and a half cents, sold it to the trade for 6 and a half or 7 cents and disposed of four to six cars a month. But their royalty basis would have to be adjusted. While they would operate at a loss for a year, Barryman was willing to put up the money and they would be in business.

> On that test with Argomite at the Sheffield place, I found that there was a great deal of grit in the stuff. In other words Argomite is not pure at all, and I have had several complaints from people saying that the first bag was fine but that the second was no good. Mr. B. told me this. So he wants to know why he should take a risk of investing another 25 or 50,000 and then be knifed in the back with one bad load of stuff from Washington.

Regarding a possible purchase of Argomite Industries, Aaron Shapiro, a lawyer, would be glad to take the case under advisement for $500.00, make a survey and try to raise the necessary capital.

> Don't misunderstand me now Lou. Read this letter a dozen times and try to get what I am thinking about. Philadelphia is out. Erie is out. Washington is not producing its quota by a long site. New York is absolutely out. Chicago according to Major Goodwin is

dead (and) Burrows can't possibly live up to his contract. So the only thing that they have left is Kansas City. I can't see how they can sell Argomite that cost them 9 and a half cents. So I am really expecting the Argomite Industries in Washington to blow up in very short order.

Please attend to this at once because I must have an answer to your conversation with Mr. Green. Do not see Mr. Glover as he does not mean much there. I am awaiting an immediate reply. With best regards, Sincerely, Dave

November 20, 1928

Just received your letter and know exactly how you feel. I feel the same way. I am doing as you suggested and am closing everything except the business and trying to drag along for a week or more and see what happens with the two or three live prospects that I really have. (He writes of a young banker who's already made 10 million dollars who might take the whole thing over and put it across, plus another interested party.)

I wrote to Barton yesterday, asking him to come to New York at once. Then if and when he comes here we will tie him down to certain definite facts and figures and if he agrees to them, thru Mr. B's son we might get together a syndicate that would take the proposition over and actually do something with it. Frankly there is no other way out. One of Mr. B's laundries wants it for not over 6 cents, and at that price would use a carload a month himself. So that is the story.

On the other hand I can't hang on too long. The kids must eat and that costs here in New York. So love to the *veibele* (wife). Your hard luck pardner, Dave

On Monday, November 26, 1928 Dave writes:

"I haven't had a night's sleep since Thursday. Early last week Doris got a bad attack of the grippe and I had to take her downtown to Leo's (Dave's brother's) office for examination. That was the day Barton got to town. I saw him and Glover on Thursday and we got every kind of a concession that we even dreamed of. We got Argomite now at 5.24 and I am going to pay for volume.

Friday Ida also became ill, and a cousin came to help out Monday. "So all in all I am having a fine time.

"Today, Mr. B. tells me that he is out. He discussed it with his wife and son and told me his son and he are trying (to) interest some outside capital and he suggested that I cut my expenses to the bone and try and pull thru another month and maybe in that time money will be forthcoming. Oh boy, if I can only remain in my senses thru the next four weeks I'll consider myself lucky. But I ain't dead yet, and where there is life there is hope. I got a hunch things will come out O.K. yet...

"I am glad to tell you that Ida is much better, as is the kid," Dave reports on November 30th. He is sending letters to all the customers informing them of the new prices and has a carload order from three of Barryman's laundries at 6 and a half cents a pound. And an Executive of a large silk mill is interested in Argomite, since there is no good silk washing product on the market.

Barryman's son got two men interested in getting an option on Washington. They along with the first fellow make three who might still pull things out. "I had one letter of encouragement today. You remember that bunch of fake orders I filled last June, well." The large wool company was interested in the new price of 7 and a half cents.

"I am pretty much down in the mouth but not yet quite out." As for his house, "Cafritz makes an additional profit of $2500 on the damn thing. The only one burned am I. But that's over.

"How is business with you? Is business so rotten that you did not get a single new client and did nothing better than to lose a few? It is one hell of a shame what kind of a pair of gazabos we both are. But don't worry Lou, old scout, I got me a hunch that Argomite will come out on top yet and we will be with it when it does..."

"In re bills," Dave replies on December 5 to a letter from Louis. "If I go out of business, Barryman would settle up all accounts so as to clear my name and prevent bankruptcy. That probably means that I will owe just that much more. I am daily losing hope. I don't know what to do any further. If I don't get any more money there is no play. I know just how you feel about the whole thing and I also know what you think of the accounting racket. But at least there is a living, a miserable one that's true. I think that I can last to the end of the month and then I am kaput without any resources. Then I start looking for a job.

"You don't know Lou, the miserable agony of sitting around all day with people hounding you for money and no possibility to do any business but I can't go and get orders when I can't buy and don't know if I am in business or not. You know, Lou it is a miserable feeling.

"Then there is one big fault that last batch of stuff we got is not at all up to standard and I have actually lost faith in the whole damn works. I have been getting complaints and what can I do about it. If I get money, we make a factory here, for the stuff is not the old stuff at all. It has some disagreeable features, such as building up a scum that it did not do in the beginning. I have stopped complaining as I am not going to order any more of it until I am settled. Well that's that. It does seem that it is almost time that the luck of G&G take a change for the better?"

December 8, 1928

Just a few words to let you know that I am still trying to remain alive and struggle. Markel, the new super salesman came in with a most unusual proposition. (He sent a letter through some intimate friends to the Board of Health and they were favorably impressed with Argomite.) He proposes to organize a sales force for the purpose of selling only to all of the city institutions and to the dairies. The whole thing hinges upon a report now being compiled at Columbia University Medical School. The salesman of this company will merely advise the various dairies to use Argomite, or be continually pestered by the board of health. The same thing will then be true of every restaurant, soda fountain and other public eating and drinking place. If this thing goes thru, we are made without any outside money at all.

Of course, Markel wanted to be compensated and, "I would be willing to split with him on a ⅓ basis. He to get ⅓ of the new profits of this particular business, if it comes thru."

Mr. B. advanced $1,000 to tide Dave over for another two months but with a nasty string attached. He had to sign a note for $3,000 while Mr. B. did not put up a cent. Barryman wanted Louis to sign, too, but

Dave refused. He has now shut everything down except for a steno and "has little stock on hand."

In one of Louis' letters, he told Dave that when his father returned home from shul, the ceiling fell down in the dining room. Fortunately, the portion just above his father's head remained intact.

December 13, 1928

I got your nice long letter yesterday. It seems that we are destined to be nothing much in this wonderful world of ours where everybody is a success (and) to lose a client after we saved a man from going to jail, and got him all straightened out, (and then) break our contract. Well that appears to be the G&G luck.

I can't quit this and walk out at this time, for if I do then I am out good and plenty. Yesterday Mr. B. told me that the men his son was working with were getting interested so he tells me to extend the option for another six months. Of course I could not help it and graciously told him sure it's O.K. But it is one hell of a shape to leave me in. He made (me) sign a note for $3,000 so that becomes my obligation and he has nothing in the business except an interest yet he wants to keep that option alive. Nu, what can I *mach*.

I made a lot of mistakes Louis, and one of them you advised me against. I let B. run this business for me against my better judgment and got myself into this mess, and then, if it had not been for this mess I never would have gotten the price as low as I did. I got a sneaking hunch somewhere that maybe something will yet turn up to salvage this wreck. It is this daily hope that is keeping me alive.

Well anyhow, I got you married off and believe me your troubles may have begun, but they are a darn sight easier to bear than they were a few months ago. Things are cockeyed, and yet when I get home the kids have so much to tell me. Oh well, Chanukah is here, the kids have received their Chanukah presents and *men lebt* (we're all living). So, loads of love from your old ponder, Dave

P.S. Please see if you can pack up the Alex. Hamilton course and ship it to my house and also the lessons and lectures as I simply can't afford to be spending the money and I have found out that so far what little knowledge I have, has done me no particular good, and that I won't need that to get a job as a janitor or something.

Dave writes again on December 19, complaining that service from Washington is pretty rotten. The bags come in late without the bill of lading, the laundries are raising Cain and he had to pay additional hauling for getting a partial shipment. Still, he opened two new accounts and hopes to struggle along for a couple of months. He is even going after laundries again with the new prices. "And as it says in the Good Book, 'Where there is Life there is Hope.'"

Dave has another idea on December 20. "Go down to one of the department stores and buy two or three small cartons of Argomite. Pack them very carefully and ship them to me. I want to see how they are glued and packed. I have several things in mind, one of them is putting up 2 and three quarters or 3 oz. containers for a special purpose."

Mr. Barryman told him a man who bought a ton of Argomite for his buildings was so impressed; he suggested getting ten men with five thousand dollars apiece for a year. Then it would be no problem getting others but Barryman had not committed himself.

"So I am now figuring out some organization in which they can come in and also where we can remain in."

December 24, 1928

'Lo Sweethearts:

Got your letter and also the two boxes of Argomite today, (but) they are all bunged up, (so) send me another one and wrap it in cotton and pad it heavily so it won't get crushed, and that is seriously meant.

Of the 20 bags I just got in I got rid of 19 today, all repeat orders over the phone. The customer who has been buying it in ton lots has made his fourth reorder. A funny thing happened, the last 10 bags he got lasted him six weeks, while since the new price went into effect it lasted 3 and a half weeks. Since it is cheaper they use it more liberally. I am going to concentrate on laundries right after the New Year, and I may be able to drag along for a little while until I can get some money. If old man B only came across now with the rest of the dough, I believe that we could drag along till the end of next year.

In the meanwhile I am still hoping and waiting and maybe something will hatch out.

December 26, 1928

Dear Lou:

I am sending you two samples of Argomite that I want you to take up personally with Dr. Barton. I have raised a half dozen complaints and have not received any answer from him.

The Argomite they are getting is not what they ordered or the same quality as the first two half carloads. "I did not want to believe that until the complaints got too strong for me to deny and I just took a sample of Argomite you sent me from Washington and believe me it is again a different proposition. You can see for yourself that there is a considerable difference between the colors of the two Argomites. Now I would not care so much about the color if the actions were identically the same. For the last two months I have received complaints, that the Argomite used, forms a foam when put into hot water. To what extent the white foam does any injury I do not know."

Ida and Mr. Grossberger note that Argomite used to keep their hands soft, but now has a hardening effect on them. The original Washington Argomite when put into hot water was a clear milky solution with no trace of film. Now it is white and flaky and foams like the devil. "I want you to talk to Dr. Barton and tell him that someone is monkeying around and we do not see why we are getting a different product, when we are paying the (same) price as Washington.

"If this film remains on the top of the water it will remain on the clothes in the laundry and after a few months it (will) leave a deposit on clothes that cannot be rinsed. It is a very serious matter, as you know we are absolutely powerless here. Please try to impress it upon Dr. Barton what is happening with the stuff."

January 2, 1929

Please notice that I got the date right the first time without any error. This is the first date I have written this year. Let me thank you very much on your nice telegram (for Dave's birthday).

Things are developing slowly and there is a hope that something will hatch out of the whole maze of indecisions, mistakes, *hartzergerness* (*hartzesseness*, heartaches) and other things. Today I am patiently awaiting the arrival of 20 more bags from Washington, as I have not a bag on hand. (I am) struggling along beautifully from hand to mouth, hoping to keep bones and skin alive. I really can't understand why Mr. B. does not come across with the balance of his bargain as he now sees that things are moving. But I suppose the Good Lord, who has taken care of me till now will not neglect me in the immediate future.

Dave asks for news about Washington. How did they pass the time? Did the Jewish Community Center close its doors? How were the rabbis and the cantors?

Louis does not seem as concerned as Dave when he writes: "January 4, 1928 (really 1929). Your letter came just in time to wake me up (re) a well deserved birthday present. I forgot all about trying to find a gold piece, for *war shicked as a gelt* (who sends money), a present of such small proportions other than in gold? Please buy something for yourself that you can call a present from me.

"I have finally and at last landed Mr. Kressin – the National Delivery Association. We compromised on $75 and a $25.00 monthly fee. I believe I told you that the Chevy Chase Laundry has gone bankrupt which means that we are definitely out the $507.50. Tough break, that.

"Got your samples of Argomite but Barton says don't let the scum worry you as it doesn't mean anything. Wish you lots of luck and don't let anything worry you. Hell mit it.

"Love from both of us to you and your famble. Hope to make an excursion trip to Newark in a week or so and then I shall want to see you at the Kanster's. Louis"

455

January 8, 1928 (really 1929)

Dear Lou:

I just had a talk with Mr. Barryman and he told me that (his son) Herman, had written to Dr. Barton and as yet received no answer. (The things that Dr. Barton agreed to were wanted in writing with the following important points): "a reduction of the royalty to one quarter cent after guaranteeing Doc a profit on the first carload which is our contract requirement, such as he is making on the stuff to-day at 5¢. In other words, we must build a factory here and pay him a royalty. Our contract calls for 1 cent which I have since found out is entirely ridiculous. Please attend to this at once.

If possible, please try to get the old lady (Note: Celia is an old lady by now) to pack up all the Alexander Hamilton Institute stuff and get it over to me as soon as possible. Business is so far rotten, thank you, but we are still hoping.

P.S. Need more envelops.

"Yesterday I talked to another banker with regards the New York organization," Dave writes on January 11, "and he promised to let me know within a week or so. Things here have been very quiet this week. One man trying to sell and finance at the same time makes it quite a difficult problem all around."

January 15, 1928 (really 1929)

Darlint Lou,

Just because I got my dates missed you get your present one day late. I had the darn thing in the shop and I thought Monday was the 13th, (Louis' birthday). Well it wasn't. I just want you to use that board to get a lot of fun out of it and particularly to lick Leo on it. I got it thick so it will last and on the next 70 birthdays of yours I want to lick you on the same board.

So far there is nothing doing here at all. It feels like a tightening noose, but somehow something will happen that will straighten the whole mess out. Only MOSSAI (Moses).

"Got your nice letter," Dave wrote two days later, "but will answer in more detail a little later. Just want to advise you that Herman

B. (Barryman) sent that letter to Dr. Barton with the dope that we have been asking about and want you to take the time necessary to drop in to see Barton and tell him to snap into it because old man Barryman said that if the letter comes back signed, he will try selling stock to 10 or 15 people."

January 21, 1929

Dear Lou,

Herman B. told me he sent Barton two letters now with regards the modifications of the contract to one quarter cent for Royalty. So far Barton has not replied. Please take the necessary time and see what's doing.

With regards a large company for national taking over, Herman told me that's out. His gang is not interested any more. My only salvation as I see it now, lies with trying to get 10 men to each give $5,000. Mr. B. might get that, but only on the basis of a quarter cent royalty. So see what's what, Lou old chap…

January 23, 1929

Dear Lou,

Just got your letter and want to say that it startles me to say the very least. I saw Mr. Barryman just yesterday and he told (me that). Herman's gang is out, and the Bonner gang is also out. The banker that I met has not evinced any interest and the rest of the crew is also dead.

The only remaining thing is Mr. B. getting 10 men to give each $5,000. Now he tells me that if he gets this letter from Barton with this one quarter cent royalty allowed, then he will start to get capital together, otherwise he won't do anything more and just call everything off except the $9,000 that I have signed up for.

If we intend to hold our laundry trade we must put the stuff up in barrels. Bags are harder to handle. For God's sake Louis, this is the most important thing that you can do at this time if you want to save this business. Why don't you see that in selling to the laundries at 6 and a half, I am not making one cent a pound and I must carry the accounts and assume all of the worry. It can't be done.

Then another thing. The stuff that we have been getting from Washington is absolutely inferior and I frankly want to be in position that I know what I am selling. So do your darndest and try (to) discuss it with Glover and Barton. Alright big boy, take care of yourself.

January 25, 1929
    Dear Dave:
    Celia and I are taking the excursion to Newark this Sunday. This means that you are directed to appear at 842 Hunterdon St., sometime Sunday for a Pow Wow with your friend and partner. Excepting between the hours of 1 PM and 3 PM (when) the gang is going out to dinner in order to avoid wasting the precious day in the kitchen.
    With love to your entire gang. Cel and Lou.

Dictated and read by Louis C. Grossberg; Typed and corrected by Celia K. Grossberg.

The problems don't let up. "It seems that we have to go through a little more before things turn our way," Dave writes on February 6. "For the past three months the stuff we have been getting from Washington is deteriorating until finally it is rotten, and I do not know where I stand. I have lost a lot of business and the laundries do not want it at any price.

"I just found out there is an excursion to Washington this Saturday night and so I sent Glover a letter that I want to see him Sunday. Get in touch with him and find out if we can meet Sunday morning and I would prefer seeing Barton also. I may take along with me our perspective sales manager, Mr. Markel.

"This means that you might have to get up before breakfast Sunday morning, but I will have to excuse you for that. With lots of love to the better $\%_{10}$ths, Yours, Dave"

Dave sent Louis a copy of a February 5 letter to Glover: "Thank you for any cooperation you have given me in the past – but what I need is some real cooperation at present. I have had some very astounding news, which has affected me very badly. I do not know what is going on in the factory in Washington but the stuff I am getting now is not the product that it ought to be."

Dave details his problems to date. Twenty real-estate buildings using Argomite C dropped out entirely since the product was no better than ordinary soap powder. Meat packers who used a ton every three and a half weeks now say it won't clean the pots and it cost him $1,500 to land that account. Laundries who used ten bags a week of Argomite C now use only two. It was not a question of price but of quality and over that he had no control. He trusted Washington to deliver what was ordered.

"Not knowing any chemical characteristics of the product, I am certainly in a dangerous position if I am unable to get the stuff I am representing."

Tests were made by dissolving some Argomite Tex in water with unsatisfactory results. "This morning, the water was absolutely clear, but on the bottom of the tin pan were two flocculent masses, one pure white and the other a nice rusty brown.

"This is not Argomite in any sense of the word. I have samples even now of the original stuff that has remained in suspension for weeks on end, sometimes slowly jelling and becoming thicker in the center or slowly settling, but the water always was milky and never clear. I noticed further that after the clothes were taken out, there was a peculiar scum left on the top that refused to be rinsed away. I would appreciate it indeed if you would personally send me fifty pounds of the finest grade of Argomite Tex that ever was made."

"Really Leo, tell me what is it all about anyway? I just opened a box of one of my first boxes that was filled with Argomite Tex and I compared it to the box Louis sent me from Washington, and the two powders are not the same. Is it possible that you are selling Dixie-Argomite, a better product than mine, under the same name?

"As you well realize, Leo, sooner or later we'll have to have a factory here in New York and then we'll have to know some of the chemical characteristics of the three products. Why doesn't Doctor Barton give us a method of analysis, and I know sufficient chemistry to conduct periodical tests on the stuff, so I'll know that I am not kidding my customers?

"I have the greatest of confidence in both you and Dr. Barton but

I am frankly afraid of the workings in the factory. As you have told me, Dr. Barton has not been well and for that reason I would like to test the stuff to be sure I am getting what I am paying for.

"I am enclosing a copy of the report of Dr. Coulter. It shows a very good coefficient for Argomite C and a remarkably good one for Argomite Blue, and having the weight of the Columbia University both products can be classed as disinfectants under government specifications. Please give this matter your immediate attention and advise me at once."

"It seems that every time I write to you it must be something wrong," Dave writes two weeks later. "I wish to God I could cut out this here monkeying and really go to work. Last week Glover was here and he saw for himself what was going on. So what does he do, he goes back and decides that Argomite C won't work and Tex is necessary. So he sends me some replacements with Tex and tells me that Tex is going to cost me 6 cents a pound. I know that Barton is crazy as hell. If Tex costs more than C, the difference does not amount to over a quarter cent if that much.

"Well brother, Glover sends me 10 bags marked Tex, and I sold mine at once and have one bag left in the place. This new Tex emulsifies O.K. (but) does not form a jelly. I have now concluded that the plant in Washington is absolutely all crazy. If the Tex they now make won't jell then Barton has forgotten how to make it or Hellert is deliberately careless. I wrote to Glover as per enclosed letter. I can't afford to pay more than 5 and a quarter for the *best* stuff they make. I can not increase my prices at all. So I absolutely demand that they sell me the old Argomite C I got in July for the price agreed upon.

"I wrote Glover of the most successful test in a laundry using the old Argomite C I got last July. The test was really remarkable and showed a saving in that plant of about $25.00 a day. They are now seriously considering Argomite at 6 and a half cents that Barryman quoted them. But if I can't get the same stuff, what can I do about it?

"You know, Lou, it is bad enough to have to sell a new product, but to be stabbed in the back and have no recourse is something altogether different. Anyhow I want you to insist that Doc go over all the cost figures with you and see if there is any justification in that price.

"I talked to a couple of fellows already who are willing to put up $5,000 cash and try and line up eight more fellows (to) build a factory, even tho we lose on every pound we sell. At least we will be able to control our product. If he'll give me Tex, real Tex at 5 and a quarter tell him to ship out 10 bags. Next week I expect to order 80 or 90 more bags but not at 6 cents.

"I have two demonstrations to make in laundries tomorrow and I can't go ahead as I can't take an order if I can't fill it. That's the story in a nut shell. It seems that Kansas City is now dead and all that's left is Chicago, and in January they sold nothing. So Argomite Industries is darn sorry I suppose."

"I have your letter of the 19th and I will be glad to return the bags I have on hand." In the copy of his letter to Glover, Dave repeats complaints from his letter to Louis. "The ten bags that you just shipped me are not Argomite Tex, no matter what you think you want to charge for it. Its emulsifying properties seem to be all right but it does not jell, and if Argomite Tex does not jell there is something wrong.

"Suffice it to say either Dr. Barton does not know what is going on in the plant, or the raw material they have been selling him is rubbish, or Hellert who does the mixing of the stuff does not know his business. I am positive the fault lies in one of these three things.

"The box that you brought down here you claimed was the oldest you could find in the place. You were probably right about that, as it was good stuff.

"I *demand* and have a right to demand that Dr. Barton furnish me the Argomite C he furnished me at that time. With that Argomite C I can do business today – that Argomite C *did* jell and did emulsify very well.

"I cannot see how there could be a difference of a whole cent between the Tex and C, but I can also exercise my rights set forth in my contract to demand Dr. Barton show me the exact costs of the two materials.

"Now we are definite on this basis. You are going to charge me a cent more for a product that is no better. It is not Tex, neither is it Argomite C, which means that there is something either left out or put in. On this I will demand an *immediate* answer because your reply definitely tells me whether I remain in business or not. I cannot raise my prices and you in Washington have ruined my business by sending me the last carload of rotten stuff.

"I am sending a copy of this letter to Louis and want you to talk it over with him as I cannot afford to make another trip to Washington."

Dave's frustration continues the next day. He sends Lou "a copy of a letter I am sending to Barton. I am in earnest now and have stopped all monkey business. The jack asses have sent me 10 bags of Argomite, which is supposed to be Tex, and is nothing. How in the devil they expect me to sell such stuff I do not know. Whatever the fault is, it is theirs today. If I do not get any satisfaction I will have to take any action I can. Barton is merely a jackass besides having a lot of nerve. Ask Barton to let you see a copy of the letter he sent me, it is too long to re-copy.

"I just made a demonstration in another laundry today which turned out very satisfactory with the old Tex we had on hand. This laundry is probably good for 40 bags a month. This is quantity production, but what good will it do me if I get the same rubbish from Washington? I am merely advising you of this if you see Barton, and I wish you would make it your business to see him."

"I have your letter of the 20th and to say the least I am astounded at it," Dave's February 21st letter to Barton begins. "When Mr. Glover was here he saw for himself what you had done to my trade. Now you tell me that I have not been living up to my agreement.

"I told you that in the commercial field my chief competitors are Oakite and Magnus. One pound of Oakite is just as effective as a pound of Argomite. This is particularly true in garages and in metal cleaning establishments. In the garage trade, Oakite is very well advertised, has a large staff of salesmen, and gives away an enormous amount of samples. The people who are using Argomite in the garage like it very much, chiefly because it is cheaper than Oakite.

"In the meat packing industry, Argomite is without question superior and while quite a little was sold at 14 and a half cents, yet the price was too high for actual use. At 9¢ they were delighted.

"Mr. Barryman bought Argomite at 6 and a half cents as a personal favor. So far, all of Mr. Barryman's laundries have suffered severe losses through the use of Argomite.

"I spent five months and $13,000 discovering that it is impossible to sell Argomite at 15 cents or 14 cents and even at 12 cents. Although it was possible to get original orders, I could not get repeats. I have finally discovered how Argomite works in laundries, through no thanks to you. All tests and experiments I had to make cost me money. I had finally started to develop a business and then your organization in Washington through extreme carelessness, lack of efficiency, and lack of even the fundamental tests of any chemical company, knifed me in the back, and yet you tell me that I have not lived up to my agreement.

"One laundry finally learned how to use it after experimenting for five months even at the price of 6 and a half cents, has not effected a saving of one nickel. The first 25 bags that we sent to another laundry, I saw their cost sheets and I discovered that it had gone up $350 or so, which was the amount of Argomite they had bought. They claim they do not want it for nothing. What kind of rubbish are you trying to hand me? You tell me further that the agreement in November was based upon an increase in production. Whose fault is it if I haven't been getting the original stuff?

"Mr. Glover brought 50 lbs. of Argomite Tex, which he claimed was the oldest in the place. On actual tests that I made with the last bag that I had left, I discovered that the stuff was not Argomite, Tex or even Argomite C. If you hadn't sent me one and a-half carloads of rubbish then I would have sent in an order for two carloads this month. As a result of your carelessness and the fact that we are entirely at your mercy, you have killed my business.

"I am not impressed when you tell me who has calculated your cost figures – the fact that he is a government accountant, is the greatest condemnation against a man, as I know too much about technical government employees, particularly accountants. I merely wanted to know the figures in case I was to build my own factory, which I hope to do.

"I told you I would try to raise capital here. Could you suggest to me how I can interest capital when I tell them that the product lies in the hands of one man, who is an absolutely honest gentleman but is as incompetent as he is honest and permits two months supplies to go out of the factory absolutely rotten? I have invested all of my capital, have borrowed heavily, and have given up eight months of my time building up this business. I will therefore demand from you, Dr. Barton, that you live up to your agreement we made November 25th and supply me quality product at the price we agreed then, and furthermore, we insist that you replace all defective material that has been shipped in order to get back in the good graces of the laundries, who are after all, *the* very large consumers.

"Specifically, Doctor, I want to know if you are in position to manufacture Argomite, the same kind that you did in June and July, and if so, will you sell it to me in accordance with our agreement of November 25th, and furthermore, will you replace all defective stuff you already shipped me?"

February 24, 1929
Dear Louis:

I am enclosing herewith the Profit & Loss Statement of the Argomite Company for the last year. The amount that I drew I am charging up to salaries and the loss will be so much bigger. I will include my salary on my tax return and on the partnership return you can split the loss for both of us.

I am not going to answer Barton today as I have to collect my wits before I can answer him intelligently. Just what recourse I have I do not know but in Washington they have very effectively done what they were always able to do and something which I could not prevent. However, my idea still remains the same. See Miss Crowlin – she has invested a lot of money in Argomite Industries and does not want to uphold Barton at the cost of her investment.

Argomite Industries has not been making any money as they have sold only to agents and these have dropped out one by one. When we started here, there was an agent in Kansas City, Pennsylvania and Chicago and now they are out. I understand that Chicago is back on its feet but if they got the same rubbish in their last carload as I got it will be a few weeks before Chicago will go under.

The last time I was down in Washington, I noticed that Barton hasn't even got the facilities to test his product. Barton tells me that all the raw materials that he buys is absolutely pure and does not have to be tested, but it is not so. I will advise you what my next step will be because I am afraid I cannot go out to sell Argomite, particularly knowing that I do not know what I am going to get.

February 24, 1929

Dear Louis,

I just received your long letter in which you urge me to apologize to that damn crook for my hasty words. There is damn little for which I have to apologize.

I am enclosing the last two letters I got from that damn fool and you can see for yourself what is going on. Barton is a damn liar when he tells you that he has made C as a special cheap product just for my benefit. If that is the case why did he charge me 8 cents a pound for the stuff on the very first order?

What in the devil is wrong with you Louis, to think that I am such a *schlemuselnim* (idiot) that I don't know what I am talking about?

I tell you that Barton has knifed me in the back. He has killed my business by sending me rubbish instead of Argomite. I know that Argomite cleans linens in a wash wheel, and the rubbish that he sent my customers did not clean it. What right had he to add more C (and) send me the stuff COD, and permit me to ship it to my customers on the chance that they might not kick? He did not send me the stuff that I had been demonstrating as samples. For Christ's sake can't you see what he has done to me? (After writing to Glover, he arranged to go to Washington to discuss the situation. Glover said not to tell Barryman so as not to 'dampen his enthusiasm in raising money.')

I came to Washington and plead before them and brought along some samples of the stuff. It was agreed that Glover come with me to New York and see what is going on, and (he) saw for himself just what had happened. He was told by a large user to get the hell out of here and to analyze the stuff, as they did not have time to monkey around with us. He was told by one laundry that they still had several bags that they did not want and were not going to use, EVEN IF ONLY 6 AND A HALF CENTS A POUND. Fine, Glover goes back promising me that he would replace the few bad bags and would ask Barton to look into the matter.

The next day I get a letter from Glover telling me that Barton will supply me with Tex instead of C at the price of 6 cents a pound. The shock of this raise at this time and in view of this last month's happenings was almost too much for my nervous system. So I wrote Glover a nice letter telling him that it was not fair for Barton to replace all of the stuff with Tex when I was satisfied with the old time C at our contract price of 5 cents.

I get an officious letter dictated by Barton (saying) they made the agreement for me to get Argomite C at 5 cents on condition that I materially increase my business and inasmuch as three months have gone by that I have not done so, the price would be 6 cents and that I could go and choke myself if I did not like it.

Why the damn cheek of it, the blooming impudence. I can't get it thru my head how in the devil a man has such unadulterated gall to tell me that. After deliberately ruining my business with rotten stuff, he has the nerve to tell me that I have not lived up to my agreement and that from now on the price is 6 cents.

On top of that he sends me some Tex and I find that it is from 35 to 40 percent less effective than the old Tex, besides not forming a Jelly. The fact that it does not jell means that it is not the same product.

Today I got a letter with yours from the Doctor in which he tells me that he had added too much C to the stuff and that as long as he got no complaints he kept on putting in more of it. Fine. He got no complaints because it takes a month or more till people start to use the stuff and decide definitely that the stuff is not any good and they throw it out. Then I kick, and then he decides that he has added too much C.

Who in the hell told him to start to make any change? Who in the hell cares if he is losing money until I get into production? What other company that is entirely unknown has the impudence to make outrageous demands on a new agent until he has gotten into development of the stuff? If the jackass had played fair with me, I would have sent in and sold two carloads of Argomite this month instead of wasting the entire month trying to find out what the hell struck me. Does the fool not know that he killed the entire month of February for me? What in the blazes is he doing anyhow? But that is now over. The question is what to do? I have several orders that I expect to get next week from new laundries.

I am absolutely afraid to get them because it is now impossible to know what *drek* they will ship me from Washington.

I would suggest that you talk to Miss Crowlin, and from her get a line on the rest of the directors and tell them what is going on. God, man can't you see what I am up against? How can I sell a product when I don't know what stuff I am getting?

Tell me. What shall I apologize for, for the junk that he sent me? For having knifed me in the back and then to show his appreciation has raised the price of the product to me so that I must go out of business, with or without my shirt? I can tell him that I am sorry that he is an incompetent man? What more shall I apologize for?

Now with regards costs. Barton showed me figures of materials for the year 1927. It cost him 3.33 cents a pound to make Tex. The difference in his high costs is because he is not selling any Argomite because (he's) charging his agents too high figures.

Well, Louis, I am sorry. I think that it is now all over. I am now taking up the matter with Mr. Barryman to see what can be done about getting some redress. I can't go out and sell any more Argomite. Use your judgment after reading this letter as to what you should do. I have nothing to advise you. I certainly can't stay in business any longer. I am sorry as the devil that this is the end of everything and God only knows now what I will do. This world is made up of the lousiest bunch of crooks and I have been fortunate enough to have been the victim of several of them. I wonder if I ever will learn. So I will close this letter to you now with best of love from your licked partner, Dave

February 25, 1929

Dear Dave:

Just got in here and saw your Special Delivery letter. I hardly know what to say excepting of course that you are absolutely right, however, that's beside the point, the real thing to do is to 'carry on.' My letter to you of the other day in which I asked you to apologize I think still holds the only solution.

I am perfectly confident in my mind that you have no redress and that on any court action you would lose for failure to prove quality. Perhaps young Barryman could enlighten you as to the difficulty proving quality such as (in) Argomite. So then the only way is to do it through niceness. Granting that the Doctor is a damn fool yet he has admitted making the mistake with his C, and it is quite likely that the new C he offers to deliver for six cents will be the same quality product that the old C was.

The other day I got a sample of the Tex that Hellert said he shipped to you. I made a jelly and while the color was not the same as the old jelly it did jell. Celia used it to wash some silks and she said it was the same as the old Tex, and it did a splendid job. If this is the same stuff you got in the last ten bags you would not raise such a rumpus even if it doesn't jell for us. I know that you are 1,000 times the aggrieved party but what can you do when he holds you in the palm of his hand? After all, the real trouble with you is lack of money, for if you only had a little money you could manufacture and be rid of all uncertainties.

Your suggestion regarding Miss Crowlin is not such a good one because from what I could understand, Dr. Barton is the real boss and the other stock holders and directors don't count. I am a great believer in pacifism where your opponent holds the gun.

The Doctor has promised me and you that he will supply quality Argomite C at six cents. I fail to see that you have any other course open than to give him the opportunity to deliver such quality product.

So far your only just complaint since Glover came back, was that they boosted your price and that the Tex he sent you doesn't jell, but if as you admit it does do a good cleaning job why worry? Your last letter to Barton caused me considerable apprehension because it ran counter to my pacific views.

As a good Jew you should be admirably fitted to be stabbed in the back and then to apologize to the stabber for not hitting your heart, so see if you can't follow my advice as outlined in my previous letter and give the Doctor a chance to ship you the goods he promised to ship.

It seems that before making delivery you might wash a little bit of soiled silks and see if you can't make a real working test before delivery. This may be poor advice but there seems to be but two courses open, either Peace or War. I am sure that War won't do because you are sure to lose, the only thing left is Peace and I have suggested your course. Lovingly-from the two of us, Louis

February 26, 1929

Dear Louis:

I got your letter today and have very little to comment upon it. I am enclosing a copy of the letter that Barryman's son wrote up to Barton. If we have breached our contract there is no question of the breach on their part also.

I just spoke to Mr. Barryman and he told me that this fellow we were talking to about getting some money, has interested one other party (and commented that a Washington share-holder was advised) that Argomite Industries is selling the patent to an individual or corporation to take over the business on a National scale and that Charles Evans Hughes has already written the contract, which is to be signed soon. You see if these facts are true then it is quite possible that Barton has been deliberately doing this to us in order to wipe us out of the picture.

I think that you have one other recourse left. You can find out who the directors are. Grant, of the Bank on 14th and G, is a big stockholder and is one of the directors. I know that Miss Crowlin has put in a lot of money in the business and also know that Argomite Industries is pretty much broke. If we were to institute suit, Argomite Industries would have to hire lawyers and also disclose the fact to the Board of Directors that something has been cock-eyed in Denmark. While I would hate a law-suit, it will be the only thing left for me to try, to get some of the money I lost. (Try) to find out more of the financial condition of Argomite Industries.

Glover said, they produced 200,000 lbs. in January, that their costs should have been over 6 cents and that they lost money that month. One of two things are obvious. Either he lied to us when he gave us the figures at which Argomite might be produced or they did not manufacture anything near that amount of the material. If they did, who bought it? In January we bought about 34,000 lbs., Chicago bought nothing, Huron might have bought, as Glover told me, 6,000 lbs., Washington used about 8,000, so I wonder where the rest of the stuff went to. It is possible that the whole story is a fake (and) the amounts sold were those I just quoted to you. If this is the case then we are not such small potatoes.

That is what you can talk over with Miss Crowlin and we want nothing which we are not entitled to. This is something, of course, that I am leaving entirely to your judgment.

February 26, 1929
   Attention Dr. Barton
   We beg to acknowledge receipt of yours of the 21st instant. For the sake of the record, may we not point out that Argomite C, while admittedly a cheaper product was cheaper according to your statement because of substitution of materials which it was claimed would not in any way hurt the efficiency or materially change its properties. The inferior product which was shipped us caused the loss of some of our best customers and certainly our best single customer. At the present time we are bending all our efforts to the retention of those customers who have kicked us out of their premises, and if possible, to secure again some of our old trade.

We recognize without quibble your right to raise the price of any of your products in accordance with the contract. At the same time you must realize that such an announcement of change of price comes most disastrously at this time when the inferior product has wiped out some of our accounts, alienated others and destroyed an imminent large contract as well as our financing negotiations.

If the price must be six cents, may we not ask that the price go into effect at some future time, let us say thirty days, so that the sales made on the basis of a five cent price may be filled at that figure. You can hardly ask us to take a loss on orders already secured.

We know that Argomite as originally shipped is good, and that we can put it over. As far as any claimed breach of the contract is concerned, we presume you mean the back moneys, which we admittedly owe you. It is simply impossible for us to pay that money within thirty days. That impossibility is in great measure due to the fatal defects in the materials lately shipped. If after mature consideration you feel that you wish to do us this injustice, we can merely say that we have grossly misjudged you. On our part you must not forget that the shipments of Argomite within the last two months have been a breach of the contract on your part.

We wish to place an order for thirty five bags of Argomite C under the old terms shipped immediately under the old price, and we have tentative orders for sixty bags more within the next few days at the old price. An immediate reply will be appreciated.

P.S. If you deem that we should take an additional loss at this time, send us the thirty five bags anyhow but please send us good stuff.

ARGOMITE INDUSTRIES, Argomite Corp. of New York, 37 East 12th Street, New York, NY. Copy for Mr. Grossberg.

February 27, 1929
> *Attention: Mr. Glushak*
> Gentlemen:
> Your order for 35 bags of Argomite powder received and we are shipping you this order tomorrow, Thursday, Feb. 28th, open shipment; but must ask same be remitted for upon arrival of goods. We have written you heretofore that all shipments would be made as is our custom, sight draft attached to bill of lading; but wishing to show you our desire to assist you in every possible manner we are making this exception. We will expect no delay in mailing us your check.

We are very sorry to learn of your continued inability to clear away the difference of nearly $1,000 now due since October; but must insist, Mr. Glushak, your remitting in full the earliest possible moment. You must acknowledge that in the matter of extending you credit we have tried to meet your every suggestion, although in every instance you have kept us waiting beyond the prescribed arrangement. Help us to have faith in you by remitting as soon as product is received. If not, then hereafter and for all time, we will be forced to send all shipments sight draft attached to shipping documents. We feel sure a word to the wise is sufficient. Sincerely yours, ARGOMITE INDUSTRIES INC. (SIGNED) E.W. Crowlin

March 1, 1929

Dear Lou:

I am enclosing herewith a letter that I got from Miss Crow-lin. That, apparently is in answer to the letter that Herman Barry-man wrote. I think in this letter, even though it is answered by her, they have given up the idea that the non-payment of the thousand dollars is a breach of contract, but that is not the point – what is worrying me is the lack of confidence I have gotten as a result of their actions.

During February, Dave sold nothing nor had he paid February's rent. Barryman hesitated dragging his friends in when they were at Barton's mercy. Still, he was trying to revive the business and of 35 bags ordered, 27 were sold.

You know that the raising of the price at this time certainly set me back considerably. For instance this order that just went through at 6 cents I make nothing, not even a cent, but it is just a straight turnover of money. The stuff was sold at the old price. It seems that if they were going to raise the price they might have given me a few weeks notice to that effect. Now, unless something happens within the next few weeks, I feel that the whole thing is definitely over. It is all well and true to say carry on, but it is a difficult story to play with that gang.

I do not know what I can advise, Lou, but if you have another *shmoos* with Glover, maybe you can find out how much Argomite they made in January and February, and to whom they sold it.

March 8, 1929

Dear Louis:

I got your letter the other day and just got back to the office after an enforced vacation with a young girl by the name of 'La Grippe' (the flu). Your letter interests me very much, particularly that your sympathies are with the Argomite Industries. You tell me how nicely they are treating me, and in spite of what took place, they are sending me stuff on open account. I think it is wonderful of them – bless their hearts.

I am trying to get Argomite back in Laundries – it is a difficult job to try to boost the price because those who have been using it so far have not been particularly wild about it. We are still trying to find out if we are alive. I will be needing some money very shortly now to buy some stuff – I do not know where I am going to get it. The fact is that all sources I know of are absolutely closed. My personal drawings for the past six weeks have just been enough to pay my grocery bills and rent and the bank account has gradually gone down to a couple of hundred dollars.

The rent for February has not yet been paid and the same is true of March. From what I understand now, brother Barton is just about on his very last legs and instead of being a man, he is trying to hold up his end as being a wealthy organization and we here who have been practically his main stay for the past few months, are only a drop in the bucket.

Lou, (are) there any friends of yours or Celie's upon whom pressure can now be brought to whom we could talk for money? Think really hard on the latter.

The stuff that they have been sending us now at 6¢ is not in my opinion good Argomite, but I suppose there is nothing we can do about it. Maybe we will drag along another couple of weeks.

The Profit and Loss Statement for Argomite Company Of New York for the period ending December 31, 1928, showed:

Sales of $11,029.03

Net Loss of 5,486.51

Dave's Drawing of 2,731.25

For a Total Loss of $8,217.76

After being in business for five years, Argomite Industries was still not successful, due to a lack of capital, inept management, lack of a uniform product, and an unwillingness to deal honestly with its agents. Dr. Barton, the inventor, did no testing to develop his product and expected his agents to do that for him.

Argomite, though superior to soap, was too expensive for most uses. Only in the meatpacking industry, garages, and where grease or fat removal was a factor, would a good cleaner be worth a higher price. The laundry business was a natural for some forms of Argomite but without adequate information as to its usage or a consistent product, the market disappeared. The same was true of silk, rayon and woolen mills.

The initial enthusiasm of agents disappeared and potential investors were wary of rescuing a company over which they had no control. It looked like salvation would only come if a factory were built in New York, so Dave continued trying to pull a rabbit out of the hat.

"If we will get a letter from Argomite Industries backed by the whole Board of Directors," he writes on March 11, 1929, "we may yet be able to salvage whatever there is from the wreck, otherwise there is practically no possibility for us to continue in business. (Tell) Mr. Grant, talk that so many people were buying in quantities has proved to be untrue. Washington has done nothing at all to cooperate with us, not even to trade marking our slogan, which they had promised to do." They should be willing to discuss a merger where their patents would be protected and be given a fair share. "For Argomite Industries as such, won't be alive much longer.

"Major Goodwin told me he had a three month's option to buy the Washington business for $150,000 stock in a new company, which was to put up $500,000 cash for the entire country. He asked me whether I would be willing to come in with the consolidation and under what terms. I told him (yes) at any reasonable terms that would protect my investment and permit me to remain with the company."

Louis is asked to see Barton and see if an option was given to Goodwin. If not, to ask what he wants for the works and try to get an option for thirty days. "And Lou, old boy I am sorry as the very devil. I did my darndest and flunked out mainly through being stabbed in the back. Anyhow, I have to start over again looking thru the want ads for a job and God only knows what I can land and when I can land it. One thing however, I will assume the entire note of $6,000. I will tell Mr. B., that that will be my debt entirely. It will have cost him $3,000 also and that will end the chapter.

"You know Lou, old chap, we have gone thru pretty much together and I have been considerable of a load on your shoulders. I had hoped that this new venture of ours would have repaid you a thousand fold and that we could have continued working together in joy and happiness. However, I feel that at least in your case, you will be able to make a living from what is left of the practice. That is the least that I can do. More I wish to God I could do.

"But I (still) believe that something will turn up. Well from now on Lou, I don't think that I will let them drag you along with me when I suppose I'll get burned again. You and I are the only honest people in this world. We have a sense of decency and fair play that the rest of the world has not got and it has done us no good at all. So I'll close this *megillah* with loads of love to Celia and yourself which I am sure Ida joins me, your waning partner, Dave."

This is Dave's letter from March 11, 1929 to Dr. L.T. Barton with copy to Louis.

> Dear Sir:
> We would like to ask you to consider the following proposition and we wish you to give us a definite reply to it after you have discussed the matter with your Board of Directors.
>
> If Dr. Barton agrees, Dave claims he has enough interested parties willing to invest capital to build a factory in New York. He would then be able to guarantee a uniform product and supply not only Washington, but other agents as well.
>
> We have been lead to believe that the sales in Washington are not very large, as the cost sheets to Mr. Grossberg have shown. We would be glad to enter into any agreement whereby if this factory were in New York, we would use the same people that are now being employed in Washington and they would be under your personal jurisdiction with somebody in this organization to keep an eye on production.
> We are asking you no favors, Dr. Barton. Such a move would be wise and would redound to the benefit of the entire Argomite Industries and the rest of the Argomite dealers…Such a move would…give us the chance to re-habilitate ourselves and actually make a success that is due to the product itself.

The occasion of Louis and Celia's first letters to each other as husband and wife was a trip to her parents that Celia made in March.

Monday Before Supper, March 11, 1929.

My Own Darling Wife!

This is the first time, dearest, that I am addressing you as wife in a letter. It sounds fine and I am quite pleased. I am sure you like it, too. So sorry, dearest, that I was incapacitated just at the moment when you were leaving. I should have liked to take you into the car and seat you properly and send you away with one of my choicest kisses. But never mind, dear, I'll be there to receive you when you return.

It was surely an unusual affair this knockout of mine and I could not understand the cause until much later in the afternoon. (Louis apparently had food poisoning from an affair that he and Celia had attended the night before with some of the DGS people.) I hope you escaped it altogether, but if you did, you were one of the very few. Mr. Kay thinks it was the chicken. If so, you should not be in the party at all as you hardly touched it. Please let me hear from you about it. I am all right now.

Have been more or less busy most of the day here and am of course planning to return to the office just as soon as I finish my supper. Incidentally that is something I should attend to at once as it isn't polite to come in after seven to eat. I suppose you want to know whether I miss you. Well, darling wifie, I am like little Georgie de Wash., I can't lie. I haven't yet had the chance to miss you since I often don't see you all day anyway. But you just wait for the night time. I can just feel it in my bones that the beautiful little apartment will not be beautiful this week and the princely bed in my boudvar won't be at all princely. In fact there isn't much reason for me to go home tonight excepting for the fact that I gotta sleep.

Monday 3 o'clock, March 11, 1929

Dearest Hubby,

I am going to call you this evening because I am worried about you. I hope you are well. Let me know – honey dear – just how you feel. I was fortunate in getting the train I did because it was equipped with the double seats you mentioned and I had one to myself. I didn't have to get a Pullman chair.

I found everybody well – and anxious to see me. Ed., Sam, Sara, Heshy and Ma met me at the appointed place. The bus had been traveling on Frelinghysen Ave. but he went on Elizabeth Ave. after I told him I expected someone to meet me. Not so bad, eh!

It is only a little after three and I miss you heaps. Gee, it is wonderful to love your husband – isn't it? Will write again tomorrow. Your wife who misses you, Cel

Other letters were exchanged during their separation. Louis wrote: "This morning. I didn't have the heart to make my own breakfast because it seemed so pointless. I just stepped into a restaurant and bought me a cup of coffee and a bun and got that off my mind. It was very sweet of you dear, to call me on the phone last night and I was surely sorry to hear that you didn't escape the effects of the banquet. They are trying to find the woman who catered the affair. She may have some trouble trying to collect the balance due her."

Celia answered: "I am feeling much better today. Ma gave me a big dose of salts and I believe it has helped me a lot. I didn't want to say anything yesterday because I didn't want you to worry, but as long as you told me about the others, I didn't mind telling you. Anyway a husband should know."

Dave writes to Louis on March 13. "Just another letter due which depends upon your results of the meetings with Barton and Grant. I have not yet heard from you regarding that last letter but am anticipating the refusal that you have gotten from that gang.

"The game is about over. The money raising possibilities are now through." Without waiting for a reply, Dave says time is running out with only two courses left. One is to close up shop and leave with a $10,000 debt. The other is to continue selling Argomite and eke out an existence if possible. But the catch is, he will have to leave his place of business and move into Barryman's without his machinery or empty boxes. However, "Washington can use both my machine and my empty boxes and my literature. They have got a market for it and as they get new suckers who want containers, why they can supply them just as I have been doing. The literature should be of value to them."

Dave owed $1,000 which he could not pay but thinks his assets are quite valuable to Washington. "I still owe $200 on my machine but it cost me $1,000 and I have over $1,500 worth of boxes and literature. So maybe Washington will be satisfied to do that, and in so far as my contract is concerned, it is worth nothing and I might be able to keep it alive and I might not. That depends upon the type and style of rubbish that they might be interested in feeding me. I won't write to Barton anymore. Tell him I am absolutely and definitely thru. Tell him that I intend to quit and throw the corporation into bankruptcy and out of that mess he'll get nothing for his efforts.

"The machine is not yet clear so that the company will take it back for non-payment of notes. Tell him that there is still some business in New York and that I might be able to sell some Argomite here. Tell him that I might actually be able to keep up with my contract requirement and hold it. Tell him that he can't annul my contract because of the money I owe, and if he doesn't believe you, let him ask his lawyer. Tell him that the worst he can do about that debt is to sue me and then throw the corporation into bankruptcy and in that way he can buy back the contract as the contract is the property of said corporation.

"Then ask him what he wants to do about it." Dave suggests that Barton come to New York about buying his machinery and empty boxes. "And then I'll decide whether I want to remain and sell Argomite all alone or chuck the whole thing. I must get out before the end of the month and I must also decide what to do long before that time arrives. Were it not for the fact I have to live and support the family in some fashion, things would be fine.

"Don't worry about Barton's trying to ask you for the $1,000. I sort of laughed when you wrote that in one of your prior letters, for this is a corporation, all done up real pretty.

"I have a safe file cabinet here on which there is still $30 due. If I have to close out, then it would pay you to have me ship it to you as it now cost $125.00. Sleep on that as well.

"Well old chap, we are having a lot of fun for our money whatever it is and now we must sing and dance together. So I am awaiting your answer to this letter with great impatience as much depends upon it."

While Dave struggles with the Argomite problems, Celia is using her New Jersey visit to increase her bank shares. On March 14 she writes: "Yesterday while at the bank I left an order to sell 70 rights at

478

the market price which was around $3.00 and with the money buy 30 shares at $15 a share. Well this morning Miss Walker calls me on the phone and tells me there is a panic down at the office because everybody wants the rights. There is a rumor of a merger. I got kind of nervous on account of the request I left to sell, so I immediately called the bank on the phone and was told my rights were not sold as yet as the vp has expected something of the sort. He is going to hold them for awhile and see what develops.

"I still think it is best to sell the rights and with the money buy more shares. I hardly think the bank will let me have any more money because I am an out-of-towner. The vp said I had enough and that it wasn't always a very good policy to get deep in debt. I will see him again tomorrow."

Thursday, March 14, 1929
     Hubby dear,
     I called the vp on the phone again and was told to see him tomorrow morning as he suggests I settle whatever I am going to do. He did not sell the rights as yet – for which I am very thankful. Read the enclosed clipping and save it for me to go over when I get back. If I can figure correctly, we get 180 shs of American for 200 shs of Bankers. If I am told to sell 60 rights at about $5 we get $600 and with that we can get 40 shs clear. Not bad, eh! I am too busy buying papers and calling the bank on the phone to do any social calling.
     I am very much pleased with the results of Bankers. How about you? Dearie, I miss you so much. Love to you, dearest of mine, Cel

Dave is not so happy, as he writes the same day. "Honestly Lou, in the past few weeks your letters to me have shown such complete incompetence on your part, that I swear if it were not you, Lou, in you own darn fool sap sense, I would have stopped writing to you altogether. I write to you one thing, and you go over to the idiots and listen to them, and then say they are right. You read my letter and then you say, I am right. In other words we are both right.
     "I took a sample of the stuff they sent me yesterday, and what do I

find, the solution is full of an insoluble scum, (that) ruins the Argomite for all cleaning purposes as it leaves this scum everywhere. They have sent me four bags of additional rotten stuff, which if I get rid of, will settle my hash again in these places. Should I pay for the four bags that I just got and which is rotten?

"You ask me to place myself in their position, and what have I to offer them and why? If they will abandon their factory and will take it over here, I believe that we will definitely get the money, (and) even if we operate at a loss for a year or two, everything would be all right, BUT WE WOULD KNOW THAT EVERY POUND OF ARGOMITE THAT LEAVES THE PLANT WILL DO JUST WHAT WE CLAIM FOR IT.

"You talk to me about how nice they are in Washington. I will tell you what I have to do here. I interviewed a laundryman yesterday who had already bought 15 bags of Argomite at 6 and a half a pound and who had thrown the stuff out as absolutely no good. I talked to him long and loud about the new stuff and how much better it is and also told him the good news that it was now 7 and a half cents a pound.

"(If) a salesman sells you a lot of ledger sheets and the holes on the side are not uniform, and one of your girls spent two days typing the names at the bottoms of the sheets and the job must be done over, and suppose that the salesman wrings another order from you at a higher price and the new stuff is just as bad or maybe worse. Tell me how far would the salesman have access to your confidence for a sale of the same stuff in the future?

"For Christ sake Louis, can't you figure that it is your $12,000 as well as mine that I am trying to protect? Can't you see that I am desperate?

"Do you know that I gave a demonstration yesterday with some old Argomite in a laundry and the job was excellent but I did not get an order simply because this fellow knew the laundryman who had used 45 bags of Argomite and it was no good. What do you want me to sell and to whom when I can't get the stuff? WASHINGTON HAS NOT GOT THE FACILITIES OR THE ABILITY TO PRODUCE A UNIFORM PRODUCT and therefore if we are to remain in business ARGOMITE MUST BE MANUFACTURED HERE.

"In so far as their success is concerned, are you of so little intelligence Lou, that you can't figure that less than two carloads in a month after five years of business is horribly rotten? I know how much that

$1,000 is worrying them. They have no market for the stuff and no car-load consumers and never will have.

"We have a letter from the American Textiles Company in which they ordered 200 bags of Argomite to be delivered at the rate of 15 bags a month. Well, we wrote to them and they answered that they have discontinued its use. I think they paid 10 cents a pound for it.

"Glover told me that Fels offered Barton $50,000 for the formula and that was all. No royalty or anything. The company could go hang. So don't get so excited about their prospects and another thing, please wake up and look at our side. To hell with their side. I want to remain in this business and develop it to the place that it deserves.

"So far, (we) have invested $12,000. I want to safeguard my family and your family and not bear them down with a crushing load caused by either deliberate crookedness or incompetence. For Christ sake wake up. Let Barton invite me to the board of directors meeting. I just dare him to do so.

"But I have decided that I am through. The test that I made today of this last shipment has definitely proven to me that they are deliberately out to kill me. I am going to take it up with Herman to find out if he can get anything out of them.

"I will send Barton a sample of the insoluble precipitate and (ask) what is he going to do about it. In the meantime I think I'll have recourse to law and you can go and sympathize with that bunch of incompetent jackasses to your heart's content, knowing that you have done nothing to try and protect our investment, when you being on the ground floor and a so-called business man could have done so.

"I am sorry Lou, old chap, that I am so damn frank in my remarks to you, you know I don't mean a word of it, but it came out as only the bursting of a damn will finally do. This last load of *drek* (junk) did the trick. Very affectionately yours, Dave"

He also writes Barton. "It may interest you to get the following comments on the last two shipments of Argomite that you shipped us.

"The Argomite C that we received on March 8th formed a good jelly and gave us an emulsion which released our standard amount of oil at a concentration of .00083 in one minute. At a concentration of .001, it released a standard amount of oil in one minute and twenty seconds, which we consider a fair proportion. This, however, does not come up to the standard of the original C we received in September (and) is one-half as effective as laundry 'Oakite.'

"The four bags we received yesterday, for which we are enclosing a check, we have the following comments to make: Jelly, good; a large insoluble scum formed in dissolving two grams of Argomite in one liter of water. The weight of this scum is over 5%. The emulsifying qualities of this Argomite is the worst we have had since you have shipped us any stuff. At a concentration of .001 it released a standard amount of oil in forty seconds, less than one-half of even the last shipment of C and one-third as effective as the old C. The other concentration of .002, at which all Argomite that we ever had would hold oil in emulsion for over three minutes, this wonderful product that you sent this time released the standard amount of oil in one minute, fifteen seconds.

"Kindly advise us what we should do with these four bags, two of which have been delivered as part order of ten, and two of which we still have on hand. Kindly note we are sending a check for same. A reply will be very much appreciated, giving us your specific comments. We are enclosing a small sample of the stuff."

March 15, 1929

Just a few words. A Mr. Shigo from Freeport, Pa. just stopped in to see me. He has the agency for Argomite for that little town. He has no contract or anything else. He bought a few empty cans from me for his use. He buys just what he needs. One bag at a time and he pays 6 cents a lb. for it. I, who must buy a half car minimum, get not a cent reduction. Think of that in connection with your friends Glover & Barton.

The last order I got was so rotten that I haven't got the nerve to go to the laundry that just got the 10 bags. I was supposed to re-demonstrate it there as it is the new stuff at one cent higher. It must be from the same load of stuff that I got here, and if it is, 'Good Night.' Well old chap it is good night. Next week I'll see Herman B. (Barryman) and see what recourse there is. Otherwise phooey $12,000.

March 15, 1929

Dear Dave,

Your long and very scorching letter reached me at a time when I simply had to get thru with the last returns, My helper Segal, who has been working for me three days a week for ten dollars disappointed me this week, and I (am) half dead. To-day is the last day and I must finish the job.

But I just couldn't work without reading your letter. No, Dave, old top, I am not in the least sore at the way you have jumped on me. I do know that you have received a rotten deal. But what could I do about it? I could have called Barton a liar and a damn incompetent and a crook and one who knows nothing of his own business, and then I should have received a coupla kicks in the pants. As it is, by soft-footedness, I still have in the reserve the kick which I can call for at any time.

From your letter of this morning one might think that it is in my power to ameliorate your condition and I refuse to do so. I feel it very much in my bones that appealing to Green or the other directors over the protest of Barton is a waste of energy and more than that, suicidal. Of course, when everything is all out and lost, then I shall be quite pleased to go over to Barton and collect that kick referred to above. At least I shall have the pleasure first of having told them all to go to hell to their faces.

To read your letter one might believe that I am very sympathetic with the Argomite Industries but you were here yourself and did all the kicking in person. What has it got you? You yourself admitted that you didn't expect anything but a refusal yet you raise hell with me because I didn't get it approved.

I don't know just what it is that you want me to do. Get you an audience before their board? I suppose that can be arranged. I could probably tell him that you want to put the factory moving proposition up to his board yourself. I seriously doubt that it will get you anything unless Barton agrees, and you will never get anywhere with him with strong arm tactics. After all, Barton is Argomite and without him they don't know anything about it.

If Barryman is willing to help raise the money for a factory why is it so all fired necessary to take the plant over there? Why can't you make your own Argomite for your own consumption and the hell with Washington? Of course, I am now guilty of the same thing that you are – *reden on dem baale bos* (talking about the boss behind his back).

If Barryman demands such an agreement before he budges, then that is a different story. It strikes me tho that Barryman is leading you by the nose plenty. Every thing he wanted from Barton, so far, he got.

I cannot shut my eyes to Barton's side of it in this moving business. Neither can I call him a liar when he tells me that he is well satisfied with the progress of the company and in no rush to turn the whole thing over to you. Maybe he is bluffing, but in a bluffing game the man in a hurry loses. And I doubt, that after you got such an agreement, Barryman would go thru with it anyway. His next demand is the formula, mark my word.

You tell me that Washington is incompetent and not capable to make a good uniform product and want me to make them agree with you. They won't do it, so what else is there? I'll see Barton to-morrow about the four poor bags and see what he has to say about it. I'll ask him about your appearance before his board of directors.

About your other letter, the one in re your giving it all up, I have to think that out. It seems to me that you should try to stick it out as long as possible even on pedal basis. Something might turn up. Now it might not be a bad idea to see what Rokeach has to offer for it. Maybe there are competitors of Rokeach who would be anxious to put out a good product under a Kosher label. When it comes to dropping out there is nothing to gain by a hasty exit. As to transferring the stock of empties you have to Barton, there isn't a chance if you antagonize him, whereas he might take it *a mit gutens* (with good relations).

And that brings us the question of the corporate proprietorship. What do you mean by saying that the company is a corporation all done up prettily. I have no knowledge of the papers having ever been filed for it. As far as I know you are operating as a de facto corporation but I don't know what that will mean if the thing busts up before it has the chance to become a legal corporation.

I think you should inquire carefully as to all about it as we have troubles enough without having to be personally liable for the remaining debts.

Celia doesn't know much about what is going on, and I see no advantage in having her worry about it. She already begins to feel the thrills of being a member of this gang, poor thing. I have been giving her two hundred a month or rather fifty a week but I am already three weeks behind and the account is flat.

The other day my bank, for the first time that I know, charged me three dollars for a new check book. Maybe it was on account of the fact that the thousand I borrowed for my furniture had to be renewed a couple of weeks ago. But I mustn't bother you with my worries. You have aplenty of your own.

"Just finished a letter to Dave and just had that wonderful talk with you over the phone," Louis tells Celia on the same day. "I am so glad you called. I wanted to hear your voice as I am quite some depressed. Guess it is strain from the heavy tax work and worries about Dave, together with your absence. I know that I miss you very much. So far I haven't touched a dish or a piece of food in the house. I haven't even wanted to be home at all. Funny, what love will do, isn't it.

"And I do love you, darling. It seems so foolish and unnecessary to say it for you know full well that I love you honey, don't you? Now I want to go home and close my eyes and imagine that you are in the next room rushing to get undressed before I can come in to kiss your little pretty you knows. I guess it is the accumulated missing of you that makes me so depressed this evening. But don't you let any of that interfere with your good time.

"About your selling the rights, I suppose that is all right. Perhaps it was just as well, not to borrow more, altho I feel that someday that stock will be of material help to us in making life happier in so far as money and an income can make life happy, which by the way, is quite some. But we owe plenty now and it is just as well to pay off some of the debts before going in deeper.

"Cities Service has been split four for one and we now have forty shares instead of ten, that is we will have as soon as we pay for them so shall say good nite, friend wifie darling, and hope that you'll come

485

home to daddy early next week. But don't change your plans on my account. I want you to have all the fun you can while you can and don't
worry about me. I'll appreciate you all the more for having missed you.
Always your beloved husband, Louis"

"Honey, dear," wrote Celia, also on the 15th. "I sold 60 rights for
$600 and turned the money into 40 shares. The VP suggested I do it now.
He said it might go up another point but he wouldn't bank on that. He
said $10 a share is nothing to cry about and since I was lucky coming
out at this time, I should be very happy with the results."

On the 16th, in a long letter about the busy tax season, mother's
day, and missing her, Louis mentions the Argomite business to Celia in
passing. "To-day I had a long conference with Barton and Glover and
the result is nothing more than it was before. But one never knows what
may yet happen." He is more excited about her pending return than her
one-hundred eighty dollars extra profit from the sale of the options.

> March 16, 1928 (really 1929)
>
> Dear Lou
>
> Just got your long letter and will answer a few questions. The
> reason we must have the factory here and a complete shutdown
> in Wash. is this. If as Barton says he makes a key product, then
> we are always at his mercy if he should ever want to sell us out. If
> he can still make Argomite in Wash., we are in the same boat as
> at present. At least we must know that no other Argomite is being
> manufactured anywhere else and that only we get the key ingre-
> dient. I now believe that if we manufacture the stuff here, I'll find
> out exactly what it is.
>
> 2nd. Knowing what you do now and who the men are that
> are at its head in Washington, would you ask your friends to in-
> vest $50,000 in it if you were always at the mercy of an unknown
> product in Washington? Your own answer is sufficient to explain
> Barryman's attitude.
>
> In re my selling. Sonny old chap, I have not yet become a gyp
> salesman. I am not interested in selling an article that I know will
> not be delivered as per sample.
>
> 10 bags were sent to one of B's laundries. If it is like the four I
> just got, I am going to return it and I am thru anyway. Don't talk to

Barton about my empty boxes as yet. If I don't get an audience with their board I am going to institute suit at once. Think it over. Dave

On Sunday, March 17, 1929, Louis writes Celia. "Dearest, Just a word. Got your Special Delivery letter and was overjoyed at the news that you are coming home to-morrow. You know what the Bible says, honey. 'And the Lord saw that it isn't good for man to live alone, so he made a woman for him.' But the Bible forgot to say what the man should do if his wife goes away to see her folks. I guess it would have said that he should follow her."

That day, Louis also writes Dave. "I would have written to you yesterday but I wanted first to test the sample of the stuff you sent to Barton which he turned over to me. He said that he had tested it for emulsion and found it to be good. I know what you mean now. I heated some of this Argomite and there formed a white foam on top. I ladled off this foam and it has dried out powderish to-day. I am going to present it to the doc with both our compliments, and would he please stuff it down his throat. Barton claims the scum does not matter. But you say it does, so then what?"

Barton made it clear that moving the plant to New York was out of the question. "He said no amount of money is able to compensate him for the continuous wrangling and worry that he has been having from New York, and were it not for the fact that we are in it for heavy money, he would advise you to drop Argomite and forget about it. All of which is blah blah. He is now (hiring) a chemist to test every batch before it is distributed.

"The doc insists that you are the only one to complain. Chicago is supposed to be quite a heavy user and has never made any complaints. Glover tells me the Chicago guy is negotiating for some sort of a buy out and says (he) asked him what sort of investment we have and Glover told him about $20 or 25,000.

"As to what now, I'll be darned if I know. If you could drag along and make a living out of it why then I would say go ahead and drag. Close up shop and store away your equipment. With no overhead you should be able to knock out a living. Somebody might like it and want to come in with money. It is bad any way you look at it. Maybe the advent of this new chemist will improve the quality of the stuff."

"I talked privately with Glover and he (is sore at) the doc for having sent him down to NY without telling him that the stuff had been over fed with C. Financially he is not interested in Argomite and I believe in a short while he may not be with them anymore.

"Miss Crowlin lives at the Raleigh Hotel and (I) may go up there and have a long *schmues* with her next week. I should be able to learn more of the weight the board has with the doc. I doubt very seriously that any amount of pressure will get the board to countenance the removal of the factory to New York. Barton tells me that they had offers to turn the factory over to others at a guaranteed yearly minimum net of fifty thousand and the Board refused. No doubt Hooey, but so he tells me. All the officers and stockholders are local people and they would hardly want to lose touch with the factory.

"I asked the doc for a reliable method of testing the stuff and he says he can give you none excepting to advise a working test. I know it is a lot of trouble but when it becomes a matter of in or out, more trouble should be expected.

"I washed my silk scarf this morning in a solution with your sample of Argomite (and) I thought it was pretty good.

"About that guy that has a sub contract to sell at the same cost as you, I don't see why you should object to that. Barton told me of that before I got your letter. He said they no longer give out the sort of contract that we got. They are making agents without any contract whatever to sell in uncontracted territory. They can cut them off at any time and no comeback. You can make some demands even tho you don't get anything for them.

"I don't know what else I can say about this. Glover has promised if Chicago means business, he'll try to make a good deal for us. I told him he wouldn't lose by it himself. So we wait."

March 18, 1929

Dear Dave,

I just reread your letter (dated March 16) and I am struck with the tone of it and particularly the failure for the first time that I can remember to say something by way of love or regards at the end of it. It seems for all the world that I could be doing something about the Argomite mess and am deliberately withholding its doing. Why damn, Dave, I'm getting sore myself now. What in Hell do you think I can do to Barton or to any of them? (Placing the factory in New York under Dave's supervision would require disclosure of the formula and that is something Barton would not do. Louis said he could understand Barton's position.)

You have now talked yourself into really believing that I am in sympathy with that gang as if there were any sense to it.

Tell me definitely if you are prepared to make a definite and for all time break with the Argomite crowd, and if so I shall proceed in the sneakiest manner possible to gather up a meeting for you before the board of directors and then we shall see what that will do for you. But remember that I have warned you that such action will mean a complete break as I cannot conceive any good results for us in strong arm methods with the doc.

He has the formula and no one else and you cannot compel its disclosure. He must manufacture his key ingredient somewhere (and) there is just the possibility that the key ingredient cannot be jazzed with. After all we don't know what it is and can't say definitely whether or not he could gyp you on that.

Louis then presented a grievance of his own. Celia had gone to Newark a few days earlier to attend to the bank loan for her stock. Since she no longer lived in Newark, the bank had begun not to like it. She was homesick and Louis had to work nights anyway.

Celia was asked to call and visit Dave as a surprise. She did call on Sunday but said, "his tone was so chilling and absent his customary cheery greetings and *schmendricky* (prickly, difficult) names, she decided not to go. Of course, I told her that you were no doubt worried about your business or other matters. Your tone must have been very cool indeed, as she felt you didn't want her to come up. Of course it doesn't matter much but it hurts me especially after the tone your letters have lately taken. I am telling you all this just because we are such friends. Celia was very much disappointed after talking with you, as she knows nothing of what is going on here excepting generally that things are rotten.

"Anyway I'm glad I told you as I feel better about it now, altho I did have strict orders from Ceal not to mention it to you.

"Well, that will be all for now. Don't think all this trouble is apple pie to me either. I am very much afraid that nothing can come of any suits at law as you have the business of proof and you better discuss this at length with good counsel before you go ahead with it.

"I got to leave now and do so with the same love and affection as ever despite the coolness of your last letter to me. Your buddy, Louis"

March 18, 1929

Dear Louis,

Got your letter and a wonderful one from Barton in which he calls me a liar. So be it. I saw Herman B. and he tells me that Barton can now not break the contract. We remain in, as we can prove that we were unable to perform because of him. The Chicago thing might be a solution. Herman is writing to Doc asking him just what he will take for the Argomite Industries as I have two real prospects who are anxious to buy out the works.

In re the rotten stuff, I am going to try it out in a laundry and see what happens. The tests here in the office show it be the rottenest stuff that we ever got. Play along with those bxxxxxds and humor them along. I am closing up shop this month and am abandoning my boxes. You may ask Barton if he wants to buy them to apply them on my account as I intend to keep on selling Argomite till Hell freezes over and to hold him responsible for the stuff that I get. He sent ten bags to one of the laundries. I am going there tomorrow and see what the results are. If good, then O.K., if no good then I will shoot the junk back on his hands.

Now that I feel assured of the strength of my contract I feel better, and I start out selling again, and collecting evidence. I want to keep in this outfit even if Chicago does buy (it) out. But that is yet to be seen. So will close then with love, Dave

March 19, 1929

Dear Louis,

I am dictating this letter to my former stenog. who for lack of a typewriter is writing it to you. For some unaccountable reason I have suddenly been put to bed again with a peculiar attack of the grippe and I am therefore a horse from combat.

Dave's doctor told him he was sicker than he thought and pre-scribed at least two days bed rest. He then addressed the matter of Celia, saying he was hurt to find that she was in town and did not call until Sunday.

"I figured that our relationship was such that it was Cel's duty to have called me up the minute she came to town probably before she even called her own sisters." He denied his voice was cool. "But she told me that they had started out on Saturday to come to our place and that a spring broke on their car. I was surprised that she had not called us up before they started. And when she told us that she had company from New York, I still figured she could have come down as she prom-ised to, and we waited for her, breaking an engagement to do so. How-ever, clear from your mind any question of lack of affection between me and you.

"First, however to business. Your letter and Barton's attitude defi-nitely settles the fate of the Argomite Corp. of New York. It is and al-ways will be impossible to ever interest capital to take over my business. However I will try to hang on for the next two or three months, if pos-sible, to see whether the Chicago offer comes through or one of the two deals I have pending here in New York.

"I am going to move over to Barryman's loft at the end of this month and next week I will advise you whether I want you to ask Barton if he wants to use my empty boxes. If he does not I will abandon them. The few full ones I will keep in Barryman's loft. All my bags will therefore be handled through a storage warehouse.

"You see, Lou, you are unable to know what a test is. If you have any more of that Argomite I sent to Barton, go down to Tech H.S. some day to the chemical lab, and take a teaspoonful and dissolve it in a 1,000 cc flask. Bring it to a boil and then fill the bottle with water. When it gets cold, look through the bottle and you will notice an undissolved flocculent white mass floating on top as well as on the bottom. I actu-ally weighed it twice by pouring the whole mess through a weighed filter paper. I have an accurate scale here from Barryman that is ac-curate to .0001 of a gram and the precipitated and undissolved matter amounted to over 5%, which is a terrific amount of dirt in a so-called soluble product.

"I saw Herman Barryman and he advised me that he would take

up the matter with Barton personally. Well, that matter is settled. I hope we can get back to work by the end of the week and see if we can still save our skins."

March 20, 1929

Dear Lou,

Got your other letter today. Am still good and sick, but because I am away from business, got an order for ten new bags.

With regard the returned sacks, I did not examine them as they were shipped direct. The bags which are dirty and wet and can't be used, naturally I don't expect credit for. I will only give credit for those that are accepted by Washington.

I am sticking along as I advised you and will let you know next week about the boxes.

March 21, 1929

Darling David:

I am awfully sorry that you should have developed into a horse of combat just at the time when you can't afford it. I do hope that you will snap out of it even sooner than you will.

I guess there is nothing more to be said on the subject of that little tiff we had as your explanation is accepted at face value in view of the fact that I know something about peculiarities of sensible women. I think you know something about it too.

I would suggest that you write Dr. Barton the same thing you told me regarding the credit on bags. Glover said that he is not showing these bags to me because he does not want to give credit, but merely to show me the sort of trash that you returned as usable bags. He of course doesn't know that these bags were not examined and shipped by you.

March 29, 1929

Dear Lou,

Still in bed. Wanted however, to advise you of the ten bags of Argomite sent to a laundry. This laundry originally used 15 bags six months ago, found the stuff O.K. but the price too high. In December when the price came down they ordered 25 bags

in December & 25 in January. Both of those two loads as you remember were rotten.

After the general mix up on Washington and the raising of
the price to me I used good salesmanship & sold him ten more
bags of the new stuff at 7 and a half cents. This ten bags he got just
four days before I got the four bags about which I complained to
Barton. Barton called me a liar, and told me that the only test is
in the wash wheel. Well, this laundryman used ten of them in the
wash wheel and he reported to Mr. Barryman that it was rubbish
and that he wants no more even at 7 and a half cents. Ask Barton
what he thinks about that.

I may stick around in the Argomite business for a few more
months until I can find something else to do, but now I can no
more finance New York Argomite Corp. Please let a fellow know
what you are doing. The main thing, however, is keep well. This
is the first time I have been flat on my back for two weeks and
prospects do not look very pleasant. At that I may consider myself
fortunate as this particular disease might have lasted six months
and left me with a bad heart. I hope with the help of God to be
well soon and then we will start our worries afresh.

In a condensed letter to the Newark clan, Louis writes again on March
31.

"Yesterday we went downtown at four thirty to get for me a haircut,
to make out my statements, and to adjust my brakes. We had to be back
home in time to eat supper and be downstairs to join our theater party
at 7:50. We stopped at the brake adjusters first and had them fixed up.
Time consumed – 20 minutes." When Celia remembered that the lights
weren't bright, Louis agreed to go across town to have them changed.
"Time out – one hour ten minutes.

"I then went across the street to my barber's and bought me a *yon-
tevdiker* (holiday) hair cut. Time out 20 minutes, money out 65 cents."
When he returned to the office it was 6:50 and he had no time to do
the billing. "Just one more hour in which to buy groceries, make supper, dress, eat, and be downstairs. The trip home alone at that congested
hour would take 20 minutes." Celia then blamed him for the lateness
of the hour. "The fact that all our time was lost in fooling around with

the lights which could have waited for another day didn't make any difference. It was my fault so I did what every wise husband should do. I accepted the blame and promptly forgot about it.

"I am right pleased to learn that you missed my weekly letter as I was under the impression that my failure to send one or two would be a welcome relief. You see, sis old top, you never answered them. From most people I write to I expect to receive an answer before I write another letter.

"The other night mother and Pauline were up to the house for supper. This was the first time that mamma was received as a supper guest at the home of her son and first daughter-in-law. It does seem much more natural for the son and the daughter to eat at the home of the mother than vice versa. *Nu, wos denkt ihr* (so, what do you think) it was quite a *shimche*. My wife was all excited and busy as a bee."

After a week of "racking her dear little *mindele* how to do the thing up the *brownste*, she made *schave* (spinach soup) that was a dream and fish and potatoes and dessert and coffee, and I tell you it was all just splendid.

"There was a phone call from the madam and she is getting all steamed up to raise hell with her innocent husband. Just because I am an hour and a half late. But even if it costs a *copp fun a herring* (head of a herring) I'm going to tell you about the soup. As I was saying that soup was cold *schave* but where I come from we call it *bottfene*.

"Friday nite papa wanted to know what it was about that soup Celia made that made mother rave so much about. Ain't marriage grand, Dear Sarah? But I may have to answer no to this last question of mine if I don't stop this at once and go on home."

> April 5, 1929
>
> Dear Lou,
>
> The sick man speaks again. I have been punished by an ailment for which I was not prepared at all, and God only knows when I will get well.
>
> Two weeks ago I asked Hymie to write Barton a letter and I don't know yet whether he wrote, but I do know Barton has not answered. Every bit of your judgment will be necessary if you have any, and if you haven't any, borrow some! (Dave now has two

interested parties with a half million or more each and wants to know if Barton would sell Argomite Industries Inc. And if so, on what basis.) Who are the outstanding agents?

We have no worry about Dixie Argomite. They have forfeited their contract years ago. Has Chicago lived up to their contract? Are there any other outstanding contracts? Don't tell Barton how much money there is involved. Merely get information. People here are interested enough to talk to me, but there is no use of my wasting their time if those idiots there want a million dollars for their plant.

However, don't forget to tell Barton that before I am finally through I will have talked to his entire Board of Directors in his presence and will have told them why Argomite Industries is the miserable flop it is today. It may be the only chance of recouping some of my losses. You can tell him that in a nice way, if I don't make a go of it in the next two months, after I am out of bed, his Board of Directors will know all about it, unless by that time they have gone bankrupt already. Well, old chap see what you can do about it. You should have no trouble getting some very definite advice as to a reorganization.

One day late to Newark clan, April 8, 1929

We surely enjoyed our company yesterday even tho the good wife did blue out something terrible after they left. It seems that I am not properly schooled in the art of greening out blue pipple. It all ended up by my forcing the little *veibele* to call up and talk to somebody at home. Please, Sarah dear, bawl out your sister for me and tell her not to get so blue just because she sees something in an encyclopedia that could happen to a person in your mother's condition.

Love to all particularly to my friend the best mother-in-law in the country. Louis

April 15, 1929

Dear Lou,

Thank God I am out again. Altho I am not yet particularly cured and probably won't be for some little time yet, I am able to do some real work again if there is any to be done, and in as much as the wife and kiddies need shoes occasionally.

Dave thought he knew more than the doctor. "So after one day extra in bed I went down town and almost wilted doing so. I of course came right back again." It was not the flu but rheumatic fever. "Now that is a pleasant little germ that starts like a cold and then progressively goes to the various joints, giving each an individual toothache action.

"For the first six days it got steadily worse until I was in a limp heap in bed with a pain from one hand right thru the shoulder thru to the other hand. The real danger was that it might affect my heart and lay me up for six months or so. However, thank God the doctor caught it in time."

On his first day out he went to his favorite laundry that was buying 50 bags a month. They said the Argomite was no good and getting worse. They needed to use so much at 6 and a half cents that their costs had gone up $75.00 a week. That finished the laundry business. While he sold 40 bags of Argomite over the phone last month, his real business was finished. It was possible he could make $25.00 a month with phone orders but needed to find other work.

"Mr. B. suggests that I try and build up an accounting practice again here, but how can you do that when you know nobody? Anyway I don't know what is going to happen.

"It is funny what the jackasses have done." The large group that was interested in buying the Washington operation lost interest when they tested the inferior Argomite Dave had recently received, as opposed to the original Argomite that was now gone. "I tell you Louis, that the Washington gang are downright crazy if they don't grab at even a straw, for they will never get a nickel on the showing that they have made, and frankly I don't know what is keeping them out of bankruptcy.

"Boy you don't know what it means to be flat on your back for a month with the knowledge that you have a business that is petering out on you and wondering how long it will be before you get out. Well I hope things will take a turn for the better.

"By the way, please find out why Wash. is not paying the $200 to Dr. Collier at Columbia for the work that he did. He has been calling up steadily and it is now over three months since he did the work."

April 16, 1929

Dear Lou,

My business is now all over, so you do not have to pay any further attention to Barton. You can now tell him to go to Hell. He can do us no good any more and can do me no harm either. So that's that.

Now you might be able to do something heroic. (He wanted Louis to apprise Grant of the situation. Three groups of investors examined Argomite, found it not uniform, and dropped out.) Tell him that Barton is absolutely an incompetent man and an *impudent liar*. I want you to show Grant how completely Dr. has the board flimflammed. That a laundry that used over 200 bags in five months time, the last at 6 and a half cents a pound, found the stuff to be too expensive.

There may be a solution. If the board realizes this truth, they can see that they are on the verge of disintegration. I would suggest two things. One is that the offer of Chicago, if they offered anything at all be grabbed, as such an offer without doubt means the shifting of the factory. The other solution be that they throw Barton out of the organization and let me get a crack at it, for I know a damn sight more about the stuff than all of the gang there. I can prove that the stuff was deteriorated and that is why I had to practically lose my shirt.

I am leaving this to you. In the meanwhile I am looking for a job and I wish you would send me a good copy of the report we wrote on J.B.S. I might use it. With loads of love & kisses, Your buddy, Dave

April 18, 1929

Darlint Lou,

Got your nice letter today and am writing to you at once. I am still fighting. You know that accountant Hoffman, well his friend is the accountant for Brillo. There is a possibility that Brillo might be interested in putting over a new line and inasmuch as they have the entire distributive field all ready, it would be a matter of small moment for them to put Argomite across, probably under their own name. All this is in the strictest QT. Hoffman and I are going to sign up some agreement between us and we are going to try and get an option on Wash, or agree to have them make us their agents to negotiate this deal. I am going to let you be the goat-between and see if maybe we can hatch something out of this mess.

I am still very much in earnest about the letter I sent you yesterday and you should be able to convince the directors that the fault of the failure of the company is in their president. It is a long gamble, Louis, but we have nothing to lose by it, and the one chance in a thousand may come thru.

April 18, 1929

Dear Dave,

I have received your letter and have been worried over it ever since. Your two propositions to the Argomite Industries don't seem to have much chance for success. Particularly does the possibility of the Argomite board firing Barton and putting you in his place, seem rather a far fetched grab at a straw. The other matter that of encouraging them to take Chicago's proposition seems a little more to the point. I don't hold out much possibility for this either. I think I shall rather first see Miss Crowlin at her home and see what I can get out of her as to where Barton stands with his board. I really think he has control and just kids them along.

Louis advises Dave to temporarily remain a salesman and fill phone orders. Another possibility was to contact N.R. Mass, Vice President of the Auto-Strop Safety Razor Company with whom they did business years ago. Louis suggests sending a letter explaining why he is no longer in the DC practice, as people don't have much faith in a man out of a job. "This is a very large concern and should have a place for a man like you. Your Washington calling card with my name on it will get you an interview."

Herman Barryman sent Louis a copy of an option agreement re: Argomite. Dave writes on Erev Pesach, April 24, 1929:

Darlint Lou,

You have gotten by now the letter from Herman with the agreement to be signed by the Argomite Co. If they are not altogether crooked, then they can have no objection at all to signing this agreement and with that in hand we can go ahead and talk to our parties here. At any rate, I had a long talk with Alex. Hamilton Inst. and they are advising me how to go about getting something else to do, but they tell me to be sure and sue Wash. even if I only get a judgment. This will protect my interests for all time and they won't be able to gyp me like they did the Detroit gang and the Cleveland outfit.

I will admit that you might have some selling to do, particularly on the lowest figure to them and the highest rate to us. You might as well talk to them pretty openly if they start talking in the millions, that they are crazy. But make a stab at it and see what happens. Anyhow the next move in this little game is now up to you…

"I got your letter and note what that Bxxx said," Dave fumes on April 29th. "So that lets the whole thing out. I won't introduce anybody to them, for altho you might still think that Barton is honorable, I KNOW different. You have so far not gone to see Grant (or) done several things that I wanted you to.

"In re Washington being up to production, that is a lie, for Philadelphia bought a car and I bought a half car, which they don't get now, and Kansas City is also all the way out. So that ends this chapter. I must sue therefore in order to protect myself even a little.

"Coming back to the Mass outfit (N.R. Mass, of the Auto Strop Safety Razor Company, mentioned earlier). The more I think it over the better I like it. (If) you send (Mr.) Mass a letter (and) he answers you with a definite affirmative, alright. If he says that he needs no-one, you lose nothing and I gain the same amount."

"Just a few words to advise you of the latest developments," Dave writes the next day, "and to put you wise to the law in our case. I just had a conference with Herman and this is how we are to proceed. We here owe Washington $1,000. This money they are not going to get yet awhile if ever.

"He tells me this. If I sue them now, they might beat the case. If we win, we get nothing except a lot of satisfaction. If they want the $1,000, then let them sue me and then we can file a countersuit. If they sell out, then we can file an injunction on them preventing the sale and sue for their breach of contract etc.

"So at any rate, I will continue to sell Argomite as I get orders, and the next move is up to them. They may go to Hell in five counties. I am thru trying to interest capital for them now.

I filed an application today with Pace placements agency and am going to start my personal selling campaign within the next few days. Have you got use for a nice safe file with insides that cost me $140.00 complete? What can you offer?

Well Pesach is on the wane, What will happen before next Pesach? We are after all very small pawns in the hands of destiny. *Nu*, old chap, we'll close with the best of love. I am your buddy, Dave"

On May 2, 1929, Celia received certificates for 140 shares of the Bankers Indemnity Insurance Company to be exchanged for stock of the American Insurance Company. She was asked to endorse the certificates and take a special note of Certificate at $498 for 100 shares."

"I am having simply a wonderful time here," Dave writes in another undated letter. "Practically nothing to do, only writing letters for jobs and as yet getting no replies. Hope that something turns up. It better.

"I am selling a little Argomite. That is I am filling orders. I am not going out on the street and hunting up orders, (as) I have no money to buy any more. I am ordering just as an order comes in and trying to borrow it from J.B. and hocking the account for it. If I had a leeway of say 20 bags, about $240 for 30 days, I might be able to peddle it for a while, but I have not got that sum of money so what can I do?"

Dave met a man at a chemical show who knew all about Barton. "He knows that he built a plant in Apollo Pa. to make that cleaning powder. You see what the bastard did, Lou? He is making and selling Launola and probably several other cleaning powders in different parts of the country at a reasonable price and just playing the Washington people and us agents as a bunch of suckers. I was surprised to learn how much outsiders know."

Dave asks Louis to send him accounting books from Pace and Pace to brush up on and says he will use some clients, including Louis, as references. Then adds, "Why don't you try and work out a system for the various grocers of the DGS and sell them a service for $10 a month. I believe that that is your best bet today. Your old buddy, Dave"

May 17, 1929

Dear Louis,

I got your letters, the one with the copy to Mass and the reply. The fact that there was no opening was no fault of yours and I am thankful just the same. But I want to tell you something right now that is absolutely on the QT even from Cel. (He then described his interview for an important position with the Shaw Walker Co., who were making a new type of visible record equipment he felt was superior to anything on the market.) I will be able to unite all of my work in devising systems and everything that goes with it. (Dave would take charge of different cities, receive a 20% commission and have a drawing account of $60 a week.)

That would still let me fill some small orders that might come in, as I still have over $1,000 debts to pay off which I would like to do without going bankrupt.

I am enclosing a letter I got from Studebaker Company where Glover sent the 200 pound bag for a sample and this is what they say. Show this letter to Glover.

The letter from Studebaker confirms receipt and their analysis of the sample. "We are attaching a copy of the report, and while we do not wish to enter into any controversy one way or the other we would like very much to receive any comments which you might wish to make. Very truly yours, Don O. Wilson (signed) General Service Manager"

Dave added a postscript: "Shoot some more envelops over. I am sending a copy to Glover. See what he says. Wash. wants me to send copies of Purchase Orders and letters of recommendation to Chicago. They can go to hell. I will not pay any attention to them.

Louis writes Newark his weekly letter on May 19, 1929. The Hamburg family has moved and Louis is chagrined that it will be harder to visit now. He now chides Sarah about her letters to them.

Just listen to this. I have a sister-in-law by name of Sarah Hamburg. She writes to my wife every day and keeps her informed and most up to date on all the scandal that happens around Newark. I suppose now we'll learn something of Caldwell, too. It is very nice of her and most appreciated. She has a wonderful memory for most every kind of happening particularly that which smacks of scandal, but she cannot seem to remember one rather – to me – important fact. That fact is that I am Celia's husband.

The regularity with which she forgets this is both astounding and amazing. I have refrained from mentioning this to you in the hope that she will one day remember it but finally it has dawned upon me that she either will not or cannot remember this, and I have begun to get sore about it. She forgets it when she writes to my wife, which as I said was every day, (but) she does have it recalled to her before she seals her letter.

You cannot help to remember that every letter without exception, I mean every letter goes on to say lots of things and comes to the customary 'love' close, without mentioning me at all. Then, as an afterthought, the thing starts up again and says, 'Love to Louis' by way of Post Script. Now, dear pipple, a Post Script, Mr. Webster says is, *A paragraph added to a letter after it is concluded and signed by the writer containing something omitted, or something new occurring to the writer.*

If this happens once or twice a month or even week I might not mind it, for after all who can be expected to remember all one's brothers-in-law all the time. But forget him every day is what I might very gently term a brazen chutzpa.

With love, affection, kind thoughts and kind wishes to everybody in Caldwell including also the Kansters, the Schiffs, and yes, even the Hamburgs despite the above *avle* (despair), I am as ever, Your son-in-law and brother-in-law (get that Sarah). Louis

May 21, 1929

Dear Lou,

Got the books yesterday, and thanks. I have decided to take that Shaw Walker job and I start in tomorrow. That allows me to take care of any sales of Argomite that come in and I may be able to pay for all of my outstanding bills. Then I'll be happy.

In filling out the application to the Shaw Walker outfit, I gave your name and Leo's name as references. I don't want the news broadcast. I am still in the Argomite business in so far as the world is concerned. It is a funny thing about this new deal. Nobody in the whole country knows anything about it (and it's) about 20% cheaper than Cardex. Well old man, be a damn nice fellow and lets not fall down on our correspondence, and lets keep on being buddies as of yore even if we are not biting out of the same apple.

"Today we step out into sassiety for the first time as Mr. and Mrs.," Louis writes his in-laws on May 26. "The banquet is a minor item. The thing that counts is our coming-out. My wife won't come right out and say so in so many woids but try and keep her away from the banquet. She is even going to taxi over to the Mayflower Hotel."

"I received your note book, for which thanks," Dave writes on June 2. "I just got a note from brother Barryman in which he advises me that there are certain forms (to be) filled out in re our corporation. In other words this outfit is a corp. and there is therefore nothing that we can do about it except think that it is to our advantage. It will therefore become necessary to re-file our tax return as a corporation and revamp our partnership return as well as personal returns. So please attend to this at once as I am filling out the franchise tax papers here in New York now. Herman so advised me.

"Tomorrow I am going out to start and see what can be done in re Shaw Walker. I am going to step into the water and see what makes millionaires of poor woiking pipples. Wish me luck.

"I am still selling a little Argomite, just what comes in over the phone and I am taking care of my liabilities, the small ones, for if I can clean up everything without going bankrupt it will be nicer I think. All right old chappee, get us straightened out for you are still the accountant, whereas I am a business man. Loads of love. Your buddy, Dave"

June 18, 1929
     Dear Lou,
     I just got your letter and want to answer you at once. Please be a man, and stop being a doggone *Kunilemmel* (jerk). I have finally discovered that rat poison is better for rats and sugar is only good for flies. For rats, sugar is no good. It makes them grow too fat, sleek and important.
     When I sent you the copy of the letter I got from Studebaker I sent a copy to Glover and told him that he probably sent them

the same 'junk' that I had been getting. So I got back a hot letter from Glover telling me that they never made any junk and that they objected to my calling it such. That the difficulties I got myself into were all of my own making and that if I persisted in writing to them my letters would not be answered.

I am not doing any business with them any more. In re this silver cleaning thing, the idiot can't understand English. I politely ask him what the hell is the matter with the latest rubbish as it won't clean silver any more. This same fellow has been buying 1 bag a month for the past 8 months and the last 4 months the stuff was getting rottener. So I promised him I would write to Barton and ask (for) an explanation.

For his benefit I wrote this letter and I got some reply today from Glover. He wants more information before he will let me have any dope. Well I won't even answer that. I have however a real kick and that is that they are using a very cheap bag today and 3 out of 5 bags come torn here and I have a damn lot of work fixing them up and sewing them as the express company won't take them. This is a pain in the neck to me.

When Glover came here he called me up and asked me 'if I wanted to see him.' I told him no, I had nothing to tell him. He did not say he had anything for me and as far as I am concerned he can go to Hell. I have lost my money. I can't lose more and I can't gain a quarter cent by having anything to do with him. I owe him no apologies and I want you to tell him so in very plain language.

Ida tells me that Barryman had a long talk with him and told him that they ruined the business and while Glover said the stuff is still O.K., B. told him a different story. Don't be a damn baby and beg for everything. If you want anything, fight for it.

This, I think, tells you just how I stand with those rats and I am asking you to do likewise. I may have some other news for you in a few days that may demand *ACTION* and *BACKBONE* not wheedling and whining. Hard words old scout but true. Think it over hard. Loads of love to Cel and you from your fighting buddy, Dave

July 1, 1929

Darlint Lou,

Sunday at Brighton means a lot in the lives of this gang. We are now full fledged members of the private beach where one pays to enjoy the business of a clean beach, clean crowd, and fewer crowd, where you get young working yourself to death in calisthenics and where one can spend a whole weeks vacation in an afternoon. After that, games, the leisurely reading of the funnies, more bathing, Esquimo pies, and home and a good supper. What more can a human being want or need, I ask you?

I only hope to God that I am at last on to something that will enable me to finally earn a living. In re Argomite, I got a letter from a lawyer wanting to sue me for the $200 due to Dr. Collier of Columbia University for the report on Argomite made at Barton's request. So they didn't have the $200 to pay him. I thought the bill was paid months ago. Anyway I told this lawyer who to sue, and let it go at that.

I told you that I might have some other news. Well it seems that I got another party interested in buying out the Wash. outfit and a letter is being sent to Barton by that parties' lawyer asking if perhaps and how much. This gang controls $58,000,000 of food products companies one of which is the Postum Cereal Co. Well here's Barton's chance if he wants it. I come in only as a possible employee if I want it and with a chance to sell my contract so I can make a little profit.

Alright then, long fellow we'll close with lots of love to Cel, and you can have what's left from your loving partner what's just recovering from a nice case of sunburn. Dave

ARGOMITE INDUSTRIES

(A Corporation)

Mr. David A. Glushak, July 1, 1929

Argomite Corp. of NY

Mr. Louis Grossberg,

Gentlemen:

Inasmuch as you have not fulfilled the terms of the License Agreement made by and between yourself and the Argomite

Industries (a corporation) and dated May 4th, 1928, and also appendages thereto dated October 15th, 1928 and February 1st, 1929, with particular reference to the stipulation regarding your purchase requirements and the payment of your account to the Argomite Industries, we hereby cancel the above mentioned contract, cancellation to take effect on September 1st, 1929.

This Notice of cancellation of your contract is given without prejudice to any claim of this company and it is not the purpose of Argomite Industries to now waive any rights it might have and it reserves the right to take such action as it deems advisable.

Very truly yours,
ARGOMITE INDUSTRIES (a corporation)
L.T. Barton, President.

THE ARGOMITE COMPANY OF NEW YORK
Distributors of Argomite,
Cleaner – Detergent – Germicide – Deodorant
Argomite Industries – a corporation,
July 11, 1929
Attention: *L.T. Barton*
Gentlemen:
In reply to yours of the 1st instant, we beg to notify you that since our failure to fulfill the terms of the License Agreement was caused by yourself, in that you shipped to us grossly inferior materials and made it impossible for us to comply with that agreement, any attempt on your part to cancel this contract will be resisted by us.

This notification is given without prejudice to any of our rights under the agreement or arising there from, and we do not hereby waive any rights therein.

Very truly yours,
ARGOMITE CORPORATION OF NEW YORK
By (Grossberg & Glushak)

July 12, 1929

> Argomite Industries, a corporation
>
> Gentlemen:
>
> Since according to your communication of the 9th instant, it is obvious that the efforts we have been trying to make to keep the Argomite products before the New York territory as far as may be possible in spite of the inferiority of the product will be fruitless, we shall of course cease such efforts and beg to inform you that you will be held strictly accountable for the breach of our contract.
>
> Very truly yours,
>
> THE ARGOMITE CORPORATION OF NEW YORK
>
> By (David Glushak)

At the bottom of this copy, Dave added:

Dear Lou,

> The ess of bees sent me a letter refusing to ship me an order of five bags that I gave them last week. The above is the answer for them to that letter as advised by Herman. Will write you a letter in more ditels soon.

July 20, 1929

> Darling Cel and you also Lou,
>
> I sent you the copies of letters I wrote to the Ess of Bees and to date I have had no replies. The fools have stopped selling me stuff and I could have sold over 15 bags already. But I canceled all orders and wrote that the stuff was spoiled and that until we got good stuff we would not ship out any more. I was particularly peeved when I turned back an order for 1,200 lbs. today. But that is that. I am definitely winding up the Argomite business for good. Can you use new visible binders? I have almost 1,000 ledger sheets unused.

Dave is having dental problems. He'll need to have two to three teeth pulled, and lose a gold crown his father paid $8.00 for in 1921. However, he enjoys his new job and adds, "I actually get a smile every time I make a demonstration.

"I just stopped to find out what else is doing. I noticed that the ocean still rested where it was yesterday, and suddenly a train crossed my point of view. A beautiful white yacht such as I expect to own someday just sailed by.

"Oh well, there aren't any more particular news. Annie Glushak went to Europe, Leo is going next month and he's still crying how broke he is. It's great to be that way. Meyer P has apparently made a killing on Wall Street at $15,000. Maybe we'll also dream such dreams. Who knows? So loads of love to you both. Your buddy, Dave"

"Three cheers for the DGS," Louis writes David on July 30. "There is an outfit that appreciates good work. I wrote a report for the President, Kay, that took him an hour and a half to read to the members, and you can imagine what it took me to write it.

"Anyhow when the enclosed letter came to me, it was ample repayment for all the work I did. I think more than anything the matter of my old wreck had to do with it. Both Kay and Vigderhouse have repeatedly asked me why don't I buy me a car. So I said that cars cost money and I can't afford to buy another. So he says one day, we'll have to see what can be done about it. (So) now I guess I gotta see about getting me another machine. Celia has often asked me to let her borrow on her stock but you know how I would feel about that. True what's hers is mine but I sort of don't want to use that money. Well, looks as if I shall have to do something now that those boys have worked me an increase. Hupmobile is coming out with a new $1,000 car. Maybe I can get a good deal thru Herson.

"Now as to the rush to write. Got a call from Miss Crowlin of the Argomite factory. It seems that a shake-up is finally due over there and a fellow by the name of John W. Terry in the Real Estate business who has an interest in the company, is due to take over the general management this Thursday if the thing goes thru.

"Miss Crowlin told me to hear what he has to say and to keep it in confidence. So, I went over to see him and he told me that Glover is no longer there. He says that he knows you got bad stuff and asks me these three things:-

"Assuming for the sake of argument that it is conceded by Washington that you got bum stuff, and (they) guarantee to give you a uniform product (and) remove Barton from control, do you want the contract reinstated? That is no. 1.

"Number 2, he wants a list of letters from your ex-customers stating just why they ceased to buy from you. He wants proof that you actually got bum stuff.

"No. 3. He understands that you owe them $1,000. He asks you to tell your story of how come you owe it and how come you don't pay it.

"He also would like to have you come up here and discuss things with him if you are agreeable. So I said I'd communicate with you and ask for (what) he wants to know. I think I can believe Miss Crowlin, and that a shake-up is finally in the brew. Terry looks like ability and money. On the face of it he seems to play square.

"I should suggest that you might give him what he wants if possible, so far as letters (are) concerned, and that you consult the matter with Barryman as to the desirability of getting the contract back. Terry says he is talking only on the basis of giving a standard product with standard merchandise.

"Write me a letter to forward to Terry. I asked Terry whether the change of management means the removal from control of Barton and he said it means just that.

"The madam is quite a help to me in this rush season. We have worked a good many nights lately. Am awfully sorry to hear about those bad teeth.

"Glad that you are so much enjoying your new job and I wonder what you could do with splitting the work as between part Argomite and part s&w if you decide to take it back. If the stuff is good, it should be possible to reinstate it in the laundries with a minimum of time wasted…"

Dave writes on August 13, using SHAW-WALKER letterhead, "As a correspondinger you are positively rotten. More than a week hath wended its way and no word from you. I will start and tell you the dope as I have it now. I tried to interest the two parties in this Argomite job and so far have not heard yet. I did hear that Barton offered Argomite to the Postum people last January and they turned it down flat. This friend of mine did likewise. Just why, my friend promised to find out for me.

"I took the letter I got from Terry over to Herman B. and he is still thinking on it. I think that we may sue now and try and recover whenever we can. It is impossible for me to regain my old customers particularly since that louse Glover refused to ship me stuff. That settled all of their hashes and I have not the time to try and resell them.

"In re the laundries, Mr. B. would not permit any further testing there for no money under the sun as he has no basis for their lasting under the new management. Maybe I can get Markel here to take a half interest in my business (but) I won't do a thing and from what he sells he gets half.

"Washington would have to advance me the stuff on 60 days and also advance some dough to start over again. Otherwise we will institute suit. If Terry wants to see me he will have to visit me here as I have not the means or the time to go to Washington.

"That's that. The month of August is approaching its end and I am expecting your coming here. It is therefore arranged that you spend a Friday, Saturday and Sunday with us. While I am not making many sales now, the future is bright."

> August 19, 1929
> Argomite Industries. Washington, DC
> Attention Mr. Terry
> Gentlemen:
> We feel, with you, that the various questions involved in the New York distribution of Argomite require a personal conference and we delayed answering your prior communication in the hope that our Mr. Glushak would be able to go to Washington to confer with you. It appears, however, that the pressure of other business will make this impossible for some time to come, and we would, therefore, suggest that one of your representatives, on his next trip to New York, call upon us to discuss the matter. If you will inform us of his coming, we will hold ourselves at his disposal.
>
> Your correspondence files should reveal the cause of our past troubles with your management; in effect the product had deteriorated to such an extent that it became impossible to secure any further orders except in isolated instances, and what few customers remained were lost through your predecessor's refusal to ship any further merchandise.

It is our intention to retain all our right under our present license agreement; we feel that the product has untold possibilities and your last frank communications lead us to believe that the present management not only understands the problems involved, but is capable of coping with them.

If, therefore, your representative will call upon us, we are sure you will find us more than willing to co-operate with you.

Very truly yours,

ARGOMITE CORPORATION OF NEW YORK

By President

August 21, 1929

Dear Dave:

In the rush of trying to get everything done before my leaving here to go North and elsewhere there seems to be practically no time left for my old buddy, but don't worry we will make it all up in personal contact. I just want to say that it will be impossible for us to see you Friday for we can't very well arrive at Caldwell at 6 or 7 o'clock in the evening and spend the evening with you.

I will call you up Friday night after 9 o'clock to tell you whether we are coming out Saturday or Sunday.

I have been considering whether or not it is wise for me to see Terry before I leave. I can't see any particular advantage, while there is the possibility of getting myself involved in commitments...

No date, copy of letter sent to Louis, on DC letterhead.

Argomite Industries, Washington, DC

Attention: Mr. Terry

Gentlemen:

Yours of the 29th is at hand. It is not our intention to indulge in recriminations. We simply wish to make our position very clear. We feel that the merits and demerits of the case cannot be omitted from any discussion. Any failure on our part to perform is the direct result of your own breach and we therefore intend to protect our rights in the matter.

As to any conference with you, we are willing and anxious to confer with you in New York City at any time; and in Washington at any time, provided we can be represented by counsel. Since however, the breach of the contract has been caused by yourselves, if we are to accommodate you by coming to Washington, we feel that you should be called upon to pay the necessary expenses therefore.

Very truly yours,

ARGOMITE CORPORATION OF NEW YORK

By Dave Glushak

(Handwritten at bottom)

Enclosed find a good knife. Price $1.00. Thought you'd call before you left. Love to Cel. Will write later. Dave

Sunday, August 31, 1929

Dear Lou, etc.

I was just on the verge of giving you a real *Alle boise chalimos* (bawling out) etc, for not having heard from you but your late letter calls for real congratulations and rejoicings. I am thrilled at the letter from Kay. For the first time since we were in business have we ever had our work approved at all. (Dave goes into a detailed discussion of cars and prices.) Do you really think that you should go $1,000 for a car? Chevrolet, Ford, and the little Whippet are truly excellent and $250 less. Even the Pontiac is a good buy.

Now as to the Argomite. It caught me unawares. The only thing I can add is this. I have a man who is anxious to float millions, (so) something may happen.

In re my coming to Wash. I have not time and can't do it. I might come on an excursion, altho this man of mine might go down there and look over the new situation. I can't see how I can go back into business now that I lost my money and it will take a large present from Wash. to rebuild the game now.

I have a suit on hand and may exercise it as soon as I feel I have some chance of getting it. Now the dogs have killed the balance of it by refusing to ship me stuff and I can't regain that without a lot of canvassing etc. I'll try and write an official letter tomorrow altho I think it best for brother Terry to visit me here. So old Jimmy *bull* Glover is out. Well he never did anything anyway and I think Barton's demise from the company may pep it up.

In re myself, things are beginning to shape up fine. I hope to start making a living soon again. I only hope we have turned the corner at last.

P.S. I have also the Dr. Rosenberg gang who wants to buy it as well as that letter I sent you with that other deal and which Barton refused to sign. Show that to Terry if you still have it...

For some reason, letters do not mention the October 29, 1929, stock market crash until January, 1930. The next letter is from Dave, Erev Christmas eve, December 24, 1929:

Dear Lou,

Very many apologiticals for not answering any sooner, but I was both busy and lazy. Thanks for the stock. I have tried to get a loan on it and I'll know in a few days. In re the extra share that can't be split, I suggest you hold it for a few weeks or so. They are going to exchange our stock for the new issue, four shares at $20 for one. Then you can let me have two of them. You know that makes our shares worth $80.00. At least that was one investment I made for both of us that turned out not so bad.

In re business, I've had a pretty rotten month of it, rather surprised me. But I am hoping for the future. I am getting old, young feller and in another month, please God, we will be married 10 years. A long time. I had hoped things would be different, but what can you *mach*. So we still pray and hope for the best and work like hell in the meantime...

Today. 3033 Coney Isl. Ave., Brooklyn, Jan. 5, 1930

Darlint Lou,

Once more we take the typewriter to hand and write to you. Your nice letter and your worries noted.

Howesomever, I want to talk to you about something else which will need your immediate attention and active co-operation.

Dr. Rosenberg called me the other day. He is the gentleman who has various people interested in our almost forgotten Argomite product. Well he now has a most definite proposition to offer.

I gave some of the Argomite to the president, the chief chemist and to the lawyer of a large concern having national as well as international distribution. These people were decidedly interested in the sample given them and are familiar with the story of the stuff here in New York and elsewhere.

They want to manufacture the product in local factories and other parts of the country and have the necessary money to advertise for an already established market. "They want the exclusive right to the formula and are willing to negotiate on the basis of a royalty only. They want to enter into a contractual agreement with the Argomite Industries INK. (to) sell them the formula for which this company will pay a royalty with a privilege or option to buy the capital stock of the company at a certain figure within a certain length of time."

Dave and Dr. Rosenberg want a minimum 12 and a half percent royalty as promoters of the deal and Louis is asked to negotiate with the board of directors. "As I see it, the Argomite outfit in Washington is now almost hors de combat and has neither the money or the guts to do anything. They need a new factory and therefore can't produce any decent stuff. They told me so when I was there. They are probably stumped now in so far as raising money is concerned on account of the Wall Street crash and money is not so free now for speculative purposes."

If this company approves the product, they can market it immediately and could use a hundred carloads a year just for cleaning buildings. Later they would expand its use.

"It means that you must arrange a conference with whatjuma-kolim, the manager and find out if he is responsive to the idea, and this time TRY and BE A SALESMAN. I think that this is the first real decent break that we have had to date. Everybody else we tried has made chemical analysis and have turned them down. This outfit is satisfied if it will clean floors and walls. And in that field alone there is enough use for the stuff to more than wipe out our obligations. The legal matters can easily be accomplished later. Lets get it off our minds at once one way or the other."

January 10, 1930

Dear Dave,

After quite a good deal of time expended and many confer-
ences held I did even better than I was commissioned to do and
the result is the Argomite crowd agrees to pay us a commission
of fifteen per cent on royalties and 10% on a straight sale. As you
requested I have had them make this up in your and Rosenberg's
names. They wanted to put my name in but I told them that the
name Glushak represents me too. This in reply to the query where
do I come in? I believe the letter as written is all that is necessary
to safeguard our interests.

Now there are several items to make clear to you. In the first
place, they will have to have some money consideration to clear
up their pressing and other debts since they cannot enter into any
agreement that does not allow for a payment of their debts. But
that, it seems, is more in the nature of something to be worked
out between the local and New York parties later.

I have told Glover that the next step will probably call for him
and Wagner to go to New York to continue the negotiations there.
Incidentally, Glover and Smith, who is now the manufacturer of
the product here, expect to be taken care of in this deal.

Let me know what is to be the next step in this Argomite
deal and don't delay as they claim to be in negotiation with others.
With best regards, I am, Your buddy, Louis

January 10, 1930

Messrs. David A. Glushak and L.B. Rosenberg,

New York City, New York.

Gentlemen:

Pursuant to action of the Executive Committee, you are
hereby advised that in the event you submit a proposition acceptable to the stockholders and the Board of Directors of Argomite
Industries, providing for the manufacture and distribution of Argomite products on a royalty basis by an organization of strength
and ability, then in that event on the actual closing of the deal, we
agree to allow you, during the term of such agreement, an amount
equal to fifteen percent of the new amount received by Argomite

Industries as such royalty and in the event a sale is by you negotiated, satisfactory to the Board of Directors and stockholders of
Argomite Industries, as to terms and responsibility of purchaser,
then in that event on the closing of such sale and the payment of
the sales price agreed upon, we agree to allow you a commission
equal to ten percent of such sales price, which shall cover all com-
missions incident to such sale.

This arrangement is proffered with the distinct understanding that it gives you no exclusive right of negotiation or sale and
with the further understanding that it extends to you no interest
whatever in any contract for manufacture and distribution or for
sale other than as such contract of manufacture and distribution
or sale shall have been actually negotiated and submitted by you.

Very truly yours,

ARGOMITE INDUSTRIES, INC.,

By: W.G. Grant, President

(No date)

Dear Lou,

A few words to advise you that I received your letter and the
signed agreement. I am going to get the wheels started at once
and we'll see what can be done. I note your comment that Glover
& Smith want to be taken care of. That will be their own lookout
entirely and if my opinion of Glover be asked I'll know what to
say. Don't forget I am after to look out for myself first, middle
and last.

In re the safe file, I am afraid I can't sell it. It contains my evidence against the Argomite Industries and I'll have to hang right
on to it until it is altogether settled. Will keep you in touch with
all developments.

January 14, 1930 (Annual birthday letter from Dave)

Darlint Lou,

By the time you receive this epistle you will have arrived at
a new milestone in your life's career. Another year has done came
and went and it is therefore with greater dignity and bearing that

you must carry your load of years upon your shoulders. Spread them there shoulders wide, for I have many many more years wishes on you to carry in the long to come future at least do a good job and carry happy and prosperous ones while you are at and about it. Them, sir, is the wishments of your far away partner.

The chances are that Celia will remember your birthday and she will give you a nice present and then you will undoubtedly retaliate by spending money on her and taking her to a show? Thus and so are happy things done.

In re our fortzun, Rosenberg suggests that you try and find out what is the lowest figure at which they will sell out entirely. Their old nice high figure is of course out as they themselves admit they are helpless. If they give us a bed rock figure, maybe we could agree to another little slice. We get 10% of the sale price. But if they give us a certain set figure at which they will sell, then we might try and get more, (like) 25% of the excess over and above their minimum. Try it out on Glover and see what happens.

"I met Dr. Dreyfuss of the West Disinfecting Company in re Argomite," Dave writes on January 24, "and gave him a pretty good sales talk. He gives no care what the stuff is made of as he does what it will do. I expect to meet the president of the above company within the next few days and he will then probably want to talk with the Wash. gang and if they can actually make the stuff and it is better than what they sell, they will be pleased to work on the agreement already suggested. They now sell a product just like Oakite all over the world and in large quantities, and they could simply replace it with Argomite if it did the trick. So you may hear from me more definitely very shortly or not, depending upon the trial they give some of the good Argomite I gave them. This Dr. Dreyfuss is the man who invented liquid soap and is a real chemist."

"In re Palestine," Dave asks about the imminent departure of Esther and the six children for Palestine. He understands it to be for financial as well as religious reasons and wonders why Pauline agreed to accompany them. "If I had all the money in the world I would not think of contributing even a nickel to such a venture. Well, Louis old boy, If he wants Pauline to go, he ought to pay for it." Harry was to join them after disposing of his business, which the stock market crash had made very difficult.

"In re other things. Here things are absolutely rotten and I don't know what to do. Prospects are beginning to look worse than ever and I am getting more and more discouraged in this job. How it will end, God only knows. Business generally is slow and companies are curtailing expenses. I am beginning to realize that after all, the life of the professional man is the best. At least he makes a living no matter what happens."

February 5, 1930

Dear Louis:

I met Mr. Marcus the president of the West Disinfectant Company this morning, his brother the VP, (and) the Doctor, who is the official chemist of the company, (and) we arrived at the following conclusion. I have arranged a meeting for the Washington representatives of Argomite to meet Mr. Marcus on Tuesday afternoon. But when they come here they must have the following information:

1. What about the formula? Is it secret or is it actually patented or patent pending? And such facts to substantiate either or the above facts.

2. If it is only secret, how has Dr. Barton been tied to prevent his divulging it to somebody else, or how is he stopped from going into a competing business?

3. Is the product non analyzable? I told them it was, but how do I know. In the meanwhile they are trying to have it tested and will know by Tuesday what the results are.

4. How are they going to take care of us? You can now tell them in plain language that we have not relinquished our contract with them; that they still owe us a plenty; and that as soon as they get some money we intend to fight for it. In plain suit we would sue for $25,000 but if they will consider settlement we would negotiate on the basis of 12 – 15,000 dollars. That will be to pay up our actual money losses and not other damage. This 15% commission they agreed to is purely as promoters of this sale, and tell them right now that if they sell out to some other company, we will stop them

from New York and New Jersey anyway, and that will be enough to put a crimp into any other type of sale they may have in mind. And if they go bankrupt, we will try and get the formula as our contract calls for. We have been advised by counsel that these are our rights and we intend to stand by them. So they will have to come to an understanding with you so that we will give them a release of our contract before these West people will do any business. Mr. Marcus is not interested in any law suits.

While I realize that they have no money, we can enter into an agreement that they can pay this debt to us from the royalties when they come, in certain installments but this agreement must be absolutely definite. You are the sec. of this corp. anyway and can act. I'll stand by any reasonable arrangement.

If the Washington crowd is prepared to divulge this information we are awaiting them on next Tuesday afternoon at 2:30. Otherwise we will call off the dogs and return to our policy of watchful waiting. I'll say this much, that if Washington Argomite consists of honest men, this is a real opportunity to put the proposition across. If they are going to try and bluff on it then they are licked from the start.

With the above parting words, old chap, get some action immediately. Lots of luck to you and Cel in your new apt. As ever your buddy, Dave

Thou Shalt Not Bear False Witness Against Thy Neighbor

February 11, 1930

Dear Louis,

Got your letter yesterday (and have) news for you which I am afraid actually cooks the goose all round. I met Dr. Dreyfus to-day and he had the sample of Argomite I gave him analyzed and discovers that far from being a non analyzable product, it is a most easy thing to analyze. Argomite contained 36% soap and some other common chemicals, some clay and some starch. Of course he did not try to put it together and see if he could produce Argomite. He is not interested in it at all. The point (is), it does not pay them to invest the capital and when it is a success, every other company will produce it.

On the face of the laboratory tests he thinks that Barton was simply a deliberate fake and he flamboozles the outfit into believing him. Of course it might have been possible to actually build up a very successful business, but we would never have gotten big, unless the name itself could have become so darn valuable, as for instance, the name *Gold Dust*. The product is both inferior and easily (duplicated), but the name is worth the entire fortune.

Barton has told me that there was no soap at all in Argomite. If that is true, then they really have something. Dr. Dreyfus is more than happy to be impressed, but being an old experienced chemist, and from Missouri, he wants to know specifically what is in the formula.

He would be willing to meet the gentlemen from Washington, PROVIDED AND IF THEY STAND PREPARED TO PROVE THAT THEY HAVE ACTUAL KNOWLEDGE THAT ARGOMITE CAN NOT BE ANALYZED. (IF) THEY REALLY HAVE GOT SOMETHING, then arrange for the best time to suit yourselves.

Other than that old chappie, there is little of newness here. Working like the devil and still trying to find the rainbow.

February 19, 1930

Darlint Lou,

I have scads of real information to write to you but I won't have time to spill it. Let Wagner know that a date has been arranged for Tuesday morning at 11 am to meet the Wests. I am enclosing the card of Dr. Rosenberg to attend the conference. There is nothing there for me anyway. Have them wire Rosenberg on Friday so that he can confirm the conference on Tuesday morning.

Have resigned with the Shaw Walker and have acquired me a new job as a controller of a chain store corp. of 50 stores. Will tell you all about it tomorrow. So lots of love (am not a millionaire yet). Yours as of always, Dave

Dave describes his new job to Louis on February 20, 1930

"I am betaking meself of the opportunity to let you (know) what has been transpiring here the past weeks." At Shaw Walker, things were going from bad to worse. Dave was worried about making a living. "So I started to look for something else and answered a scad of ads in the *New York Times*." The next day he explained his predicament and was offered the use of his office until he could find something else. All this he kept from Ida.

"Well the next day I walked into an employment agency and asked for a $5,000 job. Sure enough he hands me a ticket." However, that job was almost filled but Dave talked them into interviewing him anyway, and was able to convince them he was the man for the job.

"I reported to the office on Saturday Feb. 15, which by the way was our 10th anniversary, there was the job of comptroller of a chain store outfit with 50 installment Men's and Ladies stores all over these United States. I am to get $75 per week for the first three months and then after that some definite agreement. I have an excellent bookkeeper, two assistant bookkeepers, three comptometer operators, four record clerks, and five ledger posting clerks, besides stence, and multifarious and sundry other assistants.

"The job I got is to resystematize the whole accounting division and KEEP IT IN OPERATION. The first couple of days I was entirely in the middle of the ocean and floundering about (so) I started to look wise in order not to show my exquisite ignorance. Well old chappie, I do no sumpum. Things are beginning to open up and the old system mind is starting to click. I think that I have finally started up the steps to making a decent living." Naturally, two other jobs he had applied for contacted him. "When a guy is a multimillionaire everything comes his way. However, I'll stick to this job and see what can be done with it.

"Now, darlint Louis. Please send me the following books as I have not the dough to buy them and you are probably not using them anyway. I will really appreciate it."

February 22,

My dear Dave,

It surely was a fine letter, that one I just got from you yesterday. My sincerest congratulations and good wishes on your new incumbency, which I hope will shortly grow into something really worth while such as a presidency or something like that. And I am certain that you will do a good job as after all, your real ability is as a systematizer and there never was much of a chance in that line in this burg. I am only sorry that I could not be with you to help in the work of resystematizing. I think we two might have gotten far in straight system work if we only had the chance.

I don't seem to have much of any books left in my cases. I believe I sent you a number of them at one time.

As you probably guess I have been quite busy of late and a little desperate when I think that March 15th is so near. Last year I had Segal helping me in the closing rush but so far have tried to do without him because I can't seem to be able to spare his salary. But I guess I'll have to take him on next week.

Rosenberg will be in New York on Tuesday as scheduled.

Louis was so busy he forgot to remember Dave's anniversary. He also forgot Valentines Day, an unconscionable thing to do for a lover.

"I don't know whether I told you this before or not," Dave writes on March 3, "but with the help of the Almighty we ought to have another little daughter by the end of July. Ida is having a rather tiring time of it. (But) I have been standing it pretty good so far.

"Oh yes. Dr. Rosenberg told me that the fools and fatheads came to New York with no more information than I had, and instead of being able to talk formula or anything else, they simply wasted their car fare and there they were.

"In other words, altho they have a product that they might have made money by themselves if they had developed the business and the name, they have got nothing to sell. That then means the final end and finis to Argomite. So old chappie, we will call the dogs off.

"I had a hunch that I would hear from you very little until after March 15," Dave responds on March 27 to a letter from Louis, "and yet I don't seem to understand why you should have been so all fired busy. I wonder if you are not doing too much for your money. Mr. Barryman once gave me a darn dirty dig one day, when I told him what we did for our clients and how we were not remunerated for it. He made this wise crack. If your time is worth nothing, that's all you'll get for it. People pay what they think they can get away with and if you have time to give away, why they'll take it from you.

"Say young feller, you think you and I know accaynten. Well you don't know the half of it. You never saw so many statements in your life as I have to dig out here." He itemizes his work load in the next page and a half. The rest of the letter is small talk about having Louis' razor fixed and the weather."

April 1, 1930

Dear Lou,

Just a few lines to let you know that I remembered you before Pesach and would have written you even tho you owe me the letter.

You know Lou, old chap, you can do something nice for me. I have here a lovely chair and desk, but the office has supplied me with no sitzer on it, and it's both hard on the person and on the pants. I was almost on the verge of spending some dough on a nice leather cushion when lo and behold I remembered that there were two such in Washington, one of which I had used to such good purpose and for so many days. You know Lou, if you packed that cushion up and shipped it here, it would be almost like a breath from *der alte hein* (rear end) and bring back more and more memories. I wonder if you could do that. The rear begs for mercy.

May 14, 1930

Dear Dave:

Many thousands apologeticals. There is only one excuse I have for playing dead and that is the old worn down word 'busy.' The fact of the matter is that I have been rather burdened with this year's tax work (as) I tried to do most of my closings and tax returns without the aid of Segal – to cut expenses. The result has been the need of getting a few extensions and to submit my yearly statements as late as the traffic will bear. All of which means that you have been side tracked. The policy being to give attention in turn to those who holler loudest.

Things here are running along the same as ever, but as long as we manage to stay in good health we try to be happy. According to plan we expect to spend the last week of May in Newark. The madam has not seen her folks in six months, which for her is a very long time. I guess both of us have earned a good vacation. I shall call you at home when I get within calling distance of you. In the meantime do me the supreme favor of letting me take along what-ever junk you think you need. I was really afraid you wouldn't let me lug anything over to you.

The DGS politics are raging again and I should like it much better if I were entirely out of those politics. I try to keep neutral but my natural friendliness towards Kay makes me appear as siding with his group. I'll tell you more about it when I see you.

"Mr. Louis Grossberg," Dave writes on The Samuel Stores letterhead on June 21.

"The other day a letter addressed to the Argomite Corporation of New York, 36 East 12th Street, was forwarded to my home address. This letter was sent registered and when the postman handed it to Ida she noticed it was on an envelop of Louis Ottenberg, attorney. In order not to be annoyed with correspondence of this kind, Ida refused to accept it and informed the mailman that the corporation is no longer in existence.

"I do not know what Louis Ottenberg could have written, but I think it is of sufficient importance for you to go into this matter further. Ask Leo if it is advisable for you to go to Louis Ottenberg and ask him to forward all future correspondence to you direct as you were the Secretary of the old company, and in that way you will keep in touch with what is going on.

"This letter might have been a demand for the $1,000.00, in which case, of course, he can be laughed right out as having no claim. Then again it might have been a notification that the Argomite Industries are blowing up and advising us of certain rights. Whatever it might have been, I think it is advisable to be on the inside of it. Let me know what steps you intend taking with regard to this matter."

June 26, 1930

Dear Dave:

Your letter relative to the Louis Ottenberg letter (was) received. I discussed the matter with Leo and was informed to leave well enough alone. The fact is that I very much prefer not being mixed up in any possible litigation here in town. I am too close for comfort. Leo did express the opinion that Ida pulled a bone in rejecting the registered letter since nothing could be lost if you did know what they wanted.

Today I stopped around to Argomite offices ostensibly to say Hello. Here is what I discovered through the kindly information by

Miss Crowlin: Argomite Industries assets including formulae have been sold to a New York concern by the name of Quigley Furnace Specialties Company with offices somewhere in the neighborhood of 45th Street. What the consideration was, or whatever there may have been in the deal I don't know. The deal seems not to have been as yet completely consummated.

At present they are still loafing along in this plant making a little stuff for turnover sufficient to keep Smith, Glover, and Miss Crowlin going. I understand that in a few months from now they intend to move the plant to New York or New Jersey. I think also that the stockholders lost practically everything.

My suggestion is that you write a letter to Mr. Louis Ottenberg to the effect that it has just come to your attention that a registered letter addressed to the Argomite Corporation of New York was mailed by him and could not be delivered for lack of a proper address. Then give him the address of Argomite Corporation of New York and ask that the registered letter or any other correspondence be addressed there.

The possibilities are that Argomite Industries is serving notice on interested parties that a sale of its assets is being made and giving you the chance to make a claim or else hereafter hold your peace. What claims you are to make should my guess prove correct, I cannot tell you. You probably have to consult Barryman, Senior or Junior.

I hope that Ida is coming along as per and am looking forward to receiving a telegram notifying me of the birth of a little junior accountant.

"My first promotion came thru," Dave informs Louis on July 7, "and I believe that I am now starting to make a living for myself and family. The weather is lovely here and we are all having a wonderful time, with the exception of Ida. She is patiently counting days.

"Other than that, there is little to say. Business is simply rotten, and the more the Happiness boys talk of good times, Messers Hoover, Mellon, Lamont and Klein, the worse the market feels.

"By the way, did you do anything about the Argomite matter? Old man Barryman got nasty the other day and he and I are friends no longer. The SOB sends me a bill that his son sent him for $27.50 for services he rendered his father in settling a claim that Barryman assumed when he endorsed the Sterling advertising bill. All he did was to transfer the open account to notes of $100 per month and I paid them as they came due. For that terrible service he sent his father a bill for services. So his papa says I am to pay that bill. I figured as how it was none of my business, and inasmuch (as) he didn't pay his son anyway, why should I?

"So I sent him a lovely letter telling him my views and he didn't like it. So in so far as I am concerned, he may jump in the lake or any other convenient receptacle of H_2O and lump it. I got a bill from Himey also for $150 and $76.00 expenses in re the incorporation. I sent him a lovely letter in which I outlined the whole matter in a most masterful fashion and I don't intend to pay that either and I am on decidedly good terms with Herman yet. However if I can somehow settle the notes with this new deal, I will be most happy to do so. Well, write a letter once in a while. It will be read."

Once again Celia returns to New Jersey in July, 1930, and her correspondence commences with Louis until he joins her a week later. Argomite has faded from the picture temporarily. This may be the last time Celia sees her mother before her mother died from diabetes at the age of 47 on December 3.

By January 17, 1931, Celia is seven months pregnant. Louis sends the next letter to Dave. "I have been trying for sometime to get a few moments time in which to write you a few words but I need not tell you that I am considerably busy. However, the surprise arrival of two books, one of which – *The Great Betrayal* – I have coveted these last few weeks since I saw it advertised, makes it encumbered upon me to tear myself away from everything else and attack the typewriter. It is needless for me to say that I am thanking you for these nice books. You know, I hope that where-ever we may be, we shall remember each other's birthdays and send each other a little token of that remembrance.

"Aside from the usual and customary ailments my Madam is getting along fairly well. She had some trouble with an infected toe but thanks to the Lord and the immediate diagnosis of it as 'erysipelas' by Dr. Davis and his effective Violet Ray and other treatments, it is all better now. In the meantime get ready for an attendance of a *brith* of your newest nephew." Which turned out to be me, a niece and in no need of a *brith*.

"Things in this town are running along about the same as ever. Tomorrow we shall have our annual shul meeting with its election, etc. Next month on the 15th of February to be exact, there is to be in our shul what is termed 'A First Event in Washington.' It marks the conclusion of a cycle of study by the *Chevrae Shass* (Shass group) of which as you probably know, Pa is the moving spirit. It is officially termed a *Suim Hashass*. It represents a cycle of something like ten years and is the first of its kind in this City. Originally it was intended by Mama and a few of the others to have a little supper at the house on M Street. But somehow the new Rabbi saw the advertising possibilities in such a blowout and interested the Ladies Auxiliary in it, with the result that there will be a catered dinner at the shul at $5.00 per couple. It will be a most interesting occasion.

"The good wife has just slipped in and for the 70th time is bemoaning the fact that she owes Ida a letter but cannot seem to sit down to answering her. I am hereby inviting her to sit here and take over the wheel. Love to the family, Louis"

Dear Ida:

It is needless for me to tell you how bemuddled my head has been these last few weeks. I cannot seem to concentrate on any one thing. My mind keeps wandering all day long and even in my sleep it keeps on working. Time heals all wounds I am told so my chief job at this time is waiting for this Time they are all talking about. I still do all I can to help Lou with the work. Thank God I have something to do to keep me occupied most of the time. I don't know what I would have done being away from my folks in a time like this if it weren't for the work Lou gives me to do.

I do very little talking about my troubles and from outward appearances I am a very brave soldier. Your letter cheered me up quite a bit. Thanks.

Now about my other self. I am feeling pretty good. Every once in a while something crops (up) that causes me to wonder why this or that aches, but by the time I get to the Doctors it is all over. Dr. Davis is very nice. I understand you had him too. I have quite some time to go yet so I am just getting used to a lot of discomforts.

My father and sister Ruth are coming out to see us tomorrow. They are sailing for Palestine the 20th of February and will probably stay three or four months away from (the) U.S. My father's great desire in life was to visit his homeland so we all thought this is just the time for him to go, and since he never planned on going alone, my youngest sister Ruth is getting a four month leave of absence from the bank to make the trip. It gives us all a lot of comfort in their going. I expect them to visit me again before they leave.

I am a little tired and as it is nearing my bedtime I will close this letter with Love and Affection to you, Dave and the kiddies. Cel

The Argomite business reemerges on March 21, 1931, in this letter from Dave.

"I got a call from Herman today in which he advised me that the Quiggley Corporation is selling Argomite very actively. It seems that we may have some recourse against them (and) we want some definite information. I want you to get me copies of the official document of the sale. These copies should be gotten either from the Clerk of the Supreme Court in Washington, DC, or maybe from the City Clerk. (Leo could probably advise you just where you can get them.) I think the cost is nominal.

Also find out through Leo, or Lou Ottenberg, if you can, just what were the conditions of the sale. You see, as I understand it, the corporation was sold under the Bulk Sales Law, and, as such, it did eliminate creditors, but we weren't creditors; we were contracting parties, and, as such, they could not comfortably eliminate us in any way.

It may be possible that they may not enter into any litigation and make some settlement, which, in view of the facts, may be a darn good idea. At any rate, this is asking you for immediate action. Get all the information you can as to how the sale was transacted, besides these documents.

Please don't consider this a letter to you, because I wouldn't write one. I'm so darn mad I could bite nails. However, more of that anon. Love to Ceal. – Regards from Ida and the kids, Dave

Louis writes to Esther and Pauline, who have moved to Palestine, to catch them up on events at home, including my birth. "Erev Pesach, 11:55 PM (to be exact), March 31, 1931. From six thousand or so miles it must seem awfully queer that a brother would keep silent for months and then all of a sudden pick out midnight during which to write a few words. There happens, however, to be a real good explanation for this apparent *meshugas* (silliness). As you, Esther, no doubt know, the first two nights of Pesach each Jew is such a *held* (strong fellow) that he fears nothing. He even manages to get along on a very short *Krias sheme* (reading of the Shma Israel – declaration of faith in One God).

"Here I have let such a long time slip away without letting you hear from me that I was afraid of the scolding that was surely in store from you. Thus Pesach comes in just right. Since a good Jew writes not *um yontev* (on a holiday), I am doing the next best thing and write the night before.

"The preamble over, let me tell you once more that Ceal and I are the proud parents of a little Grossbergle. We have a very lovely little daughter. The Miss arrived – not unexpectedly – on Sunday afternoon March 22, 1931. Weight 7lbs. 10 oz. Announcement card is enclosed. I wired to my father-in-law in Jerusalem immediately after the birth, and requested in said wire that he notify you. If he has received the message and knows your address, you no doubt have heard from him a week ago. Also, I am sure mother has not overlooked spreading the news to Palestine long since.

"What do you think? The first Grossberg since Babe and the first Grossberg girl since Miriam. And what a girl! She has the tiniest little baby fingers and toes. And each little finger has the prettiest finger nails. Just the right curve to them all ready for the manicurist with the paint and file. She has a nice double chin all ready made and a dimple on each cheek. Looks just like her daddy. Poor thing. But then, they do say babies change later on. Maybe she'll get to look like her mamma. You see, I rather like her mamma. Still, she could do worse than take after the Grossberg looks. My sisters aren't so bad looking as sisters go.

"Strange how time slips by, and never does there seem any time for personal correspondence. It is really a shame that we write each other so seldom. First thing you know, you'll forget the English language. Then, they'll call you greenhorns.

"We read most of Pauline's letters and enjoy them immensely. We like to read about the things you do, and the places you visit, and the fellows you go out with. Compared to your adventures and interests we here live a very drab life.

"I'd love to pay you and Esther and Palestine a visit. But I guess lots of people would love to spread wings and fly. Unless there shows up some sort of *yerusha* (inheritance) from Lord knows where, we'll just continue to stay here.

September 9, 1931 (Western Union Telegram)
    To: Mrs. Celia K. Grossberg, 4700 Connecticut Ave Apt 509
WASH DC
    DEAR SWEETHEART FIRST I WISH YOU AND OUR DEAR DAUGHTER A NEW YEAR THAT IS GENEROUSLY SPRINKLED WITH HEALTH HAPPINESS AND JOY SECONDLY I WANT TO CONGRATULATE YOU ON YOUR BIRTHDAY MAY YOU HAVE SEVENTY MORE HAPPY BIRTHDAYS THIRDLY I WANT YOU TO KNOW THAT YOU HAVE MY LOVE FOREVER LOU

The letters between Dave and Louis dwindle, mostly containing updates on life and often "bawling out" for lack of correspondence. Dave's stationery letterhead now boasts, "Consultant, Office Management – Clerical Methods."

November 8, 1932
    Dear Louis,
    How's tricks in your burg, now that Hoover has deserted you and is about (to) leave you for good? I am listening now as the announcer is advising of the coming landslide, and he just announced that Hoover's managers have just conceded New York State to Roosevelt.

532

Will send my love to Pauline and Ceal. As ever your buddy,
Dave

September 19, 1933

Dear Dave, Ida, et-al:

So you all figured you could high hat me and sneak out on
me? Well, you caint. I hunted you right up and found you. You
have got me licked on personal contact but thank God Unc Sam's
mail is still delivering.

First of all permit me, friend David, to remind you that my
last letter to you, these many months ago, is still unanswered. But
being not at all proud I'm trying again. *Varf mir a Katz in ponim
mein ich dos es regent* (if you throw a cat in my face I'll pretend it
was rain). How come you forget to answer me? Too busy or don't
give a damn? I don't care either way, just would like to know as a
matter of simple curiosity.

A bundle of unforeseen circumstances combined to cause
me to climb aboard my ancient *scrabele* (car) last Wednesday
and wend our weary way towards the great white way technically
know as the City of New York. Circumstance number one: Mrs.
Herman Freudberg with the not unimportant aid of Mr. Herman
Freudberg gave birth last week to a handsome little Miss Freudberg. We wished to view the creation of a female of the species in
a land of males.

Circumstance number two: Mrs. Esther R. Abrams of Syracuse, New York and Tel Aviv, Palestine being in the so called dress
business found her stock so depleted that it required the addition
of at least 24 dresses to round out her stock. A trip to New York
was thus indicated.

Circumstance number three: *The Jewish Pageant*, after its
signal success in Chicago was scheduled to play on Thursday September 14th in New York. We wanted to see this marvelous work
of theatrical art.

All three circumstances coming so close together and our
annual urge for a vacation having not as yet been satisfied, we
thought this an excellent opportunity to take the trip. Accordingly,

Wednesday midnight saw our arrival in Newark. Our mistake was that we made no agreements with the God of Rain. Thursday morning was the blowout. It rained and poured as you well know. We went to New York anyway. Attended to the matter of the dresses and then I called. The first trouble was a change of phone numbers from the one you once gave me. The girl at the phone looked you up and announced that you were not there, may not be there that day and maybe not the next. Your phone? No listing. So I snuck back to Newark, the afternoon all shot to Hellenback. Friday it poured again and I stayed in Newark. Saturday it rained again and in the early afternoon we left for Philadelphia. So thus you have the whole story. What the Hell, Bill, whatahell!

So many things have happened since last I saw and talked to you that I could not write them out if I wanted to. My little Perla, *onaiinhora* (beyond the evil eye, i.e. knock wood) is growing up into a veritable little doll. She will be eighteen months and one year old in a few days, *mirtzeashem* (God willing). (This was Louis' humorous way of saying that 2.5-years-old.) She talks quite well and is as mischievous as they make them. In spunk and sheer nerve she outshines kids twice her age.

She delights to have her daddy hold her by the ankles at arms length so that she may touch the ceiling with her hands. She stands straight up as if standing on a chair. 'Do more, daddy', is her cry when her daddy gets tired. Outside of the apartment they have rigged up a swing for the kids. When Perla wants to swing nobody else better try to use it. She is fully convinced that the swing is for her especial enjoyment and no one else may use it unless she wishes him to do so. The other day I watched her from our fifth floor. We can see the swing and the playground from our bedroom. Here is her way of swinging:- With the board off, she takes the rope and gets on top of a bench that is nearby. Then she puts her foot on the rope and slides her hands upward as far as she can. Thus settled she jumps off the bench and the result, of course, is a high standing swing. My heart jumped into my throat when I saw her take a dive off that bench. But that is the way the big boys swing and that is the way Perla Grossberg does it. She has a reputation in the apartment. Everybody knows Perla. She is as fast as lightning. God bless the little honey.

And so to wish you and your good family the happiest of New Years. May the coming year bring to you and yours such health, happiness and prosperity that the past will seem to have been a mere dream, useful only as a contrast to accentuate the beauty and glory of the new life. *L'shono Tovo Tikosevu* (Happy New Year, May you be inscribed for a good year). Yours as ever, Louis

December 30, 1933

Dear Dave, Ida, Kiddies and the Cat (if any):

Here I've written, wroten, ROTTEN you three letters heretofore and nary a sign of either that you got them or didn't got them. Not only that but you even snuck out on me and left me no forwarding address.

Last week or rather two weeks ago, Sarah Hamburg was here to view the remaining carcass of her brother-in-law at which time said brother-in-law asked her to make all possible effort to find the last known address of one D.A. Glushak, Esq. As you know, when it rains it usually *plucket*. So who should slip me your address but our mutual friend Louis Novick, whom I met at mothers the other day awelcoming my sister Esther who just arrived from Palestine. But that is another story.

A few days later word reaches from Newark of the whereabouts of my once beloved friend David and famble. The occasion being not inauspicious – what with the receipt of your address in duplicate, the availability of time, and the imminent arrival of the new born year with its birthday and such – I am set forth writing of a letter.

There are so many things to be said that it is difficult with the limited typing ability at my discommand to know where to commence. First of all let me wish you, David, a very happy new birthday with all the standard as well as special wishes for the best that life can give. I understand from Novick that things with you have been very ungood in the past. Needless to say I am very sorry. Of course, the usual birthday knickknack will be forthcoming under separate cover.

Novick tells me that he told you I have recently undergone an operation for the removal of a malicious appendage. I never had an appendix pain, in fact the stomach has been thriving on the lady. I never could view my waistline with any illusions of the ultimate spectacle it would be destined to provide my grandchildren. When the ache that might have disturbed me finally showed up I paid little or no attention to it. Fact is I was ashamed to admit that I had any such ache.

The first thought that came to my mind was 'worms.' Could I, at my advancing years, be having worms? Two hours later I began to think that perhaps I have nothing to be ashamed of after all. These seemed to be no small worms. They showed every symptom of being full grown snakes. So I hied me downstairs to the drug store and applied for advice of the gentleman who has been called 'Doctor' for such a long time that he feels competent to prescribe medicine and thereby in effect to practice medicine.

He gave me a soda concoction first and told me to come back a little later if the pain is not much easier and he would really put me away. Of course he didn't say it in that many words but my doctor assures me that the effect would have been that, if I had taken the paregoric the druggist told me he would give me if I came back. Some kind providence (with a capital P) led me to call Dr. Daniel Davis, our family obstetrician (stomach trouble, you know) on the phone and to ask him if I should take the paregoric.

That phone call cost five cents and was the forerunner of costs aplenty. The doc told me not to dare take a thing but that if after resting an hour in the office the pain is not relieved I should come see him and be sure to bring the stomach along. (After further calls to the doctor, Solly and a friend took Louis to Georgetown University Hospital.)

Two hours later Dr. Davis came to the hospital and again began to toppen in all my most intimate anatomical spots. But this time there was apparent a definite greater ache on the right side and some sort of reaction by pressure that the medico pointed out to the intern, which was not there two hours before. My temperature had gone up a bit and another blood count was ordered. This time the white corpuscles in my blood were mobilized for action and the count was just double what it had been two hours before. So the good news was gently spilled to me that my girlish figure would have to be mutilated somewhat if I wished to avoid a possible funeral in my immediate family with the title role being played by me.

Now I esk you, what would you have done? Here it was about November 22 with most of the month's work done and a stomach ache that hurt like Hell. Go ahead, was the word and ahead they went. While I was trying to get in a word with my madam, the lady Ceal, whose reactions to all this is another and separate story and who was waiting outside my door, they slipped me what is technically known as an avert and before they could wheel me out of the room I was unconscious. No more the terrible after effects of ether. I tell you it is a *maichel* (wonderful thing) to be anesthetized nowadays. Hitler should try it for a couple of years.

Naturally the next thing I remember here was a nice looking young nurse in my room who was holding my hand and expressing satisfaction that at last I was awake. I never get the breaks. That sort of thing would have been a glorious treat to me in the days of my single so called blessedness. But now as an old married man possessed of a private hand holder all my own, it was practically no thrill whatever. In due time I learned that I cannot have things the usual way. I must be different.

The customary appendix operation of the present era takes about twenty minutes in the operating room and the incision is possibly two inches or less long. When the doc in his playful way slit away the obstruction to my appendix' view to give the thing an opportunity to see *wos tut sich* (what are you doing) outside, what do you think he found? Nothing, absolutely nothing. Where should have been an appendix there was no such thing. Not to be outdone by a faking appendix my doc immediately instituted a search, and after doing a little more cutting and digging all around me, he finally located the hound.

It appears that for no reason that could be immediately detected, friend appendix was in the rear instead of the front, and in place of riding free as most self respecting appendixes are satisfied to do, mine was tightly adhered to the intestines and was, as

Davis described it to me, as if you emptied a bottle of glue on your papers on the desk and you had to remove the glue.

The upshot of the matter was that I had to stay up in the operating room for two hours before they finally unhooked my appendix from me. The trouble seems to have been that the doc had to get it out whole as the skunk was badly inflamed and would have caused trouble if opened. Analysis showed that my appendix was streptococci and the condition of it so bad, that Dr. Davis was amazed that I never before had any pains from it as he assured me that I had had many previous attacks, even tho they were not painful.

Had I taken the paregoric as previously discussed, my pain would have been relieved and I would undoubtedly have gone home instead of to the hospital. I might have suffered thru the night and called the doctor in the morning. The operation might have taken place at about ten, we will say, and the funeral the next day. Davis said that it is very doubtful if the appendix could have been removed whole if it had been much worse because of the location and the adherence to the intestines. So that's that.

Everything was going along fine when on the morning of the fifteenth I got a letter and a terrific set back. The doc sent in his bill. What do you think it was, for $100 bucks? No, sir, she read $250.00. Of course, he might as well have said $2,500. I'm waiting until the new statement comes in after the first to see if it was not a typographical error before I go over to read him the law of depressions. Ceal's Cesarean operation he charged $100 and that is what I thought he would charge me. He could not think that I have money as it is only very recently that he finished collecting that hundred for Ceal's operation.

Just a word about Esther. As a surprise, her coming rates quite high. Last Saturday night they got a wire from New York at the house to the effect that Esther was in New York and on the way to Washington. I had something of a hunch as to the reason for said unexpected visit, even tho that reason was a silly one. You see, the New York Central Railroad has at last woke up and begun to make a bid for that old Canal Street property of the Abrams. They filed suit for condemnation and in the proceedings they stated that the property had a value of $75,000. They sent this document over to Palestine as well as here to me, and to the other executors and to the living partner.

Poor kid, she didn't know that even at $125,000, there are enough mortgages and other debts outstanding against the partnership to take all the money. So that's how come she is here. This will be all for the day. Love is again extended in which Ceal and our daughter join me. So let us wish you a very Happy New Year with all the trimmings. As ever, Louis

The wonderful life Esther and Harry planned to live together in Palestine never materialized. A few months before leaving to join his family, Harry took ill. Esther was summoned back to the United States and arrived shortly before he died. Afterwards, Esther decided to remain in Palestine to raise the children, since that was Harry's wish. Her son Jack told me his mother's story. As a young girl, her hands hurt from crushing tin cans in her father's junk shop and she thought she would be an old maid. She was 25 when she married.

I've heard it said, we do not remember much that occurred before the age of 5 or 6. However, I remember the apartment we lived in on Connecticut Avenue before moving into the house my parents built at 3421 Garrison Street. At least I remember the living room with its two windows facing the street. I also remember my parents bedroom, though not my own. There was a desk on the left side of their bed and to the left was the door. Pop was sitting at the desk with his head in his hands, obviously in great pain. On the desk sat a black telephone and a lamp with a glass dome casting a dim yellowish glow to the room. I remember being very upset at the time not knowing what was going on. I was then three years old.

I assumed all these years that my memory concerned his appendix. Yet in the previous letter, he said his pain began in the office. Did he really have pain before going downtown but dismissed it, as he often did, so as not to upset my mother? I can still picture the scene. Funny what we remember. I wonder if we think we remember things, but in reality have photographs we've seen in the past. But there were no photographs of the inside of that Connecticut Avenue apartment.

Within a year we moved into the new house. During its construction, I was told I had a little stool where I sat and watched the workmen. I can't say I remember doing that but my mother said the workmen got a kick out of my following them around. I do have photographs of my stool and me.

Jan. 3, 1934

Dear Louis, Ceal and baby Perla,

It is quite a long while since I last wrote you, but there has been so much water over the mill during that time, that one doesn't care to go into much retrospect about it. I saw Novick about a week or so ago. He told me that you had gone thru quite a stretch and from your letter you must have had one terrible time. Those are experiences that one can look back on with little pleasure, but with thankfulness that it is over and that you are again on the road to recovery and will soon be in the best of health again.

As for me, there is little now that can be said. The past 15 months passed like a nightmare, and in that time I was able to find out who were my friends and who were acquaintances. Were it not for the hands of a dead man I would have been in the bread lines a long time, for with all of my so called experience and abilities there was no job available at even $25.00 per week. I have just made a connection which permits me to pay for my rent and food. What the prospects are I don't know. I am only worried about this afternoon and tomorrow.

I thank you for your kind wishes regarding my birthday and I certainly want to extend to you my best wishes for your birthday, I note however that you are sending me a little token as of yore. I was unable to reciprocate last year, and I am unable to do so again this year. So I wish that you will not do so this year for I feel hesitant in accepting it.

Otherwise there is little news. The children are growing up thank God. Ida is feeling fairly well and I am also grateful to God to be in good health. So I'll close with kindest regards to you and Ceal and the baby in which I am joined by Ida and the children, Yours as ever, Dave

The birthday correspondence continues, as in this letter to Dave, December 30, 1935. "Thank God for a birthday, for if it were not for your or my birthdays, we might easily lose complete track of each other for the amount of correspondence that goes back and forth during the year. For my part I am sincerely sorry that we seem to have drifted away from each other. As you probably know your sister Fanny visited us last summer. During that time we had a lengthy heart to heart talk about which she may have told you.

"Still, here I find it unusually difficult to write to you. It seems very strange that this should be so since I can look through my files and find copies of long letters written to you bearing dates very close to each other. Yet here I am trying to write you the first letter in over a year and don't know what to say to you.

"Things here are rolling along from day to day more or less the same. Of course measured in years, things have changed a bit. For one thing, Solly has just become a Chosen, being engaged to a Philadelphia girl. Babe, our Revenue agent in the Chicago district, is visiting us for the New Year. Joe in Jacksonville is married to a Jacksonville sweetheart of my Florida days. Eleanor from Palestine has married a fellow in Palestine and recently returned to the United States with her husband and they are now making their home in Los Angeles, California, which is her husband's (family) home. Pauline is still in Palestine wishing to come back to America on account of economic conditions. Esther, poor soul, has made some very poor investments in Palestine and has now fallen almost entirely upon us for support for herself and six children."

Prior to this letter, Eleanor joined Pauline in Palestine and met and married an American, Morey Slosberg, who was supposedly in the movie business. He did not do well there and the couple returned to the United States. Even though his family had considerable means, they did nothing to help him. All the time Eleanor and Morey lived in California, the Grossberg family supported them. He pretended to be a songwriter though never published anything. Eleanor died quite young and according to my mother, Morey remarried immediately thereafter. For a while, Pauline remained in Palestine helping Esther after Eleanor and Morey left for America. She hoped to make a life for herself there.

Louis continues his update. "Kitty has suffered a great sorrow in the last seven months through the disappearance of her only son Bobby, who seven months ago left school one afternoon and did not return home. Despite efforts of the Department of Justice who are searching the entire United States for him, his disappearance is complete. We all hope that he merely ran away, although there appears no apparent reason for his doing so."

This was not the first time Bobby ran away. And when he did, the family quietly blamed his father, Al Cohen. In happier days, when the Abrams children visited Washington, Al and Kitty once took Esther's children, Shoshana, Sylvia and Ruthie, to visit Edith and Bobby at summer camp. During the drive, Al leaned over and kissed Kitty. Seeing this, Shoshana said, "My mommy and daddy don't do that!" Louis continues.

"Yours Truly has built himself a home. We were very fortunate to come in during the last stages of the depression which we now hope is on the wane. The beginning of this paragraph reminds me of the picture *Hollywood Hotel* where after many and varied happenings, one of the characters is caused to say, 'Nothing ever happens here.'

"Since we got a house I have come to understand why you always preached against the purchase of a house. Somehow expenses keep popping up to the end that I am always broke. However, we do enjoy it very much and only hope as Ceal says, 'we can keep it.'

"Our little Perla, now 4 and three quarters years old, is *onaiinhora* a very lovely child. She is a wild child but adorable. It has always been a mystery where she gets her unlimited energy. In health, Thank God we have fared right well.

"I hope you and your family are well both economically and physically. I want to wish you a very Happy Birthday and long life, much happiness, *naches* (pleasure) from your loved ones and anything else you may wish for yourself. With kindest personal regards to Ida, the daughters and yourself for a Happy & Prosperous New Year from Ceal, Perla and myself, I am, Most cordially, Louis"

I grew up and was married on Garrison Street. A fond memory I have of my parents in that house was of getting in the car every summer and driving out to farms in the Maryland countryside to buy corn. Six bushels of it. Pop would call the farmers to see if it was ripe and off we'd go. We picked up the corn early in the morning, just as it came in from the fields. The whole family then took part in an assembly line production to shuck, clean, scald, dry, and freeze the corn. Pop was especially fond of *Shoepeg* and *Country Gentleman*, both sweet white varieties with irregular kernels. Not many farmers grew them because most people preferred large kernels in straight rows, but we loved them and sought them out. In later years, they disappeared entirely.

The birthday letters continue between Louis and Dave, as they catch up with each other annually. Louis also sent letters to Celia on special occasions, as this anniversary letter.

"Congratulations on your tenth anniversary! May this milestone be the forerunner of many, many more. I sincerely hope that we shall never be less happy and genuinely in love with each other than we are right now!

"You are so wonderful! So *geroten*. Anything your dear fingers touch literally turns to gold. You are so clever and resourceful; so artistic, creative, inventive. You are a grand mother – a fine person – a wonderful wife. Truly you are a gentlewoman!

"For all the things you are and do I love you truly. May the good Lord give you long life and happiness. Your husband, Louis"

Postscript

"Pauline's husband is now working at the DGS," Louis tells Dave in his 1938 birthday letter. "Oh, did you know that they left Palestine, that is Pauline and her husband? Yes they came here in May of 1938 and after trying to find work he landed a job handling grocery boxes in the warehouse. He is a very nice fellow but without being able to talk English it is pretty tough. He was getting $18.00 a week until recently the Union got after the DGS and made them unionize the warehouse. That brought him as he puts it – twenty percent more pay and 25% less hours of work with time and one half for overtime. However, he is very grateful and with the learning of the language he will undoubtedly some day find his level in the scheme of things.

"It is hardly the right thing to try to bring a year's news into one letter especially since I have to do the writing myself. My speed on the typewriter has taken on a negative quality since my wife has become my stenographer these many years. Incidentally she is, *onaiinhora*, well and as lovely as ever. She would surely send her love and best wishes if she knew I was writing a letter to you (and) also from Perla."

In Israel, George Fodor romanced Pauline very effectively and she married him. I found a letter dated October 26, 1936, from the District of Columbia, where my father swore in an affidavit that Fodor was a responsible citizen with a family and resources, and if an immigration visa were issued to the said George Fodor, he would provide him with support, so at no time would he become a public charge. Shortly after Pauline and George came to America, it soon developed that the only reason Foder married Pauline was to come to the United States as the husband of an American citizen. Fodor worked briefly and then disappeared. There were suspicions he was a pedophile. One day my mother caught him being overly affectionate with me. Pauline got a divorce, resumed her maiden name, but never remarried.

"I hope you won't mind the intrusion in the middle of the year since we now seem to fix the custom of writing to each other the first of the year," Louis writes on June 1, 1939.

"First, let me congratulate you on your passing of the NY State CPA examination. For the first time it is quite a fine achievement particularly since being out of problem practice for so many years.

"Conditions here have slowed down to the extent where I find that I can devote considerable time to studying for my own CPA examinations. In that connection I wonder if you don't have some material or suggestions that I might use towards preparing myself for this tough tussle. I shall appreciate anything you can send me or tell me along that line."

This may be the first time my father asked Dave for anything.

June 30, 1939
Dear Louis:
Received your letter last week and just couldn't seem to get at it until now. Our shul has been running a bazaar at which I have been one of the muck-mucks – had to be there every night and the office was quite busy.

I note that you would like to work for your CPA and I believe I can give you some real hints. Tackling the CPA today is not a joke, particularly for a fellow out of school. I spent a couple of months wandering around blindly until I got myself set on this job and it's a job that has to be undertaken in a systematic manner. You have to learn to work fast, on schedule and with *ink* the whole way through and time yourself on everything you do.

Dave provides details of a recommended text and methods for studying, including devoting two hours daily to the task with no exceptions. "More than that I don't believe I can help you. Also, if you find that you don't agree with some of the answers to CPA problems worked by various authorities, you're perfectly O.K. on that because I found a number of major mistakes made by so-called experts. Today I'm old enough to know that I don't believe everything I read in the books.

"Alright, fellow, pitch right in. You'll need 6 months at least on this thing and do a job for yourself..."

"We were tremendously shocked to learn of the loss of your father," Louis writes Dave and Ida on November 1, 1939. "Only a little while ago we saw him and heard his splendid voice at the wedding of Ruthie Kanster. He looked so grand and young, so handsome and jolly, so full of life and spirit. We cannot somehow bring ourselves to believe that Rabbi Glushak has left this life for good.

"Men like your father are very rare these days. When one passes away there is no replacement. I mean from the broader point of view. His loss to the community – the Jewish world community. It must surely be a source of great consolation to you in your hour of sorrow to know that your father was the kind of man he was:- a champion of Jewish ideals, a God-fearing man, learned not only in Rabbinical lore but in worldly matters as well, beloved and revered by countless thousands of his friends in many cities and Lands.

"To us the passing of your father is a loss much more personal than to his other friends. Our entire life has been affected through our having known him. We can never forget that but for Rabbi Glushak, Mrs. Grossberg might never have been Jacob Kanster's daughter. For that alone we should feel eternally grateful, that when Rabbi Glushak passed through life on his way to eternity he touched our own lives with his magic wand.

"Please convey our condolences to your brother and to Fanny as well as to the Rabbi's grandchildren. We, too, feel the sorrow. As ever your friends, Louis and Ceal"

They also sent a condolence letter to the Rabbi's wife.

In his birthday letter to Dave that year, Louis tells that Perla, at a young age, began collecting miniatures and has acquired a discriminating taste in them. "All the things she has collected have now been put on display in her cabinet and it is no small collection. Ceal is a Notary Public and all the notary money she makes goes into the purchase of miniatures for Perla's collection. That doesn't mean that the old man isn't hit now and then for a quarter or fifty cents for some item that strikes the eye.

"Not all things that Perla has in her collection have been bought by her mother or daddy. Her friends all know that she likes to collect things and when a toy is in order they bring her an item for her collection. Recently Mr. and Mrs. I. S. Turover were in Europe – they returned two or three weeks after the war was declared – and they did not forget to bring her some lovely things from France, Geneva and from England.

"We are all, thank the good Lord, well and happy. Excepting for Esther and her kids in Palestine, Joe and his wife in Jacksonville, Eleanor and her husband in Los Angeles, Babe in Baltimore as a Revenue Agent, and Kitty and her brood in Arlington, Va. we are all together in Washington again."

This is the last mention of Kitty in the letters selected for this book. After Al's death in 1949, Kitty opened a collection agency to help her make a living, but she frequently borrowed $100 from Pop until her commissions came in at the end of the month. She never had enough spending money for a comfortable life. One day she saw an Oriental rug for $200 and bought it on credit because, as she said, "Why should I be poor without a rug? I might as well be poor with a rug." Al had bought some land in Virginia that produced no income but still required tax payments.

When Kitty was about to enter the hospital for surgery on a brain tumor, she visited with my parents in their home on Garrison Street. It was December of 1951. Kitty wanted to get her affairs in order before going to the hospital. I was newly pregnant with our first child and no one knew but my parents. For some reason I was there that same afternoon and in order to cheer her up, I told Kitty that Jules and I planned to name our baby in memory of Bobby. Jordan Robby was born in June of 1952 and we named him Jordan after Jule's grandfather, Joseph Radzin, and Robby after Robert Cohen.

Unfortunately, Kitty did not survive the operation. When she passed away in 1952 at the age of 56, her estate was valued at about $135,000 though she did not live to enjoy it. When our second son Kenneth Allen was born in 1954, we named him after Kitty and Al.

Edith's case was no happier. Pop said that Kitty's will called for her estate to be put into the "Grossberg Family Trust," initiated by my father in 1948, for needy Grossbergs. For tax reasons it was nominally created in the name of Benjamin Grossberg. Kitty's estate contained the property she owned in Virginia. Pop said that had Kitty sold the property during her lifetime, she could have lived like a princess but she was afraid to leave this real estate to her daughter Edith who was very irresponsible. Kitty knew that the Grossberg family would take care of Edith's vital interests if need be. Kitty did leave her other assets to Edith but they would only keep her in a modest style.

At the time, Edith was involved with a man Kitty did not like. He was not Jewish and besides that, he was married. It seemed that Edith went out of her way to irritate her mother. Soon after Kitty died, Edith made a handwritten will leaving all her assets to the man she was dating. One day my parents received a phone call from Edith saying she had taken an overdose of sleeping pills and felt very sick. This was not the first time Edith had pulled a stunt like this but my parents could not take a chance that she meant it this time. They rushed out of the house that night to pick up Dr. Abramson on the way but it was too late. She never recovered. Her last words were that she didn't really mean to kill herself. Her estate went to her boyfriend after much unpleasantness. Edith was probably another casualty of her father's bad parental behavior. I hardly remember her either.

Ten years after Kitty's death, Pop found a $25 Liberty Bond, payable to Katherine Cohen. As her executor, in order to cash it, he had to get approval from the Virginia Court House. The State of Virginia had been a hot bed of anti-Semitism during Kitty's time, yet she had become the President of the Women's Business League of the State of

Virginia. When Pop presented the bond to the Virginia lady official, he tried to tell her who Kitty Cohen was. "You don't have to tell us about Kitty Cohen," she said. "We never forgot her."

In 1939, civilization more or less ended at the district line, about 10 blocks north of Garrison Street. The basic Jewish population lived on two parallel streets farther east on the other side of Rock Creek Park, i.e. Georgia Avenue or 16th Street, NW. It was thought that as the city and suburban areas grew northward, more Jews would move to the Connecticut Avenue area. Unfortunately, that did not happen during my formative years. I was usually the only Jewish child in most of my classes throughout my school years.

Those were the days of rampant anti-Semitism in America. The worst incident I recall happened to me during the early years of WWII. I was 8 or 9 years old at Ben Murch Elementary School. One day the teacher had to leave the room for a few minutes. Suddenly a blackboard eraser started flying around the room. Boys were throwing it at each other when it hit me. I threw it back, just as the teacher appeared in the doorway. Her anger was palpable.

She looked at me and said, "If it weren't for the Jews, this war wouldn't have started!"

I was dumbfounded. I didn't know what she was talking about. I was afraid to tell my parents because I thought they would punish me for throwing the eraser. I also thought that somehow being a Jew caused all sorts of terrible things to happen in the world. When I did tell them I was surprised at how angry my mother became. The next day she went to school to complain. She was not embarrassed to be a Jew.

I was raised to look for the best in everyone, especially where it concerned religion. People were entitled to believe in God in their own way and one never denigrated another's beliefs. There were hardly any Jews in our area and precious few children. Across the street from our house lived a Catholic family, a mother and 6 children. None of them were allowed to play with me. I had killed Christ. Their attitude was the norm, yet I thought it was a sin to think ill of them.

On September 9, 1940, my father received a note from K.T. Sullivan of The Baltimore Salesbook Company.

Dear Mr. Grossberg:

In all of my life I have known what to say or thought I knew what to say (to) the sweet girl graduate. This time I swear I don't know what to say to a new CPA except congratulations. Certainly want to wish you continued success and I would probably have never known about this if I had not read closely this newspaper clipping attached. With kindest person regards, I am, Very sincerely yours, Kenneth

The attached Clipping was titled, "9 From Strayer College Victors in Accountancy Test."

"The board of Examiners for certified public accountants in the District of Columbia has just given notice to E. G. Purvis, vice-president of Strayer College of Accountancy, that nine candidates were successful in passing the May 1940 CPA examinations." Among those listed was Louis C. Grossberg.

This next letter from Dave, dated January 13, 1945, is a year or so after I decided to end this memoir but the information contained is of historical interest.

Dear Lou,

Lotzez and lotses of water has flown over the damn dam since last I wrote to you, and your long and breezy letter came as quite a surprise just as January 1 was beginning to fade away.

Your news was certainly very interesting. I was definitely interested in knowing that Perla is now a young woman, and from now on, young sir, you will first start experiencing an entirely new set of reactions resulting from the period called the 'adolescence period of female youth.' I know whereof I speak. But will I advise you, will I tell you what to look forward to, will I forewarn you? Who me? No sir. That is a lesson for you to learn by your lonesome.

In this town, there is a war all around us. Leo's two boys are in the service, the older one an ensign in the navy and just sent to the Pacific, the younger one still in the training school. You met Fanny's son, the marine flyer, and the latest one of our family is Phil, who after six months training was sent to England and within four weeks was in the first boat attacking Normandy on D day. Four days thereafter a shell hit the foxhole he was in, killed his four buddies, and split his head open. After six months in the hospital he is now back in this country and I believe now in Walter Reed (hospital) in Washington.

A neighbor of mine across the street has a boy, a pilot in Italy who just came back from eight missions in less than two weeks. We are praying for him. And so on and on. I just learned that Sam R, the fellow who used to live across the street from us in Washington, and whose two boys lived in our house, both fell in action in Europe. That news almost took the props out from under me.

But about this, I suppose we could speak for hours. I was happy to learn that Bobby is still safe. Let's hope to God he is released soon.

Sadly, Bobby Cohen, who ran off to join the army, did not survive. The American troops had retreated to Corregidor, an island in the Bataan Peninsula that was the last bastion of American defenses in the Philippines. When it fell to Japan, the troops captured in Bataan were marched for weeks. Most died on the way. Those that remained alive, including Bobby, were taken on a hospital ship bound for Japan. This ship did not carry any flag indicating it was a hospital ship carrying American wounded. And the Americans bombed and sank it.

"As for me, and mine, a number of things happened this past year. I left my last job for a much more impressive one and a more lucrative one. I am now the comptroller of a chain of 25 retail ladies wearing apparel stores doing a volume of over $8,000,000 a year. I have over 100 employees under my 'Jewish diction' and have already installed the famous Glushak systems therein.

"In re my daughters, I did not invite you to the wedding for many and numerous reasons, one of which was the fact that the wedding was a small one, that it was made in a hurry, and that I was none to happy with it. The war has taken strenuous toll of the young girls as well as of the young boys, and Evelyn's (young man) probably thinking me to be a man of large means started to go after the young lady hot and heavy. Despite my pleading the wedding was rushed, and off they went to Buffalo.

"In November, Evy came home on a visit and purely by accident we discovered that the guy she married wasn't a man at all. That was why the b – was deferred from the army, and he could not hold a job. That is one job of good riddance, and Evelyn is now home with us again.

"Well, this last Rosh Hashanah, I was invited again to daven in this same shuhl. The First day Rosh Hashanah went over big and we were invited to several of the members where Barbara – called Butch by everybody, sang all day, and there was plenty to eat etc, so the next morning in shuhl, Butch didn't feel so good and we balled her out for overeating etc.

"The next day she got worse and we called the doctor who diagnosed it as Polio. I'll never forget the next 14 days as long as I live. She had a very bad case of it and later I only heard that the doctor was afraid she might not pull thru. On the fourth day she lost control of all of her external muscles and her eyes. Ida worked day and night applying the Kenny packs for three days without rest of any kind till we were able to get a day nurse, and then kept up the night shift till we got hold of a night nurse as well. The fever was supposed to break in three to four days. It did not break for 12 days and by the 14th day we were able to get her into the Hospital for Joint Diseases.

"We got the best man in New York as her doctor. Thank God that now Butchy is recovering nicely and for the past three weeks has already been walking again. She has recovered the use of her arms perfectly and her legs are coming along fine. We hope to God that she will recover completely within the year. It has cost a sweet penny so far, and we just discovered that the National Polio Foundation will assist us in getting her treatments after she gets home. We hope to take her home in another 2 weeks. One of our friends wrote a song for the March of Dimes which Butch will sing."

In later years Louis and Dave continued to write each other on their birthdays. Then one year Pop did not receive his usual birthday letter. It was 1965 and Ida had not bothered to inform him of Dave's death in an automobile accident.

While my father had written about interesting events in his town, his Jewish activities and people Dave knew, of his own accomplishments, he was very circumspect. He was modest about my mother and when he mentioned me, it was with warts and all. By contrast, Dave's letters continually bragged excessively about his family and their involvement in their Jewish community. Two of these later letters from Dave contained bits that were prophetic. The first one is true and I hope the second one is not.

On January 10, 1954, he wrote: "You know, by keeping these letters over the years, one actually accumulates the life history of two families, and after a while it becomes interesting reading."

And again, January 15, 1955, "You know Louis, as I write this, and as I read your letters from time, I really believe that some day when I accumulate twenty five years work, have them copied nicely, and submit them to a publisher as the actual life history of a couple of plain guys in the U.S., you know I really believe he'll throw it out."

According to Pop, Dave was brilliant in his own way. His biggest shortcoming was a lack of patience with clients. He did not suffer fools gladly. Dave maximized his talents in the field of systemizing office records, and ultimately went into business for himself and prospered.

My father also prospered in his accounting practice that grew and continues to this day as the "Grossberg Company LLP, Certified Public Accountants" in Rockville, Maryland. It is a very respected institution throughout the area.

As for the Argomite business, I never learned what really happened in the end. Did it go out of business? Sell out? Merge with another company? Pop did not know. Time had blurred his memory and the letters do not reveal the answer decisively. The last available information here was from the letter Louis sent Dave, June 26, 1930. There he said the Quigley Furnace Specialties Company was buying the Argomite Company but the deal had not yet been consummated. Dave's last letter on the subject to Louis, March 21, 1931, said he learned the company had been sold under the "Bulk Sales Law."

The last time I spoke to Pop about it, I had more knowledge of the double-dealing than he remembered. Chances are it ultimately just faded away. I always assumed Argomite was the first attempt at producing a detergent, but in Dave's letter of August 28, 1929, he mentioned others also making detergents. Dr. Barton, through Argomite, thought he could play with the big boys but ultimately faded away, too. Unfortunately he took advantage of a lot of honest little people along the way.

In February of 2004 I tried to find out if there was any record of what really happened to the company. I wrote to the Secretary of State, Division of Corporations in the State of Delaware. I received a reply dated March 2, 2004 as follows:

Re: ARGOMITE INDUSTRIES (A CORPORATION) File number: 01815–27

Ms. Fox,

In reply to your request, we find ARGOMITE INDUSTRIES (A CORPORATION) filed a Certificate of Incorporation under the laws of the State of Delaware on March 23, 1925. However, we advise this company is no longer in existence as a Delaware corporation since its charter became void and inoperative on April 1, 1932 due to non-payment of franchise taxes.

The records of this department do not reflect the distribution of assets of void, merged or dissolved corporations. To the best of our knowledge, this information is not available through any State agency.

Sincerely,

Robert C. Mathers

Corporations Administrator

My father's biggest regret about the Argomite story was not having enough money to ride out the journey. He always thought lack of funding prevented their success. I think he was lucky not to have invested more before the roof fell in. Then again, maybe if he had had the finances, he would have become very wealthy indeed. It hardly seems important now. His life was very full and when he passed away at the age of 97, he had a nice bank account, which allowed him to continue donating to charities – a practice and desire from his youth. He also fulfilled his dream of helping his family as well as my mother's family financially, and he had a respected name in the community. But most important, he had the good fortune to have lived with the love of his life – my mother.

Erev Fifteenth Anniversary, October 26, 1943
My own sweet little wife,
Greetings.
Did I tell you I love you? For every hour I forgot to tell you that I love you I apologize most humbly. You are such a sweet wife that I should be a *melech* (king) to deserve you.

Fifteen short years. They flew by as so many hours. That means that every hour was a pleasant one, a lovely one, a dream hour.

We are at the McAlpin (Hotel). My little shy tootsie goes to bed with pants on. Then comes Rochester, New York. The crowds are celebrating Halloween and you and I are celebrating each other.

I thought then that I loved you. I didn't then know what real love is. Maybe I still don't know and will have to wait until our fiftieth anniversary to find out. I think I do know. It seems that there cannot be love greater than I have for you. But then, that's what I thought fifteen years ago. Who knows?

I think about you a lot. Many an early morning I wait quietly until you will awaken and crawl into my bed so that I may hug you and love you and kiss you.

I am jealous of the newspaper in the morning that claims your attention for many precious minutes. Would you say that is love?

What do you think, dearie? Forever your lover, Louis

Grossberg Family Album

Ship Manifest that brought
Sarah Henna and her
children to America, 1909

Book of Genesis, *Published
in Warsaw, 1865. One of three
Hebrew books Louis brought
from Latvia in 1909.*

The only things saved from the
voyage were three Hebrew Torah
books Louis brought with him
in 1909. Published in Vilna – 1834,
Warsaw – 1865 and Vienna – 1874.

Sarah Henna and Benjamin Grossberg,

Sarah Henna and Benjamin Grossberg, 1945

Louis' sister, Kitty, as a young girl

Louis' sister, Kitty Cohen, 1930

Louis' sister, Kitty and Al Cohen, 1931

Kitty and Al's son, Robert Cohen, 1937

*Kitty and Al's son, Robert Cohen,
soldier approximately 1943*

Louis' niece, Edith Cohen, 1958

557

*Rose (left) and Bella Bersh (right)
with Louis, 1925*

Louis in the Army, 1918

*Louis' sister, Esther Grossberg,
as a young girl*

*Louis' sister, Esther
Grossberg with parasol*

Louis' sister, Eleanor, and Maurie Schlossberg, approximately 1932

*Louis' brother,
William Grossberg, 1944*

*Miriam Grossberg and Alex
Freedman at the beach, 1929*

Miriam and Alex, 1954

Pauline Grossberg in the garden, 1939

*Louis' brother, Babe Grossberg,
in the garden, 1939*

Louis' brother, Sol Grossberg

Louis' brother,
Joe Grossberg, 1918

Louis' brother, Joe Grossberg,
in uniform, approximately 1944

Joe and Florence Grossberg
in Skyline Drive, Virginia, 1938

Ida Glushak, approximately 1929

Dave Glushak, 1928

Ida Glushak (left), Louis and Fanny Glushak, 1925

Celie Shultz with her sisters, Annie and Dora Freudberg, approximately 1946 [Celie on left, Annie in middle and Dora on right]

Leo and Rose Freudberg

Herman and Rose Freudberg, approximately 1950

Benjamin Grossberg's retirement. Left to right: Louis; Joseph Wilner; Benjamin, Sarah Henna; Rabbi Metz; Cantor Barkin and Sol, 1947

Kanster Family Album

Engagement picture of Pauline Berger and Jacob Kanster, 1900

Pauline and Jacob Kanster with Edith, 2, and Celia, 3 ½, 1906

Left to right, Dave Glushak visiting Louis, Celia, Pauline Kanster, Sara Hamburg, and Ruthie Kanster holding Harry Hamburg in New Jersey, 1929.

Celia, approximately 1926

*Sunburned Celia Kanster
in water, 1926*

*Fidelity Union Trust Masquerade, 1928.
Celia with head band is in second row, second from right.*

Four sisters, left to right, Edith, Celia, Sara and Ruth, 1930

Left to right, three sisters: Edith, Sara and Celia, 1928

Jacob and Pauline Kanster, 1930

Photo Louis sent Celia that she titled, "Louis, My Sweetheart," 1928

Celia and Louis, 1928

Big Sam Hamburg and
Jacob Kanster in the Kanster-
Hamburg Manufacturing
Co. workshop, 1928

Edith and Sam's car, 1928

Celia's sister, Edith,
and Sam Schiff, 1928

Ruthie Kanster, 1930s

Ruthie Kanster, 1930s

567

Big Sam Hamburg; Little Sam Schiff & Louis, 1939

New Jersey Clan, top left to right, Jacob Kanster, Ruth Kanster, Edith & Little Sam Schiff, Big Sam Hamburg. Bottom row left to right, Louis & Celia Grossberg, Pauline Kanster, Sara Hamburg with Harry, 1930

Benjamin & Sarah Henna Grossberg with Jacob Kanster, approximately 1935

Dave, Celia and Louis, 1930

Jacob Kanster Portrait, 1931, possible passport photo for trip to Palestine

Louis and Celia's wedding picture, October 28, 1928

My painting of Celia and Louis on their 50th Anniversary invitation card, 1978

About the Author

Born in Washington, DC, to Louis and Celia Grossberg, whose letters appear in this book, Perla Fox married Julius Fox. They have three children and three grandchildren. Perla authored and illustrated *The Wooodles: Stretching Your Imagination*, a children's art book. She and Jules moved to Israel with their daughter in 1972. There, they helped found ESRA, an all-volunteer non-profit in Israel. After almost 30 years in Israel, they left Israel for California to be near their grandchildren.

A watercolor artist who first exhibited in the nation's capitol in 1962, she has exhibited her painting, lithographs and serigraphs throughout the United States, Israel, Mexico, and France. She won prizes and awards from the Montgomery County, MD, Art Association, B'nai B'rith and the American Art League. The National Gallery of Art and Artexpo (New York and Los Angeles) have shown her work. Her paintings appear on greeting cards, Israeli Calendars, in annual editions of *Encyclopedia of Living Artists* and in *Israel Painters & Sculptors*. The 2004 San Diego Jewish Film Festival used her paintings. In 2008, the San Diego Gotthelf Art Gallery included her work in "Jewish Women: A Lifetime of Art." Find out more about her artwork at: www.perlafoxart.com